A DICTIONARY OF
Contemporary
American Artists

A DICTIONARY OF

Contemporary American Artists

PAUL CUMMINGS

St. Martin's Press, New York

Published in Canada by
THE MACMILLAN COMPANY OF CANADA LIMITED
70 Bond Street, Toronto 2

Acknowledgments

I would first like to express my great indebtedness to the hundreds of artists who took time to complete, and in many instances document, the long questionnaire sent them. Without their direct aid this project could not have reached its conclusion. In addition I should like to thank the many museum directors and art dealers across the country for supplying me with catalogues, photographs, and other material. I am grateful to the following museum personnel for making their time and offices available to me: Mary Joan Hall and Louise Averill Svendsen of The Solomon R. Guggenheim Museum, Bernard Karpel and his very helpful staff of the Library of The Museum of Modern Art, Janet Solinger of The Jewish Museum, the staffs of the Frick Art Reference Library and The Metropolitan Museum of Art Library, and especially to Eloise Morris and Edward Bryant of The Whitney Museum of American Art for making available the Museum's archive on American art.

I also wish to acknowledge an enormous debt to Miss Ellie Kurtz for the considerable editorial aid offered me and for the many direct contributions she made to the realization of this book. I am most grateful for her expert advice, assistance, and understanding.

Special acknowledgment must also be made to Rose Fried of the Rose Fried Gallery, to Edith Gregor Halpert of The Downtown Gallery, and to Nina Kaiden, Vice President of Ruder and Finn, Inc., for her patient understanding during the turmoil of editing this book.

To the collectors, museums, and art dealers that gave permission for works of art in their collections to be illustrated, grateful thanks.

P. C.

February, 1966
New York City

Contents

Illustrations

(All dimensions are in inches. Height precedes width.)

Josef Albers
    Homage to the Square—In and Out. 1959
    30 x 30. oil/masonite
    Courtesy Sidney Janis Gallery, New York
    Photograph by Geoffrey Clements

Alexander Archipenko
    Arabian. 1936
    26 high. bronze
    Courtesy Perls Galleries

Milton Avery
    Two Women. 1959
    50 x 60. oil/canvas
    Courtesy Grace Borgenicht Gallery Inc.
    Photograph by O. E. Nelson

Leonard Baskin
    Caprice. n.d.
    25 x $24\frac{1}{2}$ x $11\frac{3}{4}$. bronze
    Courtesy Grace Borgenicht Gallery Inc.
    Photograph by Walter Rosenblum

Robert Beauchamp
    Drawing. n.d.
    40 x 48. pencil and charcoal/paper
    Courtesy The American Gallery
    Photograph by Nathan Rabin

Elmer Bischoff
    Yellow Sun. 1963
    64 x 68. oil/canvas
    Courtesy Staempfli Gallery, New York
    Photograph by John D. Schiff

Isabel Bishop
    Subway Reading. n.d.
    $24\frac{1}{2}$ x $17\frac{3}{4}$. oil and tempera
    Collection: Dr. and Mrs. Fletcher McDowall
    Courtesy The Midtown Galleries
    Photograph by Brenwasser

Arshile Gorky
    Housatonic Falls. 1942/43
    34 x 44. oil/canvas
    Collection: Mr. and Mrs. William B. Jaffe, New York
    Courtesy Sidney Janis Gallery, New York
    Photograph by Geoffrey Clements

Adolph Gottlieb
    Emerging. 1960
    72 x 48. oil/canvas
    Collection: J. Daniel Weitzman
    Photograph by Oliver Baker Associates Inc.

Morris Cole Graves
    Spirit Bird. 1954
    $14\frac{3}{4}$ x $22\frac{3}{4}$. tempera and gold
    Collection: Mrs. Donald Strauss
    Courtesy The Willard Gallery
    Photograph by Oliver Baker Associates Inc.

Balcomb Greene
    Rocks on the Maine Coast. 1962
    44 x 36. oil/canvas
    Courtesy Saidenberg Gallery
    Photograph by John D. Schiff

Chaim Gross
    Two Sisters. 1956–60
    28 high. mahogany
    Collection: Mr. and Mrs. Lewis Garlick
    Courtesy The Forum Gallery
    Photograph by Soichi Sunami

Roy Gussow
    Mutual. 1963
    21 x $13\frac{1}{2}$ x $11\frac{1}{4}$. stainless steel
    Collection: Susan Morse Hilles
    Courtesy Grace Borgenicht Gallery Inc.

Robert Gwathmey
    Musing. 1961
    23 x $17\frac{1}{2}$. oil/canvas
    Collection: Mrs. Lewis Hoffman
    Courtesy Terry Dintenfass, Inc.
    Photograph by Oliver Baker Associates Inc.

Edward Higgins
    Untitled. 1963
    43 x 72 x 24. welded steel and epoxy
    Collection: The Art Institute of Chicago
    Courtesy Leo Castelli Inc.
    Photograph by Rudolph Burckhardt

Joseph Hirsch
    The Beach. n.d.
    26 x 39. oil/canvas
    Collection: Mrs. Daisy Shapiro
    Courtesy The Forum Gallery
    Photograph by Walter J. Russell

Hans Hofmann
    Sparks. 1951
    60 x 48. oil/canvas
    Courtesy The Kootz Gallery

Edward Hopper
    High Noon. 1949
    28 x 40. oil/canvas
    Collection: Mr. and Mrs. Anthony Haswell
    Courtesy Rehn Galleries
    Photograph by Peter A. Juley and Son

John Hultberg
    Landscape with Flag. 1958
    35 x $51\frac{1}{4}$. oil/canvas
    The Joseph H. Hirshhorn Collection, New York
    Photograph by Oliver Baker Associates Inc.

Paul Jenkins
    Phenomena Cross Purpose. 1964
    36 x 36. oil/canvas
    Collection: Dr. Paul Krooks
    Courtesy Martha Jackson Gallery
    Photograph by John D. Schiff

Jasper Johns
    Flag on Orange Field. 1957
    66 x 49. encaustic/canvas
    Collection: Ileana Sonnabend, Paris
    Courtesy Leo Castelli Inc.
    Photograph by Rudolph Burckhardt

Ben Kamihira
    Fish Tank. n.d.
    $66\frac{3}{4}$ x $77\frac{7}{8}$. oil/canvas
    Courtesy Durlacher Brothers
    Photograph by Brenwasser

Franz Kline
    Kupola. 1958
    78 x 107. oil/canvas
    Collection: Art Gallery of Toronto
    Courtesy Sidney Janis Gallery, New York
    Photograph by Geoffrey Clements

Karl Knaths
    Dunes. n.d.
    30 x 42. oil/canvas
    Courtesy P. Rosenberg and Co.

John Koch
    The Telephone. 1957
    30 x 25. oil/canvas
    Collection: Mr. F. William Carr
    Courtesy Kraushaar Galleries
    Photograph by Oliver Baker Associates Inc.

Yasuo Kuniyoshi
    Somebody Tore My Poster. 1943
    26 x 46. oil/canvas
    Collection: The Honorable and Mrs. William Benton, Southport, Connecticut
    Courtesy The Downtown Gallery

Gaston Lachaise
    Kneeling Woman. n.d.
    $19\frac{1}{2}$ x $7\frac{3}{4}$. bronze
    Estate of Isabel Lachaise, courtesy Robert Schoelkopf Gallery
    Photograph by John D. Schiff

Ibram Lassaw
    Counterpoint Castle. 1957
    38 high. bronze
    Courtesy The Kootz Gallery
    Photograph by Rudolph Burckhardt

Roy Lichtenstein
    In the Car. 1963
    68 x 80. magna/oil/canvas
    Collection: Mr. and Mrs. Robert C. Scull
    Courtesy Leo Castelli Inc.
    Photograph by Rudolph Burckhardt

Stanton Macdonald-Wright
    Embarkation. 1962
    48 x 36. oil/canvas
    Courtesy Rose Fried Gallery
    Photograph by John D. Schiff

Robert Mallary
    The Spector. 1961
    120 high. polyester/wood
    Collection: Los Angeles County Museum of Art
    Courtesy Allan Stone Gallery
    Photograph by Peter Moore

Conrad Marca-Relli
    The Blackboard. 1961
    84 x 120. paint/canvas collage
    Courtesy The Kootz Gallery

Julius Schmidt
    Untitled. 1962
    $19\frac{1}{2}$ high. bronze
    Courtesy Marlborough-Gerson Gallery Inc.
    Photograph by O. E. Nelson

Karl Schrag
    Black Trees at Noon. 1960
    40 x 20. drawing
    Courtesy Kraushaar Galleries
    Photograph by Oliver Baker Associates Inc.

Charles Sheeler
    California Industrial. 1957
    25 x 33. oil/canvas
    Collection: Mr. and Mrs. John Hilson
    Courtesy The Downtown Gallery
    Photograph by Oliver Baker Associates Inc.

David Smith
    Cubi XVII Dec. 4–63. 1963
    $107\frac{3}{4}$ high. stainless steel
    Courtesy Marlborough-Gerson Gallery Inc.

Raphael Soyer
    Nude with Self Portrait. 1960
    51 x 51. oil/canvas
    Courtesy The Forum Gallery
    Photograph by Peter A. Juley and Son

Theodoros Stamos
    Solstice Over Field. 1961
    61 x 45. oil/canvas
    Collection: William B. Tabler
    Courtesy Andre Emmerich Gallery
    Photograph by Eric Pollitzer

Richard P. Stankiewicz
    Untitled. 1960
    50 x 17 x 19. steel
    Collection: Mr. Hanford Yang
    Courtesy The Stable Gallery

Mark Tobey
    Toward the Whites. n.d.
    $44\frac{1}{2}$ x 28. tempera
    Collection: Museo Civico, Turin, Italy
    Courtesy The Willard Gallery
    Photograph by Geoffrey Clements

George Tooker
      The Table. n.d.
      24 x 28. tempera
      Collection: Dr. and Mrs. Henry H. Crapo, Boston, Massachusetts
      Photograph by Walter J. Russell

Jack Tworkov
      Thursday. 1960
      72 x 69. oil/canvas
      Courtesy Leo Castelli Inc.
      Photograph by Rudolph Burckhardt

Esteban Vicente
      Blue, Red, Black and White. 1961
      30 x 40. collage
      Courtesy Andre Emmerich Gallery
      Photograph by Eric Pollitzer

Max Weber
      Acrobats. 1946
      48 x 58. oil/canvas
      Courtesy The Downtown Gallery
      Photograph by Geoffrey Clements

H. C. Westermann
      The Suicide. 1964
      $13\frac{3}{4}$ x $10\frac{3}{4}$ x $6\frac{3}{8}$. wood and mirrors
      Sterling Holloway Collection
      Courtesy Allan Frumkin Gallery, New York
      Photograph by Nathan Rabin

William T. Wiley
      Columbus Rerouted #3. 1963
      72 x 141. oil/canvas
      Courtesy Staempfli Gallery, New York
      Photograph by John D. Schiff

James Wines
      Suspended Disc II. 1963
      $49\frac{1}{2}$ x 36. iron and cement
      Courtesy Marlborough-Gerson Gallery Inc.

Jack Youngerman
      Palma. 1964
      60 x 74. plastic paint/canvas
      Courtesy Betty Parsons Gallery
      Photograph by Rudolph Burckhardt

Wilfrid Zogbaum
      Kroeber Hall. 1962
      27 x $17\frac{1}{2}$. metal and stone
      Courtesy Grace Borgenicht Gallery Inc.

Index of Artists

and Pronunciation Guide

(A) Painter; (A$_1$) Watercolorist; (B) Sculptor; (C) Printmaker; (D) Assemblagist;
(E) Teacher; (F) Happenings; (G) Mosaicist; (H) Draftsman

1. Aach, Herb (A)
2. Acton, Arlo C. (B)
3. Adams, Clinton (A,C)
4. Adams, Patricia (Pat) (A)
5. Adler, Samuel M. (A)
6. Agostini, Peter (B)
7. Albers, Josef (A, C, E)
8. Albert, Calvin (B)
9. Albright, Ivan Le Lorraine (A)
10. Alcalay, Albert (A)
11. Alston, Charles H. (A)
12. Altman, Harold (C, A)
13. Altoon, John (A)
14. Amen, Irving (C)
15. Anderson, Guy (A)
16. Anderson, Jeremy R. (B)
17. Anderson, John S. (B)
18. Anderson, Lennart (A)
19. Andrejevic, Milet (A)
    An **dre** avic, Millet
20. Andrews, Oliver (B)
21. Antreasian, Garo (C)
    An **tray** sian
22. Anuszkiewicz, Richard (A)
    Anu **skay** vitch
23. Archipenko, Alexander (B, E)
    Ar chi **pen** ko
24. Aronson, David (A)
25. Atherton, John C. (A)
26. Ault, George C. (A)
27. Austin, Darrel (A)
28. Avery, Milton (A)
29. Baizerman, Saul (B)
30. Baringer, Richard E. (A)
31. Barnes, Robert M. (A)
32. Barnet, Will (A, C, E)
33. Baskin, Leonard (B, C, E)
34. Bayer, Herbert (A)
35. Baylinson, A. S. (A)
36. Baziotes, William A. (A, E)
37. Beal, Gifford (A)
38. Bearden, Romare H. (A)
    Roh **mayr**
39. Beattie, George (A)
40. Beauchamp, Robert (A)
    Beecham
41. Beck, Rosemarie (A)
42. Behl, Wolfgang (B)
43. Benjamin, Karl (A)
44. Benton, Thomas Hart (A, E)
45. Ben-Zion (A)
46. Berger, Jason (A)
47. Berman, Eugene (A)
48. Bertoia, Harry (B)
    Ber **toy** a
49. Bess, Forest (A)
50. Biddle, George (A, C)
51. Biederman, Charles (Karl) Joseph (B)
    Bee derman
52. Bischoff, Elmer (A)
    Bish off
53. Bishop, Isabel (A)
54. Bisttram, Emil (A, E)
55. Blackburn, Morris (C)
56. Blaine, Nell (A)
57. Blanch, Arnold (A)
58. Blaustein, Al (A)
59. Bleifeld, Stanley (A)

60. Bloch, Albert (A)
61. Bloom, Hyman (A)
62. Bluemner, Oscar (A)
    Bloom ner
63. Bluhm, Norman (A)
    Bloom
64. Blume, Peter (A)
65. Boardman, Seymour (A)
66. Bodin, Paul (A)
67. Bohrod, Aaron (A, E)
68. Bolomey, Roger (B)
    Bolo **may**
69. Bolotowsky, Ilya (A, B, E)
70. Bontecou, Lee (B)
71. Booth, Cameron (A, E)
72. Bosa, Louis (A)
73. Bothwell, Dorr (C, A)
74. Botkin, Henry (A)
75. Bouche, Louis (A, E)
    Boo **shay**
76. Bourgeois, Louise (B)
    Boo **zwah**
77. Bowman, Geoffrey (A)
78. Bowman, Richard (A)
79. Boyce, Richard (B, E)
80. Boyle, Keith (A)
81. Boynton, James W. (A)
82. Brach, Paul (A)
    Brock
83. Brackman, Robert (A)
84. Brandt, Warren (A)
85. Breinin, Raymond (A, E)
    Brennan
86. Brice, William (A)
87. Briggs, Ernest (A)
88. Broderson, Morris (Gaylord) (A)
89. Broderson, Robert M. (A)
90. Brodie, Gandy (A)
91. Broner, Robert (A, C)
    Brauner
92. Brook, Alexander (A)
93. Brooks, James (A)
94. Brown, Carlyle (A)
95. Brown, Joan (A)
96. Brown, William T. (A)
97. Browne, Byron (A, E)
98. Browning, Colleen (A)
99. Bultman, Fritz (A, B)
100. Bunce, Louis (A)
101. Burchfield, Charles (A_1)

102. Burkhardt, Hans Gustav (A)
103. Burlin, Paul (A)
104. Burliuk, David (A)
105. Cadmus, Paul (A)
106. Caesar, Doris (B)
107. Cajori, Charles (A)
108. Calcagno, Lawrence (A)
     Cal **cahn** yo
109. Calder, Alexander (B)
110. Callahan, Kenneth (A)
111. Callery, Mary (B)
112. Campoli, Cosmo (B)
113. Candell, Victor (A, E)
114. Caparn, Rhys (B)
     Ca **parn,** Reese
115. Carewe, Sylvia (A)
116. Casarella, Edmond (C)
117. Castellon, Federico (C, A)
118. Cavallon, Giorgio (A)
119. Chaet, Bernard (A)
     Chate
120. Chamberlain, Elwin (A)
121. Chamberlain, John (B)
122. Cherney, Marvin (A)
123. Chesney, Lee R., Jr. (A)
124. Chinni, Peter (B)
     Keeny
125. Christopher, William (A)
126. Chryssa (B)
     Kree sa
127. Cicero, Carmen Louis (A)
128. Cikovsky, Nicolai (A, E)
     Sih **kahv** ski
129. Cloar, Carroll (A)
     Clore
130. Clutz, William (A)
131. Congdon, William (A)
132. Conner, Bruce (D, A)
133. Conover, Robert (A)
134. Constant, George (A)
135. Cook, Howard (A)
136. Corbett, Edward (A)
137. Corbino, Jon (A)
138. Cornell, Joseph (D)
139. Cowles, Russell (A)
     Coles
140. Cramer, Konrad (A)
141. Crampton, Rollin McNeil (A)
142. Crawford, Ralston (A)

(A) Painter; (A_1) Watercolorist; (B) Sculptor; (C) Printmaker; (D) Assemblagist;
(E) Teacher; (F) Happenings; (G) Mosaicist; (H) Draftsman

143. Cremean, Robert (B)
    Cre **mee** an
144. Criss, Francis H. (A)
145. Cronbach, Robert M. (B)
146. Curry, John Steuart (A)
147. Cusumano, Stefano (A)
148. Daphnis, Nassos (A, B)
149. D'Arcangelo, Allan (A)
150. D'Arista, Robert (A)
151. Darrow, Paul Gardner (A)
152. Dasburg, Andrew (A)
153. Dash, Robert (A)
154. Davey, Randall (A)
155. Davis, Jerrold (A)
156. Davis, Stuart (A)
157. Day, (Esther) Worden (A)
158. Decker, Lindsey (B)
159. de Creeft, Jose (B)
160. Deem, George (A)
161. De Erdely, Francis (A, E)
162. De Forest, Roy Dean (A)
163. Dehn, Adolf Arthur (A, C)
164. Dehner, Dorothy (B)
165. de Kooning, Elaine (A)
166. de Kooning, Willem (A)
167. Delap, Tony (B)
168. Della-Volpe, Ralph (A)
169. De Martini, Joseph (A)
170. Demuth, Charles (A)
171. De Niro, Robert (A)
172. de Rivera, Jose (B)
173. Deshaies, Arthur (C)
    Da **shay**
174. Dickinson, Edwin (A, E)
175. Diebenkorn, Richard (A)
    Dee ben korn
176. Diller, Burgoyne (A, E)
177. Dine, Jim (A, F)
178. Di Suvero, Mark (B)
179. Dobkin, Alexander (A)
180. Dodd, Lamar (A, E)
181. Dodd, Lois (A)
182. Dole, William (A)
183. Donati, Enrico (A)
184. Dove, Arthur G. (A)
185. Doyle, Thomas J. (B)
186. Drewes, Werner (A, E)
187. Drummond, Sally Hazelet (A)
188. Du Bois, Guy Pene (A)
    Du Bwah
189. Duchamp, Marcel (A)
190. Dugmore, Edward (A)
191. Dzubas, Friedel (A)

192. Edie, Stuart (A, E)
193. Edmondson, Leonard (A)
194. Elliott, Ronnie (A)
195. Engel, Jules (A)
196. Ernst, Jimmy (A)
197. Etting, Emlen (A)
198. Evergood, Philip Howard Francis
    Dixon (A)
199. Farr, Fred (B)
200. Feeley, Paul (A, E)
201. Feininger, Lyonel (A)
202. Feitelson, Lorser (A)
203. Fenton, Alan (A)
204. Ferber, Herbert (B)
205. Ferren, John (A, E)
206. Fiene, Ernest (A)
    Fine
207. Flannagan, John (B)
208. Fleischmann, Adolf R. (A)
209. Floch, Joseph (A)
    Flack
210. Follett, Jean F. (A, D)
211. Forakis, Peter (A, B)
    For **ah** kis
212. Forst, Miles (A)
213. Fortess, Karl E. (A)
    For tess
214. Foulkes, Llyn (A)
    Folks
215. Francis, Sam (A, C)
216. Frankenthaler, Helen (A)
217. Frasconi, Antonio (C)
218. Freilicher, Jane (A)
    Fry likker
219. French, Jared (A)
    Jard
220. Friedensohn, Elias (A, B)
221. Fuller, Sue (B)
222. Gabo, Naum Neemia Pevsner (B)
223. Gallatin, Albert E. (A)
    Gal atin
224. Ganso, Emil (A)
225. Gatch, Lee (A)
226. Gechtoff, Sonia (A)
    Getch toff
227. Gelb, Jan (A)
228. George, Thomas (A)
229. Georges, Paul (A)
    George's
230. Giambruni, Tio (B)
    Jam **bru** ni
231. Gibran, Kahlil (A)

232. Gikow, Ruth (A)
    Geeko
233. Giobbi, Edward (A)
234. Girona, Julio (B)
    Ji **ro** na
235. Glackens, William (A)
236. Glarner, Fritz (A)
237. Glasco, Joseph (A)
238. Goldberg, Michael (A)
239. Goldin, Leon (A)
240. Golub, Leon (A)
241. Gonzalez, Xavier (A)
242. Goodman, Sidney (A)
243. Goodnough, Robert (A)
    Good know
244. Gorchov, Ron (A)
245. Gordin, Sidney (B)
246. Gorky, Arshile (A)
247. Goto, Joseph (B)
248. Gottlieb, Adolph (A)
249. Goulet, Lorrie (B)
    Goo **lay**
250. Graham, John D. (A)
251. Granlund, Paul (B)
252. Graves, Morris Cole (A)
253. Gray, Cleve (A)
254. Greene, Balcomb (A, E)
255. Greene, Stephen (A)
256. Grillo, John (A)
257. Grippe, Peter (B)
    Grippy
258. Grooms, Red (A, F)
259. Gropper, William (A, C)
260. Gross, Chaim (B)
261. Grosser, Maurice (A)
262. Grosz, George (A, C)
263. Guerrero, Jose (A)
264. Guglielmi, O. Louis (A)
265. Gussow, Alan (A)
266. Gussow, Roy (B)
267. Guston, Philip (A)
268. Guy, James (B, A)
269. Gwathmey, Robert (A)
270. Hadzi, Dimitri (B)
271. Haines, Richard (A)
272. Hale, Nathan Cabot (B)
273. Hale, Robert Beverly (A, E)
274. Haley, John Charles (A)
275. Hammersley, Frederick (A)
276. Hansen, James Lee (B)

277. Hansen, Robert (A)
278. Hare, David (B)
279. Hartell, John (A)
280. Hartigan, Grace (A)
281. Hartl, Leon (A)
282. Hartley, Marsden (A)
283. Harvey, James (A)
284. Harvey, Robert (A)
285. Hayes, David V. (B)
286. Hebald, Milton (B)
    Hee bald
287. Held, Al (A)
288. Heliker, John Edward (A)
289. Hendler, Raymond (A)
290. Henry, Charles T. (A)
291. Higgins, Edward (B)
292. Hillsmith, Fannie (A)
293. Hirsch, Joseph (A)
294. Hofmann, Hans (A, E)
295. Holty, Carl Robert (A)
296. Hopkins, Budd (A)
297. Hopper, Edward (A)
298. Horiuchi, Paul (A)
299. Hovannes, John (A)
300. Howard, Charles (A)
301. Hudson, Robert (B)
302. Hueter, James W. (A)
    Hooter
303. Hultberg, John (A)
304. Hunt, Richard (B)
305. Indiana, Robert (A)
306. Ippolito, Angelo (A)
    Ippo **lee** to
307. Jacobs, David (B)
308. Jarvaise, James (A)
    Zhar **vez**
309. Jenkins, Paul (A)
310. Jensen, Alfred (A)
311. Johns, Jasper (A)
312. Johnson, Ben (A)
313. Johnson, Buffie (A)
314. Johnson, Lester (A)
315. Johnston, Ynez (A)
    Eye nez
316. Jones, John Paul (A, C)
317. Kabak, Robert (A)
    Kay back
318. Kahn, Wolf (A)
319. Kaish, Luise (B)
320. Kamihira, Ben (A)

(A) Painter; (A₁) Watercolorist; (B) Sculptor; (C) Printmaker; (D) Assemblagist;
(E) Teacher; (F) Happenings; (G) Mosaicist; (H) Draftsman

321. Kamrowski, Gerome (A, E)
322. Kamys, Walter (A, E)
   Came ease
323. Kanemitsu, Matsumi (A)
324. Kantor, Morris (A, E)
325. Kaprow, Allan (A, D, F)
326. Karfiol, Bernard (A)
327. Kasten, Karl (A)
328. Katz, Alex (A)
329. Katzman, Herbert (A)
330. Kearl, Stanley Brandon (B)
   Curl
331. Kearns, James (A)
   Carns
332. Kelly, Ellsworth (A)
333. Kelly, James (A)
334. Kelly, Leon (Leon Kelly y Corrons) (A)
335. Kent, Rockwell (A)
336. Kepes, Gyorgy (A, E)
   Kep ish
337. Keyser, Robert (A)
338. Kienbusch, William (A)
   Keen bush
339. Kiesler, Frederick J. (B, A)
   Kees ler
340. King, William Rikey (B)
   Rickey
341. Kipniss, Robert (A)
342. Kipp, Lyman E. (B)
343. Kirschenbaum, Jules (A)
344. Kline, Franz (A)
345. Knaths, Karl (A)
   (*pron.* K)
346. Koch, Gerd (A)
   Coke
347. Koch, John (A)
   Coke
348. Koenig, John Franklin (A)
   Kay nig
349. Kohn, Gabriel (B)
350. Kohn, Misch (C)
351. Konzal, Joseph (B)
352. Kopman, Benjamin (A)
353. Koppelman, Chaim (C, A)
354. Krasner, Lee (A)
355. Kriesberg, Irving (A)
   Crize berg
356. Kroll, Leon (A)
357. Krushenick, Nicholas (A)
   Croosh nick
358. Kuhn, Walt (A)
   Kyuhn
359. Kuniyoshi, Yasuo (A, E)

360. Kuntz, Roger (A)
361. Kupferman, Lawrence (A, E)
362. Labaudt, Lucien (A)
   Lah bowe
363. Lachaise, Gaston (B)
   La **shey**
364. Landau, Jacob (A, C)
365. Landon, Edward (A)
366. Langlais, Bernard (B, A)
   Langley
367. Laning, Edward (A)
   Lanning
368. Lansner, Fay (A)
369. Lanyon, Ellen (A)
370. Lasansky, Mauricio (C, E)
371. Lassaw, Ibram (B)
372. Laufman, Sidney (A)
373. Laurent, John (A)
374. Laurent, Robert (B, E)
375. Lawrence, Jacob (A)
376. Lawson, Ernest (A)
377. Lebrun, Rico (A, E)
378. Lechay, James (A, E)
   Le **shey**
379. Leiber, Gerson (C)
380. Lekakis, Michael (B)
381. Leong, James C. (A)
   Lee ong
382. Leslie, Alfred (A)
383. Levee, John (A)
384. Levi, Julian (A)
385. Levine, Jack (A)
386. Levinson, Mon (A)
387. Levitan, Israel (B)
388. Lewandowski, Edmund D. (A, E)
   Lew and **ow** ski
389. Lewis, Norman (A)
390. Liberman, Alexander (A, B)
391. Lichtenstein, Roy (A)
   Lick ten stine
392. Lindner, Richard (A)
393. Lipchitz, Jacques (B)
   Lipschitz
394. Lippold, Richard (B)
395. Lipton, Seymour (B)
396. Lobdell, Frank (A)
397. Loberg, Robert W. (A)
398. Loew, Michael (A)
   Lowe
399. Loran, Erle (A, E)
400. Louis, Morris (A)
   Lewis
401. Lozowick, Louis (A)

402. Lund, David (A)
403. Lye, Len (B)
404. Lytle, Richard (A)
     Littell
405. Macdonald-Wright, Stanton (A)
406. MacIver, Loren (A)
     Mac Eye ver
407. Maldarelli, Oronzio (B)
408. Mallary, Robert (B)
409. Man Ray (A)
410. Manship, Paul (B)
411. Manso, Leo (A)
412. Marca-Relli, Conrad (A)
413. Marcus, Marcia (A)
414. Margo, Boris (A, C)
415. Marin, John (A₁)
416. Marisol (Escobar) (B)
417. Marsh, Reginald (A, E)
418. Marsicano, Nicholas (A)
419. Martin, Fletcher (A)
420. Martin, Knox (A)
421. Martinelli, Ezio (B)
422. Mason, Alice Trumbull (A)
423. Matulka, Jan (A, E)
424. Mayhew, Richard (A)
425. Mazur, Michael B. (A)
426. McChesney, Robert P. (A)
427. McClellan, Douglas Eugene (A)
428. McFee, Henry Lee (A)
429. McGarrell, James (A)
430. McLaughlin, John (A)
431. McNeil, George (A)
432. Meeker, Dean Jackson (C)
433. Meigs, Walter (A)
     Megs
434. Menkes, Sigmund (A)
     Menkeys
435. Mesibov, Hugh (B)
436. Mestrovic, Ivan (B)
437. Metcalf, James (B)
438. Miller, Kenneth Hayes (A, E)
439. Miller, Richard K. (A)
440. Millman, Edward (A)
441. Mitchell, Fred (A)
442. Mitchell, Joan (A)
443. Mitchell, Wallace (A)
444. Moholy-Nagy, Lazlo (B)
445. Moller, Hans (A)
446. Morin, Thomas (B)
447. Morris, Carl (A)

448. Morris, George L. K. (A)
449. Morris, Kyle R. (A)
450. Motherwell, Robert (A)
451. Moy, Seong (A)
452. Moyer, Roy (A)
453. Muller, Jan (A)
454. Mullican, Lee (A)
455. Murch, Walter Tandy (A)
456. Nadelman, Elie (B)
457. Nakian, Reuben (B)
458. Natkin, Robert (A)
459. Neal, Reginald (A, C)
460. Nepote, Alexander (A)
     Ne po ty
461. Neuman, Robert S. (A)
     Newman
462. Nevelson, Louise (B)
463. Nevelson, Mike (B)
464. Newbill, Al (A)
465. Newman, Barnett (A)
466. Nivola, Constantino (B)
467. Noguchi, Isamu (B)
468. Noland, Kenneth (A)
469. Nordfeldt, B. J. O. (A)
470. Nowack, Wayne K. (A)
471. O'Hanlon, Richard (B)
472. Ohashi, Yutaka (A)
473. Okada, Kenzo (A)
474. Okamura, Arthur (A)
475. O'Keeffe, Georgia (A)
476. Oldenburg, Claes Thure (A, B, F)
     Klaus
477. Olitski, Jules (A)
478. Oliveira, Nathan (A)
479. Onslow-Ford, Gordon (A)
480. Opper, John (A, E)
481. Ortman, George Earl (A)
482. Ossorio, Alfonso (A)
483. Osver, Arthur (A)
484. Pace, Stephen (A)
485. Pachner, William (A)
     Pack ner
486. Packard, David (B)
487. Padovano, Anthony (B)
488. Palmer, William C. (A)
489. Paone, Peter (A, C)
     Pay oh ni
490. Paris, Harold P. (B)
491. Park, David (A)
492. Parker, Raymond (A)

(A) Painter; (A₁) Watercolorist; (B) Sculptor; (C) Printmaker; (D) Assemblagist;
(E) Teacher; (F) Happenings; (G) Mosaicist; (H) Draftsman

493. Parker, Robert Andrew (A)
494. Pasilis, Felix (A)
    Pa **sill** iss
495. Pattison, Abbott (B)
496. Peake, Channing (A)
497. Pearlstein, Philip (A)
    Pearl steen
498. Pearson, Henry Charles (A)
499. Peirce, Waldo (A)
500. Penney, James (A)
501. Pereira, I. Rice (A)
    Per **err** a
502. Perlin, Bernard (A)
503. Peterdi, Gabor (C, A)
    Pet erdi
504. Pfriem, Bernard (A)
    Freem
505. Pineda, Marianna (B)
    (ñ)
506. Pittman, Hobson L. (A)
507. Pollack, Reginald (A)
508. Pollock, Jackson (A)
509. Ponce de Leon, Michael (C)
510. Poons, Larry (A)
511. Poor, Henry Varnum (A)
512. Porter, David (A)
513. Porter, Fairfield (A)
514. Pousette-Dart, Nathaniel (A)
515. Pousette-Dart, Richard (A)
516. Pozzatti, Rudy (C)
517. Prestopino, Gregorio (A)
518. Price, Clayton S. (A)
519. Quirt, Walter (A, E)
520. Quisgard, Liz Whitney (A)
521. Rabkin, Leo (A)
522. Racz, Andre (A, C)
    Racks
523. Raffaele, Joseph (A)
524. Rattner, Abraham (A)
525. Rauschenberg, Robert (A)
526. Reder, Bernard (B)
527. Reinhardt, Ad (A, E)
528. Reinhardt, Siegfried Gerhard (A)
529. Resnick, Milton (A)
530. Reynal, Jeanne (G)
531. Rice, Dan (A)
532. Richenburg, Robert B. (A)
533. Rickey, George (B)
534. Rivers, Larry (A, B)
535. Robinson, Boardman (A, E)
536. Robus, Hugo (B)
537. Rocklin, Raymond (B)
538. Roesch, Kurt (A, E)
    Resh
539. Rogalski, Walter (C)
540. Rohm, Robert (B)
541. Ronald, William (A)
542. Rood, John (B, E)
543. Rosati, James (B)
544. Rosenborg, Ralph M. (A)
545. Rosenquist, James (A)
546. Rosenthal, Bernard (B)
547. Roszak, Theodore (B)
548. Roth, Frank (A)
549. Rothko, Mark (A)
550. Ruben, Richards (A)
551. Ruvolo, Felix (A, E)
552. Sage, Kay (A)
553. Salemme, Attilio (A)
554. Samaras, Lucas (D)
555. Sander, Ludwig (A)
556. Sato, Tadashi (A)
557. Saul, Peter (A)
558. Saunders, Raymond (A)
559. Savelli, Angelo (A, C)
560. Scarpitta, Salvatore (A)
561. Schanker, Louis (A, C, B)
562. Schapiro, Miriam (A)
563. Schlemowitz, Abram (B)
564. Schmidt, Julius (B)
565. Schnakenberg, Henry (A)
566. Schrag, Karl (A, C)
567. Schucker, Charles (A)
568. Schueler, Jon (A)
    Shooler
569. Schwabacher, Ethel (A)
570. Schwartz, Manfred (A, E)
571. Segal, George (B)
572. Seley, Jason (B)
573. Seliger, Charles (A)
574. Seligmann, Kurt (A, C)
575. Sennhauser, John (A)
576. Serisawa, Sueo (A)
577. Shahn, Ben (A)
578. Shaw, Charles (A)
579. Sheeler, Charles (A)
580. Sheets, Millard (A)
581. Shinn, Everett (A)
582. Simon, Sidney (B)
583. Simpson, David (A)
584. Sinton, Nell (A)
585. Siporin, Mitchell (A)
586. Sloan, John (A, E)
587. Smith, David (B)
588. Smith, Hassel W., Jr. (A)

589. Smith, Leon Polk (A)
590. Snelgrove, Walter (A)
591. Solomon, Hyde (A)
592. Solomon, Syd (A)
593. Sonenberg, Jack (A)
594. Soyer, Moses (A)
595. Soyer, Raphael (A)
596. Speicher, Eugene (A)
    Spiker
597. Spohn, Clay E. (A, E)
598. Sprinchorn, Carl (A)
    Sprin corn
599. Spruance, Benton (A, C)
600. Spruce, Everett (A)
601. Squier, Jack (B)
602. Stamos, Theodoros (A)
603. Stankiewicz, Richard P. (B)
    Stan kyay vitch
604. Stasik, Andrew (C)
605. Stefanelli, Joseph (A)
606. Steg, J. L. (C)
607. Stein, Ronald (A)
608. Steinberg, Saul (H)
609. Stella, Frank (A)
610. Stella, Joseph (A)
611. Stern, Gerd (B)
612. Sternberg, Harry (C, E)
613. Sterne, Hedda (A)
614. Sterne, Maurice (A)
615. Still, Clyfford (A, E)
616. Stout, Myron S. (A)
617. Stuempfig, Walter (A)
    Stum fig
618. Sugarman, George (B)
619. Summers, Carol (C)
620. Suttman, Paul (B)
621. Suzuki, James Hiroshi (A)
622. Takai, Teiji (A)
623. Takal, Peter (C)
624. Talbot, William H. M. (B)
625. Tam, Reuben (A, E)
626. Tanguy, Yves (A, C)
    Tan ghee, Eve
627. Tania (Schreiber) (B)
628. Taubes, Frederic (A, E)
    Taubs
629. Tchelitchew, Pavel (A)
    Chel itcheff
630. Thiebaud, Wayne (A, E)
    Tee bowe

631. Thomas, Robert C. (B)
632. Tobey, Mark (A)
633. Tomlin, Bradley Walker (A)
634. Tooker, George (A)
635. Tovish, Harold (B, E)
636. Townley, Hugh (B)
637. Treiman, Joyce (A, B)
    Tree man
638. Tsutakawa, George (A, E)
639. Twardowicz, Stanley (A)
    Twardo witz
640. Twombly, Cy (A)
641. Tworkov, Jack (A, E)
642. Vander Sluis, George (B, E)
    Sluice
643. Vasilieff, Nicholas (A, E)
644. Vass, Gene (A)
645. Vicente, Esteban (A)
646. Vollmer, Ruth (B)
647. Von Weigand, Charmion (A)
    Weegand, Sharmion
648. Von Wicht, John (A)
    Vict
649. Voulkos, Peter (B, E)
    Vole kos
650. Vytlacil, Vaclav (A, E)
    Vitt la sill
651. Wald, Sylvia (A, C)
652. Waldman, Paul (A)
653. Walkowitz, Abraham (A)
654. Warshaw, Howard (A)
655. Washington, James W., Jr. (B)
656. Watkins, Franklin C. (A)
657. Watts, Robert M. (D, F)
658. Wayne, June (A, C)
659. Weber, Hugo (A)
660. Weber, Max (A)
661. Weeks, James (A)
662. Weinberg, Elbert (B)
663. Welliver, Neil (A)
    Williver
664. Wesselmann, Tom (A)
665. Westermann, H. C. (B)
666. Wieghardt, Paul (A, E)
    Wig hart
667. Wilde, John (A, E)
    Will dee
668. Wiley, William T. (A)
669. Wilke, Ulfert S. (A)
    Will ka

(A) Painter; (A₁) Watercolorist; (B) Sculptor; (C) Printmaker; (D) Assemblagist;
(E) Teacher; (F) Happenings; (G) Mosaicist; (H) Draftsman

670. Williams, Hiram (A)
671. Wilson, Jane (A)
672. Wines, James (B)
673. Woelffer, Emerson (A)
674. Wolff, Robert Jay (A, E)
675. Wolfson, Sidney (A)
676. Wonner, Paul John (A)
677. Wood, Grant (A)
678. Wyeth, Andrew (A)
679. Xceron, Jean (A)
    Zeron
680. Yektai, Manoucher (A)
    Manu shay

681. Youngerman, Jack (A)
682. Yunkers, Adja (A, C)
    Odd ya
683. Zacharias, Athos (A)
    Zacha **rye** as
684. Zajac, Jack (B)
685. Zerbe, Karl (A)
686. Zogbaum, Wilfrid (B)
687. Zorach, Marguerite (A)
688. Zorach, William (B)
689. Zox, Larry (A)

Key to Museums
and Institutions and
Their Schools

reflecting ownership of art collections in which are
represented works of the artists in this book

AAAL. American Academy of Arts and Letters, NYC
A.F.A. American Federation of Arts, NYC
ASL. Art Students League, NYC
Abbot Academy, Andover, Mass.
Abbott Laboratories
Abilene Christian College
Abraham Lincoln High School, Brooklyn, N.Y.
Achenbach Foundation for Graphic Arts, San Francisco, Calif.
Addison Gallery of Art—*see* Andover/Phillips
Aetna Oil Co.
Agricultural and Mechanical College of Texas
Ain Harod. Mishkan Le'omanuth Museum of Art, Ain Harod, Israel
Akron/AI. Akron Art Institute, Akron, Ohio
U. of Alabama
Albany/Institute. Albany Institute of History and Art, Albany, N.Y.
Albertina (Vienna)—*see* Graphische Sammlung Albertina
Albion College
Albright-Knox Art Gallery—*see* Buffalo/Albright
Alcoa. Aluminum Company of America
Allegheny College
Allen-Bradley Co. Inc.
Allentown/AM. Allentown Art Museum, Allentown, Pa.
Lyman Allyn Museum—*see* New London
Alverthorpe Gallery, Jenkintown, Pa.
American Academy, Rome
American Academy of Arts and Letters—*see* AAAL
American Airlines
American Association of University Women
American Car and Foundry Co.
American Export Isbrandtsen Lines Inc.
American Federation of Arts—*see* A.F.A.
American Life and Casualty Insurance Co.
American Locomotive Co.
American Republic Insurance Co.
American Swedish Historical Museum, Philadelphia, Pa.
American Swedish Institute, Minneapolis, Minn.
American U.
Amherst College
Amsterdam/Stedelijk. Stedelijk Museum, Amsterdam, Holland

Andover/Phillips. Phillips Academy, Addison Gallery of American Art, Andover, Mass.
  Phillips Academy
Antwerp. Musee Royal des Beaux-Arts, Antwerp, Belgium
Argentina/Nacional. Museo Nacional de Bellas Artes, Buenos Aires, Argentina
Arizona State College
Arizona State U.
U. of Arizona
U. of Arkansas (incl. Arkansas Art Center)
Art Council of Pakistan—*see* Karachi
Art Students League—*see* ASL
Art of This Century (Peggy Guggenheim), Venice, Italy
Arts Club of Chicago, Chicago, Ill.
Arts Council of Great Britain, London, England
Associated Coin Amusement Company
Atlanta/AA. Atlanta Art Association, Atlanta, Ga.
Atlanta U.
Atwater Kent Museum, Philadelphia, Pa.
Auburn U.
Aubusson. College de la Manufacture d'Aubusson, Aubusson, France
Auckland. Auckland City Art Gallery, Auckland, New Zealand
Augusta, Me./State. Maine State Museum, Augusta, Me.
Austin. Texas Fine Arts Association, Austin, Tex.
L. S. Ayres & Co.
Baker U.
Ball State Teachers College
Baltimore/MA. Baltimore Museum of Art, Baltimore, Md.
U. of Baltimore
Banden Memorial Art Gallery—*see* Fort Dodge/Banden
Bangor Public Library, Bangor, Me.
Bankers Trust Company, NYC
Barat College of the Sacred Heart
Barcelona. Museo de Arte Moderno, Barcelona, Spain
Barnard College
Barnes Foundation, Merion, Pa.
Baseball Museum, Baltimore, Md.
Basel. Kunstmuseum Basel, Basel, Switzerland
Bath-Yam Museum, Israel
Baton Rouge. State of Louisiana Art Commission, Baton Rouge, La.
Bauhaus-Archiv, Darmstadt, Germany
Beach Public School, Portland, Ore.
Belgian Ministry of National Education, Brussels, Belgium
Belgrade/National. Narodni Muzej (National Museum), Belgrade, Yugoslavia
Beloit College
Belvedere. Osterreichische Galerie im Belvedere in Wien, Vienna, Austria
Bennington College
Berea College
John Nelson Bergstrom Art Center and Museum—*see* Neenah/Bergstrom
Berkshire Atheneum—*see* Pittsfield/Berkshire
Berlin/National. Nationalgalerie, (West) Berlin, Germany
Berne. Kunsthalle Berne, Berne, Switzerland
Bethlehem Steel Corp.
Bezalel Museum, Jerusalem, Israel
Bibliotheque Nationale, Paris, France

Bibliotheque Royale de Belgique, Brussels, Belgium
Birmingham, Ala./MA. Birmingham Museum of Art, Birmingham, Ala.
Black Mountain College, Beria, N.C.
Bordighera. Galleria d'Arte Moderna, Bordighera, Italy
Borg-Warner International Corporation
Boston/MFA. Museum of Fine Arts, Boston, Mass. **Boston Museum School**
Boston Public Library, Boston, Mass.
Boston U.
Boulogne. Musee des Beaux-Arts, Boulogne, France
Bowdoin College
Bradley U.
Brandeis U.
Bremen. Kunsthalle Bremen, Bremen, Germany
Bridgeport. Museum of Art, Science and Industry, Bridgeport, Conn.
Bridgestone Museum, Tokyo, Japan
Brigham Young U.
Britannica. Encyclopaedia Britannica
U. of British Columbia, Vancouver (B.C.), Canada
British Museum, London, England
Brookgreen Gardens, Georgetown, S.C.
Brooklyn Museum, Brooklyn, N.Y. **Brooklyn Museum School**
Brooklyn College of the City University of New York
Brooks Memorial Art Gallery—*see* Memphis/Brooks
Brown U.
Brunswick. Stadtisches Museum, Brunswick, Germany
Brussels/Moderne. Musee d'Art Moderne, Brussels, Belgium
Bryn Mawr College
Budapest/National. Hungarian National Gallery, Budapest, Hungary
The Budd Co.
Buenos Aires/Municipal. Museo Municipal de Bellas Artes y Arte Nacional, Buenos Aires,
   Argentina
Buffalo/Albright. Albright-Knox Art Gallery, Buffalo, N.Y. **Albright Art School** (prior to
   1962)
Bundy Art Gallery—*see* Waitsfield/Bundy
Harry and Della Burpee Gallery—*see* Rockford/Burpee
Busch-Reisinger Museum, Cambridge, Mass.
The Butler Institute of American Art—*see* Youngstown/Butler
CIT Corporation, NYC
CSFA. California School of Fine Arts, San Francisco, Calif.
California Academy of Science, Museum and Library, San Francisco, Calif.
California Palace of The Legion of Honor, San Francisco, Calif.
California School of Fine Arts—*see* CSFA
California State Fair
California State Library
California Watercolor Society, Los Angeles, Calif.
U. of California (at Berkeley, Davis, Los Angeles, Riverside, Santa Barbara)
Canajoharie. Canajoharie Library and Art Gallery, Canajoharie, N.Y.
Capehart Corp.
Caracas. Museo de Bellas Artes de Caracas, Caracas, Venezuela
Carleton College
Carnegie. Carnegie Institute, Pittsburgh, Pa.
Carolina Art Association—*see* Charleston/Carolina
La Casa del Libro, San Juan, Puerto Rico

The Catholic U. of America
Cedar Rapids/AA.   Cedar Rapids Art Association, Cedar Rapids, Iowa
Central Florida Museum—*see* Orlando
Century Association, NYC
Ceret.   Musee d'Art Moderne, Ceret, France
Charleston/Carolina.   Carolina Art Association, Charleston, S.C.
Charlotte/Mint.   Mint Museum of Art, Charlotte, N.C.
Chase Manhattan Bank, NYC
Chattanooga/AA.   Chattanooga Art Association, Chattanooga, Tenn.
Chautauqua Institute, Chautauqua, N.Y.
Chicago/AI.   The Art Institute of Chicago, Chicago, Ill.   **Chicago Art Institute School** (and
   Junior School)
Chicago Arts Club—*see* Arts Club of Chicago
Chicago Public Schools, Chicago, Ill.
The U. of Chicago
Chico State College
Chrysler Corp.
Walter Chrysler Museum of Art—*see* Provincetown/Chrysler
Cincinnati/AM.   The Cincinnati Art Museum, Cincinnati, Ohio.   **Cincinnati Museum School**
Citizens Fidelity Bank, Louisville, Ky.
City of Claremont, Calif.
City College of the City University of New York
City of Tilburg, Holland
Clairol Inc.
Clearwater/Gulf Coast.   Florida Gulf Coast Art Center, Inc., Clearwater, Fla.
Cleveland/MA.   The Cleveland Museum of Art, Cleveland, Ohio
The Coca-Cola Co.
Cochran Memorial Park, St. Paul, Minn.
Coe College
Colby College
Colgate U.
Collection de l'Etat, Paris, France
College des Musees Nationaux de France, Paris, France
Cologne.   Wallraf-Richartz-Museum, Cologne, Germany
Colonial Williamsburg, Williamsburg, Va.
Colorado Springs/FA.   Colorado Springs Fine Arts Center, Colorado Springs, Colo.
U. of Colorado
Columbia, Mo.   State Historical Society of Missouri, Columbia, Mo.
Columbia, S.C./MA.   Columbia Museum of Art, Columbia, S.C.
Columbia Broadcasting System, NYC
Columbia U.
Columbus.   Columbus Gallery of Fine Arts, Columbus, Ohio
Concordia Teachers College
Connecticut Life Insurance Company
Connecticut College
U. of Connecticut
Container Corp. of America
Continental Grain Company
Cooperative Insurance Society, Manchester, England
Cooper Union.   The Cooper Union Museum, NYC
Copenhagen.   Statens Museum for Kunst, Copenhagen, Denmark
Corcoran.   The Corcoran Gallery of Art, Washington, D.C.   **The Corcoran School of Art**
Cordoba/Municipal.   Museo Municipal de Cordoba, Cordoba, Argentina

Cordoba/Provincial.   Museo Provincial de Bellas Artes, Cordoba, Argentina
Cornell U.
Courtauld Institute, London, England
Cranbrook.   Cranbrook Academy of Art, Bloomfield Hills, Mich.
E. B. Crocker Art Gallery—*see* Sacramento/Crocker
Crown Zellerbach Foundation, San Francisco, Calif.
Cuenca.   Museo Municipal de Arte, Cuenca, Spain
Currier.   Currier Gallery of Art, Manchester, N.H.   **Currier Gallery School**
Dallas/MFA.   Dallas Museum of Fine Arts, Dallas, Tex.   **Dallas Museum School**
Dallas Public Library, Dallas, Tex.
Darmstadt/Kunsthalle.   Kunsthalle, Darmstadt, Germany
Dartmouth College
Davenport/Municipal.   Davenport Municipal Art Gallery, Davenport, Iowa
Davidson, N.C.   Davidson Art Center, Davidson, N.C.
Dayton/AI.   Dayton Art Institute, Dayton, Ohio.   **Dayton Art Institute School**
De Beers Collection, Johannesburg, South Africa
Decatur.   Decatur Art Center, Decatur, Ill.
De Cordova and Dana Museum—*see* Lincoln, Mass./De Cordova
Delaware Art Center—*see* Wilmington
U. of Delaware
Isaac Delgado Museum of Art—*see* New Orleans/Delgado
Denison U.
Denver/AM.   Denver Art Museum, Denver, Colo.
De Pauw U.
Des Moines.   The Des Moines Art Center, Des Moines, Iowa
Detroit/Institute.   The Detroit Institute of Arts, Detroit, Mich.
de Young.   M.H. de Young Memorial Museum, San Francisco, Calif.
Dillard U.
Djakarta Museum, Djakarta, Indonesia
Downeyville Museum, Downeyville, Calif.
Downtown Community School, NYC
Drake U.
Dublin/Municipal.   Municipal Gallery of Modern Art, Dublin, Ireland
Dubuque/AA.   Dubuque Art Association, Dubuque, Iowa
Duisburg.   Stadtische Museum, Duisburg, Germany
Duke U.
Dusseldorf.   Kunstmuseum der Stadt Dusseldorf, Dusseldorf, Germany
Earlham College
Eastern Michigan U.
Eastern Oregon College
Eastland Shopping Center, Detroit, Mich.
Eaton Paper Corp.
Edinburgh/National.   National Gallery of Scotland, Edinburgh, Scotland
Eilat.   Museum of Modern Art, Eilat, Israel
Eindhoven.   Stedelijk van Abbe-Museum, Eindhoven, Holland
Equitable Life Assurance Society of the U.S.
Essen.   Museum Folkwang, Essen, Germany
Esslingen.   Stadtische Museum, Esslingen, Germany
Evansville.   Evansville Museum of Arts and Sciences, Evansville, Ind.   **Evansville Museum
   School**
Everett Junior College
Everhart Museum—*see* Scranton/Everhart
Everson Museum of Art—*see* Syracuse/Everson

Exeter.   Phillips Exeter Academy, The Lamont Art Gallery, Exeter, N.H.
Fairleigh Dickinson U.
Fairmount Park Association, Philadelphia, Pa.
Farmers Elevator Insurance Co.
William A. Farnsworth Library and Art Museum—*see* Rockland/Farnsworth
Father Judge Mission Seminary, Lynchburg, Va.
Hamilton Easter Field Foundation, Portland, Me.
57th Madison Corp., NYC
Finch College
First National Bank, Iowa City, Iowa
First National Bank, Madison, Wisc.
First National Bank of Memphis, Memphis, Tenn.
First National Bank, Minneapolis, Minn.
First National Bank of Nevada, Reno, Nev.
First National City Bank, NYC
Fisk U.
Fitchburg/AM.   Fitchburg Art Museum, Fitchburg, Mass.
525 William Penn Plaza, Philadelphia, Pa.
Flint/Institute.   Flint Institute of Arts, Flint, Mich.
Florence, Italy.   Galleria dell'Accademia, Florence, Italy
Florence, S.C., Museum.   Florence Museum, Florence, S.C.
Florida Gulf Coast Art Center, Inc.—*see* Clearwater/Gulf Coast
Florida Southern College
Florida State U.
U. of Florida
Fontana-Hollywood Corp., NYC
Ford Foundation
Ford Motor Company
Fort Dodge/Banden.   Banden Memorial Art Gallery, Fort Dodge, Iowa
Fort Wayne/AM.   Fort Wayne Art Museum, Fort Wayne, Ind.
Fort Worth.   Fort Worth Art Center, Fort Worth, Tex.
405 Park Avenue, NYC
France/National.   Musee National d'Art Moderne, Paris, France (*see also* Paris/Moderne)
Frankfurt am Main.   Stadelsches Kunstinstitut, Frankfurt am Main, Germany
Franklin Institute, Philadelphia, Pa.
Free Library of Philadelphia, Philadelphia, Pa.
French Ministry of National Education, Paris, France
Friends of Art, Uniontown, Pa.
Galerie des 20. Jahrhunderts, Berlin, Germany
Gallery of Modern Art, NYC
Gallery of Modern Art, Washington, D.C.—*see* WGMA
Galveston.   Galveston Historical Foundation Inc., Galveston, Tex.
Garcia Corp.
Garnett Public Library, Garnett, Kans.
Geigy Chemical Corp.
General Mills Inc.
General Motors Corp.
State U. of New York, **Geneseo**
George Washington U.
George Washington Carver Junior College
Georgia Institute of Technology
U. of Georgia (incl. Georgia Museum of Art)
Gettysburg College

Ghent.   Musee des Beaux-Arts, Ghent, Belgium
Gibraltar Savings & Loan Association
Gimbel Bros.
U. of Glasgow, Glasgow, Scotland
Glen Alden Corp.
Golden State Mutual Life Insurance Co.
Goucher College
Grand Rapids.   Grand Rapids Art Gallery, Grand Rapids, Mich.
Graphische Sammlung Albertina, Vienna, Austria
Greece/National.   National Museum, Athens, Greece
Grenchen.   Sammlungen der Museumgesellschaft, Grenchen, Switzerland
Grenoble.   Musee des Beaux-Arts de Grenoble, Grenoble, France
Grinnell College
Grolier Club, NYC
Grunwald Foundation for Graphic Arts, Los Angeles, Calif.
Guadalajara.   Museo de Bellas Artes, Guadalajara, Mexico
The Solomon R. Guggenheim Museum—*see* SRGM
Guild Hall, East Hampton, N.Y.
Guild Plastics Co.
Gulf Coast Art Center—*see* Clearwater/Gulf Coast
Hackley Art Center—*see* Muskegon/Hackley
Hagen.   Karl-Ernst-Osthaus-Museum, Hagen, Germany
Hagerstown/County MFA.   Washington County Museum of Fine Arts, Hagerstown, Md.
The Hague.   Haags Gemeentemuseum, The Hague, Holland
Haifa.   Museum of Modern Art, Haifa, Israel
Hallmark Collection
Hamburg.   Hamburger Kunsthalle, Hamburg, Germany
Hamilton College
Hamline U.
Hampton Institute
Hannover.   Stadtische Galerie, Hannover, Germany
Harlem Hospital, NYC
Harmon Foundation Inc., NYC
Hartford/Wadsworth.   The Wadsworth Atheneum, Hartford, Conn.
Harvard U.
Havana/Nacional.   Museo Nacional, Havana, Cuba
U. of Hawaii
Hebron Academy, Hebron, Me.
Heckscher Museum—*see* Huntington, N.Y./Heckscher
Hemisphere Club, NYC
Hempstead Bank, Hempstead, N.Y.
John Herron Art Institute—*see* Indianapolis/Herron
The Hertz Corp.
Hickory, N.C.   Hickory Museum of Art, Hickory, N.C.
Historical Society of Montana, Helena, Mont.
Hofstra U.
Hollins College
Holyoke Public Library, Holyoke, Mass.
Home Savings and Loan Association
Honolulu Academy of Arts, Honolulu, Hawaii.   **Honolulu Academy School**
Houston/MFA.   Museum of Fine Arts of Houston, Houston, Tex.   **Houston Museum School**
Howard College
Howard U.

J. L. Hudson Co.
Hunter College of the City University of New York
Huntington, N.Y./Heckscher. Heckscher Museum, Huntington, N.Y.
IBM. International Business Machines
ICA, Boston. Institute of Contemporary Art, Boston, Mass.
ICA, London. Institute of Contemporary Art, London, England
ICA, Washington, D.C. Institute of Contemporary Arts, Washington, D.C.
ILGWU. International Ladies' Garment Workers Union, NYC
Illinois State Museum of Natural History and Art—*see* Springfield, Ill./State
Illinois Wesleyan U.
Illinois State Normal U.
U. of Illinois
Immaculate Heart College
Indian Head Mills, Inc.
Indiana National Bank, Indianapolis, Ind.
Indiana State College
Indiana (Pa.) State Teachers College
Indiana U.
Indianapolis/Herron. John Herron Art Institute, Indianapolis, Ind.
Industrial Museum, Barcelona, Spain
Inland Steel Co.
Institute of Contemporary Art, Boston—*see* ICA, Boston
Institute of Contemporary Art, London—*see* ICA, London
Institute of Contemporary Arts, Washington, D.C.—*see* ICA, Washington, D.C.
Institute of International Education, London, England
International Institute for Aesthetic Research, Turin, Italy
International Minerals & Chemicals Corp.
Iowa State Education Association, Des Moines, Iowa
Iowa State Fair, Des Moines, Iowa
Iowa Wesleyan College
State College of Iowa
State U. of Iowa
Iowa State U. of Science and Technology
Jacksonville/AM. Jacksonville Art Museum, Jacksonville, Fla.
Japanese Craft Museum, Tokyo, Japan
Jay Mfg. Co.
Jesus College (Cambridge U.), Cambridge, England
Jewish Museum, NYC
Jewish Theological Seminary of America, NYC
Johannesburg/Municipal. Municipal Art Gallery, Johannesburg, South Africa
Johns Hopkins U.
S. C. Johnson & Son, Inc.
Johnson College
Joslyn Art Museum—*see* Omaha/Joslyn
Kaiserslautern Museum, Kaiserslautern, Germany
Kalamazoo/Institute. The Kalamazoo Institute of Arts, Kalamazoo, Mich.
Kamakura. Modern Art Museum of Kanagawa Prefecture, Kamakura, Japan
Kansas City/Nelson. William Rockhill Nelson Gallery of Art, Kansas City, Mo.
U. of Kansas City
Kansas State College
U. of Kansas
Karachi. Art Council of Pakistan, Karachi, Pakistan
Karlsruhe. Staatliche Kunsthalle, Karlsruhe, Germany

Kassel. Stadtische Kunstsammlungen, Kassel, Germany
U. of Kentucky
Kestner-Museum, Hannover, Germany
Knoll Associates Inc.
Krakow/National. National Museum, Krakow, Poland
Kultusministerium, Hannover, Germany
Kunsthalle, Basel, Basel, Switzerland
Kunstkredit, Basel, Switzerland
La France Art Institute, Philadelphia, Pa.
La Jolla. Art Center in La Jolla, La Jolla, Calif.
The Lamont Art Gallery—*see* Exeter
Lane Foundation, Leominster, Mass.
Lannan Foundation, NYC
La Plata. Museo de La Plata, La Plata, Argentina
Lawrence College
Layton School of Art, Milwaukee, Wisc.
League of Nations, Geneva, Switzerland
Lehigh U.
Leipzig. Museum der Bildenden Kunste Leipzig, Leipzig, Germany
Leverkusen. Stadtisches Museum Leverkusen, Leverkusen, Germany
Library of Congress, Washington, D.C.
Liege. Musee des Beaux Arts, Liege, Belgium
Lille. Palais des Beaux-Arts, Lille, France
Eli Lilly & Co.
Lima, Peru. Instituto de Arte Contemporaneo, Lima, Peru
Lincoln, Mass./De Cordova. De Cordova and Dana Museum, Lincoln, Mass.
Lincoln Life Insurance Co.
Linz. Oberosterreichisches Landesmuseum, Linz, Austria
Little Rock/MFA. Museum of Fine Arts, Little Rock, Ark.
Liverpool/Walker. Walker Art Gallery, Liverpool, England
Lodz. Muzeum Sztuki w Lodzi, Lodz, Poland
Long Beach/MA. Long Beach Museum of Art, Long Beach, Calif.
Long Beach State College
Longview Foundation
Look **Magazine**
Los Angeles/County MA. Los Angeles County Museum of Art, Los Angeles, Calif.
Los Angeles County Fair Association, Los Angeles, Calif.
Los Angeles Public Library, Los Angeles, Calif.
Lotus Club, NYC
Louisiana State U. and Agricultural and Mechanical College
Louisville/Speed. J. B. Speed Art Museum, Louisville, Ky.
U. of Louisville
The Joe and Emily Lowe Art Gallery—*see* U. of Miami
The Joe and Emily Lowe Foundation, NYC
Lucerne. Kunstmuseum Luzern, Lucerne, Switzerland
Lugano. Museo Civico di Belle Arti, Lugano, Switzerland
Luther College
Lytton Savings and Loan Association
MIT. Massachusetts Institute of Technology, Cambridge, Mass.
MMA. The Metropolitan Museum of Art, NYC
MOMA. The Museum of Modern Art, NYC. **MOMA School**
Norman MacKenzie Art Gallery—*see* Regina/MacKenzie
MacMurray College

R. H. Macy & Co.
Madrid/Nacional. Museo Nacional de Arte Contemporaneo, Madrid, Spain
Maine State Museum—*see* Augusta, Me./State
U. of Maine
Mannheim. Stadtische Kunsthalle, Mannheim, Germany
Mansfield State College
Manufacturers Hanover Trust Co., NYC
Marquette U.
Marshall Field & Co.
Marshall U.
Mary Washington College of the U. of Virginia
U. of Massachusetts
Massillon Museum, Massillon, Ohio
McCann-Erickson, Inc.
McDonald & Company
McDonnell & Co. Inc.
Marion Koogler McNay Art Institute—*see* San Antonio/McNay
Mead Corporation
Melbourne/National. National Gallery of Victoria, Melbourne (Victoria), Australia
Memphis/Brooks. Brooks Memorial Art Gallery, Memphis, Tenn.
Mendoza. Museo de Historia Natural, Mendoza, Argentina
Mestrovic Gallery, Split, Yugoslavia
Mestrovic Museum, Zagreb, Yugoslavia
Metalcraft Corp.
Meta-Mold Aluminum Co.
The Metropolitan Museum of Art, NYC—*see* MMA
Mexico City/Nacional. Museo Nacional de Arte Moderno, Mexico City, Mexico
Miami/Modern. Miami Museum of Modern Art, Miami, Fla.
U. of Miami (incl. The Joe and Emily Lowe Art Gallery)
James A. Michener Foundation, Allentown, Pa.
Michigan Consolidated Gas Co.
Michigan State U.
U. of Michigan
Milan. Civica Galleria d'Arte Moderna, Milan, Italy
Miles Laboratories Inc.
The Miller Co.
Millikin U.
Mills College
Mills College of Education
Milton Academy, Milton, Mass.
Milwaukee. Milwaukee Art Center, Milwaukee, Wisc.
Milwaukee-Downer College
Milwaukee *Journal*
Minneapolis/Institute. Minneapolis Institute of Arts, Minneapolis, Minn. **Minneapolis Institute School**
Minnesota State Historical Society, St. Paul, Minn.
U. of Minnesota (at Duluth, Minneapolis, Morris, St. Paul)
Mint Museum of Art—*see* Charlotte/Mint
Mitsui Bank of Japan
Mons. Musee des Beaux-Arts, Mons, Belgium
Montana State College
Montana State U.
Montclair/AM. Montclair Art Museum, Montclair, N.J.

Montevideo/Municipal.   Museo Municipal de Bellas Artes, Montevideo, Uruguay
Montpelier/Wood.   Thomas W. Wood Art Gallery, Montpelier, Vt.
Montreal/MFA.   Montreal Museum of Fine Arts, Montreal (Que.), Canada
Montreal Trust Co.
The Morgan Library
Morgan State College
Morristown/Junior.   Morris Junior Museum, Morristown, N.J.
Moscow/Western.   Museum of Western Art, Moscow, U.S.S.R.
Mount Holyoke College
Mt. Vernon High School, Mt. Vernon, Wash.
Muhlenberg College
Mulvane Art Museum—*see* Washburn U. of Topeka
Munich/State.   Munchner Stadtmuseum, Munich, Germany
Municipal U. of Omaha
Munson-Williams-Proctor Institute—*see* Utica
Munster.   Landesmuseum fur Kunst und Kulturgeschichte, Munster, Germany
Musee du Jeu de Paume, Paris, France
Musee de Verviers, Verviers, Belgium
Museo de Arte Moderno, Barcelona—*see* Barcelona
Museo Municipal de Bellas Artes, Montevideo—*see* Montevideo
Museo Municipal de Bellas Artes y Arte Nacional, Buenos Aires—*see* Buenos Aires
Museo Nacional de Bellas Artes, Buenos Aires—*see* Argentina
Museo Nacional de Bellas Artes, Montevideo—*see* Uruguay
Museo Nacional de Historia, Mexico City, Mexico
Museo Rosario, Santa Fe, Argentina
Museum of the City of New York
Museum of Contemporary Crafts, NYC
Museum of Living Art—*see* PMA
Museum of Military History, Washington, D.C.
Museum of Modern Art, Israel—*see* Haifa
The Museum of Modern Art, NYC—*see* MOMA
Museum of New Mexico Art Gallery—*see* Santa Fe, N.M.
Museum of Science and Industry, Chicago, Ill.
Museum of Western Art, Tokyo—*see* National Museum of Western Art, Tokyo
Museum des 20. Jahrhunderts, Vienna, Austria
Muskegon/Hackley.   Hackley Art Center, Muskegon, Mich.
NAD.   The National Academy of Design, NYC
NIAL.   National Institute of Arts and Letters, NYC
NYPL.   The New York Public Library, NYC
NYU.   New York University, NYC
Nantucket.   Artists' Association of Nantucket, Nantucket, Mass.
Nashville.   Tennessee Fine Arts Center, Nashville, Tenn.
The National Academy of Design—*see* NAD
National Academy of Sciences, Washington, D.C.
National Arts Foundation, NYC
National Gallery, Washington, D. C. (incl. Rosenwald Collection)
National Gallery of Canada—*see* Ottawa/National
National Gallery of Scotland—*see* Edinburgh/National
National Institute of Arts and Letters—*see* NIAL
National Museum, Athens—*see* Greece/National
National Museum of Israel—*see* Bezalel Museum
National Museum of Western Art, Tokyo, Japan
National Orange Show, San Bernardino, Calif.

National U.—*see* George Washington U.
Nebraska State Teachers College
U. of Nebraska
Neenah/Bergstrom. John Nelson Bergstrom Art Center and Museum, Neenah, Wisc.
William Rockhill Nelson Gallery of Art—*see* Kansas City/Nelson
U. of Nevada
Newark Museum, Newark, N.J.
Newark Public Library, Newark, N.J.
New Britain. Art Museum of the New Britain Institute, New Britain, Conn.
New Haven Public Library, New Haven, Conn.
U. of New Hampshire
New Jersey State Museum—*see* Trenton/State
New London. Lyman Allyn Museum, New London, Conn.
U. of New Mexico
New Orleans/Delgado. Isaac Delgado Museum of Art, New Orleans, La.
State U. of New York, **New Paltz**
New School for Social Research
New Trier High School, Winnetka, Ill.
New York Coliseum, NYC
New York Hilton Hotel, NYC
The New York Public Library—*see* NYPL
New York University—*see* NYU
Norfolk. Norfolk Museum of Arts and Sciences, Norfolk, Va.
North Carolina/State. North Carolina State Museum, Raleigh, N.C. (*see also* Raleigh/NCMA)
North Carolina Museum of Art—*see* Raleigh/NCMA
U. of North Carolina
U. of North Dakota
Northeast Missouri State Teachers College
Northland College
North Shore State Bank, Milwaukee, Wisc.
North Texas State U.
Northwest Missouri State College
Northwestern U.
Norton Gallery and School of Art—*see* West Palm Beach/Norton
U. of Notre Dame
Nurnberg. Stadtische Kunstsammlungen, Nurnberg, Germany
Oakland/AM. Oakland Art Museum, Oakland, Calif.
Oberlin College
Ogunquit. Museum of Art of Ogunquit, Ogunquit, Me.
Ohio Wesleyan U.
The Ohio State U.
Ohio U.
Oklahoma. Oklahoma Art Center, Oklahoma City, Okla.
Oklahoma City U.
U. of Oklahoma
Oldenburg. Oldenburger Stadtmuseum, Oldenburg, Germany
The Olsen Foundation Inc., New Haven, Conn.
Omaha/Joslyn. Joslyn Art Museum, Omaha, Neb.
Oran. Musee Demaeght, Oran, Algeria
Oregon State U.
U. of Oregon
Orlando. Central Florida Museum, Orlando, Fla.
Osaka/Municipal. Osaka Municipal Art Museum, Osaka, Japan

Oslo/National.   Nasjonalgalleriet, Oslo, Norway
Otis Art Institute, Los Angeles, Calif.
Ottawa/National.   National Gallery of Canada, Ottawa, Canada
PAFA.   The Pennsylvania Academy of the Fine Arts, Philadelphia, Pa.
PCA.   Print Council of America, NYC
PMA.   The Philadelphia Museum of Art, Philadelphia, Pa. (incl. the Museum of Living Art
   and the Rodin Museum).   **Philadelphia Museum School**
Pacific Indemnity Co.
Palm Beach—*see* Society of the Four Arts
Palos Verdes.   Palos Verdes Art Gallery, Palos Verdes, Calif.   **Palos Verdes Community Arts**
   Association
Paris/Moderne.   Musee d'Art Moderne de la Ville de Paris, Paris, France (*see also*
   France/National)
Park College
The Parrish Museum—*see* Southampton/Parrish
Pasadena/AM.   The Pasadena Art Museum, Pasadena, Calif.   **Pasadena Museum School**
Peabody Institute of the City of Baltimore
Peabody Museum, Salem, Mass.
Pendleton High School, Pendleton, Ore.
The Pennsylvania Academy of the Fine Arts—*see* PAFA
The Pennsylvania State U.
U. of Pennsylvania
Pensacola.   Pensacola Art Center, Pensacola, Fla.
The Pentagon, Washington, D.C.
Pepsi-Cola Co.
The Philadelphia Museum of Art—*see* PMA
Philbrook Art Center—*see* Tulsa/Philbrook
Phillips.   The Phillips Gallery, Washington, D.C.   **The Phillips Gallery School**
Phillips Academy, Addison Gallery of American Art—*see* Andover/Phillips
Phillips Exeter Academy, The Lamont Art Gallery—*see* Exeter
Phoenix.   Phoenix Art Center, Phoenix, Ariz.
Pittsfield/Berkshire.   Berkshire Atheneum, Pittsfield, Mass.
Pomona College
Portland, Me./MA.   Portland Museum of Art, Portland, Me.
Portland, Ore./AM.   Portland Art Museum, Portland, Ore.   **Portland (Ore.) Museum School**
Portland State College (Ore.)
Prague/National.   Narodni (National) Galerie, Prague, Czechoslovakia
Pratt Institute
Princeton Print Club, Princeton, N.J.
Princeton U.
The Print Club, Philadelphia
Print Club of Rochester, Rochester, N.Y.
Print Council of America—*see* PCA
Provincetown/Chrysler.   Walter P. Chrysler Museum of Art, Provincetown, Mass.
Prudential Lines Inc.
Publishers Printing Co.
U. of Puerto Rico
The Pure Oil Co.
Quaker Ridge School, NYC
Queens College of the City University of New York
Queens U., Kingston (Ont.), Canada
RAC.   Richmond Art Center, Richmond, Calif.
RISD.   Rhode Island School of Design, Providence, R.I.

Radio Corporation of America
Raleigh/NCMA. North Carolina Museum of Art, Raleigh, N.C. (*see also* North Carolina/State)
Randolph-Macon College
Randolph-Macon Woman's College
Ration Mfg. Co.
Readers Digest
Reading/Public. Reading Public Museum and Art Gallery, Reading, Pa.
Recklinghausen. Stadtische Kunsthalle, Recklinghausen, Germany
Red Wing. Interstate Clinic, Red Wing, Minn.
Reed College
Regina/MacKenzie. Norman MacKenzie Art Gallery, Regina (Sask.), Canada
Remington-Rand Corp.
Rennes. Musee des Beaux Arts (of the Musee de Rennes), Rennes, France
Revlon Inc.
Reynolds Metals Co.
Rhode Island School of Design—*see* RISD
Richmond Art Center—*see* RAC
Rijksmuseum Amsterdam, Amsterdam, Holland
Rijksmuseum Kroller-Muller, Otterlo, Holland
Ringling. John and Mable Ringling Museum of Art, Sarasota, Fla. **Ringling School of Art**
Rio Cuarto. Museo Municipal de Bellas Artes, Rio Cuarto, Argentina
Rio de Janeiro. Museu de Arte Moderna, Rio de Janeiro, Brazil
Ripon College
Riverside Museum, NYC
Sara Roby Foundation, NYC
Rochester/Memorial. Rochester Memorial Art Gallery, Rochester, N.Y.
U. of Rochester
Rockefeller Brothers Fund, NYC
Rockefeller Center, NYC
Rockefeller Institute, NYC
Rockford/Burpee. Harry and Della Burpee Gallery, Rockford, Ill.
Rockland/Farnsworth. William A. Farnsworth Library and Art Museum, Rockland, Me.
Rodin Museum—*see* PMA
Nicholas Roerich Museum, NYC
Will Rogers Shrine, Colorado Springs, Colo.
Rome/Nazionale. Galleria Nazionale d'Arte Moderna, Rome, Italy
U. of Rome, Rome, Italy
Rosenthal China Co., NYC
Roswell. Roswell Museum and Art Center, Roswell, N.M.
Rotterdam. Museum Boymans-van Beuningen, Rotterdam, Holland
Rouen. Musee des Beaux-Arts et de Ceramique, Rouen, France
Rumsey Hall School, Washington, Conn.
Rutgers U.
SAGA. The Society of American Graphic Artists, NYC
SFMA. San Francisco Museum of Art, San Francisco, Calif.
SRGM. The Solomon R. Guggenheim Museum, NYC
Sacramento/Crocker. E. B. Crocker Art Gallery, Sacramento, Calif.
Sacramento State College
Safad. Glicenstein Museum, Safad, Israel
St. Albans School, Washington, D.C.
St. Antony's College (Oxford U.), Oxford, England
St. Bernard's Church, Hazardville, Conn.

St. John's Abbey, Collegeville, Minn.
St. Louis/City.   The City Art Museum of St. Louis, St. Louis, Mo.
St. Mary's College (Ind.)
St. Patrick's, Menasha, Wisc.
St. Paul Gallery and School of Art, St. Paul, Minn.   **St. Paul School of Art**
St. Petersburg, Fla.   Art Club of St. Petersburg, St. Petersburg, Fla.
U. of St. Thomas (Tex.)
Salt Lake City Public Library, Salt Lake City, Utah
Salzburg.   Salzburger Museum Carolino Augusteum, Salzburg, Austria
San Antonio/McNay.   Marion Koogler McNay Art Institute, San Antonio, Tex.
San Diego.   The Fine Arts Gallery of San Diego, San Diego, Calif.   **San Diego Fine Arts**
   School
San Francisco Art Association, San Francisco, Calif.
San Francisco Municipal Art Commission, San Francisco, Calif.
San Francisco Museum of Art—*see* SFMA
San Jose Library, San Jose, Calif.
San Jose State College
Carl Sandburg Memorial Library, S.C.
Santa Barbara/MA.   Santa Barbara Museum of Art, Santa Barbara, Calif.   **Santa Barbara**
   Museum School
Santa Fe, N.M.   Museum of New Mexico Art Gallery, Santa Fe, N.M.
Sao Paulo.   Museu de Arte Moderna, Sao Paulo, Brazil
Sarah Lawrence College
U. of Saskatchewan, Saskatoon (Sask.), Canada
Savannah/Telfair.   Telfair Academy of Arts and Sciences, Inc., Savannah, Ga.
Savings Banks Association of New York State
Schwebber Electronics
Scranton/Everhart.   Everhart Museum, Scranton, Pa.
Scripps College
Seagram Collection
Seattle/AM.   Seattle Art Museum, Seattle, Wash.
Seattle Civic Center, Seattle, Wash.
Seattle Public Library, Seattle, Wash.
Shasta College
Shelburne.   Shelburne Museum Inc., Shelburne, Vt.
Shell Oil Co.
Shuttleworth Carton Co.
Silvermine Guild of Artists, New Canaan, Conn.   **Silvermine Guild School of Art**
Simmons College
The Singer Company Inc.
Sioux City Art Center, Sioux City, Iowa
Skidmore College
Skowhegan School of Painting and Sculpture, Skowhegan, Me.
W. & J. Sloane, Inc.
Smith College
Smithsonian Institution, Washington, D.C.
The Society of American Graphic Artists—*see* SAGA
Society of the Four Arts, Palm Beach, Fla.
Society of New York Hospitals
Sofu School of Flower Arrangement, Tokyo, Japan
Southampton/Parrish.   The Parrish Museum, Southampton, N.Y.
U. of South Florida
U. of Southern California

Southern Illinois U.
Southern Methodist U.
Southern Oregon College
Southwest Missouri State College
Southwestern College
J. B. Speed Art Museum—*see* Louisville/Speed
Springfield, Ill./State.   Illinois State Museum of Natural History and Art, Springfield, Ill.
Springfield, Mass./MFA.   Museum of Fine Arts, Springfield, Mass.
Springfield, Mo./AM.   Springfield Art Museum, Springfield, Mo.
Staatliche Graphische Sammlung Munchen, Munich, Germany
Stadtische Galerie im Lenbachhaus, Munich, Germany
Standard Oil Co. of New Jersey
Stanford U.
State of California
State Historical Society of Missouri—*see* Columbia, Mo.
State of Iowa
State of Louisiana Art Commission—*see* Baton Rouge
Staten Island.   Staten Island Institute of Arts and Sciences, St. George, S.I., N.Y.
Steel Service Institute, Cleveland, Ohio
Stephens College
Steuben Glass, NYC
Stockholm/National.   Moderna Museet (Nationalmuseum), Stockholm, Sweden
State U. of New York, **Stony Brook**
Storm King Art Center, Mountainville, N.Y.
Stuttgart.   Staatsgalerie Stuttgart, Stuttgart, Germany
Svest, Germany
Sweden/Goteborgs.   Goteborgs Konstmuseum, Gothenburg, Sweden
Sweet Briar College
Sheldon Swope Art Gallery—*see* Terre Haute/Swope
Syracuse/Everson.   Everson Museum of Art, Syracuse, N.Y.   **Syracuse Museum School**
Syracuse U.
Tacoma.   Tacoma Art League Gallery, Tacoma, Wash.
Taft Museum, Cincinnati, Ohio
Taos (N.M.) County Court House
Tate Gallery, London, England
Tel Aviv.   Tel Aviv Museum of Art, Tel Aviv, Israel
Telfair Academy of Arts and Sciences, Inc.—*see* Savannah/Telfair
Temple Israel, St. Louis, Mo.
Temple U.
Tennessee Fine Arts Center—*see* Nashville
U. of Tennessee
Terre Haute/Swope.   Sheldon Swope Art Gallery, Terre Haute, Ind.
Terry Art Institute, Miami, Fla.
Texas Fine Arts Association—*see* Austin
Texas Technological College
Texas Wesleyan College
Texas Western College
U. of Texas
Louis Comfort **Tiffany Foundation,** NYC
Time Inc.
Tishman Realty & Construction Co. Inc.
Tokyo/Modern.   National Museum of Modern Art, Tokyo, Japan
Tokyo U. of Arts, Tokyo, Japan

Toledo/MA. Toledo Museum of Art, Toledo, Ohio
Topeka Public Library, Topeka, Kans.
Topeka U.—*see* Washburn U. of Topeka
Toronto. Art Gallery of Toronto, Toronto (Ont.), Canada
Towner Art Gallery, Eastbourne, England
Trenton/State. New Jersey State Museum, Trenton, N.J.
Tretyakov Art Gallery, Moscow, U.S.S.R.
Harry S. Truman Library, Independence, Mo.
Tulane U. of Louisiana
Tulsa/Philbrook. Philbrook Art Center, Tulsa, Okla.
Tupperware Museum, Orlando, Fla.
Turin/Civico. Museo Civico, Turin, Italy
Turku Museum, Finland
Twentieth Century Fox Film Corp.
UCLA—*see* U. of California (at Los Angeles)
USIA. United States Information Agency
US Coast Guard
US Labor Department
US Maritime Commission
US Military Academy, West Point, N.Y.
US Navy
U.S. Rubber Co.
US State Department
US Treasury Department
Underwood-Neuhaus Corp.
Union Carbide Corp.
Union College (N.Y.)
United Aircraft Corp.
United Nations
Upjohn Co.
Uris Buildings Corp.
Uruguay/Nacional. Museo Nacional de Bellas Artes, Montevideo, Uruguay
Utah State U.
U. of Utah
Utica. Munson-Williams-Proctor Institute, Utica, N.Y.
Utica Public Library, Utica, N.Y.
VMFA. Virginia Museum of Fine Arts, Richmond, Va.
Valparaiso U. (Ind.)
Vancouver. Vancouver Art Gallery, Vancouver (B.C.), Canada
Vanderbilt U.
Vassar College
Venice/Contemporaneo. Museo dell'Arte Contemporaneo, Venice, Italy
U. of Vermont
Victoria (B.C.). Art Gallery of Greater Victoria, Victoria (B.C.), Canada
Victoria and Albert Museum, London, England
Vienna/Stadt. Museen der Stadt Wien, Vienna, Austria
Virginia Museum of Fine Arts—*see* VMFA
Virginia State College
WDAY, Fargo, N.D.
WGMA. Washington Gallery of Modern Art, Washington, D.C.
WMAA. The Whitney Museum of American Art, NYC
The Wadsworth Atheneum—*see* Hartford/Wadsworth
Waitsfield/Bundy. Bundy Art Gallery, Waitsfield, Vt.

Wake Forest College
Walker.   The Walker Art Center, Minneapolis, Minn.
Walker Art Gallery, Liverpool, England—*see* Liverpool/Walker
Warsaw/National.   Muzeum Narodwe (National Museum), Warsaw, Poland
Washburn U. of Topeka, Topeka, Kans. (incl. Mulvane Art Museum)
Washington County Museum of Fine Arts—*see* Hagerstown/County MFA
Washington Federal Bank, Miami, Fla.
Washington Gallery of Modern Art—*see* WGMA
Washington State U.
Washington U. (St. Louis)
U. of Washington
Wellesley College
Wells College
Wesleyan U. (Conn.)
Westminster Academy, Salisbury, Conn.
Westminster Foundation, Iowa City, Iowa
West Palm Beach/Norton.   Norton Gallery and School of Art, West Palm Beach, Fla.
The White House, Washington, D.C.
The Whitney Museum of American Art—*see* WMAA
Wichita/AM.   The Wichita Art Museum, Wichita, Kans.
Wiesbaden.   Stadtisches Museum Wiesbaden, Wiesbaden, Germany
Wilberfeld.   Stadtische Museum, Wilberfeld, Germany
College of William and Mary
Williams College
Wilmington.   Delaware Art Center, Wilmington, Del.
Winston-Salem Public Library, Winston-Salem, N.C.
U. of Wisconsin (at Madison, Milwaukee)
Witte.   Witte Memorial Museum, San Antonio, Tex.
Thomas W. Wood Art Gallery—*see* Montpelier/Wood
Woodward Foundation, Washington, D.C.
College of Wooster
Worcester/AM.   The Worcester Art Museum, Worcester, Mass.   **Worcester Museum School**
Wuppertal.   Staedliches Museum, Wuppertal, Germany
U. of Wyoming
Yale U.
Youngstown/Butler.   The Butler Institute of American Art, Youngstown, Ohio
Youngstown U.
Zanesville/AI.   Art Institute of Zanesville, Zanesville, Ohio
Zurich.   Kunsthaus Zurich, Zurich, Switzerland

Galleries

A. A. A. Gallery
605 Fifth Avenue
New York, N.Y.

ACA Gallery
63 East 57 Street
New York, N.Y.

American Federation of Arts
41 East 65 Street
New York, N.Y.

The Alan Gallery
766 Madison Avenue
New York, N.Y.

The Amel Gallery
831 Madison Avenue
New York, N.Y.

American Art Gallery
Lykkesholms Alle 5
Copenhagen, Denmark

The American Gallery
156 East 64 Street
New York, N.Y.

Galerie Anderson-Mayer
15, rue de l'Echaudé
Paris 6, France

Ankrum Gallery
930 No. La Cienega Boulevard
Los Angeles, Calif.

Galerie Arnaud
212, Boulevard Saint-Germain
Paris 7, France

The Babcock Gallery
805 Madison Avenue
New York, N.Y.

Esther Baer Gallery
1125 High Road
Santa Barbara, Calif.

The Banfer Gallery
23 East 67 Street
New York, N.Y.

The Bay Window Gallery
604 Main Street
Mendocino, Calif.

The Bianchini Gallery
16 East 78 Street
New York, N.Y.

Bolles Gallery
729 Sansome
San Francisco, Calif.

Grace Borgenicht Gallery Inc.
1018 Madison Avenue
New York, N.Y.

Brentano's
586 Fifth Avenue
New York, N.Y.

Bresler Galleries Inc.
729 N. Milwaukee Street
Milwaukee, Wisc.

Burliuk Gallery
Hampton Bays, N.Y.

The Byron Gallery
1018 Madison Avenue
New York, N.Y.

Haydon Calhoun Gallery
2528 Fairmount
Dallas, Tex.

Leo Castelli Inc.
4 East 77 Street
New York, N.Y.

Ceeje Galleries
968 No. La Cienega Boulevard
Los Angeles 69, Calif.

Galerie Chalette
9 East 88 Street
New York, N.Y.

Iris Clert
28, Faubourg Saint-Honoré
Paris 8, France

Cober Gallery
14 East 69 Street
New York 21, N.Y.

Comara Gallery
8475 Melrose
Los Angeles, Calif.

The Contemporaries
992 Madison Avenue
New York, N.Y.

Cordier & Ekstrom Inc.
978 Madison Avenue
New York, N.Y.

D'Arcy Gallery
1091 Madison Avenue
New York, N.Y.

Galerie de France
3, Faubourg Saint-Honoré
Paris 8, France

Peter H. Deitsch Gallery
24 East 81 Street
New York, N.Y.

Delphic Arts
929 Park Avenue
New York, N.Y.

Tibor de Nagy Gallery
149 East 72 Street
New York, N.Y.

Gallery de Tours
559 Sutter Street
San Francisco, Calif.

Dilexi Gallery
1858 Union
San Francisco, Calif.

Terry Dintenfass, Inc.
18 East 67 Street
New York, N.Y.

The Downtown Gallery
465 Park Avenue
New York, N.Y.

Galerie du Dragon
19, rue du Dragon
Paris 6, France

Durlacher Brothers
538 Madison Avenue
New York, N.Y.

Zoé Dusanne Gallery
532 Broadway E.
Seattle 2, Wash.

Dwan Gallery
10846 Lindbrook Drive
Los Angeles, Calif.

East Hampton Gallery
22 West 56 Street
New York, N.Y.

Charles Egan Gallery
41 East 57 Street
New York, N.Y.

Robert Elkon Gallery
1063 Madison Avenue
New York, N.Y.

Andre Emmerich Gallery
41 East 57 Street
New York, N.Y.

Rex Evans Gallery
748½ No. La Cienega Boulevard
Los Angeles, Calif.

Fairweather-Hardin Gallery
109 East Ontario
Chicago, Ill.

Richard Feigen Gallery
53 East Division
Chicago, Ill.

Richard Feigen Gallery
24 East 81 Street
New York, N.Y.

Feigen-Palmer Gallery
515 No. La Cienega Boulevard
Los Angeles, Calif.

Feingarten Gallery
226 East Ontario
Chicago, Ill.

Feingarten Gallery
816 No. La Cienega Boulevard
Los Angeles, Calif.

Ferus Gallery
723 No. La Cienega Boulevard
Los Angeles, Calif.

Arnold Finkel Gallery
121 South 16 Street
Philadelphia 2, Pa.

Fischbach Gallery
799 Madison Avenue
New York, N.Y.

Galerie Karl Flinker
34, rue du Bac
Paris 7, France

The Forum Gallery
1018 Madison Avenue
New York, N.Y.

Fountain Gallery
115 S. W. Fourth Street
Portland, Ore.

French & Co. Inc.
978 Madison Avenue
New York, N.Y.

Rose Fried Gallery
40 East 68 Street
New York, N.Y.

Allan Frumkin Gallery
620 No. Michigan
Chicago, Ill.

Allan Frumkin Gallery
41 East 57 Street
New York, N.Y.

Gallery 63, Inc.
721 Madison Avenue
New York, N.Y.

Gimpel Fils Ltd.
50 South Molton Street
London W.1, England

The Graham Gallery
1014 Madison Avenue
New York, N.Y.

Grand Central Moderns
8 West 56 Street
New York, N.Y.

Richard Gray Gallery
155 East Ontario
Chicago, Ill.

The Greer Gallery
35 West 53 Street
New York, N.Y.

Gres Gallery
1729 20th Street, N.W.
Washington, D.C.

The Griffin Gallery
32 East 58 Street
New York, N.Y.

Grippi and Waddell Gallery
15 East 57 Street
New York, N.Y.

Gump's Gallery
250 Post Street
San Francisco, Calif.

HCE Gallery
Provincetown, Mass.

Hamilton Galleries
8 St. George Street
Hanover Square
London W.1, England

Hanover Gallery
32A St. George Street
London W.1, England

Mary Harriman Gallery Inc.
134 Newbury Street
Boston, Mass.

Dalzell Hatfield Gallery
3400 Wilshire Boulevard
Los Angeles, Calif.

Galerie Camille Hébert
2075 Rue Bishop
Montreal, Canada

Heritage Gallery
724 No. La Cienega Boulevard
Los Angeles 69, Calif.

Fredric Hobbs Fine Art Center
425 14th Street
San Francisco, Calif.

B. C. Holland Gallery
155 East Ontario
Chicago, Ill.

Hollis Gallery
510 Clay Street
San Francisco, Calif.

J. L. Hudson Art Gallery
1206 Woodward
Detroit, Mich.

I. F. A. Gallery
2623 Connecticut Avenue, N.W.
Washington, D.C.

Galleria Il Milione
Via Bigli 2
Milan, Italy

Alexander Iolas Gallery
15 East 55 Street
New York, N.Y.

Martha Jackson Gallery
32 East 69 Street
New York, N.Y.

Sidney Janis Gallery
15 East 57 Street
New York, N.Y.

Jefferson Place Gallery
1212 Connecticut Avenue, N.W.
Washington, D.C.

Paul Kantor Gallery
348 North Camden
Beverly Hills, Calif.

Tirca Karlis Gallery
Provincetown, Mass.

Kasmin Ltd.
118 New Bond Street
London, England

K. Kazimir Gallery
156 East Ontario
Chicago, Ill.

Bob Keene
Southampton, N.Y.

M. Knoedler & Co.
14 East 57 Street
New York, N.Y.

The Kootz Gallery
655 Madison Avenue
New York, N.Y.

The Kornblee Gallery
58 East 79 Street
New York, N.Y.

Kovler Heman Gallery
952 No. Michigan
Chicago, Ill.

The Krasner Gallery
1061 Madison Avenue
New York, N.Y.

Kraushaar Galleries
1055 Madison Avenue
New York, N.Y.

Kunst Kabinett Klihm
Franz-Josef-Strasse 9
Munich 13, Germany

Lucien Labaudt Gallery
1407 Gough Street
San Francisco, Calif.

Felix Landau Gallery
702 No. La Cienega Boulevard
Los Angeles, Calif.

Lane Gallery
1027 Glendon Avenue
Los Angeles 25, Calif.

The Lanyon Gallery
700 Welch Road
Palo Alto, Calif.

Galerie Lawrence
13, rue de Seine
Paris 6, France

R. M. Light & Co., Inc.
421 Beacon Street
Boston 15, Mass.

Albert Loeb Gallery
12 East 57 Street
New York, N.Y.

Galerie Maeght
13, rue de Téhéran
Paris 8, France

Main Street Gallery
642 No. Michigan
Chicago, Ill.

The Marble Arch Gallery
135 East 79 Street
New York, N.Y.

Royal Marks Gallery
19 East 71 Street
New York, N.Y.

Marlborough-Gerson Gallery Inc.
41 East 57 Street
New York, N.Y.

Pierre Matisse Gallery
41 East 57 Street
New York, N.Y.

Doris Meltzer Gallery
38 West 57 Street
New York, N.Y.

Mickelson's Gallery
707 "G" Street, N.W.
Washington, D.C.

The Midtown Galleries
11 East 57 Street
New York, N.Y.

The Milch Gallery
21 East 67 Street
New York, N.Y.

Boris Mirski Gallery
168 Newbury Street
Boston, Mass.

Mission Gallery
Taos, N.M.

The Morris Gallery
174 Waverly Place
New York 14, N.Y.

Donald F. Morris Gallery
    —see Park Gallery

Rolf Nelson Gallery
669 No. La Cienega Boulevard
Los Angeles, Calif.

The New Art Centre
41 Sloane Street
London S.W.1, England

Nihonbashi Gallery
3-1 Nihonbashi-Tori
Tokyo, Japan

Notizie Gallery
Piazza Caesare Augusto
Turin, Italy

Frank Oehlschlaeger Gallery
107 East Oak
Chicago, Ill.

Frank Oehlschlaeger Gallery
28 Boulevard of the Presidents
St. Armands Key
Sarasota, Fla.

Ontario-East Gallery
235 East Ontario
Chicago, Ill.

The Osborne Gallery
965 Madison Avenue
New York, N.Y.

The Pace Gallery
135 Newbury Street
Boston, Mass.

The Pace Gallery
9 West 57 Street
New York, N.Y.

Park Gallery
20090 Livernois Avenue
Detroit 21, Mich.

Betty Parsons Gallery
24 West 57 Street
New York, N.Y.

The Peridot Gallery
820 Madison Avenue
New York, N.Y.

Perls Galleries
1016 Madison Avenue
New York, N.Y.

Frank Perls Gallery
350 North Camden
Beverly Hills, Calif.

Joan Peterson Gallery
216 Newbury Street
Boston, Mass.

Pogliani Gallery
Via Gregoriana 36/42
Rome, Italy

Poindexter Gallery
21 West 56 Street
New York, N.Y.

The Print Club, Philadelphia
1614 Latimer Street
Philadelphia, Pa.

The Rose Rabow Gallery
2130 Leavenworth
San Francisco, Calif.

Stephen Radich Gallery
818 Madison Avenue
New York 21, N.Y.

Rehn Galleries
36 East 61 Street
New York, N.Y.

The Reid Gallery
23 Cork Street
London W.1, England

Rina Gallery
13 Rechov Schlomzion Hamalka
Jerusalem, Israel

Esther Robles Gallery
665 No. La Cienega Boulevard
Los Angeles, Calif.

Roko Gallery
867 Madison Avenue
New York 21, N.Y.

P. Rosenberg and Co.
20 East 79 Street
New York, N.Y.

Royal Athena II
1066 Madison Avenue
New York, N.Y.

Saidenberg Gallery
1037 Madison Avenue
New York, N.Y.

The Salpeter Gallery
42 East 57 Street
New York, N.Y.

San Francisco Art Center
  —*see* Fredric Hobbs Fine Art Center

The Bertha Schaefer Gallery
41 East 57 Street
New York, N.Y.

Robert Schoelkopf Gallery
825 Madison Avenue
New York, N.Y.

Sculpture Center
167 East 69 Street
New York 21, N.Y.

Otto Seligman Gallery
4710 University
Seattle, Wash.

J. Seligmann and Co.
5 East 57 Street
New York, N.Y.

Devorah Sherman Gallery
619 No. Michigan
Chicago, Ill.

Galerie Smith
42 rue Van Eyck
Brussels, Belgium

Smolin Gallery
19 East 71 Street
New York, N.Y.

Galerie Springer
Kurfürstendamm 16
Berlin, Germany

The Stable Gallery
33 East 74 Street
New York, N.Y.

Stables Gallery
North Pueblo Road
Taos, N.M.

Staempfli Gallery
47 East 77 Street
New York, N.Y.

Allan Stone Gallery
48 East 86 Street
New York, N.Y.

David Stuart Gallery
807 No. La Cienega Boulevard
Los Angeles, Calif.

The Swetzoff Gallery
119 Newbury Street
Boston, Mass.

The Terrain Gallery
39 Grove Street
New York, N.Y.

Tokyo Gallery
5, 7-chome, Ginza Nishi
Tokyo, Japan

A. Tooth & Sons
31 Bruton Street
London W.1, England

Catherine Viviano Gallery
42 East 57 Street
New York, N.Y.

Waddington Gallery
2 Cork Street
London W.1, England

Maynard Walker Gallery
117 East 57 Street
New York, N.Y.

Ward-Nasse Gallery
118 Newbury Street
Boston, Mass.

Weyhe Gallery
794 Lexington Avenue
New York 21, N.Y.

Ruth White Gallery
42 East 57 Street
New York, N.Y.

The Willard Gallery
29 East 72 Street
New York, N.Y.

The Howard Wise Gallery
50 West 57 Street
New York, N.Y.

Gordon Woodside Gallery
803 East Union Avenue
Seattle 22, Wash.

World House Galleries
987 Madison Avenue
New York, N.Y.

The Zabriskie Gallery
36 East 61 Street
New York, N.Y.

Jake Zeitlin Gallery
815 No. La Cienega Boulevard
Los Angeles 69, Calif.

a

AACH, HERB. b. March 24, 1923, Cologne, Germany. STUDIED: Stanford U.; Brooklyn Museum School; Pratt Institute; School of Fine Arts, Cologne; Escuela de Pintura y Escultura, Mexico City (with John Ferren, Rufino Tamayo, Max Beckmann, Edwin Dickinson, Arthur Osver, Xavier Gonzalez). Traveled Europe, USA, Central America. TAUGHT: Brooklyn Museum School, 1947–51; Hazleton Art League; Kingsbridge Community Center, Bronx, N.Y. Technical consultant on colors. ADDRESS: 50 Falcourt Street, Brooklyn, N.Y. DEALER: J. Seligmann and Co. ONE-MAN EXHIBITIONS: (first) Creative Gallery, NYC, 1952; Stroudsberg Gallery; Hazleton Art League; The Pennsylvania State U.; Scranton/Everhart; Albert Landry, NYC; J. Seligmann and Co., 1964. GROUP: WMAA; PAFA; U. of Illinois, 1961; ART:USA, NYC; Scranton/Everhart; Riverside Museum. COLLECTIONS: Scranton/Everhart.

ACTON, ARLO C. b. May 11, 1933, Knoxville, Iowa. STUDIED: Washington State U., 1958, BA; California Institute of the Arts, 1959, MFA. US Army Medical Corps, 1955–57. TAUGHT: U. of California, Berkeley, 1963. AWARDS: SFMA, Edgar Walter Memorial Prize, 1961; California State Fair, 1961; Richmond (Calif.) Art Association Annual, Second Prize, 1961; San Francisco Art Association, cash award, 1964. ADDRESS: 3556 23rd Street, San Francisco, Calif. DEALER: The Lanyon Gallery. ONE-MAN EXHIBITIONS: (first) Bolles Gallery, San Francisco, 1962. GROUP: SFMA Annuals, 1960, 61, 62, 63; RAC, 1961, 62; Los Angeles/County MA, Cross-section LA—SF, 1961; Oakland/AM, 1960, 61; SFMA, Arts of San Francisco, 1962; Stanford U., Some Points of View for '62, 1962; Fort Worth, The Artist's Environment: The West Coast, 1962; WMAA, Fifty California Artists, 1962–63; Kaiser Center, Oakland, California Sculpture, 1963; III Paris Biennial, 1963. COLLECTIONS: SFMA.

ADAMS, CLINTON. b. December 11, 1918, Glendale, Calif. STUDIED: UCLA, 1940, BA; 1942, MFA. US Army, World War II. Traveled USA and Europe extensively. TAUGHT: UCLA, 1946–54; U. of Kentucky, 1954–57; U. of Florida, 1957; U. of New Mexico. Associate Director, Tamarind Lithography Workshop, 1960–61. ADDRESS: 1917 Morningside Drive, Albuquerque, N.M. DEALER: Felix Landau Gallery. ONE-MAN EXHIBITIONS: (first) UCLA, 1950; Felix Landau Gallery, 1952, 56, 58, 61; Pasadena/AM, 1954; U. of Texas, 1957; U. of Florida, 1957; Louisville/Speed, 1956; Galleria Mazzuchelli, Florence, Italy; Jonson Gallery, Albuquerque, N.M. GROUP: MOMA; MMA; Brooklyn Museum; Library of Congress; Carnegie; PAFA; Cincinnati/AM; Ringling; Oakland/AM. COLLECTIONS: Bibliotheque Nationale; Chicago/AI; Florida State U.; U. of Illinois; Los Angeles/County MA; MOMA; Pasadena/AM; Victoria and Albert Museum.

ADAMS, PATRICIA (PAT). b. 1928, Stockton, Calif. STUDIED: U. of California, with Glenn Wessels, John Haley, 1949, BA, PBK; Brooklyn Museum School, with Max Beckmann, Reuben Tam, John Ferren. Traveled Italy, France, Malta. Worked in Florence, Italy, 1951–52. AWARDS: Fulbright Fellowship (France), 1956; Yaddo Fellowship, 1954, 64.

ADDRESS: Bennington College Station, Bennington, Vt. **DEALER:** The Zabriskie Gallery. **ONE-MAN EXHIBITIONS:** (first) San Joaquin Pioneer Museum and Haggin Art Galleries, Stockton, Calif., 1950; Korman Gallery, NYC, 1954; The Zabriskie Gallery, 1954, 56, 57, 60, 62, 64; Kanegis Gallery, Boston, 1959; Wheaton College, 1959; Bennett College, 1959; Green Mountain College, 1962; Arts and Crafts Gallery, Wellfleet, Mass., 1963; Hotchkiss School, Lakeville, Conn., 1960. **GROUP:** Bordighera, Americans in Europe, 1952; WMAA Annuals, 1956, 58, 61; A.F.A., Collage in America, circ., 1957–58; MOMA, 41 Watercolorists, circ. Europe, 1957; U. of Nebraska, 1958; A.F.A., The New Landscape in Art and Science, circ., 1958–59; WMAA, Fulbright Artists, 1958; Hirschl & Adler Galleries, Inc., NYC, Experiences in Art, I & II, 1959, 60; Tanager Gallery, NYC, The Private Myth, 1961; A.F.A., Lyricism in Abstract Art, circ., 1962–63; PAFA Watercolor Annual, 1959. **COLLECTIONS:** Bordighera; WMAA. **BIBLIOGRAPHY:** Chaet.

ADLER, SAMUEL M. b. July 30, 1898, NYC. **STUDIED:** NAD, 1911. Traveled North and Central America, Europe, Africa. A professional violinist through student years. **TAUGHT:** Privately, 1935–48; U. of Illinois, 1959–60; Associate Member, Institute of Advanced Study, U. of Illinois, 1964; NYU, 1948– . Ex-member, Artists Equity, formerly Vice President and President of the New York Chapter. **AWARDS:** PAFA, J. Henry Schiedt Memorial Prize, 1951; U. of Illinois, P.P., 1952; WMAA, P.P., 1952, 63; Audubon Artists, 1956; Audubon Artists, First Hon. Men., 1957, 59; Audubon Artists, Gold Medal of Honor, 1960; Staten Island, P.P., 1962. **ADDRESS:** 45 Christopher Street, NYC. **DEALER:** Rose Fried Gallery. **ONE-MAN EXHIBITIONS:** (first) Joseph Luyber Galleries, NYC, 1948; Indiana U., 1950; Louisville Art Center Association, 1950; Charlotte/Mint, 1951; Grace Borgenicht Gallery Inc., 1952, 54; Philadelphia Art Alliance, 1954; U. of Illinois, 1959, 60; Grand Central Moderns, 1960; The Babcock Gallery, 1962. **GROUP:** AAAL; Chicago/AI; ART:USA, NYC; Atlanta/AA; Audubon Artists; Birmingham, Ala./MA; Youngstown/Butler; California Palace; Cincinnati/AM; St. Louis/City; Columbia, S.C./MA; Columbus; Corcoran; Dallas/MFA; Dayton/AI; Lincoln, Mass./De Cordova; Denver/AM; Honolulu Academy; Howard U.; Jewish Museum; Omaha/Joslyn; Los Angeles/County MA; MMA; Milwaukee; Cranbrook; Boston/MFA; Santa Barbara/MA; NAD; PAFA; Stanford U.; WMAA; Royal Academy, London. **COLLECTIONS:** Clearwater/Gulf Coast; U. of Illinois; S. C. Johnson & Son, Inc.; NYU; Norfolk; Safad; Staten Island; Utica; WMAA; Youngstown/Butler. **BIBLIOGRAPHY:** Biddle 3; Nordness, ed.; Pearson 2; Pousette-Dart, ed.

AGOSTINI, PETER. b. 1913, NYC. **STUDIED:** Leonardo da Vinci Art School, NYC. **COMMISSIONS:** New York World's Fair, 1964–65. **AWARDS:** Longview Foundation Grant, 1960, 61, 62; Brandeis U., Creative Arts Award, 1964. **ADDRESS:** 151 Avenue B, NYC. **DEALER:** Stephen Radich Gallery. **ONE-MAN EXHIBITIONS:** Galerie Grimaud, NYC, 1959; Stephen Radich Gallery, 1960, 62, 63, 64. **GROUP:** New School for Social Research; Jewish Museum, Recent American Sculpture, 1964; WMAA; MOMA; Claude Bernard, Paris, 1960; Chicago/AI, 1962; Hartford/Wadsworth, 1962; Battersea Park, London, International Sculpture Exhibition, 1963. **COLLECTIONS:** Brandeis U.; Hartford/Wadsworth; ILGWU; Kalamazoo/Institute; MIT; MOMA; U. of Southern California; U. of Texas; Union Carbide Corp.; Walker.

ALBERS, JOSEF. b. March 19, 1888, Bottrop, Westphalia, Germany. **STUDIED:** Academy of Fine Arts, Berlin, 1913–15; School of Applied Art, Essen, 1916–19; Academy of Fine Arts, Munich, 1919–20; Bauhaus, Weimar, 1920–23, where he became an instructor (Weimar-Dessau-Berlin), 1923–33. To USA 1933 to teach and head Art Department at Black Mountain College, to 1940. US citizen 1939. Headed Department of Design at Yale U., 1950–58; Visiting Critic, 1958–60. **TAUGHT:** design, drawing, color and painting. Presented courses, seminars, lecture series in Germany, Mexico, Cuba, Chile, Peru, and many American universities. **MEMBER:** American Abstract Artists; PCA. **COMMISSIONS** (murals): Harvard U.; Corning Glass Building, NYC; Time & Life Building, NYC; Pan-Am Building, NYC. **AWARDS:** Medal of the American Institute of Graphic Arts, 1964; Ford

Josef Albers
Homage to the Square—In and Out. 1959

Foundation Fellowship, 1959; German Federal Republic, Officers Cross First Class of the Order of Merit; Corcoran, William A. Clark Prize, 1954; Chicago/AI, Ada S. Garrett Prize, 1954; PMA, Citation, 1962; Hon. DFA, Yale U., 1962; Hon. DFA, U. of Hartford, 1957. ADDRESS: 8 North Forest Circle, New Haven, Conn. DEALERS: Sidney Janis Gallery; The Contemporaries. ONE-MAN EXHIBITIONS: (first) Goltz Gallery, Munich, 1919; Sidney Janis Gallery, 1949, 52, 55, 58, 59, 61, 64; MOMA, Josef Albers, circ. Latin America, 1964; Yale U., 1956; Galerie Denise Rene, Paris, 1957; Raleigh/NCMA, 1962; Cincinnati/AM, 1949; Kunstverein Freiburg im Breisgau, 1958; Amsterdam/Stedelijk, 1961; Zurich, 1960; and some 100 others. GROUP: American Abstract Artists, 1939; Herbert Herrmann Gallery, Brooklyn, 1949; Galerie Stuttgart, 1948; U. of Illinois, 1951, 52, 53; Hartford/Wadsworth, Josef and Annie Albers, 1953; Zurich, 1956; WMAA, Geometric Abstraction in America, circ., 1962; SRGM, Cezanne and Structure in Modern Painting, 1963; SRGM, Abstract Expressionists and Imagists, 1961; and some 500 others. COLLECTIONS: Amsterdam/Stedelijk; Baltimore/MA; Basel; Bennington College; Berea College; Brown U.; Buffalo/Albright; Carnegie; Chicago/AI; Corcoran; Currier; Denver/AM; Detroit/Institute; Duke U.; Essen; Hagen; Hartford/Wadsworth;

Harvard U.; Hollins College; Leverkusen; Los Angeles/County MA; U. of Louisville; MIT; MMA; MOMA; Mills College; U. of Minnesota; Morgan State College; Muhlenberg College; Munster; New London: U. of New Mexico; North Texas State U.; Park College; Portland, Ore./AM; Rio de Janeiro; SFMA; SRGM; Smith College; Smithsonian; Springfield, Mass./MFA; Stockholm/National; Svest; Toronto; Utica; VMFA; WMAA; Wesleyan U.; U. of Wisconsin; Yale U.; Zurich. BIBLIOGRAPHY: MOMA, The Albers Archive—1. "Documentation in Manuscript" (photocopy, artist's personal record of his professional chronology); 2. Writings on Art (photocopies of typescripts); 3. scrapbooks, clippings, catalogues, photographs, etc. Additional and overlapping data may be found at the Bauhaus-Archiv, Darmstadt, Germany, the Busch-Reisinger Museum, Cambridge, Mass., and the Yale U. Library, New Haven, Conn. Albers 1, 2, 3, 4, 5, 6, 7; American Abstract Artists, ed.; Baur 7; Blanchard; Blesh 1; Chaet; Cheney, M. C.; Christensen; Dorner; Eliot; Frost; Gaunt; Gerstner; Goodrich and Baur 1; Haftman; Hamilton, G. H.; Henning; Hess, T. B.; Janis and Blesh 1; Janis, S.; Kepes, ed.; Kuh 2; McCurdy, ed.; Mendelowitz; *Metro;* Morris; Motherwell 1; Neumeyer; Nordness, ed.; Pearson; Ponente; Pousette-Dart, ed.; Read 2; Ritchie 1; Rodman 2, 3; Seuphor 1.

ALBERT, CALVIN. b. November 19, 1918, Grand Rapids, Mich. STUDIED: Institute of Design, Chicago, with Lazlo Moholy-Nagy, Gyorgy Kepes, Alexander Archipenko. Traveled Europe. TAUGHT: Institute of Design, Chicago; NYU; Brooklyn College; Pratt Institute. FEDERAL A.P.: Painting, sculpture, design exhibitions. AWARDS: Detroit/Institute, The Haass Prize, 1944; ICA, London/Tate, International Unknown Political Prisoner Competition, Hon. Men., 1953; Audubon Artists, First Prize, 1954; Fulbright Fellowship, 1961; L. C. Tiffany Grant, 1963. ADDRESS: 222 Willoughby Avenue, Brooklyn, N.Y. DEALER: The Stable Gallery. ONE-MAN EXHIBITIONS: Paul Theobald Gallery, Chicago, 1941; Puma Gallery, NYC, 1944; Chicago/AI, 1945; California Palace, 1947; Grand Rapids, 1948; Laurel Gallery, NYC, 1950; Grace Borgenicht Gallery Inc., 1952, 54, 56, 57; The Stable Gallery, 1959; Galleria George Lester,

Rome, 1962; MMA, 1952; U. of Nebraska, 1955; Walker, 1954. RETROSPECTIVE: Jewish Museum, 1960. GROUP: Andover/Phillips, The American Line—100 Years of Drawing, 1959; Chicago/AI, Contemporary Drawings from 12 Countries, 1952; MMA, American Watercolors, Drawings and Prints, 1952; A.F.A., The Embellished Surface, circ., 1953–54; Contemporary Drawing from the United States, circ. France, 1954; MOMA, Recent Drawings USA, 1956; U. of Illinois, 1957; WMAA Annuals, 1954, 55, 56, 58, 60, 62; A.F.A., God and Man in Art, circ., 1958–59; Brooklyn Museum, Golden Year of American Drawing, 1956; Chicago/AI, 1962; PAFA, 1949, 53, 64. COLLECTIONS: Chicago/AI; Detroit/Institute; Jewish Museum; Kansas City/Nelson; MMA; U. of Nebraska; Provincetown/Chrysler; WMAA.

ALBRIGHT, IVAN LE LORRAINE. b. February 20, 1897, North Harvey, Ill. STUDIED: Chicago Art Institute School, 1920–23; PAFA, 1923; NAD, 1924; Northwestern U., 1915–16; Illinois School of Architecture, 1916–17; Ecole Regionale des Beaux-Arts, Nantes, 1919. US Army, 1918–19. Traveled Venezuela, USA, Europe. MEMBER: NAD; Chicago Society of Arts, Inc. COMMISSIONS (paintings): "The Portrait of Dorian Gray" for the film, 1943; "The Temptation of St. Anthony" for the film, 1943. AWARDS: Chicago/AI, Faculty Hon. Men., 1923; Chicago/AI, Hon. Men., 1926; Chicago/AI, John C. Shaffer Prize, 1928; Chicago/AI, Norman Wait Harris Medal, 1941, 43; Society for Contemporary American Art, Silver Medal, 1930, Gold Medal, 1931; Chicago/AI, First Prize, 1948; PAFA, Joseph E. Temple Gold Medal, 1942; MMA, Artists for Victory, First Prize, 1942; NAD, Benjamin Altman Prize, 1961; Corcoran, Silver Medal, 1955; Northwestern U., Centennial Award, 1951; Tate, $5,000 Dunn International Prize, 1963; NIAL, 1957. ADDRESS: 55 East Division Street, Chicago, Ill. ONE-MAN EXHIBITIONS: Walden Book Shop, Chicago, 1930; Chicago/AI, 1931; A.A.A. Gallery, NYC (two-man), 1945; A.A.A. Gallery, Chicago (two-man), 1946. RETROSPECTIVE: Chicago/AI, 1964. GROUP: Chicago/AI, 1918, 23, 26, 28, 41, 43, 48; PAFA, 1924, 42; Brussels World's Fair, 1958; WMAA; Corcoran, 1955; NAD. COLLECTIONS: Brooklyn Museum; Carnegie;

Chicago/AI; Dallas/MFA; Hartford/Wadsworth; Library of Congress; MMA; MOMA; PMA; US Labor Department. BIBLIOGRAPHY: Barker 1; Baur 7; Blesh 1; Canaday; Cheney, M.C.; Eliot; Flanagan; Flexner; Haftman; Hall; Jacobson, ed.; Kuh 1, 2; McCurdy, ed.; Mendelowitz; Newmeyer; Pearson 1, 2; Pousette-Dart, ed.; Reese; Richardson; Sweet.

ALCALAY, ALBERT. b. 1917, Paris, France. To USA 1951. TAUGHT: Harvard U., 1962– . AWARDS: Guggenheim Foundation Fellowship, 1959; Boston Arts Festival, First Prize, 1960. ADDRESS: c/o The Krasner Gallery. ONE-MAN EXHIBITIONS: Cortile Gallery, Rome, 1947; Gaetano Chiurazzi, Rome, 1950; Boston Museum School, 1951; Lincoln, Mass./De Cordova, 1954; Philadelphia Arts Club, 1951; The Krasner Gallery, 1959, 61, 62, 63; The Swetzoff Gallery, 1952, 53, 54, 56, 58; Wittenborn Gallery, NYC, 1958; The Pace Gallery, Boston, 1961, 62; Mickelson's Gallery, 1964. GROUP: Rome National Art Quadrennial, 1947; U. of Illinois, 1955, 57, 59; WMAA, 1956, 58, 60; ICA, Boston, View, 1960; PAFA, 1960; MOMA, 1955. COLLECTIONS: Andover/Phillips; Boston/MFA; Colby College; Harvard U.; Lincoln, Mass./De Cordova; MOMA; Rome/Nazionale; U. of Rome; Simmons College.

ALSTON, CHARLES H. b. November 28, 1907, Charlotte, N.C. STUDIED: Columbia U., BA; 1931, MA. TAUGHT: Joe and Emily Lowe Art School, NYC, 1949–57; ASL, 1951– . FEDERAL A.P.: Mural Supervisor; murals for Harlem Hospital, NYC; Golden State Mutual Life Insurance Co. AWARDS: Columbia U., Dow Fellow, 1930; Lessing J. Rosenwald Fund Fellowship, 1939, 40; NIAL Grant, 1958; Atlanta U., First Prize, 1941; Dillard U., P.P., 1942; Joe and Emily Lowe Foundation Award, 1960. ADDRESS: 555 Edgecombe Avenue, NYC. ONE-MAN EXHIBITIONS: John Heller Gallery, NYC, 1953, 55, 56; Feingarten Gallery, NYC, 1960. GROUP: MMA, 1950; Boston/MFA; MOMA; Brussels World's Fair, 1958; Corcoran; WMAA; Detroit/Institute; Baltimore/MA. COLLECTIONS: Abraham Lincoln High School; Atlanta U.; City College; Detroit/Institute; Ford Motor Company; Golden State Mutual Life Insurance Co.;

Harlem Hospital; IBM; U. of Illinois; MMA; WMAA; Youngstown/Butler.

ALTMAN, HAROLD. b. April 20, 1924, NYC. STUDIED: ASL, 1941–42, with George Bridgeman, Stefan Hirsch; Cooper Union, 1941–43, 1946–47, with Morris Kantor, Byron Thomas, Will Barnet; New School for Social Research, 1947–48, with Abraham Rattner; Black Mountain College, 1946, with Josef Albers; Academie de la Grande Chaumiere, 1949–52, with McAvoy. US Army, 1942–46. Traveled Europe, Mexico. TAUGHT: U. of Wisconsin; Indiana U.; U. of North Carolina; N.Y. State College of Ceramics; The Pennsylvania State U. MEMBER: SAGA; California Society of Etchers; PCA. COMMISSIONS (print editions): MOMA; Jewish Museum; New York Hilton Hotel; SAGA; Container Corp. of America "Great Ideas of Western Man" advertising series. AWARDS: Guggenheim Foundation Fellowship, 1961, 63; NIAL Grant, 1963; Chicago/AI, John Taylor Arms Medal; SAGA; PAFA; Tamarind Fellowship; Silvermine Guild; and some 75 others. ADDRESS: P.O. Box 269, Pine Grove Mills, Pa. DEALER: The Contemporaries. ONE-MAN EXHIBITIONS: (first) Galerie Huit, Paris, 1951; Martha Jackson Gallery, 1958; The Contemporaries, 1959, 63; Peter H. Deitsch Gallery, 1960; Felix Landau Gallery, 1962; Gump's Gallery, 1962; Chicago/AI, 1961; SFMA, 1961; Santa Barbara/MA, 1961; Escuela Nacional de Artes Plasticas, Mexico City, 1961; Kenmore Galleries, Inc., Philadelphia, 1963; The Goodman Gallery, Buffalo, 1961; Kasha Heman, Chicago, 1961, 63; Philadelphia Art Alliance, 1959; The Pennsylvania State U., 1963. GROUP: WMAA Annuals, MOMA, Recent Painting USA: The Figure, circ., 1962–63; PCA, American Prints Today, circ., 1959–62; Festival of Two Worlds, Spoleto; PAFA; MMA, Walter C. Baker Master Drawings Collection. COLLECTIONS: Auburn U.; Boston/MFA; Buffalo/Albright; Chicago/AI; Clairol Inc.; Cleveland/MA; Container Corp. of America; Copenhagen; Detroit/Institute; First National Bank, Minneapolis; Haifa; Hartford/Wadsworth; U. of Illinois; U. of Kentucky; Library of Congress; Los Angeles/County MA; Lytton Savings and Loan Association; MMA; MOMA; Milwaukee; Milwaukee *Journal;* NYPL; National Gallery;

New York Hilton Hotel; Norfolk; PAFA; PMA; The Pennsylvania State U.; Princeton U.; Raleigh/NCMA; San Francisco Art Association; Syracuse U.; WMAA; Walker; Woodward Foundation; Yale U.

ALTOON, JOHN. b. 1925, Los Angeles, Calif. STUDIED: Otis Art Institute, Los Angeles; Art Center School, Los Angeles; Chouinard Art Institute, Los Angeles. US Navy, World War II. Traveled France, Spain. TAUGHT: Art Center School, Los Angeles, 1956–60; Otis Art Institute, Los Angeles, 1951–62; UCLA, 1962–63; Chouinard Art Institute, Los Angeles, 1962–63; La Jolla Art Center, summer, 1962. AWARDS: SFMA, Stacy Award, 1950; Joe and Emily Lowe Foundation Award, 1955; Pasadena/AM, P.P., 1959; SFMA, James D. Phelan Award, 1961; Los Angeles/County MA, P.P., 1962. ADDRESS: 11 Sea View Terrace, Santa Monica, Calif. DEALER: David Stuart Gallery. ONE-MAN EXHIBITIONS: (first) Santa Barbara/MA, 1951; Artists' Gallery, NYC, 1953; Ganso Gallery, NYC, 1954; La Jolla, 1960; Ferus Gallery, 1958–62; de Young, 1963; David Stuart Gallery, 1964. GROUP: Carnegie, 1959; WMAA, Fifty California Artists, 1962–63; Santa Barbara Invitational, 1962; SRGM, American Drawings, 1964; SFMA, 1964. COLLECTIONS: La Jolla; Los Angeles/County MA; Pasadena/AM; Stanford U.; WMAA.

AMEN, IRVING. b. July 25, 1918, NYC. STUDIED: ASL, with Vaclav Vytlacil, William Zorach, John Hovannes; Pratt Institute; Leonardo da Vinci Art School, NYC; Academie de la Grande Chaumiere, 1950; Florence and Rome, Italy. US Air Force, 1942–45. Traveled Europe extensively, Russia, Mexico. TAUGHT: Pratt Institute, 1961; U. of Notre Dame, 1962. MEMBER: Artists Equity; Audubon Artists; Boston Printmakers; SAGA; Fellow of the International Institute of Arts and Letters, 1960. ADDRESS: 295 Seventh Avenue, NYC. DEALER: A.A.A. Gallery, NYC; Brentano's. ONE-MAN EXHIBITIONS: (first) New School for Social Research, 1948; Smithsonian, 1949; The Krasner Gallery, 1948. GROUP: USIA, Contemporary American Prints, circ. France, 1954; USIA, 20th Century American Graphics, circ., 1959–61; MOMA, Master Prints from the Museum Collection, 1949;

MOMA, Young American Printmakers, 1953; MMA, Graphic Arts, 1955; U. of Illinois, 50 Contemporary American Printmakers, 1956; ART:USA:59, NYC, 1959; Library of Congress; Brooklyn Museum; IV Bordighera Biennial, 1957; PAFA; NAD; Silvermine Guild; Audubon Artists; SAGA; American Color Print Society. COLLECTIONS: Bezalel Museum; Bibliotheque Nationale; Bibliotheque Royale de Belgique; Boston/MFA; Cincinnati/AM; Graphische Sammlung Albertina; Harvard U.; Library of Congress; MMA; MOMA; NYPL; PMA; Smithsonian; Victoria and Albert Museum; Wilberfeld.

ANDERSON, GUY. b. 1906, Edmonds, Wash. STUDIED with Eustace Zeigler. Traveled USA, Mexico. TAUGHT: Edmonds, Wash.; Spokane Art Center, 1939–40. Staff member, Seattle Art Museum, 1933–44. COMMISSIONS: Tacoma Art League, 1960; murals for: Hilton Inn, Seattle-Tacoma Airport; Seattle Opera House; Seattle World's Fair, 1962. AWARDS: L. C. Tiffany Grant, 1929; Seattle/AM, Art Award; MMA, 1952. ADDRESS: La Conner, Wash. DEALERS: Otto Seligman Gallery; Smolin Gallery. ONE-MAN EXHIBITIONS: (first) Seattle/AM, 1960; Otto Seligman Gallery; Michel Thomas Gallery, Beverly Hills, Calif.; Orris Gallery, San Diego; Smolin Gallery. GROUP: MMA, American Watercolors, Drawings and Prints, 1952; USIA, Eight American Artists, circ. Europe and Asia, 1957–58. COLLECTIONS: Melbourne/National; Mt. Vernon High School; Seattle/AM; Seattle Public Library; Washington State U.

ANDERSON, JEREMY R. b. October 28, 1921, Palo Alto, Calif. STUDIED: San Francisco Art Institute, 1946–50, with David Park, Clyfford Still, Robert Howard, Mark Rothko, S. W. Hayter. US Navy, 1941–45. Traveled France. TAUGHT: San Francisco Art Institute. COMMISSIONS: Fountain for Golden Gateway Redevelopment Project, San Francisco, to be completed 1966. AWARDS: Abraham Rosenberg Foundation Traveling Fellowship, 1950; SFMA, I. N. Walter Sculpture Prize, 1948; San Francisco Art Association, Sculpture Prize, 1959. ADDRESS: 534 Northern Avenue, Mill Valley, Calif. DEALER: Dilexi Gallery, San Francisco. ONE-MAN EXHIBITIONS: (first) Metart Gallery, San Francisco, 1949; Allan Frumkin Gallery, Chicago, 1954; The Stable Gallery, 1954; Dilexi Gallery, San Francisco, 1960, 61, 62, 64; Dilexi Gallery, Los Angeles, 1962. GROUP: SFMA Annuals, 1948, 49, 51, 52, 53, 58, 59, 63; WMAA Annual, 1956; U. of Illinois, 1955, 57; WMAA, Fifty California Artists, 1962–63; Stanford U., Some Points of View for '62, 1962; Kaiser Center, Oakland, California Sculpture, 1963. COLLECTIONS: Pasadena/AM; SFMA. BIBLIOGRAPHY: Seuphor 3.

ANDERSON, JOHN S. b. April 29, 1928, Seattle, Wash. STUDIED: Art Center School, Los Angeles, 1953–54; Pratt Institute, 1954-57, with Calvin Albert. US Army, 1951–53. Traveled Spain, Mexico, USA. TAUGHT: Pratt Institute, 1959–62. ADDRESS: c/o Dealer. DEALER: Allan Stone Gallery. ONE-MAN EXHIBITIONS: (first) Allan Stone Gallery, 1962, also 1964. GROUP: WMAA, 1964. COLLECTIONS: MOMA.

ANDERSON, LENNART. b. August 22, 1928, Detroit, Mich. STUDIED: Chicago Art Institute School, 1946–50, BFA; Cranbrook Academy of Art, 1950–52, MFA; ASL, 1954, with Edwin Dickinson. Traveled Europe; resided Rome, 1958–61. TAUGHT: Chatham College, 1961–62; Pratt Institute, 1962–64; Swain School, New Bedford, Mass., summers, 1963, 64. AWARDS: L. C. Tiffany Grant, 1957, 61; Prix de Rome, 1958–61. ADDRESS: 134 Beekman Street, NYC. DEALER: The Graham Gallery. ONE-MAN EXHIBITIONS: (first) Tanager Gallery, NYC, 1962; The Graham Gallery, 1963; Kansas City/Nelson (two-man, with Edwin Dickinson), 1964. GROUP: WMAA Annuals, 1963, 64; Boston U., 9 Realist Painters, 1964; Carnegie, 1964; Silvermine Guild, 1963; IBM Gallery of Arts and Sciences, American Heritage, 1963; Kansas City/Nelson, 1962; American Academy, Rome, 1958, 59, 60. COLLECTIONS: Detroit/Institute; J. L. Hudson Co.; WMAA.

ANDREJEVIC, MILET. b. September 25, 1925, Zrenjanin, Yugoslavia. STUDIED: School of Applied Arts, Belgrade, 1939–42; Academy of Fine Arts, Belgrade, 1942–47, BA. Traveled Europe; resided Paris, 1953–58. To USA 1958. ADDRESS: 35 West 82 Street, NYC. ONE-MAN EXHIBITIONS: (first) Belgrade/National, 1948; The Green Gallery, NYC, 1961, 63. GROUP:

Galerie Creuze, Paris, 1956–57; Corcoran, 1963; Chicago/AI, 1964; WMAA Annual, 1964; Dallas/MFA, 1962; WGMA, The Formalists, 1963. COLLECTIONS: Allentown/AM; WMAA.

ANDREWS, OLIVER. b. June 21, 1925, Berkeley, Calif. STUDIED: U. of Southern California, 1942; Stanford U., 1942–43, 1946–48, BA; U. of California, Santa Barbara, 1950–51; with Jean Helion, Paris, 1948–49. US Army, 1943–46. Traveled Europe, the Orient. Designed stage sets, 1951–52. TAUGHT: UCLA, 1957– ; San Fernando Valley State College, 1962–63. COMMISSIONS: Sculptural lighting fixtures for Yale U.: the David S. Ingalls Rink, 1958, Stiles and Morse Colleges, 1962; fountain for West Valley Professional Center, San Jose, Calif., 1963. AWARDS: Los Angeles/County MA, Junior Art Council P.P. for Sculpture, 1957, 61; U. of California Institute for Creative Work in the Arts, Travel Fellowship, 1963. ADDRESS: 408 Sycamore Road, Santa Monica, Calif. DEALERS: The Alan Gallery; Frank Perls Gallery. ONE-MAN EXHIBITIONS: Santa Barbara/MA, 1950, 56, 63; Stanford U., 1952; The Alan Gallery, 1955, 59, 61; Frank Perls Gallery, 1960, 61; Gallery Eight, Santa Barbara, 1961; Municipal Art Gallery, Los Angeles (two-man), 1963; Stanford U. (three-man), 1960. GROUP: Los Angeles/County MA, 1953, 56, 57, 59, 61; U. of Minnesota, Contemporary American Sculpture, 1955; WMAA Annual, 1956; Chicago/AI Annual, 1957; UCLA, 1959; MOMA, Recent Sculpture USA, 1959; SFMA Annuals, 1960, 61, 63; La Jolla, 1960, 61; U. of California, Riverside, Four Sculptors, 1958; WMAA, Fifty California Artists, 1962–63; SRGM, The Joseph H. Hirshhorn Collection, 1962; Long Beach State College, 1963; Hartford/Wadsworth, Smallscale Sculpture, 1960; Buffalo/Albright, Contemporary Sculpture, 1963. COLLECTIONS: Los Angeles/County MA; SFMA; Santa Barbara/MA.

ANTREASIAN, GARO. b. February 16, 1922, Indianapolis, Ind. STUDIED: John Herron Art Institute, BFA. TAUGHT: John Herron Art Institute. Technical Director, Tamarind Lithography Workshop, 1960–61. AWARDS: Hoosier Salon, 1944, 49; The Print Club, Philadelphia, 1958, 61; MOMA, 1953. ADDRESS: 615 North Payton Road, Indianapolis, Ind. ONE-MAN EXHIBITIONS: Tulane U.; U. of Notre Dame; Stephens College; Wabash College; Kalamazoo/Institute. GROUP: SFMA, 1942; NAD, 1943; Library of Congress, 1949; MMA, 1950; Boston/MFA; PMA; NYPL; USIA; ART:USA:59, NYC, 1959; PCA, 1959. COLLECTIONS: Albion College; L. S. Ayres & Co.; Boston/MFA; Bradley U.; Brooklyn Museum; Grand Rapids; Indiana National Bank; Indiana U.; U. of Minnesota; National Gallery; U. of Notre Dame; PMA; The Print Club, Philadelphia; Smith College; Southern Illinois U.; Terre Haute/Swope; US Coast Guard.

ANUSZKIEWICZ, RICHARD. b. May 23, 1930, Erie, Pa. STUDIED: Cleveland Institute of Art, 1948–53; Kent State U., 1955–56, BS.Ed.; Yale U., 1953–55, MFA. Traveled western Europe, North Africa. ADDRESS: c/o Dealer. DEALER: Sidney Janis Gallery. ONE-MAN EXHIBITIONS: Youngstown/Butler, 1955; The Contemporaries, 1960, 61, 63. GROUP: U. of Illinois, 1961, 63; NYU, 1961; PAFA, 1962; WMAA, Geometric Abstraction in America, circ., 1962; U. of Minnesota, Duluth, 1962; Silvermine Guild, 1962, 63; Allentown/AM, 1963; Lincoln, Mass./De Cordova, New Experiments in Art, 1963; MOMA, Americans 1963, circ., 1963–64; WGMA, The Formalists, 1963; WMAA, 1963; Chicago/AI, 1964; Tate, Painting and Sculpture of a Decade, 1954–64, 1964; Carnegie, 1964. COLLECTIONS: Akron/AI; Allentown/AM; Buffalo/Albright; Chicago/AI; Cleveland/MA; Corcoran; MOMA; WMAA; Yale U.; Youngstown/Butler.

ARCHIPENKO, ALEXANDER. b. May 30, 1887, Kiev, Ukraine; **d.** February 25, 1964, NYC. STUDIED: Kiev, an art school, 1902–05; Academie des Beaux-Arts, Paris, 1908. To USA 1923; citizen 1928. Traveled Europe and USA extensively. TAUGHT: U. of Washington, 1935–36; U. of Kansas; Allegheny College; opened school in Paris, 1910; opened school in NYC, 1939. ONE-MAN EXHIBITIONS: Hagen, 1910, 60; Darmstadt/Kunsthalle, circ. Germany, 1955; Grosvenor (Gallery), London, 1961; Mannheim, 1962; Andover/Phillips, 1928; Karl Nierendorf Gallery, NYC, 1944; Perls Galleries, 1957, 59; Palazzo Barberini, Rome, 1963; X Venice Biennial, 1920; A.A.A. Gallery, NYC, 110th One-Man, 1954; Dallas/MFA,

44

Alexander Archipenko   *Arabian. 1936*

100th One-Man, 1952. GROUP: Major international exhibitions. COLLECTIONS: Amherst College; Andover/Phillips; Belvedere; Brandeis U.; Chicago/AI; Cleveland/MA; Cranbrook; Darmstadt/Kunsthalle; U. of Delaware; Denver/AM; Detroit/Institute; Dusseldorf; Essen; Hagen; Hannover; Honolulu Academy; U. of Kansas City; Leipzig; MOMA; Mannheim; Miami/Modern; U. of Michigan; U. of Minnesota; Municipal U. of Omaha; Northwestern U.; Omaha/Joslyn; U. of Oregon; Osaka/Municipal; Phillips; Phoenix; Rotterdam; SFMA; SRGM; San Antonio/McNay; Seattle/AM; Tel Aviv; WMAA; Yale U. BIBLIOGRAPHY: Archipenko 1, 2; Barr 1; Baur 7; Biddle 3; Blesh 1; Brown; Brumme; Bulliet 1; Cassou; Cheney, M.C.; Christensen; Daubler and Goll; Dorner; Dreier 2; Gertz; Giedion-Welcker 1, 2; Goodrich and Baur 1; Guggenheim, ed.; Haftman; Hildebrandt; Huyghe; *Index of 20th Century Artists;* Janis and Blesh 1; Janis, S.; Langui; Lee and Burchwood; McCurdy, ed.; Mellquist; Mendelowitz; Neumeyer; Poore; Ramsden 2; Raynal 1; Ritchie 3; Rosenblum; Salvini; Selz, J.; Seuphor 3; Valentine 2; Zaidenberg, ed.; Zervos.

ARONSON, DAVID. b. October 28, 1923, Shilova, Lithuania. To USA 1929. STUDIED: Boston Museum School, with Karl Zerbe; Hebrew Teachers College, Boston. Traveled Europe, Near East. TAUGHT: Boston U., 1954– ; Boston Museum School, 1942–55. COMMISSIONS: Container Corp. of America, 1962. AWARDS: ICA, Boston, First Prize, 1944; ICA, Boston, First Popular Prize, 1955; VMFA, 1946; Boston Museum School, Traveling Fellowship, 1946; Boston Arts Festival, Grand Prize, 1952, 54; Boston Arts Festival, Second Prize, 1953; Tupperware Annual, First Prize, 1954; NIAL Grant, 1958; J. S. Guggenheim Fellowship, 1960; NIAL, P.P., 1961. ADDRESS: Brimstone Lane, Sudbury, Mass. DEALER: Boris Mirski Gallery. ONE-MAN EXHIBITIONS: (first) Niveau Gallery, NYC, 1945, also 1956; Boris Mirski Gallery, 1951, 59; The Downtown Gallery, 1953; Lee Nordness Gallery, NYC, 1960, 61, 63; Rex Evans Gallery, 1961; Westhampton Gallery, NYC, 1961. GROUP: MOMA, Fourteen Americans, circ., 1946; Chicago/AI; U. of Illinois; MMA; ICA, Boston; WMAA; Boston/MFA; Bridgestone Museum; Palazzo di Venezia, Rome. COLLEC-

TIONS: Atlanta/AA; Atlanta U.; Bryn Mawr College; Chicago/AI; Colby College; U. of Illinois; Lincoln, Mass./De Cordova; MOMA; U. of Nebraska; U. of New Hampshire; Portland, Me./MA; Tupperware Museum; VMFA; WMAA; Worcester/AM. BIBLIOGRAPHY: Baur 7; Genauer; Miller, ed. 2; Nordness, ed. Pearson 2; Soby 5.

ATHERTON, JOHN C. b. June 7, 1900, Brainerd, Minn.; d. 1952, New Brunswick, Canada. STUDIED: College of the Pacific; California School of Fine Arts, 1922–25. US Navy, 1918–19. Painter, illustrator and poster artist. AWARDS: MMA, Artists for Victory, Fourth Prize, 1942; Bohemia Club, San Francisco, First Prize, 1928; Hartford/Wadsworth, First Prize, 1922. ONE-MAN EXHIBITIONS: Julien Levy Galleries, NYC, 1938, 39, 42, 44, 46; A.A.A. Gallery, NYC, 1951. GROUP: U. of Illinois, 1950; MOMA; WMAA; PAFA; Chicago/AI. COLLECTIONS: Buffalo/Albright; Chicago/AI; Hartford/Wadsworth; MMA; MOMA; PAFA; WMAA. BIBLIOGRAPHY: Baur 7; Pousette-Dart, ed.

AULT, GEORGE C. b. October 11, 1891, Cleveland, Ohio; d. December 30, 1948, Woodstock, N.Y. STUDIED: U. of London, Slade School; St. John's Wood Art School. Resided Great Britain, 1899–1911. ONE-MAN EXHIBITIONS: Sea Chest Gallery, Provincetown, 1922; Whitney Studio Club, NYC, Bourgeois Gallery, NYC, 1923; The Downtown Gallery, 1926, 28; J. B. Neumann's New Art Circle, NYC, 1927; The Little Gallery, Woodstock, N.Y., 1943; Woodstock (N.Y.) Art Gallery, 1949; The Milch Gallery, 1950; Charlotte/Mint, 1951. RETROSPECTIVE: The Zabriskie Gallery, 1957. GROUP: Independents, NYC, 1920; WMAA. COLLECTIONS: Albany/Institute; Andover/Phillips; California Palace; Cleveland/MA; Dartmouth College; Los Angeles/County MA; MOMA; U. of Nebraska; Newark Museum; Omaha/Joslyn; PAFA; PMA; WMAA. BIBLIOGRAPHY: Baur 7; Brown; Bulliet 1; Cahill and Barr, eds.

AUSTIN, DARREL. b. July 25, 1907, Raymond, Wash. STUDIED: U. of Oregon; U. of Notre Dame and Columbia U., 1926–29; and with Emile Jacques. COMMISSIONS: Medical College of the U. of Oregon, 1933 (mural).

ADDRESS: Saw Mill Hill Road, RFD #3, New Fairfield, Conn. DEALER: Perls Galleries. ONE-MAN EXHIBITIONS: (first) Howard Putzell Gallery, Los Angeles, 1938; James Vigeveno Gallery, Los Angeles (two-man), 1949; Perls Galleries, 1940, 42, 43, 44, 45, 47, 48, 50, 55, 57, 59, 64. COLLECTIONS: Boston/MFA; Detroit / Institute; U. of Georgia; Kansas City/Nelson; Los Angeles/County MA; MMA; MOMA; Montclair/AM; U. of Nebraska; PAFA; Phillips; Portland, Ore./AM; Rochester/Memorial; Smith College. BIBLIOGRAPHY: Baur 7; Bazin; Flanagan; Frost; Miller, ed. 1; Newmeyer.

AVERY, MILTON. b. March 7, 1893, Altmar, N.Y.; d. January 3, 1964, NYC. STUDIED: Connecticut League of Art Students, briefly 1913, with C. N. Flagg. Traveled Europe, USA. AWARDS: Chicago/AI, The Mr. & Mrs. Frank G. Logan Prize, 1929; Connecticut Academy of Fine Arts, Atheneum Prize, 1930; Baltimore Watercolor Club, First Prize, 1949; Boston Arts Festival, Second Prize, 1948; ART:USA:59, NYC, $1,000 Award, 1959. "A Painter's World," a 14-min., 16mm color sound film, shows him at work. ONE-MAN EXHIBITIONS: (first) Opportunity Gallery, NYC, 1928; Gallery 144, NYC, 1932; Curt Valentine Gallery, NYC, 1935, 36, 38, 41; Phillips, 1943, 44; P. Rosenberg and Co., 1943, 44, 45, 46, 47, 50; Arts Club of Chicago, 1944; The Bertha Schaefer Gallery, 1944; Durand-Ruel Gallery, NYC, 1945, 46, 47, 49; Colorado Springs/FA, 1946; Portland, Me./MA, 1946; Laurel Gallery, NYC, 1950; M. Knoedler & Co., NYC, 1950; Grace Borgenicht Gallery Inc., 1951, 52, 54, 56, 57, 58, 59; Baltimore/MA, 1952; Boston/MFA, circ., 1952; Mills College, circ., 1956; U. of Nebraska, 1956; Felix Landau Gallery, 1956, 59; HCE Gallery, 1956, 58, 59; Otto Seligman Gallery, 1958; Philadelphia Art Alliance, 1959; Waddington Gallery, 1962. RETROSPECTIVE: A.F.A./Ford Foundation, circ., 1960. GROUP: PAFA, 1945; Carnegie, 1944; Chicago/AI; Corcoran; WMAA; U. of Illinois; Buffalo/Albright. COLLECTIONS: Andover/Phillips; Atlanta/AA; Baltimore/MA; Barnes Foundation; Brandeis U.; Brooklyn Museum; Bryn Mawr College; Buffalo/Albright; Chase Manhattan Bank; Dayton/AI; Evansville; Exeter; Honolulu Academy; Houston/MFA; U. of Illinois; MMA; MOMA; U. of Minnesota; U. of Nebraska; Newark Museum; PAFA; PMA; Phillips; Santa Barbara/MA; Smith College; Tel Aviv; Utica; WMAA; Walker; West Palm Beach/Norton; Witte; Yale U. BIBLIOGRAPHY: Bazin; Blesh 1; Eliot; Frost; Goodrich and Baur 1; Greenberg 1; Kootz 2; **Kramer;** Mellquist; Nordness, ed.; Pousette-Dart, ed.; **Wight** 2, 3.

Milton Avery   *Two Women. 1959*

b

BAIZERMAN, SAUL. b. December 25, 1889, Vitebsk, Russia; **d.** August 30, 1957, NYC. STUDIED: Imperial Art School, Odessa; NAD; Beaux-Arts Institute of Design, NYC. To USA 1910. Traveled England, Russia, Italy. Fire demolished New York studio 1931, destroying almost all his work. TAUGHT: American Artists School, NYC; U. of Southern California, summer, 1949; Baizerman Art School, NYC, 1934–40. AWARDS: PAFA, Hon. Men., 1949; AAAL Grant, 1951; Guggenheim Foundation Fellowship, 1952; PAFA, Alfred G. B. Steel Memorial Prize, 1952. ONE-MAN EXHIBITIONS: (first) Dorien Leigh Galleries, London, 1924; Eighth Street Gallery, NYC, 1933; Artists' Gallery, NYC, 1938, 48, 57; Philadelphia Art Alliance, 1949; The New Gallery, NYC, 1952, 54; World House Galleries, 1963. RETROSPECTIVE: Walker, circ., 1953; ICA, Boston, 1958; Huntington, N.Y./Heckscher, 1961. COLLECTIONS: U. of Minnesota; U. of Nebraska; PAFA; Walker; WMAA. BIBLIOGRAPHY: Baur 7; Brumme; Goodrich and Baur 1; Pearson 2.

BARINGER, RICHARD E. b. December 3, 1921, Elkhart, Ind. STUDIED: Southwestern U.; Institute of Design, Chicago, with Lazlo Moholy-Nagy, Emerson Woelffer, B.Arch.; Harvard U. Graduate School, with Walter Gropius, B.Arch., M.Arch. US Air Force, World War II. Traveled Europe, Russia, North Africa. TAUGHT: Institute of Design, Chicago; Columbia U. MEMBER: American Institute of Architects. AWARDS: Prix de Rome; Harvard U., Sheldon Traveling Fellowship; American Institute of Architects, 1958 (Residential Design); *Progressive Architecture* Magazine, 1957; *Architectural Record* Magazine, 1958. AD-DRESS: 111 East 26 Street, NYC. DEALER: The Bertha Schaefer Gallery. ONE-MAN EXHIBI-TIONS: (first) Ovington Gallery, Los Angeles, 1945; South Bend Art Center, 1946; Margaret Brown Gallery, Boston, 1949; MIT, 1950; Cambridge (Mass.) School of Design, 1950; The Bertha Schaefer Gallery, 1962, 63; Segno Gallery, Chicago, 1956; Columbia U., 1963; Nelson Taylor Gallery, East Hampton, N.Y., 1962. GROUP: U. of Illinois, 1949, 62; Arts Club of Chicago, 1955, 56, 57, 61; WGMA, The Formalists, 1963; ICA, Boston, 5 Young Americans, 1950; California Palace, 1948; Johns Hopkins U., 1941. COLLECTIONS: Busch-Reisinger Museum; Cooperative Insurance Society; Farmers Elevator Insurance Co.; Pacific Indemnity Co.; Prudential Lines Inc.

BARNES, ROBERT M. b. September 24, 1934, Washington, D.C. STUDIED: Chicago Art Institute School, 1952–56; The U. of Chicago, 1952–56, BFA; Columbia U., 1956; Hunter College, 1957–61; U. of London, Slade School, 1961–63. Traveled Great Britain, France, USA. TAUGHT: Indiana U., summers, 1960, 61; Kansas City Art Institute and School of Design, 1963–64; Indiana U., 1964– . COMMISSIONS: New York Hilton Hotel, 1962 (edition of lithographs). AWARDS: William and Noma Copley Foundation Grant, 1961; Fulbright Fellowship, 1961, renewed 1962; Chicago/AI, 67th Annual. ADDRESS: c/o Dealer. DEALER: Allan Frumkin Gallery, NYC and Chicago. ONE-MAN EXHIBITIONS: (first) Allan Frumkin Gallery, NYC, 1963; Allan Frumkin Gallery, Chicago, 1964. GROUP: Chicago/AI, Exhibition Momentum, 1952, 53, 54, 55; Chicago/AI, Prints from the Graphic Workshop,

1955; Boston Arts Festival, 1958; Chicago/AI Annuals, 1958, 60, 61, 64; State U. of Iowa, Main Current of Contemporary American Painting, 1960; Ravinia Festival, Highland Park, Ill., 1961; WMAA Annual, 1962; Yale U., 1962; Kansas City/Nelson, 1962; SFMA, 1963; MOMA, 60 Modern Drawings, 1963; Chicago/AI, Drawings, 1963. COLLECTIONS: Chicago/AI; MOMA; Pasadena/AM; WMAA.

BARNET, WILL. b. May 25, 1911, Beverly, Mass. STUDIED: Boston Museum School, with Phillip Hale; ASL, with Charles Locke. Traveled USA, Europe. TAUGHT: ASL, 1936– ; Cooper Union, 1945– ; U. of Washington, summer, 1963; Boston Museum School, 1963; Famous Artists Schools, Inc., Guiding Faculty, 1954–64. MEMBER: American Abstract Artists; Federation of Modern Painters and Sculptors. FEDERAL A.P.: Technical advisor in lithography. AWARDS: Corcoran, William A. Clark Prize; Ford Foundation/A.F.A. Artist-in-Residence. ADDRESS: 43 West 90 Street, NYC. DEALERS: Peter H. Deitsch Gallery; Mary Harriman Gallery Inc. ONE-MAN EXHIBITIONS: (first) Hudson D. Walker Gallery, NYC, 1939; Gallery St. Etienne, NYC, 1943; The Bertha Schaefer Gallery, 1947, 49, 51, 53, 55, 60, 62; Peter H. Deitsch Gallery, 1960, 63; Mary Harriman Gallery Inc., 1963; Galleria Trastevere di Topazia Alliata, Rome, 1960. RETROSPECTIVE: ICA, Boston, 1961; U. of Minnesota, Duluth, 1958; Albany/Institute, 1962. GROUP: American Abstract Artists since mid-1940's; Corcoran, 1960; PAFA, 1962; II International Biennial Exhibition of Prints, Tokyo, 1960; WMAA, Geometric Abstraction in America, circ., 1962; WMAA Annuals; MMA, American Paintings Today, 1950; Yale U., 1955; Brooklyn Museum; Carnegie; ICA, Boston; MOMA. COLLECTIONS: Boston/MFA; Brooklyn Museum; Carnegie; Cincinnati/AM; Corcoran; Harvard U.; Honolulu Academy; Library of Congress; MMA; MOMA; Montana State College; NYPL; NYU; PAFA; PMA; Phillips; SRGM; Seattle/AM; Utica; WMAA. BIBLIOGRAPHY: American Artists Congress, Inc.; Farrell; Hayter 1; Janis and Blesh 1; Nordness, ed.; Reese; Smith, A.

BASKIN, LEONARD. b. August 19, 1922, New Brunswick, N.J. STUDIED: NYU, 1939–41; Yale U., 1941–43; New School for Social Research, 1949, MA; Academie de la Grande Chaumiere, 1950; Academy of Fine Arts, Florence, Italy, 1951; privately with Maurice Glickman. US Navy, 1943–46. TAUGHT: Worcester Museum School, 1952–53; Smith College, 1953– Operates the Gehenna Press. AWARDS: Prix de Rome, Hon. Men., 1940; L. C. Tiffany Grant, 1947; Guggenheim Foundation Fellowship, 1953; Library of Congress, Pennell P.P., 1952; SAGA, Mrs. A. W. Erickson Prize, 1953; U. of Illinois, P.P., 1954. ADDRESS: Fort Hill, Northampton, Mass. DEALER: Grace Borgenicht Gallery Inc. ONE-MAN EXHIBITIONS: Glickman Studio, 1939; Boris Mirski Gallery, 1954, 55, 56; Numero Galleria d'Arte, Florence, Italy, 1951; The Little Gallery, Provincetown, 1952; Mount Holyoke College, 1952; Fitchburg/AM, 1952; The Print Club, Philadelphia, 1956; Grace Borgenicht Gallery Inc., 1954, 60; Portland, Me./MA, 1956; Wesleyan U., 1956; U. of Minnesota, 1961; U. of Louisville, 1961. RETROSPECTIVE: Bowdoin College, 1962; Rotterdam, 1961; Smith College, 1963; Worcester/AM, 1957. GROUP: MOMA; WMAA; Brooklyn Museum, 1949, 52, 53, 54, 55; Library of Congress; The Print Club, Philadelphia; SAGA, 1952, 53; Sao Paulo; Brandeis U.; Seattle/AM. COLLECTIONS: Auburn U.; Baltimore/MA; Boston/MFA; Bowdoin College; Brandeis U.; Brooklyn Museum; Chase Manhattan Bank; U. of Delaware; Detroit/Institute; Fitchburg/AM; Harvard U.; Holyoke Public Library; U. of Illinois; Library of Congress; MMA; MOMA; Mount Holyoke College; National Academy of Sciences; National Gallery; U. of Nebraska; New School for Social Research; PMA; St. John's Abbey, Collegeville, Minn.; St. Louis/City; Seattle/AM; Smith College; Utica; WMAA; Wesleyan U.; Worcester/AM. BIBLIOGRAPHY: Baskin; Chaet; Goodrich and Baur 1; Peterdi; Rodman 1, 3; Sachs.

BAYER, HERBERT. b. April 5, 1900, Haag, Austria. STUDIED: Real-Gymnasium, Linz, Austria; architecture with Prof. Schmidthammer, Linz, 1919; Bauhaus, Weimar, 1921, with Vassily Kandinsky. Traveled Europe, Central America, Japan, North Africa. To USA 1938. TAUGHT: Bauhaus, Dessau, 1925–28; New York Advertising Guild, 1939–40. Designs and plans exhibitions for museums throughout

Leonard Baskin   *Caprice.*

the world. Typographer and designer of type faces, packages, posters, books and charts. Registered Architect. MEMBER: American Abstract Artists; Alliance Graphique Internationale; American Institute of Architects; Aspen Institute for Humanistic Studies; International Institute of Arts and Letters. COMMISSIONS (architectural): Seminar Building, Aspen (Colo.) Institute for Humanistic Studies; factories, Container Corp. of America; Air Force Museum; private residences; (murals): Harvard U.; Seminar Building, Aspen (Colo.) Institute for Humanistic Studies; Colonial Williamsburg; Elementary School, West Bridgewater, Mass.; Container Corp. of America. AWARDS: Poster competitions; art director awards and medals; Milan Triennial, 1930; Medal of the City of Salzburg; Oklahoma, 4th Annual Southwest Abstract Art, First Prize. ADDRESS: P.O. Box B, Aspen, Colo. DEALERS: The Byron Gallery; Kunst Kabinett Klihm. ONE-MAN EXHIBITIONS: (first) Galerie Povolotzki, Paris, 1929; Kunstverein, Linz, 1929; Bauhaus, Dessau, 1931; Kunstlerhaus, Salzburg, 1936; The London Gallery, London, 1937; PM Gallery, NYC, 1939; Black Mountain College, 1939; Yale U., 1940; The Willard Gallery, 1943; Art Headquarters Gallery, NYC, 1943; North Texas State Teachers College, 1943; Outline Gallery, Pittsburgh, 1944; Cleveland/MA, 1952; H. Schaeffer Galleries, Inc., NYC, 1953; Galleria Il Milione, 1954; Aspen (Colo.) Institute for Humanistic Studies, 1955, 64; Kunst Kabinett Klihm, 1954, 57, 59, 62; Fort Worth, 1958; Walker, 1958; Dusseldorf, 1960; Bauhaus-Archiv, 1961;

Andrew-Morris Gallery, NYC, 1963. RET-
ROSPECTIVE: Brown U., The Way Beyond
Art, circ. USA, 1947–49; Germanisches National Museum, Nurnberg, 33 Years of Herbert
Bayer's Work, circ. Germany and Austria,
1956–57. GROUP: Julien Levy Galleries, NYC,
1931, 40; MOMA, Fantastic Art, DADA, Surrealism, 1936; MOMA, Bauhaus: 1919–28,
1938; MOMA, Art and Advertising Art, circ.,
1943; ART:USA:58, NYC, 1958; American
Abstract Artists Annuals, 1959, 60, 61, 62,
63, 64; Marlborough Fine Art Ltd., London, Bauhaus, 1962; Arts Club of Chicago,
1962. COLLECTIONS: Bauhaus-Archiv; Busch-
Reisinger Museum; Cologne; Denver/AM;
Duisburg; Dusseldorf; Essen; Fort Worth;
Graphische Sammlung Albertina; Hagen; Hannover; Harvard U.; Kaiserslautern; Leverkusen; Linz; MOMA; U. of Michigan; Museum
des 20. Jahrhunderts; Oklahoma; Oldenburg;
Omaha/Joslyn; Rome/Nazionale; SFMA;
Smith College; Stuttgart; Vassar College;
Wiesbaden. BIBLIOGRAPHY: Barr 1; Baur 7;
Bayer; Blanchard; Blesh 1; Dorner; Gaunt;
Haftman; Janis, S.; McCurdy, ed.

BAYLINSON, A. S. b. 1882, Moscow, Russia;
d. May, 1950, NYC. Studied with Lattard,
and privately with Robert Henri, Homer Boss.
TAUGHT: ASL. Secretary of Society of Inde-
pendent Artists, NYC, for 17 years. Fire destroyed studio 1930. FEDERAL A.P.: Supervisor
of Painting, 1937–39. ONE-MAN EXHIBITIONS:
Kraushaar Galleries, 1931; Uptown Gallery,
NYC, 1940; Laurel Gallery, NYC, 1946, 49;
Mount Holyoke College, 1934; ASL, Memo-
rial Exhibition, 1951; Joseph Brummer Gal-
lery, NYC (two-man), 1929; Mortimer Brandt,
NYC (four-man), 1944. GROUP: WMAA. COL-
LECTIONS: Ain Harod; Boston/MFA; MMA;
MOMA; Newark Museum; PMA. BIBLIOG-
RAPHY: Baur 7; Brown; Cheney, M. C.; Dreier
2; Huyghe; *Index of 20th Century Artists;*
Janis, S.; Pach 3; Smith, S. C. K.

BAZIOTES, WILLIAM A. b. June 11, 1912,
Pittsburgh, Pa.; **d.** June 4, 1963, NYC. STUD-
IED: NAD, 1933–36, with Leon Kroll. FED-
ERAL A.P.: Teacher, 1936–38; easel painting,
1938–41. TAUGHT: NYU, 1949–53; Brooklyn
Museum School, 1949–52; Peoples Art Center
(MOMA), 1951–53; Hunter College, 1952–63.
Co-founder of a school, "Subject of the Art-

ist," with Robert Motherwell, Barnett Newman, and Mark Rothko, NYC, 1948. AWARDS:
Chicago/AI, Abstract and Surrealist Art, First
Prize, 1948; Chicago/AI, The Mr. & Mrs.
Frank G. Logan Medal, 1961; U. of Illinois,
P.P., 1951. ONE-MAN EXHIBITIONS: (first) Art
of This Century, NYC, 1944; Galerie Maeght,
1947; The Kootz Gallery, 1946, 47, 48, 50, 51,
52, 53, 54, 56, 58, 61; Sidney Janis Gallery,
1961. GROUP: Chicago/AI, Abstract and Surrealist Art, 1948; MOMA, Fifteen Americans, circ., 1952; Brussels World's Fair, 1958;
MOMA, The New American Painting, circ.
Europe, 1958–59; I & II Sao Paulo Biennials,
1951, 53; WMAA Annuals, 1948, 50, 52, 53,
54, 55, 56, 57; California Palace, 1948; Galerie
de France, 1961; Los Angeles/County MA,
1951; U. of Illinois, 1949, 50, 51, 53, 55, 61;
U. of Minnesota, 40 American Painters, 1940–
50, 1951; U. of Nebraska, 1952, 54; Documenta II, Kassel, 1959; Walker, 60 American
Painters, 1960; WMAA, The New Decade,
1954–55; SRGM, Younger American Painters,
1954. COLLECTIONS: Baltimore/MA; Brandeis U.; Buffalo/Albright; CSFA; Chicago/AI;
Detroit/Institute; Harvard U.; U. of Illinois;
MMA; MOMA; Newark Museum; New Or-
leans/Delgado; Rochester/Memorial; SRGM;
Seattle/AM; Smith College; Tel Aviv; Vassar
College; WMAA; Walker; Washington U. BIB-
LIOGRAPHY: **Alloway;** Baur 5, 7; Bazin; Biddle
3; Blesh 1; Dorner; Eliot; Finkelstein; Flanagan; Goodrich and Baur 1; Haftman; Hunter
5; Janis and Blesh 1; Janis, S.; McCurdy, ed.;
Mendelowitz; *Metro;* Motherwell, ed.; Moth-
erwell and Reinhardt, eds.; Neumeyer; Nord-
ness, ed.; Paalen; Ponente; Pousette-Dart, ed.;
Read 2; Richardson; Ritchie 1; Rodman 2;
Soby 5.

BEAL, GIFFORD. b. January 24, 1879, NYC;
d. February 5, 1956, NYC. STUDIED: Princeton
U., 1900; privately with William M. Chase;
ASL, with Frank V. DuMond. Traveled east-
ern USA. MEMBER: NAD, 1914; President,
ASL, 1914–29. COMMISSIONS (murals): Interior
Department Building, Washington, D.C.; US
Post Office, Allentown, Pa. AWARDS: Worces-
ter/AM, Third Prize, 1903; St. Louis Exposi-
tion, 1904, Bronze Medal; NAD, Hallgarten
Prize, 1910; NAD, The Thomas B. Clarke
Prize, 1913; Chicago/AI, Hon. Men., 1913;
Corcoran, Third Prize, 1914; Panama-Pacific

Exposition, San Francisco, 1915, Gold Medal; PMA, 1917; National Arts Club, Gold Medal, 1918; NAD, Benjamin Altman Prize, 1919, 31; Chicago/AI, Watson F. Blair Prize, 1930; Corcoran, Second William A. Clark Prize, 1930; NAD Annual, Andrew Carnegie Prize, 1932; Paris World's Fair, 1937, Silver Medal; NAD, Saltus Gold Medal for Merit, 1948; NAD, Samuel F. B. Morse Gold Medal, 1954; NAD, Edwin Palmer Memorial Prize, 1955. ONE-MAN EXHIBITIONS: Kraushaar Galleries, 1920–23, 1925–27, 29, 31, 33, 34, 36, 38, 41, 45, 48, 50, 56; AAAL, Memorial Exhibition, 1957; Fitchburg/AM, 1960. RETROSPECTIVE: Century Association, 1950; Cowie Galleries, Los Angeles, circ., 1953. GROUP: Chicago/AI, 1928, 34, 37, 40, 44; Whitney Studio Club, NYC, 1929; PAFA, 1929, 30, 39, 44, 47, 51; St. Louis/City, 1930, 32; MOMA, 1930; Carnegie, 1931, 36, 51; Rochester/Memorial, 1932, 62; Phillips, 1932, 40, 54; WMAA, 1935, 45; New York World's Fair, 1939; NAD, 1942, 49, 51, 55; MMA, 1942; California Palace, 1945, 59; Youngstown/Butler, 1953; Hartford/Wadsworth, 1955. COLLECTIONS: ASL; Andover/Phillips; Arizona State College; Brooklyn Museum; Chicago/AI; Detroit/Institute; Indiana U.; Kansas City/Nelson; Lehigh U.; Los Angeles/County MA; MMA; NAD; Newark Museum; New Britain; Omaha/Joslyn; Phillips; Randolph-Macon Woman's College; Southampton/Parrish; Syracuse U.; Utica; WMAA; Washington State U. BIBLIOGRAPHY: Baur 7; Bryant; Cahill and Barr, eds.; Hall; Jackman; Kent, N.; Mather 1; McCurdy, ed.; Mellquist; Neuhaus; Pagano; Phillips 1; Reese.

BEARDEN, ROMARE H. b. September 2, 1914, Charlotte, N.C. STUDIED: NYU, BS; ASL, 1938, with George Grosz. Traveled Europe, North Africa. ADDRESS: 357 Canal Street, NYC. DEALER: Cordier & Ekstrom Inc. ONE-MAN EXHIBITIONS: (first) "G" Place Gallery, Washington, D.C., 1945; The Kootz Gallery, 1945, 46, 47; Duvuloy Gallery, Paris, 1945; Niveau Gallery, NYC, 1948; Barone Gallery, NYC, 1955; Michel Warren Gallery, NYC, 1960; Cordier & Ekstrom Inc., 1961, 64. GROUP: Carnegie; WMAA; MMA, Survey of American Art, 1951; Galerie Maeght, 6 American Painters, 1948; Chicago/AI; Dallas/MFA; Boston/MFA. COLLECTIONS: Atlanta U.;

Brooklyn Museum; Buffalo/Albright; MMA; MOMA; Princeton U.

BEATTIE, GEORGE. b. August 2, 1919, Cleveland, Ohio. STUDIED: Cleveland Institute of Art. TAUGHT: Georgia Institute of Technology, Architectural School; Atlanta Art Institute. MEMBER: Audubon Artists. COMMISSIONS: State of Georgia Agricultural Building (mural). AWARDS: NIAL Grant, 1955; Fulbright Fellowship (Italy), 1956; Atlanta/AA, Southeastern Annual, 1949; Mead Painting of the Year, 1959; Audubon Artists, Minnie R. Stern Memorial Medal, 1955. ADDRESS: 857 Woodley Drive, N. W., Atlanta 18, Ga. ONE-MAN EXHIBITIONS: Grand Central Moderns, 1954; Hirschl & Adler Galleries, Inc., NYC, 1961; Atlanta/AA, 1950, 61; Georgia Institute of Technology, 1954; Columbus, 1956; U. of Virginia, 1956. GROUP: MMA, 1952; Utica, 1955; Uffizi Loggia, Florence, Italy, International Drawing Annual, 1957; Smithsonian, 1955, 1958–59, 61; ART:USA:59, NYC, 1959; Atlanta/AA, Southeastern Annual, 1949; Mead-Southeast Annual, 1955–61. COLLECTIONS: Atlanta/AA; Atlanta U.; Columbus; Mead Corp.; Montclair/AM; WMAA. BIBLIOGRAPHY: Pousette-Dart, ed.

BEAUCHAMP, ROBERT. b. November 19, 1923, Denver, Colo. STUDIED: U. of Denver; Cranbrook Academy of Art, BFA; Colorado Springs Fine Arts Center, with Boardman Robinson; Hofmann School. US Navy 1943–46. AWARDS: Fulbright Fellowship (Italy); Walter K. Gutman Foundation Grant. ADDRESS: 168½ Delancey Street, NYC. DEALER: The American Gallery, NYC. ONE-MAN EXHIBITIONS: (first) Tanager Gallery, NYC, 1953; Great Jones Gallery, NYC, 1960, 61; Sun Gallery, Provincetown, 1961, 62, 63; The Green Gallery, NYC, 1961, 63; Richard Gray Gallery, 1963; Felix Landau Gallery, 1963. GROUP: MOMA, Recent Painting USA: The Figure, circ., 1962–63; Carnegie, 1958, 61; WMAA Annual, 1963; U. of Illinois, 1963; Corcoran; Chicago/AI; Bernault Commission, circ. Asia; MOMA, Recent American Painting and Sculpture, circ. USA and Canada, 1961–62. COLLECTIONS: Carnegie; Hartford/Wadsworth; MOMA; Provincetown/Chrysler; WMAA.

Robert Beauchamp   *Drawing.*

BECK, ROSEMARIE. b. July 8, 1923, NYC. STUDIED: Oberlin College, AB; Columbia U.; NYU. Traveled Italy. TAUGHT: Vassar College, 1957–58, 1961–62, 1963–64; Middlebury College, 1959, 60, 63. ADDRESS: 6 East 12 Street, NYC. DEALER: The Peridot Gallery. ONE-MAN EXHIBITIONS: (first) The Peridot Gallery, 1953, also 1955, 56, 59, 60, 63, 64; Vassar College, 1957, 61; Wesleyan U., 1960; New Paltz, 1962. GROUP: WMAA Annuals, 1955, 57; PAFA, 1954; U. of Michigan, 1956; U. of Nottingham (England), 1954, 57; Chicago/AI; Brooklyn Museum; Tate; Youngstown/Butler; Arts Club of Chicago; Oberlin College, 1957. COLLECTIONS: U. of Nebraska; New Paltz; Ration Mfg. Co.; WMAA. BIBLIOGRAPHY: Baur 5.

BEHL, WOLFGANG. b. April 13, 1918, Berlin, Germany. STUDIED: Academy of Fine Arts, Berlin, 1936–39; RISD, 1939–40. US citizen. Traveled Europe, Mexico, USA. TAUGHT: Perkiomen School, 1940–42; Lake Forest Academy, 1942–44; Layton School of Art, 1944–45; College of William and Mary, 1945–53; Silvermine Guild, 1955–57; U. of Hartford, 1955– . COMMISSIONS: Temple Beth El Sholom, Manchester, Conn.; St. Louis Priory, Creve Coeur, Miss.; Church of St. Timothy, West Hartford, Conn.; U. of Hartford; Willow Lawn Shopping Center, Richmond, Va.; St. Joseph's Cathedral, Hartford, Conn. AWARDS: Chicago/AI, Joseph N. Eisendrath Prize, 1944; Milwaukee, Wisconsin Prize for Sculpture, 1945; Connecticut Academy of Fine Arts, First Prize for Sculpture, 1961; NIAL Grant, 1963; Ford Foundation, P.P., 1964. ADDRESS: 179 Kenyon Street, Hartford, Conn. DEALER: The Bertha Schaefer Gallery. ONE-MAN EX-

HIBITIONS: (first) The Bertha Schaefer Gallery, 1950, also 1955; Charlotte/Mint, 1949, 50; Hollins College, 1951; Randolph-Macon Woman's College, 1951; Sweet Briar College, 1951; Amerika Haus, Schweinfurt, Wurzberg, and Munich. GROUP: U. of Illinois, 1957; Chicago/AI, 1943, 44; Milwaukee, 1945; VMFA, 1946, 47, 48, 49, 51; Boston Arts Festival, 1946, 47; Silvermine Guild, 1946, 47; Hartford/Wadsworth, 1957; Carnegie, 1962; PAFA, 1964. COLLECTIONS: Andover/Phillips; U. of Miami; New Britain.

BENJAMIN, KARL. b. December 29, 1925, Chicago, Ill. STUDIED: Northwestern U.; U. of Redlands, 1949, BA; Claremont Graduate School, with Jean Ames, 1960, MA. US Navy, 1943–46. TAUGHT: General elementary school, southern California, 1949– . ADDRESS: 675 West Eighth Street, Claremont, Calif. DEALER: Esther Robles Gallery. ONE-MAN EXHIBITIONS: (first) Pasadena/AM, 1954; U. of Redlands, 1953, 56, 62; Jack Carr Gallery, Pasadena, 1955, 56; Occidental College, 1958; Long Beach/MA, 1958; Scripps College, 1960; La Jolla, 1961; Bolles Gallery, 1961; Santa Barbara/MA, 1962; Hollis Gallery, 1964; Esther Robles Gallery, 1959, 60, 62, 64. GROUP: Fort Worth, The Artist's Environment: The West Coast, 1962; WMAA, Fifty California Artists, 1962–63; Colorado Springs/FA Annual, 1964; WMAA, Geometric Abstraction in America, circ., 1962; Los Angeles/County MA, Four Abstract Classicists, circ., 1959–61; ICA, London, West Coast Hard-Edge, 1960; Pasadena/AM, Pacific Profile, 1961; Carnegie, California Artists, 1961; A.F.A., New Talent, circ., 1959; Los Angeles/County MA Annuals; UCLA, California Painters Under 35, 1959. COLLECTIONS: City of Claremont, Haifa; La Jolla; Long Beach/MA; Los Angeles/County MA; Pasadena/AM; Pepsi-Cola Co.; SFMA; San Diego; Santa Barbara/MA; WMAA.

BENTON, THOMAS HART. b. April 15, 1889, Neosho, Mo. STUDIED: Western Military Academy, 1906–07; Chicago Art Institute School, 1907; Academie Julian, Paris, 1908–11. Gallery director and art teacher for Chelsea Neighborhood Association, NYC, 1917. US Navy, 1918–19. Traveled Europe, USA, Canada. TAUGHT: ASL, 1926–36; Kansas City Art Institute and School of Design, 1935–40; lectured at many colleges and universities. COMMISSIONS (murals): New School for Social Research, with Jose Clemente Orozco, 1928; WMAA, 1932; State of Indiana, 1933 (mural now located at U. of Indiana); Missouri State Capitol, 1935–36; "Achelous and Hercules" for Harzfeld Department Store, Kansas City, 1947 (Encyclopaedia Britannica filmed his progress on this mural); Lincoln U., 1952–53; Kansas City River Club, 1947; New York State Power Authority, Massena, 1957–61; Truman Library, Independence, Mo., 1958–61. AWARDS: Architectural League of New York, Gold Medal, 1933; Academia Argentina de Bellas Artes, Buenos Aires, Hon. Men., 1945; Accademia Fiorentina dell'Arte del Disegno, Hon. Men., 1949; Accademia Senese degli Intronati, Siena, 1949; Hon. D.Litt., Lincoln U., 1957; Hon. DFA, U. of Missouri, 1948; Hon. PBK, 1948. ADDRESS: 3616 Belleview Avenue, Kansas City, Mo. ONE-MAN EXHIBITIONS: Lakeside Press Gallery, Chicago, 1927; Ferargil Galleries, NYC, 1934, 35; Des Moines (two-man), 1939; A.A.A. Gallery, NYC, 1939, 41; A.A.A. Gallery, Chicago, 1946; U. of Arizona, circ., 1962. RETROSPECTIVE: Kansas City/Nelson, 1939; Omaha/Joslyn, 1951; New Britain, 1954; U. of Kansas, 1958. GROUP: Anderson Galleries, NYC, Forum Exhibition, 1916; The Daniel Gallery, NYC, 1919; PMA, Modern Americans, 1922; Architectural League of New York, 1924; Delphic Studios, NYC, 1928, 29; A.A.A. Gallery, NYC, 1939, 40, 42. COLLECTIONS: Andover/Phillips; Brooklyn Museum; California Palace; Canajoharie; Columbia, Mo.; Kansas City/Nelson; U. of Kansas City; MMA; MOMA; U. of Nebraska; New Britain; Omaha/Joslyn; PAFA; St. Louis/City; Terre Haute/Swope. BIBLIOGRAPHY: Baur 7; Bazin; Benton 1, 2, 3; Biddle 3; Biederman 1; Blesh 1; Boswell 1; Brown; Bruce and Watson; Bryant; Cahill and Barr, eds.; Canaday; Cheney, M. C.; Christensen; Craven 1, 2, 3; Eliot; Flanagan; Flexner; Goodrich and Baur 1; Haftman; Hall; Hunter 5; Huyghe; Index of 20th Century Artists; Kent, N.; Kootz 2; Lee and Burchwood; McCourbrey; McCurdy, ed.; Mellquist; Mendelowitz; Myers 2; Neuhaus; Newmeyer; Pagano; Pearson 1; Poore; Reese; Richardson; Ringel, ed.; Rodman 2; Smith, S. C. K.; Soby 6; Wight 2; Wright 1; Zigrosser 1.

BEN-ZION. b. July 8, 1897, Old Constantin, Ukraine. Self-taught. Traveled Europe, Mexico, USA. To USA 1920; citizen 1936. TAUGHT: Cooper Union, 1946–53; Visiting Artist, Ball State Teachers College, 1956; State U. of Iowa, 1959; Municipal U. of Omaha, 1959. FEDERAL A.P.: Teacher. A co-founder of the Expressionist group The Ten, 1935. COMMISSIONS: Drawings for *Wisdom of the Fathers,* Limited Editions Club (1960) and Heritage Press (1962). ADDRESS: 58 Morton Street, NYC. ONE-MAN EXHIBITIONS: (first) Artists' Gallery, NYC, 1936; The Willard Gallery, 1937; Buchholz Gallery, NYC; The Bertha Schaefer Gallery; Curt Valentine Gallery, NYC, 1952; Duveen-Graham Gallery, NYC, 1955–56; Baltimore/MA; Taft Museum; SFMA; State U. of Iowa; St. Louis/City; Bezalel Museum; Jewish Museum, 1948, 52; A.F.A., circ., 1953–54. RETROSPECTIVE: Jewish Museum, circ., 1959. GROUP: PAFA; NYU; Carnegie, 1945; WMAA, 1946. COLLECTIONS: Ball State Teachers College; Bezalel Museum; Chicago/AI; Jewish Museum; Kansas City/Nelson; MOMA; NYPL; Newark Museum; Phillips; St. Louis/City; Tel Aviv; WMAA; U. of Washington. BIBLIOGRAPHY: Baur 7; Pearson 2.

BERGER, JASON. b. January 22, 1924, Malden, Mass. STUDIED: Boston Museum School, 1942–43, 1946–49; U. of Alabama, 1943–44; Zadkine School of Sculpture, Paris, 1950–52. TAUGHT: Boston Museum School, 1955– . AWARDS: Boston/MFA, James William Paige Fellowship, 1957; Boston Arts Festival, Grand Prize, 1956; Boston Arts Festival, First Prize, 1961. ADDRESS: 251 St. Paul Street, Brookline, Mass. DEALER: The Peridot Gallery. ONE-MAN EXHIBITIONS: Deerfield (Mass.) Academy, 1954; The Swetzoff Gallery, 1952, 56; The Peridot Gallery, 1956, 57, 58, 61; Nova Gallery, Boston, 1960; Joan Peterson Gallery, 1962; Fitchburg/AM, 1955; The Pace Gallery, Boston, 1961. GROUP: Institute of Modern Art, Boston, 1943; Chicago/AI, 1952, 54; Salon de la Jeune Sculpture, Paris, 1952; ICA, Boston, 1952, 56, 60, 61; Boston Arts Festival, 1952, 53, 54, 55, 56, 57, 61; Boston/MFA, 1953–57; Carnegie, 1954, 55; MOMA, Young American Printmakers, 1953; MOMA, Recent Drawings USA, 1956; Library of Congress, 1954; PAFA, 1962; Silvermine Guild. COLLEC-

TIONS: Brandeis U.; MOMA; Rockefeller Institute; SRGM.

BERMAN, EUGENE. b. November 4, 1899, St. Petersburg, Russia. Studied with P. S. Naumoff, and the architect S. Grosenberg; Academie Ranson, Paris, 1919, with Edouard Vuillard, Maurice Denis; with the architect Emilio Terry, 1920. Traveled Europe. To USA 1935; first citizenship papers 1937. Became active in designing for ballet, opera, 1937. COMMISSIONS (murals): Wright Ludington, 1938; John Yeon, 1941; (theatre): Hartford Music Festival, 1936; *L'Opera de Quatre Sous,* Paris, 1936; "Icare" (ballet), NYC, 1939; "Concerto Barocco" (ballet), by George Balanchine, NYC, 1941. AWARDS: Guggenheim Foundation Fellowship, 1947, 49. ADDRESS: 107 Via del Plebicito, Rome, Italy. ONE-MAN EXHIBITIONS: (first) Galerie Granoff, Paris, 1927; Galerie de l'Etoile, Paris, 1928; Galerie Bonjean, Paris, 1929; Balzac Gallery, NYC, 1929; Galerie des Quatre Chemins, Paris, 1929; Julien Levy Galleries, NYC, 1932, 33, 35, 36, 37, 39, 41, 43, 46, 47; Galerie Pierre Colle, Paris, 1933; Zwemmer Gallery, London, 1935; Hanover Gallery, 1949; Renoir and Lolle, Paris, 1937; Galerie Montaigne, Paris, 1939; Courvoisier Gallery, San Francisco, 1941; Princeton U., 1947; Kraushaar Galleries, 1948, 49, 54, 60; MOMA, 1945. RETROSPECTIVE: Institute of Modern Art, Boston, circ., 1941. GROUP: Galerie Drouant, Paris, 1924; MOMA; Chicago/AI; WMAA; Musee du Petit Palais, Paris, 1934; Hartford/Wadsworth, 1931. COLLECTIONS: Baltimore/MA; Boston/MFA; Cincinnati/AM; Cleveland/MA; Denver/AM; Graphische Sammlung Albertina; Hartford/Wadsworth; Harvard U.; U. of Illinois; State U. of Iowa; Los Angeles/County MA; MMA; MOMA; PMA; Paris/Moderne; Phillips; St. Louis/City; Santa Barbara/MA; Smith College; Vassar College; Venice/Contemporaneo; Washington U. BIBLIOGRAPHY: Bazin; **Berman;** Canaday; Flanagan; Frost; Genauer; Holme 1, 2; Hunter 5; Huyghe; Kent, N.; **Levy;** McCurdy, ed.; Mendelowitz; Myers 2; Pearson 1, 2; Phillips 1; Richardson; Soby 1; Wight 2.

BERTOIA, HARRY. b. March 10, 1915, San Lorenzo, Italy. To USA 1930. STUDIED: Society of Arts and Crafts, Detroit; Cranbrook Academy of Art. TAUGHT: Cranbrook Academy of Art, 1937–41. COMMISSIONS: General Motors Technical Center, Detroit; MIT Chapel; Manufacturers Trust Co.; Dayton Co., Minneapolis; First National Bank of Miami; First National Bank of Tulsa; Dulles International Airport, Washington, D.C.; Kodak Pavilion, New York World's Fair, 1964–65. AWARDS: Architectural League of New York, Gold Medal; American Institute of Architects, Gold Medal; Graham Foundation Grant ($10,000), 1957. ADDRESS: RD #1, Barto, Pa. DEALERS: Staempfli Gallery; Fairweather-Hardin Gallery. ONE-MAN EXHIBITIONS: (first) Karl Nierendorf Gallery, NYC, 1940; Staempfli Gallery; Fairweather-Hardin Gallery; Museum of Non-Objective Art, NYC; Smithsonian, circ. GROUP: WMAA; MOMA; Battersea Park, London, International Sculpture Exhibition, 1963. COLLECTIONS: Buffalo/Albright; Colorado Springs/FA; Dallas Public Library; Denver/AM; MIT; MOMA; SFMA; Utica; VMFA. BIBLIOGRAPHY: Baur 7; Blesh 1; Janis, S.; *Metro;* Ragon 2; Seuphor 3.

BESS, FOREST. b. October 5, 1911, Bay City, Tex. STUDIED: Agricultural and Mechanical College of Texas, 1929–32; U. of Texas, 1932–33. Traveled Mexico, 1934–40, and USA. Corps of Army Engineers, 1940–45. ADDRESS: 1701 Avenue E, Bay City, Tex. DEALER: Betty Parsons Gallery. ONE-MAN EXHIBITIONS: Witte, 1939; Houston/MFA, 1938, 62; Betty Parsons Gallery, 1949, 54, 57, 59, 62; Andre Emmerich Gallery, Houston, 1958; Agricultural and Mechanical College of Texas; New Arts Gallery, Houston; Texas Technological College. GROUP: Corcoran, 1938; Dallas/MFA; Tulsa/Philbrook; A.F.A., Wit and Whimsey in 20th Century Art, 1962; de Young; Stanford U. COLLECTIONS: Boston/MFA; Brandeis U.; Houston/MFA; Witte.

BIDDLE, GEORGE. b. January 24, 1885, Philadelphia, Pa. STUDIED: Groton School, 1904; Harvard U., 1908, AB with honors, 1911, LLB; Academie Julian, Paris, 1911. Traveled Europe, Asia, Africa, Latin America, USA. TAUGHT: Columbia U.; U. of California; Colorado Springs Fine Arts Center; Artist-in-Residence, American Academy, Rome. MEMBER: American Society of Painters, Sculptors and Gravuers; National Society of Mural Painters;

NIAL. COMMISSIONS (murals): Justice Department, Washington, D.C.; Supreme Court Building, Mexico City; National Library, Rio de Janeiro. AWARDS: Yaddo, MacDowell Colony, and Huntington Hartford Foundation Fellowships. ADDRESS: Croton-on-Hudson, N.Y. DEALER: Cober Gallery. ONE-MAN EXHIBITIONS: (first) The Milch Gallery, 1919; more than 100 in USA, Europe, Japan, India. RETROSPECTIVE: USIA, Prints, circ., 1950. COLLECTIONS: Berlin/National; Mexico City/Nacional; Provincetown/Chrysler; Tokyo/Modern; Youngstown/Butler. BIBLIOGRAPHY: American Artists Congress, Inc.; American Artists Group Inc. 3; **Biddle 1, 2, 3;** Birchman; Boswell 1; Brown; Bruce and Watson; Cheney, M. C.; *Index of 20th Century Artists;* Nordmark; Pagano; Parkes; Pearson 2; Poore; Reese; Sachs; Zigrosser 1.

BIEDERMAN, CHARLES (Karl) JOSEPH. b. August 23, 1906, Cleveland, Ohio. STUDIED: Chicago Art Institute School, 1926–29, with Henry Poole, van Papelandam, John W. Norton. Resided Prague, Paris, New York. AWARDS: Amsterdam/Stedelijk, Sikkens Award, 1962. ADDRESS: Route 2, Red Wing, Minn. ONE-MAN EXHIBITIONS: (first) Chicago Art Institute School; a movie theater lobby in Chicago, 1930; Pierre Matisse Gallery, 1936; Arts Club of Chicago, 1941; Katharine Kuh Gallery, Chicago, 1941; St. Paul Gallery, 1954; Columbia U. School of Architecture, 1962; Georgia Institute of Technology, 1962. GROUP: Buffalo/Albright, 1936; Reinhardt Galleries, NYC, 1936; Galerie Pierre, Paris, 1936; Amsterdam/Stedelijk, 1962; Kunstgewerbemuseum, Zurich, 1962; Marlborough-Gerson Gallery Inc., 1964. COLLECTIONS: Chicago Public Schools; MOMA; PMA; Red Wing; U. of Saskatchewan. BIBLIOGRAPHY: **Biederman 1, 2;** Seuphor 3.

BISCHOFF, ELMER. b. July 9, 1916, Berkeley, Calif. STUDIED: U. of California, Berkeley, with Margaret Peterson, Erle Loran, John Haley, 1939, MA. US Air Force, 1942–46. TAUGHT: San Francisco Art Institute, 1946–52, 1956–63; U. of California, Berkeley, 1963– ; Yuba College, 1964; Skowhegan School, 1961. AWARDS: Oakland/AM, P.P., 1957; Ford Foundation Grant, 1959; NIAL Grant, 1963; Chicago/AI, Norman Wait Harris Medal, 1964;

Elmer Bischoff   *Yellow Sun. 1963*

RAC, First Prize, 1955. **ADDRESS:** 2415½ Curtis Street, Berkeley, Calif. **DEALER:** Staempfli Gallery. **ONE-MAN EXHIBITIONS:** (first) California Palace, 1947; King Ubu Gallery, San Francisco, 1953; Paul Kantor Gallery, 1955; SFMA, 1956; de Young, 1961; Sacramento/Crocker, 1964; Staempfli Gallery, 1960, 62, 64; Achenbach Foundation (three-man drawing show), 1963. **GROUP:** San Francisco Art Association Annuals, 1942, 46, 52, 56, 57, 59, 63; Chicago/AI, 1947, 59, 64; California Palace, 1948, 50, 60, 61, 62, 63; Los Angeles/County MA, 1951; RAC, 1955, 56; Oakland/AM, 1957; ART:USA:59, NYC, 1959; Minneapolis/Institute, American Painting, 1945–57, 1957; A.F.A., New Talent, circ., 1958; A.F.A., West Coast Artists, circ., 1959–60; U. of Illinois, 1959, 61; WMAA, 1959, 61, 63; Denver/AM, 1960; Youngstown/Butler, 1960; SFMA, Fifty California Artists, circ., 1962; MOMA, Recent Painting USA: The Figure, circ., 1962–63; PAFA, 1962; Corcoran, 1963; Auckland, Painting from the Pacific, 1961; Fort Worth, The Artist's Environment: The West Coast, 1962; NIAL, 1963; Art:USA:Now, circ., 1962– **COLLECTIONS:** Chase Manhattan Bank; S. C. Johnson & Son, Inc.; MOMA; Oakland/AM; Rockefeller Institute; SFMA; Sacramento/Crocker; WMAA. **BIBLIOGRAPHY:** Goodrich and Baur 1; Nordness, ed.

BISHOP, ISABEL. b. March 3, 1902, Cincinnati, Ohio. **STUDIED:** New York School of Applied Design; ASL, with Kenneth Hayes Miller. **TAUGHT:** ASL, 1937. **MEMBER:** NAD; NIAL; SAGA; Audubon Artists. **FEDERAL A.P.:** US Post Office, New Lexington, Ohio (mural). **AWARDS:** NAD, Isaac N. Maynard Prize; NAD, The Adolph and Clara Obrig Prize, 1942; NAD Annual, Andrew Carnegie Prize, 1945; Corcoran, Second William A. Clark Prize, 1945; AAAL Grant, 1943; PAFA, Walter Lippincott Prize, 1953; NAD, Benjamin Altman Prize, 1955; Library of Congress, Pennell P.P., 1946; NAD, Joseph S. Isidora Gold Medal, 1957; Hon. DFA, Moore Institute. **ADDRESS:** 857 Broadway, NYC. **DEALER:** The Midtown Galleries. **ONE-MAN EXHIBITIONS:** The Midtown Galleries, 1932, 35, 36, 39, 49, 55, 60; VMFA (two-man), 1960; Pittsfield/Berkshire, 1957. **GROUP:** Carnegie; VMFA; Corcoran; PAFA; New York World's

Isabel Bishop   *Subway Reading.*

Fair, 1939; Chicago/AI; WMAA; MOMA; St. Louis/City; NAD. **COLLECTIONS:** Andover/Phillips; Atlanta U.; Brooklyn Museum; Clearwater/Gulf Coast; Columbus; Corcoran; Cranbrook; Des Moines; Kansas City/Nelson; Library of Congress; MMA; NYPL; U. of Nebraska; Newark Museum; New Britain; PAFA; PMA; Phillips; Springfield, Mass./MFA; Tel Aviv; Terre Haute/Swope; Utica; VMFA; WMAA; Youngstown/Butler. **BIBLIOGRAPHY:** Baur 7; Boswell 1; Brown; Cheney, M. C.; Goodrich and Baur 1; Kent, N.; McCurdy, ed.; Mellquist; Mendelowitz; Nordness, ed.; Pagano; Reese; Richardson.

BISTTRAM, EMIL. b. April 7, 1895, Hungary. **STUDIED:** NAD; Cooper Union; New York School of Fine and Applied Art (with Ivan Olinsky, Leon Kroll, William Dodge, Jay Hambridge, Howard Giles). **TAUGHT:** New York School of Fine and Applied Art; Master Institute of United Arts, Inc., NYC; Bisttram School, Taos, N.M. **COMMISSIONS** (murals): Justice Department, Washington, D.C.; US Post Office, Ranger, Tex. **AWARDS:** Phila-

delphia Watercolor Club, First Prize, Gold Medal, 1926; Guggenheim Foundation Fellowship, 1931; California Palace, Hon. Men., 1936. **ADDRESS:** Box 46, Taos, N.M. **ONE-MAN EXHIBITIONS:** Philadelphia Watercolor Club; Delphic Gallery, NYC; Stendahl Gallery, Los Angeles, 1945. **GROUP:** PAFA; Chicago/AI; XV Venice Biennial, 1930; WMAA, 1933. **COLLECTIONS:** Buffalo/Albright; Nicholas Roerich Museum; Taos (N.M.) County Court House. **BIBLIOGRAPHY:** Allen, ed.; Bruce and Watson; Cheney, M. C.; Coke; *Index of 20th Century Artists;* Pearson 1, 2.

BLACKBURN, MORRIS. b. October 13, 1902, Philadelphia, Pa. **STUDIED:** PAFA, with Arthur B. Carles, Jr., Henry McCarter, Daniel Garber. Traveled Europe, Mexico. **TAUGHT:** Philadelphia Museum School, 1933–45; Bryn Mawr College, 1947–48; Stella Elkins Tyler School of Fine Arts, Temple U., 1945– ; PAFA, 1952– . **FEDERAL A.P.:** Mural and easel painting. **MEMBER:** Philadelphia Watercolor Club; Audubon Artists; The Print Club, Philadelphia; American Watercolor Society. **AWARDS:** Guggenheim Foundation Fellowship, 1952; PAFA, Cresson Fellowship, 1928, 29; PAFA, Gold Medal, 1946; PAFA, H. S. Morris Prize, 1951; PAFA, Thornton Oakley Prize, 1955. **ADDRESS:** 2104 Spring Street, Philadelphia, Pa. **DEALER:** Mission Gallery. **ONE-MAN EXHIBITIONS:** (first) Warwick Gallery, Philadelphia, 1930; PAFA; The Print Club, Philadelphia, Woodmere Art Gallery, Philadelphia; Philadelphia Art Alliance; Newman Gallery, Philadelphia; Joseph Luyber Galleries, NYC; National Serigraph Society, NYC; Pennsylvania Art Center. **RETROSPECTIVE:** Woodmere Art Gallery, Philadelphia, 1956. **GROUP:** PAFA Annuals since 1937; NAD; Audubon Artists; New York World's Fair, 1939; Chicago/AI; Carnegie; Brooklyn Museum; WMAA; Library of Congress; USIA traveling print exhibitions; Youngstown/Butler. **COLLECTIONS:** Clearwater/Gulf Coast; Free Library of Philadelphia; Library of Congress; Memphis/Brooks; Montana State U.; PAFA; PMA; The Pennsylvania State U.; USIA; Youngstown/Butler. **BIBLIOGRAPHY:** Bethers.

BLAINE, NELL. b. July 10, 1922, Richmond, Va. **STUDIED:** Richmond (Va.) School of Art,

1939–43; Hofmann School, 1943–44; Atelier 17, NYC, with S. W. Hayter; New School for Social Research, 1952–53. Traveled Europe, Near East. TAUGHT: Great Neck (N.Y.) Public Schools, 1943–63. MEMBER: American Abstract Artists, 1944–57; Jane Street Group, 1945–49. COMMISSIONS: Revlon Inc. (murals); New York Hilton Hotel (lithographs). AWARDS: Norfolk, First Prize, Watercolor, 1945; Longview Foundation Grant, 1964; Yaddo Fellowship, 1957, 58, 64; MacDowell Colony Fellowship, 1957. ADDRESS: 210 Riverside Drive, NYC. DEALER: Poindexter Gallery. ONE-MAN EXHIBITIONS: (first) Jane Street Gallery, NYC, 1945, also 1948; VMFA, 1947, 54; Southern Illinois U., 1949; Tibor de Nagy Gallery, 1953, 54; Poindexter Gallery, 1956, 58, 60; New Paltz, 1959; Stewart Richard Gallery, San Antonio, 1961; Philadelphia Art Alliance, 1961; Yaddo, 1961; Longwood College, 1962. GROUP: Art of This Century, NYC, The Women, 1944; Chicago/AI; Baltimore/MA; WMAA; PAFA; Corcoran; VMFA; ART:USA:59, NYC, 1959; Festival of Two Worlds, Spoleto; MOMA, Hans Hofmann and His Students, circ., 1963–64; Hartford/Wadsworth, Figures, 1964; Salon des Realites Nouvelles, Paris, 1950; MOMA, Abstract Watercolors and Drawings: USA, circ. Latin America and Europe, 1961–62. COLLECTIONS: Chase Manhattan Bank; Colgate U.; Hallmark Collection; New Paltz; Revlon Inc.; Southern Illinois U.; Union Carbide Corp.; VMFA; WMAA; Worcester/AM.

BLANCH, ARNOLD. b. June 4, 1896, Mantorville, Minn. STUDIED: Minneapolis Institute School; ASL, 1916–17, 1919–21, with Kenneth Hayes Miller, Boardman Robinson, John Sloan. Traveled USA. TAUGHT: California School of Fine Arts, 1930–31; ASL, 1915–21, 1935–39, 1947– ; Woodstock, N.Y., 1950–61; Colorado Springs Fine Arts Center, summers, 1939–41; Michigan State U., 1964; Florida Gulf Coast Art Center, Inc., 1950–51; Ohio U., summers, 1952, 56; U. of Minnesota, 1949, 52; U. of Hawaii, 1955; Minneapolis Institute School, 1954; Norton Gallery and School of Art, 1961–62; Rollins College, 1950. COMMISSIONS: US Post Offices, Fredonia, N.Y., Norwalk, Conn., and Columbus, Wisc. (murals). AWARDS: SFMA, P.P., 1931; California Palace, 1931; Chicago/AI, Norman Wait Harris Prize, 1929; PAFA, Medal, 1938; Guggenheim Foun-

dation Fellowship, 1933; Carnegie, Medal, 1938; Syracuse/Everson, National Ceramic Exhibition, 1949, 51; Silvermine Guild. ADDRESS: Woodstock, N.Y. DEALER: The Krasner Gallery. ONE-MAN EXHIBITIONS: The Krasner Gallery, 1954, 58, 59, 61; Rehn Galleries, 1923, 25; Walden-Dudensing Gallery, Chicago, 1930; A.A.A. Gallery, NYC, 1943, 55, 63; West Palm Beach/Norton, 1961; Philadelphia Art Alliance; Dudensing Gallery, NYC, 1928, 30; Ulrich Gallery, Minneapolis, 1930; Des Moines, 1952; Beaux Arts Gallery, San Francisco, 1930; Walker, 1952. RETROSPECTIVE: U. of Minnesota, 1949. GROUP: Corcoran, 1931–45; WMAA, 1931–46, 1948–52; PAFA, 1931–45, 1948–52; Chicago/AI, 1930–43; New York World's Fair, 1939; MOMA; Carnegie; VMFA; MMA; Library of Congress; ART:USA, NYC. COLLECTIONS: Abbott Laboratories; U. of Arizona; Britannica; Brooklyn Museum; California Palace; Carnegie; Cincinnati/AM; Clearwater/Gulf Coast; Cleveland/MA; Colorado Springs/FA; Cranbrook; Denver/AM; Detroit/Institute; Library of Congress; MMA; U. of Minnesota, Duluth; U. of Nebraska; U. of Oklahoma; PAFA; St. Louis/City; Utica; WMAA; Youngstown/Butler. BIBLIOGRAPHY: American Artists Congress, Inc.; Baur 7; **Blanch 1, 2, 3;** Boswell 1; Cheney, M. C.; *Index of 20th Century Artists;* Jewell 2; Pagano; Pearson 1; Reese; Richardson; Zaidenberg, ed.

BLAUSTEIN, AL. b. January 23, 1924, NYC. STUDIED: Cooper Union, with Morris Kantor; Skowhegan School. US Air Force, 3 years. Traveled Mexico, Africa, the Orient; resided Rome, 1954–57. TAUGHT: Pratt Institute; Yale U. COMMISSIONS: Drawings for *Life* Magazine and British Overseas Food Corporation, 1948–49; fresco mural for South Solon (Me.) Meeting House, 1953. AWARDS: Prix de Rome, 1954–57; Guggenheim Foundation Fellowship, 1958, 61; AAAL Grant, 1958; PAFA, Alice McFadden Eyre Medal, 1959; ART:USA:59, NYC, Graphic Prize, 1959; SAGA, First Prize, 1962; Audubon Artists, Gold Medal of Honor, 1962; Youngstown/Butler, First Prize, 1961. ADDRESS: 603 Sixth Avenue, NYC. ONE-MAN EXHIBITIONS: (first) Lee Nordness Gallery, NYC, 1959, also 1961, 62; U. of Nevada, 1961. GROUP: MMA, 1950; A.F.A., 1951; Buffalo/Albright, Expressionism in American Painting,

1952; U. of Illinois, 1957; Carnegie, 1952; WMAA Annuals, 1953, 57; The Downtown Gallery, Americans in Europe, 1956; Brooklyn Museum, 1957; NIAL, 1958; SAGA, 1962. COLLECTIONS: Hartford/Wadsworth; Library of Congress; MMA; Norfolk; PAFA; Scranton/Everhart; WMAA; Youngstown/Butler. BIBLIOGRAPHY: Chaet; Nordness, ed.

BLEIFELD, STANLEY. b. August 28, 1924, Brooklyn, N.Y. STUDIED: Stella Elkins Tyler School of Fine Arts, Temple U., with Raphael Sabatini, 1949, BFA, BS.Ed., 1950, MFA. US Navy, 1944–46. Traveled Israel, Mexico; resided Rome, 1962–63. TAUGHT: Weston (Conn.) Public Schools, 1950–53; New Haven State Teachers College, 1953–55; Danbury State College, 1955–63. MEMBER: National Sculpture Society. COMMISSIONS: Vatican Pavilion, New York World's Fair, 1964–65. AWARDS: Tyler Annual, First Prize, 1951; National Sculpture Society, John Gregory Award, 1964; elected Tyler Fellow, 1964. ADDRESS: Spring Valley Road, Weston, Conn. DEALER: The Peridot Gallery. ONE-MAN EXHIBITIONS: The Peridot Gallery, 1963; Hoffman Fuel Co., Danbury, Conn., 1962. GROUP: Silvermine Guild; Stella Elkins Tyler School of Fine Arts, Temple U.; International Arts Festival, Newport, R.I. COLLECTIONS: Silvermine Guild; Temple U.

BLOCH, ALBERT. b. August 2, 1882, St. Louis, Mo.; **d.** December 9, 1961, Lawrence, Kans. STUDIED: Washington U. School of Fine Arts, 1898–1900; New York and Europe. TAUGHT: Chicago Art Institute School, 1922–23; U. of Kansas School of Fine Arts, 1941–47 (Prof. Emeritus). ONE-MAN EXHIBITIONS: Chicago/AI, 1915; St. Louis/City, 1915; Kansas City/Nelson (three-man), 1927; Arts Club of Chicago, 1927; Germany; Switzerland; Sweden; The Daniel Gallery, NYC, 1921, 26; Renaissance Society, Chicago; The U. of Chicago, 1956; The Willow Gallery, NYC, 1948. RETROSPECTIVE: U. of Kansas, 1955; Tulsa/Philbrook, 1961–62. GROUP: Der Blaue Reiter, Munich, 1911–14; Neue Sezession, Munich, 1916; Cologne; A Century of Progress, Chicago, 1933–34; New York World's Fair, 1939; Der Sturm, Berlin, 1913, 18. COLLECTIONS: Baker U.; Chicago/AI; Columbus; Kansas State College; U. of Kansas; Phillips; Stadtische Galerie im Lenbachhaus; Yale U. BIBLIOGRAPHY: Baur 7; Brown; Cheney, M. C.; Selz, P. 1.

BLOOM, HYMAN. b. April, 1913, near Riga, Latvia. To USA 1920. STUDIED: West End Community Center, Boston, with Harold Zimmerman; Harvard U., with Denman W. Ross. FEDERAL A.P.: Easel painting. ADDRESS: 9 Irvington Street, Boston, Mass. DEALER: Durlacher Brothers. ONE-MAN EXHIBITIONS: (first) Durlacher Brothers, 1946, 48, 54; WMAA; Stuart Gallery, Boston, 1945; ICA, Boston; Boris Mirski Gallery, 1949; The Swetzoff Gallery, 1957. RETROSPECTIVE: Buffalo/Albright, 1954, circ. GROUP: MOMA, Americans 1942, circ., 1942; Boston/MFA; WMAA. COLLECTIONS: Andover/Phillips; Harvard U.; MOMA; Smith College; WMAA. BIBLIOGRAPHY: Barker 1; Baur 7; Biddle 3; Chaet; Eliot; Goodrich 1; Hess, T. B.; Hunter 5; Kootz 2; Miller; Miller, ed. 1; Newmeyer; Pousette-Dart, ed.; Richardson; Rodman 2, 3; Soby 5; Wight 2; **Wight and Goodrich.**

BLUEMNER, OSCAR. b. 1867, Hannover, Germany; **d.** 1938, South Braintree, Mass. STUDIED: Academy of Fine Arts, Berlin. To USA 1892. Practicing architect, 1894–1912. ONE-MAN EXHIBITIONS: Berlin, 1885, 1912; Stieglitz Gallery, NYC, 1915; Mrs. Liebman's Art Room, NYC, 1926; Stieglitz's Intimate Gallery, NYC, 1928; Whitney Studio Club, NYC, 1929; Marie Harriman Gallery, NYC, 1935; U. of Minnesota, 1939; Today's Gallery, Boston, 1945; The Graham Gallery, 1956, 60. GROUP: Anderson Galleries, NYC, Forum Exhibition, 1916; Bourgeois Gallery, NYC, 1917, 18, 19, 20, 21, 22, 23; J. B. Neumann Gallery, NYC, 1924–36; WMAA, Pioneers of Modern Art in America, 1946; WMAA, Juliana Force Memorial Exhibition, 1949. COLLECTIONS: MOMA; Phillips; WMAA. BIBLIOGRAPHY: Baur 7; Brown; Cheney, M. C., Frank, ed.; Goodrich and Baur 1; Hunter 5; Janis, S.; Mellquist; Wright 1.

BLUHM, NORMAN. b. March 28, 1920, Chicago, Ill. STUDIED: Illinois Institute of Technology, 1936, 1945–47, with Mies van der Rohe. US Air Force, 1941–45. Resided Paris, 1947–56. ADDRESS: 333 Park Avenue South, NYC. DEALERS: Galerie Anderson-Mayer; Notizie Gallery; Galerie Smith. ONE-

MAN EXHIBITIONS: (first) Leo Castelli Inc., 1957, also 1960; Galleria d'Arte del Naviglio, Milan, 1959; Notizie Gallery, 1961; David Anderson Gallery, NYC, 1962; Galerie Semiha Huber, Zurich, 1963; The American Gallery, NYC, 1963; Galerie Anderson-Mayer, 1963; Galerie Smith, 1964. GROUP: Carnegie, 1958; Documenta II, Kassel, 1959; ICA, Boston, 100 Works on Paper, circ. Europe, 1959; Walker, 60 American Painters, 1960; WMAA Annual, 1960; Chicago/AI Annual, 1961; SRGM, The G. David Thompson Collection; SRGM, Abstract Expressionists and Imagists, 1961; Salon du Mai, Paris, 1964. COLLECTIONS: Baltimore/MA; Dallas/MFA; Dayton/AI; Kansas City/Nelson; MIT; U. of Massachusetts; NYU; Phillips; Reed College; Stony Brook; Vassar College; WMAA. BIBLIOGRAPHY: Metro.

BLUME, PETER. b. October 27, 1906, Russia. To USA 1911. STUDIED: Educational Alliance, NYC; ASL; Beaux Arts Academy, NYC. FEDERAL A.P.: US Post Offices, Cannonsburg, Pa., Rome, Ga., and Geneva, N.Y. (murals). AWARDS: Guggenheim Foundation Fellowship, 1932, 36; Carnegie, First Prize, 1934; NIAL Grant, 1947; MMA, Artists for Victory, 1942. ADDRESS: Sherman, Conn. DEALER: Durlacher

Brothers. ONE-MAN EXHIBITIONS: (first) The Daniel Gallery, NYC, 1930; The Downtown Gallery, 1941; 47; Durlacher Brothers, 1949, 54, 58; Julien Levy Galleries, NYC, 1937. GROUP: WMAA; MOMA; Corcoran. COLLECTIONS: Boston/MFA; Columbus; Hartford/Wadsworth; MMA; Newark Museum; Randolph-Macon College; Williams College. BIBLIOGRAPHY: Barker 1; Barr 3; Baur 7; Boswell 1; Brown; Cahill and Barr, eds.; Canaday; Cheney, M. C.; Eliot; Flanagan; Goodrich and Baur 1; Haftman; Hunter 5; *Index of 20th Century Artists;* Janis, S.; Jewell 2; Kootz 1, 2; Kuh 1; McCurdy, ed.; Mellquist; Mendelowitz; Neumeyer; Nordness, ed.; Pearson 2; Poore; Pousette-Dart, ed.; Richardson; Ringel, ed.; Sachs; Smith, S. C. K.; Soby 5, 6; Wight 2.

BOARDMAN, SEYMOUR. b. December 29, 1921, Brooklyn, N.Y. STUDIED: City College of New York, 1946–51, BS; Academie des Beaux-Arts, Paris; Academie de la Grande Chaumiere; Atelier Fernand Leger, Paris. US Army, 1942–46. Resided Paris, 1946–52. TAUGHT: Wagner College, 1957–58. AWARDS: Longview Foundation Grant, 1963. ADDRESS: 334 East 30 Street, NYC. ONE-MAN EXHIBITIONS: (first) Salon du Mai, Paris, 1951; Martha Jackson

Peter Blume   *Winter. 1964*

Gallery, 1955, 56; Dwan Gallery, 1960; Stephen Radich Gallery, 1960, 61, 62. GROUP: WMAA, 1955, 61; Youngstown/Butler, 1955; SFMA, 1955; U. of Nebraska, 1956; Santa Barbara/MA, 1964; Carnegie, 1955. COLLECTIONS: Geigy Chemical Corp.; Newark Museum; Santa Barbara/MA; Union Carbide Corp.; WMAA; Walker.

BODIN, PAUL. b. October 30, 1910, NYC. STUDIED: NAD; ASL, with Boardman Robinson. Traveled USA extensively. FEDERAL A.P.: Easel painting and art teacher. AWARDS: Longview Foundation Grant, 1959; ART:USA:58, NYC, Special Distinction Award, 1958. ADDRESS: 207 West 86 Street, NYC. ONE-MAN EXHIBITIONS: (first) Playhouse Gallery, NYC, 1936; Theodore A. Kohn Gallery, NYC, 1937; Artists' Gallery, NYC, 1942; Laurel Gallery, NYC, 1948, 50; The New Gallery, NYC, 1952; Betty Parsons Gallery, 1959, 61. GROUP: New York World's Fair, 1939; American-British Art Center, NYC, 1943, 44, 45; Yale U., 1949; Santa Barbara/MA, 1949; Philadelphia Art Alliance, 1949; Brooklyn Museum, 1949, 59; MMA, American Watercolors, Drawings and Prints, 1952; NAD, 1954; ART:USA:58, NYC, 1958; ART:USA:59, NYC, 1959. COLLECTIONS: Buffalo/Albright; Dallas/MFA.

BOHROD, AARON. b. November 21, 1907, Chicago, Ill. STUDIED: Crane Junior College, 1925–26; Chicago Art Institute School, 1927–29; ASL, 1930–32, with Boardman Robinson, John Sloan, Richard Lahey. Traveled USA, Europe, South Pacific. TAUGHT: Illinois State Normal U., 1941–42; Ohio U., summers, 1949, 54; U. of Wisconsin, 1948– . MEMBER: NAD, Academician, 1952. FEDERAL A.P.: Easel painting. Artist War Correspondent for *Life* Magazine, 1942–45. COMMISSIONS: Eli Lilly & Co. (7 paintings, Medical Disciplines); *Look* Magazine (14 paintings, Great Religions of America). AWARDS: Corcoran, William A. Clark Prize and Corcoran Silver Medal ($1,500); MMA, Artists for Victory, $1,000 Prize; Guggenheim Foundation Fellowship, 1936, renewed, 1937; Chicago/AI, The Mr. & Mrs. Frank G. Logan Prize, 1937, 45; Illinois State Fair, First Award, 1955; PAFA, First Watercolor Prize, 1942; Carnegie International; NAD, Saltus Gold Medal for Merit, 1961; AAAL, Childe Hassam Award, 1962;

Hon. DFA, Ripon College, 1960. ADDRESS: 4811 Tonyawatha Trail, Madison, Wisc. DEALERS: The Milch Gallery; Frank Oehlschlaeger Gallery. ONE-MAN EXHIBITIONS: (first) Rehn Galleries, *ca.* 1935; The Milch Gallery, 1957, 59, 61; A.A.A. Gallery, NYC, 1939, 41, 43, 45, 46, 49, 52, 55. GROUP: WMAA; Milwaukee; MMA; Boston/MFA; PAFA; Chicago/AI; Corcoran; Brooklyn Museum. COLLECTIONS: Abbott Laboratories; U. of Arizona; Beloit College; Boston/MFA; Britannica; Brooklyn Museum; Chicago/AI; Corcoran; Cranbrook; Davenport/Municipal; Detroit/Institute; Finch College; Gallery of Modern Art, NYC; Lawrence College; MMA; New Britain; PAFA; San Antonio/McNay; Savannah/Telfair; Springfield, Mass./MFA; Terre Haute/Swope; Syracuse U.; WMAA; Walker; West Palm Beach/Norton; Youngstown/Butler. BIBLIOGRAPHY: American Artists Group Inc. 2; Baur 7; Bethers; Bruce and Watson; Cheney, M. C.; Christensen; Flanagan; McCurdy, ed.; Mendelowitz; Pagano; Pearson 1; Reese; Richardson; Wight 2.

BOLOMEY, ROGER. b. 1918, Torrington, Conn. STUDIED: Academy of Fine Arts, Florence, Italy; California College of Arts and Crafts; privately with Alfredo Cini in Switzerland. Resided Switzerland, Italy. Between 1958 and 1960, changed from painting to sculpture. COMMISSIONS: San Jose State College Art Building. AWARDS: Waitsfield, Bundy Sculpture Competition, First Prize, 1963; SFMA, P.P., 1960; Walnut Creek (Calif.) Pageant, First Prize, 1962. ADDRESS: c/o Dealer. DEALER: Royal Marks Gallery. ONE-MAN EXHIBITIONS: (first) SFMA, 1950; Sacramento/Crocker, 1950; Passedoit Gallery, NYC, 1951; Santa Barbara/MA, 1953; de Young, 1954; California Palace, 1958; Royal Marks Gallery, 1964. GROUP: SFMA Annuals, 1950, 60, 61, 62, 63; ICA, Boston, 100 Works on Paper, circ. Europe, 1959; Chicago/AI, 1963; Salon du Mai, Paris, 1964; Carnegie, 1964; WMAA Annual, 1964. COLLECTIONS: Chase Manhattan Bank; Fontana-Hollywood Corp.; San Jose State College; WMAA.

BOLOTOWSKY, ILYA. b. July 1, 1907, Petrograd, Russia. To USA 1923; citizen 1929. STUDIED: College St. Joseph, Istanbul; NAD, with Ivan Olinsky. US Air Force, 1942. Trav-

Roger Bolomey   *Hoboken # 10. 1964*

eled Russia, Europe, North America. **TAUGHT:** Black Mountain College, 1946–48; U. of Wyoming, 1948–57; Brooklyn College, 1954–56; New Paltz, 1957– ; Hunter College, 1954–56, 1963–64. **FEDERAL A.P.:** Master easel and mural artist, teacher. **MEMBER:** co-founder, charter member, and former President of American Abstract Artists; co-founder and charter member of Federation of Modern Painters and Sculptors. Produced 16mm experimental films. Began constructivist painted columns 1961. **COMMISSIONS** (murals): Cinema I, NYC, 1962; Hospital for Chronic Diseases, NYC, 1941; Theodore Roosevelt High School, NYC, 1941; New York World's Fair, 1939; Williamsburgh Housing Project, NYC, 1936 (one of the first abstract murals). **AWARDS:** Sharon (Conn.) Art Foundation, First Prize for Painting, 1959; S. R. Guggenheim Fellowship, 1941; Yaddo Fellowship, 1935; L. C. Tiffany Grant, 1930, 31; NAD, Hallgarten Prize for Painting, 1929, 30; NAD, First Prize Medal for Drawing, 1924, 25; The U. of Chicago, Midwest Film Festival, First Prize (for "Metanois"); State U. of New York Grant, for film research, 1959, 60. **ADDRESS:** 69 Tiemann Place, NYC. **DEALER:** Grace Borgenicht Gallery Inc. **ONE-MAN EXHIBITIONS:** (first) G.R.D. Studios, NYC, 1930; J. B. Neumann's New Art Circle, NYC, 1946, 52; Rose Fried Gallery, 1947, 49; Pratt Institute, 1949; Grace Borgenicht Gallery Inc., 1954, 56, 58, 59, 61, 63; New Paltz, 1960; Dickinson College, 1960; Elmira College, 1962. **GROUP:** American Abstract Artists Annuals; Federation of Modern Painters and Sculptors Annuals; Seattle World's Fair, 1962; Corcoran, 1963; WMAA Annuals; WMAA, Geometric Abstraction in America, circ., 1962; SRGM. **COLLECTIONS:** Brandeis U.; Ceret; Chase Manhattan Bank; Continental Grain Company; MOMA; The Miller Co.; NYU; New London; PMA; Phillips; Provincetown/Chrysler; RISD; SRGM; Union Carbide Corp.; Utica; WMAA; Yale U. **BIBLIOGRAPHY:** Blanchard; Goodrich and Baur 1.

BONTECOU, LEE. b. January 15, 1931, Providence, R. I. **STUDIED:** Bradford Junior College, with Robert Wade; ASL, 1952–55, with William Zorach, John Hovannes. Traveled Europe. **COMMISSIONS:** New York State Theater, Lincoln Center for the Performing Arts, NYC. **AWARDS:** Fulbright Fellowship

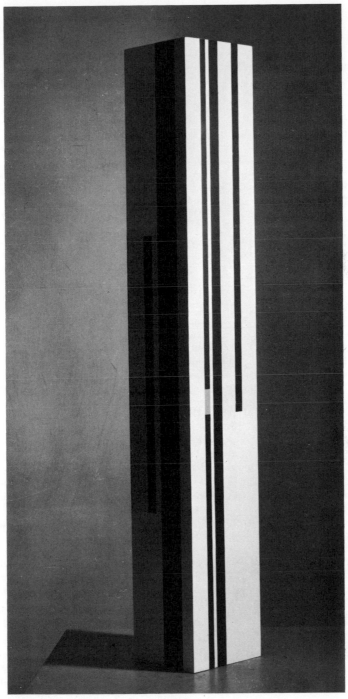

Ilya Bolotowsky   *Column October. 1964*

(Rome), 1957, 58; L. C. Tiffany Grant, 1959. ADDRESS: 147 Wooster Street, NYC. DEALER: Leo Castelli Inc. ONE-MAN EXHIBITIONS: (first) "G" Gallery, NYC, 1959; Leo Castelli Inc., 1960, 62. GROUP: Festival of Two Worlds, Spoleto, 1958; Martha Jackson Gallery, New Media—New Forms, I & II, 1960, 61; WMAA Annuals, 1961, 63, 64; Carnegie, 1961; MOMA, The Art of Assemblage, circ., 1961; VI Sao Paulo Biennial, 1961; Chicago/AI, 1962, 63; Seattle World's Fair, 1962; Corcoran, 1963; MOMA, Americans 1963, circ., 1963–64; Buffalo/Albright, Mixed Media and Pop Art, 1963. COLLECTIONS: Amsterdam/Stedelijk; Buffalo/Albright; Chase Manhattan Bank; Chicago/AI; Corcoran; Cornell U.; Dallas/MFA; Houston/MFA; MOMA; PAFA; The Singer Company Inc.; Smith College; WGMA; WMAA. BIBLIOGRAPHY: Janis and Blesh 1; *Metro;* Seitz 2.

BOOTH, CAMERON. b. March 11, 1892, Erie, Pa. STUDIED: Fargo College, 1912; Chicago Art Institute School, 1912–17; Hofmann School, Munich and Capri, 1927–28; Academie Andre Lhote, Paris, 1927. Traveled Europe extensively. TAUGHT: Minneapolis Institute School, 1921–25; St. Paul School of Art, 1929–40; ASL, 1944–48; Queens College, summers, 1946, 47; U. of California, Berkeley, 1935; Chicago Art Institute School, 1940; U. of Minnesota, 1947–50. MEMBER: Federation of Modern Painters and Sculptors. AWARDS: Chicago/AI, J. Q. Adams Traveling Scholarship, 1917; J. S. Guggenheim Fellowship, 1942; Hon. Ph.D., Hamline U. ADDRESS: 3408 47th Avenue South, Minneapolis, Minn. DEALER: The Howard Wise Gallery, NYC. ONE-MAN EXHIBITIONS: (first) Howard Putzell Gallery, San Francisco, 1936; Paul Elder Gallery, San Francisco, 1935; Denver/AM, 1936; Chicago/AI, 1942; Mortimer Brandt, NYC, 1943; The Bertha Schaefer Gallery, 1950; The Howard Wise Gallery, NYC, 1960. RETROSPECTIVE: A.F.A./Ford Foundation, circ. USA, 1961–64. GROUP: Many in 1920's and 1930's; WMAA, 1958; Carnegie. COLLECTIONS: U. of California; Denver/AM; MMA; MOMA; Minneapolis/Institute; Newark Museum; PAFA; Phillips; SFMA; SRGM; Walker. BIBLIOGRAPHY: Cheney, M. C.; Hall; Pousette-Dart, ed.

BOSA, LOUIS. b. April 2, 1905, Codroipo, Italy. To USA 1923; became a citizen. STUD-IED: Academy of Fine Arts, Venice, with Mazotti; ASL, with John Sloan. Traveled Europe extensively. TAUGHT: ASL, 1942–53; Parsons School of Design, 1950–53; Syracuse U.; U. of Notre Dame, summer, 1960; Cleveland Institute of Art, 1956– . MEMBER: NAD; ASL; Audubon Artists. FEDERAL A.P.: Easel painting. AWARDS: Portrait of America, NYC, $1,500 Prize, 1944; NAD, Hon. Men., 1944; Rockport (Mass.) Art Association, $100 Award, 1945; Mead Painting of the Year ($500), 1947; AAAL, $1,000 Award, 1948; Los Angeles County Fair, First Prize ($700), 1948; Pepsi-Cola $500 Award, 1948; U. of Illinois, P.P. ($900), 1949; Audubon Artists, Gold Medal of Honor, 1949; Hallmark International Competition, $750 Award, 1949; NAD, Gold Medal, 1957; Hallmark International Competition, $900 Award, 1958; New Hope, Pa., First Prize, 1959, 62; Legionnaires of Pennsylvania, First Prize and Gold Medal, 1959; Youngstown/Butler, First Prize ($1,000); NAD, $400 Prize, 1961. ADDRESS: 2549 Kenilworth Road, Cleveland, Ohio. DEALERS: The Milch Gallery; Frank Oehlschlaeger Gallery, Chicago and Sarasota. ONE-MAN EXHIBITIONS: (first) Contemporary Arts Gallery, NYC, 1930; The Milch Gallery; Springfield, Mass./MFA; Coy Gallery, Miami; Cleveland Institute of Art; Frank Oehlschlaeger Gallery, Chicago; Kleemann Gallery, NYC. GROUP: MMA; MOMA; WMAA; Carnegie; Corcoran; PMA; Boston/MFA; Toledo/MA; Buffalo/Albright; New Orleans/Delgado; Worcester/AM; Montclair/AM; Wilmington; Audubon Artists; Atlanta/AA; Cleveland/MA; Chicago/AI; Kansas City/Nelson; Argentina/Nacional; PAFA; NAD. COLLECTIONS: AAAL; Atlanta/AA; Britannica; Clearwater/Gulf Coast; Hartford/Wadsworth; IBM; U. of Illinois; Indianapolis/Herron; MMA; Montclair/AM; New Orleans/Delgado; U. of Notre Dame; PMA; Rochester/Memorial; San Diego; Springfield, Mass./MFA; Syracuse U.; Toronto; VMFA; WMAA; Wilmington; Worcester/AM; Youngstown/Butler. BIBLIOGRAPHY: Kent, N.; Pagano; Watson 2.

BOTHWELL, DORR. b. May 3, 1902, San Francisco, Calif. STUDIED: U. of Oregon; California School of Fine Arts; Rudolph Schaeffer School of Design, San Francisco. Traveled Europe, American Samoa. TAUGHT: California School of Fine Arts, 1945–61; Parsons School of Design, 1952; Rudolph Schaeffer School of Design, San Francisco, 1958–61; Mendocino (Calif.) Art Center, 1961– . FEDERAL A.P.: Painter; also designed murals for Visual Education, State Exhibition Building, Los Angeles, Calif.; Pomona (Calif.) High School, 1934. AWARDS: National Serigraph Society, First Prize, 1948; Abraham Rosenberg Foundation Traveling Fellowship, 1949. ADDRESS: P.O. Box 27, Mendocino, Calif. DEALER: The Bay Window Gallery. ONE-MAN EXHIBITIONS: (first) The Modern Gallery, San Francisco, 1927; El Prado Gallery, San Diego, 1929; San Diego, 1930; San Francisco Art Association, 1940, 41; Albatross Bookshop Gallery, San Francisco, 1942; Art in Action Gallery, San Francisco, 1943; Rotunda Gallery, San Francisco, 1946, 52; California Palace, 1947; National Serigraph Society, NYC, 1948, 52, 54; Sacramento/Crocker, 1948; Smithsonian, 1952; de Young, 1957, 63; Doris Meltzer Gallery, NYC, 1958; Mendocino Art Center, 1963. GROUP: San Francisco Art Association, 1925; California Palace, California Artists, 1930; San Diego Annuals, 1927–40; Golden Gate International Exposition, San Francisco, 1939; San Francisco Art Association Annuals, 1941– ; Denver/AM Annual, 1945; National Serigraph Society, NYC, Serigraph Annuals; WMAA Annual, 1950; SFMA, The New Decade, 1955; III Sao Paulo Biennial, 1955. COLLECTIONS: Achenbach Foundation; Bibliotheque Nationale; Brooklyn Museum; MMA; MOMA; SFMA; Sacramento/Crocker; San Diego; Santa Barbara/MA; Victoria and Albert Museum; WMAA; U. of Wisconsin.

BOTKIN, HENRY. b. April 5, 1896, Boston, Mass. STUDIED: Massachusetts School of Art, 1915–19, with Joseph de Camp, Ernest Major; ASL, with George Bridgeman. Traveled Europe, USA; resided Paris, eight years. TAUGHT privately. Active as a lecturer, writer, and organizer of exhibitions. MEMBER: Artists Equity (President, 1951–52); American Abstract Artists (President, 1954–55); Federation of Modern Painters and Sculptors (President, 1957–61); Fellow of the International Institute of Arts and Letters; Audubon Artists; International Association of Plastic Arts. AWARDS: Audubon Artists, First Prize (2); Mead Painting of the Year, $500 Prize. ADDRESS: 56 West 11 Street, NYC. DEALER: Rehn Galleries. ONE-MAN EXHIBITIONS: (first) Billiet

Gallery, Paris, 1927; The Downtown Gallery; Marie Harriman Gallery, NYC; Carstairs Gallery, NYC; J. Seligmann & Co.; A.A.A. Gallery, NYC; Otto Gerson Gallery, NYC; Riverside Museum; Denver/AM; Phillips; Arts Club of Chicago. GROUP: Tate; Cleveland/MA; de Young; Carnegie; Chicago/AI; SFMA; MMA; WMAA; Boston/MFA; Brooklyn Museum; NIAL; PAFA; Detroit/Institute; Corcoran; Stadtische Kunstsammlungen, Bonn; Munich/State. COLLECTIONS: Abbott Laboratories; Ain Harod; Akron/AI; Bath-Yam Museum; Boston/MFA; Brooklyn Museum; Colby College; Dallas/MFA; Denver/AM; Hartford/Wadsworth; MMA; MOMA; Mount Holyoke College; Munich/State; NYU; U. of Nebraska; Newark Museum; Norfolk; U. of Oklahoma; Phillips; Provincetown/Chrysler; Riverside Museum; Rochester/Memorial; Smith College; Tel Aviv; WMAA; Walker; West Palm Beach/Norton; Youngstown/Butler.

BOUCHE, LOUIS. b. March 18, 1896, NYC. STUDIED: Academie Colarossi; Academie de la Grande Chaumiere; Academie des Beaux-Arts, Paris, 1910–15, with Jules Bernard, Frank V. DuMond, Bernard Naudin; ASL, 1915–16. TAUGHT: ASL; NAD, 1951– . COMMISSIONS (murals): New Interior Department Building, Washington, D.C.; Justice Department Building, Washington, D.C.; US Post Office, Ellenville, N.Y.; Radio City Music Hall, NYC; Bar Lounge cars, Pennsylvania Railroad (4); Eisenhower Center, Abilene, Kans. AWARDS: NAD, Saltus Gold Medal for Merit, 1915; Guggenheim Foundation Fellowship, 1933; PAFA, Carol H. Beck Gold Medal, 1944; MMA, Artists for Victory, Third Prize, 1944; NAD, The Adolph and Clara Obrig Prize, 1951; NAD, Benjamin Altman Prize, 1955, 62. ADDRESS: 20 West 10 Street, NYC. DEALER: Kraushaar Galleries. ONE-MAN EXHIBITIONS: Kraushaar Galleries, 1936, 38, 40, 42, 44, 46, 49, 51, 54, 58, 62, 64; Des Moines. RETROSPECTIVE: Temple U. GROUP: Independents, NYC, 1917; The Daniel Gallery, NYC, 1918–31; Carnegie, 1937, 39; NAD; PAFA, 1941, 42, 45; Cincinnati/AM, 1948. COLLECTIONS: AAAL; Britannica; Cincinnati/AM; Columbus; Cranbrook; Des Moines; Fort Dodge/Banden; Lehigh U.; Los Angeles/County MA; MMA; U. of Nebraska; New Britain; U. of Oklahoma; PAFA; PMA; Phillips; US State Department; WMAA; Walker; Wichita/AM; Worcester/AM. **Bibliography:** Bethers; Bruce and Watson; Goodrich and Baur 1; Kent, N.; Pousette-Dart, ed.; Richardson; Watson 2.

BOURGEOIS, LOUISE. b. December 25, 1911, Paris, France. Studied: Lycee Fenelon, 1932, baccalaureate; Sorbonne, 1932–35; Ecole du Louvre, 1936–37; Academie des Beaux-Arts, Paris, 1936–38; Atelier Bissiere, Paris, 1936–37; Academie de la Grande Chaumiere, 1937–38; Academie Julian, Paris, 1938; Atelier Fernand Leger, Paris, 1938. Traveled Europe extensively. To USA 1938. Taught: Docent at the Louvre, 1937–38; Academie de la Grande Chaumiere, 1937, 38; Great Neck (N.Y.) Public Schools, 1960; Brooklyn College, 1963. Address: 347 West 20 Street, NYC. Dealer: The Stable Gallery. One-man Exhibitions: The Bertha Schaefer Gallery, 1945; Norlyst Gallery, NYC, 1947; The Peridot Gallery, 1949, 50, 53; Allan Frumkin Gallery, Chicago, 1953; Cornell U., 1959; The Stable Gallery, 1964; Rose Fried Gallery, 1964. Group: MOMA, 1943, 49, 51, 62; WMAA, 1945, 46, 53, 55, 57, 60, 62; MMA, 1943; SFMA, 1944; Los Angeles/County MA, 1945; Rochester/Memorial, 1945; Brooklyn Museum, 1945; Walker, 1954; U. of Illinois, 1957; Dallas/MFA, 1960; Claude Bernard, Paris, 1960. Collections: MOMA; WMAA. Bibliography: Baur 5; Giedion-Welcker 1; Goodrich and Baur 1; Motherwell and Reinhardt, eds.; Seuphor 3.

BOWMAN, GEOFFREY. b. December 29, 1928, San Francisco, Calif. Studied: City College of San Francisco, 1951, AA; San Francisco State College, with John Ihle, Seymour Locks, Alexander Nepote, John Gutman, Waldermar Johanssen, 1945, BA, 1957, MA; San Francisco Art Institute, graduate study with Henry Takemoto, 1960. US Navy, 1946–48. Taught: California State Prison, San Quentin, 1957–60 full time, 1960– , part time. Member: California Society of Etchers. Address: 429 West Richmond Avenue, Point Richmond, Calif. Dealer: The Lanyon Gallery. One-man Exhibitions: (first) The East-West Gallery, San Francisco, 1957; Yakima Valley Junior College, 1959; David Cole Gallery, San Francisco, 1962; The Lanyon Gallery, 1963; RAC, 1964. Group: SFMA, Small

Format, 1963; U. of Illinois, 1963; California Society of Etchers Annuals, 1960, 61, 62, 63, 64; Brooklyn Museum, Print Biennial; California Palace, 50th Anniversary of the California Society of Etchers, 1964; Denver/AM Annual, 1964; California Palace Annuals, 1961, 62, 64; SFMA, 1961; Santa Barbara Invitational, 1962; California Palace, James D. Phelan Art Awards, 1959. Collections: Lannan Foundation; SFMA.

BOWMAN, RICHARD. b. March 15, 1918, Rockford, Ill. Studied: Chicago Art Institute School, 1938–42, BFA; State U. of Iowa, 1947–49, MFA. Traveled Mexico, USA. Taught: Chicago Art Institute School, 1944–47, including summer school, 1944, 45; North Park College, 1944–46; State U. of Iowa, 1947–49; Stanford U., 1949–50, 1957, 58, 63; U. of Manitoba, 1950–54; Washburn-White Art Center, Palo Alto, Calif., 1954. Awards: Chicago/AI, Scholarship, 1939–41; Rockford/Burpee Annual, First Prize, 1940; Edward L. Ryerson Traveling Fellowship, 1942; Chicago/AI, William R. French Memorial Gold Medal, 1945; Iowa State Fair, Second Prize, 1948; Montreal/MFA Annual, 1952; Oakland/AM, Hon. Men., 1955. Address: 178 Springdale Way, Redwood City, Calif. Dealer: The Rose Rabow Gallery. One-man Exhibitions: Beloit College, 1941; Rockford/Burpee, 1941, 47; Ras-Martin Gallery, Mexico City, 1943; The Pinacotheca, NYC, 1945; Chicago/AI, 1945; Milwaukee, 1946; U. of Illinois, 1947; The Swetzoff Gallery, 1949; Pen and Palette Gallery, St. Louis, 1949; Contemporary Gallery, Sausalito, Calif., 1949, 50; Stanford U., 1950; Bordelon Gallery, Chicago, 1950; Kelly Gallery, Vancouver, B.C., 1954; The Rose Rabow Gallery, 1959, 61, 64; SFMA (two-man, with Gordon Onslow-Ford), 1959; SFMA, 1961. Retrospective: Stanford U., 1956; Washington State U., circ., 1957. Group: Chicago/AI, 1940, 44, 45; SFMA, 1941, 49, 50, 55, 60; Cincinnati/AM, 1941; Art of This Century, NYC, 1945; Chicago/AI, Abstract and Surrealist Art, 1948; Chicago/AI, Exhibition Momentum, 1948; Omaha/Joslyn, 1948, 49; Iowa State Fair, 1948; Philadelphia Print Club Annual, 1949; Walker, 1949; Brooklyn Museum, 1949; Canadian Society of Graphic Arts Annual, Toronto, 1952; Ottawa/National, Canadian Painters 1953, 1953; II Sao Paulo

Biennial, 1953; Royal Ontario Museum, 1954; Oakland/AM, 1955; Stanford U., 50 Contemporary American Painters, 1956; SFMA, After Surrealism, circ., 1959; USIA, Contemporary American Prints, circ. Latin America, 1959–60; California Palace, 1960, 61, 62, 63, 64; Carnegie, 1961, 64; WMAA, Fifty California Artists, 1962–63; Stanford U., Some Points of View for '62, 1962.

BOYCE, RICHARD. b. June 11, 1920, NYC. US Army, 1940–44. STUDIED: Boston Museum School, 1945–49, with Karl Zerbe (highest honors in painting). Assistant to O. Kokoschka, summer, 1948, Pittsfield, Mass. Traveled Europe, southern Mexico. TAUGHT: Boston Museum School, 1946–49; Wellesley College, 1953–62; Visiting Lecturer, Boston U., 1959–61; UCLA, 1963–64. MEMBER: Artists Equity. AWARDS: Boston/MFA, James William Paige Fellowship, 1949–51; Boston/MFA, Bartlett Grant, 1959, 60. ADDRESS: 11981 Kiowa Avenue, Los Angeles, Calif. DEALERS: The Alan Gallery; The Swetzoff Gallery; Felix Landau Gallery. ONE-MAN EXHIBITIONS: Boris Mirski Gallery, 1952; The Swetzoff Gallery, 1956, 59, 61, 62; The Zabriskie Gallery, 1961; Brattle Gallery, Cambridge, 1956; The Alan Gallery, 1963. GROUP: U. of Illinois, 1957; Chicago/AI Annual, 1960; WMAA, 1963; PAFA Annual, 1964; Johns Hopkins U., Three Young Americans, 1948; Worcester/AM, 1959; ICA, Boston, 1948, 52, 56, 62, 64. COLLECTIONS: Andover/Phillips; Harvard U.; Lincoln, Mass./De Cordova; RISD; WMAA; Wellesley College; Worcester/AM.

BOYLE, KEITH. b. February 15, 1930, Defiance, Ohio. STUDIED: State U. of Iowa, with James Lechay, BFA; Ringling School of Art, with Fred Sweet, Andrew Sanders. Traveled Europe; resided Rome. TAUGHT: Lake Forest College, 1956; Barat College, 1957, 59; Sacramento State College, 1960; Stanford U., 1962– . AWARDS: State of Iowa, Department of Education, P.P., 1952; Indiana (Pa.) State Teachers College, 1953; Springfield, Mo./AM, 1955; The Pennsylvania State U., 1955; Chicago/AI, The Mr. & Mrs. Frank G. Logan Medal ($1,500), 1958; California Palace, Patrons of Art and Music Award, 1964. ADDRESS: 3322 St. Michael Drive, Palo Alto, Calif. DEALER: The Lanyon Gallery. ONE-MAN

EXHIBITIONS: (first) Feingarten Gallery, Chicago, 1958, also 1959; Feingarten Gallery, San Francisco, 1960; Triangle Art Gallery, San Francisco, 1960; The Lanyon Gallery, 1963; de Young, 1964; SFMA, 1964; Stanford U., 1964. GROUP: Springfield, Mo./AM, 1952, 53, 54, 55; Des Moines, 1953; Denver/AM, 1953; Walker, 1954; Washburn U. of Topeka, 1955; Youngstown/Butler, 1955, 56, 58; Omaha/Joslyn, 1956; Chicago/AI, 1957, 58, 59, 60; Ravinia Festival, Highland Park, Ill., 1957; PAFA, 1958, 60, 62; SFMA, 1960, 62, 64; California Palace, 1964; Chicago/AI, 53 Chicago Artists, circ. France and Germany, 1957; Buffalo/Albright, 1960. COLLECTIONS: Barat College; Indiana (Pa.) State Teachers College; The Pennsylvania State U.; SFMA; Springfield, Mo./AM; State of Iowa.

BOYNTON, JAMES W. b. January 12, 1928, Fort Worth, Tex. STUDIED: Texas Christian U., BFA, MFA. TAUGHT: U. of Houston, 1955–57. AWARDS: Denver/AM, P.P., 1952, 54, 58; Texas State Fair, P.P., 1953; Fort Worth, P.P., 1951, 52, 54, 55; Houston/MFA, P.P., 1955; Texas Watercolor Society, First P.P., 1951, 53, 54, 55; Underwood-Neuhaus Corp., 1957; ART:USA:59, NYC, Hon. Men., 1959; Youngstown/Butler, 1957. ADDRESS: 4037 Browning Street, Houston 5, Tex. ONE-MAN EXHIBITIONS: Fort Worth, 1955; La Escondida, Taos, N.M., 1956; Andre Emmerich Gallery, Houston, 1957; Fairweather-Hardin Gallery, 1958; Barone Gallery, NYC, 1958; Bolles Gallery, San Francisco. GROUP: Fort Worth, 1950, 51, 52, 53, 54, 55; WMAA, Young America; SRGM, Younger American Painters, 1954; MOMA, Recent Drawings USA, 1956; Houston/MFA, 1955, 57; Santa Fe, N.M., 1957; SFMA, After Surrealism, circ., 1959; Yale U.; Corcoran; Colorado Springs/FA, 1953, 54, 57; Denver/AM, 1952, 54, 55, 56, 58; Carnegie, 1955; Youngstown/Butler, 1957; Chicago/AI, 1957, 58; Brussels World's Fair, 1958. COLLECTIONS: Dallas/MFA; Denver/AM; Fort Worth; Hartford/Wadsworth; Houston/MFA; Inland Steel Co.; Underwood-Neuhaus Corp.; WMAA; Witte; Youngstown/Butler. BIBLIOGRAPHY: MacAgy.

BRACH, PAUL. b. March 13, 1924, NYC. STUDIED: Fieldston School, NYC; State U. of Iowa, 1941–42, 1945–48, BA, MA. US Army,

1942–45. **Taught:** U. of Missouri; Cooper Union; Parsons School of Design; New School for Social Research. **m.** Miriam Schapiro. **Address:** 235 West 76 Street, NYC. **Dealer:** Cordier & Ekstrom Inc. **One-man Exhibitions:** (first) Leo Castelli Inc., 1957, also 1959; Union College (N.Y.), 1958; Dwan Gallery, 1960; Cordier and Warren, NYC, 1962; Cordier & Ekstrom Inc., 1964. **Group:** WMAA; MOMA; Chicago/AI; Corcoran; Baltimore/MA; St. Louis/City; Jewish Museum. **Collections:** Albion College; NYPL; U. of Nebraska; St. Louis/City. **Bibliography:** Blesh 1.

BRACKMAN, ROBERT. b. September 25, 1898, Odessa, Russia. **Studied:** Ferrer School, San Francisco; NAD; and with George Bellows, Robert Henri. **Taught:** ASL, 1934– ; American Art School, NYC, 1951– ; Brooklyn Museum School, 1936–38. **Awards:** NAD, The Thomas B. Clarke Prize, 1932; Chicago/AI, 1929; NAD, Saltus Gold Medal for Merit, 1941; Noel Flagg Prize, 1936; Connecticut Academy of Fine Arts, First Award, 1947; Carnegie, Hon. Men., 1949; PAFA, Carol H. Beck Gold Medal, 1958; Audubon Artists, p.p., 1960. **Address:** Noank, Conn. **One-man Exhibitions:** Macbeth Gallery, NYC, 1930, 31, 33, 34, 36, 40, 44; Grand Central, NYC, 1946. **Group:** NAD; Connecticut Academy of Fine Arts; PAFA; Audubon Artists; Montclair/AM. **Collections:** Atlanta/AA; Britannica; Brooklyn Museum; Bryn Mawr College; Canajoharie; The U. of Chicago; Colonial Williamsburg; Connecticut Life Insurance Company; U. of Connecticut; Davenport/Municipal; U. of Georgia; Harvard U.; Honolulu Academy; Houston/MFA; IBM; MMA; Memphis/Brooks; Milton Academy; Minneapolis/Institute; Montclair/AM; Newark Museum; New Britain; New Haven Public Library; Pasadena/AM; The Pentagon; Princeton U.; RISD; Radio Corporation of America; Rochester/Memorial; Rockford/Burpee; Toledo/MA; US Military Academy; US State Department; West Palm Beach/Norton; Wilmington; Yale U. **Bibliography: Bates;** Bazin; Boswell 1; Cheney, M. C.; Hall; Jewell 2, 3; Watson 1.

BRANDT, WARREN. b. February 26, 1918, Greensboro, N.C. **Studied:** Pratt Institute, 1935–37; ASL, 1946, with Yasuo Kuniyoshi; Washington U., with Philip Guston, Max Beck-mann, 1947–48, BFA with honors; U. of North Carolina, 1953, MFA. Traveled Mexico, Europe. **Taught:** School of Visual Arts, NYC, 1962–63; Southern Illinois U., 1959–61; U. of Mississippi, 1957–59; Guilford College, 1952–56; Pratt Institute, 1950–52; Salem College, 1949–50. **Awards:** John T. Milliken Traveling Fellowship. **m.** Grace Borgenicht. **Address:** 138 East 95 Street, NYC. **Dealer:** Grippi and Waddell Gallery. **One-man Exhibitions:** (first) Sacramento State College, 1943; Nonagon Gallery, NYC, 1959; Memphis State U., 1960; New Gallery, Provincetown, 1960; Michigan State U., 1961; The American Gallery, NYC, 1961; Esther Stuttman Gallery, Provincetown, 1962; Grippi Gallery, NYC, 1963; Obelisk Gallery, Washington, D.C., 1963; Grippi and Waddell Gallery, 1964. **Group:** MMA, American Watercolors, Drawings and Prints, 1952; WMAA; Brooklyn Museum, Print Biennials; VMFA, Virginia Artists Biennial; PAFA; A.F.A. **Collections:** Michigan State U.; Provincetown/Chrysler; Southern Illinois U.; WGMA.

BREININ, RAYMOND. b. November 30, 1910, Vitebsk, Russia. **Studied:** Chicago Academy of Fine Arts, with Uri Penn. **Taught:** Southern Illinois U.; U. of Minnesota; Breinin School of Art, Chicago; ASL. Costumes and settings for Ballet Theatre's "Undertow." **Awards:** U. of Illinois; ART:USA:58, NYC, 1958; Chicago/AI, Watson F. Blair Prize, 1942; Chicago/AI, Norman Wait Harris Silver Medal, 1942; MMA, p.p., 1942. **Address:** 48 West 20 Street, NYC. **One-man Exhibitions:** (first) The Downtown Gallery, 1939, also 1943; Indiana U., 1942; Chicago/AI, 1942. **Group:** MOMA, Twelve Americans, circ., 1956; WMAA. **Collections:** AAAL; Boston/MFA; Britannica; Brooklyn Museum; Capehart Corp.; Chicago/AI; Cranbrook; Edinburgh/National; Harvard U.; U. of Illinois; Indianapolis/Herron; Eli Lilly & Co.; MMA; MOMA; Newark Museum; Phillips; SFMA; San Diego; Williams College; Zanesville/AI. **Bibliography:** Baur 7; Frost; Genauer; Halpert; Miller, ed. 1.

BRICE, WILLIAM. b. April 23, 1921, NYC. **Studied:** ASL; Chouinard Art Institute, Los Angeles. **Taught:** Jepson Art Institute, Los Angeles; UCLA, 1953– . **Address:** 427 Beloit Street, Los Angeles, Calif. **Dealers:** Frank Perls Gallery; The Alan Gallery. **One-man**

EXHIBITIONS: Santa Barbara/MA, 1958; Frank Perls Gallery, 1952, 55, 56, 62; The Alan Gallery, 1955, 56, 64; The Downtown Gallery, 1949. GROUP: MMA, 1952; MOMA, 1952, 56; Chicago/AI, 1952, 56; Paris/Moderne, 1954; Carnegie, 1948, 49, 54; U. of Illinois; WMAA, 1947, 50, 51; California Palace, 1951, 52; SFMA; de Young; Los Angeles/County MA, 1947, 48, 49, 50, 51; Sao Paulo; Santa Barbara/MA, 1945. COLLECTIONS: AAAL; Andover/Phillips; Chicago/AI; U. of Illinois; Los Angeles/County MA; MMA; MOMA; U. of Nebraska; Santa Barbara/MA; WMAA; Wichita/AM. BIBLIOGRAPHY: Pousette-Dart, ed.

BRIGGS, ERNEST. b. 1923, San Diego, Calif. STUDIED: California School of Fine Arts, with Clyfford Still, David Park, Mark Rothko. US Army, 1943–45. A co-founder of Metart Gallery, San Francisco, 1949. TAUGHT: U. of Florida, 1958; Pratt Institute, 1961– . AWARDS: CSFA, Albert M. Bender Fellowship, 1951; SFMA, Anne Bremer Memorial Prize, 1953. ADDRESS: 128 West 23 Street, NYC. DEALER: The Howard Wise Gallery, NYC. ONE-MAN EXHIBITIONS: (first) Metart Gallery, San Francisco, 1949; The Stable Gallery, 1954, 55; CSFA, 1956; The Howard Wise Gallery, NYC, 1960, 62, 63. GROUP: San Francisco Art Association Annuals, 1948, 49, 53; WMAA Annuals, 1955, 56, 61; California Palace, Five Bay Area Artists, 1953; MOMA, Twelve Americans, circ., 1956; Corcoran, 1961; Dallas/MFA, "1961," 1962; Carnegie, 1961; SFMA, 1962, 63. COLLECTIONS: Carnegie; Michigan State U.; Rockefeller Institute; SFMA; WMAA.

BRODERSON, MORRIS (Gaylord). b. November 4, 1928, Los Angeles, Calif. STUDIED: Pasadena Museum School; U. of Southern California, with Francis De Erdely; Jepson Art Institute, Los Angeles. AWARDS: Pasadena Museum School, Scholarship, 1943; Los Angeles/County MA, P.P.; Los Angeles Art Festival, 1961; Carnegie International, 1961; *Art In America* (Magazine), New Talent, 1959. ADDRESS: 344 Huntley Drive, Los Angeles, Calif. DEALER: Ankrum Gallery. ONE-MAN EXHIBITIONS: Stanford U., 1958; Santa Barbara/MA, 1958; U. of California, Riverside, 1959; Dixi Hall Studio, Laguna Beach, Calif., 1954; Bertha Lewinson Gallery, Los Angeles, 1959, 60; Ankrum Gallery, 1961, 62; The Downtown Gallery, 1963. GROUP: Youngstown/Butler, 1959, 60; PAFA, 1959; Ringling, 1960; WMAA, 1960; Carnegie, 1961, 62; Santa Barbara/MA, 1958; Los Angeles/County MA, 1958, 59; U. of Illinois, 1963; San Diego, 1961; de Young, 1960; California Palace. COLLECTIONS: Boston/MFA; Home Savings and Loan Association; Kalamazoo/Institute; Los Angeles/County MA; Phoenix; SFMA; Santa Barbara/MA; Stanford U.; WMAA.

BRODERSON, ROBERT M. b. July 6, 1920, West Haven, Conn. STUDIED: Duke U., 1947–50, AB; State U. of Iowa, 1952, MFA, with Mauricio Lasansky, James Lechay, Stuart Edie. US Air Force, 1941–45. Traveled Europe, USA. TAUGHT: Duke U., 1957–64. AWARDS: AAAL, Childe Hassam Award; Ford Foundation, P.P.; AAAL, 1962; Guggenheim Foundation Fellowship. ADDRESS: c/o Dealer. DEALER: Catherine Viviano Gallery. ONE-MAN EXHIBITIONS: (first) Charlotte/Mint, 1951; Raleigh/NCMA, 1957, 60; Catherine Viviano Gallery, 1961, 63, 64. GROUP: PAFA, 1951, 53, 62; MMA, 1952; Corcoran Biennials, 1953, 57, 61; WMAA, 1961; U. of Illinois, 1963; Southwestern Annual, 1950, 54, 60. COLLECTIONS: Charlotte/Mint; Colorado Springs/FA; Des Moines; Hartford/Wadsworth; NIAL; Princeton U.; WMAA.

BRODIE, GANDY. b. May 20, 1924, NYC. STUDIED: Art history courses with Meyer Schapiro; self-taught as artist. Traveled Mexico, Europe. TEACHES privately. AWARDS: Ingram Merrill Foundation Grant, 1961; Mark Twain Contest ($1,000), 1959. ADDRESS: West Townshend, Vt. DEALER: Saidenberg Gallery. ONE-MAN EXHIBITIONS: (first) Urban Gallery, NYC, 1954; Durlacher Brothers, 1955, 57, 59, 61, 63; Saidenberg Gallery, 1964. GROUP: WMAA, Recent Acquisitions, 1957; MOMA, 1957, 61; Phillips. COLLECTIONS: Baltimore/MA; Charlotte/Mint; MIT; MOMA; Phillips; Provincetown/Chrysler; Sarah Lawrence College; WMAA.

BRONER, ROBERT. b. March 10, 1922, Detroit, Mich. STUDIED: Wayne State U., 1940–46, BFA, MFA; U. of California; Society of Arts and Crafts, Detroit, 1942–45, with Sarkis Sarkisian; Atelier 17, NYC, 1949–52, with S. W. Hayter; New School for Social Research, 1949–50, with Stuart Davis. TAUGHT: New

York Community College, 1963–64; Society of Arts and Crafts, Detroit. Detroit *Times*, 1958–60 (art critic); Birmingham *Eccentric*, 1962–63 (art critic); *Craft Horizons* (Magazine), 1961–63 (correspondent); *Art In America* (Magazine), 1958–63 (correspondent); *Pictures on Exhibit* (Magazine), 1963–64 (reviewer). AWARDS: Brooklyn Museum, Print Biennial, P.P.; Los Angeles Art Festival, Bronze Medal, 1948. ADDRESS: 58 Glendale Avenue, Highland Park, Mich. ONE-MAN EXHIBITIONS: (first) Anna Werbe Gallery, Detroit, 1953; Wellons Gallery, NYC, 1954; Philadelphia Art Alliance, 1956; Garelick's Gallery, Detroit, 1956, 61; Michigan State U., 1957; Drake U., 1961; Society of Arts and Crafts, Detroit, 1962; Feingarten Gallery, Chicago, 1962; Raven Gallery, Birmingham, Mich., 1963. GROUP: USIA, circ. Europe, 1959–60 (prints); SAGA, 1962, 63; MMA, American Watercolors, Drawings and Prints, 1952; MOMA, Young American Printmakers, 1953; Brooklyn Museum, Print Biennials; PAFA, 1959, 60; Pasadena/AM, 1962; PCA, circ. USA and France, 1959–60. COLLECTIONS: Brooklyn Museum; Chicago/AI; Cincinnati/AM; Detroit/Institute; Los Angeles/County MA; MOMA; NYPL; National Gallery; PMA; SRGM; Smithsonian; Walker.

BROOK, ALEXANDER. b. July 14, 1898, Brooklyn, N.Y. STUDIED: ASL, 1913–17, with R. W. Johnson, Frank V. DuMond, George Bridgeman, Dimitri Romanovsky, Kenneth Hayes Miller. Assistant Director, Whitney Studio Club, NYC. COMMISSIONS: US Post Office, Washington, D.C. (mural). AWARDS: Chicago/AI, The Mr. & Mrs. Frank G. Logan Medal, 1929; Carnegie, Second Prize, 1930; PAFA, Joseph E. Temple Gold Medal, 1931; Guggenheim Foundation Fellowship, 1931; Carnegie, First Prize, 1939; Los Angeles/County MA, First Prize, 1934; Paris World's Fair, 1937, Gold Medal; SFMA, Medal of Award, 1938. ADDRESS: Point House, Sag Harbor, New York. DEALER: Rehn Galleries. ONE-MAN EXHIBITIONS: ACA Gallery; Dayton/AI, 1942; The Downtown Gallery, 1934, 37; M. Knoedler & Co., NYC, 1952; Rehn Galleries, 1947, 60; Curt Valentine Gallery, NYC, 1930. RETROSPECTIVE: Chicago/AI, 1929. GROUP: WMAA; Rochester/Memorial, 1937; Brooklyn Museum; Carnegie; MMA; Toledo/MA; Buffalo/Albright; Chicago/AI; Newark Museum. COLLECTIONS:

Boston/MFA; Britannica; Brooklyn Museum; Buffalo/Albright; California Palace; Carnegie; Chicago/AI; Columbus; Corcoran; Detroit/Institute; de Young; Hartford/Wadsworth; IBM; Kansas City/Nelson; MMA; MOMA; Michigan State U.; U. of Nebraska, Newark Museum; SFMA; St. Louis/City; Toledo/MA; WMAA. BIBLIOGRAPHY: Baur 7; Bethers; Biddle 3; Boswell 1; **Brook;** Cahill and Barr, eds.; Cheney, M. C.; Eliot; Flexner; Goodrich and Baur 1; Hall; *Index of 20th Century Artists;* **Jewell 1,** 2; Kent, N.; Mellquist; Mendelowitz; Pagano; Pearson 1; Pousette-Dart, ed.; Richardson.

BROOKS, JAMES. b. October 18, 1906, St. Louis, Mo. STUDIED: Southern Methodist U., 1923–25; Dallas Art Institute, 1925–26, with Martha Simkins; ASL, 1927–31, with Kimon Nicolaides, Boardman Robinson; privately with William Harrison. FEDERAL A.P.: 1937–42. US Army in Middle East, 1942–45. Traveled Italy. TAUGHT: Pratt Institute, 1947–59; Columbia U., 1947–48; Yale U., 1955–60; Artist-in-Residence, American Academy, Rome, 1963. COMMISSIONS (murals): Woodside, N.Y., Library; La Guardia Airport; US Post Office, Little Falls, N.Y. AWARDS: Carnegie, Fifth Prize, 1952; Chicago/AI, The Mr. & Mrs. Frank G. Logan Medal, 1957; Chicago/AI, Norman Wait Harris Silver Medal and Prize, 1961; Ford Foundation, P.P., 1962. ADDRESS: 500 West Broadway, NYC. DEALER: The Kootz Gallery. ONE-MAN EXHIBITIONS: (first) The Peridot Gallery, 1950, also 1951, 52, 53; Grace Borgenicht Gallery Inc., 1954; The Stable Gallery, 1957, 59; The Kootz Gallery, 1961, 62. RETROSPECTIVE: WMAA, circ., 1963–64. GROUP: WMAA Annuals from 1950's; Galerie de France, American Vanguard, 1952; SRGM, Younger American Painters, 1954; WMAA, The New Decade, 1954–55; MOMA, Twelve Americans, circ., 1956; IV Sao Paulo Biennial, 1957; MOMA, The New American Painting, circ. Europe, 1958–59; Documenta II, Kassel, 1959; II Inter-American Paintings and Prints Biennial, Mexico City, 1960; Carnegie, 1952, 55, 58; 61; SRGM, Abstract Expressionists and Imagists, 1961; Seattle World's Fair, 1962; Cleveland/MA, 1963; SFMA, 1963; Tate, Dunn International, 1964. COLLECTIONS: Allentown/AM; Brandeis U.; Brooklyn Museum; Buffalo/Albright; Carnegie; Chase Manhattan Bank; Detroit/Institute; Hartford/Wadsworth;

James Brooks   *Ealand II. 1963*

Houston/MFA; MMA; MOMA; U. of Nebraska; PAFA; SRGM; The Singer Company Inc.; Tate; Union Carbide Corp.; WMAA; Walker. **BIBLIOGRAPHY:** Chaet; Flanagan; Goodrich and Baur 1; Haftman; Hess, T. B.; Hunter 1, **3**, 5; McCurdy, ed.; *Metro;* Motherwell and Reinhardt, eds.; Ponente; Pousette-Dart, ed.; Ritchie 1; Rodman 2.

BROWN, CARLYLE. b. 1919, Los Angeles, Calif.; **d.** December 21, 1964. **STUDIED:** Rudolph Schaeffer School of Design, San Francisco, 1939–40. US Navy, 1942–46. **AWARDS:** U. of Illinois, **P.P.**, 1952. **ONE-MAN EXHIBITIONS:** Durlacher Brothers, 1947; Catherine Viviano Gallery, 1950, 51, 53, 55, 57, 59; The Banfer Gallery, 1964; de Young, 1947; L'Obelisco, Rome, 1954. **GROUP:** WMAA; Detroit/Institute; U. of Illinois; Carnegie, 1950. **COLLECTIONS:** California Palace; U. of Illinois; MMA; PAFA; WMAA. **BIBLIOGRAPHY:** Goodrich and Baur 1; McCurdy, ed.; Newmeyer; Pousette-Dart, ed.

BROWN, JOAN. b. 1938, San Francisco, Calif. **STUDIED:** California School of Fine Arts, 1955; with Elmer Bischoff, Frank Lobdell, Sonia

Gechtoff, Richard Diebenkorn, Manuel Neri, Robert Howard, 1957–62. **TAUGHT:** San Francisco Art Institute, 1961– ; Raymond Wilkins High School, San Francisco, 1959. **m.** Manuel Neri. **ADDRESS:** 555-A Lombard Street, San Francisco, Calif. **DEALER:** Staempfli Gallery. **ONE-MAN EXHIBITIONS:** Spasta Gallery, San Francisco, 1958; Staempfli Gallery (two-man), 1960; Batman Gallery, San Francisco, 1961; Staempfli Gallery, 1961, 64; Ferus Gallery, 1962. **GROUP:** Oakland/AM; RAC; SFMA; WMAA; PAFA.

BROWN, WILLIAM T. b. April 7, 1919, Moline, Ill. **STUDIED:** Yale U., 1941, BA; U. of California, Berkeley, 1952, MA. Traveled Europe. **TAUGHT:** U. of California, Berkeley and Davis; California School of Fine Arts. **ADDRESS:** 1920 Mason Street, San Francisco, Calif. **DEALER:** Felix Landau Gallery. **ONE-MAN EXHIBITIONS:** SFMA, 1957; Felix Landau Gallery, 1958, 60, 63; Barone Gallery, NYC, 1961; The Kornblee Gallery, 1962. **GROUP:** Oakland/AM Annuals, 1952–58; RAC Annuals, 1952–58; Minneapolis/Institute, American Painting, 1945–57, 1957; Oakland/AM, Contemporary Bay Area Figurative Painting, 1957; Santa Barbara/MA,

II & III Pacific Coast Biennials, 1957, 59; SFMA Annuals, 1952, 53, 54, 55, 56, 57, 58; SFMA, West Coast Artists, circ., 1957, 59; The Zabriskie Gallery, East-West, 1960; California Palace, 1959. COLLECTIONS: Oakland/AM; SFMA.

BROWNE, BYRON. b. 1907, Yonkers, N.Y.; d. December 25, 1961. STUDIED: NAD, 1924–28, with C. W. Hawthorne, Ivan Olinsky. TAUGHT: ASL, 1948–61. Charter MEMBER, American Abstract Artists. AWARDS: U. of Illinois, P.P.; PAFA, P.P.; NAD, Hallgarten Prize, 1928; La Tausca Competition, Third Prize. ONE-MAN EXHIBITIONS: (first) New School for Social Research, 1936, also 1937; Artists' Gallery, NYC, 1939; The Pinacotheca, NYC, 1943, 44; The Kootz Gallery, 1946, 47, 48; Grand Central, NYC, 1949, 50, 53; Grand Central Moderns, 1950, 51, 52, 54, 55, 57, 58, 61, 62; Syracuse U., 1952; Tirca Karlis Gallery, 1960; ASL, Memorial Exhibition, 1962. GROUP: Chicago/AI; Carnegie; WMAA; Corcoran; MOMA; MMA; ART:USA, NYC; U. of Illinois; PAFA. COLLECTIONS: Brown U.; Dallas/MFA; U. of Georgia; NIAL; U. of Nebraska; Newark Museum; U. of Oklahoma; PAFA; Rio de Janeiro; Roswell; San Antonio/McNay; Tel Aviv; VMFA; WMAA; Youngstown/Butler. BIBLIOGRAPHY: Baur 7; Blesh 1; Cheney, M. C.; Janis, S.; Kootz 2; Pousette-Dart, ed.; Ritchie 1.

BROWNING, COLLEEN. b. May 18, 1927, Fermoy, County Cork, Ireland. STUDIED: Privately, and U. of London, Slade School. Traveled the world extensively. TAUGHT: City College of New York. Illustrated many children's books. AWARDS: NAD; Carnegie International; Edwin Austin Abbey Fellowship; Tupperware National Competition; Yaddo Fellowship. ADDRESS: 100 La Salle Street, NYC. DEALER: J. Seligmann and Co. ONE-MAN EXHIBITIONS: Hewitt Gallery, NYC, 1951, also 1952, 54; Robert Isaacson Gallery, NYC; Little Gallery, London, 1949; galleries in Los Angeles, Chicago. GROUP: A.F.A., 20th Century Realists; WMAA Annual; Chicago/AI; PAFA; NAD; NIAL; ART:USA, NYC; Walker; Carnegie; Festival of Two Worlds, Spoleto; Youngstown/Butler; Brandeis U.; Rochester/Memorial; U. of Illinois. COLLECTIONS: California Palace; Columbia, S.C./MA; Corcoran; Detroit/Institute; Rochester/Memorial; Williams College; Youngstown/Butler.

BULTMAN, FRITZ. b. 1919, New Orleans, La. STUDIED: Privately with Morris Graves, 1931; New Orleans Arts and Crafts School; Munich Preparatory School; Hofmann School, NYC and Provincetown, 1938–41; New Bauhaus, Chicago, 1937–38. TAUGHT: Hunter College, 1959–60; Pratt Institute, 1958–59. AWARDS: Italian Government Scholarship, 1950; Fulbright Fellowship, 1951. ADDRESS: 176 East 95 Street, NYC. DEALER: Tibor de Nagy Gallery. ONE-MAN EXHIBITIONS: (first) Hugo Gallery, NYC, 1947, also 1950; The Kootz Gallery, 1952; Martha Jackson Gallery, 1959; Galerie Stadler, Paris, 1960; The Stable Gallery, 1958; Tibor de Nagy Gallery, 1963; New Orleans/Delgado, 1959; Michel Warren Gallery, NYC, 1960; Gallery Mayer, NYC, 1960. GROUP: WMAA, 1950, 53. BIBLIOGRAPHY: Pousette-Dart, ed.

BUNCE, LOUIS. b. August 13, 1907, Lander, Wyo. STUDIED: Portland (Ore.) Museum School, 1925–26; ASL, 1927–30, with Boardman Robinson, William Von Schlegell. Traveled USA, Mexico, Europe extensively. TAUGHT: Salem (Ore.) Art Museum, 1937–38; Portland (Ore.) Museum School, 1946– ; U. of California, Berkeley, 1960; U. of British Columbia, 1960. FEDERAL A.P.: Mural Division, NYC, 1940–41. COMMISSIONS: Federal Building, Grants Pass, Ore., 1936–37 (mural); Portland (Ore.) International Airport, 1958 (mural); Portland (Ore.) Hilton Hotel, 1963 (637 serigraphs). AWARDS: SFMA, E. Walter Prize, 1961; Seattle/AM, P.P., 1936, 62; Portland, Ore./AM, P.P., 1952; Northwest Printmakers Annual, 1948; U. of Washington, P.P., 1950; Ford Foundation, P.P., 1964. ADDRESS: 1109 N.W. Gilson Street, Portland, Ore. DEALERS: Fountain Gallery; Gordon Woodside Gallery; Comara Gallery. ONE-MAN EXHIBITIONS: Seattle/AM, 1936, also 1953; Washburn U. of Topeka, 1937; Hollins College, 1941, 58; Portland, Ore./AM, 1945, 47, 56; Reed College, 1947, 51; U. of Washington, 1947; Harvey Welch Gallery, Portland, Ore., 1947; National Serigraph Society, NYC, 1947; Willamette U., 1948; Santa Barbara/MA, 1948; Kharouba Gallery, Portland, Ore., 1950, 52; Cincinnati/AM, 1952; Grants Pass (Ore.) Art League, 1953, 54; John Heller Gallery, NYC, 1953; Fountain Gallery, 1962, 64; Comara Gallery, 1964; Artists Gallery, Seattle, 1958; Salem (Ore.) Art Association, 1955; Morrison Street Gallery, Portland, Ore., 1955; Doris Meltzer Gallery, 1956,

57, 59, 60; U. of California, Berkeley, 1960; Gordon Woodside Gallery, 1964. RETROSPECTIVE: Portland, Ore./AM, 1955. GROUP: Chicago/AI, Abstract and Surrealist Art, 1948; Worcester/AM, 1949; WMAA Annuals, 1951, 53, 54, 59, 60; Grand Rapids, 1961; Colorado Springs/FA, Artists West of the Mississippi, 1951, 53, 56, 59; Corcoran, 1953; U. of Colorado, 1953; Los Angeles/County MA, 1953; VMFA, 1954; Des Moines, 1954; U. of Nebraska, 1954, 57; PAFA, 1958; Carnegie Annual, 1955; Denver/AM Annual, 1955, 56, 59, 62; Detroit/Institute, 1958; Santa Barbara/MA, 1957; Stanford U., Fresh Paint, 1958; Sao Paulo, 1955, 56; Golden Gate International Exposition, San Francisco, 1939; New York World's Fair, 1939; MMA, American Paintings Today, 1950; Seattle World's Fair, 1962. COLLECTIONS: AAAL; American Association of University Women; Auburn U.; Colorado Springs/FA; Hollins College; Library of Congress; MMA; U. of Michigan; National Gallery; PMA; Portland, Ore./AM; Reed College; SFMA; Seattle/AM; Springfield, Mo./AM; US State Department; Utica; WMAA; U. of Washington; Youngstown/Butler. BIBLIOGRAPHY: Bunce.

BURCHFIELD, CHARLES. b. April 9, 1893, Ashtabula Harbor, Ohio. STUDIED: Cleveland Institute of Art, 1912, with Henry G. Keller, F. N. Wilcox, William J. Eastman; NAD. US Army, 1918–19. TAUGHT: U. of Minnesota, Duluth, 1949; Art Institute of Buffalo, 1949–52; Ohio U., summer, 1950; U. of Buffalo, summers, 1950, 51; Buffalo Fine Arts School, 1951–52. MEMBER: American Academy of Arts and Sciences; NIAL; NAD. COMMISSIONS: *Fortune* Magazine, 1936, 37. AWARDS: U. of Buffalo, Chancellor's Medal, 1944; Cleveland/MA, First Prize and Penton Medal, 1921; PAFA, Jennie Sesnan Gold Medal, 1929; Carnegie, Second Prize, 1935; International Arts Festival, Newport, R.I., First Prize, 1936; PAFA, Dana Watercolor Medal, 1940; Chicago/AI, Watson F. Blair Prize, 1941; NIAL,

Charles Burchfield   *Song of the Redbird. 1917–60*

Award of Merit Medal, 1942; Carnegie, Second Hon. Men., 1946; PAFA, Dawson Memorial Medal, 1947; PAFA, Special Award, 1950; MMA, 1952 ($500); Buffalo/Albright, J. C. Evans Memorial Prize, 1952; Buffalo/Albright, Satter's Prize, 1955; Buffalo Historical Society, Red Jacket Medal, 1958; Hon. LHD, Kenyon College, 1944; Hon. DFA, Harvard U., 1948; Hon. DFA, Hamilton College, 1948; Hon. LLD, Valparaiso U., 1951. **ADDRESS:** 3574 Clinton Street, West Seneca, N.Y. **DEALER:** Rehn Galleries. **ONE-MAN EXHIBITIONS:** (first) Sunwise Turn Bookshop, NYC, 1916; Cleveland Institute of Art, 1916, 17, 21, 44; Laukhuff's Bookstore, Cleveland, 1918; Garrick Theater Library, NYC, 1919; Little Theatre, Cleveland, 1919; H. Kevorkian, NYC, 1920; Chicago/AI, 1921; Grosvenor (Gallery), London, 1923; Montross Gallery, NYC, 1924, 26, 28; Eastman-Bolton Co., Cleveland, 1928; Rehn Galleries, 1930, 31, 34, 35, 36, 39, 41, 43, 46, 47, 50, 52, 54–64; MOMA, 1954; Rochester/Memorial, 1932; Phillips, 1934; Philadelphia Art Alliance, 1937; Town and Country Gallery, Cleveland, 1948; State U. of New York, Buffalo, 1963. **RETROSPECTIVE:** Carnegie, 1938; Buffalo/Albright, 1944, 63; Cleveland/MA, 1953 (drawings); WMAA, 1956. **GROUP:** WMAA Annuals; Chicago/AI; U. of Illinois; MOMA; MMA; Carnegie. **COLLECTIONS:** Boston/MFA; Brooklyn Museum; Buffalo/Albright; Carnegie; Chase Manhattan Bank; Chicago/AI; Cleveland/MA; Detroit/Institute; Harvard U.; IBM; U. of Illinois; Indianapolis / Herron; Kalamazoo / Institute; Kansas City/Nelson; MMA; MOMA; Muskegon/Hackley; Newark Museum; New Britain; PAFA; Phillips; RISD; St. Louis/City; San Diego; Santa Barbara/MA; Sweet Briar College; Syracuse/Everson; Terre Haute/Swope; Utica; VMFA; Valparaiso U.; WMAA; Wichita/AM; Wilmington; Youngstown/Butler. **BIBLIOGRAPHY:** Barr 3; **Baur 1,** 7; Bazin; Beam; Blesh 1; Boswell 1; Brown; **Burchfield 1, 2, 3;** Cahill and Barr, eds.; Canaday; Cheney, M. C.; Christensen; Craven 1, 2; *The Drawings of Charles E. Burchfield;* Eliot; Flanagan; Flexner; Gallatin 1; Goodrich 1; Goodrich and Baur 1; Haftman; Hall; Hunter 5; *Index of 20th Century Artists;* Jewell 2; Lee and Burchwood; McCurdy, ed.; Mellquist; Mendelowitz; Newmeyer; Nordness, ed.; Pagano; Pearson 1; Phillips 1; Poore; Pousette-Dart, ed.; Richardson; Ringel, ed.; Sachs; Soby 5; Sutton; Watson 1; Wight 2.

BURKHARDT, HANS GUSTAV. b. December 20, 1904, Basel, Switzerland. To USA 1924. **STUDIED:** Cooper Union, 1924–25; Grand Central School, NYC, 1928–29, with Arshile Gorky; and privately with Gorky, 1930–35. Resided Mexico, 1950–52. **TAUGHT:** Long Beach State College, summer, 1959; U. of Southern California, 1959–60; UCLA, 1962–63; California Institute of the Arts, 1962–64; San Fernando Valley State College, 1963– . **AWARDS:** California State Fair, P.P., 1954; California State Fair, Second Prize, 1962; California Watercolor Society, P.P., 1962; Los Angeles All-City Show, P.P., 1957, 60, 61; Los Angeles/County MA, First P.P., 1946; Santa Barbara/MA, Ala Story Purchase Fund, 1957. **ADDRESS:** 1914 Jewett Drive, Los Angeles, Calif. **ONE-MAN EXHIBITIONS:** (first) Stendahl Gallery, Los Angeles, 1939; Open Circle Gallery, 1943, 44; Chabot Gallery, Los Angeles, 1946, 47, 49; U. of Oregon, 1947; Hall of Art, Beverly Hills, 1948; Los Angeles/County MA, 1946, 62; Fraymont Gallery, Los Angeles, 1951, 52; Guadalajara, 1951; Paul Kantor Gallery, 1953; Escuela de Bellas Artes, San Miguel de Allende, Mexico, 1956, 61; Esther Robles Gallery, 1957, 58, 59; Comara Gallery, 1959; Long Beach State College, 1959; Glendale (Calif.) Public Gallery, 1960; Whittier (Calif.) Art Association, 1960; SFMA, 1961; La Jolla, 1962; Ankrum Gallery, 1961, 63; Fresno Art Center, 1962; Palm Springs Desert Museum, 1964. **RETROSPECTIVE:** Falk-Raboff (Gallery), Los Angeles, 1954; Pasadena/AM (10-year), 1957; Santa Barbara/MA (30-year), 1961. **GROUP:** Los Angeles/County MA Annuals, 1940, 45, 46, 53, 54, 57, 59; Los Angeles Art Association Annuals, 1940–63; Long Beach/MA, 1958, 60, 64; Denver/AM, 1949, 53, 54; U. of Illinois, 1951; Corcoran, 1947, 51, 53; PAFA, 1951, 52, 53; MMA, 1951; WMAA Annuals, 1951, 55, 58; III Sao Paulo Biennial, 1955. **COLLECTIONS:** The Coca-Cola Co.; Columbia, S.C./MA; Downeyville Museum; Guadalajara; Home Savings and Loan Association; La Jolla; Long Beach/MA; Los Angeles/County MA; Lucerne; U. of Miami; Pasadena/AM; Santa Barbara/MA; State of California; Stockholm/National.

BURLIN, PAUL. b. September 10, 1886, NYC. Self-taught in art. Traveled Europe, North Africa, USA; resided Paris, 1921–32. TAUGHT: U. of Minnesota, 1949; Washington U., 1949–54; U. of Colorado, 1951; U. of Wyoming, 1952; UCLA, 1954; Union College (N.Y.), 1954–55; Chicago Art Institute School, 1960. FEDERAL A.P.: Easel painting. AWARDS: Portrait of America, First Prize ($2,500), 1945; ART:USA:59, NYC, First Prize, 1959; Chicago/AI, Watson F. Blair Prize ($2,000), 1960; PAFA, J. Henry Schiedt Memorial Prize, 1963. ADDRESS: 54 West 74 Street, NYC. DEALER: Grace Borgenicht Gallery Inc. ONE-MAN EXHIBITIONS: (first) The Daniel Gallery, NYC, 1913, also 1914–20; Kraushaar Galleries, 1926, 27; Westheim Gallery, Berlin, 1927; de Hauke Gallery, NYC, 1942; A.A.A. Gallery, NYC, 1942, 43, 44; Vincent Price Gallery, Los Angeles, 1944; The Downtown Gallery, 1946, 49, 52, 53; U. of Minnesota, 1949; Southern Illinois U., 1950, 60; U. of Wyoming, 1952; Washington U., circ., 1954; The Stable Gallery, 1954; Poindexter Gallery, 1958, 59; The Alan Gallery, 1959; Chicago/AI, 1960; Holland-Goldowsky Gallery, Chicago, 1960; Grace Borgenicht Gallery Inc., 1963, 64. RETROSPECTIVE: A.F.A., circ., 1962. GROUP: The Armory Show, 1913; WMAA Annuals; Carnegie; PAFA; WMAA, Pioneers of American Art, 1946; Walker; Corcoran; U. of Nebraska; nationally since 1913. COLLECTIONS: Auburn U.; Britannica; Brooklyn Museum; Carleton College; Exeter; Hartford/Wadsworth; IBM; S. C. Johnson & Son, Inc.; MOMA; U. of Minnesota; Newark Museum; Southern Illinois U.; Tel Aviv; WMAA; Washington U.; Wichita/AM. BIBLIOGRAPHY: Baur 7; Biddle 3; Cheney, M. C.; Coke; Genauer; Goodrich and Baur 1; Kootz 2; Nordness, ed.; Pagano; Passloff; Pearson 1, 2; Pousette-Dart, ed.; Richardson; Zaidenberg, ed.

BURLIUK, DAVID. b. July 22, 1882, Kharkov, Ukraine. STUDIED: Art schools in: Kazan, 1898–1902, Odessa, 1911, Munich, Moscow, 1914; Bayerische Akademie der Schonen Kunst, Munich; Academie des Beaux-Arts, Paris. To USA 1922; citizen 1930. Traveled Europe, the Orient, USA. TAUGHT: Painting, art history. FEDERAL A.P.: Easel painting. A founder (with W. Mayakovsky and W. Kamiensky) of Futurist art movement in Russia, 1911. A founder-member of Der Blaue Reiter and Der Sturm groups, 1910–14. Co-founder and publisher (with Marussia Burliuk) of art magazine *Color Rhyme*, 1930– . Owns and operates Burliuk Gallery, Hampton Bays, N.Y. AWARDS: Pepsi-Cola, 1946. ADDRESS: Hampton Bays, Long Island, N.Y. DEALERS: ACA Gallery; Burliuk Gallery. ONE-MAN EXHIBITIONS: (first) Cherson, South Russia, 1904; galleries in Moscow and St. Petersburg, 1907; Societe Anonyme, NYC, 1924; J. B. Neumann Gallery, NYC, 1927; Morton Gallery, NYC, 1928; Dorothy Paris Gallery, NYC, 1933, 34, 35; California Palace, 1931; Boyer Gallery, NYC, 1935, 36, 37, 38, 39; Phillips, 1937; ACA Gallery, 1941–50, 1952, 53, 54, 56, 58, 60, 63; Havana/Nacional, 1955; Galerie Maeght, Der Blaue Reiter, 1962; Galerie Stangl, Munich, 1962; Leonard Hutton Gallery, NYC, Der Blaue Reiter, 1963. GROUP: Brooklyn Museum, 1923, 26; PMA, 1926. COLLECTIONS: Boston/MFA; Brooklyn Museum; MMA; Phillips; WMAA; Yale U. BIBLIOGRAPHY: Baur 7; Dreier 1; Richardson; Selz, P. 1.

C

CADMUS, PAUL. b. December 17, 1904, NYC. STUDIED: NAD, 1919–26; ASL, 1929–31, with Joseph Pennell, Charles Locke. Traveled Europe, the Mediterranean. FEDERAL A.P.: Easel painting, 1934. Designed sets and costumes for Ballet Caravan, 1938. COMMISSIONS (mural); US Post Office, Richmond, Va., 1938. AWARDS: NIAL Grant, 1961. ADDRESS: 5 St. Luke's Place, NYC. DEALER: The Midtown Galleries. ONE-MAN EXHIBITIONS: The Midtown Galleries, 1937, 49; Baltimore/MA (three-man), 1942. GROUP: MOMA; MMA; WMAA, 1934, 36, 37, 38, 40, 41, 45; Chicago/AI, 1935; Hartford/Wadsworth; Williams College; PAFA, 1941; Carnegie, 1944, 45; Corcoran; Golden Gate International Exposition, San Francisco, 1939. COLLECTIONS: Andover/Phillips; Baltimore/MA; Cranbrook; Hartford/Wadsworth; Library of Congress; MMA; MOMA; Milwaukee; Sweet Briar College; WMAA; Williams College. BIBLIOGRAPHY: American Artists Congress, Inc.; American Artists Group Inc. 3; Baur 7; Bazin; Boswell 1; Goodrich and Baur 1; Hall; Kent, N.; McCurdy, ed.; Nordness, ed.; Pagano; Reese.

CAESAR, DORIS. b. November 8, 1892, NYC. STUDIED: ASL; Archipenko School of Art; privately with Rudolph Belling. MEMBER: Federation of Modern Painters and Sculptors; Sculptors Guild; Architectural League of New York; New York Society of Women Artists; National Association of Women Artists; Audubon Artists. ADDRESS: Litchfield, Conn. DEALER: Weyhe Gallery. ONE-MAN EXHIBITIONS: Weyhe Gallery, 1933, 35, 37, 47, 53, 57, 59, 61, 64; Curt Valentine Gallery, NYC, 1943; Musee du Petit Palais, Paris, 1950; Argent Gallery, NYC, 1948; Margaret Brown Gallery, Boston, 1956; WMAA, 1959; Katonah (N.Y.) Art Gallery, 1955; Gallery Fifteen, NYC, 1940; Hartford/Wadsworth, 1960. GROUP: MMA, 1955; City of Philadelphia, Sculpture International, 1940–50; New Burlington Galleries, London, 1956; A.F.A., circ., 1953–54; I International Religious Art Biennial, Salzburg, 1958; WMAA, circ., 1959; Memphis/Brooks, 1960. COLLECTIONS: Albion College; Andover/Phillips; Atlanta/AA; Busch-Reisinger Museum; La Casa del Libro; Cleveland/MA; Colby College; Colorado Springs/FA; Connecticut College; Dayton/AI; U. of Delaware; Father Judge Mission Seminary; Fort Worth; Grand Rapids; Hartford/Wadsworth; Harvard U.; Howard U.; Indiana U.; State U. of Iowa; Kansas City/Nelson; Memphis/Brooks; Minneapolis/Institute; U. of Minnesota; NYU; Newark Museum; PAFA; Pasadena/AM; Phoenix; Portland, Me./MA; Rockland/Farnsworth; St. Bernard's Church, Hazardville, Conn.; St. John's Abbey, Collegeville, Minn.; Utica Public Library; WMAA; Williams College. BIBLIOGRAPHY: Brumme; **Goodrich and Baur 2.**

CAJORI, CHARLES. b. March 9, 1921, Palo Alto, Calif. STUDIED: Colorado College, 1939–40, with Boardman Robinson; Cleveland Institute of Art, 1940–42; Columbia U., 1946–48, with John Heliker, Henry Poor; Skowhegan School, summers, 1947, 48. US Air Force, 1942–46. A co-organizer of the Tanager Gallery, NYC, 1952. Traveled Europe. TAUGHT: College of Notre Dame of Maryland, 1950–56; American U., 1955–56; Philadelphia Museum

School, 1956–57; U. of California, Berkeley, 1959–60; Cornell U., summers, 1961, 63; Cooper Union, 1956– ; Yale U., 1963–64; U. of Washington, 1964; Pratt Institute, 1961–62. AWARDS: Fulbright Fellowship (Italy), 1952; Yale U., Distinction in Arts Award, 1959; Longview Foundation Grant, 1962; Ford Foundation, P.P., 1962. ADDRESS: 205 West 14 Street, NYC. DEALER: The Howard Wise Gallery, NYC. ONE-MAN EXHIBITIONS: (first) Tanager Gallery, NYC, 1956, also 1961; The Bertha Schaefer Gallery, 1958; Watkins Gallery, Washington, D.C., 1956; Oakland/AM, 1959; Cornell U., 1961; The Howard Wise Gallery, NYC, 1963; U. of Washington, 1964. GROUP: Walker, Vanguard, 1955; WMAA, 1957; U. of Kentucky, 1957, 61; U. of Nebraska, 1958; Festival of Two Worlds, Spoleto, 1958; Corcoran, 1959; Brooklyn Museum, 1959; ICA, Boston, 100 Works on Paper, circ. Europe, 1959; MOMA, Abstract Watercolors and Drawings: USA, circ. Latin America and Europe, 1961–62; Chicago/AI, 1964; WMAA Annuals, 1957, 62. COLLECTIONS: Kalamazoo/Institute; U. of Kentucky; WMAA; Wake Forest College; Walker.

CALCAGNO, LAWRENCE. b. March 23, 1913, San Francisco, Calif. US Air Force, 1941–45. STUDIED: California School of Fine Arts, 1947–50. Traveled Mexico, 1945–47; Europe, North Africa, 1950–55; Peru. TAUGHT: U. of Alabama, 1955–56; State U. of New York, Buffalo, 1956–58; U. of Illinois, 1958–59; NYU, 1960. ADDRESS: 215 Bowery, NYC. DEALER: The Osborne Gallery. ONE-MAN EXHIBITIONS: (first) The Little Gallery, New Orleans, 1945; College of the Pacific, 1948; Lucien Labaudt Gallery, 1948, 54; Numero Galleria d'Arte, Florence, Italy, 1951–52; Galeria Clan, Madrid, 1955; Studio Paul Facchetti, Paris, 1955; Martha Jackson Gallery, 1955, 58, 60, 62; U. of Alabama, 1956; Howard College, 1956; Macon (Ga.) Art Association, 1956; Buffalo/Albright, 1956; Lima, 1957; U. of Illinois, 1959; Fairweather-Hardin Gallery, 1959; Philadelphia Art Alliance, 1960; New Arts Gallery, Houston, 1960; Mexico City U., 1961; Tirca Karlis Gallery, 1961; McRoberts & Tunnard Gallery, London, 1961; Galerie Kobenhavn, Denmark, 1962. GROUP: Art:USA:Now, circ., 1962– . COLLECTIONS: U. of Alabama; Buffalo/Albright; California

Palace; Carnegie; Chase Manhattan Bank; Dayton/AI; ICA, Boston; U. of Illinois; Lima; MOMA; McCann-Erickson, Inc.; NYU; U. of Nebraska; Phoenix; Provincetown/Chrysler; RISD; Reynolds Metals Co.; SFMA; Union Carbide Corp.; WMAA; Walker. BIBLIOGRAPHY: Baur 5; Blesh 1; Nordness, ed.

CALDER, ALEXANDER. b. July 22, 1898, Philadelphia, Pa. STUDIED: Stevens Institute of Technology, 1915–19; ASL, 1923–26, with George Luks, Guy Du Bois, Boardman Robinson, John Sloan. Traveled Europe, USA, Latin America, India. To Paris 1928. The subject of three films: "Alexander Calder: Sculpture and Constructions" (MOMA, 1944); "Alexander Calder" (Burgess Meredith and Herbert Matter, 1951); "Calder's Circus" (Pathé, 1961). Two Calder sequences are in the film "Dreams That Money Can Buy" (Hans Richter, 1948). Designed sets for: "Horizons" and "Four Movements" (by Martha Graham, NYC, 1936); *Balloons* (by Padraic Colum, Boston, 1946); "Socrates" (by Eric Satie, 1936); *Happy as Larry* (by Donagh MacDonagh, NYC, 1946); "Symphonic Variations" (by Tatiana Leskova, 1949). COMMISSIONS: Spanish Pavilion, Paris World's Fair, 1937; New York World's Fair, 1939; Terrace Plaza Hotel, Cincinnati, 1945; General Motors Corp., 1954; New York International Airport, 1958; UNESCO, Paris, 1958; Hotel Avila, Caracas, 1940; Aula Magna, University City, Caracas, 1952. AWARDS: XXVI Venice Biennial, 1952, First Prize; Sao Paulo, 1953; Carnegie, First Prize, 1958; Architectural League of New York, Gold Medal, 1960; City of Philadelphia, Outstanding Citizen Award, 1955; Stevens Institute of Technology, Medal, 1956; Brandeis U., Creative Arts Award, 1962; MOMA, First Prize, Plexiglas Sculpture Competition, 1939. ADDRESS: Roxbury, Conn.; Sache (Indre-et-Loire), France. DEALERS: Perls Galleries; Galerie Maeght. ONE-MAN EXHIBITIONS: (first) Weyhe Gallery, 1928 (wire sculpture); Billiet Gallery, Paris, 1929; Galerie Percier, Paris, 1931; Neumann-Nierendorf Gallery, Berlin, 1929; 56th Street Gallery, NYC, 1930; Galerie Vignon, Paris, 1932 (first mobiles exhibited); Julien Levy Galleries, NYC, 1932; Pierre Matisse Gallery, 1934, 36, 37, 39, 40, 41, 42, 43; Mayor Gallery, London, 1937; The Willard Gallery, 1940 (first jewelry exhibited), 1941, 42;

Alexander Calder   *Yellow Dot in the Air and Polychrome. 1961*

Buchholz Gallery, NYC, 1944, 45, 47, 49; The Kootz Gallery, 1945; Galerie Louis Carre, Paris, 1946; Cincinnati/AM, 1946; Amsterdam/Stedelijk, 1947 (two-man), 1950, 59; Berne (two-man), 1947; Margaret Brown Gallery, Boston, 1949; Galerie Maeght, 1949, 64; Galerie Pierre Colle, Paris, 1933; The U. of Chicago, 1935; Arts Club of Chicago, 1935; Honolulu Academy, 1937; Arts and Crafts Club, New Orleans, 1941; SFMA, 1942; Andover/Phillips, 1943; Brazilian Ministry of Education, Rio de Janeiro, 1948; Sao Paulo, 1948; Gallery R. Hoffman, Hamburg, 1954; Galerie Blanche, Stockholm, 1950; MIT, 1950; Lefevre Gallery, London, 1951; Palais des Beaux Arts, Brussels, 1960; Kunstgewerbemuseum, Zurich, 1960; Galerie d'Art Moderne, Basel, 1962; Galleria d'Arte del Naviglio, Milan, 1964. **RETROSPECTIVE:** Springfield, Mass./MFA, 1938; MOMA, 1943; Tate, 1962; SRGM, 1964. **GROUP:** Artists' Gallery, NYC, 1926 (first paintings exhibited); Salon des Humoristes, Paris, 1927; Salon des Artistes Independants, Paris, 1929, 30; MOMA, Painting and Sculpture, 1930; Salon des Surindependants, Paris, 1930; WMAA; Chicago/AI; SFMA; Cincinnati/AM, 1942; Berne, 1947; Documenta III, Kassel, 1964; Yale U., 1950; Kestner-Gesellschaft, Hannover, 1954. **COLLECTIONS:** Amsterdam/Stedelijk; Andover/Phillips; U. of Arkansas; Arts Club of Chicago; Basel; Chicago/AI; Dallas/MFA; Frankfurt am Main; Hartford/Wadsworth; Honolulu Academy; Lodz; MMA; MOMA; Mannheim; Marshall Field & Co.; Montreal/MFA; Moscow/Western; Museum of Science and Industry, Chicago; PAFA; Phillips; Pittsfield/Berkshire; SRGM; St. Louis/City; U. of St. Thomas; Sao Paulo; Smith College; Stockholm/National; Toronto; VMFA; WMAA; Washington U.; Yale U. **BIBLIOGRAPHY:** Baldinger; Barr 1; Baur 5, 7; Beam; Biederman 1; Blesh 1; Breton 3; Brion 1; Brumme; **Calder; Calder and Liedl;** Canaday; Cheney, M. C.; Christensen; Evans, ed.; Flanagan; Gaunt; Gertz; Giedion-Welcker 1, 2; Goodrich and Baur 1; Guggenheim, ed.; Haftman; Hayter 2; Henning; Hess, T. B.; Hunter 5; Jakovski; Janis and Blesh 1; Janis, S.; Kuh 1, 2; Langui; Lowry; McCurdy, ed.; Mellquist; Mendelowitz; *Metro;* Myers 2; Neumeyer; Paalen; Pearson 2; Ragon 1, 2; Ramsden 1, 2; Read 1, 4, 5; Ritchie 1, 3; Rodman 1, 3; Sachs; Seuphor 2, 3; Soby 1, 5; Sutton; **Sweeney 1;** Valentine 2; "What Abstract Art Means to Me"; Wilenski.

CALLAHAN, KENNETH. b. October 30, 1907, Spokane, Wash. Self-taught in art. Traveled USA, Europe, Central America, Mexico. **TAUGHT:** Privately and as Visiting Artist in various parts of the USA. **COMMISSIONS** (murals):

Marine Hospital, Seattle; US Post Offices, Centralia and Anacostes, Wash., and Rugby, N.D.; Washington State Library, Olympia, Wash. AWARDS: J. S. Guggenheim Fellowship, 1954. ADDRESS: 740 35th, Seattle, Wash. DEALER: Maynard Walker Gallery. ONE-MAN EXHIBITIONS: (first) American-British Art Center, NYC, 1944; Maynard Walker Gallery, 11 exhibitions 1946–64; SFMA; Santa Barbara/MA; La Jolla; Colorado Springs/FA; Phoenix; Roswell; Williams College; Columbia, S.C./MA; U. of Arkansas; Rochester/Memorial; Detroit/Institute; Renaissance Society, Chicago; Seattle/AM; Portland, Ore./AM; Spokane Art Center of Washington State U.; Tacoma; Galerie George Giraux, Brussels, 1947. RETROSPECTIVE: Emily Winthrop Miles Collection, circ., 1961–64. GROUP: Japan; Formosa; Korea; Philippines; Australia; New Zealand; Brazil; USA; Great Britain; France; Italy; Sweden; Denmark; Yugoslavia; Germany. COLLECTIONS: Andover/Phillips; Beloit College; Brooklyn Museum; Chicago/AI; Colby College; Columbus; Detroit/Institute; Fort Worth; Garnett Public Library; MMA; MOMA; U. of Michigan; U. of Nebraska; PAFA; PMA; Phillips; Portland, Ore./AM; SFMA; SRGM; St. Louis/City; Santa Barbara/MA; Seattle/AM; Springfield, Mo./AM; Tacoma; Utica; WMAA; Washington State U.; U. of Washington; Wichita/AM. BIBLIOGRAPHY: Baur 7; Bruce and Watson; Cheney, M. C.; Eliot; Nordness, ed.; Pousette-Dart, ed.; Richardson; Ritchie 1.

CALLERY, MARY. b. June 19, 1903, NYC. STUDIED: ASL, with Edward McCarten; privately in Paris with Jacques Loutchansky. Resides in Paris part of each year. COMMISSIONS: Aluminum Co. of America, 1953; P.S. 34, NYC, 1954; Gen. George W. Wingate High School, Brooklyn, N.Y., 1955. ADDRESS: 168 East 68 Street, NYC. DEALER: M. Knoedler & Co., NYC. ONE-MAN EXHIBITIONS: (first) Buchholz Gallery, NYC, 1944; Curt Valentine Gallery, NYC, 1947, 49, 50, 52, 55; Arts Club of Chicago, 1946; Salon du Mai, Paris, 1949; Margaret Brown Gallery, Boston, 1951; Galerie des Cahiers d'Art, Paris, 1954; M. Knoedler & Co., NYC, 1957, 61; M. Knoedler & Co., Paris, 1962. GROUP: Salon des Tuileries, Paris; Brussels World's Fair, 1958; MOMA; WMAA; Chicago/AI; St. Louis/City, 1946;

Houston/MFA, 1939; Utica, 1956; Dallas/MFA, 1958; PMA, 1949. COLLECTIONS: Alcoa; Andover/Phillips; CIT Corporation; Cincinnati/AM; Detroit/Institute; Eastland Shopping Center, Detroit; 525 William Penn Plaza; Hartford/Wadsworth; MOMA; NYU; Publishers Printing Co.; SFMA; Toledo/MA. BIBLIOGRAPHY: Baur 7; Gertz; Giedion-Welcker 1; Ramsden 2; Ritchie 3; Seuphor 3; Valentine 2; Zervos and Radams.

CAMPOLI, COSMO. b. 1922, South Bend, Ind. STUDIED: Chicago Art Institute School, 1950–52. Traveled France, Spain, Italy. TAUGHT: Institute of Design, Chicago; Contemporary Art Workshop, Chicago. AWARDS: Ford Foundation Grant; Chicago/AI, James Nelson Raymond Traveling Fellowship, 1950; Chicago/AI, 16 Sculptors, First Prize. ADDRESS: 5307 University, Chicago, Ill. DEALER: Ontario-East Gallery. ONE-MAN EXHIBITIONS: Allan Frumkin Gallery, NYC and Chicago; Contemporary Art Workshop, Chicago; Institute of Design, Chicago. GROUP: Beloit College, 1958; Michigan State U.; Lake Forest College, 1960; MOMA, New Images of Man, 1959; Galerie du Dragon, Eight Chicago Artists, 1962; U. of Colorado, 1962; Silvermine Guild, 1962; Chicago/AI, Exhibition Momentum. COLLECTIONS: A.F.A.; MOMA; VMFA.

CANDELL, VICTOR. b. May 11, 1903, Budapest, Hungary. To USA 1921; citizen 1927. Self-taught. Resided Paris, 1928–31. TAUGHT: Brooklyn Museum School, 1946–54; Cooper Union, 1954– ; Provincetown Workshop, summers; and privately since 1940. MEMBER: International Institute of Arts and Letters. AWARDS: Audubon Artists, 1952; Audubon Artists, Emily Lowe Prize, 1956; Audubon Artists, The Lamont Award, 1961. ADDRESS: 460 Riverside Drive, NYC. DEALERS: Grand Central Moderns; HCE Gallery. ONE-MAN EXHIBITIONS: Grand Central Moderns, 1954–59, 64; Philadelphia Art Alliance, 1958; Hofstra College, 1959; Silvermine Guild, 1962; Scranton/Everhart; Mortimer Brandt, NYC. GROUP: WMAA Annuals, 1951–61; Carnegie, 1952, 55; Brooklyn Museum, 1953, 55; PAFA, 1964; U. of Illinois, 1952, 55, 57; Corcoran, UNESCO Exhibition; Audubon Artists; U. of Nebraska; MOMA, American Painting, circ. Europe, 1956–57. COLLECTIONS: Brandeis U.;

Carnegie; Corcoran; U. of Illinois; MMA; Montclair/AM; Mount Holyoke College; NIAL; NYU; U. of Nebraska; Newark Museum; US Treasury Department; Utica; WMAA. **BIBLIOGRAPHY:** American Artists Congress, Inc.

CAPARN, RHYS. b. July 28, 1909, Onteora Park, N.Y. **STUDIED:** Bryn Mawr College; privately in Paris with Edouard Navellier; privately in New York with Alexander Archipenko. Traveled Europe; resided France. **TAUGHT:** Dalton School, NYC, 1946–55, 1960–ᅳ; Master Institute of United Arts, Inc., NYC, 1963–ᅳ. **MEMBER:** Federation of Modern Painters and Sculptors; Sculptors Guild; American Abstract Artists; Architectural League of New York; International Institute of Arts and Letters. **COMMISSIONS:** Brooklyn Botanic Garden; Wollman Library, Barnard College; National Furniture Mart, NYC; private portrait commissions. **AWARDS:** MMA, American Sculpture, Second Prize, 1951; New York State Fair, First Prize for Sculpture, 1958; National Association of Women Artists, Medal of Honor for Sculpture, 1960, 61. **ADDRESS:** 333 West 57 Street, NYC. **ONE-MAN EXHIBITIONS:** (first) Delphic Studios, NYC, 1933, also 1935; Architectural League of New York, 1941; New York Zoological Park (Bronx), 1942; Wildenstein & Co., NYC, 1944, 47; Dartmouth College, 1949, 55; John Heller Gallery, NYC, 1953; Doris Meltzer Gallery, 1956, 59, 60; Riverside Museum, 1961. **GROUP:** MOMA, Fifteen Sculptors, circ., 1941; WMAA Annuals, 1941, 53, 54, 56, 60; Musee du Petit Palais, Paris, 1950; PAFA, 1951, 52, 53, 60, 64; ICA, London/Tate, International Unknown Political Prisoner Competition, 1953; USIA, American Drawings, Prints, and Watercolors, circ. Europe, 1957; Silvermine Guild, 1956; VMFA, American Sculpture Today, 1958; Claude Bernard, Paris, 1960. **COLLECTIONS:** Barnard College; Bryn Mawr College; Colorado Springs/FA; Corcoran; Dartmouth College; Harvard U.; La Jolla; Raleigh/NCMA; Riverside Museum; St. Louis/City; WMAA; Youngstown/Butler. **BIBLIOGRAPHY:** Seuphor 3.

CAREWE, SYLVIA. b. February 22, 1914, NYC. **STUDIED:** Columbia U.; Atelier 17, NYC; New School for Social Research, with Yasuo Kuniyoshi; Hofmann School. Traveled Europe extensively; Mexico; St. Thomas. **COMMISSIONS:** First American artist to be commissioned by the College de la Manufacture d'Aubusson, 1957; several portrait commissions. Lectures. **ADDRESS:** 544 East 86 Street, NYC. **DEALER:** French & Co. Inc. **ONE-MAN EXHIBITIONS:** (first) ACA Gallery, 1948, also 1951, 53, 54, 56, 58, 61; Barnett Aden Gallery, Washington, D.C., 1950; Three Arts Gallery, Poughkeepsie, 1947, 52, 54; Galerie Granoff, Paris, 1957; Condon Riley Gallery, NYC, 1959; Indiana U., circ., 1955; Youngstown/Butler, 1960; French & Co. Inc., 1962. **GROUP:** MOMA; WMAA; Brooklyn Museum; Boston/MFA; Bruge, Belgium; Smith College; Silvermine Guild; The Print Club, Philadelphia. **COLLECTIONS:** Brandeis U.; Djakarta Museum; Howard U.; Paris/Moderne; Tel Aviv; Youngstown/Butler.

CASARELLA, EDMOND. b. September 3, 1920, Newark, N.J. **STUDIED:** Cooper Union, 1938–42; Brooklyn Museum School, 1949–51, with Gabor Peterdi. US Army, 1944–46. Traveled Italy and Greece, 1951–52, 1960–61. **TAUGHT:** Brooklyn Museum School, 1956–60; Yale-Norfolk Summer Art School, 1958; Pratt Graphic Art Center, 1964; NYU, 1962; Hunter College, 1963–ᅳ; Columbia U., summers, 1963, 64; Yale U., 1964–ᅳ; Rutgers U., 1964–ᅳ; Pratt Institute, 1964–ᅳ. **MEMBER:** SAGA. National Youth Administration: Designed posters. **AWARDS:** Fulbright Fellowship (Italy), 1951; L. C. Tiffany Grant, 1955; Guggenheim Foundation Fellowship, 1960; PCA, 1959; Brooklyn Museum, Print and Watercolor Biennials; Library of Congress, 1955, 56, 58; Bay Printmakers Society, 1955, 57; The Print Club, Philadelphia, 1956; U. of Illinois, Graphic Art exhibitions, P.P., 1954, 56; Boston Printmakers, 1957; Northwest Printmakers Annual, 1956; New York State Fair, 1958; SAGA, 100 Prints of the Year, 1962, 63. **ADDRESS:** 83 East Linden Avenue, Englewood, N.J. **ONE-MAN EXHIBITIONS:** (first) The Zabriskie Gallery, 1953, also 1956; Obelisk Gallery, Washington, D.C., 1956, 61; Louisiana State U., 1957; U. of Mississippi, 1957; U. of Kentucky, 1964; Rutgers U., 1964; Brooklyn Museum (two-man), 1952. **GROUP:** The Print Club, Philadelphia, 1956; St. Louis/City, 1964; Philadelphia Art Alliance, 1960; Memphis/Brooks, 1960, 61, 62; A.A.A. Gallery, NYC, 100 Prints of the Year, 1962; New York Foundation/USIA, American Prints

Around the World, circ., 1963; Los Angeles/County MA, 1963; American Academy, Rome, 1960, 61; Riverside Museum, 1963; The Pennsylvania State U., 10 American Printmakers, 1959; Yale U., 1960; Trenton/State, Contemporary Printmakers, 1959; Jewish Museum, 100 Contemporary Prints, 1964; New York World's Fair, 1964–65; Brooklyn Museum, Print Biennials; PAFA, 1953, 59, 63; Corcoran, 1955, 56, 58, 59, 63; Boston/MFA, 1957; Library of Congress, 1955, 56, 58; International Print Exhibition, Salzburg, 1952, 58; Brooklyn Museum, Watercolor Biennials; WMAA, American Painting, 1961; WMAA, American Prints Today, 1959, 62; WMAA, New York Hilton Hotel Collection, 1963; Bay Printmakers Society, Oakland, 1955, 56, 57; U. of Illinois, 50 Contemporary American Printmakers, 1956; Grenchen, Graphics International, 1958; I Inter-American Paintings and Prints Biennial, Mexico City, 1958; Victoria and Albert Museum, 1959; USIA, Graphic Arts—USA, circ. U.S.S.R., 1963; Cincinnati/AM, 1960; Gallery of Modern Art, Ljubljana, Yugoslavia, III & IV International Exhibitions of Prints, 1959, 61. **COLLECTIONS:** Brooklyn Museum; U. of Illinois, Library of Congress. **BIBLIOGRAPHY:** Chaet; Peterdi.

CASTELLON, FEDERICO. b. September 14, 1914, Almeria, Spain. Self-taught in art. Traveled Europe and Latin America extensively; resided Spain, 1914–21, 1961–62; France, 1934–36, 1962–63. US citizen 1943. **TAUGHT:** Columbia U., 1948–61; Pratt Institute, 1951–61, 1964– ; Queens College, 1964; NAD, 1964– . **MEMBER:** SAGA; NAD. **COMMISSIONS:** Illustrations for numerous books and magazines; two prints for International Graphic Arts Society. **AWARDS:** Four-year Fellowship from the Spanish Republic, 1933; Guggenheim Foundation Fellowship, 1940, 50; NIAL Grant, 1950; Chicago/AI, The Mr. & Mrs. Frank G. Logan Prize, ca. 1940; PAFA, Alice McFadden Eyre Medal, 1940; Library of Congress, First Pennell P.P., 1949; A.A.A. Gallery, NYC, National Print Competition, First Prize, 1948; SAGA, 1963. **ADDRESS:** 432 West 22 Street, NYC. **DEALERS:** Terry Dintenfass, Inc.; Weyhe Gallery; The Print Club, Philadelphia. **ONE-MAN EXHIBITIONS:** (first) Raymond and Raymond, Inc., NYC; Weyhe Gallery, 1934, 35, 36, 37, 38, 39, 40, 41; A.A.A. Gallery, NYC, 1947, 48,

49, 50, 51, 52; Bucknell U.; Philadelphia Art Alliance; Albany/Institute; Bennington College; Swarthmore College; Princeton U.; Columbia U.; California Palace; Madrid/Nacional, Caracas; La Paz, Bolivia; Argentina/Nacional; Asuncion, Paraguay; Montevideo/Municipal; a gallery in Paris; Bombay. **GROUP:** College d'Espagne, Paris, 1934; Corcoran; Chicago/AI; Brooklyn Museum; PAFA; WMAA; SAGA. **COLLECTIONS:** Brooklyn Museum; Chicago/AI; Dartmouth College; U. of Georgia; Kalamazoo/Institute; Library of Congress; MMA; U. of Minnesota; Montclair/AM; NYPL; PAFA; PMA; Princeton U.; Syracuse U.; Utica; WMAA; Yale U. **BIBLIOGRAPHY:** American Artists Group Inc. 3; Baur 7; Frost; Goodrich and Baur 1; Mendelowitz; Pearson 1; Reese; Zigrosser 1.

CAVALLON, GIORGIO. b. March 3, 1904, Sorio, Vicenza, Italy. To USA 1920. **STUDIED:** NAD, 1925–30; with C. W. Hawthorne, ca. 1929; Hofmann School 1935–36. Resided Italy, 1930–33. **TAUGHT:** Pratt Institute, 1952, 54 (woodworking); U. of North Carolina, 1964; Visiting Critic, Yale U., 1964. **MEMBER:** American Abstract Artists, 1936–57. **FEDERAL A.P.:** Mural project assistant to Arshile Gorky, and easel painting. **AWARDS:** L. C. Tiffany Grant, 1929. **ADDRESS:** 178 East 95 Street, NYC. **DEALER:** The Kootz Gallery. **ONE-MAN EXHIBITIONS:** (first) Bottege d'Arte, Vicenza, Italy, 1932; ACA Gallery, 1934; Eighth Street Playhouse, NYC, 1940; Charles Egan Gallery, 1946, 48, 51, 54; The Stable Gallery, 1957, 59; The Kootz Gallery, 1961, 63; U. of North Carolina, 1964. **GROUP:** MOMA, Abstract Painting and Sculpture in America, 1951; MMA, American Watercolors, Drawings and Prints, 1952; Salon des Realites Nouvelles, Paris, 1950; U. of Nebraska, 1955; Carnegie, 1959, 61; Documenta II, Kassel, 1959; Chicago/AI, 1959; WMAA, 1947, 48, 59, 61; Walker, 1960; SRGM, Abstract Expressionists and Imagists, 1961; U. of Illinois, 1963; MOMA, 60 Modern Drawings, 1963. **COLLECTIONS:** Buffalo/Albright; Continental Grain Company; James A. Michener Foundation; NYU; SRGM; The Singer Company Inc.; Tishman Realty & Construction Co. Inc.; Union Carbide Corp.; WMAA. **BIBLIOGRAPHY:** Blesh 1; Hess, T. B.; McCurdy, ed.; Pousette-Dart, ed.; Ritchie 1.

CHAET, BERNARD. b. March 7, 1924, Boston, Mass. STUDIED: Tufts U., BS.Ed.; Boston Museum School, with Karl Zerbe. Traveled Europe. TAUGHT: Yale U., 1951– . AWARDS: Yale U., Senior Faculty Fellowship, 1962; St. Paul Art Center, Drawing USA, Merit Award, 1963; Silvermine Guild Award, 1955. ADDRESS: 141 Cold Spring Street, New Haven, Conn. DEALER: Boris Mirski Gallery. ONE-MAN EXHIBITIONS: (first) Boris Mirski Gallery, 1946, also 1951, 54, 57, 59, 61; The Bertha Schaefer Gallery, 1954; The Stable Gallery, 1959, 61; Cornell U., 1961. GROUP: U. of Illinois, 1951, 53, 61; PAFA; Los Angeles/County MA; Phillips; Chicago/AI; U. of Nebraska; ICA, Boston, 6 New England Painters, 1954; Corcoran; Contemporary American Drawings, circ. France, 1957–58; Hartford/Wadsworth, 8 From Connecticut, 1961; Detroit/Institute; MOMA; Brooklyn Museum. COLLECTIONS: Andover/Phillips; Brandeis U.; Brooklyn Museum; UCLA; Lincoln, Mass./De Cordova; Worcester/AM. BIBLIOGRAPHY: Chaet.

CHAMBERLAIN, ELWIN. b. May 19, 1928, Minneapolis, Minn. STUDIED: Minneapolis Institute School; U. of Idaho, BA; U. of Wisconsin, MA. US Navy, 1944–46. ADDRESS: 2 East 12 Street, NYC. ONE-MAN EXHIBITIONS: Hewitt Gallery, NYC, 1953, 56; "G" Gallery, NYC, 1959; Lee Nordness Gallery, NYC, 1961. GROUP: Boston/MFA; Bresler Galleries Inc.; Lincoln, Mass./De Cordova; Denver/AM, 1955; Layton School of Art; PAFA, 1953; Philadelphia Art Alliance; Princeton U.; RISD; Walker; WMAA; Yale U., 1955, 57; Festival of Two Worlds, Spoleto, 1958. COLLECTIONS: Sara Roby Foundation; WMAA. BIBLIOGRAPHY: Nordness, ed.

CHAMBERLAIN, JOHN. b. 1927, Rochester, Ind. STUDIED: Chicago Art Institute School, 1950–52; Black Mountain College, 1955–56. ADDRESS: c/o Dealer. DEALER: Leo Castelli Inc. ONE-MAN EXHIBITIONS: (first) Wells Street Gallery, Chicago, 1957; Davida Gallery, Chicago, 1958; Martha Jackson Gallery, 1960; Dilexi Gallery, Los Angeles, 1962; Dilexi Gallery, San Francisco, 1962; The Pace Gallery, Boston, 1963; Leo Castelli Inc. (two-man), 1962; Robert Fraser Gallery, London (two-man), 1963; Leo Castelli Inc., 1964. GROUP: WMAA Annuals, 1960, 62; MOMA, Recent Sculpture USA, 1959; Martha Jackson Gallery, New Media—New Forms, I & II, 1960, 61; Galerie Rive Droite, Paris, Le Nouveau Realisme, 1961; VI Sao Paulo Biennial, 1961; MOMA, The Art of Assemblage, circ., 1961; Carnegie, 1961; Chicago/AI, 1961; Buenos Aires Museum of Modern Art, International Sculpture Exhibition, 1960; Seattle World's Fair, 1962; SRGM, The Joseph H. Hirshhorn Collection, 1962; Battersea Park, London, International Sculpture Exhibition, 1963; Musee Cantonal des Beaux-Arts, Lausanne, I Salon International de Galeries Pilotes, 1963; Pasadena/AM, New American Sculpture, 1964; New York World's Fair, 1964–65. COLLECTIONS: Buffalo/Albright; MOMA. BIBLIOGRAPHY: Janis and Blesh 1; *Metro;* Seitz 2; Seuphor 3.

CHERNEY, MARVIN. b. November 1, 1925, Baltimore, Md. STUDIED: Maryland Institute; School for Art Studies, NYC, with Maurice Glickman, Sol Wilson, Isaac Soyer. Traveled Europe, USA. TAUGHT: Brooklyn Museum School; South Shore Arts Workshop, 1953–58. AWARDS: Baltimore/MA, Freeland Award, 1951; Brooklyn Museum, First Prize, 1954; Baltimore/MA, First Prize (Artists Award), 1955; Silvermine Guild, Lucille Lortel Award, 1958; L. C. Tiffany Grant, 1959, 60; NIAL Grant, 1960; NAD, Isaac N. Maynard Prize, 1961. ADDRESS: 112 East 17 Street, NYC. DEALER: ACA Gallery. ONE-MAN EXHIBITIONS: (first) AFI Gallery, NYC, 1953; The Babcock Gallery, 1958; Capitol Art Gallery, Washington, D.C., 1959; Washington Irving Gallery, NYC, 1960; Garelick's Gallery, Detroit, 1961, 63; Bernard Crystal Gallery, NYC, 1961; Arnold Finkel Gallery, Philadelphia, 1961, 64; Mary Washington College, 1961; Bucknell U., 1962; Swarthmore College, 1962; Athena Gallery, New Haven, 1963. GROUP: NAD, 1950; Chicago/AI, 1961; U. of Nebraska, 1957; PAFA, 1957; WMAA, 1960; MOMA, Recent Drawings USA, 1956; Smithsonian; Brooklyn Museum, 1954, 56, 58. COLLECTIONS: Kalamazoo/Institute; PAFA; Reading/Public; Syracuse U.; WMAA; Youngstown/Butler.

CHESNEY, LEE R., JR. b. June 1, 1920, Washington, D.C. STUDIED: U. of Colorado, with James Boyle, BFA; State U. of Iowa, with Mauricio Lasansky, James Lechay, MFA; Universidad Michoacana, Morelia, Mexico, with

Alfredo Zalce. **Taught:** U. of Illinois, 1950– . **Awards:** PMA, 1953; Chicago/AI, John Taylor Arms Medal, 1955; Library of Congress, 1954, 58; Seattle/AM, 1959, 61; Silvermine Guild, 1959; Youngstown/Butler, 1959; Pasadena/AM, 1960; Oklahoma, 1960; SAGA, 1961; Brooklyn Museum, p.p., 1953, 56; U. of Southern California, p.p., 1953, 54; Dallas/MFA, p.p., 1953, 54; Denver/AM, p.p., 1954, 59, 60, 61; Bradley U., p.p., 1953; Washington U., p.p., 1955; Texas Wesleyan College, p.p., 1955; Michigan State U., p.p., 1956; Oakland/AM, p.p., 1957; Fulbright Fellowship, 1956–57. **Address:** 207 West Vermont Street, Urbana, Ill. **Group Exhibitions:** Brooklyn Museum, 1948, 50, 52, 54, 56, 58; Library of Congress, 1950, 54, 56, 58; The Print Club, Philadelphia, 1947, 49, 50, 53, 55, 58; Seattle/AM, 1947, 48, 49, 50, 51, 53, 54, 55, 56; SFMA, 1949, 50, 53, 54; Bradley U., 1950, 52, 53, 54, 55; Denver/AM, 1949, 52, 55, 56; Des Moines, 1947, 48, 49, 50; International Biennial Exhibition of Paintings, Tokyo; U. of Illinois; IV Bordighera Biennial, 1957. **Collections:** Albion College; Bibliotheque Nationale; Bradley U.; Brooklyn Museum; Dallas/MFA; Denver/AM; Illinois Wesleyan U.; Library of Congress; MOMA; Michigan State U.; Milwaukee-Downer College; National Gallery; Oakland/AM; The Ohio State U.; PMA; Seattle/AM; Stockholm/National; Tate; Texas Wesleyan College; Tokyo/Modern; Tokyo U. of Arts; Victoria and Albert Museum.

CHINNI, PETER. b. 1928, Mt. Kisco, N.Y. **Studied:** ASL, 1947, with Edwin Dickinson, Kenneth Kayes Miller, Julian Levi; Academy of Fine Arts, Rome, 1949–50, with Emilio Sorrini. **Member:** Sculptors Guild. **Commissions:** Denver Art Museum (bronze mural). **Awards:** Silvermine Guild, First Prize, 1958, 60, 61; Denver/AM, Second Prize, 1960. **Address:** 389 Broome Street, NYC. **One-man Exhibitions:** (first) Fairleigh Dickinson U., 1951; Galleria San Marco, Rome, 1955; Il Torcoliere, Rome, 1956; Kipnes Gallery, Westport, Conn., 1956; R. R. Gallery, Denver, 1957; Galleria Schneider, Rome, 1957; Janet Nessler Gallery, NYC, 1959, 61; Royal Marks Gallery, 1964. **Group:** Audubon Artists Annuals, 1958, 59, 61, 62; Corcoran, 1962; Galleria Pagani del Grattacielo, Milan, 1962; WMAA, 1960, 62; Boston Arts Festival, 1960, 62; Festival of Two Worlds, Spoleto, 1960; Sculptors Guild, 1963; Carnegie,

1964; Connecticut Academy of Fine Arts, 1960, 62. **Collections:** Denver/AM; Fontana-Hollywood Corp.

CHRISTOPHER, WILLIAM. b. 1924, Columbus, Ga. **Studied:** Sorbonne; Ecole des Beaux-Arts, Fontainebleau; Academie Julian, Paris; with Ossip Zadkine, Paris; with Amedee Ozenfant, NYC. Traveled Europe, Latin America. Changed from sculpture to painting in Paris, 1948. **Taught:** Polytechnic Preparatory School, Brooklyn (woodworking), 1956–60. **Awards:** Brooklyn Museum, Shiva Award, 1956; Silvermine Guild, Painting Award, 1962. **Address:** Hartland, Vt. **Dealer:** Joan Peterson Gallery. **One-man Exhibitions:** (first) Roko Gallery, 1952; Nexus Gallery, Boston, 1957, 59, 60; Joan Peterson Gallery, 1961, 62; The Amel Gallery, 1961; Dartmouth College, 1964; Boston Architectural Center, 1963; Harvard U., 1959. **Group:** Corcoran, 1961, 63; WMAA; Smithsonian; Brooklyn Museum; Boston/MFA; Sorbonne; Harvard U.; Andover/Phillips; A.F.A. **Collections:** Boston/MFA; Lincoln, Mass./De Cordova; WMAA.

CHRYSSA. b. 1933, Athens, Greece. **Studied:** Academie de la Grande Chaumiere, 1953–54; California School of Fine Arts, 1954–55. US citizen 1955. Traveled Europe, USA. **Address:** 863 Broadway, NYC. **One-man Exhibitions:** (first) Betty Parsons Gallery, 1961; SRGM, 1961; Cordier & Ekstrom Inc., 1962; Robert Fraser Gallery, London, 1962. **Group:** MOMA, Americans 1963, circ., 1963–64; VII Sao Paulo Biennial, 1963; WMAA Annuals; Carnegie; Martha Jackson Gallery, New Media—New Forms, I, 1960; Boston Arts Festival, 1960; Seattle World's Fair, 1962. **Collections:** Buffalo/Albright; Chase Manhattan Bank; MOMA; SRGM; WMAA.

CICERO, CARMEN LOUIS. b. August 14, 1926, Newark, N.J. **Studied:** Newark State Teachers College, 1947–51, BA; Hunter College, 1953–55, with Robert Motherwell; Hofmann School, NYC. **Awards:** Guggenheim Foundation Fellowship, 1958; Ford Foundation, p.p., 1962. **Address:** 355 Mountain Road, Englewood, N.J. **Dealer:** The Peridot Gallery. **One-man Exhibitions:** The Peridot Gallery, 1956, 57, 59, 61, 62, 64; Arts Club of Chicago, 1958. **Group:** Corcoran, 1953; WMAA, 1955,

57; MOMA, 1953, 55; U. of Nebraska, 1957; Chicago/AI, 1957; Worcester/AM, 1958; PAFA; Brooklyn Museum. **COLLECTIONS:** Brooklyn Museum; Cornell U.; MOMA; U. of Michigan; NYU; U. of Nebraska; Newark Museum; SRGM; Toronto; WMAA; Worcester/AM.

CIKOVSKY, NICOLAI. b. December 10, 1894, Russia. **STUDIED:** Royal Art School, Vilna; Technical Institute of Arts, Moscow. To USA 1923. **TAUGHT:** The Corcoran School of Art; Chicago Art Institute School; ASL. **COMMISSIONS** (murals): Interior Department, Washington, D.C.; US Post Offices, Towson and Silver Springs, Md. **AWARDS:** Chicago/AI, The Mr. & Mrs. Frank G. Logan Medal, 1933; Worcester/AM, First Prize, 1933; Chicago/AI, Norman Wait Harris Bronze Medal, 1932; PAFA, Lambert P.P., 1937. **ADDRESS:** 500 West 58 Street, NYC. **ONE-MAN EXHIBITIONS:** A.A.A. Gallery, NYC, 1944, 46, 49, 52, 56; The Downtown Gallery, 1933, 38; Whyte Gallery, Washington, D.C., 1939. **GROUP:** Toledo/MA; MOMA; Chicago/AI, 1932, 33, 60, 61; Newark Museum; U. of Glasgow; Walker; Carnegie; Corcoran; Brooklyn Museum; Boston/MFA; Worcester/AM; Cleveland/MA; Los Angeles/County MA; NAD, 1959. **COLLECTIONS:** Brooklyn Museum; Chicago/AI; Cleveland/MA; Kansas City/Nelson; Los Angeles/County MA; MOMA; PAFA; Phillips; WMAA; Worcester/AM. **BIBLIOGRAPHY:** American Artists Group Inc. 2, 3; Bethers; Cheney, M. C.; Hall; Mellquist; Pagano.

CLOAR, CARROLL. b. January 18, 1913, Earle, Ark. **STUDIED:** Memphis Academy of Arts; ASL, with William C. McNulty, Harry Sternberg; Southwestern College, BA. US Air Force, World War II, three years. Traveled Central and Latin America, Europe. **TAUGHT:** Memphis Academy of Arts, 1956. **MEMBER:** Artists Equity. **AWARDS:** MacDowell Traveling Fellowship, 1940; Guggenheim Foundation Fellowship, 1946; Youngstown/Butler, P.P.; Hon. PBK. **ADDRESS:** 235 S. Greer, Memphis, Tenn. **DEALER:** The Alan Gallery. **ONE-MAN EXHIBITIONS:** (first) Memphis/Brooks, 1955, also 1957; The Alan Gallery, 1956, 58, 60, 62, 64; U. of Arkansas, 1956, 61; Fort Worth, 1963. **RETROSPECTIVE:** Memphis/Brooks, 1960. **GROUP:** PAFA; MMA; Carnegie; MOMA;

WMAA; Brooklyn Museum; Dallas/MFA; U. of Nebraska. **COLLECTIONS:** Abbott Laboratories; Brandeis U.; Bridgeport; Brooklyn Museum; Chase Manhattan Bank; Corcoran; First National Bank of Memphis; Hartford/Wadsworth; Library of Congress; MMA; MOMA; Memphis/Brooks; Newark Museum; St. Petersburg, Fla.; Southwestern College; WMAA; Youngstown/Butler.

CLUTZ, WILLIAM. b. March 19, 1933, Gettysburg, Pa. **STUDIED:** Mercersburg Gallery, 1948–51; State U. of Iowa, with James Lechay, Stuart Edie, 1951–55, BA; ASL, 1956, with Robert Brackman. **TAUGHT:** Artist-in-Residence, Bucknell U., 1957. **ADDRESS:** 485 Central Park West, NYC. **DEALER:** The Bertha Schaefer Gallery. **ONE-MAN EXHIBITIONS:** (first) Penn Hall Junior College and Preparatory School, Chambersburg, Pa., 1954; Bucknell U., 1957; Mercersburg Academy, 1958, 59; Condon Riley Gallery, NYC, 1959; David Herbert Gallery, NYC, 1962; The Bertha Schaefer Gallery, 1963. **GROUP:** MOMA, Recent Painting USA: The Figure, circ., 1962–63; Houston/MFA, The Emerging Figure, 1961; A.F.A., The Figure, circ., 1960; MOMA, Recent Drawings USA, 1956; PAFA Annual, 1964. **COLLECTIONS:** Ball State Teachers College; Chase Manhattan Bank; Hagerstown/County MFA; NYU; Newark Museum; St. Paul Gallery.

CONGDON, WILLIAM. b. April 15, 1912, Providence, R.I. **STUDIED:** Yale U., BA; Cape School of Art, with Henry Hensche; PAFA; Folly Cove School of Art, with George Demetrios. American Field Service, World War II. Active in post-war Italy with American Friends Service Committee. Traveled Mexico, North Africa, India, Cambodia, Central America, Europe. **AWARDS:** RISD, 1949, 50; PAFA, Joseph E. Temple Gold Medal, 1951; U. of Illinois, P.P., 1951; Corcoran, William A. Clark Prize, 1952; International Novara, Trieste, Gold Medal, 1961. **ADDRESS:** Via Ancaiani, 20, Assissi, Italy. **DEALER:** Betty Parsons Gallery. **ONE-MAN EXHIBITIONS:** (first) Betty Parsons Gallery, 1949, also 1950, 52, 53, 54, 56, 59, 62; ICA, Boston, 1951; Margaret Brown Gallery, Boston, 1951, 56; Phillips, 1952; L'Obelisco, Rome, 1953, 58; Providence (R.I.) Art Club, 1953; Santa Barbara/MA, 1954; UCLA, 1954; Arts Club of Chicago, 1954; Art of This Century

(Peggy Guggenheim), 1957; Denver/AM, 1957; Michigan State U., 1959; MIT, 1958; Arthur Jeffress Gallery, London, 1958; Pro-Civitate Christiana, Assisi, 1961; Palazzo Reale, Milan, 1962; U. of Notre Dame, circ., 1964–65; Vatican Pavilion, New York World's Fair, 1964–65. GROUP: NAD, 1939; PAFA, 1936, 37, 38, 51, 52, 53, 56, 58, 60; Carnegie, 1940, 52, 58; WMAA, 1950, 51, 53, 56, 58; Andover/Phillips, 1941; Chicago/AI, 1952, 54, 57; Walker, Expressionism, 1900–1955, 1956; Buffalo/Albright, 1952; California Palace, 1952; U. of Illinois, 1952, 53, 55, 57, 59; MMA, American Painters Under 35, 1950; XXVI & XXIX Venice Biennials, 1952, 58; WMAA, The New Decade, 1954–55; Hartford/Wadsworth; Cincinnati/AM; Lincoln, Mass./De Cordova. COLLECTIONS: Andover/Phillips; Boston/MFA; Carnegie; Cleveland/MA; Detroit/Institute; Hartford/Wadsworth; Houston/MFA; U. of Illinois; MMA; MOMA; Phillips; RISD; Rochester/Memorial; St. Louis/City; Santa Barbara/MA; Toledo/MA; Venice/Contemporaneo; WMAA. BIBLIOGRAPHY: McCurdy, ed.; Nordness, ed.; Pousette-Dart, ed.; Rodman 2.

CONNER, BRUCE. b. November 18, 1933, McPherson, Kans. STUDIED: U. of Nebraska, BFA; U. of Wichita; Brooklyn Museum School, with Reuben Tam; Kansas City Art Institute and School of Design; U. of Colorado. AWARDS: The U. of Chicago, Midwest Film Festival, First Prize; SFMA, Nealie Sullivan Award, 1963; Ford Foundation Grant, 1964. ADDRESS: 83

Bruce Conner   *Child. (detail)* 1959

Francis Street, Brookline, Mass. DEALERS: The Alan Gallery; Ferus Gallery. ONE-MAN EXHIBITIONS: Robert Fraser Gallery, London, 1964; The Alan Gallery, 1960, 61, 63, 64; Batman Gallery, San Francisco; Ferus Gallery, 1963; The Swetzoff Gallery, 1963. GROUP: U. of Illinois, 1961; MOMA, The Art of Assemblage, circ., 1961; WMAA, Fifty California Artists, 1962–63; The Hague, 1964; SFMA; WMAA, 1963; IV International Art Biennial, San Marino (Europe), 1963. COLLECTIONS: MOMA; SFMA. BIBLIOGRAPHY: Janis and Blesh 1.

CONOVER, ROBERT. b. July 3, 1920, Trenton, N.J. STUDIED: Philadelphia Museum School, 1938–42; ASL, with Morris Kantor, Cameron Booth, Will Barnet; Brooklyn Museum School, with Max Beckmann, John Ferren, Reuben Tam, William Kienbusch, William Baziotes. Corps of Army Engineers, World War II. Traveled Europe, Canada. TAUGHT: New School for Social Research. MEMBER: American Abstract Artists; SAGA. FEDERAL A.P.: National Youth Act, Philadelphia, 1939–41. COMMISSIONS: International Graphic Arts Society, 1957, 62 (woodcuts); New York Hilton Hotel, 1963; *Business Week* Magazine, 1963. AWARDS: MacDowell Colony Fellowship; Brooklyn Museum, P.P., 1951, 56; The Print Club, Philadelphia, P.P.; PAFA, Samuel S. Fleisher Memorial P.P. ADDRESS: 263 East Seventh Street, NYC. DEALERS: The Terrain Gallery; Ruth White Gallery, Peter H. Deitsch Gallery. ONE-MAN EXHIBITIONS: (first) Laurel Gallery, NYC, 1949; The New Gallery, NYC, 1951, 53, 55; The Zabriskie Gallery, 1957, 59, 61. GROUP: WMAA Annuals, 1950, 51, 53, 54, 55, 61; PAFA, 1951, 53; Chicago/AI; Cincinnati/AM; Brooklyn Museum, 1952, 54, 56, 58, 60, 62, 64; MOMA, Abstract Painting and Sculpture in America, 1951; Newark Museum; Los Angeles/County MA; Memphis/Brooks; MOMA, Young American Printmakers, 1953; ART:USA:59, NYC, 1959; American Abstract Artists, Tokyo; International Graphic Arts Exhibition, Zagreb; WMAA, American Prints Today, 1958; WMAA, Landscape in American Art; Walker, The Classic Tradition, 1953; New York World's Fair, 1964–65. COLLECTIONS: Baltimore/MA; Brooklyn Museum; Cincinnati/AM; U. of Illinois; MOMA; National Gallery; PAFA; PMA. BIBLIOGRAPHY: Baur 5; Ritchie 1.

CONSTANT, GEORGE. b. April 2, 1892, Greece. STUDIED: Washington U., 1912; Chicago Art Institute School, 1914–18; and with George Bellows, C. W. Hawthorne. Traveled Europe, USA. TAUGHT: Dayton Art Institute School, 1920–22. MEMBER: Federation of Modern Painters and Sculptors; Audubon Artists. FEDERAL A. P.: Easel painting and graphic art. AWARDS: MMA, Alexander Shilling Prize, 1939, 45, 56; Library of Congress, Pennell P.P., 1947; Chicago/AI, The Mr. & Mrs. Frank G. Logan Prize, 1943; Audubon Artists, 1946; Southampton/Parrish, 1950, 51; Greek Government, Cross of the Phoenix Brigade, 1963. ADDRESS: 187 East Broadway, NYC. ONE-MAN EXHIBITIONS: (first) Arts Club of Chicago, 1929; Albert Roullier Gallery, Chicago; J. B. Neumann Gallery, NYC; Contemporary Arts Gallery, NYC; Boyer Gallery, NYC, 1939; Marquie, NYC; Boyer Gallery, Philadelphia, 1937; Dikram Kelekian Gallery, NYC; Weyhe Gallery; Ferargil Galleries, NYC, 1944, 45, 46, 47, 48, 50, 51; Grace Borgenicht Gallery Inc., 1952, 55; Philadelphia Art Alliance; Valentine-Dudensing Gallery, NYC; College Art Association Exhibit, circ., 1932–35; and some 30 others. GROUP: Victoria and Albert Museum; Brooklyn Museum; WMAA; Chicago/AI; MMA; PAFA; Carnegie; Amsterdam/Stedelijk; Minneapolis/Institute; Paris/Moderne; Corcoran; Library of Congress; Walker, 1944, 48; New York World's Fair, 1939, 1964–65; State U. of Iowa; Brooklyn Museum, 10 Years of American Prints —1947–56, 1956; Golden Gate International Exposition, San Francisco, 1939; USIA, 1956–57, 1960–61; ART:USA:59, NYC, 1959; USIA, 20th Century Highlights, circ., 1957–58. COLLECTIONS: Amsterdam/Stedelijk; Andover/Phillips; Auburn U.; Baltimore/MA; Brandeis U.; Brooklyn Museum; Dayton/AI; Detroit/Institute; Library of Congress; MMA; U. of Nebraska; New Orleans/Delgado; PAFA; PMA; Tel Aviv; US State Department; Walker; Youngstown/Butler.

COOK, HOWARD. b. July 16, 1901, Springfield, Mass. STUDIED: ASL, 1919–21, with George Bridgeman, Wallace Morgan, Joseph Pennell, Andrew Dasburg, Maurice Sterne. Artist War Correspondent, South Pacific, World War II. Traveled extensively, USA, North Africa, the Orient, Europe. TAUGHT: U. of New Mexico, 1947; U. of Texas, 1942–43; U. of California, Berkeley, 1948; Scripps College, 1951; Minneapolis Institute School, 1945–50; Colorado Springs Fine Arts Center, 1949; Washington U., 1954; New Mexico Highlands U., 1957. MEMBER: NAD; SAGA. FEDERAL A.P.: Mural painting. COMMISIONS (murals): Hotel Tasqueno, Taxco, Mexico; Law Library, Springfield, Mass.; Federal Court House, Pittsburgh, Pa.; US Post Offices, Alamo Plaza (San Antonio) and Corpus Christi; Mayo Clinic, Rochester, Minn. AWARDS: Two Guggenheim Foundation Fellowships; Architectural League of New York, Gold Medal; NAD, Samuel F. B. Morse Gold Medal; MMA, P.P., 1942; PMA, P.P.; Denver/AM, P.P.; Tupperware National Competition, P.P., 1956; Orlando, P.P.; Oklahoma, First Painting Award; Tucson Fine Arts Association, Art Prize. ADDRESS: Ranchos de Taos, N.M. DEALER: Grand Central Moderns. ONE-MAN EXHIBITIONS: (first) Denver/AM, 1928; Weyhe Gallery, 1929, 31, 34, 37, 41; Rehn Galleries, 1945, 50; Kennedy Gallery, NYC, 1942, 44; Grand Central Moderns, 1951, 53, 56, 60;

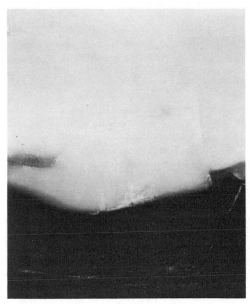

Edward Corbett   *Provincetown # 10. 1960*

Springfield, Mass./MFA, 1936; G. W. V. Smith Art Museum, Springfield, Mass., 1954; The Print Club, Philadelphia, 1937; San Diego, 1952; Raymond Burr Gallery, Los Angeles, 1962, 63; Santa Barbara/MA, 1952; de Young, 1952; Dallas/MFA, 1945, 53; Houston/MFA, 1954; Dartmouth College, 1954; Minneapolis/Institute, 1950; Carnegie Institute of Technology, 1958; National Gallery, 1944; Montclair/AM, 1954; Kansas City/Nelson, 1953; Omaha/Joslyn, 1953. COLLECTIONS: Baltimore/MA; Chicago/AI; Dallas/MFA; Dartmouth College; Denver/AM; de Young; Harvard U.; MMA; MOMA; Minneapolis/Institute; Oklahoma; Omaha/Joslyn; Orlando; PMA; Rochester/Memorial; Santa Barbara/MA; Santa Fe, N.M.; WMAA. BIBLIOGRAPHY: American Artists Congress, Inc.; American Artists Group Inc. 1, 3; Bethers; Bruce and Watson; Cheney, M. C.; Coke; Hall; Kent, N.; Mellquist; Pearson 1; Pousette-Dart, ed.; Reese; Wheeler; Zigrosser 1.

CORBETT, EDWARD. b. August 22, 1919, Chicago, Ill. STUDIED: California School of Fine Arts, two years. Traveled Mexico, USA, Philippines. US Army, US Navy, Merchant Marine, 1941–44. TAUGHT: San Francisco State Teachers College, 1947; California School of Fine Arts, 1947–50; U. of California, Berkeley, 1950; U. of

Minnesota, 1960–61; U. of New Mexico, 1955; Mount Holyoke College, 1953– . AWARDS: Abraham Rosenberg Foundation Fellowship, 1951. ADDRESS: 249 Pearl Street, South Hadley, Mass. DEALER: Grace Borgenicht Gallery Inc. ONE-MAN EXHIBITIONS: Grace Borgenicht Gallery Inc., 1956, 59, 61, 64. GROUP: California Palace, 1947, 50; Riverside Museum, 1948; Chicago/AI, American Abstract Artists, 1948; de Young, 1951; MOMA, Fifteen Americans, circ., 1952; U. of Illinois, 1954; U. of Nebraska, 1955; WMAA Annuals, 1953, 55, 58, 61, 63; Walker, 1961; Sao Paulo, 1962; Corcoran, 1956; Carnegie, 1955. COLLECTIONS: Bankers Trust Company; Buffalo/Albright; Chase Manhattan Bank; Chicago/AI; MOMA; Mount Holyoke College; Newark Museum; SFMA; Tate; WMAA; Walker.

CORBINO, JON. b. April 3, 1905, Vittoria, Sicily; **d.** July 10, 1964, Sarasota, Fla. To USA 1913. STUDIED: PAFA, with Daniel Barber; ASL, with George Luks, Frank V. DuMond, William Von Schlegell. TAUGHT: NAD, 1945; ASL, 1938–56. MEMBER: NAD; ASL; Lotus Club; PAFA; Philadelphia Watercolor Club; Audubon Artists. FEDERAL A.P.: US Post Office, Long Beach, N.Y. (mural). AWARDS: Chicago/AI, The M. V. Kohnstamm Prize, 1937; PAFA, Walter Lippincott Prize and Purchase, 1938; NAD, The Adolph and Clara Obrig Prize, 1938; Lotus Club, Drawing Award, 1938; New Rochelle Art Association, Silver Medal, 1940; NIAL, Painting Award, 1941; Leonardo da Vinci Art School, NYC, Da Vinci Silver Medal, 1942; Chicago/AI, Watson F. Blair Prize, 1944; NAD, Saltus Gold Medal for Merit, 1944; Audubon Artists, Gold Medal of Honor, 1945; Salmagundi Club, NYC, P.P., 1945; Pepsi-Cola, 1945; La Tausca Competition, 1946; Rockport (Mass.) Art Association, Hayward Neidringhause Memorial Prize, 1950; National Arts Club, Gold Medal, 1950; NAD, Ellen P. Speyer Prize, 1961. ONE-MAN EXHIBITIONS: (first) Oberlin College, 1927, also 1939; Contemporary Arts Gallery, NYC, 1934; Goodman Walker, Inc., Boston, 1935; Macbeth Gallery, NYC, 1937, 38, 40; A.A.A. Gallery, NYC, 1937, Corcoran, 1938; Warner Gallery, Los Angeles, 1939; Carnegie, 1939; Grace Horne Galleries, Boston, 1939; J. Seligmann and Co., 1942; Kleemann Gallery, NYC, 1944, 45; Marshall Field & Co., Chicago, 1948; Rehn Galleries, 1948, 51, 55, 59; Boris Mirski Gallery, 1950; The Manor Club, Pelham, N.Y., 1952; Frank Oehlschlaeger Gallery, Chicago, 1953, 56, 60; Ringling, 1963; Cowie Galleries, Los Angeles, 1959; O'Briens Art Emporium, Scottsdale, Ariz., 1960; Art Center, Bradenton, Fla., 1961; Harmon Gallery, Naples, Fla., 1964. GROUP: Chicago/AI, 1926, 36, 43, 44; Brooklyn Museum, 1931, 39, 43; Andover/Phillips, 1936; Carnegie, 1936, 37, 38, 40, 42, 50; U. of Minnesota, 1936; WMAA, 1937, 38, 40, 49, 52; PAFA, 1937, 50; Detroit/Institute, 1937; Worcester/AM, 1938, 42; St. Louis/City, 1938; NAD, 1938, 39, 44, 47; VMFA, 1938, 44; Toledo/MA, 1938, 40, 41; Golden Gate International Exposition, San Francisco, 1939; Cranbrook, 1940; New York World's Fair, 1939; MMA, 1941, 42, 50; Audubon Artists, 1945; Los Angeles/County MA, 1945; U. of Illinois, 1948; Sao Paulo, 1960; U. of South Florida, 1962. COLLECTIONS: ASL; Amherst College; Andover/Phillips; Ball State Teachers College; Brigham Young U.; Britannica; Brooklyn Museum; Canajoharie; Carnegie; Chicago/AI; Clearwater/Gulf Coast; Davenport/Municipal; Downtown Community School; Hebron Academy; Hickory, N.C.; Howard U.; IBM; Indianapolis/Herron; Kalamazoo/Institute; Kansas City/Nelson; Lotus Club; MMA; Memphis/Brooks; Montclair/AM; Mount Holyoke College; Municipal U. of Omaha; NAD; New Britain; Northwest Missouri State College; PAFA; Pasadena/AM; Portland, Me./MA; Quaker Ridge School; Ripon College; San Diego; Society of the Four Arts; Southampton/Parrish; Sweet Briar College; Toledo/MA; WMAA; Walker; Worcester/AM; Youngstown/Butler. BIBLIOGRAPHY: Baur 7; Boswell 1; Cheney, M. C.; Flexner; Genauer; Hall; Kent, N.; Pagano.

CORNELL, JOSEPH. b. December 24, 1903, Nyack, N.Y. Self-taught in art. ADDRESS: 3708 Utopia Parkway, Flushing, N.Y. ONE-MAN EXHIBITIONS: (first) Julien Levy Galleries, NYC, 1932, also 1933, 39, 40; Hugo Gallery, NYC, 1946; Copley Gallery, Hollywood, 1948; Charles Egan Gallery, 1949, 50; Allan Frumkin Gallery, Chicago, 1953; The Stable Gallery, 1957; Bennington College, 1959; Richard Feigen Gallery, Chicago (three-man), 1960. GROUP: MOMA, Fantastic Art, DADA, Surrealism, 1936; Galerie des Beaux Arts, Paris, Exposition Internationale du Surrealisme, 1938; Art of This Century, NYC, 1942; Carnegie, 1958; MOMA, The Art of Assemblage, 1961; WMAA Annual, 1962. COLLECTIONS: MOMA; WMAA. BIBLIOGRAPHY: Baur 7; Blesh 1; Breton 2; Flanagan; Guggenheim, ed.; Hunter 5; Janis and Blesh 1; Janis, S.; *Metro;* Seitz 2; Seuphor 3.

COWLES, RUSSELL. b. October 7, 1887, Algona, Iowa. STUDIED: Dartmouth College; ASL; American Academy, Rome; NAD (assistant to Douglas Volk and Barry Faulkner in mural painting). Traveled Europe and Asia extensively. US Army Intelligence, 1917. AWARDS: Prix de Rome, 1915; Chicago/AI, Norman Wait Harris Silver Medal, 1926; Denver/AM, Yetter Prize, 1936; Hon. DFA, Dartmouth College, 1951; Hon. DFA, Grinnell College, 1945; Hon. DFA, Cornell U., 1958. ADDRESS: 135 East 71 Street, NYC. DEALER: Kraushaar Galleries. ONE-MAN EXHIBITIONS: Des Moines, 1955; Dartmouth College, 1948, 63; Kraushaar Galleries, 1939, 41, 44, 46, 48, 50, 54, 59; Dayton/AI (three-man), 1942; Dalzell Hatfield Gallery, 1939, 43; Los Angeles/County MA, 1937; Ferargil Galleries, NYC, 1935. GROUP: Carnegie; PAFA; WMAA; Los Angeles/County MA; Des Moines; Architectural League of New York; Chicago/AI; California

Joseph Cornell   A Pantry Ballet for Jacques Offenbach. 1942

Palace; Wichita/AM; Corcoran. **COLLECTIONS:** Andover/Phillips; Britannica; Dartmouth College; Denver/AM; Des Moines; Fort Dodge/Banden; Los Angeles/County MA; Minneapolis/Institute; New Britain; PAFA; Santa Barbara/MA; Terre Haute/Swope; Wichita/AM. **BIBLIOGRAPHY: Baer;** Bethers; Cheney, M. C.; Hall; Kent, N.; Pearson 2; Watson 2; Wheeler.

CRAMER, KONRAD. b. November 9, 1888, Wurzburg, Germany. **STUDIED:** Academy of Fine Arts, Karlsruhe, Germany. **TAUGHT:** Bard College, 1940; founder, Woodstock (N.Y.) School of Photography, 1936. **ADDRESS:** Woodstock, N.Y. **ONE-MAN EXHIBITIONS:** Woodstock (N.Y.) Art Gallery, 1952; Long Island U., 1958. **GROUP:** Corcoran, 1938, 39; Carnegie, 1937, 38; WMAA, 1946; PAFA, 1936; Woodstock (N.Y.) Art Gallery. **COLLECTIONS:** MMA; MOMA; WMAA. **BIBLIOGRAPHY:** Baur 7; Brown; Janis, S.

CRAMPTON, ROLLIN McNEIL. b. March 9, 1886, New Haven, Conn. **STUDIED:** Yale U., with Lanzetell, Thompson; ASL, with Thomas Fogarty, Renterdahl. **FEDERAL A.P.:** Mural Supervisor. **AWARDS:** AAAL Grant; Longview Foundation Grant; Louisiana State U., P.P. **ADDRESS:** Woodstock, N.Y. **DEALER:** The Stable Gallery. **ONE-MAN EXHIBITIONS:** (first) Woodstock (N.Y.) Art Gallery; The Stable Gallery, 1961, 64; The Krasner Gallery, 1960; The Peridot Gallery, 1958. **COLLECTIONS:** Buffalo/Albright; Hartford/Wadsworth; Kalamazoo/Institute; Louisiana State U.; MIT; MMA; New Paltz; U. of Texas; WMAA; Walker. **BIBLIOGRAPHY:** Read 3; Zaidenberg, ed.

CRAWFORD, RALSTON. b. September 5, 1906, St. Catherines (Ont.), Canada. **STUDIED:** Otis Art Institute, Los Angeles, 1926–27; PAFA, 1927–30, with Henry Breckenridge, Henry McCarter; Barnes Foundation, 1927–30; Academie Colarossi and Academie Scandinave, Paris, 1932–33; Columbia U., 1933. Traveled Europe, USA, Mediterranean. **TAUGHT:** Art Academy of Cincinnati, 1940–41, 1949; Buffalo Fine Arts Academy, 1942; Honolulu Academy School, summer, 1947; Brooklyn Museum School, 1948–49; U. of Minnesota; Louisiana State U., 1949–50; U. of Colorado, summer, 1953; New School for Social Research, 1952–57; U. of Michigan, summer, 1953; Hofstra College, 1960–62; U. of Southern California, summer,

1961; lecture tour of USA for American Association of Colleges, 1956. **AWARDS:** MMA, P.P., 1942; L. C. Tiffany Grant, 1931; Mary Curtis Bok Foundation Fellowship, 1937; Wilmington, 1933. **ADDRESS:** 60 Gramercy Park, NYC. **ONE-MAN EXHIBITIONS:** (first) Maryland Institute, 1934; Philadelphia Art Alliance, 1938; Flint/Institute, 1942; Boyer Gallery, Philadelphia, 1937; Boyer Gallery, NYC, 1939; U. of Alabama, 1953; The Downtown Gallery, 1943, 44, 46, 50; Arts Club of Chicago (three-man), 1945; Cincinnati/AM, 1941; Milwaukee, 1958; Grace Borgenicht Gallery Inc., 1954, 56, 58; Louisiana State U., 1956; Hofstra College, 1952; Lee Nordness Gallery, NYC, 1961, 63; Artists' Gallery, Philadelphia, 1943; Portland, Ore./AM, 1946; Santa Barbara/MA, 1946; Howard U., 1947; MacMurray College, 1949. **RETROSPECTIVE:** U. of Alabama, 1953; Milwaukee, 1958; U. of Kentucky, 1961; U. of Minnesota, 1961. **GROUP:** PAFA; WMAA; MOMA; MMA; Corcoran; Phillips; Chicago/AI. **COLLECTIONS:** American Export Isbrandtsen Lines Inc.; Auburn U.; Baton Rouge; Buffalo/Albright; Cincinnati/AM; Flint/Institute; U. of Georgia; Hamline U.; Hofstra U.; Honolulu Academy; Houston/MFA; Howard College; Illinois Wesleyan U.; Library of Congress; MMA; MOMA; MacMurray College; The Miller Co.; U. of Minnesota; U. of Oklahoma; Phillips; Toledo/MA; Vassar College; WMAA; Walker; Wesleyan U.; Youngstown/Butler. **BIBLIOGRAPHY:** Baur 7; Boswell 1; Frost; Halpert; Janis, S.; Kootz 2; McCurdy, ed.; Nordness, ed.; Pagano; Reese; Ritchie 1; Rodman 2.

CREMEAN, ROBERT. b. September 28, 1932, Toledo, Ohio. **STUDIED:** Alfred U., 1950–52; Cranbrook Academy of Art, 1954, BA, 1956, MFA. **TAUGHT:** The Detroit Institute of Arts; UCLA, 1956–57; Art Center in La Jolla, 1957–58. **AWARDS:** Fulbright Fellowship (Italy), 1954. **ADDRESS:** c/o Dealer. **DEALER:** Esther Robles Gallery. **ONE-MAN EXHIBITIONS:** Esther Robles Gallery, 1960, 61, 62, 63, 64. **GROUP:** Detroit/Institute, 1956; Houston/MFA, 1957; Santa Barbara/MA, 1957; U. of Nebraska, 1958; Chicago/AI, 1960, 61; Los Angeles/County MA, The Image Retained, 1961; SFMA, Bay Area Artists, 1961; U. of Illinois, 1961, 63; California Palace, 1961; WMAA Annuals, 1961, 62; WMAA, Fifty California Artists, 1962–63; Western Association of Art Museum Directors,

Light, Space, Mass, circ., 1962. **COLLECTIONS:** UCLA; Cleveland/MA; Detroit/Institute; Los Angeles/County MA; U. of Miami; U. of Nebraska; St. Louis/City; Santa Barbara/MA; Toledo/MA.

CRISS, FRANCIS H. b. April 26, 1901, London, England. **STUDIED:** PAFA; ASL; with Jan Matulka. **TAUGHT:** Brooklyn Museum School; Albright Art School; ASL; Graphic Sketch Club, Philadelphia. **AWARDS:** PAFA, Cresson Fellowship; Guggenheim Foundation Fellowship, 1934. **ADDRESS:** 440 West 57 Street, NYC. **ONE-MAN EXHIBITIONS:** (first) Contemporary Arts Gallery, NYC; Philadelphia Art Alliance, 1953; Mellon Galleries, Philadelphia, 1933, 34. **GROUP:** Corcoran, 1939; PAFA, 1939, 41, 43, 45; Carnegie, 1944, 45; WMAA, 1936, 37, 38, 40, 42, 51; Chicago/AI, 1942, 43; MMA, 1941. **COLLECTIONS:** Kansas City/Nelson; La France Art Institute; National Gallery; PMA; WMAA. **BIBLIOGRAPHY:** Baur 7; Pagano.

CRONBACH, ROBERT M. b. February 10, 1908, St. Louis, Mo. **STUDIED:** Washington U. School of Fine Arts, 1926, with Victor Holm; PAFA, 1927–30, with Charles Grafly, Albert Laesslie; assistant in Paul Manship Studio, NYC and Paris, 1930. Traveled Europe extensively. **TAUGHT:** Adelphi College, 1947–62; Skowhegan School, summers, 1959, 60, 64; North Shore Community Art Center, 1949–54. **MEMBER:** Sculptors Guild; Architectural League of New York; Artists Equity. **FEDERAL A.P.:** Willerts Park Housing Project, Buffalo, N.Y., 1939 (sculpture). **COMMISSIONS** (architectural): St. Louis (Mo.) Municipal Auditorium, 1933; Social Security Building, Washington, D.C., 1940; Cafe Society Uptown, NYC, 1940; Hopping Phillips Motor Agency, Newark, N.J., 1948; Hotel Hollenden, Cleveland, 1946; 240 Central Park South, NYC, 1954; Dorr-Oliver Building, Stamford, Conn., 1957; Adelphi College, 1958; Ward School, New Rochelle, N.Y., 1959; National Council for U.S. Art, 1960 (a gift to the United Nations); Temple Chizuk Amuno, Baltimore, 1962; Federal Building, St. Louis, 1964; Temple Israel, St. Louis, 1964. **AWARDS:** PAFA, Stewardson Prize, 1938; PAFA, Cresson Fellowship, 1929, 30; National Sculpture Competition for Social Security Building, Washington, D.C., First Award, 1939. **ADDRESS:** 170 Henry Street, Westbury, N.Y. **DEALER:** The Bertha Schaefer

Gallery. ONE-MAN EXHIBITIONS: (first) Hudson D. Walker Gallery, NYC, 1939; The Bertha Schaefer Gallery, 1951 (two-man), 1952, 1960 (two-man). GROUP: New York World's Fair, 1939, 1964–65; Sculptors Guild, 1939, 40, 41, 42, 1945–62; City of Philadelphia, Sculpture International, 1940, 49; MMA, 1943; Denver/AM, The Modern Artist and His World, 1947; Brussels World's Fair, 1958; Riverside Museum, 1957; Silvermine Guild, 1957, 58, 60; WMAA Annuals, 1948, 56, 57, 58, 59; ART:USA:59, NYC, 1959; PAFA; Architectural League of New York; Brooklyn Museum; St. Louis/City; Houston/MFA; MOMA. COLLECTIONS: U. of Minnesota; Rosenthal China Co.; St. Louis/City; Springfield, Mo./AM; Walker. BIBLIOGRAPHY: Baur 7.

CURRY, JOHN STEUART. b. November 14, 1897, Dunavant, Kans.; d. 1946, Madison, Wisc. STUDIED: Kansas City Art Institute and School of Design, 1916; Chicago Art Institute School, 1916–18, with E. J. Timmons, John W. Norton; Geneva College, 1918–19; Studio of B. Schoukhaieff, Paris, 1926–27. Traveled France. TAUGHT: U. of Wisconsin, 1936; Cooper Union, 1932–34; ASL, 1932–36. COMMISSIONS (murals): Justice Department, Washington, D.C., 1936–37; Kansas State Capitol, 1938–40; U. of Wisconsin, 1940–42. AWARDS: MMA, Artists for Victory, Second Prize, 1942; Carnegie, 1933; PAFA, Gold Medal, 1941. ONE-MAN EXHIBITIONS: (first) Whitney Studio Club, NYC, 1930; U. of Kansas, 1957; U. of Wisconsin, 1937; Milwaukee, 1946; A.A.A. Gallery, NYC, 1947; Ferargil Galleries, NYC, 1933, 35; Hudson D. Walker Gallery, NYC, 1938; Syracuse U., 1956. GROUP: WMAA; Chicago/AI; Wichita/AM; Milwaukee. COLLECTIONS: Andover/Phillips; Britannica, Chicago/AI; First National Bank, Madison; Kansas State College; MMA; Muskegon/Hackley; U. of Nebraska; St. Louis/City; WMAA; Wichita/AM. BIBLIOGRAPHY: American Artists Group Inc. 1; Baur 7; Bazin; Biddle 3; Blesh 1; Boswell 1; Brown; Bruce and Watson; Cahill and Barr, eds.; Canaday; Cheney, M. C.; Christensen; Craven 1; Curry 1, 2, 3; Flanagan; Flexner; Goodrich and Baur 1; Hall; Hunter 5; *Index of 20th Century Artists;* Jewell 2; McCurdy, ed.; Mellquist; Mendelowitz; Newmeyer; Pagano; Pearson 1; Reese; Richardson; Schmeckebier; Wight 2.

CUSUMANO, STEFANO. b. February 5, 1912, Tampa, Fla. STUDIED: Metropolitan Art School, with Arthur Schiewder; Cooper Union. Traveled Europe. TAUGHT: Leonardo da Vinci Art School, NYC, 1932–40; Art Career School, 1945–54; NYU, 1954– ; Cooper Union, 1956– . AWARDS: Ford Foundation, P.P., 1963. ADDRESS: 170 West 73 Street, NYC. DEALER: Gallery 63, Inc., NYC and Rome. ONE-MAN EXHIBITIONS: (first) Montross Gallery, NYC, 1942; G. Binet Gallery, NYC, 1946, 47, 48, 50; Passedoit Gallery, NYC, 1953, 56, 57, 59; Gallery 63, Inc., NYC, 1963; Philadelphia Art Alliance, 1948; Woodmere Art Gallery, Philadelphia, 1950; Tampa Art Institute, 1949; Oregon State College, 1951; Washington State U., 1951; Gallery 63, Inc., Rome, 1964; Mari Gallery, Woodstock, N.Y., 1962. GROUP: U. of Illinois, 1950; PAFA, 1951, 52; WMAA, 1947; Carnegie, 1949; Corcoran, 1951; NIAL, 1952, 61. COLLECTIONS: Brooklyn Museum; Florida State U.; U. of Illinois; Johns Hopkins U.; MMA; National Gallery; Newark Museum; PMA; Pensacola; WMAA; Wesleyan U.

d

DAPHNIS, NASSOS. b. July 23, 1914, Krockeai, Greece. To USA 1930. Self-taught. Traveled USA, Greece, Italy, France. **TAUGHT:** Horace Mann School, Riverdale, N.Y., 1953–58. **MEMBER:** American Abstract Artists. **ADDRESS:** 11 Bangs Street, Provincetown, Mass. **DEALER:** Leo Castelli Inc. **ONE-MAN EXHIBITIONS:** (first) Contemporary Arts Gallery, NYC, 1938, also 1947, 49; Leo Castelli Inc., 1959, 60, 61, 63; Charlotte/Mint, 1949; Galerie Colette Allendy, Paris, 1950; Galleria Toninelli, Milan, 1961; Iris Clert, 1962. **GROUP:** Carnegie, 1955, 58, 61; Seattle World's Fair, 1962; WMAA Annuals, 1960, 61, 62, 63; Musee Cantonal des Beaux-Arts, Lausanne, I Salon International de Galeries Pilotes, 1963; Corcoran Annual, 1959; Walker, Purist Painting, 1961; American Abstract Artists Annual, 1961; SRGM, Abstract Expressionists and Imagists, 1961; WMAA, Geometric Abstraction in America, circ., 1962. **COLLECTIONS:** Baltimore/MA; MOMA; Provincetown/Chrysler; RISD; Tel Aviv; Union Carbide Corp.; Utica; WMAA.

D'ARCANGELO, ALLAN. b. June 16, 1930, Buffalo, N.Y. **STUDIED:** U. of Buffalo, 1948–52, BA (History and Government); City College of New York; New School for Social Research, 1953–54; Mexico City College, 1957–59, with Dr. John Golding, Fernando Belain; studio work with Boris Lurie, NYC, 1955–56. Traveled Mexico, USA. **TAUGHT:** School of Visual Arts, NYC, 1963– . **COMMISSIONS:** Transportation and Travel Pavilion, New York World's Fair, 1964–65 (mural). **ADDRESS:** 76 West 69 Street, NYC. **DEALER:** Fischbach Gallery. **ONE-MAN EXHIBITIONS:** (first) Long Island U., 1961; Thibaut Gallery, NYC, 1963; Fischbach Gallery,

1964; Galeria Genova, Mexico City (two-man), 1958. **GROUP:** Sarah Lawrence College, Popular Imagery, 1963; ICA, London, 1963; Salon du Mai, Paris, 1964; Dwan Gallery, Boxes, 1964; Oakland/AM, Pop Art USA, 1963; The Hague, New Realism, 1964; Buffalo/Albright, Mixed Media and Pop Art, 1963; Salon des Comparaisons, Paris, 1964. **COLLECTIONS:** The Hertz Corp.

D'ARISTA, ROBERT. b. July 2, 1929, Pelham, N.Y. **STUDIED:** NYU, with Philip Guston; Columbia U., with John Heliker; American Art School, NYC; Academie de la Grande Chaumiere. Traveled France, Italy. **TAUGHT:** American U., 1961– . **AWARDS:** Fulbright Fellowship, 1956. **ADDRESS:** 2208 Tunlaw Road, N.W., Washington, D.C. **DEALER:** Jefferson Place Gallery. **ONE-MAN EXHIBITIONS:** (first) The Alan Gallery, 1955, also 1956, 60; Grippi Gallery, NYC, 1962; Lee Nordness Gallery, NYC, 1964; Jefferson Place Gallery, 1962. **GROUP:** Carnegie, 1956, 59; WMAA Annuals, 1956, 57, 59; Chicago/AI; PAFA, 1954, 60; Brooklyn Museum; U. of Illinois, 1955; U. of Nebraska, 1955, 56, 57; Columbia, S.C./MA Annual; Bogota, Colombia; SRGM; Detroit/Institute, 1955, 58. **COLLECTIONS:** American U.; S. C. Johnson & Son, Inc.; Smith College; Toledo/MA; Yale U. **BIBLIOGRAPHY:** Nordness, ed.

DARROW, PAUL GARDNER. b. October 31, 1921, Pasadena, Calif. **STUDIED:** Art Center School, Los Angeles; Colorado Springs Fine Arts Center, with Boardman Robinson; Claremont Graduate School, with Millard Sheets, Sueo Serisawa, Henry McFee, Howard Cook. **TAUGHT:** Brigham Young U., 1954; Coronado

School of Fine Arts, summers, 1953, 55; Scripps College, 1954–55; Otis Art Institute, Los Angeles; Claremont Graduate School. COMMISSIONS (murals): Richmond (Calif.) Youth Center, 1952; Convair Aircraft, San Diego, 1953; National American Insurance Co., Los Angeles, 1954; Kaiser Aluminum, Disneyland, Calif., 1955; Broadway Dept. Stores, Anaheim and Van Nuys, Calif., 1955; Gourmet Shop, Hollywood, 1955; Air France, 1960–61. AWARDS: Los Angeles/County MA, 1954; Pasadena/AM, 1954; California State Fair, 1950. ADDRESS: 403 Blaisdell Drive, Claremont, Calif. ONE-MAN EXHIBITIONS: Philadelphia Art Alliance, 1948. GROUP: Sao Paulo, 1955; Smithsonian, circ., 1955–56; PAFA, 1954; Los Angeles/County MA, 1951, 52, 53, 54; Denver/AM, 1954; Youngstown/Butler, 1953, 54; Corcoran, 1954; U. of Vienna, 1951; SFMA, 1952, 53; Seattle/AM, 1953; Santa Barbara/MA, 1952, 53, 54, 55; Long Beach/MA, 1958, 59, 60, 61; Oakland/AM. COLLECTIONS: Palos Verdes; Pasadena/AM.

DASBURG, ANDREW. b. May 4, 1887, Paris, France. To USA 1892. STUDIED: ASL, with Kenyon Cox, Frank V. DuMond; privately with Birge Harrison; also with Robert Henri. AWARDS: Pan-American Exhibition, Los Angeles, 1925; Carnegie, 1927, 31; Guggenheim Foundation Fellowship, 1932; Ford Foundation Grant. ADDRESS: Ranchos de Taos, N.M. ONE-MAN EXHIBITIONS: Dallas/MFA, 1957; Rehn Galleries, 1958. RETROSPECTIVE: A.F.A./Ford Foundation, circ., 1959. GROUP: WMAA; SFMA; MMA; Denver/AM; Santa Fe, N.M. COLLECTIONS: Barnes Foundation; California Palace; Cincinnati/AM; Colorado Springs/FA; Dallas/MFA; Denver/AM; Los Angeles/County MA; MMA; SFMA; Santa Barbara/MA; Santa Fe, N.M.; WMAA. BIBLIOGRAPHY: Baur 7; Brown; Bywaters 1, 2; Cahill and Barr, eds.; Cheney, M. C.; Coke; Goodrich and Baur 1; Hunter 5; *Index of 20th Century Artists;* Janis, S.; McCurdy, ed.; Neuhaus; Richardson; Wright 1.

DASH, ROBERT. b. June 8, 1932, NYC. STUDIED: U. of New Mexico, BA (Anthropology and English). Traveled Italy, Mexico, USA. AWARDS: New York State Board of Regents Scholarship. ADDRESS: 302 Elizabeth Street, NYC. DEALER: The Osborne Gallery. ONE-MAN EXHIBITIONS: (first) The Kornblee Gallery, 1961, also 1962, 63; The Osborne Gallery, 1964. GROUP: Yale U., The New York Season, 1961; MOMA, Eight American Painters of the Landscape, circ., 1964; Corcoran; U. of Colorado. COLLECTIONS: Chase Manhattan Bank; First National Bank of Memphis.

DAVEY, RANDALL. b. May 24, 1887, East Orange, N.J. STUDIED: Cornell U., 1905–07; in Europe with Robert Henri, 1908–09. Traveled USA, Europe. TAUGHT: Chicago Art Institute School, 1920; U. of New Mexico, 1945–46; Kansas City Art Institute and School of Design, 1921–24; Broadmoor Art Academy, Colorado Springs, 1924–31. COMMISSIONS (murals): US Post Offices, Vinita and Claremore, Okla., 1939. AWARDS: NAD, 1939; NAD, The Thomas B. Clarke Prize, 1938; NAD, Hallgarten Prize, 1915; SFMA, Hon. Men., 1915. ADDRESS: Canyon Road, Santa Fe, N.M. ONE-MAN EXHIBITIONS: California Palace; San Diego; U. of New Mexico; Vassar College; Vose Gallery, Boston; Whitney Studio Club, NYC; Ferargil Galleries, NYC, 1933, 34; Grand Central, NYC, 1941; Kraushaar Galleries, 1938; Macbeth Gallery, NYC, 1916; Montross Gallery, NYC, 1922; Rehn Galleries, 1930; Santa Fe, N.M., 1946; Buffalo/Albright; Chicago/AI; Symphony Hall, Boston; Broadmoor Art Academy, Colorado Springs; Carnegie; Carroll Gallery, NYC; Kleemann Gallery, NYC. RETROSPECTIVE: Santa Fe, N.M., 1957. GROUP: Corcoran; Chicago/AI; WMAA; Kansas City/Nelson; Santa Fe, N.M.; Taos, N.M. COLLECTIONS: Chicago/AI; Cleveland/MA; Corcoran; Detroit/Institute; Kansas City/Nelson; Montclair/AM; Will Rogers Shrine; Santa Fe, N.M.; US Navy; WMAA. BIBLIOGRAPHY: Bryant; Cheney, M. C.; Coke; Davey; Hall; Jewell 2; Neuhaus.

DAVIS, JERROLD. b. November 2, 1926; Chico, Calif. STUDIED: U. of California, Berkeley, BA, 1953, MA. Traveled Latin America, Mexico, Europe. AWARDS: Sigmund Martin Heller Traveling Fellowship, 1953; Guggenheim Foundation Fellowship, 1958; Ford Foundation Artist-in-Residence, 1964. ADDRESS: 66 Twain, Berkeley, Calif. DEALER: Esther Robles Gallery. ONE-MAN EXHIBITIONS: (first) California Palace, 1957; Instituto Brasil-Estados-Unidos, Rio de Janeiro, 1951; Everett Ellin Gallery, Los Angeles, 1958; The Rose Rabow

Gallery, 1963; Esther Robles Gallery, 1964. **GROUP:** I Sao Paulo Biennial, 1951; Oberlin College, 3 Young Painters, 1958; U. of Illinois, 1959, 61, 63; California Palace, 1960, 61, 62, 63, 64; Carnegie, 1958; Flint/Institute, 1964; Phoenix, 1964. **COLLECTIONS:** Carnegie; Flint/Institute; Los Angeles/County MA; Santa Barbara/MA.

DAVIS, STUART. b. December 7, 1894, Philadelphia, Pa.; **d.** June 25, 1964, NYC. STUDIED with Robert Henri, 1910–13. US Army Intelligence, World War I. Traveled Europe, Cuba, USA. **TAUGHT:** ASL, 1931–32; New School for Social Research, 1940–50; lectured at museums and universities. FEDERAL A.P.: 1933–39. Editor: *Art Front* Magazine. **COMMISSIONS** (murals): Radio City Music Hall, NYC, 1932; Indiana U., 1938; New York World's Fair, 1939; Municipal Broadcasting Co., NYC, 1939; Drake U., 1955; Heinz Research Center, Pittsburgh, 1957. **AWARDS:** Pepsi-Cola, 1944; Carnegie, Hon. Men., 1944; PAFA, J. Henry Schiedt Memorial Prize, 1945; PAFA, Hon. Men., 1956; Chicago/AI, Norman Wait Harris Silver Medal, 1948; Chicago/AI, Ada S. Garrett Prize, 1951;

Stuart Davis   *Standard Brand. 1961*

Chicago/AI, Flora Mayer Witkowsky Prize, 1961; La Tausca Competition, P.P., 1948; VMFA, John Barton Payne Medal, 1950; Guggenheim Foundation Fellowship, 1952; Hallmark International Competition, 1956; Brandeis U., Creative Arts Award, 1957; Guggenheim International, 1958, 60. **ONE-MAN EXHIBITIONS:** Sheridan Square Gallery, NYC, 1917; Ardsley Gallery, 1918; Newark Museum, 1925; Whitney Studio Club, NYC, 1926, 29; The Downtown Gallery, 1927, 30, 31, 32, 34, 43, 46, 52, 54, 56, 60, 62; Curt Valentine Gallery, NYC, 1928; Crillon Galleries, Philadelphia, 1931; Katherine Kuh Gallery, Chicago, 1939; Modern Art Society, Cincinnati (two-man), 1941; Arts Club of Chicago, 1945; Baltimore/MA, 1946; XXVI Venice Biennial, 1952; Brandeis U., 1957; Santa Barbara/MA (three-man), 1949; MOMA, 1945; Contemporary Arts Gallery, NYC, 1955, 59. **RETROSPECTIVE:** Walker, 1957. **GROUP:** The Armory Show, 1913; Independents, NYC, 1916; Golden Gate International Exposition, San Francisco, 1939; Tate, American Painting, 1946; I Sao Paulo Biennial, 1951; MOMA, 12 Modern American Painters and Sculptors, circ. Europe, 1953–55; MOMA, Modern Art in the United States, circ. Europe, 1955–56; American Painting and Sculpture, Moscow, 1959; I Inter-American Paintings and Prints Biennial, Mexico City, 1958. **COLLECTIONS:** AAAL; Andover/Phillips; Arizona State College; U. of Arizona; Baltimore/MA; Bezalel Museum; Brandeis U.; Britannica; Brooklyn Museum; Buffalo/Albright; Carnegie; Chicago/AI; Cincinnati/AM; Cranbrook; Dartmouth College; U. of Georgia; Hartford/Wadsworth; Harvard U.; Honolulu Academy; IBM; U. of Illinois; State U. of Iowa; U. of Kentucky; Library of Congress; Los Angeles/County MA; MMA; MOMA; Milwaukee; Minneapolis/Institute; U. of Nebraska; Newark Museum; New Trier High School; Ogunquit; U. of Oklahoma; PAFA; PMA; The Pennsylvania State U.; Phillips; Randolph-Macon Woman's College; Sara Roby Foundation; Rochester/Memorial; Roswell; SFMA; SRGM; St. Louis/City; San Diego; Seattle/AM; Utica; VMFA; Vassar College; WMAA; Walker; Washington U.; Wellesley College; Wichita/AM; Yale U. **BIBLIOGRAPHY: Arnason 3;** Barker 1; Barr 3; Baur 5, 7; Bazin; Beekman; Biddle 3; Biederman 1; **Blesh** 1, **2;** Brown; Cahill and Barr, eds.; Cheney, M. C.; Christensen; Coke; **Davis;** Eliot;

Elliott; Flanagan; Flexner; Frost; Genauer; Goodrich and Baur 1; **Goossen 1;** Haftman; Halpert; Hess, T. B.; Hunter 1, 5; Huyghe; Janis, S.; Kepes 2; Kootz 2; Kuh 2; Lee and Burchwood; McCurdy, ed.; Mendelowitz; Munsterberg; Newmeyer; Nordness, ed.; Pagano; Pearson 1; Phillips 1; Pousette-Dart, ed.; Read 2; Richardson; Ringel, ed.; Ritchie 1; Rodman 2; Rosenblum; Sachs; Seuphor 1; Sutton; **Sweeney 3;** "What Abstract Art Means to Me"; Wheeler; Wight 2.

DAY, (Esther) WORDEN. b. June 11, 1916, Columbus, Ohio. STUDIED: Randolph-Macon Woman's College, BA; NYU, MA; with Maurice Sterne, Jean Charlot, Vaclav Vytlacil, Hans Hofmann, S. W. Hayter in NYC. Traveled USA, North Africa, Europe. TAUGHT: U. of Wyoming; Pratt Institute; State U. of Iowa; New School for Social Research. MEMBER: SAGA; Audubon Artists. FEDERAL A.P.: Taught book illustration and lithography, 1938–39. Included in USIA film, "Printmaking, USA." COMMISSIONS: International Graphic Arts Society, 1964. AWARDS: VMFA Fellowship, 1940; Lessing J. Rosenwald Fund Fellowship, 1942–44; Guggenheim Foundation Fellowship, 1951, 52; Brooklyn Museum, P.P.; Library of Congress, Pennell P.P. ADDRESS: 522 Valley Road, Upper Montclair, N.J. DEALERS: Grand Central Moderns; Weyhe Gallery. ONE-MAN EXHIBITIONS: (first) Perls Galleries, 1940; VMFA, 1940; The Bertha Schaefer Gallery, 1948, 51; Cincinnati/AM; Norfolk; Baltimore/MA; The Krasner Gallery, 1959; Grand Central Moderns, 1961. GROUP: U. of Illinois, 1950; WMAA; MOMA; Chicago/AI; Brooklyn Museum; MMA; USIA, 10 American Artists of Woodcut, circ. COLLECTIONS: Bradley U.; Brooklyn Museum; Carnegie; Detroit/Institute; U. of Illinois; Library of Congress; U. of Louisville; MMA; MOMA; Mills College; U. of Minnesota; Montclair/AM; NYPL; National Gallery; U. of Nebraska; Newark Museum; Norfolk; PMA; Rutgers U.; St. Louis/City; VMFA; Walker; U. of Wyoming; Yale U. BIBLIOGRAPHY: Ritchie 1.

DECKER, LINDSEY. b. 1923, Lincoln, Neb. STUDIED: American Academy of Art, Chicago, 1942–43; State U. of Iowa, 1946–50, BFA, MFA. Subject of a film, "The World of Lindsey Decker," on drawings and sculpture (11 min., color). COMMISSIONS: Eastland Center, Detroit,

1957; Atomic Energy Commission, Oak Ridge, Tenn. AWARDS: Italian Government Fellowship for work in creative sculpture, 1957; Fulbright Fellowship (Italy), 1957; Detroit/Institute, P.P., 1956; Detroit/Institute, Dr. & Mrs. Meyer O. Cantor Prize, 1956. ADDRESS: 113 Bedford Street, NYC. DEALER: The Zabriskie Gallery. ONE-MAN EXHIBITIONS: Chiku-Rin Gallery, Detroit; Michigan State U.; Kalamazoo/Institute; Los Artesantos Gallery, Las Vegas, N.M.; The Zabriskie Gallery, 1959, 60. GROUP: Chicago/AI, Exhibition Momentum, 1950, 51, 52, 53, 54; Philadelphia Art Alliance, 1954; WMAA Annuals, 1956, 60; Houston/MFA, Irons in the Fire, 1957; A.F.A., New Talent, circ., 1957; MOMA, Recent Sculpture USA, 1959; A.F.A., Contemporary Sculpture, 1960; PAFA, 1960; Cincinnati/AM, Midwest Sculpture, 1960. COLLECTIONS: Albion College; Cranbrook; Detroit/Institute.

DE CREEFT, JOSE. b. November 27, 1884, Guadalajara, Spain. STUDIED: Atelier of Don Augustin Querol, Barcelona, 1906; apprenticed to Idalgo de Caviedas; Academie Julian, Paris, 1906; Maison Greber, Paris, 1910–14. To USA 1929; citizen 1940. TAUGHT: ASL, 1934–62; New School for Social Research, 1932–48, 1957–62. MEMBER: Artists Equity (founding member); Audubon Artists; National Sculpture Society; NIAL, 1955; Federation of Modern Painters and Sculptors (President, 1943); NAD, 1964; Sculptors Guild. COMMISSIONS: Saugues (Puy de Dome), France, 1918 (World War I Memorial); Fortress of Ramonje, Mallorca, 1932 (200 pieces of sculpture); Fairmount Park, Philadelphia, 1950; Central Park, NYC, 1959 (Alice in Wonderland group); Bronx (N.Y.) Municipal Hospital, 1962 (mosaic for nurses' residence). AWARDS: Officier de l'Instruction Publique, France; MMA, Artists for Victory, First Prize, 1942; PAFA, George D. Widener Memorial Gold Medal, 1945; Audubon Artists, Gold Medal of Honor, 1954, 57; Ford Foundation Traveling Retrospective, 1960. m. Lorrie Goulet. ADDRESS: Kirby Lane North, Rye, N.Y. DEALER: The Contemporaries. ONE-MAN EXHIBITIONS: (first) El Circulo de Bellas Artes, Madrid, 1903; Seattle/AM, 1929; Ferargil Galleries, NYC, 1929; Arts Club of Chicago, 1930; Philadelphia Art Alliance, 1933; Santa Barbara/MA, 1937; St. Paul Gallery, 1943; College of William and Mary, 1944; West Palm

Jose de Creeft   *La Nina.*

Beach/Norton, 1949, 50; Passedoit Gallery, NYC, 1936, 1938–49; The Contemporaries, 1956, 58, 60, 64. **Retrospective:** A.F.A./Ford Foundation, circ., 1960. **Group:** Chicago/AI Annuals, 1939–51; MMA, National Sculpture Exhibition, 1942, 51; Carnegie; MOMA, Sculpture of the XXth Century, 1953; PAFA Annuals, 1944–62; WMAA Annuals, 1942–57; Worcester/AM; Brooklyn Museum; Sculptors Guild Annuals; Audubon Artists Annuals; Federation of Modern Painters and Sculptors; Artistes Francais; Societe Nationale des Beaux Arts, Paris; Salon des Artistes Independants, Paris; Salon d'Automne, Paris, 1910–29. **Collections:** Bezalel Museum; Brooklyn Museum; Columbia U.; IBM; MMA; MOMA; U. of Nebraska; New Paltz; PAFA; U. of Puerto Rico; SFMA; Seattle/AM; Utica; WMAA; West Palm Beach/Norton; Wichita/AM. **Bibliography:** Baur 7; Brumme; **Campos;** Cheney, M. C.; de

Creeft; **Devree;** Goodrich and Baur 1; Mc-Curdy, ed.; Pearson 2; Ritchie 3; Selz, J.; Seuphor 3.

DEEM, GEORGE. b. August 18, 1932, Vincennes, Ind. STUDIED: Vincennes U.; The U. of Chicago; Chicago Art Institute School, with Paul Wieghardt, Boris Margo, 1958, BFA. US Army, two years. **ADDRESS:** 65 Fulton Street, NYC. **DEALER:** Allan Stone Gallery. **ONE-MAN EXHIBITIONS:** (first) Allan Stone Gallery, 1962, also 1963. **GROUP:** Corcoran; Chicago/AI, 1963; Baltimore/MA, 1962; Buffalo/Albright, 1962; MOMA; Barnard College; Silvermine Guild. **COLLECTIONS:** The Singer Company Inc.

DE ERDELY, FRANCIS. b. 1904, Budapest, Hungary; **d.** 1959, Los Angeles, Calif. STUDIED: Academy of Fine Arts, Budapest; Real Academia de Bellas Artes de San Fernando, Madrid; Sorbonne; Ecole du Louvre. **TAUGHT:** Royal Netherlands Art Academy, The Hague; Pasadena Museum School, 1944–46; U. of Southern California, 1945–59. **ONE-MAN EXHIBITIONS:** Hungarian Relief Library, NYC, 1939; de Young; Santa Barbara/MA; Pasadena/AM, 1950, 60; Bonestell Gallery, NYC, 1940; Laguna Beach (Calif.) Art Gallery; Sacramento/Crocker; San Joaquin Pioneer Museum and Haggin Art Galleries, Stockton, Calif.; La Jolla; Oakland/AM, 1950; Seattle/AM; Kansas City/Nelson; Lane Gallery, 1960; Los Angeles/County MA, Memorial Exhibition, 1960. **COLLECTIONS:** Antwerp; Brussels/Moderne; Carnegie; Chicago/AI; Colorado Springs/FA; Corcoran; Denver/AM; Detroit/Institute; Ghent; The Hague; Los Angeles/County MA; MMA; Melbourne/National; Mons; Oakland/AM; PAFA; Pasadena/AM; San Diego; Youngstown/Butler. **BIBLIOGRAPHY:** Watson 2.

DE FOREST, ROY DEAN. b. February 11, 1930, North Platte, Neb. STUDIED: Yakima Valley Junior College; California School of Fine Arts, with Edward Corbett, Hassel Smith, David Park; San Francisco State College, with Seymour Locks, Alexander Nepote (AA, BA, MA). **TAUGHT:** California College of Arts and Crafts; Bayview High School (San Quentin Prison); San Francisco State College; Contra Costa College; Yakima Valley Junior College. **AWARDS:** SFMA, Nealie Sullivan Award, 1962; Bay Printmakers Society, Oakland, P.P., 1956; San Fran-cisco Art Association, 1956. **ADDRESS:** 1700 Bissell, Richmond, Calif. **DEALER:** Dilexi Gallery, San Francisco. **ONE-MAN EXHIBITIONS:** (first) The East-West Gallery, San Francisco, 1955, also 1958; Dilexi Gallery, San Francisco, 1960, 63; Dilexi Gallery, Los Angeles, 1962; San Francisco Art Association, 1962; Stonecourt Gallery, Yakima, Wash., 1960. **GROUP:** Reed College, 1957; SFMA, 1952, 63, 64; Cincinnati/AM, 1952; Sao Paulo, 1955; California Palace, 1960, 63; WMAA, 1962; Buffalo/Albright, 1963; Walker, 1963; U. of Illinois, 1964; Pasadena/AM, 1962. **COLLECTIONS:** Oakland/AM; Omaha/Joslyn; SFMA. **BIBLIOGRAPHY:** Janis and Blesh 1.

DEHN, ADOLF ARTHUR. b. November 22, 1895, Waterville, Minn. STUDIED: Minneapolis Institute School; ASL. **TAUGHT:** Famous Artists Schools, Inc. **MEMBER:** NAD. **AWARDS:** Guggenheim Foundation Fellowship, 1939, 51; Chicago/AI, 1943; Philadelphia Art Alliance, 1936; The Print Club, Philadelphia, 1939; Library of Congress, Pennell P.P., 1946. **ADDRESS:** 443 West 21 Street, NYC. **ONE-MAN EXHIBITIONS:** Brooklyn Public Library, 1944; Macbeth Gallery, NYC, 1933; Dayton/AI, 1946; A.A.A. Gallery, NYC, 1941, 51; The Milch Gallery, 1957, 60; FAR Gallery, NYC, 1964. **GROUP:** MMA; MOMA; NYPL; Brooklyn Museum; Chicago/AI; Boston/MFA; WMAA. **COLLECTIONS:** Boston/MFA; Brooklyn Museum; Chicago/AI; Cincinnati/AM; Cleveland/MA; Indianapolis/Herron; Lehigh U.; MMA; MOMA; Minneapolis/Institute; NYPL; Newark Museum; Standard Oil Co.; US Navy; Utica; WMAA. **BIBLIOGRAPHY:** American Artists Group Inc. 1, 2, 3; Brown; **Dehn;** Goodrich 1; Goodrich and Baur 1; *Index of 20th Century Artists;* Mellquist; Mendelowitz; Pagano; Pearson 1, 2; Pousette-Dart, ed.; Reese; Zigrosser 1.

DEHNER, DOROTHY. b. December 23, 1908, Cleveland, Ohio. STUDIED: UCLA; Skidmore College, BS (Art); Pasadena Playhouse, with Gilmor Brown; ASL, with Kimon Nicolaides, Boardman Robinson, Jan Matulka, Kenneth Hayes Miller. Traveled Europe, Russia. Began as a painter, became a sculptor in 1955. **TAUGHT:** Barnard School, NYC, and privately. **MEMBER:** Federation of Modern Painters and Sculptors; Sculptors Guild. **AWARDS:** Audubon Artists, First Prize, 1949; ART:USA:59, NYC, Second

Prize for Sculpture, 1959; Tamarind Fellowship. **ADDRESS:** 33 Fifth Avenue, NYC. **DEALER:** The Willard Gallery. **ONE-MAN EXHIBITIONS:** (first) Rose Fried Gallery, 1952; The Willard Gallery, 1955, 57, 59, 61, 63; Chicago/AI, 1955; Gres Gallery, Washington, D.C., 1959; Wittenborn Gallery, NYC, 1956; Columbia U., 1961; Albany/Institute, 1954; U. of Virginia, 1954; Philadelphia Art Alliance, 1962; Howard U., 1954; Cornell U., 1964; U. of Michigan, 1963; Skidmore College, 1948, 53, 59; Albany/Institute (two-man, with David Park), *ca.* 1944. **GROUP:** MMA, 1953; MOMA, 1962, 64; WMAA Annuals, 1950, 51, 54, 60, 63; Brooklyn Museum; Sculptors Guild Annuals; Carnegie, 1961; Baltimore/MA; Los Angeles/County MA; Utica; PAFA; Walker; Hartford/Wadsworth; New Sculpture Group, NYC; SFMA, 1944. **COLLECTIONS:** Columbus; Free Library of Philadelphia; Hemisphere Club; MMA; MOMA; US State Department; Utica. **BIBLIOGRAPHY:** Read 1.

DE KOONING, ELAINE. b. March 20, 1920, NYC. **STUDIED:** Leonardo da Vinci Art School, NYC, 1937; American Artists School, NYC, 1938, with Conrad Marca-Relli; privately with Willem de Kooning, 1938–43. **TAUGHT:** U. of New Mexico, 1959; The Pennsylvania State U., 1960. **ADDRESS:** 827 Broadway, NYC. **DEALER:** The Graham Gallery. **ONE-MAN EXHIBITIONS:** The Stable Gallery, 1954, 56; Tibor de Nagy Gallery, 1957; U. of New Mexico, 1958; Santa Fe, N.M., 1959; Gump's Gallery, 1959; Dord Fitz Gallery, Amarillo, 1959; Holland-Goldowsky Gallery, Chicago, 1960; The Howard Wise Gallery, Cleveland, 1960; Ellison Gallery, Fort Worth, 1960; The Graham Gallery, 1960, 61, 64; De Aenlle Gallery, NYC, 1961; Tanager Gallery, NYC, 1960. **RETROSPECTIVE:** New London, 1959. **GROUP:** The Kootz Gallery, New Talent, 1950; International Biennial Exhibition of Paintings, Tokyo; MOMA, Younger American Painters, circ., 1957–59; Walker, Expressionism, 1900–1955, 1956; A.F.A., Sports in Art, 1957; Carnegie, 1956; Jewish Museum, The New York School, Second Generation, 1957; Houston/MFA, Action Painting, 1958; Walker, 60 American Painters, 1960; Hallmark Art Award, 1960. **COLLECTIONS:** MOMA. **BIBLIOGRAPHY:** Blesh 1; Hunter 5; Janis and Blesh 1.

DE KOONING, WILLEM. b. April 24, 1904, Rotterdam, Holland. **STUDIED:** Academie voor Beeldende Kunsten ed Technische Wetenschappen, Amsterdam, 1916–24. To USA 1926. **FEDERAL** A.P.: Mural painting, 1935–39. **TAUGHT:** Yale U., 1950–51; Black Mountain College, 1948. **COMMISSIONS** (murals): New York World's Fair, 1939; French Line Pier, NYC (with Fernand Leger); Williamsburgh Housing Project, NYC. **AWARDS:** State Academy Medal, Rotterdam; Academy of Plastic Arts, Rotterdam, Silver Medal; Chicago/AI, The Mr. & Mrs. Frank G. Logan Medal, 1951. **ADDRESS:** Springs, East Hampton, N.Y. **ONE-MAN EXHIBITIONS:** (first) Charles Egan Gallery, 1948, also 1951; Arts Club of Chicago, 1951; Sidney Janis Gallery, 1953, 56, 59, 62; Boston Museum School, 1953; Martha Jackson Gallery, 1955; Workshop Art Center, Washington, D.C., 1953; Paul Kantor Gallery, 1961; Allan Stone Gallery, 1964; The Goodman Gallery, Buffalo, 1964. **GROUP:** XXV, XXVI, & XXVIII Venice Biennials, 1950, 54, 56; Sao Paulo, 1951, 53; WMAA, The New Decade, 1954–55; MOMA, The New American Painting, circ. Europe, 1958–59; MOMA, New Horizons in American Art, 1936; WMAA Annuals, 1948, 50, 51; VMFA, American Painting, 1950; California Palace, 1950; MOMA, Abstract Painting and Sculpture in America, 1951; Chicago/AI, 1951, 54; Buffalo/Albright, Expressionism in American Painting, 1952; Carnegie, 1952, 55; WMAA, Nature in Abstraction, 1958; Brussels World's Fair, 1958; Baltimore/MA, 1953. **COLLECTIONS:** Baltimore/MA; Brooklyn Museum; Buffalo/Albright; Carnegie; Chicago/AI; Kansas City/Nelson; MMA; MOMA; U. of Nebraska; U. of North Carolina; Phillips; SRGM; Vassar College; WMAA; Washington U. **BIBLIOGRAPHY:** Barr 3; Baur 5, 7; Biddle 3; Blesh 1; Brion 1; Canaday; Eliot; Elsen; Flanagan; Goodrich and Baur 1; Greenberg 1; Haftman; Henning; Hess, T. B.; Hunter 1, 5; **Janis and Blesh** 1, **2**; Janis, S.; Langui; McCourbrey; McCurdy, ed.; Mendelowitz; *Metro;* Motherwell and Reinhardt, eds.; Neumeyer; Nordness, ed.; Ponente; Pousette-Dart, ed.; Ragon 1; Read 2; Richardson; Ritchie 1; Rodman 1, 2, 3; Rothschild; Seitz 1, 2; Seuphor 1; Soby 6; "What Abstract Art Means to Me."

DELAP, TONY. b. November 4, 1927, Oakland, Calif. **STUDIED:** California College of Arts and Crafts; Menlo Junior College; Academy of Art, San Francisco; Claremont Graduate School, AA. Traveled Europe for 3 months, 1954. **TAUGHT:** Academy of Art, San Francisco;

Willem de Kooning   *A Tree Grows in Naples.*

California College of Arts and Crafts; U. of Wisconsin; Scripps College; U. of California, Davis; San Francisco Art Institute. Art Commissioner, San Francisco Municipal Art Commission. **COMMISSIONS:** Brooks Hall, San Francisco. **AWARDS:** SFMA, Nealie Sullivan Award; San Francisco Art Festival, First Prize, Mural Competition, 1957; and others. **ADDRESS:** 3410 California Street, San Francisco, Calif. **DEALERS:** Dilexi Gallery, San Francisco; Robert Elkon Gallery; Felix Landau Gallery. **ONE-MAN EXHIBITIONS:** (first) Gump's Gallery; SFMA; Oakland/AM; RAC; Dilexi Gallery, San Francisco. **GROUP:** Stanford U., 1961; Kaiser Center, Oakland, Sculpture Today, 1964; Carnegie, 1964; WMAA, 1964; Chicago/AI, 1964; MOMA, 1964. **COLLECTIONS:** San Francisco Municipal Art Commission; State of California.

DELLA-VOLPE, RALPH. b. May 10, 1923, New Jersey. **STUDIED:** NAD; ASL, with Edwin Dickinson, Will Barnet, Harry Sternberg. Traveled USA extensively. **TAUGHT:** Bennett College, 1949– . **AWARDS:** MacDowell Colony Fellowship, 1963; Library of Congress, Pennell P.P.; NIAL, Drawing Prize, 1963, 64. **ADDRESS:** Bennett College, Millbrook, N.Y. **DEALER:** The Babcock Gallery. **ONE-MAN EXHIBITIONS:** (first) Three Arts Gallery, Poughkeepsie, 1951; The Babcock Gallery, 1960, 62, 63; Artists' Gallery, NYC, 1959; Bennett College, 1949–63; Lehigh U., 1963; Mansfield State College, 1964; Pittsfield/Berkshire, 1964. **GROUP:** PAFA; Library of Congress; NIAL; American Color Print Society; Youngstown/Butler; Bradley U.; Brooklyn Museum; Hartford/Wadsworth; San Antonio/McNay. **COLLECTIONS:** ASL; Library of Congress; Mansfield State College; Wichita/AM.

DE MARTINI, JOSEPH. b. July 20, 1896, Mobile, Ala. **STUDIED:** NAD. **TAUGHT:** U. of Georgia, 1952–53. **FEDERAL A.P.:** Easel painting. **AWARDS:** Pepsi-Cola, 1944; U. of Illinois,

P.P., 1948; Guggenheim Foundation Fellowship, 1951; NAD, 1950; PAFA, Gold Medal, 1952. **ADDRESS:** 103 West 27 Street, NYC. **ONE-MAN EXHIBITIONS:** Eighth Street Gallery, NYC, 1935; Macbeth Gallery, NYC, 1941, 43, 47; Hudson D. Walker Gallery, NYC, 1942; Dorothy Paris Gallery, NYC, 1935. **GROUP:** MOMA, 1941, 42, 43; Carnegie, 1941, 43, 44, 46; WMAA, 1934, 42, 43, 44, 45; Corcoran, 1941, 43, 45; St. Louis/City, 1938, 41, 42, 46; PAFA, 1940, 42, 43, 44, 45; Chicago/AI, 1941, 42; New York World's Fair, 1939; Worcester/AM, 1945; de Young, 1941, 43; VMFA, 1942, 44, 46; Colorado Springs/FA, 1942; Brooklyn Museum, 1943; Indianapolis/Herron, 1945; U. of Nebraska, 1945, 46. **COLLECTIONS:** Andover/Phillips; U. of Arizona; Boston/MFA; Canajoharie; IBM; MMA; MOMA; Memphis/Brooks; U. of Nebraska; New Britain; Pepsi-Cola Co.; Phillips; Rochester/Memorial; Rockland/Farnsworth; St. Louis/City; US State Department; WMAA; Walker; Wichita/AM. **BIBLIOGRAPHY:** Baur 7; Cheney, M. C.; Frost; Genauer.

DEMUTH, CHARLES. b. November 8, 1883, Lancaster, Pa.; **d.** October 23, 1935. **STUDIED:** Franklin and Marshall College; Drexel Institute of Technology, 1901; Pennsylvania School of Industrial Art, Philadelphia; PAFA, 1905–08, with Thomas Anshutz, Henry McCarter; Academie Colarossi, Academie Moderne, and Academie Julian, Paris, 1912–14. Traveled Europe, eastern USA. **ONE-MAN EXHIBITIONS:** (first) The Daniel Gallery, NYC, 1915, also 1916, 17, 18, 20, 22, 23, 24, 25; Stieglitz's Intimate Gallery, NYC, 1926, 29; An American Place (Gallery), NYC, 1931; The Downtown Gallery, 1931, 50, 54, 58; Smith College, 1934; WMAA, 1935; WMAA, Memorial Exhibition, 1937; U. of Minnesota, 1937; Franklin and Marshall College, 1941, 48; Cincinnati/AM, 1941; Phillips, 1942; PMA, 1944; The U. of Chicago, 1946; Graphische Sammlung Albertina, 1949; Ogunquit, 1959. **RETROSPECTIVE:** MOMA, 1949. **GROUP:** MOMA; WMAA; MMA; PAFA; Phillips; Pomona College, Stieglitz Circle, 1958. **COLLECTIONS:** Amherst College; Andover/Phillips; Arizona State College; Baltimore/MA; Barnes Foundation; Boston/MFA; Brooklyn Museum; Buffalo/Albright; Chicago/AI; Cleveland/MA; Columbus; Detroit/Institute; Fisk U.; Hartford/Wadsworth; Harvard U.; Honolulu Academy; MMA; MOMA; Milwau-

kee; National Gallery; U. of Nebraska; Newark Museum; New Britain; Ogunquit; PMA; Phillips; Princeton U.; RISD; San Antonio/McNay; Santa Barbara/MA; Toledo/MA; Utica; WMAA; Walker; Wellesley College; West Palm Beach/Norton; Wichita/AM; Worcester/AM; Yale U. **BIBLIOGRAPHY:** Barnes; Baur 7; Bazin; Biddle 3; Blesh 1; Born; Brown; Cahill and Barr, eds.; Cheney, M. C.; Christensen; Eliot; Frank, ed.; Frost; Gallatin 1; Goodrich and Baur 1; Haftman; Hall; Hunter 5; Huyghe; *Index of 20th Century Artists;* Janis, S.; Jewell 2; Kootz 1, 2; Lane; Mather 1; McCourbrey; McCurdy, ed.; **Murrell 1;** Neuhaus; Phillips 2; Poore; Richardson; Ringel, ed.; **Ritchie 2;** Rosenblum; Sachs; Soby 5; Sutton; Wight 2.

DE NIRO, ROBERT. b. May 3, 1922, Syracuse, N.Y. **STUDIED:** Syracuse Museum School, 1935–39; Hofmann School, Provincetown, summers, 1939, 40; Black Mountain College, with Josef Albers. Traveled France; resided Paris. **AWARDS:** V Hallmark International Competition; Longview Foundation Grant. **ADDRESS:** 219 West 14 Street, NYC. **DEALER:** The Zabriskie Gallery. **ONE-MAN EXHIBITIONS:** (first) Art of This Century, NYC, 1946; Charles Egan Gallery, 1950, 52, 54; Poindexter Gallery, 1955, 56; The Zabriskie Gallery, 1958, 60 (2), 62; Ellison Gallery, Fort Worth (two-man), 1959. **GROUP:** WMAA Annuals; Jewish Museum, The New York School, Second Generation, 1957; ICA, Boston, 100 Works on Paper, circ. Europe, 1959; U. of Nebraska, 1960; A.F.A., The Figure, circ., 1960; Felix Landau Gallery, Los Angeles-New York 1960; Colorado Springs/FA Annual, 1961; MOMA, Recent Painting USA: The Figure, circ., 1962–63; Illinois Wesleyan U. Annual, 1962. **COLLECTIONS:** Longview Foundation.

DE RIVERA, JOSE. b. September 18, 1904, West Baton Rouge, La. **STUDIED:** Studio School, Chicago, with John W. Norton, 1928–30. Traveled USA, Europe, Mediterranean, North Africa. **FEDERAL A.P.:** Mural painting, 1937–38. US Army Air Corps, 1942–43. **TAUGHT:** Brooklyn College, 1953; Yale U., 1954–55; North Carolina School of Design, Raleigh, 1957–60. **COMMISSIONS:** Cavalry Monument, El Paso, 1938–40; Newark Airport, 1938; Soviet Pavilion, New York World's Fair, 1939; Wm. Kaufman Inc., NYC, 1955; Hotel Statler-Hilton, Dallas, 1956; Moore-McCormack Lines Inc., SS *Argen-*

Jose de Rivera   *Construction #87. 1964*

tina, 1958; Reynolds Metals Co., 1958. **Awards:** Chicago/AI, Watson F. Blair Prize, 1957; NIAL Grant, 1959. **Address:** 346 East 34 Street, NYC. **Dealer:** Grace Borgenicht Gallery Inc. **One-man Exhibitions:** (first) Mortimer Levitt Gallery, NYC, 1946; Grace Borgenicht Gallery Inc., 1952, 56, 57, 58, 59, 60; Walker, 1957; Harvard U. (two-man, with Burgoyne Diller), 1945. **Retrospective:** A.F.A./Ford Foundation, circ., 1961. **Group:** Chicago/AI, 1934; MOMA, Twelve Americans, circ., 1956; Brooklyn Museum, 1938; Brussels World's Fair, 1958; American Painting and Sculpture, Moscow, 1959; MOMA, Recent Sculpture USA, 1959; WMAA Annuals, 1938– . **Collections:** Chicago/AI; Fort Dodge/Banden; MMA; MOMA; Newark Museum; Rochester/Memorial; SFMA; St. Louis/City; Utica; VMFA. **Bibliography:** Baur 7; Brumme; Flanagan; Gertz; Goodrich and Baur 1; McCurdy, ed.; Mendelowitz; Ritchie 1, 3; Rodman 3; Seuphor 3.

DESHAIES, ARTHUR. b. July 6, 1920, Providence, R.I. **Studied:** Cooper Union, 1939–42; RISD, 1947–48, BFA; Indiana U., 1948–50,

MFA; self-taught as printmaker. Traveled Mexico, USA, Europe. **Taught:** RISD, 1947–48; Indiana U., 1949–56; Pratt Institute, 1956–57; Pratt Graphic Art Center, 1962; Florida State U., 1963–64; lectures and writes extensively on art and printmaking. **Awards:** Indiana U., Faculty Research Grant for Painting, 1950; Fulbright Fellowship, 1952; MacDowell Colony Fellowship, summers, 1959, 60, 61, 62; Yaddo Fellowship, 1960; L. C. Tiffany Grant, 1960; Guggenheim Foundation Fellowship, 1961; Brooklyn Museum; Bradley U.; Oklahoma Print Society; Indianapolis/Herron; U. of Kentucky, p.p.; Otis Art Institute, Los Angeles; Memphis/Brooks, p.p. **Address:** 14 Taunton Avenue, Norton, Mass. **One-man Exhibitions:** Philadelphia Art Alliance; The Little Gallery, Tallahassee, 1964. **Group:** PCA, American Prints Today, circ., 1959–62; Brooklyn Museum; III International Biennial Exhibition of Prints, Tokyo, 1962; Otis Art Institute, Los Angeles; WMAA. **Collections:** Bradley U.; Brooklyn Museum. **Bibliography:** Hayter 1; Peterdi.

DICKINSON, EDWIN. b. October 11, 1891, Seneca Falls, N.Y. **Studied:** Pratt Institute, 1910–11; ASL, 1911–12, with William M. Chase; Provincetown, summers, 1912, 13, 14, with C. W. Hawthorne. US Navy, 1917–19. Traveled Europe, Near East, North Africa. **Taught:** ASL, 1922–23, 1944– ; Cooper Union, 1945– ; Brooklyn Museum School, 1949– . **Member:** NAD; NIAL; AAAL; Audubon Artists; The Patteran Society. **Federal A.P.:** Easel painting, 1934. **Awards:** NAD, Benjamin Altman Prize, 1929, 58; Benjamin West Medal; NAD, First Prize, 1949; Century Association, Medal; Brandeis U., Creative Arts Medal, 1959; Ford Foundation Grant, 1959; NIAL Grant, 1954. **Address:** 420 West 119 Street, NYC. **Dealer:** The Graham Gallery. **One-man Exhibitions:** (first) Buffalo/Albright, 1927; The Graham Gallery, 1961; Worcester/AM; Boston/MFA; Houston/MFA; Rochester/Memorial; Cornell U.; Provincetown/Chrysler; Passedoit Gallery, NYC, 1939; Wellesley College, 1940; MOMA (circ. only), 1961; Kansas City/Nelson (two-man, with Lennart Anderson), 1964. **Group:** MOMA; WMAA; Brooklyn Museum; Boston/MFA; PMA; PAFA; Carnegie; Rochester/Memorial. **Collections:** Atlanta/AA; Bowdoin College; Brooklyn Museum; Buffalo/Albright; Chicago/AI; Cornell U.; MMA; MOMA; Montpelier/Wood; NAD; U. of Nebraska; Sara Roby Foundation; Springfield, Mass./MFA; Syracuse U.; Yale U. **BIBLIOGRAPHY: Goodrich 2;** Goodrich and Baur 1; Haftman; Kuh 2; McCurdy, ed.; Mellquist; Nordness, ed.; Pousette-Dart, ed.

DIEBENKORN, RICHARD. b. 1922, Portland, Ore. STUDIED: Stanford U., 1940–43; U. of California, 1943–44; California School of Fine Arts, 1946. TAUGHT: California School of Fine Arts, 1947–50; California College of Arts and Crafts; Stanford U., 1963–64; U. of Illinois; U. of Colorado. AWARDS: CSFA, Albert M. Bender Fellowship, 1946. ADDRESS: c/o Poindexter Gallery. DEALERS: Poindexter Gallery; Paul Kantor Gallery. ONE-MAN EXHIBITIONS: (first) California Palace, 1948, also 1960; Paul Kantor Gallery, 1952, 54; Los Angeles/County MA, 1952, 54, 57, 60; Oakland/AM, 1957; Pasadena/AM, 1960; Phillips, 1958, 61; Carnegie, 1961; Poindexter Gallery, 1955, 58, 61, 63; Allan Frumkin Gallery, Chicago; de Young, 1963. GROUP: SRGM, Younger American Paint-

ers, 1954; Brussels World's Fair, 1958; WMAA Annuals, 1955, 58, 61; Carnegie, 1955, 58, 61; IV Sao Paulo Biennial, 1957; MOMA, New Images of Man, 1959. COLLECTIONS: Buffalo/Albright; Carnegie; Kansas City/Nelson; Los Angeles/County MA; Oakland/AM; Oberlin College; PAFA; Phillips; Phoenix; *Readers Digest;* SFMA; Toronto; WMAA. BIBLIOGRAPHY: Blesh 1; Mendelowitz; Neumeyer; Nordness, ed.; Read 2.

DILLER, BURGOYNE. b. 1906, NYC; **d.** January 30, 1965, NYC. STUDIED: Michigan State College; ASL. US Navy, World War II. TAUGHT: Brooklyn College, 1945–64; Pratt Institute, 1945–64. MEMBER: American Abstract Artists. FEDERAL A.P.: Head, Mural Division, 1935–40; Assistant Technical Director, New York Art Project, 1940–41; Director, New York City Art Section, 1939–42. AWARDS: Ford Foundation, P.P., 1963. ONE-MAN EXHIBITIONS: The Pinacotheca, NYC, 1946; Galerie Chalette, 1961, 64; Harvard U. (two-man, with Jose de Rivera), 1945. GROUP: American Abstract Art-

Richard Diebenkorn   *Woman on a Porch. 1958*

Burgoyne Diller   *First Theme. 1964*

ists Annuals to 1940; VII Sao Paulo Biennial, 1963; WMAA, Geometric Abstraction in America, circ., 1962; Corcoran, 1963. **COLLECTIONS:** Corcoran; MMA; MOMA; NYU; WMAA;

Yale U. **BIBLIOGRAPHY:** Blesh 1; Hess, T. B.; Janis and Blesh 1; Janis, S.; McCurdy, ed.; Ritchie 1; Seuphor 1, 3.

DINE, JIM. b. June 16, 1935, Cincinnati, Ohio. **STUDIED:** U. of Cincinnati; Boston Museum School; Ohio U., 1957, BFA, and 1958. An early creator of Happenings and Environments. **ADDRESS:** 470 West End Avenue, NYC. **DEALER:** Sidney Janis Gallery. **ONE-MAN EXHIBITIONS:** Reuben Gallery, NYC, 1960; Martha Jackson Gallery, 1962; Galleria dell'Ariete, Milan, 1962; Sidney Janis Gallery, 1963, 64; Ileana Sonnabend (Gallery), Paris, 1963; Palais des Beaux Arts, Brussels, 1963; Judson Gallery, NYC (two-man, with Claes Oldenburg), 1959; Car Crash (Happening), NYC, 1960. **GROUP:** Cornell U., Young Americans, 1960; Martha Jackson Gallery, New Media—New Forms, I, 1960; USIA Gallery, London, Modern American Painting, 1961; Dallas/MFA, "1961," 1961; Sidney Janis Gallery, The New Realists, 1962; Philadelphia YM-YWHA Arts Council, Art, A New Vocabulary, 1962; Pasadena/AM, New Paintings of Common Objects, 1962; International Biennial

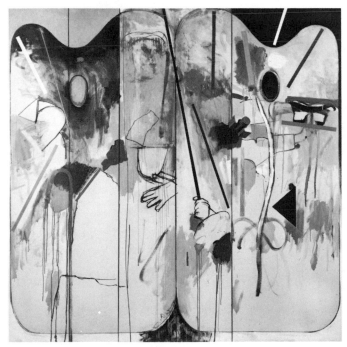

Jim Dine   *Two Palettes. 1963*

Exhibition of Paintings, Tokyo; SRGM, Six Painters and The Object, circ., 1963; Houston/MFA, Pop Goes the Easel, 1963; WGMA, The Popular Image, 1963; ICA, London, The Popular Image, 1963; Buffalo/Albright, 1963; Cincinnati/AM, An American Viewpoint, 1963; Jewish Museum, Black and White, 1963; Hartford/Wadsworth, Black, White, and Gray, 1964; Chicago/AI, 1964; Tate, Gulbenkian International, 1964. COLLECTIONS: Ball State Teachers College; Brandeis U.; Buffalo/Albright; MOMA; NYU; SRGM; WGMA; Woodward Foundation. BIBLIOGRAPHY: Janis and Blesh 1; *Metro*.

DI SUVERO, MARK. b. September 18, 1933, Shanghai, China. To USA 1941. STUDIED: U. of California, BA. Traveled USA, Mexico. AWARDS: Longview Foundation Grant; Walter K. Gutman Foundation Grant; Chicago/AI, 1963. ADDRESS: 195 Front Street, NYC. ONE-MAN EXHIBITIONS: (first) The Green Gallery, NYC, 1960. GROUP: Hartford/Wadsworth, Continuity and Change, 1962; March Gallery, NYC (three-man); The Green Gallery, NYC, 1961, 62, 63; 79 Park Place Gallery, NYC, 1963, 64; Chicago/AI, 1963. COLLECTIONS: Hartford/Wadsworth; NYU.

DOBKIN, ALEXANDER. b. May 1, 1908, Genoa, Italy. STUDIED: City College of New York, BS; Columbia U., MA; ASL, with George Bridgeman, Dimitri Romanovsky, Jose Clemente Orozco. Traveled Europe, Scandinavia, Israel; resided Paris. TAUGHT: Lecturer, A Century of Progress, Chicago, 1933–34; New Art School, NYC, 1937–41; City College of New York; Art Director, Educational Alliance, NYC, 1934– . MEMBER: Artists Equity. FEDERAL A.P.: Easel painting for public buildings. AWARDS: Augustus Saint-Gaudens Medal from Cooper Union, 1930; Roosevelt Memorial Award, 1936; AAAL, Childe Hassam Award, 1947; AAAL, P.P., 1956; Library of Congress, Pennell P.P., 1949, 55. ADDRESS: 737 Greenwich Street, NYC. DEALER: The Forum Gallery. ONE-MAN EXHIBITIONS: (first) ACA Gallery, 1935, also 1938, 47, 51, 58; The Forum Gallery, 1962; A.A.A. Gallery, NYC, 1960; Philadelphia Art Alliance, 1957; Michel Galerie, Paris, 1959; Garelick's Gallery, Detroit, 1957. GROUP: A Century of Progress, Chicago, 1933–34; New York World's Fair, 1964–65; ART:USA:58, NYC,

1958; Brooklyn Museum; Chicago/AI; MOMA; PMA; PAFA; Carnegie; Corcoran; Festival of Two Worlds, Spoleto; Library of Congress. COLLECTIONS: Library of Congress; MOMA; Newark Museum; PMA; Phoenix; Tel Aviv; Youngstown/Butler.

DODD, LAMAR. b. September 22, 1909, Fairburn, Ga. STUDIED: Georgia Institute of Technology, 1926–27; ASL, 1929–33, with George Luks, Boardman Robinson, John Steuart Curry, Jean Charlot, George Bridgeman; LHD, DFA. Traveled USA, Europe. TAUGHT: Five Points, Ala., 1927–28; U. of Georgia, 1937– . MEMBER: NAD, Audubon Artists. FEDERAL A.P.: Easel painting. AWARDS: Pepsi-Cola, 1947, 48; VMFA, Virginia Artists Biennial, P.P., 1948; NIAL Grant, 1950; NAD, Edwin Palmer Memorial Prize, 1953; Chicago/AI, 1936; PAFA, P.P., 1958; WMAA, P.P., 1958. ADDRESS: 590 Springdale, Athens, Ga. DEALER: Grand Central Moderns. ONE-MAN EXHIBITIONS: (first) Ferargil Galleries, NYC, 1933; Grand Central Moderns. GROUP: New York World's Fair, 1939; WMAA Annuals, 1937–57; U. of Nebraska; Carnegie, 1936; Golden Gate International Exposition, San Francisco, 1939; PAFA; NIAL; Audubon Artists; Chicago/AI; Corcoran; Boston/MFA; NAD; U. of Illinois; Santa Barbara/MA. COLLECTIONS: Atlanta/AA; Chicago/AI; Cranbrook; U. of Georgia; IBM; MMA; Montclair/AM; PAFA; Pepsi-Cola Co.; Rochester/Memorial; Savannah/Telfair; VMFA; WMAA; Wilmington. BIBLIOGRAPHY: Baur 7; Bethers; Cheney, M. C.; Wheeler.

DODD, LOIS. b. April 22, 1927, Montclair, N.J. STUDIED: Cooper Union, with Byron Thomas, Peter Busa. Traveled Italy, France, Switzerland. TAUGHT: Wagner College. A co-founder of the Tanager Gallery, NYC. COMMISSIONS: New York Hilton Hotel (lithographs). AWARDS: Italian Government Scholarship, 1959–60; Longview Foundation Grant, 1962. ADDRESS: 30 East Second Street, NYC. DEALER: The Graham Gallery. ONE-MAN EXHIBITIONS: (first) Tanager Gallery, NYC, 1954, also 1957, 58, 61, 62. GROUP: The Stable Gallery Annuals, 1956, 58; USIA, Americans in Rome, Rome, 1960; Yale U., Drawings and Watercolors, 1964; U. of Kentucky, Drawings, 1961. COLLECTIONS: Brooklyn Museum; Kalamazoo/Institute; New York Hilton Hotel; WMAA.

DOLE, WILLIAM. b. September 2, 1917, Angola, Ind. STUDIED: Olivet College, 1937, AB; U. of California, Berkeley, 1947, MA; Mills College, 1940, 49. TAUGHT: U. of California, Berkeley, 1947– ; U. of California, Santa Barbara, 1947– . ADDRESS: 29 Calle Crespis, Santa Barbara, Calif. ONE-MAN EXHIBITIONS: Santa Barbara/MA, 1952, 58; de Young, 1951; Mills College, 1951; Geddis-Martin Studios, Santa Barbara, 1952; La Jolla, 1954; Rotunda Gallery, San Francisco, 1954; Galerie Springer, 1956; Eric Locke Gallery, San Francisco, 1956; Galleria Sagittarius, Rome, 1957; Duveen-Graham Gallery, NYC, 1958, 60; U. of California, Santa Barbara, 1958; Bertha Lewinson Gallery, Los Angeles, 1955; Esther Baer Gallery, 1960; Galeria Antonio Souza, Mexico City, 1961; Rex Evans Gallery, 1961; The Thacher School, Ojai, Calif., 1961. GROUP: California Palace, 1947, 52; SFMA, 1948, 49, 50, 51; PAFA, 1950; Hallmark Art Award, 1953; Denver/AM, 1948; California State Fair, 1950, 51; Los Angeles County Fair, 1951; Santa Barbara/MA, 1955, 57; Los Angeles/County MA, 1958. COLLECTIONS: Amherst College; Mills College; Phoenix; Rockefeller Institute; Santa Barbara/MA.

DONATI, ENRICO. b. 1909, Milan, Italy. To USA 1934; citizen 1945. STUDIED: New School for Social Research; ASL. Traveled Europe, India, USA. TAUGHT: Yale U., 1960–62. MEMBER: Advisory Board of Brandeis U., 1956– ; Jury of Fulbright Program, 1954–56, 1963; Yale U. Council for Arts and Architecture, 1962; belonged to the Surrealist group of Andre Breton, to 1950. ADDRESS: 222 Central Park South, NYC. DEALER: Staempfli Gallery. ONE-MAN EXHIBITIONS: New School for Social Research, 1942; Passedoit Gallery, NYC, 1942, 44; Arts Club of Chicago, 1944, 59; Durand-Ruel Gallery, NYC, 1945, 46, 47, 49; Galerie Drouant, Paris, 1947; Syracuse U., 1958; P. Rosenberg and Co., 1950; L'Obelisco, Rome, 1950; Galleria Il Milione, 1950; Alexander Iolas Gallery, 1952; Galleria del Cavallino, Venice, 1952; Galleria d'Arte del Naviglio, Milan, 1953; Betty Parsons Gallery, 1954, 55, 57, 59, 60; Neue Galerie, Munich, 1962; Staempfli Gallery, 1962, 64. RETROSPECTIVE: Palais des Beaux Arts, Brussels, 1961. GROUP: Carnegie, 1950, 52, 54, 56, 58, 61; Venice Biennial; Sao Paulo, 1953; International Biennial Exhibition of Paintings,

Tokyo; A.F.A., The Embellished Surface, circ., 1953–54; Chicago/AI, 1954, 57; WMAA Annuals, 1954, 56, 58, 59, 61, 62; Santa Barbara/MA, 1954; SRGM, Younger American Painters, 1954; Utica, 1955; SFMA, 1955; Indiana U., 1957, 59; PAFA, 1957; VMFA, American Painting, 1958; I Inter-American Paintings and Prints Biennial, Mexico City, 1958; U. of Illinois, 1959; Lincoln, Mass./De Cordova, Decade in Review, 1959; A.F.A., V International Exhibition, 1959; Corcoran, 1960; St. Paul Gallery, 1960; Walker, 60 American Painters, 1960; SRGM, Abstract Expressionists and Imagists, 1961. COLLECTIONS: American Republic Insurance Co.; Baltimore/MA; Brussels/Moderne; Buffalo/Albright; Chase Manhattan Bank; Detroit/Institute; Houston/MFA; J. L. Hudson Co.; IBM; Indian Head Mills, Inc.; International Institute for Aesthetic Research; MIT; MOMA; Michigan Consolidated Gas Co.; U. of Michigan; Milan; Newark Museum; Oslo/National; Rockefeller Institute; Rome/Nazionale; St. Louis/City; Turin/Civico; WMAA. BIBLIOGRAPHY: Breton 2, 3; Goodrich and Baur 1; Read 2.

DOVE, ARTHUR G. b. August 2, 1880, Canandaigua, N.Y.; **d.** November, 1946, Centerport, N.Y. STUDIED: Cornell U., 1903. Commercial illustrator, 1903–07. Traveled Europe, 1907–09, with Alfred Maurer and Arthur B. Carles, Jr. Met Alfred Stieglitz 1910. ONE-MAN EXHIBITIONS: (first) Photo-Secession, NYC, 1912; Scott Thurber Gallery, Chicago, 1912; Stieglitz's Intimate Gallery, NYC, 1926, 27, 29; An American Place (Gallery), NYC, annually, 1930–46; Springfield, Mass./MFA, 1933; Phillips, 1937; The Downtown Gallery, 1949, 52, 54, 55, 56; Vanbark Studios, Studio City, Calif., 1947; Utica, 1947; Houston/MFA, 1951; Walker, 1954; Deerfield (Mass.) Academy, 1956; Paul Kantor Gallery, 1956. RETROSPECTIVE: The Downtown Gallery, 1947; UCLA, circ., 1958–59; Cornell U., 1954. GROUP: Salon d'Automne, Paris, 1908, 09; National Arts Club Annual, NYC, 1914; Anderson Galleries, NYC, Forum Exhibition, 1916; Society of Independent Artists, NYC, 1917; PAFA, 1921; Wildenstein & Co., NYC, Tri-National Art, 1926; Brooklyn Museum, International Exhibition of Modern Art (assembled by Societe Anonyme), 1926; Salons of America, NYC, 1929; MOMA, Paintings by 19 Living Americans, 1929; Cleve-

Arthur G. Dove   *Out the Window.*

land/MA Annuals, 1931, 32, 35; WMAA Annuals, 1932, 34; A.F.A., Abstraction, 1932; A Century of Progress, Chicago, 1933–34; WMAA, Abstract Painting in America, 1935; Buffalo/Albright, 1935; U. of Minnesota, 1937; Cleveland/MA, American Painting from 1860 Until Today, 1937; Worcester/AM, 1938; Musee du Jeu de Paume, Trois Siecles d'Art aux Etats-Unis, 1938; MOMA, Art in Our Time: 10th Anniversary Exhibition, 1939; Boston/MFA, 10 American Watercolor Painters, 1939; Golden Gate International Exposition, San Francisco, 1939; Cornell U., 1940; MOMA, Cubist and Abstract Art, 1942; PMA, History of An American, Alfred Stieglitz: "291" and After, 1944. COLLECTIONS: American U.; Andover/Phillips; Arizona State College; Baltimore/MA; Boston U.; Britannica; Brooklyn Museum; Buffalo/Albright; Carnegie; Chicago/AI; Colorado Springs/FA; Columbus; Cornell U.; Des Moines; Detroit/Institute; Fisk U.; Fort Worth; Hartford/Wadsworth; Honolulu Academy; IBM; Inland Steel Co.; MMA; MOMA; Milwaukee; U. of Minnesota; National Gallery; U. of Nebraska; Omaha/Joslyn; PMA; Phillips; Phoenix; Randolph-Macon Woman's College; Rochester/Memorial; SFMA; Smith College; Springfield, Mass./MFA; Utica; WMAA; Washington U.; Wellesley College; West Palm Beach/Norton; Wichita/AM; Wilmington; Yale U. BIBLIOGRAPHY: Barr 3; Baur 5, 7; Blanchard; Blesh 1; Brown; Cahill and Barr,

eds.; Cheney, M. C.; Eliot; Frank, ed.; Frost; Goodrich and Baur 1; Haftman; Hess, T. B.; Hunter 5; Janis and Blesh 1; Janis, S.; Kootz 1; Mather 1; McCurdy, ed.; Mellquist; Mendelowitz; Neuhaus; Newmeyer; Phillips 1, 2; Poore; Read 2; Richardson; Ringel, ed.; Ritchie 1; Rodman 2; Seitz 2; Sutton, Wight 2; Wright 1.

DOYLE, THOMAS. b. May 23, 1928, Jerry City, Ohio. STUDIED: Miami U.; The Ohio State U., with Roy Lichtenstein, Stanley Twardowicz, BFA, MA. Traveled Europe. TAUGHT: Brooklyn Museum School; New School for Social Research. AWARDS: Ohio State Fair, 2 First and 2 Second Prizes. ADDRESS: 134 Bowery, NYC. ONE-MAN EXHIBITIONS: (first) The Ohio State U., 1956; Allan Stone Gallery, 1961, 62. GROUP: Cornell U., 1960; Oberlin College, 1961; Martha Jackson Gallery, New Media—New Forms, I & II, 1960, 61; Seattle World's Fair, 1962; Carnegie, 1961. COLLECTIONS: Carnegie.

DREWES, WERNER. b. July 27, 1899, Canig, Germany. STUDIED: Gymnasium, Brandenburg/Havel, 1909–17; Charlottenburg Technische Hochschule, Berlin, 1919; Stuttgart School of Architecture, 1920; Stuttgart School of Arts and Crafts, 1921; Bauhaus, Weimar, 1921–22, with Josef Itten, Paul Klee; Bauhaus, Dessau, 1927–28, with Vassily Kandinsky, Lyonel Feininger; Brooklyn Museum School,

1934–36. Resided Italy, 1923–30. To USA 1930; citizen 1936. Traveled Europe, Mexico, Peru, USA. **TAUGHT:** Columbia U., 1937–40; Master Institute of United Arts, Inc., NYC, 1940; Brooklyn College, 1944; Institute of Design, Chicago, 1945; Washington U., 1946– . **MEMBER:** American Artists Congress; co-founder, American Abstract Artists, 1936. **FEDERAL A.P.:** Director, Graphic Art Project, 1940–41. **COMMISSIONS:** International Graphic Arts Society, 1954, 57. **AWARDS:** PAFA, P.P., 1933; MOMA, Plexiglas Sculpture Competition, Third Prize, 1939; MOMA, Textile Design Competition, First and Second Prizes, 1941; The Print Club, Philadelphia, Hon. Men., 1946; A.A.A. Gallery, NYC, P.P., 1959; St. Louis Artists' Guild, Bader Art Prize, 1960; 50 Best Prints of the Year, 1932, 44. **ADDRESS:** 7135 Northmoor, St. Louis, Mo. **DEALERS:** Weyhe Gallery; Kraushaar Galleries; A.A.A. Gallery, NYC. **ONE-MAN EXHIBITIONS:** Madrid/Nacional, 1923; Montevideo/Municipal, 1924; St. Louis Public Library, 1924; Gump's Gallery, 1926; Flechtheim and Kahnweiler, Frankfurt, 1928; Galerie del Vecchio, Leipzig, 1929; Morton Gallery, NYC, 1932, 33; New School for Social Research, 1935; Artists' Gallery, NYC, 1939, 41; Lilienfeld Gallery, NYC, 1945; Indiana U., 1945; Kleemann Gallery, NYC, 1945, 46, 47, 49; Smithsonian, 1948; Pen and Palette Gallery, St. Louis, 1949; Lutz and Meyer Gallery, Stuttgart, 1951; Argent Gallery, NYC, 1951; Neue Galeries Gurlitt, Linz, 1952; St. Louis Artists' Guild, 1953; Beloit College, 1954; Los Angeles/County MA, 1956; Memphis/Brooks, 1957; Springfield, Mo./AM, 1958; Oregon State College, circ., 1959; Cleveland/MA, 1961; Schermahorn Gallery, Beloit, 1955, 56; Princeton U. (four-man), 1946. **GROUP:** Carnegie; Brooklyn Museum; Chicago/AI; MMA; USIA; WMAA; U. of Illinois; PAFA; SRGM; Bennington College. **COLLECTIONS:** U. of Alabama; Andover/Phillips; Beloit College; Bennington College; Bibliotheque Nationale; Boston Public Library; Brooklyn Museum; Chicago/AI; Cleveland/MA; Frankfurt am Main; Harvard U.; Honolulu Academy; U. of Illinois; Kansas City/Nelson; Library of Congress; Los Angeles/County MA; MOMA; Memphis/Brooks; Mills College; NYPL; Newark Public Library; Oregon State U.; PAFA; RISD; SFMA; SRGM; St. Louis/City; Seattle/AM; Springfield, Ill./State; Springfield, Mo./AM;

Trenton/State; Victoria and Albert Museum; Washington U.; Wells College; Wichita/AM; Worcester/AM; Yale U. **BIBLIOGRAPHY:** American Artists Congress, Inc.; Baur 7; Bazin; Cheney, M. C.

DRUMMOND, SALLY HAZELET. b. June 4, 1924, Evanston, Ill. **STUDIED:** Rollins College, 1942–44; Columbia U., with John Heliker, Peppino Mangravite, 1946–48, BA; Institute of Design, Chicago, 1949–50, with Hugo Weber, Emerson Woelffer; U. of Louisville, with Ulfert Wilke, 1950–52, MA. Traveled Italy, France, England. A co-organizer of the Tanager Gallery, NYC. **AWARDS:** Fulbright Fellowship (Italy), 1952. **ADDRESS:** One Wilton Road, East Ridgefield, Conn. **ONE-MAN EXHIBITIONS:** (first) Hadley Gallery, Louisville, 1952, also 1961; Art Center Association, Louisville, 1955; Tanager Gallery, NYC, 1955, 57, 60; The Green Gallery, NYC, 1962. **GROUP:** American Embassy, Rome, 1953; WMAA Annual, 1960; MOMA, Americans 1963, circ., 1963–64; Bordighera, 1953; A.F.A., Fulbright Artists, circ., 1958; Houston/MFA, 1959; A.F.A., Lyricism in Abstract Art, circ., 1962–63. **COLLECTIONS:** MOMA; Union Carbide Corp.

DU BOIS, GUY PENE. b. January 4, 1884, Brooklyn, N.Y.; **d.** July 18, 1958, Boston, Mass. **STUDIED:** W. M. Chase School, NYC, 1899–1905, with J. C. Beckwith, Frank V. DuMond, Robert Henri, Kenneth Hayes Miller; Academie de la Grande Chaumiere, with Theophile A. Steinlen. Traveled USA, Europe. Reporter and critic for New York *American,* New York *Tribune,* New York *Evening Post;* Editor of *Arts and Decoration* Magazine for seven years. **AWARDS:** Pan-American Exhibition, Los Angeles, 1925, Third Prize; Chicago/AI, Norman Wait Harris Silver Medal, 1930; NAD, Benjamin Altman Prize, 1936; Corcoran, Second William A. Clark Prize, 1937. **ONE-MAN EXHIBITIONS:** The Graham Gallery, 1961, 63; Kraushaar Galleries, 1922, 24, 30, 32, 35, 36, 38, 42, 43, 46; Staten Island, 1954. **RETROSPECTIVE:** Hagerstown/County MFA, 1940. **GROUP:** Salon des Beaux-Arts, Paris, 1906; Corcoran; Chicago/AI; PAFA; WMAA. **COLLECTIONS:** Amherst College; Andover/Phillips; Baltimore/MA; Barnes Foundation; Brooklyn Museum; Chicago/AI; Cleveland/MA; Detroit/Institute; Los Angeles/County MA;

MMA; MOMA; Milwaukee; Newark Museum; New Britain; PAFA; PMA; Phillips; San Diego; Toledo/MA; WMAA. **BIBLIOGRAPHY:** Baur 7; Bazin; Brown; Bruce and Watson; Cahill and Barr, eds.; Cheney, M. C.; **Cortissoz 2; Du Bois 1, 2, 3, 4, 5, 6;** Ely; Glackens; Goodrich and Baur 1; Hall; Hunter 5; *Index of 20th Century Artists;* Jewell 2; Kent, N.; Mather 1; McCourbrey; **Medford;** Mellquist; Neuhaus; Pagano; Pearson 1; Phillips 2; Poore; Richardson; Ringel, ed.; Smith, S. C. K.

DUCHAMP, MARCEL. b. July 28, 1887, Blainville, near Rouen, France. STUDIED: Academie Julian, Paris, 1904. To USA 1915; citizen 1955. Traveled Europe, Argentina, USA. Founding MEMBER, Society of Independent Artists, 1916. Co-founder (with Man Ray and Francis Picabia) of DADA group, NYC, 1917. Co-organizer (with Katherine S. Dreier and Man Ray) of Societe Anonyme (Museum of Modern Art), 1920. Published one issue of *New York DADA* with Man Ray, 1921. Produced a film, "Anemic Cinema," 1925. **ADDRESS:** c/o Dealer. **DEALER:** Cordier & Ekstrom Inc. **ONE-MAN EXHIBITIONS:** (first) Arts Club of Chicago, 1937; Montross Gallery, NYC (four-man), 1916; SRGM (three-man), 1957; Sidney Janis Gallery, 1958, 59; La Hune, Paris, 1959; Rose Fried Gallery (three-man), 1952; Pasadena/AM, 1963; Eva de Buren Gallery, Stockholm, 1963; Galerie de l'Institute, Paris, 1957. **GROUP:** Salon des Artistes Independants, Paris, 1909–12; Salon d'Automne, Paris, 1909–12; Salon de la Section d'Or, 1912; The Armory Show, 1913; Societe Anonyme, NYC, 1920; Salon DADA, Paris, 1920; A Century of Progress, Chicago, 1933–34; MOMA, Cubism and Abstract Art, 1936; MOMA, Fantastic Art, DADA, Surrealism, 1936; WMAA, European Artists in America, 1945; MOMA, Eleven Europeans, 1946; XXIV Venice Biennial, 1948; California Palace, 1948; Chicago/AI, 1949. **COLLECTIONS:** MOMA; PMA; Yale U. **BIBLIOGRAPHY:** Barr 1, 3; Baur 7; Biddle 3; Biederman 1; Blesh 1; Breton 2; Brion 2; Brown; Bulliet 1, 2; Canaday; Cassou; Christensen; Davidson 1; Dorival; Dorner; Dreier 2; **Duchamp 1, 2;** Elsen; Flanagan; Frost; Gascoyne; Gaunt; Giedion-Welcker 1, 2; Guggenheim, ed.; Haftman; **Hamilton, R.;** Hunter 5; Huyghe; Janis and Blesh 1; Janis, S.; Kepes 2; Kuh 1, 2; Kyrou; Langui; **Lebel;** Lee and Burchwood; Lowry; McCurdy, ed.; Mellquist; *Metro;* Motherwell 1; Neumeyer; Newmeyer; Pach 2, 3; Ramsden 1; Raynal 3, 4; Read 2; Richardson; Rosenblum; Seitz 2; Seuphor 1, 3; Soby 1, 5, 6; **Sweeney 2;** Valentine 2; Waldberg 2, 3.

DUGMORE, EDWARD. b. February 20, 1915, Hartford, Conn. STUDIED: U. of Guadalajara, 1951–52, MA; California School of Fine Arts, 1948–50, with Clyfford Still; Hartford Art School, 1934–38. US Marine Corps, 1943–44. Traveled Mexico, USA extensively. **TAUGHT:** St. Joseph College, 1946–49; Southern Illinois U. A co-founder of Metart Gallery, San Francisco. **AWARDS:** Chicago/AI, The M. V. Kohnstamm Prize, 1962. **ADDRESS:** 100 West 14 Street, NYC. **DEALER:** The Howard Wise Gallery, NYC. **ONE-MAN EXHIBITIONS:** (first) Metart Gallery, San Francisco, 1949; The Stable Gallery, 1953, 54, 56; Holland-Goldowsky Gallery, Chicago, 1959; The Howard Wise Gallery, Cleveland, 1960; The Howard Wise Gallery, NYC, 1960, 61, 63. **GROUP:** Carnegie, 1955; Walker, Vanguard, 1955; WMAA Annual, 1959; SRGM, Abstract Expressionists and Imagists, 1961; Chicago/AI Annual, 1962; SFMA, Directions—Painting U.S.A., 1963; U. of Texas, Recent American Painting, 1964. **COLLECTIONS:** Buffalo/Albright; Southern Illinois U.; Walker.

DZUBAS, FRIEDEL. b. April 20, 1915, Berlin, Germany. STUDIED with Paul Klee in Dusseldorf. To USA 1939. Traveled Europe extensively. **TEACHES** occasionally; Artist-in-Residence, Dartmouth College, 1962. **ADDRESS:** 147 Wooster Street, NYC. **DEALERS:** Robert Elkon Gallery; Kasmin Ltd. **ONE-MAN EXHIBITIONS:** Tibor de Nagy Gallery, 1952; Leo Castelli Inc., 1958; French & Co. Inc., 1959; Dwan Gallery, 1960; Robert Elkon Gallery, 1961, 62, 63, 64; Kasmin Ltd., 1964. **GROUP:** Chicago/AI Annuals, 1942, 43, 44; The Kootz Gallery, New Talent, 1960; MMA, American Painters Under 35, 1950; Ninth Street Exhibition, NYC, 1951; WMAA Annuals, 1958, 59, 64; Corcoran, 1959, 63; Carnegie, 1961; SRGM, Abstract Expressionists and Imagists, 1961; Dayton/AI, 1963; Jewish Museum, Black and White, 1963; Los Angeles/County MA, Post Painterly Abstraction, 1964. **COLLECTIONS:** Baltimore/MA; Dayton/AI; Phillips; SRGM; WMAA; Yale U.

e

EDIE, STUART. b. November 10, 1908, Wichita Falls, Tex. Studied: Kansas City Art Institute and School of Design; ASL, with Thomas Hart Benton, Boardman Robinson, John Sloan. Traveled Europe, Mexico, North Africa, Canada, West Indies. Taught: State U. of Iowa, 1944– . Federal A.P.: Easel painting; mural for US Post Office, Honeoye Falls, N.Y. Awards: L. C. Tiffany Grant; Walker; Missouri Valley Annual; Omaha/Joslyn, The Midwest; Des Moines. Address: 111 South Summit Street, Iowa City, Iowa. One-man Exhibitions: (first) An American Group (Gallery), NYC, 1932; galleries in Des Moines, Kansas City, Iowa City. Group: PAFA; Corcoran; NAD; WMAA; Chicago/AI; Brooklyn Museum; MMA; MOMA. Collections: ASL; U. of Arizona; Des Moines; U. of Georgia; Grinnell College; State College of Iowa; State U. of Iowa; Kansas City/Nelson; MMA; Newark Museum; Omaha/Joslyn; Syracuse U.; Toledo/MA; WMAA; Washburn U. of Topeka. Bibliography: Zaidenberg, ed.

EDMONDSON, LEONARD. b. June 21, 1916, Sacramento, Calif. Studied: Los Angeles City College, 1934–37; U. of California, Berkeley, 1937–42, BA (1940), MA (1942). US Army Intelligence, 1942–46. Taught: Los Angeles County Art Institute, 1954–56; Pasadena City College, 1947–54, 1956–64; U. of California, Berkeley, summers, 1960, 64; Pratt Institute, summer, 1961; Los Angeles State College, 1964– . Commissions (prints): International Graphic Arts Society, 1960; New York Hilton Hotel, 1962. Awards: L. C. Tiffany Grant, 1952, 55; J. S. Guggenheim Fellowship, 1960; SFMA, First p.p., 1946; SFMA, Second Prize, 1951, 52; SFMA, p.p., 1957; Los Angeles/County MA, Patronnaires Prize, 1957; SFMA, James D. Phelan Award, 1951, 53; California State Fair, First Prize for Etching, 1951; California State Fair, Second p.p., 1952, 56; Brooklyn Museum, 1951, 56; Seattle/AM, p.p., 1952, 53, 54, 59; Oakland/AM, First Prize, Etching, 1952; Pasadena/AM, p.p., 1952, 54, 57, 58, 59, 62; MMA, $500; U. of Illinois, p.p., 1954, 55; Library of Congress, Pennell p.p., 1957, 63; American Color Print Society, Prize for Etching, 1954, 55; and many others. Address: 714 Prospect Boulevard, Pasadena, Calif. One-man Exhibitions: (first) Felix Landau Gallery, 1950, also 1953, 55, 58, 60; de Young, 1952; Pasadena/AM, 1953; SFMA, 1956; Santa Barbara/MA, 1953; The Gallery, Denver, 1963; Comara Gallery, 1963; Laguna Beach (Calif.) Art Gallery, 1964; Oklahoma City U., 1964. Group: MMA, 1952; Corcoran, 1957, 59; WMAA, 1952, 53, 55, 56, 58; U. of Illinois, 1953, 55, 58; SRGM, Younger American Painters, 1954; Carnegie, 1955; Sao Paulo, 1955; SFMA, Art in the Twentieth Century, 1955; U. of Illinois, 50 Contemporary American Printmakers, 1956; Chicago/AI, 1957; VMFA, 1958; PCA, American Prints Today, circ., 1959–62; USIA, 30 Contemporary American Prints, circ., 1964; New York World's Fair, 1964–65. Collections: Bibliotheque Nationale; Brooklyn Museum; Dallas/MFA; U. of Illinois; Karachi; Library of Congress; Los Angeles/County MA; MMA; NYPL; National Gallery; Oakland/AM; PMA; Pasadena/AM; SFMA; State of California; VMFA; Victoria and Albert Museum.

ELLIOTT, RONNIE. b. December 16, 1916, NYC. Studied: Hunter College; NYU; ASL. Traveled Europe extensively. Federal A.P.:

Easel and mural painting; also mosaic and stained glass windows. AWARDS: New Orleans Arts and Crafts Society, First Prize for Sculpture, 1935. ADDRESS: 68 East Seventh Street, NYC. DEALER: Grand Central Moderns. ONE-MAN EXHIBITIONS: (first) Delphic Gallery, NYC, 1937; Marquie, NYC, 1942, 43, 44; Norlyst Gallery, NYC, 1947; Carlebach Gallery, NYC, 1948; Galerie Creuze, Paris, 1948; Galerie Colette Allendy, Paris, 1952; Rose Fried Gallery, 1957, 58; Grand Central Moderns, 1963; Granville Gallery, NYC, 1964. GROUP: PAFA, 1933, 34, 39; Golden Gate International Exposition, San Francisco, 1939; Corcoran, 1939, 41; NAD, 1941; Carnegie, 1941; MMA, Contemporary American Art, 1942; Museum of Non-Objective Art, NYC, 1946; MOMA, Collage, 1948; Salon des Realites Nouvelles, Paris, 1948, 49, 51; A.F.A., Cross-Currents, circ., 1958; Houston/MFA, 1958; A.F.A., Collage in America, circ., 1957–58; WMAA Annual, 1964; U. of Nebraska. COLLECTIONS: Carnegie; NYU; Wellesley College. BIBLIOGRAPHY: Janis and Blesh 1.

ENGEL, JULES. b. 1915, Budapest, Hungary. STUDIED: Chouinard Art Institute, Los Angeles. AWARDS: SFMA, P.P., 1950, 51; Los Angeles/County MA, P.P., 1951; Ford Foundation Grant, 1960. ADDRESS: c/o Dealer. DEALER: Esther Robles Gallery. ONE-MAN EXHIBITIONS: Paul Kantor Gallery, 1952, 54, 56, 58, 60, 63; Forsyth Gallery, Los Angeles, 1950; The New Gallery, NYC, 1951; Esther Robles Gallery, 1961, 62. GROUP: WMAA, 1951, 52; Chicago/AI, 1949; MMA, 1952; de Young, 1945–53; Denver/AM; Santa Barbara/MA; Pasadena/AM; Sao Paulo, 1955. COLLECTIONS: Los Angeles/County MA; SFMA.

ERNST, JIMMY. b. June 24, 1920, Cologne, Germany. STUDIED: Cologne-Lindenthal Real-Gymnasium; Altona Arts and Crafts School. To USA 1938. TAUGHT: U. of Colorado, summers, 1954, 56; Museum of Fine Arts of Houston, 1956; Brooklyn College, 1951– ; Pratt Institute; lectures extensively. Sent by US State Department to U.S.S.R., 1961. COMMISSIONS: *Fortune* Magazine, 1955, 61 (paintings); Abbott

Jimmy Ernst   *Due East. 1961*

Laboratories, 1955; General Motors Technical Center, Detroit (10-ft. mural); NBC-TV, "Producers' Showcase," 1954 (plastic sculpture signature); NBC-TV, "Playwrights '56" (welded steel sculpture signature, with Albert Terris); American President Lines, *USS President Adams*, 1956 (mural); Continental National Bank, Lincoln, Neb., 1956 (96-ft. mural); Envoy Towers, 300 East 46 Street, NYC, 1960 (relief mural). AWARDS: Brandeis U., Creative Arts Award, 1957; Chicago/AI, Norman Wait Harris Bronze Medal, 1954; WMAA, Juliana Force Memorial P.P., 1951; Pasadena/AM, Hattie Brooks Stevens Memorial P.P., 1946; Guggenheim Foundation Fellowship, 1961. ADDRESS: Ponus Ridge, New Canaan, Conn. DEALER: Grace Borgenicht Gallery Inc. ONE-MAN EXHIBITIONS: (first) Norlyst Gallery, NYC, 1941; Grace Borgenicht Gallery Inc., 1951, 52, 53, 54, 55, 57, 61, 62; Walker, 1954; Philadelphia Art Alliance, 1948; Silvermine Guild, 1955; Houston/MFA, 1956; Brandeis U., 1957; Detroit/Institute, 1963. GROUP: XXVIII Venice Biennial, 1956; American Embassy, Paris, American Drawing, 1954; Brussels World's Fair, 1958; WMAA, Young America, 1955; SRGM, Younger American Painters, 1954; MMA, 100 Years of American Painting, 1954; *Life* Magazine, Painters Under 35, NYC, 1954; Chicago/AI, Directions in American Painting, 1960; Carnegie, 1955; Brooklyn Museum, Golden Years of American Drawing, 1957; U. of Illinois, 1957; U. of Nebraska, 1956; Brooklyn Museum, Watercolor Biennial; California Palace, 1952; Toledo/MA, 1954, 55; U. of Colorado, 1953, 54, 56; Toronto, 1954; Pasadena/AM, 1946; PAFA, 1959; Detroit/Institute, 1953, 59; NIAL, 1958, 60. COLLECTIONS: Allentown/AM; Brooklyn Museum; Buffalo/Albright; Chicago/AI; Clearwater/Gulf Coast; U. of Colorado; Cranbrook; Detroit/Institute; Hartford/Wadsworth; Houston/MFA; S. C. Johnson & Son, Inc.; Lehigh U.; MMA; MOMA; Michigan State U.; U. of Michigan; U. of Nebraska; PAFA; Pasadena/AM; SFMA; SRGM; Southern Illinois U.; Toledo/MA; Toronto; Utica; VMFA; WMAA; Walker. BIBLIOGRAPHY: Baur 7; Beekman; Blesh 1; Goodrich and Baur 1; Guggenheim, ed.; McCurdy, ed.; Janis and Blesh 1; Janis, S.; Mendelowitz; Motherwell and Reinhardt, eds.; Nordness, ed.; Pousette-Dart, ed.; Read 2; Ritchie 1.

ETTING, EMLEN. b. 1905, Philadelphia, Pa. STUDIED: Harvard U., 1928; Academie de la Grande Chaumiere; privately with Andre Lhote in Paris. TAUGHT: Philadelphia Museum School. COMMISSIONS (murals): Market Street National Bank, Philadelphia; Italian Consulate, Philadelphia. AWARDS: Italian Star of Solidarity. ADDRESS: 1927 Panama Street, Philadelphia, Pa. DEALER: The Midtown Galleries. ONE-MAN EXHIBITIONS: The Midtown Galleries, 1940, 43, 44, 46, 48, 50, 51, 57; ICA, Boston; Cleveland/MA; Warwick Gallery, Philadelphia; Artists' Gallery, Philadelphia, 1946. GROUP: WMAA; Corcoran; PAFA; Florida Southern College; VMFA; NAD; Audubon Artists; St. Louis/City; Philadelphia Art Alliance; Youngstown/Butler; Dayton/AI; Indiana U.; Illinois Wesleyan U.; West Palm Beach/Norton. COLLECTIONS: Andover/Phillips; Atwater Kent Museum; La France Institute; PAFA; WMAA. BIBLIOGRAPHY: Etting; Frost; Hall.

EVERGOOD, PHILIP HOWARD FRANCIS DIXON. b. October 26, 1901, NYC. STUDIED: Eton College, England, 1914–18; Trinity Hall, Cambridge, 1918–20; U. of London, Slade School, 1920–23, with Henry Tonks; ASL, 1923–25, with George Luks, William Von Schlegell; Academie Julian, Paris, 1925, with Jean Paul Laurens, Andre Lhote. Traveled North Africa, USA and Europe extensively. TAUGHT: The Kalamazoo Institute of Arts; American Artists School, NYC; Contemporary School of Art, NYC; U. of Minnesota, Duluth, 1955; Iowa State College, 1952–58; Muhlenberg College; Settlement Music School, Philadelphia; extensive lecturing. Wrote for *Art Front* and *Direction* Magazines. MEMBER: NIAL; Artists Equity. FEDERAL A.P.: Mural painting; Managing Supervisor, Easel Painting Division; mural for Richmond Hill (N.Y.) Public Library. COMMISSIONS (murals): Kalamazoo College; US Post Office, Jackson, Ga. AWARDS: Chicago/AI, The M. V. Kohnstamm Prize, 1935; MMA, P.P., 1942; Chicago/AI, W. H. Tuthill P.P., 1946; Carnegie, Second Prize, 1949; Corcoran, Second Prize, 1951; PAFA, Carol H. Beck Gold Medal, 1949; PAFA, Joseph E. Temple Gold Medal, 1958; AAAL Grant, 1956; Carnegie, Hon. Men., 1945; Ford Foundation, P.P., 1962. ADDRESS: RFD #1, Bridgewater, Conn. DEALER: Gallery 63, Inc., NYC. ONE-MAN EXHIBITIONS: (first)

Philip Evergood   *Woman at Piano. 1955*

Dudensing Gallery, NYC, 1927; Montross Gallery, NYC, 1929, 33, 35; Balzac Gallery, NYC, 1931; Denver/AM, 1936; Atheneum Gallery, Melbourne, 1937; Gallery 63, Inc., Rome, 1963; Gallery 63, Inc., NYC, 1964; ACA Gallery, 1938, 40, 42, 44, 46, 48, 51, 53, 55–62; Halkins College, 1953; Tulane U., 1957; Kalamazoo/Institute, 1941; Norlyst Gallery, NYC, 1948; Garelick's Gallery, Detroit, 1953, 55; State U. of Iowa; Utica; Hartford/Wadsworth. **Retrospective:** U. of Minnesota, Duluth, 1955; WMAA, 1960. **Group:** An American Group (Gallery), NYC; American Society of Painters, Sculptors and Gravuers; Salon d'Automne, Paris, 1924; NAD; Independent Artists, NYC; WMAA Annuals since 1934; PAFA; Chicago/AI; Brooklyn Museum; Corcoran; Carnegie; Venice Biennial. **Collections:** Arizona State College; Atlanta/AA; Baltimore/MA; Boston/MFA; Britannica; Brooklyn Museum; Carnegie; Chicago/AI; Corcoran; Cornell U.; Dallas/MFA; Denver/AM; Free Library of Philadelphia; Grolier Club; Hartford/Wadsworth; Harvard U.; IBM; U. of Illinois; Kalamazoo/Institute; Lehigh U.; Library of Congress; Los Angeles/County MA; U. of Louisville; MMA; MOMA; Melbourne/National; Muhlenberg College; PAFA; Pepsi-Cola Co.; Santa Fe, N.M.; Smith College; Syracuse U.; WMAA; Youngstown/Butler. **Bibliography:** American Artists Congress, Inc.; **Baur 6, 7**; Biddle 3; Cheney, M. C.; Eliot; Finkelstein; Genauer; Goodrich and Baur 1; Haftman; Kootz 2; McCurdy, ed.; Mendelowitz; Nordness, ed.; Pagano; Pousette-Dart, ed.; Reese; Richardson.

f

FARR, FRED. b. August 9, 1914, St. Petersburg, Fla. STUDIED: U. of Oregon; ASL; American Artists School, NYC. Traveled Mexico. TAUGHT: Brooklyn Museum School, 1950– ; MOMA School, 1947; Hunter College, 1954; Dalton Schools, NYC, 1950; U. of Colorado; Dayton Art Institute School; U. of Oregon, 1948. MEMBER: Artists Equity. FEDERAL A.P.: Social Security Building, Washington, D.C. (mural). COMMISSIONS: Moore-McCormack Lines Inc., SS *Argentina* (mural). AWARDS: Port-au-Prince Bicentennial Exposition, 1950, Haiti Silver Medal. ADDRESS: 526 East Fifth Street, NYC. DEALER: P. Rosenberg and Co. ONE-MAN EXHIBITIONS: (first) The Bertha Schaefer Gallery; P. Rosenberg and Co., 1957, 58, 61. GROUP: MOMA, 1946; Springfield, Mass./MFA, 1947; Walker, 1948; Utica; U. of Michigan; Ohio U.; The Ohio State U.; U. of Delaware, 1948; RISD, 1949; WMAA; U. of New Hampshire; Northwestern U.; U. of Tennessee; U. of Wisconsin; Port-au-Prince (Haiti) Bicentennial Exposition, 1950; Walters Art Gallery, Baltimore, 1953; U. of Illinois, 1961; ART:USA:59, NYC, 1959. COLLECTIONS: Ball State Teachers College; Detroit/Institute; U. of Illinois; Phillips; Portland, Me./MA.

FEELEY, PAUL. b. July 27, 1913, Des Moines, Iowa. STUDIED: Menlo Junior College; privately with Hobart Jacobs in California and Cecilia Beaux in NYC; ASL, with Thomas Hart Benton, George Bridgeman; Beaux-Arts Institute of Design, NYC. Traveled Spain, Morocco, Greece, USA. TAUGHT: Cooper Union, 1936–39; Bennington College, 1940– . US Marine Corps, 1943–46. MEMBER: National Society of Mural Painters. ADDRESS: Bennington, Vt. DEALER: Betty Parsons Gallery. ONE-MAN EXHIBITIONS: (first) Palo Alto (Calif.) Public Library, 1929; New School for Social Research, 1948; Santa Barbara/MA, 1950; The Rose Rabow Gallery, 1951; Stanford U., 1951; Mills College, 1951; SFMA, 1951; Tibor de Nagy Gallery, 1955, 57, 58; Betty Parsons Gallery, 1960, 62, 63, 64; Kasmin Ltd., 1964. GROUP: ICA, Boston, 1952; PAFA; The Kootz Gallery, New Talent, 1954; Walker, 1950; Chicago/AI; Lincoln, Mass./De Cordova, New Experiments in Art, 1963; Los Angeles/County MA, Post Painterly Abstraction, 1964; SRGM, American Drawings, 1964.

FEININGER, LYONEL. b. July 17, 1871, NYC; **d.** January 13, 1956. Studied the violin with his father and played in concerts from the age of 12; went to Germany in 1880 to study music, but changed to painting. STUDIED: Kunstgewerbeschule, Hamburg; Academy of Fine Arts, Berlin, with Ernst Hancke, Woldemar Friedrich; Jesuit College, Liege, Belgium, 1887–91; Academie Colarossi, Paris, 1892–93. Traveled Europe, USA. TAUGHT: Bauhaus, Weimar, 1919–24; Bauhaus, Dessau, 1925–33; Mills College, summers, 1936, 37. Cartoonist and illustrator for *Ulk* and *Lustige Blatter*, Berlin, 1893–1906, *Le Temoin*, Paris, 1906–07, and Chicago *Sunday Tribune*. A member of the Blue Four, 1924 (with Vassily Kandinsky, Paul Klee, and Alexej von Jawlensky). COMMISSIONS: New York World's Fair, 1939 (murals for Marine Transport Building and Masterpieces of Art Building). ONE-MAN EXHIBITIONS: Emil Richter Gallery, Dresden, 1919; Anger-Museum, Erfurt, Germany, 1920, 27, 29, 30; Kunst und Bucherstube, Erfurt, 1921; Goldschmidt-Wallerstein, Berlin, 1922, 25; Wiesbaden, 1925; Neue Kunst-

Lyonel Feininger   *Headland. 1950*

fides, Dresden, 1925, 26, 31; Brunswick, 1926; Kassel, 1927; Staatliche Galerie Moritzburg, Halle, Germany, 1928; Anhalt Gallery, Dessau, 1929; Kunstverein, Prague, 1930; Anderson Galleries, NYC, 1923; Mills College, 1936, 37; SFMA, 1937; Los Angeles/County MA, 1937; Karl Nierendorf Gallery, NYC, 1943; Seattle/AM, circ., 1937; Andover/Phillips, 1938; Dalzell Hatfield Gallery, 1944; Buchholz Gallery, NYC, 1941, 43, 44; The Willard Gallery, 1943, 44; Harvard U., 1958; Detroit/Institute, 1964; Fort Worth, 1956; Curt Valentine Gallery, NYC, 1941, 44, 46, 48, 50, 52, 54. RETROSPEC-TIVE: Berlin, 1931; MOMA (two-man), 1944; ICA, Boston, 1949; Print Club of Cleveland, 1951; SFMA, circ., 1959–61; Jeanne Bucher, Paris, circ. Europe, 1950–51; Hannover, circ. Europe, 1954–55. GROUP: Der Sturm, Berlin, 1917; Salon des Artistes Independants, Paris, 1911; Documenta I, Kassel, 1955; WMAA; Tate; Mannheim. COLLECTIONS: Baltimore/MA; Buffalo/Albright; Chicago/AI; Cranbrook; Kansas City/Nelson; Lehigh U.; MOMA; U. of Michigan; Milwaukee; Phillips; RISD; Raleigh/NCMA; SRGM; San Antonio/McNay;

Seattle/AM; Toledo/MA; Utica; WMAA. BIBLIOGRAPHY: Barr 1; Baur 5, 7; Bazin; Beekman; Biddle 3; Blanchard; Blesh 1; Born; Brion 2; Brown; Bulliet 1; Cassou; Cheney, M. C.; Eliot; Flanagan; Frost; Goodrich and Baur 1; Haftman; **Hess, H.;** Hess, T. B.; Hunter 5; Huyghe; Janis, S.; Kouvenhoven; Kuh 1; Langui; Lee and Burchwood; McCurdy, ed.; Mendelowitz; Munsterberg; Neumeyer; Newmeyer; Pousette-Dart, ed.; Raynal 3, 4; Read 2; Richardson; Ritchie 1; Rosenblum; Sachs; Selz, P. 1; Sutton; Valentine 2; Wight 2.

FEITELSON, LORSER. b. 1898, Savannah, Ga. TAUGHT: Art Center School, Los Angeles. ADDRESS: c/o Dealer. DEALER: Ankrum Gallery. ONE-MAN EXHIBITIONS: The Daniel Gallery, NYC, 1924; California Palace, 1928, 32; San Diego, 1928; Los Angeles/County MA, 1929, 44; SFMA, 1944; San Antonio/McNay, 1955; Paul Rivas Gallery, Los Angeles (two-man), 1959; Ankrum Gallery, 1964. RETROSPEC-TIVE: Pasadena/AM, 1952. GROUP: Brooklyn Museum, 1936; SFMA, 1936; MOMA, Fantastic Art, DADA, Surrealism, 1936; Chicago/AI,

Abstract and Surrealist Art, 1948; U. of Illinois, 1950, 51, 53; Sao Paulo, 1955; WMAA, 1955. **BIBLIOGRAPHY:** Baur 7; Flanagan.

FENTON, ALAN. b. July 29, 1927, Cleveland, Ohio. STUDIED: Pratt Institute, with Jack Tworkov, Adolph Gottlieb, BFA; ASL, with Richard Bove. US Merchant Marine, World War II. Traveled Europe, Mexico, Canada, USA. AWARDS: Cleveland/MA, First Prize, 1960, 61; City Center Gallery, NYC, Hon. Men., 1958. ADDRESS: 333 Park Avenue South, NYC. DEALER: The Pace Gallery, New York and Boston. ONE-MAN EXHIBITIONS: (first) The Pace Gallery, NYC, 1963. GROUP: ART:USA:58, NYC, 1958; SFMA, 1963; New York World's Fair, 1964–65; Cleveland/MA, 1959, 60, 61; Artists of the Western Reserve, circ., 1961. COLLECTIONS: Baltimore/MA; Stony Brook.

FERBER, HERBERT. b. April 30, 1906, NYC. STUDIED: City College of New York, 1923–26; Columbia U. School of Dental and Oral Surgery, 1927, BS, 1930, DDS; Beaux-Arts Institute

Herbert Ferber
Caligraph Cee III. 1964

of Design, NYC, 1927–30; NAD, 1930. Traveled Italy, France, Mexico, Great Britain. TAUGHT: U. of Pennsylvania, 1963–64; Columbia U. School of Dental and Oral Surgery. COMMISSIONS: B'nai Israel Synagogue, Millburn, N.J., 1950; Brandeis U., Jewish Chapel, 1955; Temple Anshe Chesed, Cleveland, 1955; Temple of Aaron, St. Paul, 1955; WMAA, Sculpture as Environment, 1961. AWARDS: L. C. Tiffany Grant, 1930; Beaux-Arts Institute of Design, NYC, Paris Prize, 1929; MMA, Artists for Victory, $1,000 Prize, 1942; ICA, London/Tate, International Unknown Political Prisoner Competition, 1953. ADDRESS: 454 Riverside Drive, NYC. DEALER: Andre Emmerich Gallery, NYC. ONE-MAN EXHIBITIONS: (first) The Midtown Galleries, 1937, also 1943; Betty Parsons Gallery, 1947, 50, 53; The Kootz Gallery, 1955, 57; Andre Emmerich Gallery, NYC, 1960, 62; Columbia U., 1960. RETROSPECTIVE: Bennington College, 1958; WMAA, 1961. GROUP: NAD, 1930; Brooklyn Museum; PAFA, 1931, 42, 43, 45, 46, 54, 58; Corcoran, 1932; Philadelphia Art Alliance, 1933; American Artists Congress, 1936, 40; Musee du Jeu de Paume, 1938; Sculptors Guild, 1938–42, 1944, 48, 64; WMAA Annuals, 1940, 42, 1945– ; Golden Gate International Exposition, San Francisco, 1939; New York World's Fair, 1939; Chicago/AI, 1940, 41, 45; Federation of Modern Painters and Sculptors, 1941–49; A.F.A., Sculpture in Wood, 1941; MMA, 1942; Sao Paulo, 1951; Tate, 1953; U. of Illinois, 1955, 59; MOMA, Abstract Painting and Sculpture in America, 1951; MOMA, Fifteen Americans, circ., 1952; Brussels World's Fair, 1958; Carnegie, 1958; A.F.A., God and Man in Art, circ., 1958–59; WMAA, The New Decade, 1954–55; Documenta II, Kassel, 1959; St. Paul Gallery, Drawings, USA, 1961; Baltimore/MA; Cranbrook; Musee Rodin, Paris. COLLECTIONS: Bennington College; Buffalo/Albright; Cranbrook; Detroit/Institute; Grand Rapids; MMA; MOMA; NYU; Newark Museum; WMAA; Williams College. BIBLIOGRAPHY: Baur 5, 7; Blesh 1; Brumme; Flanagan; Giedion-Welcker 1; Goodrich and Baur 1; **Goossen 2;** Henning; Hunter 5; McCurdy, ed.; Motherwell and Reinhardt, eds.; Ritchie 1, 3; Seuphor 3.

FERREN, JOHN. b. October 17, 1905, Pendleton, Ore. STUDIED: Academie de la Grande Chaumiere; Sorbonne; U. of Florence; U. of

Salamanca; Academie Ranson, Paris; Academie Colarossi, Paris. Traveled Europe, USA, Middle East; resided, worked in Paris, 1931–38. Civilian employee of War Department and OWI, 1941–45: Psychological Warfare Division, SHAEF (Propaganda Chief, Italian Radio Section); Algiers headquarters (Chief of Publications for France); received Bronze Star. TAUGHT: Brooklyn Museum School, 1946–50; Art Center School, Los Angeles, summer, 1948; Cooper Union, 1947–54; UCLA, summer, 1953; privately in New York; Queens College; U. of Saskatchewan, summer, 1960; Yale U., summer, 1962; lectures extensively and publishes essays. Advisory work on "The Trouble with Harry" (1955) and "Vertigo" (1958), films directed by Alfred Hitchcock. MEMBER: Advisory Council to the School of Art and Architecture, Yale U., 1959–62. ADDRESS: 15 West 73 Street, NYC. DEALER: Rose Fried Gallery. ONE-MAN EXHIBITIONS: Art Center, San Francisco, 1930; Galerie Zak, Paris, 1932; Galerie Pierre, Paris, 1936; Pierre Matisse Gallery, 1936, 37, 38; Minneapolis/Institute, 1936; Howard Putzell Gallery, Hollywood, 1936; SFMA, 1936, 52; Arts Club of Chicago, 1937; Galerie Beaune, Paris, 1938; The Willard Gallery, 1942; Art Project Gallery, Hollywood, 1942; Kleemann Gallery, NYC, 1947, 49; Santa Barbara/MA, 1952; Tacoma, 1952; Portland (Ore.) Arts Club, 1952; Alexander Iolas Gallery, 1953; UCLA, 1953; U. of Washington, 1953; The Stable Gallery, 1954, 55, 56, 57, 58; Phillips, 1958; U. of Wisconsin, 1959; Glassboro State College, 1959; Trenton State College, 1959; Rose Fried Gallery, 1962; Queens College, 1963; Beirut, Lebanon, 1964. GROUP: California Palace, 1931; Los Angeles/County MA Annuals, 1925–29; SFMA Annuals, 1925–29; American Abstract Artists, 1934, 35, 37; Musee du l'Orangerie, Paris, 1937; Salon des Surindependants, Paris, 1937; Royal Institute of the Arts, Copenhagen, 1937; Corcoran, 1940; Chicago/AI, 1947; Brooklyn Museum, 1949; U. of Minnesota, Pioneers in American Abstract Art, 1951; Ninth Street Exhibition, NYC, 1951; WMAA Annuals, 1952, 55, 56; MOMA, Abstract Painting and Sculpture in America, 1951; Carnegie, 1955; MOMA, 7 American Watercolorists, circ. Europe, 1956; Chicago/AI, 1956; U. of Illinois, 1957; WMAA, Nature in Abstraction, 1958; U. of Kentucky, Graphics, 1958, 59; Pasadena/AM, A Decade in the Contemporary Gallery, 1959; ART:USA:59,

NYC, 1959; A.F.A., Affinities, circ., 1962; SRGM, Abstract Expressionists and Imagists, 1961; Walker, 60 American Painters, 1960; PAFA, 1964. COLLECTIONS: Allentown/AM; Art of This Century (Peggy Guggenheim); Birmingham, Ala./MA; Brandeis U.; Buffalo/Albright; California Palace; U. of California, Berkeley; Cleveland/MA; Detroit/Institute; Hartford/Wadsworth; MOMA; NYU; U. of Nebraska; PMA; Phillips; Provincetown/Chrysler; SFMA; SRGM; Scripps College; Tel Aviv; WGMA; WMAA; Washington U.; Yale U. BIBLIOGRAPHY: Baur 5, 7; Eliot; Frost; Goodrich and Baur 1; Guggenheim, ed.; Hayter 2; Janis, S.; Passloff; Ritchie 1.

FIENE, ERNEST. b. November 2, 1894, Eberfeld, Germany; d. August 10, 1965, Paris, France. To USA 1912; citizen 1928. STUDIED: NAD, 1914–18; Beaux-Arts Institute of Design, NYC, 1916–18; ASL, 1923; Academie de la Grande Chaumiere, 1929; Florence, Italy (fresco painting), 1932. Traveled Europe, Mexico, USA. TAUGHT: Cooper Union, 1938–39; ASL, 1938–65; NAD, 1960–65; Famous Artists Schools, Inc., 1956–65; Westchester County Center, 1930–31; Colorado Springs Fine Arts Center, 1935; Ogunquit School of Painting, 1950–51. MEMBER: Artists Equity (Hon. President); NAD; Century Association; ASL. COMMISSIONS (portraits): Columbia U.; New York Hospital; Ohio U.; Abbott Laboratories; (series of paintings): Scruggs, Vandervoort and Barney; Gimbels, Philadelphia; Central Needle Trades High School of New York; (murals): International Ladies' Garment Workers Union, NYC; Abraham Lincoln High School, Brooklyn (2); US Post Office, Canton, Mass.; New Interior Building, Washington, D.C. AWARDS: Guggenheim Foundation Fellowship, 1932; Chicago/AI, Norman Wait Harris Prize, 1937; Corcoran, William A. Clark Prize, 1938; Carnegie, Hon. Men., 1938; Chicago/AI, Ada S. Garrett Prize, 1940; Library of Congress, Pennell P.P., 1940; Library of Congress, First Pennell P.P., 1944; NAD, Edwin Palmer Memorial Prize, 1961. ONE-MAN EXHIBITIONS: (first) Whitney Studio Club, NYC, 1923; The New Gallery, NYC, 1924; Kraushaar Galleries, 1927; The Downtown Gallery, 1928, 33, 36; Rehn Galleries, 1930–32; A.A.A. Gallery, NYC, 1938–41, 45; M. Knoedler & Co., 1949–51; The Midtown Galleries, 1959; Stonington Gallery, Conn.,

1963; Bay Head Art Center, 1964; Western Association of Art Museum Directors, circ., 1938. GROUP: WMAA, 1930–45; Carnegie, 1930–45; PAFA, 1930–45; Corcoran, 1931–45; NAD; MOMA; Youngstown/Butler; Chicago/AI, 1930–33, 1936–45; MMA; Boston/MFA. COLLECTIONS: ASL; Abbott Laboratories; Boston/MFA; Bowdoin College; Britannica; Brooklyn Museum; California Palace; Chicago/AI; Cleveland/MA; Columbia U.; Dartmouth College; Denver/AM; Detroit/Institute; Drake U.; Library of Congress; Los Angeles/County MA; MIT; MMA; MOMA; NAD; NYPL; U. of Nebraska; Newark Museum;Ogunquit; Ohio U.; PAFA; Phillips; SFMA; Syracuse U.; Tel Aviv; Terre Haute/Swope; Tulsa/Philbrook; WMAA; Yale U. BIBLIOGRAPHY: American Artists Congress, Inc.; American Artists Group Inc. 1, 2, 3; Cahill and Barr, eds.; Goodrich and Baur 1; Hall; Pearson 1; Phillips 1; Reese; Richardson.

FLANNAGAN, JOHN. b. April 7, 1895, Fargo, N.D.; **d.** January 6, 1942, NYC. STUDIED: Minneapolis Institute School, 1914–17, with R. Koehler. US Merchant Marine, 1914–17. Traveled Ireland, USA, France. AWARDS: Guggenheim Foundation Fellowship, 1932; MMA, Alexander Shilling Prize, 1940. ONE-MAN EXHIBITIONS: (first) Weyhe Gallery, 1927, also 1928, 30, 31, 34, 36, 38; Whitney Studio Club, NYC, 1925; Arts Club of Chicago, 1934; Vassar College, 1936; Bard College, 1937; Buchholz Gallery, NYC, 1942 (2); VMFA, 1946; A.F.A., circ., 1959. RETROSPECTIVE: MOMA, 1942. GROUP: WMAA; MOMA; MMA; Brooklyn Museum. COLLECTIONS: Andover/Phillips; Cincinnati/AM; Cleveland/MA; Detroit/Institute; Dublin/Municipal; Harvard U.; Honolulu Academy; MMA; U. of Nebraska; Oberlin College; Vassar College; WMAA; Wichita/AM. BIBLIOGRAPHY: Baur 7; Brumme; Cheney, M. C.; Fierens; Goodrich and Baur 1; Hunter 5; Jackman; McCurdy, ed.; Mellquist; Mendelowitz; **Miller, ed. 3;** Ritchie 3; Seuphor 3; Seymour; **Valentine 1, 2;** Wheeler.

FLEISCHMANN, ADOLF R. b. March 18, 1892, Esslingen, Germany. STUDIED: Academy of Fine Arts, Stuttgart; Academy of Fine Arts, Munich, with Carl Caspar. Traveled Europe extensively. TAUGHT: Palma de Mallorca, 1933–36; and privately. To USA 1952. MEMBER: American Abstract Artists; Groupe Espace, Paris; Salon des Realites Nouvelles, Paris. ADDRESS: 1482 First Avenue, NYC. DEALER: The Stable Gallery. ONE-MAN EXHIBITIONS: (first) Kunsthaus Schaller, Stuttgart; Galerie Creuze, Paris, 1948; Galerie Colette Allendy, Paris, 1950, 51; Lutz and Meyer Gallery, Stuttgart, 1952, 60, 62; Johannesburg/Municipal, 1953; Rose Fried Gallery, 1955, 57; Galerie Weiss, Kassel, 1959; Parma Gallery, NYC, 1961; Apiaw (Gallery), Liege, 1962; Kunstverein Freiburg im Breisgau, 1962; The Stable Gallery, 1963; Hessisches Landesmuseum, Kassel, circ., 1964. GROUP: Neue Sezession, Munich; Salon des Realites Nouvelles, Paris, 1946; Groupe Espace, Paris, 1946; American Abstract Artists Annuals; WMAA, Geometric Abstraction in America, circ., 1962; SFMA; Yale U.; Chicago/AI. COLLECTIONS: Boulogne; Busch-Reisinger Museum; Ceret; Esslingen; Grenoble; Harvard U.; Kassel; New London; Stuttgart; Union Carbide Corp.; WMAA; Wellesley College. BIBLIOGRAPHY: Read 2; Seuphor 1.

FLOCH, JOSEPH. b. November 5, 1895, Vienna, Austria. STUDIED: Academy of Fine Arts, Vienna, MA. Traveled Europe; resided Paris, twenty years. To USA 1941. TAUGHT: New School for Social Research. MEMBER: Federation of Modern Painters and Sculptors; NAD; Salon d'Automne, Paris; Salon des Tuileries, Paris. COMMISSIONS: French Government, 1939 (murals); costumes and stage sets (with Louis Jouvet) for the Jean Giraudoux play *Judith.* AWARDS: Chevalier of the Order of Arts and Letters (France); Paris World's Fair, 1937, Gold Medal; William Palmer Memorial Prize; PAFA, Walter Lippincott Prize. ADDRESS: 61 West 74 Street, NYC. DEALER: The Forum Gallery. ONE-MAN EXHIBITIONS: (first) a gallery in Vienna, 1917; Galerie Berthe Weill, Paris; A.A.A. Gallery, NYC; Toledo/MA; de Young. GROUP: MMA; WMAA; New York World's Fair, 1939; Paris World's Fair, 1937. COLLECTIONS: Belvedere; Bezalel Museum; de Young; Graphische Sammlung Albertina; Grenoble; Kansas City/Nelson; Lille; MMA; MOMA; Montclair/AM; Musee du Jeu de Paume; Paris/Moderne; Southampton/Parrish; Springfield, Mass./MFA; Tel Aviv; Toledo/MA; Vienna/Stadt; WMAA. BIBLIOGRAPHY: Huyghe; Pagano.

FOLLETT, JEAN F. b. June 5, 1917, St. Paul, Minn. STUDIED: U. of Minnesota; St. Paul School of Art, with Cameron Booth; Hofmann School; Atelier Fernand Leger, Paris. US Army, 1943–46. TAUGHT: St. Paul School of Art, 1942–43. AWARDS: Longview Foundation Grant, 1961; Marie Hofmann Grant, 1963. ADDRESS: 982 Case Avenue, St. Paul, Minn. ONE-MAN EXHIBITIONS: (first) Hansa Gallery, NYC, 1952, also 1953, 56, 57. GROUP: The Stable Gallery Annual, 1957; Carnegie, 1958; MOMA, Recent Sculpture USA, 1959; Claude Bernard, Paris, 1960; Houston/MFA, 1957; Cornell U., 1958; WMAA Annual, 1961; Martha Jackson Gallery, New Media—New Forms, I, 1960. COLLECTIONS: Houston/MFA; MIT; MOMA; WMAA. BIBLIOGRAPHY: Seitz 2.

FORAKIS, PETER. b. October 2, 1927, Hanna, Wyo. STUDIED: San Francisco Art Institute, with Bud Dixon, Thomas Hardy, Nathan Oliveira, 1954–57, BA. TAUGHT: Brooklyn Museum School. COMMISSIONS: Mural for a motion picture theater, San Francisco, 1956. ADDRESS: 10 Little West 12 Street, NYC. DEALER: Tibor de Nagy Gallery. ONE-MAN EXHIBITIONS: (first) Gallery Six, San Francisco, 1955, also 1956, 58; Tibor de Nagy Gallery, 1962, 64; David Anderson Gallery, NYC (two-man), 1961; Spasta Gallery, San Francisco, 1959. GROUP: SFMA, 1955, 56, 57, 58; Oakland/AM, 1957; Martha Jackson Gallery, New Media—New Forms, I, 1960; Uiano Museum, Tokyo, 1952, 53; SRGM, Drawings and Prints, 1964.

FORST, MILES. b. August 18, 1923, Brooklyn, N.Y. STUDIED: New School for Social Research; Veterans Art Center, MOMA, with Mervin Jules; ASL, with Morris Kantor; Hofmann School, NYC. Traveled Europe, Mexico. TAUGHT: Assistant to Hans Hofmann at his School, 1952–53; Great Neck (N.Y.) Adult Education Program, 1958, 59, 60. A co-founder of Hansa Gallery, NYC. AWARDS: Dolia Laurian Fund Award, 1954; Walter K. Gutman Foundation Grant, 1960; Longview Foundation Grant, 1961, 62. ADDRESS: 129 Spring Street, NYC. ONE-MAN EXHIBITIONS: (first) Hansa Gallery, NYC, 1953, also 1954, 55, 58; Wittenborn Gallery, NYC, 1955; The Drawing Shop, NYC, 1964. GROUP: Chicago/AI, 1953; SRGM, 1954; A.F.A., Collage in America, circ., 1957–58; Carnegie, 1959; A.F.A., The Figure, circ., 1960;

MOMA, Hans Hofmann and His Students, circ., 1963–64; Hartford/Wadsworth, 1964; Cornell U., 1958; U. of Illinois. COLLECTIONS: Bowdoin College; Charlotte/Mint; Dillard U.; MIT; Newark Museum; Tulane U.

FORTESS, KARL E. b. October 13, 1907, Antwerp, Belgium. STUDIED: Chicago Art Institute School; ASL; Woodstock School of Painting, with Yasuo Kuniyoshi. US citizen 1923. TAUGHT: ASL; Brooklyn Museum School; Louisiana State U.; American Art School, NYC; Boston U. AWARDS: AAAL, Childe Hassam Award, 1952; Guggenheim Foundation Fellowship, 1946; Carnegie, First Hon. Men., 1941; Woodstock Artists Association, E. Keith Memorial Award, 1935. ADDRESS: 96 Bay State Road, Boston, Mass. DEALER: A.A.A. Gallery, NYC. ONE-MAN EXHIBITIONS: Boris Mirski Gallery; A.A.A. Gallery, NYC, 1948, 51; Ganso Gallery, NYC; Vose Gallery, Boston; Sawkill Gallery, Woodstock, N.Y.; Bucknell U.; Louisiana State U.; U. of Georgia; The Krasner Gallery. GROUP: NIAL; Chicago/AI; Carnegie; U. of Illinois; Boston Arts Festival; Corcoran; MOMA; NAD; PAFA; WMAA. COLLECTIONS: U. of Arizona; Brooklyn Museum; Colby College; MOMA; Montpelier/Wood; Newark Museum; Rochester/Memorial; Youngstown/Butler. BIBLIOGRAPHY: Cheney, M. C.; Pearson 2; Zaidenberg, ed.

FOULKES, LLYN. b. November 17, 1934, Yakima, Wash. STUDIED: Central Washington College; U. of Washington, 1952–54; Chouinard Art Institute, Los Angeles, 1957–59, with Richards Ruben, Emerson Woelffer, Don Graham. US Army, Germany, 1954–56. Traveled Europe, North Africa, USA. ADDRESS: 6010 Eucalyptus Lane, Los Angeles, Calif. DEALERS: Rolf Nelson Gallery; The Lanyon Gallery; Allan Frumkin Gallery, NYC and Chicago. ONE-MAN EXHIBITIONS: (first) Ferus Gallery, 1961; Pasadena/AM, 1962; Rolf Nelson Gallery, 1963, 64; Oakland/AM, 1964. GROUP: Los Angeles/County MA Annuals, 1960, 61, 63; Pomona College, Object Makers, 1961; SFMA, West Coast Artists, circ., 1961; Pasadena/AM, Directors Choice, 1964; SFMA, Directions—Painting U.S.A., 1963; Sao Paulo, 1964. COLLECTIONS: Los Angeles/County MA; Oakland/AM; Pasadena/AM.

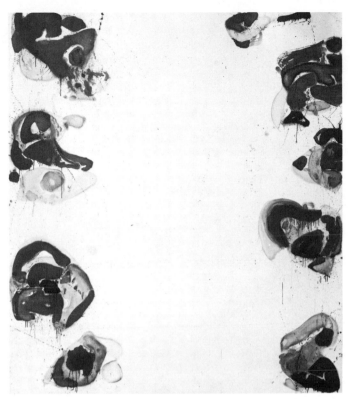

Sam Francis   *Blue in Motion. 1960*

FRANCIS, SAM. b. 1923, San Mateo, Calif. STUDIED: U. of California, Berkeley, 1941–43; 1949, BA; 1950, MA. US Air Force, 1943–45. Began painting under the encouragement of David Park while hospitalized in 1945. Traveled Europe, Japan, USA; resided and worked in Paris, seven years. COMMISSIONS (murals): Kunsthalle Berne, 1957; Sofu School of Flower Arrangement, Tokyo, 1957; Chase Manhattan Bank, NYC, 1959. AWARDS: III International Biennial Exhibition of Prints, Tokyo, 1962, First Prize; Tate, $5,000 Dunn International Prize. ADDRESS: c/o Martha Jackson Gallery. DEALERS: Martha Jackson Gallery; Gimpel Fils Ltd. ONE-MAN EXHIBITIONS: (first) Galerie Nina Dausset, Paris, 1952; Galerie Rive Droite, Paris, 1955, 56; Martha Jackson Gallery, 1956, 58, 63; Gimpel Fils Ltd., 1957; Klipstein & Kornfeld, Berne, 1957, 59; Zoé Dusanne Gallery, 1957; Tokyo Department Store Gallery, 1957; Kintetsu Department Store Gallery, Osaka, 1957; Phillips, 1958; Esther Baer Gallery, 1962; Seattle/AM, 1959; SFMA, 1959; Galerie Engelberts, Geneva, 1962; Galerie Pauli, Lausanne, 1962. RETROSPECTIVE: Kestner-Gesellschaft, Hannover, 1963. GROUP: Salon du Mai, Paris, 1950; Studio Paul Facchetti, Signifiants de l'Informal, 1952; Studio Paul Facchetti, Un Art Autre, 1953; ICA, London, Opposing Forces, 1953; Berne, Tendences Actuelles, 1955; Carnegie, 1955; MOMA, Twelve Americans, circ., 1956; International Biennial Exhibition of Paintings, Tokyo; Arts Council Gallery, London, New Trends in Painting, 1957; Brussels World's Fair, 1958; MOMA, The New American Painting, circ. Europe, 1958–59; American Cultural Center, Paris, 3 Americans, 1958; III International Biennial Exhibition of Prints, Tokyo, 1962; Chicago/AI, 1962; Tate, Dunn International, 1964; Musee Cantonal des Beaux-Arts, Lausanne, I Salon International de Galeries Pilotes, 1963; WMAA Annual, 1964; Tate, Gulbenkian International, 1964; Flint/Institute, The Coming of Color, 1964; Brooklyn Museum,

1959; Sao Paulo, 1959. **Collections:** Berne; Buffalo/Albright; Dayton/AI; MOMA; SRGM; Sofu School of Flower Arrangement; Tate; Zurich. **Bibliography:** Blesh 1; Haftman; Hunter 1; Langui; McCurdy, ed.; *Metro;* Nordness, ed.; Ponente; Read 2; Restany 2; Seuphor 1; Tapie 1.

FRANKENTHALER, HELEN. b. December. 12, 1928, NYC. **Studied:** Dalton School, NYC, with Rufino Tamayo; Bennington College, with Paul Feeley, 1945–49, BA; ASL, with Vaclav Vytlacil, 1946; with William Harrison, NYC, 1948; with Hans Hofmann, 1950. Traveled Europe extensively. **Taught:** NYU; Hunter College, 1962. **Commissions:** Temple of Aaron, St. Paul (ark curtain tapestry). **Awards:** I Paris Biennial, First Prize, 1959. **m.** Robert Motherwell. **Address:** 173 East 94 Street, NYC. **Dealers:** Andre Emmerich Gallery, NYC; Galerie Lawrence. **One-man Exhibitions:** (first) Tibor de Nagy Gallery, 1951, also 1952, 53, 54, 56, 57, 58; Andre Emmerich Gallery, NYC, 1959, 60, 61, 62, 63; Jewish Museum, 1960; Everett Ellin Gallery, Los Angeles, 1961; Bennington College, 1962; Galerie Lawrence, 1961, 63; Galleria dell'Ariete, Milan, 1962. **Group:** The Kootz Gallery, New Talent, 1951; Ninth Street Exhibition, NYC, 1951; WMAA, Nature in Abstraction, 1958; International Biennial Exhibition of Paintings, Tokyo; WMAA, Young America, 1957; Documenta II, Kassel, 1959; Carnegie, 1955, 58, 61; Sao Paulo, 1958; SRGM, Abstract Expressionists and Imagists, 1961; Seattle World's Fair, 1962; WMAA Annuals, 1955, 58. **Collections:** Brooklyn Museum; Buffalo/Albright; Carnegie; Hartford/Wadsworth; MOMA; Milwaukee; Newark Museum; WMAA. **Bibliography:** Baur 5; Friedman, ed.; Goodrich and Baur 1; Hunter 1, 5; Janis and Blesh 1; *Metro.*

FRASCONI, ANTONIO. b. April 28, 1919, Montevideo, Uruguay. **Studied:** Circulo de Bellas Artes, Montevideo; ASL, 1946, with Yasuo Kuniyoshi; New School for Social Research, 1947, with Camilio Egas. To USA 1945. **Taught:** New School for Social Research, 1951–52; Brooklyn Museum School; Pratt Institute; Vassar College; Atlanta Art Institute. **Awards:** Guggenheim Foundation Fellowship, 1952; US Post Office Department, Design Competition, 1963; NIAL Grant, 1954; Grand Prix, Venice International Film Festival, 1960, for "The Neighboring Shore" (15 min., more than 100 woodcuts). **Address:** 20 Dock Road, South

Helen Frankenthaler   *Gliding Figure. 1961*

Norwalk, Conn. **DEALERS:** Terry Dintenfass, Inc.; Weyhe Gallery. **ONE-MAN EXHIBITIONS:** Ateneo Gallery, Montevideo, 1939; Asociacion Cristiana de Jovenes, Montevideo, 1940; Agrupacion Intelectual, Montevideo, 1944; Santa Barbara/MA, 1946, 50, 51, 55; Brooklyn Museum, 1946; San Jose State College Art Gallery, 1946; Pasadena/AM, 1946; New School for Social Research, 1947; Weyhe Gallery, 1948, 49, 50, 51, 52, 53, 54, 56, 60; Philadelphia Art Alliance, 1948; Pan-American Union, Washington, D.C., 1949; Utica, 1949; San Diego, 1950; Princeton Print Club, 1950, 52; SFMA, 1950; Honolulu Academy, 1950; Art Association, Madison, Wisc., 1951; Prang Institute, NYC, 1951; U. of Delaware, 1951; Bennington College, 1952; Louisville/Speed, 1953; Detroit/Institute, 1953; Los Angeles/County MA, 1953; Currier, 1955; Chattanooga/AA, 1955; Fort Worth, 1955; Wesleyan U., 1956; U. of Maine, 1956; Scripps College, 1958; Berea College, 1958; Collectors Art Center, Tallahassee, 1958; Atlanta/AA, 1959; Carnegie Institute of Technology, 1959; San Antonio/McNay, 1959; Terry Dintenfass, Inc., 1962, 63, 64; The Print Club, Philadelphia, 1963; The Pennsylvania State U., 1963; Ankrum Gallery, 1963. **RETROSPECTIVE:** Baltimore/MA, 1963; Cleveland/MA, 1952; Smithsonian, circ., 1953–55; Montevideo/Municipal, 1961. **GROUP:** Brooklyn Museum; Corcoran; Boston/MFA; Detroit/Institute; Hartford/Wadsworth; PAFA; Newark Museum; MOMA; Carnegie; St. Louis/City; San Diego; Baltimore/MA. **COLLECTIONS:** Akron/AI; Albion College; Allegheny College; Alverthorpe Gallery; U. of Arizona; Arts Council of Great Britain; Atlanta/AA; Baltimore/MA; Boston/MFA; Boston Public Library; Brandeis U.; Brooklyn Museum; U. of California, Berkeley; Carnegie; La Casa del Libro; Chicago/AI; Cincinnati/AM; Cleveland/MA; Dartmouth College; U. of Delaware; Des Moines; Detroit/Institute; Fort Worth; Geneseo; Grand Rapids; Hamilton College; Hartford/Wadsworth; Harvard U.; Honolulu Academy; Hunter College; State College of Iowa; Kalamazoo/Institute; U. of Kentucky; Lawrence College; Library of Congress; Louisville/Speed; MMA; MOMA; U. of Maine; Memphis/Brooks; U. of Michigan; U. of Minnesota; Montclair/AM; Montevideo/Municipal; NYPL; Newark Museum; New Britain; New Paltz; U. of Notre Dame; Omaha/Joslyn; PAFA; PMA; The Penn-

Antonio Frasconi   *Portrait of Brecht. 1960*

sylvania State U.; Princeton U.; RISD; Rochester/Memorial; Rutgers U.; St. Louis/City; San Diego; Santa Barbara/MA; Seattle/AM; Smith College; Springfield, Mo./AM; Uruguay/Nacional; Utica; Washington U.; Wesleyan U.; College of William and Mary; Williams College. **BIBLIOGRAPHY:** Sachs.

FREILICHER, JANE. b. November 29, 1924, NYC. **STUDIED:** Brooklyn College, BA; Columbia U., MA; Hofmann School. Traveled Europe, Morocco. **TAUGHT:** Great Neck (N.Y.) Adult Education Program; New Jersey public schools. **AWARDS:** Hallmark International Competition, 1960; *Art News* (Magazine), 10 Best Shows of 1962. **ADDRESS:** 16 West 11 Street, NYC. **DEALER:** Tibor de Nagy Gallery. **ONE-MAN EXHIBITIONS:** (first) Tibor de Nagy Gallery, 1952, also 1953–64. **GROUP:** RISD, Four Young Americans, 1955; WMAA Annual, 1958; PAFA, 1961; MOMA, Recent Drawings USA, 1956; U. of Nebraska, 1963; MOMA, Hans Hofmann and His Students, circ., 1963–64; Chicago/AI; Brooklyn Museum; Yale U.; Corcoran. **COLLECTIONS:** Brooklyn Museum; Hampton Institute; NYU; RISD.

FRENCH, JARED. b. February 4, 1905, Ossining, N.Y. Studied: ASL, with Thomas Hart Benton, Boardman Robinson, Kimon Nicolaides; Amherst College, BA. Traveled Europe, northeastern USA. Federal A.P.: US Post Offices, Richmond, Va., and Plymouth, Pa., 1935–39 (murals). Address: 5 St. Luke's Place, NYC. Dealer: The Banfer Gallery. One-man Exhibitions: (first) Julien Levy Galleries, NYC, 1939; Hewitt Gallery, NYC, 1950; Robert Isaacson Gallery, NYC. Group: Arts Club of Chicago; PAFA; WMAA; Chicago/AI; Carnegie; NAD; Walker. Collections: Baltimore/MA; Baseball Museum; Dartmouth College; WMAA. Bibliography: Baur 7; Goodrich and Baur 1.

FRIEDENSOHN, ELIAS. b. December 12, 1924, NYC. Studied: Stella Elkins Tyler School of Fine Arts, Temple U., 1942–43, with Rafael Sabatini; Queens College, with Cameron Booth, 1946–48, AB; NYU, Institute of Fine Arts; privately with Gabriel Zendel in Paris. Traveled Europe. Taught: Queens College. Awards: Guggenheim Foundation Fellowship, 1960; Fulbright Fellowship (Italy), 1957; Joe and Emily Lowe Foundation Award, 1951; U. of Illinois, p.p., 1957; National Arts Club Annual, NYC, Stephens Award, 1958. Address: 43–44 149th Street, Flushing, N.Y. Dealers: The Contemporaries; Feingarten Gallery, Los Angeles. One-man Exhibitions: (first) Roko Gallery, 1951; Hewitt Gallery, NYC, 1955, 57, 59; Robert Isaacson Gallery, NYC, 1960; Feingarten Gallery, NYC, San Francisco, Los Angeles and Chicago, 1961, 62; Feingarten Gallery, Los Angeles, 1964; Vassar College, 1958. Group: Galleria Schneider, Rome, Fulbright Artists, 1958; Festival of Two Worlds, Spoleto, 1958; Audubon Artists Annual, 1957; WMAA, Young America, 1957; WMAA, Fulbright Artists, 1958; WMAA Annuals, 1958, 59, 60, 62; Chicago/AI Annuals, 1957, 59; National Arts Club Annual, NYC, 1958; Corcoran Annuals, 1960, 62; Denver/AM, 1962; U. of Illinois, 1957, 59, 61, 63. Collections: Chicago/AI; U. of Illinois; The Joe and Emily Lowe Foundation; Sara Roby Foundation; WMAA.

FULLER, SUE. b. August 11, 1914, Pittsburgh, Pa. Studied: Carnegie Institute of Technology, 1936, BA; Teachers College, Columbia U., 1939, MA; special studies with Hans Hofmann, 1934; with S. W. Hayter, 1943–44; privately with Josef Albers, T. Tokuno. Traveled Europe, Africa, Japan. Taught: U. of Minnesota, 1950; Stourbridge (England) School of Arts and Crafts, 1951; U. of Georgia, 1951, 52; Teachers College, Columbia U., 1958. Awards: Charles M. Rosenbloom Prize, 1942; Northwest Printmakers Annual, p.p., 1945; The Print Club, Philadelphia, 1944, 45; Society of American Etchers and Engravers, NYC, 1947; L. C. Tiffany Grant, 1948; The Print Club, Philadelphia, Charles M. Lea Prize, 1949; Guggenheim Foundation Fellowship, 1949; NIAL Grant, 1950. Address: 44 East 63 Street, NYC. Dealer: The Bertha Schaefer Gallery. One-man Exhibitions: Village Art Center, NYC, 1947; Corcoran, 1951; U. of Georgia, 1951; The Bertha Schaefer Gallery, 1952, 55, 56, 61; Nishi Machi School, Tokyo, 1954; Fort Worth, 1956; Currier, 1956; San Antonio/McNay, 1956; Grand Rapids, 1957; Grinnell College, 1960; Chatham College, 1960; Charlotte/Mint, 1957. Group: MOMA, Master Prints from the Museum Collection, 1949; SAGA, 1951; I Sao Paulo Biennial, 1951; MOMA, Abstract Painting and Sculpture in America, 1951; WMAA Annuals, 1951, 53, 54, 56; Salon du Mai, Paris, 1952; PMA, A Decade of American Print Making, 1952; III Biennial of Spanish-American Art, Barcelona, 1955; Brooklyn Museum, 14 Painter Printmakers, 1955; WMAA, The New Decade, 1954–55; Chicago/AI Annual, 1957; USIA, American Prints, circ. Middle East, 1957–59; A.F.A., 14 Painter-Printmakers, circ., 1957; A.F.A., Collage in America, circ., 1957–58; A.F.A., The New Landscape in Art and Science, circ., 1958–59; A.F.A., Explorers of Space, circ., 1961–62; A.F.A., Hayter and Atelier 17, circ., 1961–62; USIA, Plastics—USA, circ. U.S.S.R., 1961; Corcoran, 1963; WMAA, Geometric Abstraction in America, circ., 1962. Collections: Albion College; Andover/Phillips; Baltimore/MA; Boston/MFA; Brooklyn Museum; CIT Corporation; Carnegie; Chase Manhattan Bank; Chicago/AI; Des Moines; Ford Foundation; Hartford/Wadsworth; Harvard U.; Indianapolis/Herron; MMA; MOMA; NYPL; National Gallery; PMA; Peabody Institute; Union Carbide Corp.; WMAA. Bibliography: Hayter 2; Janis and Blesh 1; Newmeyer; Reese; Ritchie 1.

g

GABO, NAUM NEEMIA PEVSNER. b. August 5, 1890, Briansk, Russia. Studied: U. of Munich, medical faculty, 1910, natural science, 1911; Polytechnic Engineering School, Munich, 1912. Traveled Italy, Scandinavia, Great Britain, USA, Russia. To USA 1946; citizen 1952. Taught: Harvard U., 1953–54. Designed set for "La Chatte" (Ballet Russe, 1926). Edited *Circle* (with Leslie Martin and Ben Nicholson), 1937. Commissions: Bijenkorf Building, Rotterdam, 1955; U.S. Rubber Co. Building, NYC, 1956. Awards: ICA, London/Tate, International Unknown Political Prisoner Competition, Second Prize, 1953; Guggenheim Foundation Fellowship, 1954; Chicago/AI, The Mr. & Mrs. Frank G. Logan Medal, 1954. Address: Breakneck Hill, Middlebury, Conn. Dealer: Marlborough-Gerson Gallery Inc. One-man Exhibitions: Galerie Percier, Paris, 1924; Little Review Gallery, NYC, 1926; Kestner-Gesellschaft, Hannover, 1930; Arts Club of Chicago, 1934, 1952 (two-man); Lefevre Gallery, London, 1936; Musee du Jeu de Paume, 1937; The London Gallery, London, 1937; Julien Levy Galleries, NYC, 1938; Museum of the City of London, 1942; MOMA, 1948; Baltimore/MA, 1950; MIT, 1952; Pierre Matisse Gallery, 1953; Hartford/Wadsworth, 1938, 53. Group: Golden Gate International Exposition, San Francisco, 1939; MOMA; WMAA; Chicago/AI; Paris/Moderne. Collections: MOMA; U.S. Rubber Co.; WMAA. Bibliography: Baldinger; Barr 1; Baur 7; Biederman 1; Blanchard; Blesh 1; Canaday; Cassou; Flanagan; **Gabo;** Gaunt; Gertz; Giedion-Welcker 1, 2; Goodrich and Baur 1; Guggenheim, ed.; Henning; Hess, T.B.; Janis and Blesh 1, Janis, S.; Kepes 2; Kepes, ed.; Kuh 1, 2; Langui; Lowry; McCurdy, ed.; **Martin, Nichol-** son and Gabo, eds.; Mendelowitz; *Metro;* Myers 2; Neumeyer; Newmeyer; Newton 2; **Olson and Chanin;** Ramsden 1, 2; Read 1, 5; **Read and Martin;** Ritchie 3; Selz, J.; Selz, P. 1; Seuphor 3; Seymour; Valentine 2; Zervos.

GALLATIN, ALBERT E. b. 1882, Villanova, Pa.; **d.** June 17, 1952. Studied: Cutler School, Vermont; New York Law School. Traveled Europe, USA. Founder of Museum of Living Art, now housed at The Philadelphia Museum of Art. One-man Exhibitions: (first) Galerie Pierre, Paris, 1938; Passedoit Gallery, NYC, 1938, 42; Pittsfield/Berkshire, 1939; Mortimer Brandt, NYC, 1945; The Willard Gallery, 1941; J. Seligmann and Co. (three-man), 1939; Durand-Ruel Gallery, NYC, 1947, 48; The Pinacotheca, NYC, 1950. Retrospective: Rose Fried Gallery. Group: American Abstract Artists Annuals, 1938–48; New York World's Fair, 1939; Salon des Surindependants, Paris, 1938; Arts Club of Chicago, 1940; SFMA, 1940; MOMA, 1942; Federation of Modern Painters and Sculptors, 1943; PMA, 1945; Corcoran, 1947. Collections: Black Mountain College; MMA; MOMA; PMA; Phillips; Pittsfield/Berkshire; SFMA; SRGM. Bibliography: American Abstract Artists, ed.; Baur 7; Bazin; Blesh 1; Frost; **Gallatin 1, 2, 3, 4, 5, 6, 7, 8;** McCurdy, ed.; Morris; Ritchie 1.

GANSO, EMIL. b. April 14, 1895, Halberstadt, Germany; **d.** April 18, 1941, Iowa City, Iowa. To USA 1912. Studied: NAD. Taught: Lawrence College, 1940; State U. of Iowa, 1941. Awards: Guggenheim Foundation Fellowship, 1933. One-man Exhibitions: Washington Irving Gallery, NYC, 1960; Weyhe Gallery, 1926,

27, 28, 30, 31, 32, 33, 34, 35, 36, 44, 46. **Retro-**
spective: WMAA, 1941; Brooklyn Museum,
1944. **Group:** WMAA; Salons of America, NYC;
Brooklyn Museum; Chicago/AI; Cleve-
land/MA; PAFA; Corcoran; NAD. **Collec-**
tions: Boston/MFA; Dartmouth College;
Denver/AM; MMA; Rochester/Memorial;
WMAA. **Bibliography:** American Artists
Group Inc. 1, 3; Cahill and Barr, eds.; Cheney,
M. C.; Hall; *Index of 20th Century Artists;*
Jewell 3; Mellquist; Pearson 1; Reese; Ringel,
ed.; Zigrosser 1.

GATCH, LEE. b. September 10, 1902, Baltimore, Md. **Studied:** Maryland Institute, 1924;
Academie Moderne, Paris, 1924, with Andre
Lhote, Moise Kisling. Traveled France, Italy.
Commissions (murals): US Post Offices, Mullins,
S.C., and Elizabethtown, Pa. **Awards:** Chi-
cago/AI, Watson F. Blair Prize, 1957; Corcoran, 1960. **Address:** Lambertville, N.J. **Dealer:**
Staempfli Gallery. **One-man Exhibitions:**
(first) J. B. Neumann's New Art Circle, NYC,
1927, also 1932, 37, 46, 49; The Willard Gal-
lery, 1943; Grace Borgenicht Gallery Inc., 1954;
Phillips, 1954, 56, 60; World House Galleries,
1958; Staempfli Gallery, 1963. **Retrospective:**
WMAA, 1960. **Group:** Santa Barbara/MA,
1952; XXV & XXVIII Venice Biennials, 1950,
56; Detroit/Institute, 1959; U. of Illinois, 1961.
Collections: Andover/Phillips; Atlanta U.;
Baltimore/MA; Boston/MFA; Detroit/Insti-
tute; Hartford/Wadsworth; U. of Illinois; Los
Angeles/County MA; MMA; MOMA; U. of
Nebraska; PAFA; PMA; Phillips; St. Louis/City;
Utica; WMAA; Washington U. **Bibliography:**
Baur 5; Blesh 1; Eliot; Frost; Goodrich and
Baur 1; Hess, T. B.; Janis and Blesh 1; Janis, S.;
McCurdy, ed.; Nordness, ed.; Pousette-Dart,
ed.; Richardson.

GECHTOFF, SONIA. b. September 25, 1926,
Philadelphia, Pa. **Studied:** Philadelphia Mu-
seum School, BFA. **Taught:** California School
of Fine Arts, 1957–58; NYU, 1961– . **Awards:**
SFMA, p.p.; Santa Barbara/MA, p.p.; Tama-
rind Fellowship, 1963. **m.** James Kelly. **Ad-**
dress: 361 Canal Street, NYC. **Dealer:** East
Hampton Gallery. **One-man Exhibitions:** (first)
Dubin Gallery, Philadelphia, 1949; Lucien
Labaudt Gallery, 1952, 53; Gallery Six, San
Francisco, 1955; de Young, 1957; Ferus Gallery,
1957, 59; Poindexter Gallery, 1959, 60; East

Hampton Gallery, 1963. **Group:** SFMA Annuals, 1952–58; SRGM, Younger American Painters, 1954; Brussels World's Fair, 1958; Carnegie,
1958; I Paris Biennial, 1959; Walker, 60 American Painters, 1960; VI Sao Paulo Biennial, 1961;
WMAA Annual, 1959; WMAA, Young America,
1960; MOMA, Abstract American Drawings
and Watercolors, circ. Latin America, 1961–63.
Collections: UCLA; Oakland/AM; SFMA;
San Francisco Art Association; The Singer Company Inc.; Woodward Foundation.

GELB, JAN. b. July 18, 1906, NYC. **Studied:**
Yale U., 1928; Atelier Sigrid Skou, NYC and
Brittany, 1928–29; ASL occasionally, 1930–34;
NAD. **Taught:** Elementary schools, 1928-early
1960's. **Member:** SAGA (Vice President); Mac-
Dowell Colony. **Awards:** The Print Club,
Philadelphia, p.p., 1958; Boston Arts Festival,
Second Prize. **m.** Boris Margo. **Address:** 749
West End Avenue, NYC. **Dealer:** Ruth White
Gallery. **One-man Exhibitions:** (first) West
Haven (Conn.) Public Library, 1929 or 1930;
Delphic Studios, NYC, 1940; Weyhe Gallery,
1948, 50; Research Studio, Maitland, Fla., 1948,
50; Ganso Gallery, NYC, 1954; Artists' Gallery,
Provincetown, 1955, 56; New Brunswick (N.J.)
Art Center, 1957; Ruth White Gallery, 1957, 59,
61, 62, 64; Esther Robles Gallery, 1958; Galerie
A. G., Paris, 1960; Piccadilly Gallery, London,
1960; Shore Galleries, Provincetown, 1961.
Retrospective: Smithsonian, 1963. **Group:**
WMAA Annuals; PAFA; Brooklyn Museum,
Print Biennials; MMA, American Watercolors,
Drawings and Prints, 1952; Boston Arts Festival;
NAD; Oakland/AM; SAGA; Brooklyn Museum,
14 Painter Printmakers, 1955; A.F.A. and USIA
circ. exhibitions; WMAA, Nature in Abstraction,
1958. **Collections:** Abbot Academy; Balti-
more/MA; U. of Delaware; Howard U.; Library
of Congress; MMA; MOMA; PMA; WMAA.
Bibliography: Baur 5.

GEORGE, THOMAS. b. July 1, 1918, NYC.
Studied: Dartmouth College, 1940, BA; ASL;
Academie de la Grande Chaumiere; Academy
of Fine Arts, Florence, Italy. US Navy, 1942–46.
Awards: Brooklyn Museum, p.p., 1955; Rocke-
feller Foundation Grant, 1957; Ford Founda-
tion, p.p., 1962, 63. **Address:** Old Mill Road,
Valley Cottage, N.Y. **Dealers:** Betty Parsons
Gallery; The Reid Gallery. **One-man Exhibi-**
tions: Ferargil Galleries, NYC, 1951, 53; Kor-

man Gallery, NYC, 1954; Dartmouth College, 1956; The Contemporaries, 1956; Bridgestone Museum, 1957; Diamaru, Osaka, 1957; Betty Parsons Section Eleven (Gallery), NYC, 1959; The Reid Gallery. GROUP: MOMA, Recent Drawings USA, 1956; WMAA Annuals, 1960, 61, 62; Carnegie, 1958, 61; PAFA, 1962; Corcoran, 1963; International Biennial Exhibition of Paintings, Tokyo; Lincoln, Mass./De Cordova, 1963; San Antonio/McNay, 1964. COLLECTIONS: Bridgestone Museum; Brooklyn Museum; Buffalo/Albright; Dartmouth College; Library of Congress; Riverside Museum; Tate; WGMA; WMAA.

GEORGES, PAUL. b. 1923, Portland, Ore. STUDIED: U. of Oregon; Hofmann School; Atelier Fernand Leger in Paris, 1949–52. Traveled France, USA. TAUGHT: U. of Colorado, 1960; Dartmouth College, 1961; Yale U. AWARDS: Longview Foundation Grant; Hallmark International Competition, P.P., 1961; PAFA, Carol H. Beck Gold Medal, 1964. ADDRESS: 654 Broadway, NYC. DEALER: Allan Frumkin Gallery, NYC and Chicago. ONE-MAN EXHIBITIONS: Reed College, 1948, 56, 61; Tibor de Nagy Gallery, 1955, 57; Great Jones Gallery, NYC, 1960, 61; Allan Frumkin Gallery, NYC and Chicago, 1962; Allan Frumkin Gallery, NYC, 1964; The Zabriskie Gallery, 1959. GROUP: Salon du Mai, Paris, 1949; PAFA, 1952, 64; Corcoran, 1962; WMAA, 1962, 63; MOMA; U. of Colorado; Chicago/AI, 1962; The Kootz Gallery, New Talent, 1952; U. of Kentucky, Drawings, 1963; Boston U., 1964; MOMA, Hans Hofmann and His Students, circ., 1963–64; Silvermine Guild, 1964; Youngstown/Butler, 1964. COLLECTIONS: 57th Madison Corp.; Hallmark Collection; MIT; U. of Massachusetts; NYU; Newark Museum; Reed College.

GIAMBRUNI, TIO. b. August 30, 1925, San Francisco, Calif. STUDIED: U. of California, Berkeley, with Glenn Wessels, John Haley, Jacques Schnier, Richard O'Hanlon, BA, MA. US Army. TAUGHT: Modesto (Calif.) High School, 1951–52; Liberty High School, 1953–56; Miramonte (Calif.) High School, 1956–59; California College of Arts and Crafts, 1959–60; U. of California, Davis, 1960– . COMMISSIONS: Golden Gateway Redevelopment Project, San Francisco, to be completed 1966. AWARDS: SFMA, Patrons of Music and Art Award, 1959.

ADDRESS: 1718 Jaynes Street, Berkeley, Calif. ONE-MAN EXHIBITIONS: (first) Nevada Art Gallery, Reno, 1958; RAC, 1960; Barrios Art Gallery, Sacramento, 1963; Mills College, 1963; Berkeley Gallery, Berkeley, 1963, 64. GROUP: SFMA, Tradition and Invention, 1962; New School for Social Research, The Artist's Reality, 1964; Museum of Contemporary Crafts, Creative Casting, 1963; New Orleans/Delgado, Bay Area Artists, 1963; SFMA, Molten Image— Seven Sculptors, 1962; Stanford U., Some Points for View for '62, 1962; Santa Barbara/MA, 1959; SFMA Annuals since 1951.

GIBRAN, KAHLIL. b. November 29, 1922, Boston, Mass. STUDIED: Boston Museum School, 1940–43, with Karl Zerbe. Changed from painting to sculpture, 1953–54. AWARDS: Guggenheim Foundation Fellowship, 1959, 60; NIAL Award, 1961; PAFA, George D. Widener Memorial Gold Medal, 1958. ADDRESS: 160 West Canton Street, Boston, Mass. ONE-MAN EXHIBITIONS: (first) Stuart Gallery, Boston, 1944; Mortimer Levitt Gallery, NYC; Margaret Brown Gallery, Boston; U. of Kansas; Lee Nordness Gallery, NYC, 1962 (sculpture). GROUP: WMAA Annual, 1960; Boston Arts Festival; Carnegie; Dallas/MFA; NAD; Chicago/AI; ICA, Boston. COLLECTIONS: Norfolk; PAFA; Provincetown/Chrysler. BIBLIOGRAPHY: Pousette-Dart, ed.

GIKOW, RUTH. b. 1914, Russia. STUDIED: Cooper Union, 1932–35, with John Steuart Curry, Raphael Soyer. Traveled Europe, Mexico. TAUGHT: New School for Social Research. Illustrated: *Crime and Punishment* (World Publishing Co.) and *History of the Jews in America* (Jewish Theological Seminary). Subject of a film demonstrating the cutting and printing of linoleum blocks, produced by Walter O. Gutjohn, 1943. MEMBER: Artists Equity. FEDERAL A.P.: Mural painter and graphic artist; mural for Bronx County Hospital, 1940. COMMISSIONS (murals): New York World's Fair, 1939; Rockefeller Center, 1943. AWARDS: NIAL Grant, 1961. m. Jack Levine. ADDRESS: 231 West 11 Street, NYC. ONE-MAN EXHIBITIONS: (first) National Serigraph Society, 1943, also 1947; Weyhe Gallery, 1946; Grand Central Moderns, 1948, 50; Philadelphia Art Alliance, 1949; Ganso Gallery, NYC, 1952, 53, 54; Rehn Galleries, 1956, 57, 59; Lee Nordness Gallery, NYC, 1961,

63. **GROUP:** Carnegie; Corcoran; Utica; Youngstown/Butler; MMA; MOMA; U. of Nebraska; PAFA; Springfield, Mass./MFA; WMAA; State U. of Iowa; SFMA; Toledo/MA; San Diego. **COLLECTIONS:** Brandeis U.; Colby College; S. C. Johnson & Son, Inc.; MMA; MOMA; NIAL; NYU; PMA; Portland, Me./MA; Smithsonian; Springfield, Mass./MFA; Syracuse/Everson; Terre Haute/Swope; WMAA. **BIBLIOGRAPHY:** Bethers; Nordness, ed.

GIOBBI, EDWARD. b. 1926, Waterbury, Conn. US Army, 1944–46. **STUDIED:** Whitney School of Art, 1946, 47; Vesper George School of Art, 1947–50; ASL, 1950–51; Academy of Fine Arts, Florence, Italy, 1951–54, 1955–56. Traveled Europe. **TAUGHT:** Memphis Academy of Arts, 1960–61 (Artist-in-Residence). **AWARDS:** Yaddo Fellowship, 1957; Joe and Emily Lowe Foundation Award, 1951, and Special Grant, 1952. **ADDRESS:** 161 Croton Lake Road, Katonah, N.Y. **DEALERS:** The Contemporaries; Tirca Karlis Gallery; The New Art Centre. **ONE-MAN EXHIBITIONS:** (first) Ward Eggleston Gallery, NYC, 1952; Artists' Gallery, NYC, 1956; John Heller Gallery, NYC, 1957, 58; The Contemporaries, 1960, 61, 63; Memphis Academy, 1962; Memphis/Brooks, 1961; Katonah (N.Y.) Art Gallery, 1963; The New Art Centre, 1964. **GROUP:** Galerie An Der Reuss, Lucerne (two-man), 1953; Nexus Gallery, Boston (two-man), 1956; WMAA, Young America, 1961; WMAA, Forty Artists Under Forty, circ., 1962; WMAA Annuals, 1957, 61; MOMA, Recent Drawings USA, 1956; MOMA, Recent Painting USA: The Figure, circ., 1962–63; PAFA, 1961. **COLLECTIONS:** Baltimore/MA; Chicago/AI; Detroit/Institute; Florence, Italy; Memphis/Brooks; U. of Michigan; San Antonio/McNay; Syracuse U.; Tate; WMAA.

GIRONA, JULIO. b. December 29, 1914, Manzanillo, Cuba. **STUDIED:** Escuela San Alejandro, Havana, 1930–34; Academie Ranson, Paris, 1935–36; ASL, 1950–56, with Morris Kantor. Traveled Europe extensively, Mexico. To USA 1941. **TAUGHT:** Werkkunstschule, Krefeld, Germany, 1963–64. **COMMISSIONS:** Colegio Medicos,

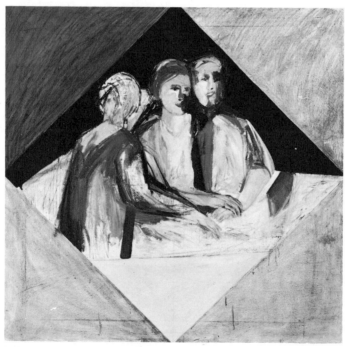

Edward Giobbi   *The Family. 1962*

Havana (5 murals). **Awards:** Newark Museum, First Prize; Havana/Nacional. **Address:** 53 Genesee Avenue, Teaneck, N.J. **Dealer:** The Bertha Schaefer Gallery. **One-man Exhibitions:** (first) Colegio de Arquitectos, Havana, 1934; Havana/Nacional, 1947, 54; Artists' Gallery, NYC, 1953; The Bertha Schaefer Gallery, 1956, 59, 61, 63; Galerie Gunar, Dusseldorf, 1958; Recklinghausen, 1959; Galerie Seide, Hannover, 1960; Werkkunstschule, Krefeld, Germany, 1963. **Group:** Venice Biennial; Baltimore/MA, 1956, 59, 60; Chicago/AI, 1957; Minneapolis/Institute, American Painting, 1945–57, 1957; Ball State Teachers College, 1958, 60; MOMA, 1958, 60; Brooklyn Museum, 1959; U. of Nebraska, 1958, 59; Buffalo/Albright, 1959, 60; Argentina/Nacional; MMA; Houston/MFA; SFMA; Newark Museum; Denver/AM. **Collections:** Argentina/Nacional; Havana/Nacional; Newark Museum; Recklinghausen; Union Carbide Corp. **Bibliography:** Janis and Blesh 1.

GLACKENS, WILLIAM. b. March 13, 1870, Philadelphia, Pa.; **d.** May 22, 1938, Westport, Conn. Studied: Central High School, Philadelphia, BA; PAFA. Traveled France, Spain, Canada. Newspaper illustrator for many years. **Member:** Society of Independent Artists, NYC (First President, 1916–17); The Eight; NAD, 1937 (Associate, 1896); NIAL. **Awards:** Buffalo/Albright, Gold Medal, 1901; St. Louis Exposition, 1904, Silver and Bronze Medals; Carnegie, Hon. Men., 1905; Panama-Pacific Exposition, San Francisco, 1915, Bronze Medal; PAFA, Joseph E. Temple Gold Medal, 1924; Carnegie, Second Prize, 1929; PAFA, Carol H. Beck Gold Medal, 1933; PAFA, Jennie Sesnan Gold Medal, 1936; Paris World's Fair, 1937, Grand Prix; PAFA, J. Henry Schiedt Memorial Prize, 1938. **One-man Exhibitions:** (first) New Arts Club, NYC; Kraushaar Galleries, 1925, 28, 35, 42, 57; Andover/Phillips, 1936; Academy of Fine Arts, Berlin, 1910; Louisville/Speed, 1939; 10 West Ninth Street, NYC, Memorial Exhibition, annually, 1939–49. **Retrospective:** WMAA, 1938; Carnegie, 1939; Kraushaar Galleries, 1949; Dartmouth College, 1960. **Group:** Paris Salon, 1895, 1900; Macbeth Gallery, NYC, The Eight, 1908; Independents, NYC, 1910; The Armory Show, 1913; Brooklyn Museum, The Eight, 1943; WMAA, New York Realists, 1937; PMA, Artists of the Philadelphia Press,

1945; Renaissance Society, Chicago, 1955; Syracuse/Everson, The Eight, 1958. **Collections:** Andover/Phillips; Barnes Foundation; Boston/MFA; Buffalo/Albright; Chicago/AI; Columbus; Detroit/Institute; MMA; U. of Nebraska; Newark Museum; PMA; Sweet Briar College; WMAA. **Bibliography:** Barnes; Bazin; Biddle 3; Born; Bulliet 1; Canaday; Cheney, M. C.; **Du Bois 5, 6;** Gallatin 2; **Glackens;** Hall; Hartmann; Huyghe; *Index of 20th Century Artists;* Jackman; Kent, N.; McCourbrey; McCurdy, ed.; Neuhaus; Pach 1; Perlman; Phillips 2; Poore; Ringel, ed.; Sachs; **Watson, F.**

GLARNER, FRITZ. b. July 20, 1899, Zurich, Switzerland. **Studied:** Academy of Fine Arts, Naples. To USA 1936. **Commissions:** Time & Life Building lobby, NYC, 1960 (mural). **Awards:** Corcoran, 1957. **Address:** R.D. #2, Huntington, N.Y. **One-man Exhibitions:** Galerie Povolotzki, Paris, 1930; Civic Club, NYC, 1931; The Kootz Gallery, 1945; Rose Fried Gallery, 1949, 51; Galerie Louis Carre, Paris, 1952, 55. **Group:** Buffalo/Albright, 1931; American Abstract Artists, 1938–44; Chicago/AI, 1947, 58; Toronto, 1949; VMFA, 1950, 58; California Palace, 1950; WMAA, 1950, 51, 53, 54, 55; MOMA, 1951, 52, 54, 55; Sao Paulo, 1951; Brooklyn Museum, 1951; U. of Illinois, 1952; U. of Minnesota, 1951; U. of Nebraska, 1955; Carnegie, 1952, 58; Corcoran, 1955, 57; Documenta I, Kassel, 1955; SRGM, 1954; Tokyo/Modern, 1953; Zurich, 1956; Musee Neuchatel, 1957; Kunstverein, Winterthur, 1958; Congresshalle, Berlin, 1958. **Collections:** Baltimore/MA; Boston/MFA; Brandeis U.; MOMA; Phillips; WMAA; Walker; Yale U.; Zurich. **Bibliography:** Baur 7; Biddle 3; Blesh 1; Haftman; Hess, T. B.; Janis, S.; McCurdy, ed.; Neumeyer; Pousette-Dart, ed.; Read 2; Ritchie 1; Seuphor 1; "What Abstract Art Means to Me."

GLASCO, JOSEPH. b. January 19, 1925, Paul's Valley, Okla. **Studied:** U. of Texas, 1941–43; Jepson Art Institute, Los Angeles; Art Center School, Los Angeles, 1946–48; privately with Rico Lebrun, 1946–48; Escuela de Bellas Artes, San Miguel de Allende, Mexico, 1948; ASL, 1949. US Army Air Force, 1943–45, Infantry, 1945–46. Traveled Mexico, Europe, Africa. **Commissions:** Amarillo (Tex.) Air Field (mural). **Address:** c/o Dealer. **Dealer:** Catherine

Viviano Gallery. ONE-MAN EXHIBITIONS: (first) Perls Galleries, 1950; Catherine Viviano Gallery, 1951, 52, 53, 54, 56, 58, 61, 63; Arts Club of Chicago, 1954, 57. GROUP: MOMA, New Talent; MMA; WMAA; Corcoran; SRGM; Brooklyn Museum; Chicago/AI; Dallas/MFA; Detroit/Institute; Los Angeles/County MA; U. of Illinois; U. of Nebraska; Carnegie, 1958; PAFA. COLLECTIONS: Brooklyn Museum; Buffalo/Albright; MMA; MOMA; Newark Museum; Princeton U.; WMAA. BIBLIOGRAPHY: Goodrich and Baur 1; Mendelowitz; Rodman 1; Tapie 1.

GOLDBERG, MICHAEL. b. 1924, NYC. STUDIED: ASL, 1938–42, 1946, with Jose de Creeft; City College of New York, 1940–42, 1946–47; Hofmann School, 1941–42, 1948–50. US Army, 1942–46. TAUGHT: U. of California, 1961–62. ADDRESS: c/o Dealer. DEALER: Martha Jackson Gallery. ONE-MAN EXHIBITIONS: (first) Tibor de Nagy Gallery, 1953; Poindexter Gallery, 1956, 58; Martha Jackson Gallery, 1960, 64; Paul Kantor Gallery, 1960; B. C. Holland Gallery, 1961; Galerie Anderson-Mayer, 1963; Holland-Goldowsky Gallery, Chicago (two-man), 1960; Bob Keene, 1963. GROUP: Ninth Street Exhibition, NYC, 1951; The Stable Gallery Annuals, 1952, 53, 54, 55, 56, 57; Sidney Janis Gallery, Four Younger Americans, 1956; Carnegie, 1958; WMAA Annual, 1958; Gutai 9, Osaka, 1958; Turin Art Festival, 1959; V Sao Paulo Biennial, 1959; Documenta II, Kassel, 1959; Walker, 60 American Painters, 1960; Columbus, Contemporary American Painting, 1960; MOMA, Hans Hofmann and His Students, circ., 1963–64; Musee Cantonal des Beaux-Arts, Lausanne, I Salon International de Galeries Pilotes, 1963. COLLECTIONS: Baltimore/MA; Buffalo/Albright; Cornell U.; Lincoln, Mass./De Cordova; Provincetown/Chrysler; Walker. BIBLIOGRAPHY: Janis and Blesh 1.

GOLDIN, LEON. b. January 16, 1923, Chicago, Ill. STUDIED: State U. of Iowa, with Mauricio Lasansky, 1948, BFA, 1950, MFA; Chicago Art Institute School, with Robert Von Neuman. Traveled Europe extensively; resided Paris, 1952–53, Rome, 1955–58. TAUGHT: Philadelphia Museum School, 1960–62; Cooper Union, 1961–64; Queens College; Columbia U.; California College of Arts and Crafts, 1950–52, 1954–55. AWARDS: L. C. Tiffany Grant, 1951; Fulbright Fellowship (France), 1952; Prix de Rome, 1955, renewed 1956–57; Guggenheim Foundation Fellowship, 1959; Ford Foundation, P.P., 1960; SFMA, H. S. Crocker Co. Award, 1952; and many print awards. ADDRESS: 313 East Sixth Street, NYC. DEALER: Kraushaar Galleries. ONE-MAN EXHIBITIONS: (first) Oakland/AM, 1955; Felix Landau Gallery, 1956, 57, 59; Galleria L'Attico, Rome, 1958; Kraushaar Galleries, 1960, 64. GROUP: MMA, American Paintings Today, 1950; MOMA, Contemporary American Painting, 1953; MOMA, Recent Drawings USA, 1956; Corcoran, 1963; Carnegie, 1964; PAFA, 1951, 60, 61, 62, 63, 64; Chicago/AI Annuals, 1946, 48; SFMA Annuals, 1948, 51, 52, 53, 54; Los Angeles/County MA, 1949, 50; Santa Barbara/MA, 1955. COLLECTIONS: Andover/Phillips; Arts Council of Great Britain; Brooklyn Museum; Cincinnati/AM; S. C. Johnson & Son, Inc.; Los Angeles/County MA; Morgan State College; Oakland/AM; PAFA; RAC; St. Louis/City; Santa Barbara/MA; U. of Southern California; Worcester/AM. BIBLIOGRAPHY: Nordness, ed.

GOLUB, LEON. b. January 23, 1922, Chicago, Ill. Studied: The U. of Chicago, 1942, BA; Chicago Art Institute School, with Paul Wieghardt, Kathleen Blackshear, Robert Lifuendahl, 1949, BFA, 1950, MFA. US Army, 1942–46. Traveled Europe; resided Paris, 1959–64, Italy, 1956–57. TAUGHT: Indiana U., 1957–59; Wright Junior College; Northwestern U.; Illinois Institute of Technology, 1955–56. AWARDS: Ford Foundation Grant, 1960; Chicago/AI, Watson F. Blair Prize; II Inter-American Paintings and Prints Biennial, Mexico City, 1960, Hon. Men.; Chicago/AI, Florsheim Memorial Prize, 1954. ADDRESS: 299 East 10 Street, NYC. DEALERS: Allan Frumkin Gallery, NYC and Chicago; Felix Landau Gallery; Iris Clert; Hanover Gallery. ONE-MAN EXHIBITIONS: (first) Contemporary Gallery, Chicago, 1950; Purdue U., 1951; Wittenborn Gallery, NYC, 1952, 57; Kerrigan-Hendricks Gallery, Chicago, 1954; Artists' Gallery, NYC, 1954; Feigl Gallery, NYC, 1955, 56; Chicago Public Library, 1956; Allan Frumkin Gallery, Chicago, 1955, 60, 64; Allan Frumkin Gallery, NYC, 1959, 61, 63; Pomona College, 1956; Pasadena/AM, 1956; Indiana U., 1958; ICA, London, 1957; Gallery A, Melbourne, 1963; American Cultural Center, Paris, 1960; Iris Clert, 1962; Hanover Gallery, 1962.

RETROSPECTIVE: Temple U., 1964. GROUP:
Documenta II, Kassel, 1959; Ghent, Figuration
d'Aujourd'hui, 1964; Premio Marzotto; Carnegie, 1955, 64; Mythologiques Quitidiennes,
Paris, 1964; Chicago/AI, Exhibition Momentum, 1948–58; SRGM, Younger American Painters, 1954; Chicago/AI, 1954, 62; U. of Illinois,
1957, 61, 63; MOMA, New Images of Man,
1959; Sao Paulo, 1962; MOMA, Recent Painting
USA: The Figure, circ., 1962–63; Corcoran,
1962; Salon des Realites Nouvelles, Paris, 1962;
Art:USA:Now, circ., 1962–   ; Tate, Dunn International, 1964; SFMA, Directions—Painting
U.S.A., 1963; PAFA, 1964; Smithsonian, Graphics, circ. USA, 1963. COLLECTIONS: Chase Manhattan Bank; Chicago/AI; S. C. Johnson & Son,
Inc.; Kansas City/Nelson; La Jolla; MOMA;
Nashville; Tel Aviv. BIBLIOGRAPHY: Nordness, ed.

GONZALEZ, XAVIER. b. February 15, 1898,
Almeria, Spain. US citizen 1930. TAUGHT:
H. Sophie Newcomb Memorial College; Brook-
lyn Museum School; Western Reserve U.,
1953–54; Summer School of Art, Wellfleet,
Mass. AWARDS: AAAL Grant; Guggenheim
Foundation Fellowship, 1947; PAFA, Dawson
Memorial Medal, 1946; Audubon Artists, Gold
Medal of Honor. ADDRESS: 222 Central Park
South, NYC. ONE-MAN EXHIBITIONS: Grand
Central Moderns, 1951, 52, 53; Widdifield Gal-
lery, NYC, 1958; Philadelphia Art Alliance,
1949; Arts and Crafts Club, New Orleans, 1948;
Joseph Luyber Galleries, NYC, 1946, 47; Nor-
lyst Gallery, NYC; The Milch Gallery, 1960, 63;
Shore Studio, Boston; The Howard Wise Gal-
lery, Cleveland, 1958. GROUP: PAFA; Cor-
coran; U. of Nebraska; Carnegie; Brooklyn
Museum; WMAA; Indianapolis/Herron. COL-
LECTIONS: Wellesley College. BIBLIOGRAPHY:
Biddle 3; Cheney, M. C.; Pearson 2; Pousette-
Dart, ed.

GOODMAN, SIDNEY. b. January 19, 1936,
Philadelphia, Pa. STUDIED: Philadelphia Mu-
seum School, 1958, with Jacob Landau, Larry
Day, Morris Berd. US Army, 1958–59. Traveled
Europe. TAUGHT: Philadelphia Museum School.
AWARDS: PAFA, First Watercolor Prize, 1961;
Guggenheim Foundation Fellowship, 1963;
Ford Foundation, P.P.; Yale-Norfolk Art Sum-
mer School Fellowship. ADDRESS: High School
Road and Harrison Avenue, Elkins Park, Pa.

DEALER: Terry Dintenfass, Inc. ONE-MAN EXHI-
BITIONS: (first) The Print Club, Philadelphia,
1958, also 1963; Terry Dintenfass, Inc., 1961, 63,
64. GROUP: Corcoran, 1963; MOMA, 1962;
WMAA Annuals, 1962, 63, 64; Brooklyn Museum, 1963; PAFA, 1960, 61, 62, 63, 64; NAD,
1962; WMAA, Forty Artists Under Forty, circ.,
1962; MOMA, Recent Painting USA: The Figure, circ., 1962–63. COLLECTIONS: Library of
Congress; MOMA; PMA; WMAA.

GOODNOUGH, ROBERT. b. October 23,
1917, Cortland, N.Y. STUDIED: Syracuse U.,

Robert Goodnough
Standing Man with Hat. 1964

BFA; NYU, MA; New School for Social Research; Hofmann School; Ozenfant School of Art, NYC. TAUGHT: Cornell U.; NYU; Fieldston School, NYC. Critic for *Art News* Magazine, 1950–57. Secretary, *Documents of Modern Art* (edited by Robert Motherwell), 1951. AWARDS: Syracuse U., Hiram Gee Fellowship; Chicago/AI, Ada S. Garrett Prize, 1962; Ford Foundation, P.P., 1962. ADDRESS: 237 West Fourth Street, NYC. DEALER: Tibor de Nagy Gallery. ONE-MAN EXHIBITIONS: (first) Tibor de Nagy Gallery, 1952, and annually thereafter; RISD, 1956; Nova Gallery, Boston, 1961; Jefferson Place Gallery, 1960; Ellison Gallery, Fort Worth, 1960; Dwan Gallery, 1959, 60, 61, 62; U. of Minnesota; U. of Notre Dame, 1964; Arts Club of Chicago, 1964. GROUP: The Kootz Gallery, New Talent, 1950; Sidney Janis Gallery, Four Younger Americans, 1956; MOMA; WMAA; Yale U.; Carnegie; Chicago/AI; NIAL, 1964. COLLECTIONS: Baltimore/MA; Birmingham, Ala./MA; Buffalo/Albright; Chase Manhattan Bank; Chicago/AI; Hartford/Wadsworth; MOMA; NYU; Newark Museum; RISD; Raleigh/NCMA; SRGM; WMAA. BIBLIOGRAPHY: Baur 5; Blesh 1; Friedman, ed.; Goodrich and Baur 1; **Guest and Friedman;** Janis and Blesh 1; Nordness, ed.; Seitz 2.

GORCHOV, RON. b. April 5, 1930, Chicago, Ill. STUDIED: U. of Mississippi; Roosevelt College; Chicago Art Institute School; U. of Illinois. Traveled USA, Europe. TAUGHT: Hunter College, 1962– . Designed stage sets for Theatre Club of New York production of Lorca's *Shoemaker's Prodigious Wife*, 1957. AWARDS: Ingram Merrill Foundation Grant, 1959; National Arts Club Annual, NYC, Hon. Men., 1959. ADDRESS: 74 Grand Street, NYC. DEALER: Tibor de Nagy Gallery. ONE-MAN EXHIBITIONS: Tibor de Nagy Gallery, 1960, 63. GROUP: The Stable Gallery, Invitational, 1958; National Arts Club Annual, NYC, 1959; WMAA, Young America, 1960; Carnegie, 1961; Brooklyn Museum, 1962. COLLECTIONS: Glen Alden Corp.; Hartford/Wadsworth.

GORDIN, SIDNEY. b. October 24, 1918, Cheliabinsk, Russia. STUDIED: Cooper Union, 1937–41, with Morris Kantor, William Harrison, Leo Katz. TAUGHT: Pratt Institute, 1953–58; Sarah Lawrence College, 1957–58; Brooklyn College, 1955–58; New School for Social Research, 1956–58; U. of California, Berkeley, 1958– . COMMISSIONS (sculpture): Temple Israel, Tulsa, 1959; Envoy Towers, NYC, 1960. ADDRESS: 725 Greenwich Street, San Francisco, Calif. DEALER: Grace Borgenicht Gallery Inc. ONE-MAN EXHIBITIONS: (first) Grace Borgenicht Gallery Inc., 1953, also 1955, 58, 60, 61; Dilexi Gallery, San Francisco, 1959, 63; Los Angeles/County MA, 1963; Bennington College, 1951; Peter Cooper Gallery, NYC, 1951; de Young, 1962; New School for Social Research, 1957. GROUP: MMA, 1951; WMAA Annuals, 1952–57; MOMA; Chicago/AI; PAFA, 1954, 55; Brooklyn Museum; Newark Museum; SFMA; Oakland/AM; Tulsa/Philbrook, 1960. COLLECTIONS: Chicago/AI; Newark Museum; Provincetown/Chrysler; Southern Illinois U.; WMAA. BIBLIOGRAPHY: Goodrich and Baur 1; Mendelowitz; Seuphor 3.

GORKY, ARSHILE (Vosdanig Manoog Adoian). b. 1905, Khorkom Vari Haiyotz Dzor, Armenia; **d.** July 21, 1948, Sherman, Conn. To USA 1920. STUDIED: Polytechnic Institute, Tiflis, 1916–18; RISD; Providence (R.I.) Technical High School; New School of Design, Boston, 1923; NAD, 1925. TAUGHT: New School of Design, Boston, 1924; Grand Central School, NYC, 1925–31. FEDERAL A.P.: Newark (N.J.) Airport, 1935–38 (mural). COMMISSIONS: Aviation Building, New York World's Fair, 1939 (mural). Fire destroyed 27 paintings in his studio, January, 1946. ONE-MAN EXHIBITIONS: (first) Guild Art Gallery, NYC, 1932, also 1935, 36; Mellon Galleries, Philadelphia, 1934; Boyer Gallery, Philadelphia, 1935; Boyer Gallery, NYC, 1938; Julien Levy Galleries, NYC, 1945, 46, 47, 1948 (two-man, with Howard Warshaw); The Kootz Gallery, 1942, 50, 51; WMAA, Memorial Exhibition, 1951; Princeton U., 1952; Paul Kantor Gallery, 1952; Sidney Price Gallery, NYC, 1952, 55, 57. RETROSPECTIVE: SFMA, 1941; MOMA, 1963. GROUP: WMAA Annuals; MOMA, Fourteen Americans, circ., 1946; MOMA, 46 Painters and Sculptors Under 35 Years of Age, 1930; WMAA, Abstract Painting in America, 1935; Galerie Maeght, 6 Surrealists in 1947, 1947; XXIV & XXV Venice Biennials, 1948, 50; Galerie de France, 1952; MOMA, The New American Painting, circ. Europe, 1958–59. COLLECTIONS: U. of Arizona; Buffalo/Albright; MMA; MOMA; Oberlin College; SFMA; Utica; WMAA; Washington U. BIBLIOGRAPHY: Barr 3;

Arshile Gorky   *Housatonic Falls. 1942/43*

Baur 5, 7; Blesh 1; Breton 2, 3; Calas; Cheney, M. C.; Eliot; Flanagan; Goodrich and Baur 1; Greenberg 1; Haftman; Hess, T. B.; Hunter 1, 5; Janis, S.; Langui; McCourbrey; McCurdy, ed.; Miller, ed. 2; Myers 2; Neumeyer; Newmeyer; Passloff; Ponente; Pousette-Dart, ed.; Ragon 1; Read 2; Richardson; Ritchie 1; Rodman 2; **Rosenberg; Schwabacher;** Seitz 1; Seuphor 1; Soby 6; Waldberg 3.

GOTO, JOSEPH. b. January 7, 1920, Hilo, Hawaii. STUDIED: Chicago Art Institute School; Roosevelt U. AWARDS: Chicago/AI, P.P., 1957; Graham Foundation Fellowship, 1957; John Hay Whitney Fellowship; Chicago/AI, Watson F. Blair Prize; Chicago/AI, The Mr. & Mrs. Frank G. Logan Prize; Chicago/AI, Pauline Palmer Prize. ADDRESS: 17 Sixth Street, Providence, R.I. DEALER: Stephen Radich Gallery. ONE-MAN EXHIBITIONS: Allan Frumkin Gallery,

NYC and Chicago, 1962; Stephen Radich Gallery, 1964. **GROUP:** Chicago/AI; Carnegie; U. of Illinois; Louisville/Speed; VMFA, 1958; WMAA; Chicago/AI, Exhibition Momentum; Denver/AM; Houston/MFA, 1957. **COLLEC-TIONS:** Chicago/AI; Indiana U.; MOMA; U. of Michigan; Union Carbide Corp.

GOTTLIEB, ADOLPH. b. March 14, 1903, NYC. STUDIED: ASL, 1919, with John Sloan, Robert Henri; Academie de la Grande Chaumiere, 1921; Parsons School of Design, 1923. Exhibited with The Ten, NYC, 1935–40. President, Federation of Modern Painters, 1944–45. TAUGHT: Pratt Institute, 1958; UCLA, 1958. AWARDS: Winner of Dudensing National Competition, 1929; US Treasury Department, Mural Competition, 1939; Brooklyn Museum, First Prize, 1944; U. of Illinois, P.P., 1951; Carnegie, Third Prize, 1961; Sao Paulo Biennial, First

Prize. **ADDRESS:** 206 West 23 Street, NYC. **DEALER:** Marlborough-Gerson Gallery Inc. **ONE-MAN EXHIBITIONS:** (first) Dudensing Gallery, NYC, 1930; Uptown Gallery, NYC, 1934; Theodore A. Kohn Gallery, NYC, 1934; Artists' Gallery, NYC, 1942, 43; Wakefield Gallery, NYC, 1944; "67" Gallery, NYC, 1945; Karl Nierendorf Gallery, NYC, 1945; The Kootz Gallery, 1947, 50, 51, 52, 53, 54; J. Seligmann and Co., 1949; Area Arts Gallery, San Francisco, 1953; Williams College, 1954; The Kootz Gallery, Provincetown, 1954; Martha Jackson Gallery, 1957; HCE Gallery, 1957; Andre Emmerich Gallery, NYC, 1958, 59; Galerie Rive Droite, Paris, 1959; Paul Kantor Gallery, 1959; ICA, London, 1959; French & Co. Inc., 1960; Sidney Janis Gallery, 1960, 62; Galleria dell'Ariete, Milan, 1961; Galerie Handschin, Basel, 1961; Marlborough-Gerson Gallery Inc., 1964; Walker, 1963. **RETROSPECTIVE:** Bennington College, 1954; Jewish Museum, 1957. **GROUP:** WMAA Annuals, 1944, 45, 46, 48, 51, 53, 55, 61; PAFA; Walker; SRGM; Documenta II, Kassel, 1959; MOMA, The New American Painting, circ. Europe, 1958–59; Chicago/AI, Abstract and Surrealist Art, 1948; WMAA, The New Decade, 1954–55; SRGM, Younger American Painters, 1954; Carnegie, 1952, 55, 58, 61; Seattle World's Fair, 1962; Tate, Dunn International, 1964. **COLLECTIONS:** Andover/Phillips; Atlanta/AA; Ball State Teachers College; Brandeis U.; Buffalo/Albright; Carnegie; Chicago/AI; Columbia U.; Cornell U.; Des Moines; Detroit/Institute; Hartford/Wadsworth; U. of Illinois; Jewish Museum; Los Angeles/County MA; MMA; MOMA; U. of Miami; NYU; U. of Nebraska; U. of Nevada; New Orleans/Delgado; Pasadena/AM; Phillips; SRGM; San Jose Library; Santa Barbara/MA; Seagram Collection; Smith College; Society of the Four Arts; Tel Aviv; VMFA; WMAA; Walker; Yale U.; Youngstown/Butler. **BIBLIOGRAPHY:** Barr 3; Baur 5, 7; Blesh 1; Eliot; **Friedman;** Goodrich and Baur 1; Greenberg 1; Haftman; Hess, T. B.; Hunter 1, 5; Janis, S.; Kootz 2; Mendelowitz; *Metro;* Motherwell and Reinhardt, eds.; Myers 2; Neumeyer; Nordness, ed.; Pousette-Dart, ed.; Read 2; Richardson; Rodman 1, 2, 3; Seuphor 1; Soby 5; Wight 2.

GOULET, LORRIE. b. August 17, 1925, Riverdale, N.Y. **STUDIED:** Black Mountain College, 1943–45, with Josef Albers, Jose de Creeft. Traveled USA, Europe. **TAUGHT:** Scarsdale Art Workshop and privately, 1957–61; MOMA School, 1957– ; New School for Social Research, 1961– . **MEMBER:** Sculptors Guild; Artists Equity. **COMMISSIONS:** Grand Concourse (Bronx) Public Library, 1958 (ceramic relief); Nurses Residence and School, Bronx Municipal Hospital Center, 1961 (relief). **AWARDS:** West Palm Beach/Norton, First Prize, 1949, 50. **m.** Jose de Creeft. **ADDRESS:** Kirby Lane North, Rye, N.Y. **DEALER:** The Contemporaries. **ONE-MAN EXHIBITIONS:** (first) Clay Club, NYC, 1948; Sculpture Center, 1955; The Contemporaries, 1959, 62. **GROUP:** PAFA, annually since 1948; Audubon Artists, annually since 1948; WMAA Annuals, 1948, 49, 50, 53, 55; A.F.A., Mother and Child in Modern Art, circ., 1963; Sculptors Guild, annually since 1960; Philadelphia Art Alliance, 1950; MMA, 1951; AAAL, 1961. **COLLECTIONS:** WMAA.

GRAHAM, JOHN D. b. 1881, Kiev, Russia; **d.** 1961, London, England. **STUDIED:** U. of Kiev,

Adolph Gottlieb   *Emerging. 1960*

degree in Law, 1911; ASL, 1921, with John Sloan. To USA 1920; became a citizen. Traveled Europe, Asia, Africa, USA. ONE-MAN EXHIBITIONS: (first) Baltimore/MA, 1926; Societe Anonyme, NYC, 1931; Galerie Zborowski, Paris, 1929; The Stable Gallery, 1954; Gallery Mayer, NYC, 1960; Dudensing Gallery, NYC; The Pinacotheca, NYC, 1946; Artists' Gallery, NYC, 1941; Eighth Street Gallery, NYC, 1933; U. of Minnesota, 1964; Arts Club of Chicago. GROUP: MOMA; WMAA; U. of Minnesota; Societe Anonyme, NYC. COLLECTIONS: MOMA; Nashville; Phillips; WMAA. BIBLIOGRAPHY: Baur 7; George 2; Graham; Hunter 5; Janis, S.; Kootz 2; Passloff; Phillips 1.

GRANLUND, PAUL. b. October 6, 1925, Minneapolis, Minn. STUDIED: Gustavus Adolphus College, 1952, BA; U. of Minnesota; Cranbrook Academy of Art, 1954, MFA. TAUGHT: Cranbrook Academy of Art, 1954; Minneapolis Institute School, 1955– ; U. of California, summer, 1959. AWARDS: Cranbrook, George A. Booth Scholarship, 1953; Fulbright Fellowship, 1954; Guggenheim Foundation Fellowship, 1957, 58. ADDRESS: 5320 Russell Avenue, South, Minneapolis, Minn. DEALER: Allan Frumkin Gallery, NYC and Chicago. ONE-MAN EXHIBITIONS: Minnesota State Fair, 1957; Minneapolis/Institute, 1959; Walker, 1956; Gustavus Adolphus College, 1956, 60; Allan Frumkin Gallery, Chicago, 1959; Allan Frumkin Gallery, NYC, 1960, 63; Esther Robles

Gallery, 1962; California Palace, 1962; Gethsemane Lutheran Church, Seattle, 1962. GROUP: American Academy, Rome, 1959; U. of Illinois, 1961; Cincinnati/AM, 1961; Corcoran, 1961; U. of Colorado, 1962; Buffalo/Albright, 1962; VMFA, 1962; Louisiana State U., 1964. COLLECTIONS: American Swedish Institute; Cranbrook; Minneapolis/Institute; VMFA; Walker.

GRAVES, MORRIS COLE. b. August 28, 1910, Fox Valley, Ore. STUDIED with Mark Tobey. Traveled Europe, the Orient, USA. FEDERAL A.P.: Easel painting, 1936–39. US Army, 1943. AWARDS: Seattle/AM, Northwest Annual, $100 Award, 1933; Guggenheim Foundation Fellowship, 1946; Chicago/AI, Norman Wait Harris Medal, 1947; Chicago/AI, Watson F. Blair Prize, 1949; U. of Illinois, P.P., 1955; NIAL Grant, 1956; Windsor Award, 1957. ADDRESS: c/o Dealer. DEALER: The Willard Gallery. ONE-MAN EXHIBITIONS: (first) Seattle/AM, 1936, also 1956; Arts Club of Chicago, 1943; U. of Minnesota, 1943; Detroit/Institute, 1943; Phillips, 1943, 54; Philadelphia Art Alliance, 1946; Santa Barbara/MA, 1948; Los Angeles/County MA, 1948; Chicago/AI, 1948; Margaret Brown Gallery, Boston, 1950; Beaumont (Tex.) Art Museum, 1952; Kunstnernes hus, Oslo, 1955; The Willard Gallery, 1942, 44, 45, 48, 53, 54, 55, 59; La Jolla, 1957; Roswell, 1961; Bridgestone Museum, 1957; Phoenix, 1960; Kalamazoo/Institute, 1961. RET-

Morris Cole Graves   *Spirit Bird. 1954*

ROSPECTIVE: California Palace, 1948; WMAA, circ., 1956; Pavilion Gallery, Balboa, Calif., 1963. GROUP: Seattle/AM; WMAA; U. of Illinois; Chicago/AI; MOMA, Americans 1942, circ., 1942; Seattle World's Fair, 1962; Brussels World's Fair, 1958; Houston/MFA, 1956; ICA, London, 1957; Phillips. COLLECTIONS: Baltimore/MA; Boston/MFA; Buffalo/Albright; U. of California; Chicago/AI; Cincinnati/AM; Cleveland/MA; Detroit/Institute; Fort Wayne/AM; Hartford/Wadsworth; Harvard U.; U. of Illinois; MMA; MOMA; Milwaukee; NIAL; U. of Nebraska; Pasadena/AM; Phillips; Portland, Ore./AM; SFMA; Santa Barbara/MA; Seattle/AM; Toronto; Wilmington; Worcester/AM. BIBLIOGRAPHY: Baldinger; Barker 1; Barr 3; Baur 7; Bazin; Beekman; Blesh 1; Canaday; Flanagan; Flexner; Frost; Goodrich and Baur 1; Haftman; Hunter 5; Janis, S.; Kootz 2; Kuh 1, 2; Langui; McCurdy, ed.; Mendelowitz; Miller, ed. 1; Munsterberg; Neumeyer; Nordness, ed.; Pousette-Dart, ed.; Ragon 1; Read 2, 3; Richardson; Rodman 1, 2; Sachs; Soby 5; Sutton; Valentine 2; Wight 2; **Wight, Baur and Phillips.**

GRAY, CLEVE. b. September 22, 1918, NYC. STUDIED: Princeton U., 1940, BA summa cum laude, PBK; Academie Andre Lhote; privately with Jacques Villon in Paris. US Army, 1943–46. Traveled Europe, USA. MEMBER: Century Association. AWARDS: U. of Illinois, P.P.; Ford Foundation, P.P. ADDRESS: Cornwall Bridge, Conn. ONE-MAN EXHIBITIONS: (first) J. Seligmann and Co., 1947, also 1948, 49, 50, 52, 54, 57, 59; Staempfli Gallery, 1960, 62, 64; Galleria Pagani del Grattacielo, Milan, 1963; Jerrold Morris Gallery, Toronto, 1963; Oklahoma, 1963. GROUP: WMAA Annuals, 1946– ; Chicago/AI; SRGM, Abstract Expressionists and Imagists, 1961; Hartford/Wadsworth; PAFA; El Retiro Parquet, Arte de America y España, 1963. COLLECTIONS: Andover/Phillips; Columbus; Hartford/Wadsworth; U. of Illinois; MMA; Nashville; U. of Nebraska; U. of Notre Dame; Oklahoma; SRGM; St. Paul Gallery; Vanderbilt U.; WMAA; Williams College. BIBLIOGRAPHY: Goodrich and Baur 1.

GREENE, BALCOMB. b. May 22, 1904, Shelby, N.Y. STUDIED: Syracuse U., 1922–26, AB; Columbia U., 1927; U. of Vienna, 1926–27; NYU, 1943, MA; self-taught in art. Traveled Europe extensively. TAUGHT: Dartmouth College (English), 1928–31; Carnegie, 1942–59. Editor, *Art Front* (Magazine), 1935–36. Fire in New York studio, 1941, destroyed many early paintings. MEMBER: American Abstract Artists

Balcomb Greene   *Rocks on the Maine Coast. 1962*

(First Chairman, 1936–37, 1938–39, 1940–41); International Institute of Arts and Letters; Cosmopolitan Club, NYC. FEDERAL A.P. (Mural Division): New York World's Fair, 1939, Federal Hall of Medicine (mural); Bronx (N.Y.) High School of Science (stained glass window); Williamsburgh Housing Project, Brooklyn, 1939 (mural). AWARDS: *Art News* (Magazine) Critics Choice, 1950, 53, 55, 56; PAFA, Carol H. Beck Gold Medal, 1961. ADDRESS: 332 East 53 Street, NYC. DEALER: Saidenberg Gallery. ONE-MAN EXHIBITIONS: (first) a gallery in Paris, 1932; J. B. Neumann's New Art Circle, NYC, 1947; Arts and Crafts Center, Pittsburgh, 1953; The Bertha Schaefer Gallery, 1952, 54, 55, 56, 58, 59, 61; American U., 1957; Brookhaven (Long Island) National Laboratory, 1959; American Cultural Center, Paris, 1960; Saidenberg Gallery, 1962, 63; Feingarten Gallery, Los Angeles, 1963, 64; La Jolla, 1964. RETROSPECTIVE: WMAA/A.F.A., circ., 1961. GROUP: American Abstract Artists Annuals; WMAA Annuals; U. of Illinois; Chicago/AI; Walker; SRGM; Brooklyn Museum; Carnegie. COLLECTIONS: Ball State Teachers College; Baltimore/MA; Brooklyn Museum; Carnegie; Chicago/AI; Corcoran; Guild Hall; Hartford/Wadsworth; Indianapolis/Herron; S. C. Johnson & Son, Inc.; MIT; MMA; MOMA; U. of Nebraska; Omaha/Joslyn; PAFA; Portland, Ore./AM; SRGM; WMAA; Walker; Youngstown/Butler. BIBLIOGRAPHY: Baur 5, 7; Flanagan; Frost; Goodrich and Baur 1; Hess, T. B.; Janis, S.; Kootz 2; Newmeyer; Nordness, ed.; Pousette-Dart, ed.; Read 2; Richardson; Ritchie 1; Rodman 3.

GREENE, STEPHEN. b. September 19, 1918, NYC. STUDIED: ASL, 1937; State U. of Iowa, with Philip Guston, 1939–42, 1944–45, BFA, MA. Traveled Europe, North Africa. TAUGHT: Parsons School of Design; ASL, 1959– ; NYU; Princeton U., 1956; Columbia U., 1961–62, 1964– . AWARDS: Prix de Rome, 1949. ADDRESS: Box 408-A, RD 1, Valley Cottage, N.Y. DEALER: Staempfli Gallery. ONE-MAN EXHIBITIONS: (first) Durlacher Brothers, 1947, also 1949, 52; Grace Borgenicht Gallery Inc., 1955, 57, 58; Staempfli Gallery, 1961 (circ. 1964). RETROSPECTIVE: Corcoran, 1963; Lincoln, Mass./De Cordova, 1953. GROUP: MMA, American Paintings Today, 1950; Chicago/AI, Contemporary Drawings from 12 Countries, 1952;

Walker, Reality and Fantasy, 1954; Paris/Moderne, American Drawings, 1954; WMAA, The New Decade, 1954–55; MOMA, Recent Drawings USA, 1956; I International Religious Art Biennial, Salzburg, 1958; VI Sao Paulo Biennial, 1961; WMAA Annuals; SRGM, Abstract Expressionists and Imagists, 1961; Corcoran; Carnegie; Chicago/AI. COLLECTIONS: Andover/Phillips; Brandeis U.; Chicago/AI; Detroit/Institute; Hamline U.; Hartford/Wadsworth; Harvard U.; U. of Illinois; Indiana U.; Indianapolis/Herron; Kansas City/Nelson; MMA; MOMA; NYU; Nashville; New Orleans/Delgado; Princeton U.; SRGM; St. Louis/City; Santa Barbara/MA; Tate; Utica; VMFA; WMAA. BIBLIOGRAPHY: Baur 7; Bazin; Genauer; Mendelowitz; Sachs; Soby 5.

GRILLO, JOHN. b. July 4, 1917, Lawrence, Mass. STUDIED: Hartford Art School, 1935–38; California School of Fine Arts, 1946; Hofmann School, NYC, 1949–50. US Armed Forces, 1944–46. TAUGHT: School of Visual Arts, NYC, 1961; Southern Illinois U., 1960; New School for Social Research, 1962; U. of California, Berkeley, 1962–63; Tamarind Lithography Workshop, 1964. AWARDS: CSFA, Albert M. Bender Fellowship, 1947. ADDRESS: 500 Third Avenue, NYC. DEALER: The Howard Wise Gallery, NYC. ONE-MAN EXHIBITIONS: Daliel Gallery, Berkeley, 1947; Artists' Gallery, NYC, 1948; Tanager Gallery, NYC, 1952, 60; Tibor de Nagy Gallery, 1953; The Bertha Schaefer Gallery, 1955, 57, 59; HCE Gallery, 1959, 62; The Howard Wise Gallery, NYC, 1961, 62, 63; Ankrum Gallery, 1962; U. of California, Berkeley, 1962; East End Gallery, Provincetown, 1963. GROUP: The Kootz Gallery, Fifteen Unknowns, 1950; Walker, Vanguard, 1955; WMAA Annual, 1959; Walker, 60 American Painters, 1960; SRGM, Abstract Expressionists and Imagists, 1961; Yale U., Contemporary Painting, 1961; Dallas/MFA, 1961, 62; Seattle World's Fair, 1962; MOMA, Hans Hofmann and His Students, circ., 1963–64; SFMA, Directions—Painting U.S.A., 1963. COLLECTIONS: Baton Rouge; Bennington College; Brooklyn Museum; Hartford/Wadsworth; James A. Michener Foundation; Newark Museum; The Olsen Foundation Inc.; Provincetown/Chrysler; SRGM; Smith College; Southern Illinois U.; WMAA; Waitsfield/Bundy; Walker. BIBLIOGRAPHY: Blesh 1.

GRIPPE, PETER. b. August 8, 1912, Buffalo, N.Y. STUDIED: Albright Art School; Buffalo Fine Arts Academy, with E. Wilcox, Edwin Dickinson, William Ehrich; Atelier 17, NYC. TAUGHT: Black Mountain College, 1948; Pratt Institute, 1949–50; Smith College, 1951–52; Atelier 17, NYC, 1951–52; Brandeis U., 1953– . FEDERAL A.P.: Taught sculpture and drawing, 1939–42. COMMISSIONS: Theo. Shapiro Forum, Brandeis U., 1963 (sculpture); Puerto Rican Information Center, NYC, 1958 (2 sculpture murals); Creative Arts Award Medallion design for Brandeis U., 1954. AWARDS: Brooklyn Museum, P.P., 1947; National Council for United States Art, $1,000 Sculpture Award, 1955; The Print Club, Philadelphia, Charles M. Lea Prize, 1953; MMA, $500 Print Prize, 1952; Boston Arts Festival, First Prize for Sculpture, 1955; Guggenheim Foundation Fellowship, 1964; Rhode Island Arts Festival, Sculpture Award, 1961. ADDRESS: 1190 Boylston Street, Newton 64, Mass. ONE-MAN EXHIBITIONS: (first) Orrefors Galleries, NYC, 1942; The Willard Gallery, 1944, 45, 46, 48; Brandeis U., 1957; The Peridot Gallery, 1957, 59; Lee Nordness Gallery, NYC, 1960, 63. GROUP: MMA, Contemporary American Art, 1942; WMAA Annuals, 1944, 45, 47, 48, 50, 51, 52, 54, 56, 57, 60, 62; Federation of Modern Painters and Sculptors, 1944, 45, 52; American Abstract Artists Annuals, 1946, 47, 49; Detroit/Institute, Origins of Modern Sculpture, 1948; Chicago/AI, Abstract and Surrealist Art, 1948; A.F.A., Tradition and Experiment in Modern Sculpture, circ., 1950–51; Carnegie, 1946, 48; Brooklyn Museum, 1947, 48, 49, 53, 56, 58; MMA, National Sculpture Exhibition, 1951; MOMA, Abstract Painting and Sculpture in America, 1951; Ninth Street Exhibition, NYC, 1951; MOMA, From Sketch to Sculpture, 1952; PAFA, 1952, 59; U. of Illinois, 50 Contemporary American Printmakers, 1956; ART:USA:59, NYC, 1959; PCA, American Prints Today, circ., 1959–62; ICA, Boston, View, 1960; U. of Illinois, 1961; Chicago/AI, 1961; Smithsonian, Drawings by Sculptors, circ. USA, 1961–63; A.F.A., Hayter and Atelier 17, circ., 1961–62; Hartford/Wadsworth, Eleven New England Sculptors, 1963. COLLECTIONS: Andover/Phillips; Brandeis U.; Brooklyn Museum; Buffalo/Albright; Fort Dodge/Banden; U. of Georgia; Library of Congress; MMA; MOMA; U. of Michigan; Milwaukee-Downer College; NYPL; National Gallery; PCA; PMA; The Print Club, Philadelphia; Provincetown/Chrysler; Raleigh/NCMA; Tel Aviv; Toledo/MA; USIA; WMAA; Walker; Washington U. BIBLIOGRAPHY: Baur 7; Blesh 1; Brumme; Flanagan; Hayter 1; Mendelowitz; Motherwell and Reinhardt, eds.; Ritchie 1; Seuphor 3.

GROOMS, RED. b. June 2, 1937, Nashville, Tenn. STUDIED: Peabody Institute; Chicago Art Institute School; Hofmann School, Provincetown. Traveled Europe, Near East. Movie with Rudi Burckhardt, "Shoot the Moon," 1963. COMMISSIONS: Center of Modern Culture, Florence, Italy (mural, with Mimi Gross). ADDRESS: 234 West 26 Street, NYC. DEALER: Tibor de Nagy Gallery. ONE-MAN EXHIBITIONS: (first) Sun Gallery, Provincetown, 1958; Reuben Gallery, NYC, 1960; Tibor de Nagy Gallery, 1963; Artists Guild, Nashville, 1962. HAPPENINGS: Fire, NYC, 1958; Burning Building, NYC, 1958. GROUP EXHIBITIONS: Chicago/AI, 1964; Delancey Street Museum, NYC, 1959, 60; Provincetown/Chrysler. COLLECTIONS: Nashville; Provincetown/Chrysler; Raleigh/NCMA. BIBLIOGRAPHY: Janis and Blesh 1.

GROPPER, WILLIAM. b. December 3, 1897, NYC. STUDIED: NAD, 1913–14; Ferrer School, San Francisco, 1912–13, with Robert Henri, George Bellows; New York School of Fine and Applied Art, 1915–18, with Howard Giles, Jay Hambridge. Traveled Europe, USA. Staff Artist, New York *World*, 1925–27; New York *Tribune*, 1919–21. TAUGHT: American Art School, NYC, 1946–48. MEMBER: Artists Equity. COMMISSIONS: New Interior Building, Washington, D.C.; Northwestern Postal Station, Detroit; US Post Office, Freeport, N.Y.; Schenley Industries, Inc., NYC. AWARDS: Young Israel Prize; Los Angeles/County MA, P.P.; Indianapolis/Herron, Prize for Lithography; J. S. Guggenheim Fellowship, 1937; Carnegie, Third Prize; *Collier's* (Magazine) Prize for Illustration, 1920; Harmon Foundation Award, 1930; MMA, Artists for Victory, Lithography Prize, 1942. ADDRESS: Mt. Airy Road, Croton-on-Hudson, N.Y. DEALERS: ACA Gallery; Gallery de Tours, San Francisco. ONE-MAN EXHIBITIONS: (first) ACA Gallery, 1936, also 1939, 42, 44; A.A.A. Gallery, NYC, 1945, 51, 52; Kleemann Gallery,

NYC, 1943; Smith College, 1941; de Young, 1945. **Group:** MMA; WMAA; Chicago/AI; MOMA; Los Angeles/County MA. **Collections:** Abbott Laboratories; U. of Arizona; Britannica; Chicago/AI; Hartford/Wadsworth; Harvard U.; Library of Congress; Los Angeles/County MA; MMA; MOMA; Newark Museum; PAFA; Phillips; St. Louis/City; WMAA; Walker. **Bibliography:** American Artists Congress, Inc.; Barr 3; Baur 7; Bazin; Boswell 1; Brown; Canaday; Cheney, M. C.; Christensen; Goodrich and Baur 1; Hall; Kootz 2; McCurdy, ed.; Mellquist; Mendelowitz; Pagano; Pearson 1; Reese; Richardson; Wight 2.

GROSS, CHAIM. b. March 17, 1904, Kolomea, East Austria. To USA 1921. **Studied:** Kunstgewerbe Schulle; Educational Alliance, NYC; Beaux-Arts Institute of Design, with Elie Nadelman; ASL, with Robert Laurent. Traveled Europe, Israel, Turkey. **Taught:** Educational Alliance, NYC; New School for Social Research. **Member:** Sculptors Guild (President); Artists Equity; Federation of Modern Painters and Sculptors; NIAL. **Federal A.P.:** Teacher, supervisor, sculptor. **Commissions:** Main Post Office, Washington, D.C., 1936; Federal Trade Commission Building, Washington, D.C., 1938; France Overseas Building, New York World's Fair, 1939; US Post Office, Irwin, Pa., 1940; Reiss-Davis Child Guidance Clinic, Beverly Hills, 1961; Hadassah Hospital, Jerusalem, 1964; Temple Sharaay Tefila, NYC, 1964. **Awards:** L. C. Tiffany Grant, 1933; Paris World's Fair, 1937, Silver Medal; MMA, Artists for Victory, $3,000 Second Prize, 1942;

Chaim Gross   *Two Sisters. 1956–60*

Boston Arts Festival, Third Prize for Sculpture, 1954; PAFA, Hon. Men., 1954; Audubon Artists, Prize for Sculpture, 1955; NIAL Grant, 1956; Boston Arts Festival, First Prize, 1963; NIAL, Award of Merit Medal, 1963. ADDRESS: 526 West Broadway, NYC. DEALER: The Forum Gallery. ONE-MAN EXHIBITIONS: (first) Gallery 144, NYC, 1932; Boyer Gallery, Philadelphia, 1935; Boyer Gallery, NYC, 1937; A.A.A. Gallery, NYC, 1942; Massillon Museum, 1946; Akron/AI, 1946; Youngstown/Butler, 1946; New Paltz, 1952; Jewish Museum, 1953; Shore Studios, Boston, 1954; Muriel Latow Gallery, Springfield, Mass., 1956; Duveen-Graham Gallery, NYC, 1957; WMAA, circ., 1959; The Marble Arch Gallery, Miami Beach, 1961; Anna Werbe Gallery, Detroit, 1962; The Forum Gallery, 1962, 64; Irving Galleries, Inc., Milwaukee, 1963. GROUP: WMAA Sculpture Annuals; Sculptors Guild Annuals; PAFA; New York World's Fair, 1964–65; A.F.A., Sculpture in Wood, circ., 1941–42; American Painting and Sculpture, Moscow, 1959; MOMA, The Making of Sculpture, circ., 1961–62; Smithsonian, Drawings by Sculptors, circ. USA, 1961–63. COLLECTIONS: Ain Harod; Andover/Phillips; Atlanta/AA; Baltimore/MA; Bezalel Museum; Boston/MFA; Brandeis U.; Brooklyn Museum; Bryn Mawr College; Chicago/AI; Colby College; Dayton/AI; Des Moines; Fairleigh Dickinson U.; U. of Georgia; Haifa; Jewish Museum; Kalamazoo/Institute; Kansas City/Nelson; La Jolla; MMA; MOMA; Massillon Museum; Milwaukee; U. of Minnesota; Newark Museum; Ogunquit; PAFA; PMA; Phoenix; Queens College; Reading/Public; Reed College; Rutgers U.; Scranton/Everhart; Scripps College; Smith College; Tel Aviv; WMAA; Walker; West Palm Beach/Norton; Worcester/AM; Youngstown/Butler. BIBLIOGRAPHY: Baur 7; Brumme; Cheney, M. C.; Flanagan; **Goodrich and Baur** 1, **2; Gross; Lombardo;** McCurdy, ed.; Mendelowitz; Sutton; Wheeler.

GROSSER, MAURICE. b. October 23, 1903, Huntsville, Ala. STUDIED: Harvard U., 1920–24, with M. Mower. Traveled Europe, USA, Latin America, Africa. ADDRESS: 219 West 14 Street, NYC. DEALER: The Banfer Gallery. ONE-MAN EXHIBITIONS: Grand Central Palace, NYC, 1928; Grace Horne Galleries, Boston, 1925; Carstairs Gallery, NYC, 1957, 60, 62; The Banfer Gallery, 1964; Galerie Vignon, Paris, 1931;

Galerie des Quatre Chemins, Paris, 1933, 39; Hendrix, Inc. (Gallery), NYC, 1935; Arts Club of Chicago, 1939; Julien Levy Galleries, NYC, 1940, 41, 44, 47; Houston/MFA, 1942; Hugo Gallery, NYC, 1954; Alexander Iolas Gallery, 1955; Carlen Gallery, Philadelphia, 1958. GROUP: U. of Minnesota; MOMA; WMAA; Cleveland/MA; VMFA. COLLECTIONS: Cleveland/MA; Columbus; MOMA; U. of Minnesota; Rockland/Farnsworth; Springfield, Mass./MFA; VMFA. BIBLIOGRAPHY: **Grosser** 1, 2.

GROSZ, GEORGE. b. July 26, 1893, Berlin, Germany; **d.** July 6, 1959, Berlin, Germany. STUDIED: Royal Saxon Academy of Fine Art, Dresden, 1909–11, with R. Muller, O. Schindler, R. Sterl, R. Wehle; School of Fine and Applied Arts, Berlin, 1911, with E. Orlik; Academie Colarossi, Paris, 1913. German Army, 1914–16, 1917–18. Traveled Russia, Europe, USA. To USA 1932; citizen 1938. TAUGHT: ASL, 1933–36, 1940–42, 1943–44, 1950–53; Columbia U., 1941–42; Maurice Sterne School, NYC, 1933. Designed sets for Max Reinhardt Theatre, 1920–30. COMMISSIONS: A. Harris & Co., Dallas (portfolio of drawings entitled *Impressions of the City*). AWARDS: Guggenheim Foundation Fellowship, 1937; PAFA, Carol H. Beck Gold Medal, 1940; Chicago/AI, Watson F. Blair Prize, 1931, 40; Carnegie, Second Prize, 1945. ONE-MAN EXHIBITIONS: (first) Goltz Gallery, Berlin, 1918; Weyhe Gallery, 1931; Gallery A. Flechtheim, Berlin, 1926; M. Wasservogel, Berlin, 1926; An American Group (Gallery), NYC, 1933; Raymond and Raymond, Inc., NYC, 1933; Arts Club of Chicago, 1933; A.A.A. Gallery, NYC, 1926, 41, 43, 46, 48, 54; Crillon Galleries, Philadelphia, 1933; Milwaukee, 1933; Mayor Gallery, London, 1934; An American Place (Gallery), NYC, 1935; Contemporary Arts Gallery, NYC, 1935; Smith College (three-man), 1936; Currier, 1939; Harvard U., 1935, 49; Leicester Gallery, London, 1946; Municipal U. of Omaha, 1936; Chicago/AI, 1938; Hudson D. Walker Gallery, NYC, 1938 (2), 41; MOMA, 1941; Denver/AM, 1943; Baltimore/MA, 1944; Print Club of Cleveland, 1949; The Swetzoff Gallery, 1950; Dallas/MFA, 1952; Paul Kantor Gallery, 1964; Vera Lazuk, Cold Spring Harbor, N.Y., 1959; Arts Council of Great Britain, circ., 1963; The Forum Gallery, 1963; E. V. Thaw, NYC, 1963.

RETROSPECTIVE: WMAA, 1954. GROUP: WMAA Annuals; MOMA; Chicago/AI; Los Angeles/County MA; SFMA; Newark Museum; St. Louis/City; Dallas/MFA. COLLECTIONS: Berlin/National; Boston/MFA; Chicago/AI; Cleveland/MA; Detroit/Institute; Essen; Galerie des 20. Jahrhunderts; Harvard U.; Huntington, N.Y./Heckscher; MOMA; Newark Museum; Stuttgart; WMAA. BIBLIOGRAPHY: Ballo, ed.; Baur 2, 7; Bazalgette; Bazin; Biddle 3; Bittner; Blesh 1; Bulliet 1, 2; Canaday; Cassou; Cheney, M. C.; Christensen; Craven 1, 2; Davidson 2; Flanagan; Frost; Genauer; Goodrich and Baur 1; Grosz 1, 2, 3, 4, 5; Haftman; Hess, T. B.; Huyghe; Janis, S.; Kent, N.; Kouvenhoven; Kuh 1; Langui; McCurdy, ed.; Mehring; Mendelowitz; Newmeyer; Pagano; Pearson 1, 2; Pousette-Dart, ed.; Read 2; Richardson; Rodman 3; Sachs; Salvini, Seitz 2; Selz, P. 1; Tavolato.

GUERRERO, JOSE. b. October 27, 1914, Granada, Spain. STUDIED: Escuela de Artes y Oficios Artisticos, Granada, 1930–34; Real Academia de Bellas Artes de San Fernando, Madrid, 1940–44; Academie des Beaux-Arts, Paris, 1945–46. Traveled Europe, 1947–49. To USA 1949; citizen 1952. TAUGHT: New School for Social Research, 1962– . AWARDS: *Art In America* (Magazine), New Talent, 1958; Graham Foundation Grant, 1958–59; Chevalier of the Order of Arts and Letters (France), 1959; Society for Contemporary American Art annual prize donation to The Art Institute of Chicago, 1959. ADDRESS: 406 West 20 Street, NYC, and Cuenca, Spain. ONE-MAN EXHIBITIONS: (first) Galleria Secolo, Rome, 1948; Lou Cosyn Gallery, Brussels, 1948; Buchholz Gallery, Madrid, 1950; Betty Parsons Gallery, 1954, 57, 58, 60, 63; Rose Fried Gallery, 1964; Galeria Juana Mordo, Madrid, 1964; Galerie Altarriba, Paris (two-man), 1946; St. George's Gallery, London (two-man), 1949; Arts Club of Chicago (two-man), 1954. GROUP: SRGM, Younger American Painters, 1954; Galerie de France, 10 Jeune Peintres de l'Ecole de Paris, 1956; Salon des Realites Nouvelles, Paris, 1957; WMAA Annuals, 1958, 59, 62; Worcester/AM, 1958; Dallas/MFA, 1958; Rome-New York Foundation, Rome, 1958; Buffalo/Albright, 1958; Carnegie International, 1958, 61, 63; Corcoran, 1959; American Abstract Artists, 1958, 61, 62; I Inter-American Paintings and Prints Biennial, Mexico City, 1958. COLLECTIONS: Belgian Ministry of National Education; Beloit College; Buffalo/Albright; Carnegie; Chase Manhattan Bank; Chicago/AI; Cuenca; French Ministry of National Education; Friends of Art; Houston/MFA; Madrid/Nacional; PAFA; RISD; SRGM; Toronto; WMAA; Yale U.

GUGLIELMI, O. LOUIS. b. April 9, 1906, Cairo, Egypt; d. September 3, 1956, Amagansett, N.Y. To USA 1914. STUDIED: NAD, 1920–25. Corps of Army Engineers, 1943–45. TAUGHT: Louisiana State U., 1952–53; New School for Social Research, 1953. FEDERAL A.P.: Easel painting. AWARDS: L. C. Tiffany Grant, Yaddo Fellowship, and MacDowell Colony Fellowship, 1925–32; Chicago/AI, Ada S. Garrett Prize, 1943; Pepsi-Cola, Hon. Men., 1944; Carnegie, Hon. Men., 1944; AAAL Grant, 1946; PAFA, Joseph E. Temple Gold Medal, 1952. ONE-MAN EXHIBITIONS: (first) The Downtown Gallery, 1938, also 1942, 46, 47, 51; New Art Center, NYC; J. Seligmann and Co.; Julien Levy Galleries, NYC; Lee Nordness Gallery, NYC, 1958, 61, 62. GROUP: Musee du Jeu de Paume; New York World's Fair, 1939; MOMA, Americans 1943: Realists and Magic-Realists, circ., 1943; WMAA, The Precisionists, 1961; Chicago/AI, 1943; PAFA; Pepsi-Cola Co.; Newark Museum; U. of Minnesota; Denver/AM; PMA. COLLECTIONS: Auburn U.; Britannica; Chicago/AI; Cornell U.; Cranbrook; U. of Georgia; MMA; MOMA; Newark Museum; SFMA; Tel Aviv; WMAA; Walker. BIBLIOGRAPHY: Baur 7; Bethers; Blesh 1; Genauer; Goodrich and Baur 1; Haftman; Hall; Halpert; Janis, S.; McCurdy, ed.; Pagano.

GUSSOW, ALAN. b. May 8, 1931, NYC. STUDIED: Middlebury College, 1952, AB; Cooper Union, 1952–53, with Morris Kantor; Atelier 17, NYC. Traveled Europe; resided Rome, two years. TAUGHT: Parsons School of Design, 1956– , Chairman, Department of Fashion Illustration, 1959– ; Sarah Lawrence College, 1958–59. COMMISSIONS: Skidmore, Owings and Merrill, Architects (mural). AWARDS: Prix de Rome, 1953–54, renewed 1954–55. ADDRESS: 121 New York Avenue, Congers, N.Y. DEALER: The Peridot Gallery. ONE-MAN EXHIBITIONS: (first) Hagerstown/County MFA, 1961; The Peridot Gallery, 1962, 63; Middlebury College, 1961. **Group:** Maine State Art Festival, 1961– ; Youngstown/Butler, 1963; III Mostra di Pittura Americana, Bordighera, 1955; U. of Nebraska.

GUSSOW, ROY. b. November 12, 1918, Brooklyn, N.Y. **Studied:** New York State Institute of Applied Agriculture (Farmingdale), 1938; Institute of Design, Chicago, 1945, with Lazlo Moholy-Nagy, and 1946, with Alexander Archipenko, 1948, BS. Traveled Europe and USA extensively. **Taught:** Bradley U., 1948; Colorado Springs Fine Arts Center, 1949–51; North Carolina State College, 1951–62; Pratt Institute, 1962– . **Commissions:** US Commerce Department Trade Fair, circ. Bangkok and Tokyo, 1956 (American Pavilion); Lenoir-Rhyne College, 1957; Cooperative Savings & Loan Association, Wilmington, N.C., 1959; North Carolina State College, 1961; North Carolina State College Faculty Club, 1962; San Francisco Museum of Science and Indus-

Roy Gussow   *Mutual. 1963*

try, 1962; Phoenix-Mutual Building, Hartford, Conn., 1963 (8-ft. stainless steel sculpture commissioned by Max Abramovitz). **Awards:** PAFA, Hon. Men., 1958; Raleigh/NCMA, P.P., 1957, 61; Ford Foundation, P.P., 1960, 62; National Gold Medal Exhibition for the Building Arts, NYC, 1962. **Address:** c/o Dealer. **Dealer:** Grace Borgenicht Gallery Inc. **One-man Exhibitions:** (first) Design Associates Gallery, Greensboro, N.C., 1952; The Pennsylvania State U., 1959; Grace Borgenicht Gallery Inc., 1964. **Group:** Chicago/AI, 1947, 48, 49; U. of Arkansas, 1948; Omaha/Joslyn, 1949, 50; Oakland/AM, 1959; Denver/AM, 1949, 50, 51; SFMA, 1951; PAFA, annually 1951–59; MMA, 1951; Raleigh/NCMA, annually 1952–61; WMAA, 1956, 63. **Collections:** Atlanta/AA; Brooklyn Museum; California Academy of Science; Equitable Life Assurance Society; U. of North Carolina; Raleigh/NCMA.

GUSTON, PHILIP. b. June 27, 1913, Montreal, Canada. To USA 1916. **Studied:** Otis Art Institute, Los Angeles, for 3 months, 1930. Traveled Spain, Italy, France, USA. **Taught:** State U. of Iowa, 1941–45; Washington U., 1945–47; U. of Minnesota, 1950; NYU, 1951–59; Pratt Institute, 1953–57; Yale U., 1963. **Federal A.P.:** 1935–40, murals: WPA Building, New York World's Fair, 1939 (façade); Queensbridge Housing Project, 1940; Forestry Building, Laconia, N.H., 1941. Section of Fine Arts (murals): Social Security Building, Washington, D.C., 1942; US Post Office, Commerce, Ga., 1938. **Awards:** Carnegie, First Prize, 1945; Guggenheim Foundation Fellowship, 1947; Prix de Rome, 1948; AAAL Grant, 1948; Ford Foundation Grant, 1948; $10,000 Ford Foundation Grant, 1959. **Address:** Woodstock, N.Y. **Dealer:** Marlborough-Gerson Gallery Inc. **One-man Exhibitions:** (first) The Midtown Galleries, 1945; Boston Museum School, 1947; Utica, 1947; U. of Minnesota, 1950; The Peridot Gallery, 1952; Charles Egan Gallery, 1953; Sidney Janis Gallery, 1956, 58, 60, 61; Dwan Gallery, Los Angeles (two-man, with Franz Kline), 1962. **Retrospective:** V Sao Paulo Biennial, 1959; XXX Venice Biennial, 1960; SRGM, 1962. **Group:** U. of Illinois, 1944; U. of Minnesota, 40 American Painters, 1940–50, 1951; Baltimore/MA, Abstract Expressionists, 1953; MOMA, Twelve Americans, circ., 1956; MOMA, The New American Painting, circ.

Europe, 1958–59; Sao Paulo, 1957; I Inter-American Paintings and Prints Biennial, Mexico City, 1958; WMAA, 18 Living American Artists, 1959; Documenta II, Kassel, 1959; Ringling, 1961; SRGM/USIA, American Vanguard, circ. Europe, 1961–62; Tate, Painting and Sculpture of a Decade, 1954–64, 1964; MOMA, Abstract Painting and Sculpture in America, 1951; Walker, Contemporary American Painting, 1950; WMAA, Nature in Abstraction, 1958; St. Louis/City, Modern American Painting, 1959; WMAA Annuals; PAFA; Carnegie; SFMA; Chicago/AI; Corcoran. COLLECTIONS: Allentown/AM; Baltimore/MA; Buffalo/Albright; Chicago/AI; Cleveland/MA; U. of Illinois; State U. of Iowa; MMA; MOMA; Minneapolis/Institute; Phillips; SRGM; St. Louis/City; Utica; Worcester/AM; Yale U. BIBLIOGRAPHY: Arnason 2; Ashton 2; Baur 5; Bazin; Biddle 3; Blesh 1; Canaday; Genauer; Goodrich and Baur 1; Haftman; Henning; Hunter 1, 5; McCourbrey; McCurdy, ed.; Nordness, ed.; Ponente; Read 2; Ritchie 1; Seuphor 1.

GUY, JAMES. b. 1910, Middletown, Conn. STUDIED: Hartford Art School, with Albertus Jones, Kimon Nicolaides. Traveled Mexico, Europe, USA. Articles on fishing for leading outdoor publications. FEDERAL A.P.: Easel painting; mural for Hartford (Conn.) High School. ADDRESS: 171 Main Street, Middletown, Conn. DEALER: Rose Fried Gallery. ONE-MAN EXHIBITIONS: (first) Boyer Gallery, NYC, 1939, also 1940; Ferargil Galleries, NYC, 1941, 42, 44; a gallery in Hollywood, Calif., 1945; Lehigh U., 1945; Bennington College, 1947; Carlebach Gallery, NYC, 1949, 50; MacMurray College, 1949; St. Louis/City, 1952; Hartford College for Women, 1960; Wesleyan U., 1961; Rose Fried Gallery. GROUP: Paris World's Fair, 1937; New York World's Fair, 1939; Golden Gate International Exposition, San Francisco, 1939; WMAA Annuals; MOMA; MMA; Chicago/AI. COLLECTIONS: Hartford/Wadsworth; The Miller Co.; The Olsen Foundation Inc.; SRGM; Society of the Four Arts. BIBLIOGRAPHY: Hall.

GWATHMEY, ROBERT. b. January 24, 1903, Richmond, Va. STUDIED: North Carolina State College, 1924–25; Maryland Institute, 1925–26; PAFA, 1926–30, with George Harding, Daniel Garber. Traveled Europe, Carib-

Robert Gwathmey   *Musing. 1961*

bean. TAUGHT: Beaver College, 1931–37; Carnegie Institute of Technology, 1938–52; Cooper Union, 1942– . MEMBER: Artists Equity. COMMISSIONS: US Post Office, Eutaw, Ala. AWARDS: PAFA, Cresson Fellowship, 1929, 30; US Government 48 State Mural Competition winner, 1939; San Diego, First Prize, Watercolors, 1940; Carnegie, Second Prize, 1943; Lessing J. Rosenwald Fund Fellowship, 1944; AAAL Grant, 1946; Corcoran, Fourth Prize, 1957. ADDRESS: 304 East 73 Street, NYC. DEALER: Terry Dintenfass, Inc. ONE-MAN EXHIBITIONS: (first) ACA Gallery, 1940, also 1946, 49; VMFA; Terry Dintenfass, Inc. GROUP: WMAA Annual; Corcoran; PAFA; MMA; Boston/MFA. COLLECTIONS: Auburn U.; Birmingham, Ala./MA; Boston/MFA; Brandeis U.; Brooklyn Museum; California Palace; Carnegie; U. of Georgia; IBM; U. of Illinois; Los Angeles/County MA; U. of Nebraska; U. of Oklahoma; PAFA; Rochester/Memorial; San Diego; Sao Paulo; Savannah/Telfair; Springfield, Mass./MFA; U. of Texas; VMFA; WMAA; Youngstown/Butler. BIBLIOGRAPHY: Baldinger; Baur 7; Bazin; Goodrich and Baur 1; McCurdy, ed.; Mendelowitz; Nordness, ed.; Pousette-Dart, ed.; Reese.

h

HADZI, DIMITRI. b. March 21, 1921, NYC. STUDIED: Polytechnic Institute of Brooklyn; Cooper Union; Polytechneion, Athens; Museo Artistico Industriale, Rome; Brooklyn Museum School. US Air Force, 1943. COMMISSIONS: MIT; Philharmonic Hall, Lincoln Center for the Performing Arts, NYC; sculpture for the Reynolds Metals Co. Memorial Award. AWARDS: Fulbright Fellowship (Greece), 1950; L. C. Tiffany Grant, 1955; Guggenheim Foundation Fellowship, 1957; NIAL, 1962. ADDRESS: c/o Dealer. DEALER: Stephen Radich Gallery. ONE-MAN EXHIBITIONS: Galleria Schneider, Rome, 1958, 60; Seiferheld Gallery, NYC, 1959; Galerie Van der Loo, Munich, 1961; Stephen Radich Gallery, 1961; Gallery Hella Nebelung, Dusseldorf, 1962; MIT, 1963. GROUP: MOMA, New Talent, 1956; Middleheim Park, Antwerp, International Outdoor Sculpture Exhibition, 1957, 59; Carnegie, 1958, 61; MOMA, Recent Sculpture USA, 1959; Smith College, New Sculpture Now, 1960; WMAA, Business Buys American Art, 1960; RISD, Bronze Figure Sculpture Today, 1960; U. of Nebraska, 1960; Claude Bernard, Paris, Aspects of American Sculpture, 1960; Boston Arts Festival, 1961; WMAA Annuals, 1960, 63; XXXI Venice Biennial, 1962; Seattle World's Fair, 1962; Battersea Park, London, International Sculpture Exhibition, 1963; New York World's Fair, 1964–65. COLLECTIONS: Andover/Phillips; Chase Manhattan Bank; City of Tilburg; MIT; MOMA; New School for Social Research; Princeton U.; RISD; SRGM; Smith College; Union Carbide Corp.; U. of Vermont; WMAA; Yale U.

HAINES, RICHARD. b. December 29, 1906, Marion, Iowa. STUDIED: Minneapolis Institute School, 1932–34. Traveled Europe. TAUGHT: Minneapolis Institute School, 1941; Chouinard Art Institute, Los Angeles, 1945–54; Otis Art Institute, Los Angeles, 1954– . MEMBER: California Watercolor Society. FEDERAL A.P.: 1937–41, murals: Fort Snelling, Minn.; Sebeka (Minn.) High School; City Armory, Willmar, Minn.; US Post Offices in Wichita, Neb., Cresco, Iowa, Hastings, Minn., Clinton, Mo., Berwyn, Ill., Shelton, Wash. AWARDS: Vanderlip Traveling Scholarship, 1933; Los Angeles/County MA, First Award, 1944, Third Award, 1945; Oakland/AM, 1947; Denver/AM, Hon. Men., 1947; California State Fair, First P.P., 1948; California Watercolor Society, First P.P., 1948; SFMA, Artists Council Prize, 1948; Society of Etchers, Engravers and Lithographers, NYC, First Prize, Lithography, 1948; California State Fair, Second Award, 1949; Los Angeles Centennial, Second P.P., 1949; SFMA, Art Association Prize, 1949; Corcoran, Third Award, 1951; Los Angeles County Fair, First P.P., 1951; Tupperware National Competition, $600 P.P., 1957. ADDRESS: 247 Amalfi Drive, Santa Monica, Calif. DEALER: Dalzell Hatfield Gallery. ONE-MAN EXHIBITIONS: (first) Dalzell Hatfield Gallery, 1948, also 1958, 62, 64; Pasadena/AM, 1960; Santa Barbara/MA, 1959; Rutherford Gallery, San Francisco, 1957. GROUP: SFMA; Oakland/AM; Los Angeles/County MA; MMA; Dallas/MFA; Corcoran; San Diego; Kansas City/Nelson; California State Fair. COLLECTIONS: Arizona State College; Britannica; California State Fair;

California Watercolor Society; Corcoran; Dallas/MFA; Kansas City/Nelson; Library of Congress; Los Angeles/County MA; Los Angeles County Fair; MMA; San Diego; Santa Barbara/MA; U. of Utah. **BIBLIOGRAPHY:** Pousette-Dart, ed.

HALE, NATHAN CABOT. b. July 5, 1925, Los Angeles, Calif. **STUDIED:** Chouinard Art Institute, Los Angeles, 1945; ASL, 1945–50; Santa Monica City College, 1952. Traveled Mexico, Europe, South Pacific, USA. **TAUGHT:** Los Angeles City Art Education and Recreation Program, 1956–57; Pratt Institute, 1963–64. Designed sets for off-Broadway production of *The Affairs of Anatole*, 1958. **MEMBER:** Architectural League of New York. **COMMISSIONS:** Architectural and portraits. **AWARDS:** Los Angeles/County MA, P.P. for Sculpture, 1953. **ADDRESS:** 321 East 10 Street, NYC. **DEALER:** The Midtown Galleries. **ONE-MAN EXHIBITIONS:** (first) Felix Landau Gallery, 1957; Washington Irving Gallery, NYC, 1960; Feingarten Gallery, NYC and Chicago, 1961; The Midtown Galleries, NYC, 1964. **GROUP:** Roko Gallery, 1948, 49, 50; J. Seligmann and Co., 1947, 48, 49; Hirschl & Adler Galleries, Inc., NYC, Continuing Traditions of Realism in American Art, 1962; Los Angeles/County MA, 1953, 54, 55; Buffalo/Albright, 1963; Corcoran, 1963, 64; Colorado Springs/FA, 1961; Lehigh U., 1963; Wayne State U., 1964. **COLLECTIONS:** Los Angeles/County MA.

HALE, ROBERT BEVERLY. b. January 29, 1901, Boston, Mass. **STUDIED:** Columbia U. School of Architecture, 1923, AB; Ecole des Beaux-Arts, Fontainebleau; ASL, with George Bridgeman, William C. McNulty. Traveled Europe. **TAUGHT:** ASL, 1942– ; Columbia U., 1946– . Associate Editor, *Art News* (Magazine), 1941–49. **ADDRESS:** 2 West 67 Street, NYC. **DEALER:** Staempfli Gallery. **ONE-MAN EXHIBITIONS:** (first) Stamford (Conn.) Museum and Nature Center, 1959; Staempfli Gallery, 1960. **COLLECTIONS:** U. of Arizona; WMAA. **BIBLIOGRAPHY:** Biddle 3; **Hale.**

HALEY, JOHN CHARLES. b. September 21, 1905, Minneapolis, Minn. **STUDIED:** Minneapolis Institute School, with Cameron Booth; Hofmann School, Munich and Capri; Scuola

Mosaico, Ravenna, Italy. US Navy, World War II. Traveled Europe, USA. **TAUGHT:** U. of California, Berkeley. **FEDERAL A.P.:** Fresco painter, briefly. **COMMISSIONS:** Stained glass in churches in St. Paul, Duluth, Rochester, and Benson, Minn.; a fresco at Government Island. **AWARDS:** San Francisco Art Association, 1936, 39, 44, 51, 53, 56; California State Fair, 1950, 51; RAC, 1956, 58. **ADDRESS:** P.O. Box 31, Pt. Station, Richmond, Calif. **ONE-MAN EXHIBITIONS:** (first) SFMA, mid-1930's; Mortimer Levitt Gallery, NYC, 1949, 52; U. of California Worth Ryder Gallery, 1962; de Young, 1962; Chico State College, 1963. **GROUP:** SFMA Annuals, 1932– ; California Palace Annuals; III & VI Sao Paulo Biennials, 1955, 61; Chicago/AI; MMA; U. of Illinois Annuals, 1948, 49, 50, 51; PAFA; Dallas/MFA; Denver/AM; RAC; Pasadena/AM; Colorado Springs/FA; Santa Barbara/MA; St. Louis/City; MOMA, circ. **COLLECTIONS:** Chico State College; First National Bank of Nevada; IBM; Mills College; Phillips; SFMA.

HAMMERSLEY, FREDERICK. b. January 5, 1919, Salt Lake City, Utah. **STUDIED:** U. of Idaho, 1936–38; San Francisco Junior College, 1938–39; Academy of Advertising Art, San Francisco, 1939–40; Chouinard Art Institute, Los Angeles, 1940–42, 1946–47, with Henry McFee; Jepson Art Institute, Los Angeles, 1947–49, with Rico Lebrun; Academie des Beaux-Arts, Paris, 1945. US Army, 1942–46. **TAUGHT:** Jepson Art Institute, Los Angeles, 1949–51; Pomona College, 1953–62; Pasadena Museum School, 1956–61 (children's painting class), 1963– (adult classes); occasional private lessons. **AWARDS:** Laguna Beach Art Gallery, First Prize, 1949; Youngstown/Butler, P.P., 1961; City of Claremont, First Prize, 1960. **ADDRESS:** 905¾ Sanborn Avenue, Los Angeles, Calif. **DEALER:** Heritage Gallery. **ONE-MAN EXHIBITIONS:** (first) Fullerton (Calif.) Art Museum, 1959; Pasadena/AM, 1961; Heritage Gallery, 1961, 63; Occidental College, 1962; California Palace, 1962; La Jolla, 1963. **GROUP:** SFMA, Abstract Classicists (circ. to Los Angeles/County MA; ICA, London; Queens U., Belfast, 1959–60); Western Association of Art Museum Directors, circ., 1960–61; WMAA, Geometric Abstraction in America, circ., 1962; A.F.A., Purist Painting, circ., 1960–61; WMAA,

Fifty California Artists, 1962–63; USIA, Draw-
ings from California, circ. Europe, 1958–59.
COLLECTIONS: City of Claremont; US Navy;
Youngstown/Butler. BIBLIOGRAPHY: Seuphor 1.

HANSEN, JAMES LEE. b. June 13, 1925,
Tacoma, Wash. STUDIED: Portland (Ore.)
Museum School. TAUGHT: Oregon State U.,
1957–58; U. of California, Berkeley, 1958;
Portland (Ore.) State College, 1964. Founder
of The Fine Arts Collaborative, 1959. COM-
MISSIONS: Vancouver (Wash.) Federal Savings
and Loan Building; Land Title Building, Van-
couver, Wash.; Sacred Heart Nurses Dormi-
tory, Eugene, Ore.; Corvallis (Ore.) First Fed-
eral Savings and Loan; Alder Way Building,
Portland, Ore.; St. Louise Church, Bellevue,
Wash.; Providence Heights College, Pine Lake,
Wash.; St. Mary's Mission, Pioneer, Wash.;
Fresno (Calif.) Civic Mall. AWARDS: SFMA,
First P.P., 1952, 60; Seattle/AM, First P.P.,
1952; SFMA, American Trust Co. Award,
1956; Seattle/AM, Norman Davis P.P., 1958;
Fellow of the International Institute of Arts
and Letters. ADDRESS: 4115 "Q" Street, Vancouver, Wash. DEALERS: The Morris Gallery;
Fountain Gallery. ONE-MAN EXHIBITIONS:
Kraushaar Galleries, 1952; Dilexi Gallery, San
Francisco; The Morris Gallery, 1961. GROUP:
WMAA, 1953; San Diego; The Morris Gallery,
1961; Seattle/AM, 1952, 53, 54, 55, 56, 57, 59,
60; Denver/AM, 1952, 61; SFMA, 1952, 56,
60; Portland, Ore./AM, 1951–60; Santa Bar-
bara/MA; Fort Worth; U. of Oregon; U. of
Washington. COLLECTIONS: U. of Oregon; Portland, Ore./AM; SFMA; Seattle/AM.

HANSEN, ROBERT. b. January 1, 1924, Osce-
ola, Neb. STUDIED: U. of Nebraska, with Kady
Faulkner, Dwight Kirsch, 1948, AB, BFA;
Escuela de Bellas Artes, San Miguel de Allende, Mexico; Universidad Michoacana, Morelia, Mexico, with Alfredo Zalce. US Army,
1943–46. Resided Mexico, Hawaii, India.
TAUGHT: Bradley U., 1949–55; U. of Hawaii,
1955–56; Occidental College, 1956– . COM-
MISSIONS (murals): Public School and State
Library, Morelia, Mexico. AWARDS: Fulbright
Fellowship (India), 1961; Guggenheim Foundation Fellowship, 1961. ADDRESS: 1974 Addi-
son Way, Los Angeles, Calif. DEALER: Comara
Gallery. ONE-MAN EXHIBITIONS: (first) Peoria

(Ill.) Art Center, 1951; Occidental College,
1957; Ferus Gallery, 1958; Bertha Lewinson
Gallery, Los Angeles, 1959; Huysman Gallery,
Los Angeles, 1961; Comara Gallery, 1963.
GROUP: UCLA, California Painters Under 35,
1959; Carnegie, 1961, 64; MOMA, Recent
Painting USA: The Figure circ., 1962–63;
WMAA, Fifty California Artists, 1962–63;
Pasadena/AM, Pacific Profile, 1960; Pasa-
dena/AM, Ten Californians, 1964; SFMA
Annuals, 1957, 58, 59; Oakland/AM Annuals,
1958, 60; U. of Nebraska, 1958; Ball State
Teachers College Annuals, 1957, 58, 60; Beloit
College, 1963. COLLECTIONS: Long Beach/MA;
MOMA.

HARE, DAVID. b. March 10, 1917, NYC.
STUDIED in New York, Arizona, Colorado
(majored in experimental color photography).
Researched and published a portfolio of color
photographs on the American Indian, in collaboration with Dr. Clark Whistler of the American Museum of Natural History, 1940. Editor,
VVV (surrealist magazine), 1942–44. Lectured
extensively. COMMISSIONS (sculpture): NYC;
Massachusetts; Rhode Island; Illinois. ADDRESS:
34 Leroy Street, NYC. ONE-MAN EXHIBITIONS:
(first) Hudson D. Walker Gallery, NYC, 1939;
Art of This Century, NYC, 1946, 47; Julien
Levy Galleries, NYC, 1946; The Kootz Gallery,
1946, 48, 51, 52, 55, 56, 58, 59; SFMA, 1947;
Galerie Maeght, 1948; Saidenberg Gallery,
1960–63. GROUP: MOMA, Fourteen Ameri-
cans, circ., 1946; I & IV Sao Paulo Biennials,
1951, 57; WMAA, The New Decade, 1954–55;
MOMA, Modern Art in the United States, circ.
Europe, 1955–56; Musee Rodin, Paris, Inter-
national Sculpture, 1956; Seattle/AM, circ.
Far East and Europe, 1958; Brussels World's
Fair, 1958; Chicago/AI, 1961; Seattle World's
Fair, 1962; Pittsburgh Bicentennial, 1962;
WMAA, 1962. COLLECTIONS: Brandeis U.;
Buffalo/Albright; Carnegie; Hartford/Wads-
worth; MMA; MOMA; SFMA; SRGM;
WMAA; Washington U.; Yale U. BIBLIOGRA-
PHY: Baur 5; Biddle 3; Blesh 1; Breton 3;
Brumme; Calas; Giedion-Welcker 1; Goodrich
and Baur 1; Goossen 2; Hess, T. B.; Hunter 5;
Janis and Blesh 1; Janis, S.; McCurdy, ed.;
Mendelowitz; Miller, ed. 2; Motherwell and
Reinhardt, eds.; Paalan; Ritchie 3; Rodman 1;
Seuphor 3.

HARTELL, JOHN. b. January 30, 1902, Brooklyn, N.Y. STUDIED: Cornell U. (Architecture), 1925; Royal Academy of Fine Arts, Stockholm. Traveled Europe. TAUGHT: Clemson College (Architecture), 1927–28; U. of Illinois, 1928–30; Cornell U., 1930– , Chairman, Department of Art, 1939–61. AWARDS: Illinois Wesleyan U., 1950; Utica, 1948, 52; New York State Fair, 1951; Rochester/Memorial, 1953; Fellow of the American Scandinavian Foundation. ADDRESS: 319 The Parkway, Ithaca, N.Y. DEALER: Kraushaar Galleries. ONE-MAN EXHIBITIONS: Kleemann Gallery, NYC, 1937; Kraushaar Galleries, 1943, 45, 49, 53, 57, 63; Cornell U., 1943, 46, 53, 57, 62; Wells College, 1945, 49, 55; Utica, 1952; Rochester/Memorial, 1954. GROUP: Architectural League of New York, 1932; Rochester/Memorial, 1943, 53, 54; WMAA, 1946, 50, 53; Carnegie, 1945, 46, 47; ICA, Boston; Cincinnati/AM, 1945; U. of Illinois, 1951; St. Louis/City, 1945; PAFA, 1953; Illinois Wesleyan U., 1950, 57; Utica, 1948, 51, 52, 54. COLLECTIONS: Cornell U.; Illinois Wesleyan U.; U. of Nebraska; Utica; Wake Forest College.

HARTIGAN, GRACE. b. March 28, 1922, Newark, N.J. STUDIED with Isaac Lane Muse, NYC, mid-1940's. Traveled Europe; resided Mexico, 1949. Designed set for *Red Riding Hood*, by Kenneth Koch, for the Artists Theater, NYC, 1953. ADDRESS: 209 Edgevale Road, Baltimore, Md. DEALER: Martha Jackson Gallery. ONE-MAN EXHIBITIONS: (first) Tibor de Nagy Gallery, 1951, also 1952, 53, 54, 55, 57, 59; Vassar College, 1954; Gres Gallery, Washington, D.C., 1960; Chatham College, 1960; Carnegie, 1961; Martha Jackson Gallery, 1962, 64; U. of Minnesota, 1963; Franklin Siden Gallery, Detroit, 1964. GROUP: Ninth Street Exhibition, NYC, 1951; U. of Minnesota, Rising Talent, 1955; MOMA, Modern Art in the United States, circ. Europe, 1955–56; MOMA, Twelve Americans, circ., 1956; Jewish Museum, The New York School, Second Generation, 1957; International Biennial Exhibition of Paintings, Tokyo; IV Sao Paulo Biennial, 1957; MOMA, The New American Painting, circ. Europe, 1958–59; Brussels World's Fair, 1958; ART:USA:59, NYC, 1959; Documenta II, Kassel, 1959; Walker, 60 American Painters, 1960; SRGM, Abstract Expressionists and Imagists, 1961; SRGM/USIA, American Vanguard, circ. Europe, 1961–62; PAFA, 1963; WMAA Annual, 1963. COLLECTIONS: Baltimore/MA; Brandeis U.; Brooklyn Museum; Buffalo/Albright; Carnegie; Chicago/AI; Kansas City/Nelson; MMA; MOMA; Minneapolis/Institute; New Paltz; RISD; Raleigh/NCMA; Vassar College; WGMA; WMAA; Walker; Washington U. BIBLIOGRAPHY: Friedman, ed.; Goodrich and Baur 1; Haftman; Hunter 1, 5; McCurdy, ed.; *Metro*; Nordness, ed.; Read 2.

HARTL, LEON. b. January 31, 1889, Paris, France. To USA 1912; citizen 1922. Self-taught. Expert on aniline dyes. MEMBER: Artists Equity. FEDERAL A.P.: Easel painting. AWARDS: NIAL, Marjorie Peabody Waite Award, 1959; Youngstown/Butler, Hon. Men., 1960. ADDRESS: 56 Seventh Avenue, NYC. DEALER: The Peridot Gallery. ONE-MAN EXHIBITIONS: (first) Whitney Studio Club, NYC, 1925, also 1926; Curt Valentine Gallery, NYC, 1927, 30, 36; Joseph Brummer Gallery, NYC, 1934, 38; The Peridot Gallery, 1954, 55, 58, 60, 62, 64. Group: Youngstown/Butler; Carnegie; Chicago/AI; Corcoran; Independent Artists, NYC, 1917, 18, 19; NIAL; Palazzo del Parco, Bordighera; PAFA; U. of Nebraska. COLLECTIONS: Hallmark Collection; Hartford/Wadsworth; U. of Nebraska; Phillips; Society of New York Hospitals; WMAA.

HARTLEY, MARSDEN. b. January 4, 1877, Lewiston, Me.; d. September 2, 1943, Ellsworth, Me. STUDIED: Cleveland Institute of Art, 1892, with C. Yates, N. Waldeck, C. Sowers; privately with John Semon; W. M. Chase School, NYC, 1898–99, with Frank V. DuMond, William M. Chase, F. L. Mora; NAD, 1900, with F. C. Jones, E. M. Ward, G. W. Maynard, E. H. Blashfield, F. J. Dillman, F. S. Hartley. Traveled USA extensively; Germany, France, Mexico. FEDERAL A.P.: Easel painting. AWARDS: Guggenheim Foundation Fellowship, 1931. ONE-MAN EXHIBITIONS: (first) Photo-Secession, NYC, 1909, also 1912, 14; The Daniel Gallery, NYC, 1915; Anderson Galleries, NYC, 1921; Montross Gallery, NYC, 1920; Stieglitz's Intimate Gallery, NYC, 1926, 29; Arts Club of Chicago, 1928, 45; An American Place (Gallery), NYC, 1930, 36, 37; The Downtown Gallery, 1932; Galeria de la Escuela Nacional de Artes Plasticas, Mexico City, 1933; Hudson D. Walker Gallery, NYC, 1938, 39, 40; Carlen Gallery, Philadelphia, 1938; Symphony Hall, Boston, 1939; Portland, Ore./AM, 1940; California Palace, 1940; Walker, 1940; P. Rosenberg and Co., 1944, 47, 48, 50, 55; Phillips, 1943; Macbeth Gallery, NYC, 1945; M. Knoedler & Co., NYC, 1942, 44; U. of Minnesota, 1952; Indianapolis/Herron, 1946; The Babcock Gallery, 1959, 60, 61; Santa Fe, N.M., 1958; The Bertha Schaefer Gallery, 1948, 56. RETRO-SPECTIVE: Cincinnati/AM, 1941; MOMA, 1944; A.F.A., circ., 1960. GROUP: The Armory Show, 1913; The Forum Gallery, 1916; Brooklyn Museum, 1926; WMAA, 1935, 38; Baltimore/MA, 1942; U. of Minnesota, 1937. COL-LECTIONS: MMA; MOMA; U. of Minnesota; WMAA; Walker. BIBLIOGRAPHY: Barker 1; Baur 7; Bazin; Biddle 3; Blesh 1; Born; Brown; Cahill and Barr, eds.; Canaday; Coke; Eliot; Flexner; Frank, ed.; Frost; Goldwater and Treves, eds.; Goodrich and Baur 1; Haftman; **Hartley;** Hunter 5; *Index of 20th Century Artists;* Janis, S.; Kootz 1, 2; **McCausland;** McCourbrey; McCurdy, ed.; Mellquist; Mendelowitz; Phillips 2; Read 2; Richardson; Ritchie 1; Rodman 2; Soby 6; Sutton; **Well, ed.;** Wight 2; Wright 1.

HARVEY, JAMES. b. March 9, 1929, Toronto (Ont.), Canada; **d.** July 15, 1965, NYC. STUDIED: Chicago Art Institute School, with Paul Wieghardt, BFA. Traveled Middle East, Europe, Russia. AWARDS: Fulbright Fellowship (Egypt), 1953; Yaddo Fellowship, 1960. ONE-MAN EXHIBITIONS: (first) Roko Gallery, 1953; Cairo, Egypt, 1954; Parma Gallery, NYC, 1956, 58; The Graham Gallery, 1959, 60, 61, 63. GROUP: WMAA Annual, 1952; MMA, American Paintings Today, 1950; WMAA, Fulbright Artists, 1958; Baltimore/MA, 1958; WMAA, Young America, 1960; Yale U., 1961; Corcoran, 1960. COLLECTIONS: Toronto.

HARVEY, ROBERT. b. September 16, 1924, Lexington, N.C. STUDIED: Ringling School of Art, with Elmer Harmes, Georgia Warren; San Francisco Art Institute, with Nathan Oliveira, Sonia Gechtoff. Traveled Great Britain, France, North Africa. AWARDS: Corcoran, Hon. Men. and Ford Foundation Purchase, 1963; San Francisco Art Festival, Award of Merit, 1963.

ADDRESS: 3340 Folsom Street, San Francisco, Calif. DEALER: Gump's Gallery. ONE-MAN EXHIBITIONS: (first) Saidenberg Gallery, 1954; Gump's Gallery, 1959, 61, 63, 64; Terry Dintenfass, Inc., 1963; La Escondida, Taos, N.M., 1962; Bedell Gallery, Santa Fe, N.M., 1962; Phoenix, 1964; Jefferson Gallery, La Jolla, 1964. GROUP: Corcoran, 1963; de Young, New Images of San Francisco; Oakland/AM; California Palace; Kansas City/Nelson; Denver/AM; Santa Barbara/MA; Phoenix; Santa Fe, N.M.; Raleigh/NCMA. COLLECTIONS: Corcoran; Crown Zellerbach Foundation; Storm King Art Center.

HAYES, DAVID V. b. March 15, 1931, Hartford, Conn. STUDIED: U. of Notre Dame, 1949–53, AB; Indiana U., with Robert Laurent, David Smith, 1955, MFA; Ogunquit School of Painting. US Navy, 1955–57. Traveled USA, Europe. AWARDS: Fulbright Fellowship, 1961; Guggenheim Foundation Fellowship, 1961; Chicago/AI, The Mr. & Mrs. Frank G. Logan Medal, 1961; Silvermine Guild, Sculpture Award, 1958. ADDRESS: c/o Dealer. DEALER: The Willard Gallery. ONE-MAN EXHIBITIONS: (first) Indiana U., 1955; Wesleyan U., 1958; New London, 1959; The Willard Gallery, 1961, 63, 64. GROUP: MOMA, New Talent; SRGM, 1958; MOMA, Recent Sculpture USA, 1959; Chicago/AI, 1961; Boston Arts Festival, 1960; Claude Bernard, Paris, 1960. COLLECTIONS: Andover/Phillips; Carnegie; Currier; Dallas/MFA; Hartford/Wadsworth; MOMA; SRGM.

HEBALD, MILTON. b. May 24, 1917, NYC. STUDIED: ASL, 1927–28; NAD, 1931–32; Master Institute of United Arts, Inc., NYC, 1931–34; Beaux-Arts Institute of Design, NYC, 1932–35. US Army, 1944–46. Traveled Europe, Near East, North Africa; resided Rome, nine years. TAUGHT: Brooklyn Museum School, 1946–51; Cooper Union, 1946–53; U. of Minnesota, 1949; Skowhegan School, summers, 1950, 51, 52. FEDERAL A.P.: Taught sculpture and worked on sculpture project, three years. COMMISSIONS: US Post Office, Toms River, N.J., 1940 (relief); Ecuador Pavilion, New York World's Fair, 1939 (façade); Republic Aviation Trophy, 1942; Isla Verde Aeroport, San Juan, P.R., 1954; East Bronx (N.Y.) TB Hospital, 1954; AAAL, 1957 (portrait bust of Archibald

MacLeish); Pan American Airways Terminal, NYC, 1957–58 (110-ft. bronze relief, "Zodiac"); 333 East 79 Street Building, NYC, 1962 (bronze fountain); U. of North Carolina, 1962. AWARDS: Prix de Rome, 1955–59; Brooklyn Museum, First Prize, 1950; ACA Gallery Competition, Exhibition Prize, 1937. ADDRESS: Viale Trastevere 60, Rome, Italy. ONE-MAN EXHIBITIONS: ACA Gallery (prize show), 1937, also 1940; Grand Central Moderns, 1949, 52; Lee Nordness Gallery, NYC, 1959, 60, 61, 63; Galleria Schneider, Rome, 1957, 63; Mickelson's Gallery, 1963. GROUP: Sculptors Guild, 1937–46; WMAA Annuals, 1937–63; PAFA, 1938–64. COLLECTIONS: AAAL; U. of Arizona; Bezalel Museum; Little Rock/MFA; U. of Notre Dame; PAFA; PMA; WMAA; Yale U. BIBLIOGRAPHY: Brumme; Cheney, M. C.

HELD, AL. b. October 12, 1928, NYC. STUDIED: ASL; Academie de la Grande Chaumiere. Traveled France, USA. TAUGHT: Yale U. ADDRESS: 182 Fifth Avenue, NYC. ONE-MAN EXHIBITIONS: (first) Poindexter Gallery, 1959, also 1961, 62; Galeria Bonino, Buenos Aires, 1961; Poindexter Gallery (two-man), 1958. GROUP: SRGM, Abstract Expressionists and Imagists, 1961; Marlborough Fine Art Ltd., London, 1961; ICA, Boston, 1961; Dallas/MFA, 1961, 62; WMAA, Geometric Abstraction in America, circ., 1962; Yale U., 1962; Carnegie, 1961; Corcoran, 1962; Jewish Museum, Toward a New Abstraction, 1963; MOMA, Abstract American Drawings and Watercolors, circ. Latin America, 1961–63; Chicago/AI, 1963, 64. COLLECTIONS: Brandeis U.; Geigy Chemical Corp.; Kunsthalle, Basel.

HELIKER, JOHN EDWARD. b. January 16, 1909, Yonkers, N.Y. STUDIED: ASL, 1927–29, with Kimon Nicolaides, Thomas Hart Benton, Kenneth Hayes Miller, Boardman Robinson. Traveled Europe; resided Italy, two years. TAUGHT: Colorado Springs Fine Arts Center; Columbia U. FEDERAL A.P.: Easel painting. AWARDS: Prix de Rome, 1948; NAD, The Adolph and Clara Obrig Prize, 1948; Guggenheim Foundation Fellowship, 1952; Corcoran, First Prize, 1941; NIAL Award, 1957; Ford Foundation, P.P., 1960, 61; Pepsi-Cola, 1946. ADDRESS: 865 West End Avenue, NYC. DEALER: Kraushaar Galleries. ONE-MAN EXHI-

BITIONS: (first) Maynard Walker Gallery, 1936, also 1938, 41; Kraushaar Galleries, 1945, 51, 54. GROUP: Chicago/AI, 1942, 43, 45; Carnegie, 1943, 44, 45; MMA; MOMA; PAFA, 1944, 46; U. of Illinois, 1961; WMAA, 1941–46, 1955, 56, 57; Brussels World's Fair, 1958; Toledo/MA, 1942, 43, 45; WMAA. The New Decade, 1954–55; Corcoran; VMFA. COLLECTIONS: Arizona State College; Atlanta U.; Brooklyn Museum; Chicago/AI; Cleveland/MA; Corcoran; Currier; Denver/AM; Des Moines; Hartford/Wadsworth; Harvard U.; Illinois Wesleyan U.; U. of Illinois; Kansas City/Nelson; MMA; U. of Miami; U. of Nebraska; PAFA; PMA; RISD; Rochester/Memorial; SFMA; Savannah/Telfair; Utica; WMAA; Walker; Washington U.; Wichita/AM. BIBLIOGRAPHY: Baur 5, 7; Goodrich and Baur 1; Kent, N.; Nordness, ed.; Pagano; Pousette-Dart, ed.; Ritchie 1.

HENDLER, RAYMOND. b. February 22, 1923, Philadelphia, Pa. STUDIED: Academie de la Grande Chaumiere; Contemporary School of Art, NYC; Temple U.; PAFA; Philadelphia Museum School; Graphic Sketch Club, Philadelphia, intermittently 1938–51. US Army in Europe, 1942–45. Traveled Europe extensively; resided Paris. TAUGHT: Assistant to Moses Soyer in NYC; adult classes, Philadelphia public school system; Samuel S. Fleisher Art Memorial, Philadelphia; Minneapolis Institute School; Moore Institute of Art, Science and Industry, Philadelphia; Parsons School of Design; Pratt Institute. A co-organizer of Galerie Huit, Paris. Director of the Hendler Gallery, Philadelphia, 1952–54. AWARDS: Longview Foundation Grant, 1963. ADDRESS: 4 Peter Cooper Road, NYC. DEALER: Rose Fried Gallery. ONE-MAN EXHIBITIONS: (first) Galerie Huit, Paris, 1951; Dubin Gallery, Philadelphia, 1952; Hendler Gallery, Philadelphia, 1953; Minneapolis/Institute, 1959; Rose Fried Gallery, 1962, 64. GROUP: Newark Museum; Paris/Moderne; Salon d'Art Libre, Paris; U. of Pennsylvania; U. of South Carolina; Montreal/MFA; Stanford U.; U. of Manitoba; Massillon Museum; Houston/MFA; Minneapolis/Institute; Walker; NYU. COLLECTIONS: NYU; Walker.

HENRY, CHARLES T. b. February 7, 1902, Niagara Falls, N.Y. STUDIED: Kirksville State College, BS.Ed.; ASL, with Thomas Hart Benton, George Grosz. Traveled Canada, Mexico, New Zealand, USA. TAUGHT privately intermittently. Life MEMBER, ASL. FEDERAL A.P.: Easel painting, 1934–37; taught for US Bureau of Prisons, Atlanta, Ga., 1938–39; murals for US Labor Department, Washington, D.C., and US Post Office, Cornelia, Ga. AWARDS: L. C. Tiffany Grant, 1929. ADDRESS: 1094 South Alfred, Los Angeles, Calif. ONE-MAN EXHIBITIONS: (first) Eighth Street Playhouse, NYC, 1934; Theodore A. Kohn Gallery, NYC, 1934; Kirksville State College, 1936; Atlanta/AA, 1939; Laurel Gallery, NYC, 1949; Havenstrite Gallery, Los Angeles, 1949; Chabot Gallery, Los Angeles, 1951. GROUP: City of Los Angeles Annuals, 1957, 59; Los Angeles/County MA; San Diego; Oakland/AM; WMAA; PAFA; NAD; Carnegie. COLLECTIONS: Northeast Missouri State Teachers College; Tiffany Foundation.

HIGGINS, EDWARD. b. 1930, Gaffney, S.C. STUDIED: U. of North Carolina, 1954, BA. TAUGHT: Parsons School of Design, 1962–63; Philadelphia Museum School, 1963. COMMISSIONS (sculpture): Cameron Building, NYC, 1962; New York State Theater, Lincoln Center for the Performing Arts, NYC, 1964. AWARDS: L. C. Tiffany Grant, 1962. ADDRESS: Old Philadelphia Road, RFD #4, Easton, Pa. DEALER: Leo Castelli Inc. ONE-MAN EXHIBITIONS: (first) Leo Castelli Inc., 1960, also 1963. GROUP: MOMA, Americans 1963, circ., 1963–64; Pasadena/AM, New American Sculpture, 1964;

WMAA, 1960, 62; SRGM, The Joseph H. Hirshhorn Collection, 1962; Carnegie, 1961; MOMA, Recent Sculpture USA, 1959; Tate, Gulbenkian International, 1964; Chicago/AI, 1961; Houston/MFA, 1961; Cornell U., 1959; Claude Bernard, Paris, 1960; New York World's Fair, 1964–65; Seattle World's Fair, 1962. COLLECTIONS: Buffalo/Albright; Chase Manhattan Bank; Chicago/AI; Dallas/MFA; MOMA; SRGM; WMAA. BIBLIOGRAPHY: Baur 7; Brown; Janis and Blesh 1; *Metro.*

HILLSMITH, FANNIE. b. March 13, 1911, Boston, Mass. STUDIED: Boston Museum School, with Burns, Guthrie; U. of London, Slade School, 1930–34; ASL, 1934–35, with Alexander Brook, Yasuo Kuniyoshi, William Zorach, John Sloan; Atelier 17, NYC, 1946–50, with S. W. Hayter. TAUGHT: Black Mountain College, 1945; Cornell U., 1963. AWARDS: Boston Museum School, Traveling Scholarship, 1958; Boston Arts Festival, First Prize, 1957, 63; Portland, Me./MA, First Prize, 1958. ADDRESS: 74 Middle Street, Lexington, Mass. DEALER: The Peridot Gallery. ONE-MAN EXHIBITIONS: Norlyst Gallery, NYC, 1943; Charles Egan Gallery, 1949, 54; The Swetzoff Gallery, 1949, 50, 54, 57, 63; The Peridot Gallery, 1957, 58, 62; Colby College, 1950; Lincoln, Mass./De Cordova, 1954, 58; Santa Barbara/MA, 1950; ICA, Boston, 1954; Dayton/AI, 1954; Milton Academy, 1952; Currier, 1954. GROUP: Art of This Century, NYC; Walker, 1953, 54; SRGM, 1954; American Abstract Artists, 1946–58;

Edward Higgins   *Untitled. 1963*

Joseph Hirsch   *The Beach.*

Carnegie, 1955; Corcoran; Phillips; A.F.A.; MOMA; Chicago/AI, 1947, 48, 54; Boston/MFA; AAAL; Brooklyn Museum; The Print Club, Philadelphia; Federation of Modern Painters and Sculptors, 1956, 57, 58; U. of Illinois, 1955, 57, 59; WMAA, 1949, 51, 55. **COLLECTIONS:** Andover/Phillips; Boston/MFA; Harvard U.; MOMA; NYPL; PMA. **BIBLIOGRAPHY:** Janis, S.

HIRSCH, JOSEPH. b. April 25, 1910, Philadelphia, Pa. **STUDIED:** Philadelphia Museum School, 1927–31; privately with Henry Hensche in Provincetown; with George Luks in NYC. Traveled Europe, the Orient, USA; resided France, five years. **TAUGHT:** Chicago Art Institute School; American Art School, NYC; U. of Utah; ASL, 1959–   . Artist war correspondent, 1943–44. **MEMBER:** Artists Equity (founder and first Treasurer); NAD; Philadelphia Watercolor Club. **FEDERAL A.P.:** Easel painting; first WPA murals in Philadelphia, for Amalgamated Clothing Workers Building and Municipal Court. **AWARDS:** Scholarship from the City of Philadelphia; PAFA, Walter Lippincott Prize; American Academy, Rome; New York World's Fair, 1939, First Prize; International Institute of Education Fellowship, 1935–36; NIAL Grant, 1947; Guggenheim Foundation Fellowship, 1942, 43; Carnegie, Second Prize, 1947; Library of Congress, Pennell P.P., 1944, 45; Chicago/AI, Watson F. Blair Prize; Fulbright Fellowship, 1949; NAD, Benjamin

Altman Prize, 1959; MMA, 1950. **ADDRESS:** 90 Riverside Drive, NYC. **DEALER:** The Forum Gallery. **ONE-MAN EXHIBITIONS:** ACA Gallery, Philadelphia; A.A.A. Gallery, NYC, 1946, 48, 54; The Forum Gallery. **GROUP:** WMAA; Newark Museum; Walker; MMA; Kansas City/Nelson; PAFA. **COLLECTIONS:** AAAL; Andover/Phillips; U. of Arizona; Boston/MFA; Bridgeport; Britannica; Brown U.; Chrysler Corp.; Coe College; Corcoran; Dallas/MFA; Dartmouth College; U. of Georgia; IBM; Kansas City/Nelson; Library of Congress; MMA; MOMA; Museum of Military History; NAD; U. of Oklahoma; PMA; Southampton/Parrish; Springfield, Mass./MFA; Harry S. Truman Library; WMAA; Walker; College of Wooster. **BIBLIOGRAPHY:** Baur 7; Cheney, M. C.; Genauer; Miller, ed. 1; Nordness, ed.; Pagano; Phillips 2; Reese; Richardson; Wight 2.

HOFMANN, HANS. b. March 21, 1880, Weissenberg, Bavaria, Germany; **d.** February 17, 1966, NYC. **STUDIED:** Gymnasium, Munich; Academie de la Grande Chaumiere, 1904. Resided Paris, 1904–14, with the patronage of Phillip Freudenberg, department store owner and art collector. **TAUGHT:** Opened first art school, 1915, in Munich; held summer sessions at Ragusa, 1924, Capri, 1925–27, Saint-Tropez, 1928, 29; Chouinard Art Institute, Los Angeles, 1930; U. of California, Berkeley, summer, 1930; ASL, 1932–33; Thurn School, Provincetown, summers, 1932, 33; opened own

Hans Hofmann   *Sparks. 1951*

school in NYC, 1933, own summer school in Provincetown, 1934. Stopped teaching 1958, to devote full time to painting. US citizen 1941. AWARDS: U. of Illinois, P.P., 1950; Society for Contemporary American Art, Chicago, P.P., 1952; PAFA, J. Henry Schiedt Memorial Prize, 1952; Chicago/AI, Flora Mayer Witkowsky Prize, 1959; II Inter-American Paintings and Prints Biennial, Mexico City, 1960, Hon. Men.; Chicago/AI, Ada S. Garrett Prize, 1961; Chicago/AI, The Mr. & Mrs. Frank G. Logan Medal, 1953; elected to the NIAL, 1964; Dartmouth College, hon. degree, 1962; U. of California, hon. degree, 1964. ONE-MAN EXHIBITIONS: (first) Paul Cassirer Gallery, Berlin, 1910; California Palace, 1931; New Orleans/Delgado, 1940; Art of This Century, NYC, 1944; "67" Gallery, NYC, 1944, 45; Betty Parsons Gallery, 1946, 47; Galerie Maeght, 1949; Boris Mirski Gallery, 1954; Baltimore/MA, 1954; Rutgers U., 1956; Dartmouth College, 1962; The Kootz Gallery, 1947, 49, 50, 51, 52, 53, 54, 55, 57, 58, 60, 61, 62, 63, 64. RETROSPECTIVE: Arts Club of Chicago, 1944; Andover/Phillips, 1948; Bennington College, 1955; Philadelphia Art Alliance, 1956; WMAA, circ., 1957; Germanisches National Museum, Nurnberg, circ. Germany, 1962; MOMA, circ. USA, Latin America, and Europe, 1963; The Kootz Gallery, 1959. GROUP: Chicago/AI; MOMA; U. of Illinois; Carnegie; Documenta II, Kassel, 1959; XXX Venice Biennial, 1960. COLLECTIONS: Abbott Laboratories; Andover/Phillips; Art of This Century (Peggy Guggenheim); Baltimore/MA; Buffalo/Albright; U. of California (Museum Hofmann); Chicago/AI; Cleveland/MA; Columbia Broadcasting System; Dallas/MFA; Dayton/AI; Fort Dodge/Banden;

Grenoble; U. of Illinois; Indianapolis/Herron; International Minerals & Chemicals Corp.; MMA; MOMA; Montreal/MFA; U. of Nebraska; Newark Museum; PMA; Rochester/Memorial; SRGM; Santa Barbara/MA; Toronto; WMAA; Walker; Washington U.; Yale U. **BIBLIOGRAPHY:** Barker 1; Baur 5, 7; Biddle 3; Blesh 1; Brion 1; Cheney, M. C.; Eliot; Goodrich and Baur 1; **Greenberg** 1, **2;** Haftman; Henning; Hess, T. B.; **Hofmann; Hunter** 1, **2,** 5; Janis and Blesh 1; Janis, S.; Kuh 2; **Loran 2;** McCurdy, ed.; Mendelowitz; *Metro;* Motherwell and Reinhardt, eds.; Newmeyer; Nordness, ed.; Ponente; Pousette-Dart, ed.; Read 2; Richardson; Ritchie 1; Rothschild; **Seitz** 1, **3;** Tapie 1; **Wight 1.**

HOLTY, CARL ROBERT. b. June 21, 1900, Freiburg, Germany. To USA 1900; citizen 1906. US Army, 1917–18. STUDIED: Marquette U., 1918–19; NAD, 1920–22; Academy of Fine Arts, Munich, 1925–26; Hofmann School, Munich. Traveled Europe. TAUGHT: ASL, 1939–40, 1950–51; U. of Georgia, 1948–50; U. of Florida, 1952–53; U. of California, Berkeley, summer, 1951; Brooklyn College, 1955–60; U. of Wisconsin, 1961; U. of Louisville, 1962–63; lectures extensively. MEMBER: American Abstract Artists. AWARDS: Ford Foundation, 1963. ADDRESS: 1245 Madison Avenue, NYC. DEALER: The Graham Gallery. ONE-MAN EXHIBITIONS: J. B. Neumann Gallery, NYC, 1936–44; Karl Nierendorf Gallery, NYC, 1938; The Kootz Gallery, 1946, 48; J. B. Neumann's New Art Circle, NYC, 1951, 52; Duveen-Graham Gallery, NYC, 1956; The Graham Gallery. GROUP: WMAA; PAFA; Corcoran; Chicago/AI; MMA; St. Louis/City; Los Angeles/County MA; Cincinnati/AM; Columbus. COLLECTIONS: Chattanooga/AA; Exeter; U. of Illinois; Milwaukee; SRGM; St. Louis/City; WMAA; Youngstown/Butler. BIBLIOGRAPHY: Baur 7; Blesh 1; Hess, T. B.; Janis, S.; Kootz 2; McCurdy, ed.; Passloff; Ritchie 1; Seuphor 1.

HOPKINS, BUDD. b. June 15, 1931, Wheeling, W.Va. STUDIED: Oberlin College, 1949–53, BA. Traveled Europe. COMMISSIONS: Walter P. Chrysler Museum of Art, Provincetown, 1958 (large painting). ADDRESS: 246 West 16 Street, NYC. DEALER: Poindexter Gallery. ONE-MAN EXHIBITIONS: (first) Poindexter Gallery, 1956, also 1962, 63; Tirca Karlis Gallery, 1958, 60,

62, 63, 64; The Zabriskie Gallery, 1959; Kasha Heman, Chicago, 1962, 63; Art Galleries Ltd., Washington, D.C., 1963; Athena Gallery, New Haven, 1964. GROUP: Wagner College, 1957; Oberlin College, 3 Young Painters, 1957; WMAA, 1958, 63; WMAA, Young America, 1960; Festival of Two Worlds, Spoleto, 1958; Charlotte/Mint, 1960; PAFA, 1964. COLLECTIONS: Historical Society of Montana; Norfolk; Provincetown/Chrysler; United Aircraft Corp.; WMAA.

HOPPER, EDWARD. b. July 22, 1882, Nyack, N.Y. STUDIED: New York School of Art, 1900–06, with Kenneth Hayes Miller, Robert Henri, George Luks, A. B. Davies; a commercial art school, NYC, 1899–1900; Paris, 1906–07, 1909–10. Traveled USA, France. AWARDS: Los Angeles/County MA, W. A. Bryan Prize, 1923; Chicago Society of Etchers, The Mr. & Mrs. Frank G. Logan Medal, 1923; US Shipping Board, Poster Prize, 1918; Baltimore/MA, Hon. Men., 1931; PAFA, Joseph E. Temple Gold Medal, 1935; NIAL, Gold Medal; Chicago/AI, Ada S. Garrett Prize, 1942; Worcester/AM, First P.P., 1935; Brooklyn Museum, 1931; Corcoran, William A. Clark Prize, 1937; Chicago/AI, The Mr. & Mrs. Frank G. Logan Medal, 1945; Chicago/AI, Hon. Men., 1946; Hallmark International Competition, 1957; Hon. DFA, Chicago/AI, 1950; Hon. Litt.D., Rutgers U., 1953. ADDRESS: 3 Washington Square North, NYC. DEALER: Rehn Galleries. ONE-MAN EXHIBITIONS: (first) Whitney Studio Club, NYC, 1919, also 1922; PAFA, 1925; Rehn Galleries, 1924, 27, 29, 46, 48; Currier, 1959; Carnegie, 1937; U. of Arizona, 1963; Arts Club of Chicago, 1934. RETROSPECTIVE: WMAA, 1960, 64; MOMA, 1933. GROUP: The Armory Show, 1913; WMAA; Cincinnati/AM, 1948; Smith College, Five Americans, 1934; Chicago/AI; Boston/MFA; PAFA; Corcoran. COLLECTIONS: Andover/Phillips; U. of Arizona; Boston/MFA; Brooklyn Museum; California State Library; Carnegie; Chicago/AI; Cleveland/MA; Corcoran; Hartford/Wadsworth; Harvard U.; IBM; Indianapolis/Herron; Kansas City/Nelson; Library of Congress; MMA; MOMA; Montclair/AM; Muskegon/Hackley; NYPL; U. of Nebraska; Newark Museum; New Orleans/Delgado; PAFA; Phillips; Randolph-Macon College; Terre Haute/Swope; Toledo/MA; Victoria and Albert Museum; WMAA;

Edward Hopper   *High Noon. 1949*

Walker; West Palm Beach/Norton; Wichita/AM; Worcester/AM; Yale U.; Youngstown/Butler. **BIBLIOGRAPHY:** Barker 1; **Barr 2,** 3; Baur 7; Bazin; Blesh 1; Boswell 1; Brown; Canaday; Cheney, M. C.; Christensen; Coke; **Du Bois 2;** Eliot; Flexner; Goldwater and Treves, eds.; **Goodrich 1, 3, 4;** Goodrich and Baur 1; Haftman; Hall; **Hopper;** Hunter 5; *Index of 20th Century Artists;* Jewell 2; Kuh 1, 2; Langui; McCourbrey; McCurdy, ed.; Mellquist; Mendelowitz; Neuhaus; Newmeyer; Nordness, ed.; Pagano; Pearson 1; Phillips 1, 2; Poore; Pousette-Dart, ed.; Print Council of America; Reese; Richardson; Ringel, ed.; Rodman 1; Sachs; Soby 5, 6; Sutton; Wight 2.

HORIUCHI, PAUL. b. April 12, 1906, Japan. Self-taught. Traveled Europe, Japan. **COMMISSIONS:** Seattle World's Fair, 1962 (free-standing mural). **AWARDS:** Ford Foundation, P.P.; Tupperware National Competition; and some 30 others. **ADDRESS:** 1547 32nd Avenue, South, Seattle, Wash. **DEALERS:** Felix Landau Gallery; Zoé Dusanne Gallery. **ONE-MAN EXHIBITIONS:** (first) Seattle/AM, 1954, also 1958; Little Rock/MFA, 1958; Zoé Dusanne Gallery, 1959, 63; Everett Junior College, 1960; U. of Arizona, 1962; Lee Nordness Gallery, NYC, 1963; Felix Landau Gallery, 1963; Reed College, 1964. **GROUP:** Carnegie, 1961; Rome-New York Foundation, Rome, 1959; ART:USA:59, NYC, 1959; Seattle World's Fair, 1962; Rikkikai (Group), Tokyo, 1963; SFMA Annuals; Denver/AM;

Seattle/AM. **COLLECTIONS:** U. of Arizona; Denver/AM; Everett Junior College; Fort Worth; Hartford/Wadsworth; Harvard U.; U. of Oregon; Santa Barbara/MA; Seattle/AM; Seattle Civic Center; Seattle Public Library; Tacoma.

HOVANNES, JOHN. b. December 31, 1900, Smyrna, Turkey. **STUDIED:** RISD. **TAUGHT:** Cooper Union, 1945–46; ASL, 1945–46. **AWARDS:** Guggenheim Foundation Fellowship, 1940; Eugene Meyer Award, 1941; MMA, Artists for Victory, 1942. **ADDRESS:** 24 West 30 Street, NYC. **ONE-MAN EXHIBITIONS:** Robinson Galleries, NYC, 1941. **GROUP:** PAFA, 1942, 43, 45, 46; Chicago/AI, 1942, 43; MMA, 1942, 51; NAD, 1943; Riverside Museum, 1943; WMAA, 1942–46; U. of Nebraska, 1945; New York World's Fair, 1939. **COLLECTIONS:** Newark Museum; Society of the Four Arts; Tel Aviv. **BIBLIOGRAPHY:** Baur 7; Brumme.

HOWARD, CHARLES. b. January 2, 1899, Montclair, N.J. **STUDIED:** U. of California, Berkeley, 1921; Harvard U.; Columbia U. Traveled USA, Europe. **TAUGHT:** Camberwell School, London, 1959– . **FEDERAL A.P.:** Design Supervisor, mural at US Naval Air Station, Alameda, Calif. **AWARDS:** SFMA, P.P., 1940; SFMA, 1942; MMA, Artists for Victory, 1942; California Palace, First Prize; La Tausca Competition, P.P., 1947; Pasadena/AM, Third Prize, 1946. **ADDRESS:** The End Cottage, Helions Bumpstead, Essex, England. DEALER: The Howard Wise Gallery, NYC. ONE-MAN EXHIBITIONS: (first) Whitney Studio Club, NYC, 1926; Julien Levy Galleries, NYC, 1933; Bloomsbury Gallery, London, 1935; Guggenheim Jeune (Gallery), London, 1939; Courvoisier Gallery, San Francisco, 1941; U. of California, Berkeley, 1941; SFMA, 1942; Karl Nierendorf Gallery, NYC, 1946; Santa Barbara/MA, 1953; Hanover Gallery, 1949; Heller Gallery, Cambridge, England, 1951; St. George's Gallery, London, 1958. RETROSPECTIVE: California Palace, 1946; Whitechapel Art Gallery, London, 1956. GROUP: MOMA, Americans 1942, circ., 1942; Salons of America, NYC, 1933; New Burlington Galleries, London, International Surrealist Exhibition, 1936; Sao Paulo, 1938; SFMA, 1940, 41, 42, 43, 44, 45, 46; Carnegie, 1941, 46; MMA, 1942, 52; Chicago/AI, 1942, 46, 48; WMAA, 1943, 44, 45, 46; Corcoran, 1943, 47; California Palace, 1945, 46, 47, 48, 49; Tate, American Painting, 1946; Salon des Realites Nouvelles, Paris, 1949. COLLECTIONS: Chicago/AI; Container Corp. of America; Dallas/MFA; Jesus College; MMA; Pasadena/AM; SFMA; SRGM. BIBLIOGRAPHY: Baur 7; Blesh 1; Frost; Genauer; Guggenheim, ed.; Howard; Janis, S.; McCurdy, ed.; Miller, ed. 1; Ragon 2; Read 2; Richardson; Ritchie 1; Robertson 1.

HUDSON, ROBERT. b. September 8, 1938, Salt Lake City, Utah. STUDIED: San Francisco Art Institute, 1962–63. AWARDS: RAC, 1959; San Francisco Art Festival, P.P., 1961; SFMA, 1963; San Jose State College, P.P., 1964. ADDRESS: c/o Dealer. DEALER: Allan Frumkin Gallery, NYC. ONE-MAN EXHIBITIONS: RAC, 1961; Batman Gallery, San Francisco, 1961; Bolles Gallery, San Francisco, 1962. GROUP: RAC, 1959, 60, 61; Oakland/AM, 1961, 63; La Jolla, 1961; SFMA. COLLECTIONS: SFMA.

HUETER, JAMES W. b. May 15, 1925, San Francisco, Calif. STUDIED: Pomona College, BA, MFA; Claremont Graduate School, with Henry McFee, Sueo Serisawa, Millard Sheets, Albert Stewart. TAUGHT: Mount San Antonio College; Pomona College, 1959–60. AWARDS: Pasadena/AM, 1953; Los Angeles County Fair, 1951; Los Angeles/County MA, 1955; California State Fair, P.P., 1957; Long Beach State College, 1960, 61. ADDRESS: 439 Arrow Highway, Claremont, Calif. ONE-MAN EXHIBITIONS:

Mount San Antonio College, 1952; First National Bank, Ontario, Calif., 1954; Pasadena/AM, 1955; Long Beach State College, 1957; Whittier (Calif.) Art Association, 1959; Monrovia (Calif.) Public Library, 1961. GROUP: Youngstown/Butler, 1955, 58, 59; Los Angeles County Fair, 1949, 51, 52; Chaffey College, 1951, 55, 59, 60; Denver/AM, 1954; Los Angeles/County MA, 1952, 54, 55, 57, 58, 61; Pasadena/AM, 1950, 51, 52, 53, 54; California State Fair, 1950, 51, 52, 53, 54, 55, 58; Newport Harbor, 1950, 54, 55; Palos Verdes, 1953, 55; Long Beach/MA, 1960; Mount San Antonio College, 1961; Pomona College, 1961; RAC, 1960; Long Beach State College, 1960, 61; California Palace, 1960. COLLECTIONS: California State Fair; Long Beach State College; Los Angeles County Fair Association; National Orange Show; Pasadena/AM; Scripps College.

HULTBERG, JOHN. b. February 8, 1922, Berkeley, Calif. STUDIED: Fresno State College, 1939–43, BA; ASL, 1941–51, with Morris Kantor; California School of Fine Arts, with Clay Spohn, Richard Diebenkorn, David Park, Clyfford Still, Mark Rothko. US Navy, 1943–46. TAUGHT: ASL, summer, 1960; Boston Museum School, 1958. COMMISSIONS: *Fortune* Magazine (portfolio of drawings of Newport News Shipbuilding Co.) AWARDS: CSFA, Albert M. Bender Fellowship, 1949; Corcoran, First Prize, 1955; Congress for Cultural Freedom, First Prize, 1955; Carnegie, Hon. Men., 1955; Guggenheim Foundation Fellowship, 1956; Hallmark International Competition, 1957; Chicago/AI, Norman Wait Harris Medal, 1962; Ford Foundation/A.F.A. Artist-in-Residence, 1964. ADDRESS: 473½ Vallejo Street, San Francisco, Calif. DEALER: Martha Jackson Gallery. ONE-MAN EXHIBITIONS: (first) Contemporary Gallery, Sausalito, Calif., 1949; Korman Gallery, NYC, 1953; Martha Jackson Gallery, 1955, 58, 59, 61, 63; ICA, London, 1956; Galerie Rive Droite, Paris, 1957; Galerie du Dragon, 1957, 59; The Swetzoff Gallery, 1957; Phoenix, 1957; Numero Galleria d'Arte, Florence, Italy, 1958; Main Street Gallery, 1959; David Anderson Gallery, NYC, 1961; Piccadilly Gallery, London, 1961; Museum of Malmo, Sweden, 1962; Esther Baer Gallery, 1962, 64; Roswell, 1963. GROUP: California Palace, 1947; MOMA, New Talent; Corcoran, 1955; WMAA Annuals, 1955, 64; XXVIII Venice Biennial, 1956; Gutai 9, Osaka,

John Hultberg   *Landscape with Flag. 1958*

1958; Carnegie, 1958; ART:USA:59, NYC, 1959; Chicago/AI, 1962; Brooklyn Museum, 1964. **COLLECTIONS:** Eindhoven; MMA; MOMA; Stockholm/National; WMAA. **BIBLIOGRAPHY:** Blesh 1; Janis and Blesh 1; Nordness, ed.

HUNT, RICHARD. b. September 12, 1935, Chicago, Ill. **STUDIED:** U. of Illinois; The U. of Chicago; Chicago Art Institute School, 1959, BA.Ed. US Army, 1958–60. Traveled Europe. **TAUGHT:** U. of Illinois, 1960–62; Chicago Art Institute School, 1960–61; Yale U., 1964; Chouinard Art Institute, Los Angeles, 1964–65. **COMMISSIONS:** Louisiana State U., 1960. **AWARDS:** Chicago/AI, James Nelson Raymond Traveling Fellowship, 1957; Guggenheim Foundation Fellowship, 1962. **ADDRESS:** 1503 No. Cleveland Avenue, Chicago, Ill. **DEALERS:** B. C. Holland Gallery; Felix Landau Gallery. **ONE-MAN EXHIBITIONS:** (first) The Alan Gallery, 1958, also 1960, 63; B. C. Holland Gallery, 1961, 63; Stewart Richard Gallery, San Antonio, 1960, 64; U. of Tulsa, 1964; Wesleyan College, 1964. **GROUP:** New Sculpture Group, NYC, 1960, 61; U. of Illinois; MOMA; WMAA; Michigan State U.; Smith College, Yale U.; Newark Museum; Carnegie; Seattle World's Fair, 1962. **COLLECTIONS:** Bezalel Museum; Buffalo/Albright; Chicago/AI; Cleveland/MA; MOMA; WMAA.

i

INDIANA, ROBERT. b. September 13, 1928, New Castle, Ind. STUDIED: U. of Edinburgh; John Herron Art Institute; Munson-Williams-Proctor Institute, Utica, N.Y.; Chicago Art Institute School, BFA. Traveled USA, Mexico, Europe. COMMISSIONS: New York State Pavilion, New York World's Fair, 1964–65 (mural); New York State Theater, Lincoln Center for the Performing Arts, NYC (poster). AWARDS: Chicago/AI, Traveling Fellowship, 1953. ADDRESS: 25 Coenties Slip, NYC. DEALER: The Stable Gallery. ONE-MAN EXHIBITIONS: (first) The Stable Gallery, 1962, also 1964; Walker (two-man, with Richard Stankiewicz), 1964. GROUP: WMAA, New Directions in American Painting, 1963; MOMA, The Art of Assemblage, circ., 1961; ICA, London, The Popular Image, 1963; Chicago/AI Annual, 1963; WMAA Annual, 1964; MOMA, Americans 1963, circ., 1963–64; Bertrand Russell Peace Foundation, Woburn Abbey, England, 1963; Tate, Dunn International, 1964; Tate, Painting and Sculpture of a Decade, 1954–64, 1964. COLLECTIONS: Allentown/AM; Brandeis U.; Buffalo/Albright; MOMA; Toronto; WMAA; Walker. BIBLIOGRAPHY: Seitz 2.

IPPOLITO, ANGELO. b. November 9, 1922, St. Arsenio, Italy. STUDIED: Ozenfant School of Art, NYC, 1946–47; Brooklyn Museum School, 1948; Instituto Meschini, Rome, 1949–50. Traveled Europe. TAUGHT: Cooper Union, 1956–59, 1962–64; Sarah Lawrence College, 1957; U. of California, Berkeley, 1961–62; Queens College, 1963–64; Visiting Critic, Yale U., 1961. A co-founder of the Tanager Gallery, NYC. COMMISSIONS: New York Hilton Hotel, 1963. AWARDS: Fulbright Fellowship (Italy), 1959. ADDRESS: 224 East 17 Street, NYC. DEALER: Grace Borgenicht Gallery Inc. ONE-MAN EXHIBITIONS: (first) Galleria della Rotondo, Bergamo, 1950; Tanager Gallery, NYC, 1954, 62; The Bertha Schaefer Gallery, 1956, 58; HCE Gallery, 1957, 61; Massillon Museum; Canton (Ohio) Museum; Cleveland Institute of Art, 1960; U. of California, 1961; Michigan State U., 1962; Grace Borgenicht Gallery Inc., 1963; Bolles Gallery, San Francisco, 1962. GROUP: Arts Club of Chicago, 1953; Walker, Vanguard, 1955; WMAA Annuals, 1955, 57, 59, 62; Utica, 1955, 57; WMAA, Young America, 1957; A.F.A., Collage in America, circ., 1957–58; WMAA, Nature in Abstraction, 1958; USIA, 20th Century Graphics, circ., 1956–58; VI Sao Paulo Biennial, 1961; Silvermine Guild, 1963. COLLECTIONS: CIT Corporation; MMA; Massillon Museum; Michigan State U.; U. of Michigan; Montreal Trust Co.; Provincetown/Chrysler; Sarah Lawrence College; Utica; WMAA. BIBLIOGRAPHY: Baur 5; Goodrich and Baur 1; Janis and Blesh 1.

JACOBS, DAVID, b. March 1, 1932, Niagara Falls, N.Y. STUDIED: Orange Coast College, 1951–53; Los Angeles State College of Applied Arts and Sciences, 1953–57. TAUGHT: The Ohio State U., 1957–62; Hofstra U., 1963– . ADDRESS: c/o Dealer. DEALER: The Kornblee Gallery. ONE-MAN EXHIBITIONS: Barone Gallery, NYC, 1961; The Kornblee Gallery, 1963, 64. GROUP: MOMA, 1961; SRGM; SFMA; Dayton/AI; Vassar College; Indianapolis/Herron; Akron/AI, 1964. COLLECTIONS: The Ohio State U.; SRGM; VMFA.

JARVAISE, JAMES. b. February 26, 1925, Indianapolis, Ind. STUDIED: U. of Southern California, 1947–52, BFA, MFA. Traveled Europe; resided Spain, France. TAUGHT: U. of Southern California, 1955–62; The Pennsylvania State U. ADDRESS: 2697 Tanoble Drive, Altadena, Calif. DEALER: Felix Landau Gallery. ONE-MAN EXHIBITIONS: (first) Felix Landau Gallery, 1952, also 1955, 58, 60, 61, 62, 64; Thibaut Gallery, NYC, 1961; Gump's Gallery (two-man), 1961. GROUP: Oakland/AM, 1951, 57; Santa Barbara/MA, 1951, 57; Seattle/AM, 1951; MMA, 1953; Denver/AM, 1953, 54, 58; Corcoran, 1953; U. of Illinois, 1953, 57; Long Beach/MA, Fifteen Americans, circ., 1956; U. of Nebraska, 1958; MOMA, Sixteen Americans, circ., 1959; Carnegie, 1959; El Retiro Parquet, Madrid, Arte de America y España, 1963. COLLECTIONS: Andover/Phillips; Buffalo/Albright; Carnegie; Los Angeles/County MA; MOMA; Youngstown/Butler.

JENKINS, PAUL. b. 1923, Kansas City, Mo. STUDIED: Kansas City Art Institute and School of Design, 1938–41; ASL, 1948–51. Resides Paris, New York. ADDRESS: 831 Broadway, NYC. DEALERS: Martha Jackson Gallery; Galerie Karl Flinker; A. Tooth & Sons. ONE-MAN EXHIBITIONS: (first) Studio Paul Facchetti, Paris, 1954; Zimmergaleries Franck, Frankfurt am Main, 1954; Zoé Dusanne Gallery, 1955; Martha Jackson Gallery, 1956, 58, 60, 61, 64; Galerie Stadler, Paris, 1957, 59; Galerie Karl Flinker, 1960, 61, 63; A. Tooth & Sons, 1960, 63; Esther Robles Gallery, 1963; Galleria Toninelli, Milan, 1962; Galerie Charles Leinhard, Zurich, 1962; Galleria Odyssia, Rome, 1962; Kunstverein, Cologne, 1962; Eva de Buren Gallery, Stockholm, 1963; Kestner-Gesellschaft, Hannover, 1964; Tokyo Gallery, 1964. GROUP: Musee du Petit Palais, Paris, 1955; MOMA, Recent Drawings USA, 1956; Arts Council Gallery, London, New Trends in Painting, 1957; WMAA, Young America, 1957; Carnegie, 1958, 61; WMAA, Nature in Abstraction, 1958; Corcoran, 1958; SRGM, Abstract Expressionists and Imagists, 1961; Salon du Mai, Paris, 1962; WMAA Annual, 1962; Seattle World's Fair, 1962; Art:USA:Now, circ., 1962– ; Salon des Realites Nouvelles, Paris, 1963; Tate, Painting and Sculpture of a Decade, 1954–64, 1964. COLLECTIONS: Amsterdam/Stedelijk; Bezalel Museum; Buffalo/Albright; Busch-Reisinger Museum; France/National; S. C. Johnson & Son, Inc.; Liverpool/Walker; Phoenix; Provincetown/Chrysler; SRGM; WMAA; Walker. BIBLIOGRAPHY: Baur 5; **Jenkins, P. and E., eds.;** *Metro;* Nordness, ed.; Read 2; **Sawyer.**

JENSEN, ALFRED. b. December 11, 1903, Guatemala City, Guatemala. STUDIED: San Diego Fine Arts School, 1925; Hofmann School,

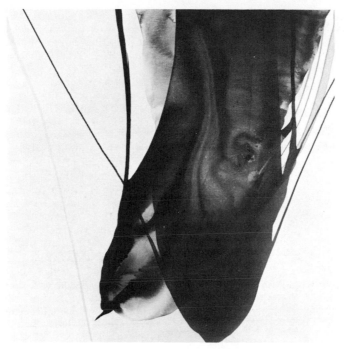

Paul Jenkins   *Phenomena Cross Purpose. 1964*

Munich, 1927–28; Academie Scandinave, Paris, with Charles Despiau, Charles Dufresne, Othon Friesz, Marcel Gromaire, Andre Masson. Traveled USA, Europe. **TAUGHT:** Maryland Institute, 1958. **COMMISSIONS:** Time Inc. (mural). **ADDRESS:** 284 East 10 Street, NYC. **DEALER:** The Graham Gallery. **ONE-MAN EXHIBITIONS:** (first) John Heller Gallery, NYC, 1952; The Bertha Schaefer Gallery, 1957; Martha Jackson Gallery, 1957; The Graham Gallery, 1963; Klipstein & Kornfeld, Berne, 1964; Rolf Nelson Gallery, 1964; Tanager Gallery, NYC, 1955. **GROUP:** San Diego; Baltimore/MA; MOMA; WMAA. **COLLECTIONS:** Baltimore/MA; MOMA; SRGM; San Diego.

JOHNS, JASPER. b. May, 1930, Allendale, S.C. **STUDIED:** U. of South Carolina. **ADDRESS:** 340 Riverside Drive, NYC; 128 Front Street, NYC. **DEALER:** Leo Castelli Inc. **ONE-MAN EXHIBITIONS:** Leo Castelli Inc., 1958, also 1960, 61, 63; Galerie Rive Droite, Paris, 1959, 61; Galleria d'Arte del Naviglio, Milan, 1959; Columbia, S.C./MA, 1960; U. of Minnesota, 1960; Ferus Gallery (two-man), 1960; Ileana

Sonnabend (Gallery), Paris, 1962; Everett Ellin Gallery, Los Angeles, 1962. **RETROSPECTIVE:** Jewish Museum, 1964. **GROUP:** Jewish Museum, The New York School, Second Generation, 1957; Houston/MFA, Collage International, 1958; Carnegie, 1958, 61; XXIX Venice Biennial, 1958; A.F.A., Collage in America, circ., 1957–58; Daniel Cordier, Paris, Exposition InteRnatiOnale de Surrealisme, 1959; Houston/MFA, Out of the Ordinary, 1959; Columbus, Contemporary American Painting, 1960; Martha Jackson Gallery, New Media—New Forms, I & II, 1960, 61; A.F.A., School of New York—Some Younger American Painters, 1960; WMAA Annuals, 1960, 61, 62, 64; SRGM/USIA, American Vanguard, circ. Europe, 1961–62; SRGM, Abstract Expressionists and Imagists, 1961; MOMA, Modern American Drawings, circ. Europe, 1961–62; MOMA, Abstract Watercolors and Drawings:USA, circ. Latin America and Europe, 1961–62; Chicago/AI, 1962; Dallas/MFA, 1961–62; Stockholm/National; Amsterdam/Stedelijk; Berne, 4 Americans, 1962; Salon du Mai, Paris, 1962; Seattle World's Fair, 1962; III International

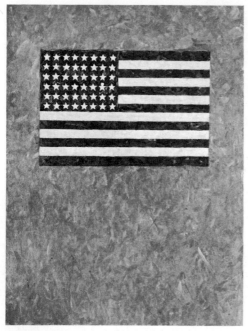

Jasper Johns   *Flag on Orange Field. 1957*

Biennial of Prints, Tokyo, 1962; MOMA, Lettering by Hand, 1962; SRGM, Six Painters and The Object, circ., 1963; WGMA, The Popular Image, 1963; Musee Cantonal des Beaux-Arts, Lausanne, I Salon International de Galeries Pilotes, 1963; Tate, Dunn International, 1964; ICA, London, The Popular Image, 1963; Buffalo/Albright, Mixed Media and Pop Art, 1963; El Retiro Parquet, Madrid, Arte de America y España, 1963; Jewish Museum, Black and White, 1963; Hartford/Wadsworth, Black, White, and Gray, 1964. COLLECTIONS: Buffalo/Albright; Hartford/Wadsworth; MOMA; Stockholm/National; Tate. BIBLIOGRAPHY: Friedman, ed.; Janis and Blesh 1; *Metro;* Rodman 3; Seitz 2; **Steinberg, L.**

JOHNSON, BEN. b. September 11, 1902, NYC. STUDIED: Pratt Institute. AWARDS: Two L. C. Tiffany Grants, 1930–33; Saratoga Springs Centennial, First Prize, 1963. ADDRESS: P.O. Box 104, Bearsville, N.Y. DEALER: Gallery 63, Inc., NYC. ONE-MAN EXHIBITIONS: (first) Jumble Shop Restaurant, NYC, 1930; Parnassus Square Gallery, Woodstock, N.Y.; Advanced Gallery, NYC; The Zabriskie Gallery, 1957, 59; Cober Gallery, 1960; The Kornblee Gallery, 1963; David Stuart Gallery, 1963; Gallery 63, Inc., NYC, 1964. GROUP: WMAA, 1963; Chicago/AI, 1964; Brooklyn Museum, Watercolor Biennials; WGMA; A.F.A., Mother and Child in Modern Art, circ., 1963.

JOHNSON, BUFFIE. b. February 20, 1912, NYC. STUDIED: ASL; Atelier 17, Paris, with S. W. Hayter (engraving); UCLA, MA. Traveled extensively, Europe, Mexico, USA. TAUGHT: Parsons School of Design, 1946–50; US State Department lecturer. COMMISSIONS: Astor Theater, NYC, 1959 (murals). ADDRESS: East Hampton, N.Y. ONE-MAN EXHIBITIONS: (first) Jake Zeitlin Gallery, 1937; Galerie Rotge, Paris, 1939; Wakefield Gallery, NYC, 1939; Vose Gallery, Boston, 1942; Caresse Crosby, Washington, D.C., 1944; "67" Gallery, NYC, 1945; Ringling, 1948; Galleria del Cavallino, Venice, 1948; Hanover Gallery, 1949; Galerie Colette Allendy, Paris, 1949; Betty Parsons Gallery, 1950; Choate School, Wallingford, Conn., 1951; Galeries Bing, Paris, 1956, 60; Bodley Gallery, NYC, 1960; Thibaut Gallery, NYC, 1961; Granville Gallery, NYC, 1964; Galeria Antonio Souza, Mexico City, 1964. GROUP: Salon des Realites Nouvelles, Paris, 1949, 50; Baltimore/MA; Walker; Brooklyn Museum, 1950, 54; WMAA; Carnegie, 1941; Art of This Century, NYC, 1943; U. of Illinois, 1955. COLLECTIONS: Baltimore/MA; Boston/MFA; Cincinnati/AM; Cornell U.; U. of Illinois; Layton School of Art; U. of Michigan; NYU; Newark Museum; RISD; Santa Barbara/MA; Utica; WMAA; Walker; Yale U.

JOHNSON, LESTER. b. January 27, 1919, Minneapolis, Minn. STUDIED: Minneapolis Institute School, St. Paul School of Art, Chicago Art Institute School (1942–47, with Cameron Booth, Alexander Masley, Glen Mitchel). TAUGHT: Yale U., 1964. AWARDS: Alfred Pillsbury Scholarship; St. Paul Gallery Scholarship; Midwestern Artists Competition, First Prize, 1942. ADDRESS: 154 Old Stone Road, East Hampton, N.Y. DEALER: Martha Jackson Gallery. ONE-MAN EXHIBITIONS: (first) Artists' Gallery, NYC, 1951; Korman Gallery, NYC, 1954; The Zabriskie Gallery, 1955, 57, 58, 59, 61; Minneapolis/Institute, 1961; B. C. Holland Gallery, 1962; Dayton/AI, 1962; Fort Worth; The Ohio State U.; City Gallery, NYC, 1959;

Sun Gallery, Provincetown, 1956, 57, 58, 59; HCE Gallery, 1960, 62; Martha Jackson Gallery, 1962, 63. GROUP: PAFA; Minneapolis/Institute; Jewish Museum, The New York School, Second Generation, 1957; Minneapolis/Institute, American Painting, 1945–57, 1957; Baltimore/MA, Critics Choice, 1958; WMAA, 1958; ICA, Boston, 100 Works on Paper, circ. Europe, 1959; A.F.A., The Figure, circ., 1960; ICA, Boston, Future Classics, 1960; A.F.A., Graphics '60, 1960; MOMA, Recent Painting USA:The Figure, circ., 1962–63; MOMA, Recent American Painting and Sculpture, circ. USA and Canada, 1961–62; Chicago/AI, Recent Trends in Painting, USA, 1962; Carnegie, 1961. COLLECTIONS: Dayton/AI; MOMA; Provincetown/Chrysler.

JOHNSTON, YNEZ. b. May 12, 1920, Berkeley, Calif. STUDIED: U. of California, Berkeley, BA, 1946, MA. Traveled Europe, USA. TAUGHT: U. of California, Berkeley, 1950–51; Colorado Springs Fine Arts Center, summers, 1945, 55. COMMISSIONS: International Graphic Arts Society, 1958, 60. AWARDS: Guggenheim Foundation Fellowship, 1952; L. C. Tiffany Grant, 1955; MMA, 1952; SFMA, James D. Phelan Award, 1958. ADDRESS: 2009 Third Street, Santa Monica, Calif. ONE-MAN EXHIBITIONS: O'Hara Gallery, London, 1958; Paul Kantor Gallery, 1952, 53, 57, 58, 59, 64; American Contemporary Gallery, Hollywood, 1948; Pasadena/AM, 1954; Chicago/AI (two-man), 1952; Fraymont Gallery, Los Angeles, 1952; SFMA, 1943; U. of Redlands, 1947; Santa Barbara/MA, 1952, 57; Colorado Springs/FA, 1955; California Palace, 1956. GROUP: Carnegie, 1955; WMAA, 1951–55; U. of Illinois, 1951–54; SFMA; Los Angeles/County MA;

MOMA, New Talent. COLLECTIONS: Albion College; Hartford/Wadsworth; U. of Illinois; La Jolla; Los Angeles/County MA; MMA; MOMA; Michigan State U.; U. of Michigan; PMA; Pasadena/AM; St. Louis/City; San Diego; Santa Barbara/MA; Tulsa/Philbrook; WMAA. BIBLIOGRAPHY: Pousette-Dart, ed.

JONES, JOHN PAUL. b. November 18, 1924, Indianola, Iowa. STUDIED: State U. of Iowa, 1949, BFA, 1951, MFA. AWARDS: L. C. Tiffany Grant, 1951; Guggenheim Foundation Fellowship, 1960; and more than 40 others. ADDRESS: c/o Dealer. DEALER: Felix Landau Gallery. ONE-MAN EXHIBITIONS: Iowa Wesleyan College, 1951; Des Moines, 1951; Fort Dodge/Banden, 1951; San Antonio/McNay, 1951; U. of Oklahoma, 1952; Los Angeles/County MA (two-man), 1954; Kalamazoo/Institute, 1955; Felix Landau Gallery, 1956, 58, 62; Oakland/AM, 1956; Laguna Blanca School, Santa Barbara, 1958; Santa Barbara/MA, 1958; Pasadena/AM, 1959; Taft College, 1959; Galleria Cadario, Milan, 1961; Arizona State U., 1962. GROUP: Youngstown/Butler; U. of Illinois; State U. of Iowa; MOMA; WMAA; Oakland/AM; Santa Barbara/MA; SFMA; Pasadena/AM; Library of Congress; Brooklyn Museum; U. of Minnesota. COLLECTIONS: Ball State Teachers College; Bibliotheque Nationale; Bradley U.; Brooklyn Museum; California State Fair; UCLA; Dallas/MFA; Des Moines; Fort Dodge/Banden; U. of Illinois; Iowa State Fair; Iowa Wesleyan College; State U. of Iowa; Kalamazoo/Institute; Kansas State College; Karachi; La Jolla; Library of Congress; Los Angeles/County MA; Michigan State U.; Omaha/Joslyn; Utica.

KABAK, ROBERT. b. February 15, 1930, NYC. Studied: Brooklyn College, with Burgoyne Diller, Mark Rothko, Ad Reinhardt, Alfred Russell, Robert Wolff, 1952, BA; Yale U., with Josef Albers, Abraham Rattner, Ad Reinhardt, 1954, MFA. Traveled France, Great Britain, Netherlands, USA. Taught: Greenport (N.Y.) Public Schools, 1953–54; P. S. 108, Queens (N.Y.), 1954–56; High School of Music and Art, NYC, 1956–60; Brooklyn College, 1960–62; U. of California, Berkeley, 1962– . Awards: MacDowell Colony Fellowship, 1956, 57, 59, 60, 61, 62; Huntington Hartford Foundation, 1960, 61, 63; Yaddo Fellowship, 1961. Address: 5273 College Avenue, Oakland, Calif. One-man Exhibitions: The Salpeter Gallery, 1958; Nonagon Gallery, NYC, 1960; Angeleski Gallery, NYC, 1960, 61; Osgood Gallery, NYC, 1962; Gump's Gallery, 1963; SFMA (two-man), 1964. Group: MOMA, New Talent; WMAA Annuals, 1956, 58; U. of Illinois, 1959; California Palace, 1964; State U. of Iowa; U. of Nebraska; Southern Illinois U. Collections: MOMA.

KAHN, WOLF. b. October 4, 1927, Stuttgart, Germany. To Great Britain 1939; to USA 1940. Studied: Hofmann School, 1947–49; The U. of Chicago, 1950–51, BA. Traveled Europe, Mexico, USA. Taught: U. of California, Berkeley, 1960; Cooper Union, 1961–62. Awards: Fulbright Fellowship, 1962, 64; Ford Foundation, p.p., 1962. Address: 813 Broadway, NYC. Dealer: Grace Borgenicht Gallery Inc. One-man Exhibitions: (first) Hansa Gallery, NYC, 1953, also 1954; Grace Borgenicht Gallery Inc., 1956, 58, 60, 61, 62; U. of California, 1960; Union College (N.Y.), 1960; Michigan State U.,

1963; Stewart Richard Gallery, San Antonio, 1964; Ellison Gallery, Fort Worth, 1961; RISD, 1961. Group: ART:USA:59, NYC, 1959; WMAA, Young America, 1960; Utica, 1959; WMAA Annuals, 1958, 60, 61; The Stable Gallery Annuals, 1954, 55; American Art Gallery, Copenhagen, 1963; International Biennial Exhibition of Paintings, Tokyo; PAFA, 1961; SFMA, 1961; MOMA, Hans Hofmann and His Students, circ., 1963–64. Collections: Brandeis U.; Chase Manhattan Bank; Dallas/MFA; Houston/MFA; U. of Illinois; MOMA; Michigan State U.; U. of Nebraska; St. Louis/City; VMFA; WMAA. Bibliography: Blesh 1.

KAISH, LUISE. b. September 8, 1925, Atlanta, Ga. Studied: Syracuse U., with Ivan Mestrovic, BFA, MFA; Escuela de Pintura y Escultura, Mexico City, with Alfredo Zalce, J. G. Galvan. Traveled Europe and Scandinavia extensively. Member: Sculptors Guild; Audubon Artists. Commissions: Temple B'rith Kopesh, Rochester, N.Y.; Container Corp. of America; Syracuse U.; Amoco Building, NYC. Awards: Guggenheim Foundation Fellowship; L. C. Tiffany Grant; Audubon Artists, Medal; Ball State Teachers College, p.p.; Joe and Emily Lowe Foundation Award; National Association of Women Artists; Rochester/Memorial; Syracuse/Everson. Address: 50 King Street, NYC. Dealer: Sculpture Center. One-man Exhibitions: (first) Sculpture Center, 1955, also 1958; Rochester/Memorial, 1959; Manhattanville College of the Sacred Heart, 1958. Group: MMA, National Sculpture Exhibition, 1951; MOMA, Recent Sculpture USA, 1959; WMAA, 1955, 62, 64; PAFA; U. of Illinois; U. of Nebraska; Ball State Teachers College; U. of

Notre Dame; Ohio U.; NAD; Sculptors Guild; Buffalo/Albright; AAAL. **Collections:** Rochester/Memorial; Syracuse U.

KAMIHIRA, BEN. b. March 16, 1925, Yakima, Wash. **Studied:** Art Institute of Pittsburgh; PAFA, 1948–52. US Army, 1944–47. **Taught:** PAFA; The Pennsylvania State U.; Philadelphia Museum School. **Awards:** NAD, Hallgarten Prize, 1952; PAFA, Walter Lippincott Prize, 1958; NAD, Benjamin Altman Prize, 1958, 62; Corcoran, First William A. Clark Prize, 1961; PAFA, Cresson Fellowship, 1951; PAFA, J. Henry Schiedt Scholarship, 1952; L. C. Tiffany Grant, 1952, 58; Guggenheim Foundation Fellowship, 1955, 56. **Address:** 909 Green Lane, Primos, Pa. **Dealer:** Durlacher Brothers. **One-man Exhibitions:** Dubin Gallery, Philadelphia, 1952; Philadelphia Art Alliance, 1954; PAFA, 1956; Janet Nessler Gallery, NYC, 1961; Durlacher Brothers, 1964. **Group:** NAD, 1952, 54, 56, 58, 61; PAFA, 1954, 58, 60; Corcoran, 1961; Youngstown/Butler, 1953, 58, 59, 60, 61; WMAA, 1958. **Collections:** NAD; PAFA; Ringling; WMAA. **Bibliography:** Goodrich and Baur 1.

KAMROWSKI, GEROME. b. January 29, 1914, Warren, Minn. **Studied:** St. Paul School of Art, with L. Turner, Cameron Booth; ASL; Hofmann School. **Taught:** U. of Michigan, 1946– . **Federal A.P.:** Mural painting in Minnesota and New York. **Awards:** Guggenheim Foundation Fellowship; Cranbrook, Horace H. Rackham Research Grant, 1957; Detroit/Institute, 1949, 54, 55, 61. **Address:** 1501 Beechwood Drive, Ann Arbor, Mich. **One-man Exhibitions:** Mortimer Brandt, NYC, 1946; Betty Parsons Gallery, 1948; Alexander Iolas Gallery; Galerie Creuze, Paris, 1950, 58; Hugo Gallery, NYC, 1951; U. of Michigan, 1952, 59, 61; The Saginaw Museum, 1954; Jackson Art Association; Cranbrook, 1947; Gallery Mayer, NYC, 1961. **Group:** Galerie Maeght, 6 American Painters, 1947; WMAA Annuals, 1947, 48, 51, 53; U. of Illinois, 1950, 52; Chicago/AI, 1945, 46; Buffalo/Albright, 1946; Sidney Janis Gallery, Surrealist and Abstract Art; MOMA; SRGM; Detroit/Institute, 1948, 50, 52, 54, 58. **Collections:** Detroit/Institute; Knoll Associates Inc.; Phillips. **Bibliography:** Baur 7; Breton 3; Calas; Janis, S.; Ritchie 1.

Ben Kamihira　　*Fish Tank*.

KAMYS, WALTER. b. June 8, 1917, Chicago, Ill. STUDIED: Chicago Art Institute School, 1943, with Hubert Ropp, Boris Anisfeld; privately in Mexico with Gordon Onslow-Ford, 1944. Traveled Mexico, Europe. TAUGHT: The Putney School, Vermont, 1945; G. W. V. Smith Art Museum, Springfield, Mass., 1947–60; U. of Massachusetts, 1960– . AWARDS: Prix de Rome, 1942; Chicago/AI, Anna Louise Raymond Fellowship, 1942–43; Chicago/AI, Paul Trebilcock P.P., 1943; Chicago/AI, James Nelson Raymond Traveling Fellowship, 1943–44; Boston Arts Festival, Second Prize, 1955. ADDRESS: Cave Hill Farm, Montague, Mass. DEALER: Ward-Nasse Gallery. ONE-MAN EXHIBITIONS: (first) Cliff Dwellers Club, Chicago, 1944; Dartmouth College, 1946; Margaret Brown Gallery, Boston, 1949; The Little Gallery, Springfield, Mass., 1951; Mortimer Levitt Gallery, NYC, 1954; Muriel Latow Gallery, Springfield, Mass., 1954; The Bertha Schaefer Gallery, 1955, 57, 61; Deerfield (Mass.) Academy, 1956; Concordia College, 1957; Springfield, Mass./MFA, 1948, 59; New Vision Center, London, 1960; Univision Gallery, London, 1960; U. of Massachusetts, 1961; Stanhope Gallery, Boston, 1963; Deerfield (Mass.) Academy, A Painter with a Camera (abstract photos), 1960. GROUP: Chicago/AI; Salon des Realites Nouvelles, Paris; PAFA; Carnegie; USIA, 20th Century American Graphics, circ.; Corcoran; ICA, Boston, Younger New England Graphic Artists, 1954; MOMA, Recent Drawings USA, 1956; ICA, Boston, View, 1960. COLLECTIONS: Albion College; Harvard U.; U. of Massachusetts; Mount Holyoke College; NYU; Smith College; WDAY; Yale U. BIBLIOGRAPHY: Janis and Blesh 1.

KANEMITSU, MATSUMI. b. May 5, 1922, Ogden, Utah. STUDIED: Atelier Fernand Leger, Paris (painting); ASL, with Yasuo Kuniyoshi, Harry Sternberg, C. P. Austin, Byron Browne; privately with Karl Metzler in Baltimore (sculpture). US Army, 1941–46. Traveled Europe, USA, the Orient. AWARDS: Ford Foundation Grant for Tamarind, 1961; Longview Foundation Grant, 1962, 64; Ford Foundation/A.F.A. Artist-in-Residence, 1964. ADDRESS: 158 West 22 Street, NYC. ONE-MAN EXHIBITIONS: (first) Gallery 77, New Haven, 1953; Western Maryland College, 1954; Baltimore/MA, 1954; Zoé Dusanne Gallery, 1955;

The New Gallery, NYC, 1957; Widdifield Gallery, NYC, 1959; Dwan Gallery, 1960, 61, 63; Stephen Radich Gallery, 1961, 62; Southern Illinois U., 1961; i Gallery, La Jolla, 1963; Akron/AI, 1964. GROUP: Baltimore/MA, 1948, 49, 50, 51, 52; Corcoran, 1950; Chicago/AI, 1952; Academy of Fine Arts, Berlin, 1954; MOMA, 1956; WMAA, 1956; Dallas/MFA, 1960; WMAA Annual, 1962; MOMA, Art in Embassies, circ. internationally, 1963–64; MOMA, Americans 1963, circ., 1963–64. COLLECTIONS: Akron/AI; U. of Arizona; Baltimore/MA; UCLA; Chicago/AI; Dillard U.; Kansas City/Nelson; Los Angeles/County MA; MOMA; Provincetown/Chrysler; Worcester/AM.

KANTOR, MORRIS. b. April 15, 1896, Minsk, Russia. STUDIED: Independent School of Art, with Homer Boss. TAUGHT: ASL, 1934– ; U. of Michigan, 1958; Michigan State U., 1960; U. of Colorado, 1962; U. of Illinois, 1963; U. of Minnesota, Duluth, 1963; U. of New Mexico, 1964. MEMBER: Federation of Modern Painters and Sculptors. FEDERAL A.P.: Supervisor in Rockland County, N.Y. (about 6 months). AWARDS: Chicago/AI, The Mr. & Mrs. Frank G. Logan Medal, 1931; Corcoran, Third Prize, 1939; PAFA, Joseph E. Temple Gold Medal, 1940; U. of Illinois, P.P., 1951; Riverside Museum, P.P., 1960. ADDRESS: 45 South Mountain Road, New City, N.Y. DEALER: The Bertha Schaefer Gallery. ONE-MAN EXHIBITIONS: (first) Rehn Galleries, 1930, also 1932, 35, 38, 40, 43, 45, 47, 49, 53, 59; The Bertha Schaefer Gallery, 1959, 62; Chicago/AI, 1932; U. of Michigan, 1958; U. of Illinois, 1963; U. of Minnesota, Duluth, 1963; Comara Gallery, 1962. GROUP: Society of Independent Artists, annually since 1920; MMA; WMAA; MOMA; Brooklyn Museum; PAFA; Newark Museum; Chicago/AI; Corcoran; XXIV Venice Biennial, 1948; III International Biennial Exhibition of Prints, Tokyo, 1962. COLLECTIONS: U. of Arizona; Chicago/AI; Detroit/Institute; U. of Illinois; MMA; MOMA; U. of Michigan; U. of Nebraska; Newark Museum; PAFA; Phillips; Riverside Museum; Santa Barbara/MA; Utica; Wilmington; Worcester/AM. BIBLIOGRAPHY: Baur 7; Brown; Cahill and Barr, eds.; Cheney, M. C.; Flanagan; Goodrich and Baur 1; Huyghe; *Index of 20th Century Artists;* Janis, S.; Jewell 2; Kootz 1; Mellquist; Pagano; Pearson

1; Phillips 1; Poore; Pousette-Dart, ed.; Wheeler; Wight 2.

KAPROW, ALLAN. b. August 23, 1927, Atlantic City, N.J. Studied: NYU, 1945–49, BA; Columbia U., with Meyer Schapiro, 1950–52, MA (Art History); Hofmann School, NYC, 1947–48; privately with John Cage in NYC, 1956–58. Traveled Europe, USA. Taught: Rutgers U., 1953–61; Pratt Institute, 1960–61; State U. of New York, Stony Brook, 1961– . A co-founder of Hansa Gallery, NYC, 1952, and Reuben Gallery, NYC, 1959. Designed sets and costumes for Eileen Passloff Dance Co., 1958. Initiated the first Environments and Happenings, 1958. Awards: Katherine White Foundation Grant, 1951; Rutgers U. Research Fund Grant, 1957; William and Noma Copley Foundation Grant, 1962. Address: 791 Glen Cove Avenue, Glen Head, N.Y. One-man Exhibitions: (first) Hansa Gallery, NYC, 1953, also 1955, 57; Rutgers U., 1953, 55; Urban Gallery, NYC, 1955, 56; Sun Gallery, Provincetown, 1957. Environments: Hansa Gallery, NYC, 1958; Judson Gallery, NYC, 1960; Martha Jackson Gallery, 1961; U. of Michigan, 1961; Rijksmuseum Amsterdam and Stockholm/National, 1961; Smolin Gallery and State U. of New York, Stony Brook, 1962; Smolin Gallery, 1964. Happenings: Douglass College, 1958; Reuben Gallery, NYC, 1959, 61; Walker, 1962; Judson Memorial Church, NYC, 1960; U. of Michigan, 1961; Maidman Playhouse, NYC, 1962; Theatre des Nations, Paris, 1963; Southern Illinois U., 1964; Edinburgh, Scotland, 1963; Miami, Fla., 1964; U. of California, Berkeley, 1964; Cornell U., 1964. Group Exhibitions: Boston Arts Festival, 1957; Cornell U., 1958; Carnegie, 1958; A.F.A., Collage in America, circ., 1957–58; A.F.A., New Talent, circ., 1958; Rijksmuseum Amsterdam and Stockholm/National, 1960; MOMA, Hans Hofmann and His Students, circ., 1963–64. Bibliography: Janis and Blesh 1; *Metro*.

KARFIOL, BERNARD. b. May 6, 1886, Budapest, Hungary; **d.** 1952. Studied: Academie Julian, Paris, 1901, with Jean Paul Laurens; Academie des Beaux-Arts, Paris; Pratt Institute, 1899; NAD, 1900. Traveled Mexico, Europe, West Indies. Awards: Pan-American Exhibition, Los Angeles, 1925; Carnegie, 1927, 29; Corcoran, First William A. Clark Prize and Corcoran Gold Medal, 1928; Fort Dodge/Banden, p.p., 1940; VMFA, p.p., 1942. One-man Exhibitions: (first) Joseph Brummer Gallery, NYC, 1924, also 1925, 27; The Downtown Gallery, 1931, 33, 35, 41, 43, 46, 50, 56; Baltimore/MA, 1939; Vanbark Studios, Studio City, Calif., 1946; Grover Cronin Gallery, Waltham, Mass., 1957; Carnegie, 1939. Group: The Armory Show, 1913; MOMA, Paintings by 19 Living Americans, 1929; Carnegie; Corcoran; Grand Salon, Paris, 1903; Salon d'Automne, Paris, 1904; Baltimore/MA, Six Americans, 1939. Collections: AAAL; Andover/Phillips; Baltimore/MA; Brandeis U.; Britannica; Brooklyn Museum; California Palace; Carnegie; Corcoran; Dartmouth College; Detroit/Institute; Fisk U.; Fort Dodge/Banden; Los Angeles/County MA; MMA; MOMA; Newark Museum; New Britain; New London; Ogunquit; Phillips; Southampton/Parrish; Upjohn Co.; VMFA; WMAA; Wellesley College; Wichita/AM. Bibliography: Bethers; Blesh 1; Brown; Cahill and Barr, eds.; Cheney, M. C.; Goodrich and Baur 1; Hall; Halpert; Huyghe; *Index of 20th Century Artists;* Jewell 2; **Karfiol;** Kootz 1, 2; McCurdy, ed.; Mellquist; Neuhaus; Pagano; Phillips 2; Pousette-Dart, ed.; Richardson; Ringel, ed.; **Slusser;** Wight 2.

KASTEN, KARL. b. March 5, 1916, San Francisco, Calif. Studied: U. of California, with Worth Ryder, John Haley, Erle Loran; State U. of Iowa, with Mauricio Lasansky; Hofmann School; San Francisco Art Institute (AB, MA). Traveled France, Germany. Taught: San Francisco Art Institute, 1941; U. of Michigan, 1946–47; San Francisco State College, 1947–50; U. of California, 1950– . Member: California Society of Etchers. Commissions: North American Tile Co., Berkeley, Calif. (mural). Address: 1884 San Lorenzo Avenue, Berkeley, Calif. Dealer: Hollis Gallery. One-man Exhibitions: (first) U. of Michigan, 1946; SFMA; Galerie Breteau, Paris; Rennes; California Palace; The Lanyon Gallery; Hollis Gallery; St. Mary's College (Ind.); Oakland/AM; Lanai Gallery; Chico State College. Group: de Young; SFMA; WMAA; MMA; Chicago/AI; Detroit/Institute; Seattle/AM; Pasadena/AM; Oakland/AM; I & III Sao Paulo Biennials, 1951, 55; U. of Illinois, 50 Contemporary American Printmakers, 1956; Pomona College, California Drawing, 1957. Collections: Achenbach

Foundation; Auckland; U. of California; de Young; Mills College; Pasadena/AM; Rennes; SFMA; US State Department; Victoria and Albert Museum.

KATZ, ALEX. b. July 24, 1927, NYC. STUDIED: Cooper Union; Skowhegan School. TAUGHT: Yale U., 1960–61; Brooklyn Museum School, 1959; Skowhegan School, 1959. ADDRESS: 182 Fifth Avenue, NYC. DEALER: Fischbach Gallery. ONE-MAN EXHIBITIONS: Roko Gallery, 1954, 57; The Pennsylvania State U., 1957; Sun Gallery, Provincetown, 1958; Tanager Gallery, NYC, 1959, 62; The Stable Gallery, 1960; Martha Jackson Gallery, 1962; Thibaut Gallery, NYC, 1963; Fischbach Gallery, 1964; Tanager Gallery, NYC (two- and three-man shows), 1953, 57, 60. GROUP: New York Art Alliance, Younger Artists, 1959; PAFA, 1960; WMAA, Young America, 1960; Chicago/AI, 1961, 62, 64; Houston/MFA, 1961; Colby College, Maine and Its Artists, 1963; Swarthmore College, Two Generations of American Art, 1964. COLLECTIONS: Bowdoin College; Brandeis U.; Colby College; MOMA; NYU; US State Department; WMAA.

KATZMAN, HERBERT. b. January 8, 1923, Chicago, Ill. STUDIED: Chicago Art Institute School, 1946. Traveled Great Britain; resided Paris, Florence. TAUGHT: Rockland Foundation, 1952–53; Pratt Institute; School of Visual Arts, NYC. AWARDS: Chicago/AI, Traveling Fellowship, 1946; Fulbright Fellowship, 1956; AAAL Grant, 1958; Chicago/AI, Campana Prize, 1951; PAFA, J. Henry Schiedt Memorial Prize, 1954. ADDRESS: 258 Riverside Drive, NYC. DEALER: Terry Dintenfass, Inc. ONE-MAN EXHIBITIONS: (first) The Alan Gallery, 1954, also 1957, 59; Terry Dintenfass, Inc., 1962, 64. GROUP: MOMA, Fifteen Americans, circ., 1952; WMAA, Forty Artists Under Forty, circ., 1962; U. of Illinois; WMAA, The New Decade, 1954–55; Carnegie, 1953, 55; XXVIII Venice Biennial, 1956; Chicago/AI, 1951; PAFA, 1952. COLLECTIONS: Chicago/AI; S. C. Johnson & Son, Inc.; MOMA; WMAA. BIBLIOGRAPHY: Nordness, ed.; Pousette-Dart, ed.

KEARL, STANLEY BRANDON. b. December 23, 1913, Waterbury, Conn. STUDIED: Yale U., 1941, BFA, 1942, MFA; State U. of Iowa, 1948, Ph.D. Traveled the world extensively; resided

Rome, nine years. TAUGHT: U. of Minnesota, Duluth, 1947–48. FEDERAL A.P.: Easel painting. AWARDS: Fulbright Exchange Professor to Rome U., Italy, 1949–50; Institute of Contemporary Arts, Florence, Italy, 1952; Connecticut Academy Sculpture Prize, 1958. ADDRESS: 344 Sprain Road, Scarsdale, N.Y. DEALER: D'Arcy Gallery. ONE-MAN EXHIBITIONS: (first) L'Obelisco, Rome, 1950; Galerie d'Art Moderne, Basel, 1951; Samlaren Gallery, Stockholm, 1951; Marbach Galerie, Berne, 1952; Galerie 16, Zurich, 1952; Beaux Arts Gallery, London, 1956; Obelisk Gallery, Washington, D.C., 1958; Galleria Selecta, Rome, 1957; Wakefield Gallery, NYC, 1961; D'Arcy Gallery, 1962; Hudson River Museum, Yonkers, N.Y., 1964. GROUP: WMAA Annual, 1962; PAFA, 1959; Hudson River Museum, Yonkers, N.Y., 1963; XXVI Venice Biennial, 1952; MOMA, 1961. COLLECTIONS: State U. of Iowa; U. of Minnesota, Duluth; Northland College; Rome/Nazionale; Stockholm/National; Sweden/Goteborgs. BIBLIOGRAPHY: Seuphor 3.

KEARNS, JAMES. b. August 7, 1924, Scranton, Pa. STUDIED: Chicago Art Institute School, DePaul U., The U. of Chicago, 1946–50 (BFA). TAUGHT: School of Visual Arts, NYC, 1959– ; Skowhegan School, summers, 1961– ; Fairleigh Dickinson U., 1962– . Illustrated *Can These Bones Live*, by Edward Dahlberg (New Directions, 1960), and *The Heart of Beethoven*, by Selman Rodman (Shorewood Press, 1962). AWARDS: NIAL Grant in Art, 1959; Montclair/AM, First Prize for Painting, 1961. ADDRESS: 452 Rockaway Road, Montclair, N.J. ONE-MAN EXHIBITIONS: (first) Grippi Gallery, NYC, 1956, also 1957, 60, 62; Lee Nordness Gallery, NYC, 1964; Fairleigh Dickinson U., 1962; Scranton/Everhart, 1963. GROUP: WMAA Annuals, 1959, 60, 61; A.F.A., Drawings, 1959; A.F.A., New Talent, circ., 1960; A.F.A., Private Worlds, 1961; Newark Museum, Survey of American Sculpture, 1962. COLLECTIONS: Colby College; S. C. Johnson & Son, Inc.; MMA; MOMA; Topeka Public Library; WMAA. BIBLIOGRAPHY: Nordness, ed.; Rodman 1, 3.

KELLY, ELLSWORTH. b. May 31, 1923, Newburgh, N.Y. STUDIED: Boston Museum School; Academie des Beaux-Arts, Paris. US Army, 1943–46. Traveled France, 1948–54.

COMMISSIONS: Transportation Building, Philadelphia, 1957 (sculpture); Eastmore House, NYC (mural); New York State Pavilion, New York World's Fair, 1964–65 (sculpture). AWARDS: Carnegie International, 1962, 64; Brandeis U., 1962; International Biennial Exhibition of Paintings, Tokyo. ADDRESS: One West 67 Street, NYC. DEALERS: Sidney Janis Gallery; Galerie Maeght. ONE-MAN EXHIBITIONS: (first) Galerie Arnaud, 1951; Betty Parsons Gallery, 1956, 57, 59, 61, 63; Galerie Maeght, 1958, 64; A. Tooth & Sons, 1962; WGMA, 1964; ICA, Boston, 1964. GROUP: Galerie Maeght, Tendence, 1951, 62; MOMA, Sixteen Americans, circ., 1959; Salon des Realites Nouvelles, Paris, 1950, 51; Carnegie, 1958, 62, 64; Brussels World's Fair, 1958; Seattle World's Fair, 1962; VI Sao Paulo Biennial, 1961; SRGM, Abstract Expressionists and Imagists, 1961; Los Angeles/County MA, Post Painterly Abstraction, 1964; Jewish Museum, Toward a New Abstraction, 1963; Chicago/AI, 1961, 62; Tate, Gulbenkian International, 1964; Documenta III, Kassel, 1964; SRGM, American Drawings, 1964. COLLECTIONS: Brandeis U.; Buffalo/Albright; Carnegie; Chicago/AI; Cleveland/MA; Dartmouth College; MMA; MOMA; Pasadena/AM; Tate; Toronto; WGMA; WMAA; Worcester/AM. BIBLIOGRAPHY: Gaunt; Nordness, ed.; Seuphor 1.

KELLY, JAMES. b. 1913, Philadelphia, Pa. STUDIED: Philadelphia Museum School, 1937; PAFA, 1938; Barnes Foundation, 1941; California School of Fine Arts, 1951–54. US Air Force, 1941–45. TAUGHT: U. of California, Berkeley, 1957. AWARDS: Ford Foundation Grant for Tamarind, 1963. m. Sonia Gechtoff. ADDRESS: 361 Canal Street, NYC. DEALER: East Hampton Gallery. ONE-MAN EXHIBITIONS: (first) California Palace, 1954; SFMA, 1956; The Stryke Gallery, NYC, 1963. GROUP: A.F.A., West Coast Artists, circ., 1959–60; PAFA, 1951; SFMA Annuals, 1955, 56, 57, 58; U. of Minnesota, California Painters, 1956; Minneapolis/Institute, American Painting, 1945–57, 1957; Santa Barbara/MA, II Pacific Coast Biennial, 1957. COLLECTIONS: UCLA; Chicago/AI; U. of Massachusetts; SFMA.

KELLY, LEON (Leon Kelly y Corrons). b. October 1, 1901, Perpignan (Pyrenees-Orientales), France. STUDIED: Philadelphia Museum School; PAFA; privately with Arthur B. Carles, Jr., and Earl Herter. Traveled Europe, North Africa, USA; resided Paris, 1924–30. FEDERAL A.P.: Supervisor of Artists in Philadelphia; mural and easel painting. COMMISSIONS: Portraits. AWARDS: PAFA, Cresson Fellowship, 1924; William and Noma Copley Foundation Grant, 1959. ADDRESS: Harvey Cedars, N.J. DEALER: Alexander Iolas Gallery. ONE-MAN EXHIBITIONS: (first) Gallery of Contemporary Art, Philadelphia, 1925, also 1932; Galerie du Printemps, Paris, 1926; Contemporary Arts Gallery, NYC, 1933; Julien Levy Galleries, NYC, 1942, 44, 45; Hugo Gallery, NYC, 1950; Hewitt Gallery, NYC, 1956; Alexander Iolas Gallery, 1959, 61; Philadelphia Art Alliance, 1943; The Zabriskie Gallery, 1963; Galleria Amici di Francia, Milan, 1954. GROUP: European International, 1927; A Century of Progress, Chicago, 1933–34; WMAA Annuals; Carnegie; U. of Nebraska; PMA; Chicago/AI; Corcoran. COLLECTIONS: Allentown/AM; Andover/Phillips; Clearwater/Gulf Coast; Hartford/Wadsworth; La France Art Institute; MMA; MOMA; Museo Nacional de Historia; National Arts Foundation; U. of Nebraska; PAFA; PMA; The Pennsylvania State U.; Steuben Glass; Tel Aviv; Utica; WMAA. BIBLIOGRAPHY: Janis, S.

KENT, ROCKWELL. b. June 21, 1882, Tarrytown Heights, N.Y. STUDIED: Columbia U., 1906–10, with William M. Chase, Robert Henri, Kenneth Hayes Miller, Abbott Thayer. Traveled Canada, USA, Europe, Latin America, Greenland. COMMISSIONS (murals): US Post Office, Washington, D.C.; Federal Building, Washington, D.C. ADDRESS: Au Sable Forks, N.Y. ONE-MAN EXHIBITIONS: Macbeth Gallery, NYC, 1934; Wildenstein & Co., NYC, 1925, 42; Clausen Galleries, NYC, 1908, 19. RETROSPECTIVE: Wildenstein & Co., NYC, 1924; Syracuse/Everson, 1937. GROUP: NAD, 1905; Academy of Fine Arts, Berlin, 1910; Century Association, 1940; Cleveland/MA; WMAA. COLLECTIONS: American Car and Foundry Co.; Andover/Phillips; Baltimore/MA; Boston/MFA; British Museum; Brooklyn Museum; Chicago/AI; Cleveland/MA; Columbus; Corcoran; Detroit/Institute; Harvard U.; Honolulu Academy; Houston/MFA; Indianapolis/Herron; Library of Congress; MMA; NYPL; Newark Museum; Phillips; Victoria and Albert

Museum; WMAA; Yale U. **BIBLIOGRAPHY:** American Artists Congress, Inc.; American Artists Group Inc. 1, 3; **Armitage;** Baur 7; Biddle 3; Birchman; Blesh 1; Brown; Cahill and Barr, eds.; Cheney, M. C.; Finkelstein; Goodrich and Baur 1; Hall; Hartmann; *Index of 20th Century Artists;* Jackman; Kent, N.; **Kent, R. 1, 2, 3; Kent, R., ed.,** Lee and Burchwood; Mather 1; Mellquist; Narodny; Neuhaus; Pagano; Pearson 1; Phillips 1, 2; Reese; Richardson; Ringel, ed.; Ritchie 1; Smith, S. C. K.; Zigrosser 1.

KEPES, GYORGY. b. October 4, 1906, Selyp, Hungary. STUDIED: Academy of Fine Arts, Budapest, 1924–28. TAUGHT: MIT, 1946– ; New Bauhaus, Chicago, 1937–43; a founding collaborator, with Lazlo Moholy-Nagy and Robert Wolff, of the Institute of Design, Chicago, 1938–42. Co-director, Rockefeller Foundation Research Project: Perceptual Form of Cities. COMMISSIONS (murals): Harvard U. Graduate Center; KLM Royal Dutch Airlines, NYC; Travelers Insurance Companies, Los Angeles; Sheraton Hotels, Dallas and Chicago; Children's Library, Fitchburg, Mass.; American Housing Exhibit, Paris, 1946. AWARDS: Guggenheim Foundation Fellowship, 1960–61; American Institute of Graphic Arts, 1944, 49; Art Directors Club, Chicago, 1963; U. of Illinois, P.P., 1954. ADDRESS: 90 Larchwood Drive, Cambridge, Mass. ONE-MAN EXHIBITIONS: Katherine Kuh Gallery, Chicago, 1939; Chicago/AI, 1944, 54; SFMA, 1952, 54; San Diego, 1952; Outline Gallery, Pittsburgh, 1945; Margaret Brown Gallery, Boston, 1951, 55; Royal Academy, Copenhagen, 1950; Amsterdam/Stedelijk, 1952; Long Beach/MA, 1952; U. of California, Berkeley, 1952; Currier, 1953; ICA, Boston, 1954; Syracuse/Everson, 1957; Houston/MFA, 1958; Cranbrook, 1954; Dallas/MFA, 1958; L'Obelisco, Rome, 1958; Baltimore/MA, 1959; The Howard Wise Gallery, Cleveland, 1959; Ivrea Gallery, Florence, Italy, 1958; Saidenberg Gallery, 1960. GROUP: Chicago/AI, 1951, 53, 57; MOMA, 1947, 52; SFMA; Cranbrook; Dallas/MFA; Andover/Phillips; U. of Illinois, 1952, 53; San Diego; WMAA; Carnegie, 1955; Denver/AM, 1953. COLLECTIONS: Andover/Phillips; Boston/MFA; Buffalo/Albright; Chase Manhattan Bank; Cranbrook; Dallas/MFA; Des Moines; Houston/MFA; U. of Illinois; Indianapolis/Her-

ron; Lincoln, Mass./De Cordova; MIT; MOMA; SFMA; San Diego; VMFA; WMAA. **BIBLIOGRAPHY: Alfieri;** Janis and Blesh 1; Janis, S.; **Kepes 1, 2; Kepes, ed.;** Kuh 1; Nordness, ed.; Pearson 1.

KEYSER, ROBERT. b. July 27, 1924, Philadelphia, Pa. STUDIED: U. of Pennsylvania; Atelier Fernand Leger, Paris, 1949–51. US Navy, World War II (three years). Traveled Europe, North Africa (two years). TAUGHT: Philadelphia Museum School, 1963– . ADDRESS: P.O. Box 76, Sugar Loaf, N.Y. DEALER: P. Rosenberg and Co. ONE-MAN EXHIBITIONS: (first) Galerie Huit, Paris, 1951; Hendler Gallery, Philadelphia, 1952; Parma Gallery, NYC, 1954, 56, 58; P. Rosenberg and Co., 1959, 60, 62; Gimpel Fils Ltd., 1962. GROUP: PAFA Annual; WMAA Annual; A.F.A., Collage in America, circ., 1957–58; Joachim Gallery, Chicago, 1960; U. of Illinois, 1961; Salon du Mai, Paris; Salon d'Automne, Paris; Salon des Realites Nouvelles, Paris. COLLECTIONS: New London; Phillips; Utica.

KIENBUSCH, WILLIAM. b. April 13, 1914, NYC. STUDIED: Princeton U., 1936, BA, PBK (Fine Arts major); ASL, 1936–37; Colorado Springs Fine Arts Center, with Henry Poor; Academie Colarossi, Paris; privately with Abraham Rattner in Paris; with Anton Refregier and Stuart Davis in New York. US Army, World War II. TAUGHT: Brooklyn Museum School, 1948– . AWARDS: Brooklyn Society of Artists Annual, First Prize, 1952; MMA, Drawing Prize, 1952; Columbia, S.C./MA, First P.P., Watercolors, 1957; Guggenheim Foundation Fellowship, 1961; Ford Foundation, P.P., 1961; Boston Arts Festival, First Prize for Watercolor, 1961. ADDRESS: 44 Greenwich Avenue, NYC. DEALER: Kraushaar Galleries. ONE-MAN EXHIBITIONS: U. of Maine, 1956; Cornell U., 1958; Princeton U., 1962; Fort Worth (two-man), 1964; Kraushaar Galleries, 1949, 52, 56, 59, 63. RETROSPECTIVE: Carnegie (two-man, with Dioda), 1954. GROUP: Buffalo/Albright; Chicago/AI; MMA, 1952; MOMA, Twelve Americans, circ., 1956; Walker; WMAA, The New Decade, 1954–55; Brussels World's Fair, 1958; Brooklyn Museum, 1953, 59; Carnegie, 1955; WMAA, 1955. COLLECTIONS: Atlanta U.; Boston/MFA; Bowdoin College; Brooklyn Museum; Buffalo/Albright; Carnegie; Colorado Springs/FA; Columbia, S.C./MA; Dartmouth College; U. of Delaware; Des Moines; Detroit/Institute; Fort Worth; Hartford/Wadsworth; Houston/MFA; Kansas City/Nelson; Lehigh U.; MMA; MOMA; U. of Maine; U. of Michigan; U. of Minnesota; Montclair/AM; U. of Nebraska; Newark Museum; New Britain; PAFA; PMA; Portland, Me./MA; Provincetown/Chrysler; Rochester/Memorial; Toledo/MA; Toronto; Utica; VMFA; WMAA; Wichita/AM; Williams College. **BIBLIOGRAPHY:** Baur 5; Eliot; Goodrich and Baur 1; McCurdy, ed.; Nordness, ed.; Pousette-Dart, ed.; Ritchie 1; Seitz 2.

KIESLER, FREDERICK J. b. 1896, Vienna, Austria; **d.** December 27, 1965, NYC. To USA 1926; became a citizen. Scenic Director, Juilliard School of Music, NYC, 1933–57. Registered Architect; designed and built the Art of This Century Gallery, NYC (1940), the Galerie Maeght, Paris (1947), the World House Galleries, NYC (1957) and the Kamer Gallery, NYC (1959). **ONE-MAN EXHIBITIONS:** MOMA, 1951 (sculpture); MOMA, Endless House, 1960; U. of Houston, Architectural Plans, 1960; Leo Castelli Inc., 1961, 62; SRGM, Environmental Sculptures, 1964. **GROUP:** WMAA; A.F.A., Universal Theater, circ., 1961–64. **COLLECTIONS:** MOMA. **BIBLIOGRAPHY:** Arp; Barr 1; Blesh 1; Breton 3; Calas; Janis and Blesh 1; Janis, S.; *Metro;* Seuphor 3.

KING, WILLIAM RIKEY. b. February 25, 1925, Jacksonville, Fla. **STUDIED:** U. of Florida, 1942–44; Cooper Union, 1945–48, with Milton Hebald, John Hovannes; Brooklyn Museum School, 1948–49, with Hebald; Central School of Arts and Crafts, London, 1952. Traveled Italy, Greece. **TAUGHT:** Brooklyn Museum School, 1953–60. **COMMISSIONS** (murals): SS *United States,* 1952; Bankers Trust Company, NYC, 1961. **AWARDS:** Fulbright Fellowship (Italy), 1949; Augustus Saint-Gaudens Medal from Cooper Union, 1964; Moorehead Patterson Award (sculpture/to AMF Company), 1960. **ADDRESS:** 17 Commerce Street, NYC. **DEALER:** Terry Dintenfass, Inc. **ONE-MAN EXHIBITIONS:** (first) The Alan Gallery, 1954, also 1955, 58, 60; Terry Dintenfass, Inc., 1962, 63, 64. **GROUP:** WMAA Annuals, 1950, 51, 52, 53, 54, 55, 56, 58, 59, 60, 62, 63; MOMA, New Talent; City of Philadelphia, Sculpture Inter-

national, 1949; MOMA, Recent Sculpture USA, 1959; Carnegie, 1958; New Sculpture Group, NYC, 1957–60; U. of Illinois, 1954, 56, 63; Newark Museum, Survey of American Sculpture, 1962; SRGM, The Joseph H. Hirshhorn Collection, 1962; Brooklyn Museum, 1949, 50, 54, 55, 57, 58. **COLLECTIONS:** American Export Isbrandtsen Lines Inc.; Andover/Phillips; Bankers Trust Company. **BIBLIOGRAPHY:** Seuphor 3.

KIPNESS, ROBERT. b. February 1, 1931, NYC. **STUDIED:** Wittenberg College, 1948–50; State U. of Iowa, 1950–54, BA (English Literature), MFA (Painting and Art History). US Army, 1956–58. **ADDRESS:** 9 East 97 Street, NYC. **ONE-MAN EXHIBITIONS:** (first) The Salpeter Gallery, 1953; The Contemporaries, 1959, 60; Alan Auslander Gallery, NYC, 1963. **GROUP:** A.F.A., circ., 1963–65; Indianapolis/Herron, 1964; U. of Minnesota, Duluth; Youngstown/Butler, 1951; Columbus, 1958; A.F.A., New Talent, circ., 1961; Utah State Institute of Fine Arts, Salt Lake City, 1964; Cornell U., 1964; Cranbrook, 1964.

KIPP, LYMAN E. b. December 24, 1929, Dobbs Ferry, N.Y. **STUDIED:** Pratt Institute, 1950–54; Cranbrook Academy of Art, 1952–53. **TAUGHT:** Harvey School, Hawthorne, N.Y.; Cranbrook Academy of Art; Bennington College. **ADDRESS:** 67 Second Avenue, NYC. **DEALER:** Betty Parsons Gallery. **ONE-MAN EXHIBITIONS:** Cranbrook, 1954; Betty Parsons Gallery, 1954, 56, 58, 60, 62; Bennington College, 1961; Myrtle Todes Gallery, Glencoe, Ill., 1957, 60; Arizona State College, 1957. **GROUP:** WMAA Annuals, 1956, 60, 62; RISD, Four Young Americans, 1955; Pensacola, Freedom of Inspiration, 1958; Claude Bernard, Paris, 1960; Carnegie, 1961, 62; U. of Illinois, 1961; Chicago/AI, 1961, 62; Sao Paulo, 1963. **COLLECTIONS:** Buffalo/Albright; Cranbrook; WMAA. **BIBLIOGRAPHY:** Seuphor 3.

KIRSCHENBAUM, JULES. b. March 25, 1930, NYC. **STUDIED:** Brooklyn Museum School, 1948–50. **AWARDS:** Joe and Emily Lowe Foundation Award, 1950; PAFA, Dana Watercolor Medal, 1952; NAD, Hallgarten Prize, 1953; NAD, Isaac N. Maynard Prize, 1954; NAD, S. J. Wallace Truman Prize, 1955; Fulbright Fellowship (Italy), 1956; PAFA, Hon. Men.,

1957; AAAL, Childe Hassam Award, 1957; Youngstown/Butler, First Prize, 1957; NAD, First Prize, Figure Painting, 1960. **ADDRESS:** Meshoppen, Pa. **DEALER:** The Forum Gallery. **ONE-MAN EXHIBITIONS:** The Salpeter Gallery, 1955, 56. **GROUP:** MMA, 1952; MOMA, WMAA, 1953–57; Brooklyn Museum; NYU; Chicago/AI, 1957; U. of Illinois, 1957; Corcoran; PAFA, 1952, 53, 54, 57; Festival of Two Worlds, Spoleto, 1958; Youngstown/Butler, 1957; Santa Barbara/MA; Pasadena/AM; Houston/MFA; Dallas/MFA. **COLLECTIONS:** U. of Nebraska; WMAA; Youngstown/Butler.

KLINE, FRANZ. b. May 23, 1910, Wilkes-Barre, Pa.; **d.** May 13, 1962, NYC. **STUDIED:** Girard College; Boston U., 1931–35; Heatherley School of Fine Art, London, 1937–38. **TAUGHT:** Black Mountain College, 1952; Pratt Institute, 1953; Philadelphia Museum School, 1954. **AWARDS:** Chicago/AI, 1957; NAD, S. J. Wallace Truman Prize, 1944; XXX Venice Biennial, 1960. **ONE-MAN EXHIBITIONS:** (first) Charles Egan Gallery, 1950, also 1951, 54; Institute of Design, Chicago, 1954; Margaret Brown Gallery, Boston, 1952; Allan Frumkin Gallery, Chicago, 1954; Sidney Janis Gallery, 1956, 58, 60, 61, 63; Arts Club of Chicago, 1961; La Tartaruga, Rome, 1958; Galleria d'Arte del Naviglio, Milan, 1958; XXX Venice

Biennial, 1960; Collectors Gallery, NYC, 1961; New Arts Gallery, Atlanta, 1961; Galerie Lawrence, 1962; Dwan Gallery (two-man, with Philip Guston), 1962. **RETROSPECTIVE:** WGMA, 1962; Whitechapel Art Gallery, London, 1964. **GROUP:** MOMA, The New American Painting, circ. Europe, 1958–59; NAD, 1942, 43, 44, 45; WMAA, The New Decade, 1954–55; MOMA, Twelve Americans, circ., 1956; Galerie de France, 1952; 10th Inter-American Conference, Caracas, 1954; XXVIII & XXX Venice Biennials, 1956, 60; Tate, 1956; Sao Paulo, 1957; Baltimore/MA, 1960; SRGM, 1961; Hartford/Wadsworth, 1962. **COLLECTIONS:** Baltimore/MA; Buffalo/Albright; Carnegie; Houston/MFA; International Minerals & Chemicals Corp.; Kansas City/Nelson; MMA; MOMA; Provincetown / Chrysler; Raleigh / NCMA; Rockefeller Institute; SRGM; Toronto; Utica; WMAA. **BIBLIOGRAPHY:** Baur 5; Blesh 1; **Breeskin;** Eliot; Elsen; Flanagan; Gaunt; Goodrich and Baur 1; Greenberg 1; Haftman; Henning; Hess, T. B.; Hunter 1, 5; Janis and Blesh 1; Kuh 2; Langui; McCourbrey; McCurdy, ed.; Mendelowitz; Neumeyer; Nordness, ed.; **O'Hara 1;** Ponente; Pousette-Dart, ed.; Read 2; Rodman 1, 3; Seuphor 1.

KNATHS, KARL. b. October 21, 1891, Eau Claire, Wisc. **STUDIED:** Chicago Art Institute

Franz Kline   *Kupola. 1958*

Karl Knaths   *Dunes.*

School. **TAUGHT:** The Phillips Gallery School; Bennington College. **MEMBER:** Audubon Artists. **FEDERAL A.P.** (murals): Falmouth (Mass.) High School; US Post Office, Rehoboth Beach, Del.; Provincetown (Mass.) Town Hall. **AWARDS:** Chicago/AI, Norman Wait Harris Prize, 1928; Boston Tercentenary Art Exhibit, Gold Medal; Carnegie, First Prize, 1946; Carnegie International, Third Hon. Men., 1950; Brandeis U., Creative Arts Award, 1961; NAD Annual, Andrew Carnegie Prize, 1962; Hon. DFA, Chicago Art Institute School, 1951; elected to NIAL, 1955. **ADDRESS:** 8 Commercial Street, Provincetown, Mass. **DEALER:** P. Rosenberg and Co. **ONE-MAN EXHIBITIONS:** (first) The Phillips Gallery and The Daniel Gallery, NYC (concurrently); P. Rosenberg and Co., 1946– . **GROUP:** WMAA; Corcoran; Chicago/AI; Carnegie; U. of Illinois; PAFA; MMA. **COLLECTIONS:** Boston/MFA; Brooklyn Museum; Buffalo/Albright; California Palace; Chicago/AI; Corcoran; Currier; Dayton/AI; Des Moines; Ford Foundation; Hartford/Wadsworth; U. of Illinois; Indianapolis/Herron; Los Angeles/County MA; MMA; MOMA; Mary Washington College; U. of Nebraska; PAFA; PMA; Phillips; Rochester/Memorial; Rockefeller Institute; St. Louis/City; Santa Barbara/MA; Stanford U.; Toledo/MA; Utica; WMAA; Walker; West Palm Beach/Norton; Wilmington; Woodward Foundation; Worcester/AM.

BIBLIOGRAPHY: American Abstract Artists, ed.; Baur 5, 7; Bazin; Bethers; Blanchard; Blesh 1; Cheney, M. C.; Eliot; Frost; **Goodrich and Baur** 1, **2**; Hess, T. B.; Janis, S.; Jewell 2; Kootz 2; Leepa; McCurdy, ed.; Mellquist; **Mocsanyi**; Morris; Nordness, ed.; Pearson 1; Phillips 1, 2; Pousette-Dart, ed.; Read 2; Richardson; Ringel, ed.; Ritchie 1; Wight 2.

KOCH, GERD. b. January 30, 1929, Detroit, Mich. **STUDIED:** Wayne State U., with David Mitchell, David Smith, L. J. Nobili, 1951, BFA; UCLA Graduate School, with Sam Amato. Traveled Europe, USA extensively. **TAUGHT:** Palos Verdes Community Arts Association, 1953– ; Ventura College, 1959–60. **AWARDS:** Los Angeles/County MA, First P.P., 1959; California Watercolor Society, M. Grumbacher P.P., 1956, 60; Palos Verdes Invitational, 1960; California Watercolor Society, Lytton P.P., 1962; California State Fair, P.P., 1963; Bay Printmakers Society, Oakland, Adell Hyde Morrison Memorial Medal, 1960, and others. **ADDRESS:** Route 1, Box 60-K, Ojai, Calif. **DEALER:** Esther Robles Gallery. **ONE-MAN EXHIBITIONS:** (first) Ojai Music Festival, 1956; Pasadena/AM, 1958; Santa Monica (Calif.) Art Gallery, 1958; Santa Barbara/MA, 1960; Esther Robles Gallery, 1959, 61, 63; Long Beach/MA, 1961; La Jolla, 1962; Esther Baer Gallery, 1964. **GROUP:** Pasadena/AM, A Decade in the Contemporary Gallery, 1959; California Water-color Society, 1955–60, 62, 63; Occidental College, Art and Anti-Art, 1964; Los Angeles Art Association, 7 Artists, 1955; Los Angeles/County MA, 1957, 59, 60, 61; SFMA, 1957, 62, 63; La Jolla, 1961, 62; San Diego, 1961, 62; Oakland/AM, 1960; Tucson Art Center, 1960; SFMA, New Paintings, 1964. **COLLECTIONS:** California State Fair; Long Beach/MA; Los Angeles/County MA; Palos Verdes; Pasadena/AM; Santa Barbara/MA.

KOCH, JOHN. b. August 18, 1909, Toledo, Ohio. Self-taught in art. Traveled France, Great Britain; resided Paris, 1929–33. **TAUGHT:** ASL, 1944–45; Chairman of the School Committee, NAD. **MEMBER:** NAD; Century Association; Lotus Club; Audubon Artists. **AWARDS:** Salon de Printemps, Paris, Hon. Men., 1929; Carnegie, First Hon. Men., 1943; NAD, 1952; NAD,

Benjamin Altman Prize, 1959; NAD, 137th Annual, Saltus Gold Medal for Merit; Youngstown/Butler, Dr. John J. McDonough Award, 1962; Lotus Club, 1964. **ADDRESS:** 300 Central Park West, NYC. **DEALER:** Kraushaar Galleries. **ONE-MAN EXHIBITIONS:** (first) Bonestell Gallery, Detroit, 1927; Curt Valentine Gallery, NYC, 1935; Kraushaar Galleries, 1939, 41, 43, 46, 49, 51, 54, 58, 61; Kansas City/Nelson, 1940; J. L. Hudson Art Gallery, 1941; Whyte Gallery, Washington, D.C., 1944; Philadelphia Art Alliance, 1945; Portraits, Inc., NYC; Syracuse/Everson, 1951; Cowie Galleries, Los Angeles, 1951; 460 Park Avenue Gallery, NYC, 1951. **RETROSPECTIVE:** Suffolk Museum, Stony Brook, N.Y., 1951; Museum of the City of New York, 1963; Pittsfield/Berkshire, 1963; VMFA, 1962. **GROUP:** Salon de Printemps, Paris, 1929; Salon des Tuileries, Paris, 1929; NAD, 1939– . **COLLECTIONS:** Bennington College; Bos-

John Koch   *The Telephone. 1957*

ton/MFA; Brooklyn Museum; U. of Georgia; Kansas City/Nelson; Newark Museum; New Britain; Southampton/Parrish. **BIBLIOGRAPHY:** Eliot; **Koch.**

KOENIG, JOHN FRANKLIN. b. October 24, 1924, Seattle, Wash. STUDIED: U. of California, Berkeley; Washington State College; U. of Washington, 1948, BA; U. of Biarritz; Sorbonne, BA (Romance languages). US Army, 1943–45. Traveled Europe and the Orient extensively. General Secretary, *Cimaise* (art magazine), Paris, 1953–58. COMMISSIONS: Hopital St. Antoine, Paris, 1964. AWARDS: Paris/Moderne, (Third) Prix des Peintres Etrangers, 1959; I Paris Biennial, 1959; Prix des Critiques d'Art de la Presse Parisienne. ADDRESS: 8 rue Madame, Paris 6, France. DEALERS: Galerie Arnaud; The Willard Gallery; Galerie Camille Hébert; Gordon Woodside Gallery; Tokyo Gallery. ONE-MAN EXHIBITIONS: (first) Galerie Arnaud, 1952 (collages), also 1953, 55, 57, 59, 60, 61, 63; Librairie Selection, Paris, 1948; La Cittadella d'Arte Internazionale e d'Avanguardia, Ascona, Switzerland, 1955, 57; Galleria del Cavallino, Venice, 1957; Palais des Beaux Arts, Brussels, 1957; Grange (Gallery), Lyon, 1958; Zoé Dusanne Gallery, 1958, 60; Seattle/AM, 1960; Tokyo Gallery, 1960, 62; Gordon Woodside Gallery, 1962; Musee de Verviers, 1963; San Antonio/McNay, 1963. GROUP: International Congress of Museums, Marseilles, 1953; ICA, London, Collages and Objects, 1954; Palais des Beaux Arts, Brussels, 1954; Amsterdam/Stedelijk, 1956; Palais des Beaux-Arts, Charleroi, Belgium, L'Art de XXIeme Siecle, 1958; Salon des Realites Nouvelles, Paris; Artistes Americains en France, circ. France, 1960; ICA, Boston, 100 Works on Paper, circ. Europe, 1959; Tate, Ecole de Paris, 1962; Havana/Nacional. COLLECTIONS: Grenoble; Houston/MFA; Musee de Verviers; National Museum of Western Art, Tokyo; Salzburg; San Antonio/McNay; Seattle/AM; Tokyo/Modern; Venice/Contemporaneo. BIBLIOGRAPHY: Ragon 1; Read 3; **Restany 1, 2.**

KOHN, GABRIEL. b. 1910, Philadelphia, Pa. STUDIED: Cooper Union, 1929; Beaux-Arts Institute of Design, NYC, 1930–34; Zadkine School of Sculpture, Paris, 1946. AWARDS: Augustus Saint-Gaudens Medal from Cooper Union, 1925; Beaux-Arts Institute of Design,

NYC, 14 awards in sculpture, 1929–32, and a Silver Medal, 1932; Nicholas Roerich Society, First Prize, 1932; Cranbrook, George A. Booth Scholarship, 1952; ICA, London/Tate, International Unknown Political Prisoner Competition, 1953; Ford Foundation Grant, 1960. ADDRESS: 1356 Main Street, Sarasota, Fla. DEALER: Marlborough-Gerson Gallery Inc. ONE-MAN EXHIBITIONS: Atelier Mannucci, Rome, 1948; Galleria Zodiaco, Rome, 1950; Cranbrook, 1953; Tanager Gallery, NYC, 1958; Leo Castelli Inc., 1959; Otto Gerson Gallery, NYC, 1963; Ringling, 1964. GROUP: Pershing Hall, Paris, American Veterans in Paris, 1948; Salon de la Jeune Sculpture, Paris, 1950; Los Angeles/County MA, 1950; Salon d'Art Libre, Paris, 1951; MMA, National Sculpture Exhibition, 1951; PAFA, 1953; WMAA Annuals, 1953, 60, 62; II Sculpture Biennial, Antwerp, 1953; MOMA, New Talent; MOMA, Recent Sculpture USA, 1959; Sao Paulo, 1959; Claude Bernard, Paris, Aspects of American Sculpture, 1960; New School for Social Research, Mechanism and Organism, 1961; Seattle World's Fair, 1962; MOMA, Americans 1963, circ., 1963–64; Ringling, 1964. COLLECTIONS: Buffalo/Albright; Cranbrook; MOMA; Ringling; WMAA. BIBLIOGRAPHY: Goodrich and Baur 1; Seuphor 3.

KOHN, MISCH. b. March 26, 1916, Kokomo, Ind. STUDIED: John Herron Art Institute, 1939; in Mexico, 1943–44, with Jose Clemente Orozco, Mendez, Diego Rivera. TAUGHT: Institute of Design, Chicago; Illinois Institute of Technology, 1949–   ; Indiana U. AWARDS: The Print Club, Philadelphia, 1950, 51, 55, 56, 58; Chicago/AI, 1951, 52, 58; Indianapolis/Herron, 1952, 56; Seattle/AM, P.P., 1950; Brooklyn Museum, P.P., 1950, 51; NAD, 1955; Guggenheim Foundation Fellowship, 1952, 54; PAFA, Pennell Memorial Medal, 1952; PAFA, Alice McFadden Eyre Medal, 1949; Gallery of Modern Art, Ljubljana, Yugoslavia, IV International Exhibition of Prints, 1961; Tamarind Fellowship, 1961; Ford Foundation Grant; Salon du Mai, Paris, 1960. ADDRESS: 1200 East Madison Park, Chicago, Ill. ONE-MAN EXHIBITIONS: Weyhe Gallery; Philadelphia Art Alliance; Chicago/AI; Los Angeles/County MA; Kansas City/Nelson. RETROSPECTIVE: A.F.A./Ford Foundation, 1961. GROUP: Salon du Mai, Paris, 1952, 53; PAFA, 1949, 52, 56; Brooklyn Museum, 1949–57; The Print Club, Philadelphia,

1949–58; Boston/MFA; Seattle/AM; Chicago/AI, 1949–58. COLLECTIONS: Brooklyn Museum; Chicago/AI; Library of Congress; MOMA; NYPL; National Gallery; PMA; Rio de Janeiro; Stockholm/National. BIBLIOGRAPHY: Hayter 1; Peterdi.

KONZAL, JOSEPH. b. May 11, 1905, Milwaukee, Wisc. STUDIED: Layton School of Art, 1927; ASL, 1926–30, with Max Weber, Walt Kuhn, Robert Laurent; Beaux-Arts Institute of Design, NYC, 1928–30. TAUGHT: Brooklyn Museum School, 1949–64; Adelphi College, 1954–64; Newark (N.J.) Public School for Fine and Industrial Art, 1960–64. MEMBER: Sculptors Guild; Federation of Modern Painters and Sculptors. FEDERAL A.P.: Supervised Federal Art Project Gallery; architectural sculpture project. AWARDS: Brooklyn Museum Biennial, 2 First Prizes. ADDRESS: 254 Warren Street, Brooklyn, N.Y. DEALER: The Bertha Schaefer Gallery. ONE-MAN EXHIBITIONS: (first) Eighth Street Playhouse, NYC, 1938; Contemporary Arts Gallery, NYC, 1950, 52, 55; The Bertha Schaefer Gallery, 1960, 63. GROUP: Chicago/AI, 1938; New York World's Fair, 1939; Riverside Museum, 14 Sculptors, 1958; WMAA, Geometric Abstraction in America, circ., 1962; Carnegie, 1961; WMAA Annuals, 1960, 62, 63; Federation of Modern Painters and Sculptors Annuals; Sculptors Guild Annuals; Silvermine Guild Annuals, 1954–63; Brooklyn Museum, 1950, 52, 54, 56, 58, 60; MOMA, Subway Art, 1938; PAFA, 1953, 54, 58, 64; MOMA, Recent Sculpture USA, 1959; Newark Museum, 1961, 64; New York World's Fair, 1964–65. COLLECTIONS: Garcia Corp.; R. H. Macy & Co.; New School for Social Research; Union Carbide Corp.; WMAA.

KOPMAN, BENJAMIN. b. December 25, 1887, Vitebsk, Russia; d. December 3, 1965, Teaneck, N.J. To USA 1903; citizen 1913. STUDIED: NAD. Illustrated *Crime and Punishment* (Random House, 1956). MEMBER: Artists Equity. FEDERAL A.P.: Paintings, lithographs. AWARDS: PAFA, Gold Medal for Landscape, 1947, 53; MMA, Fourth Prize for Etching. ONE-MAN EXHIBITIONS: (first) Scott Thurber Gallery, Chicago; Macbeth Gallery, NYC, 1912; ACA Gallery; J. B. Neumann Gallery, NYC; The Milch Gallery; John Heller Gallery, NYC;

Newhouse Gallery, NYC; The Forum Gallery; Phillips. GROUP: NAD; PAFA; Carnegie; Corcoran; Phillips; Youngstown/Butler; Ringling; MMA; MOMA; La Napoule Art Foundation, Paris. COLLECTIONS: Atlanta U.; Brooklyn Museum; Carnegie; Colgate U.; Kansas City/Nelson; MMA; U. of Michigan; New Paltz; PAFA; PMA; Syracuse U.; Tel Aviv; WMAA; Worcester/AM. BIBLIOGRAPHY: Baur 7; Brown; Cheney, M. C.; Ignatoff; Kootz 1; Mellquist; Poore; Reese; Ringel, ed.

KOPPELMAN, CHAIM. b. 1920, Brooklyn, N.Y. STUDIED: Brooklyn College, 1938; Educational Alliance, NYC, 1938; American Artists School, NYC, 1939, with Eugene Morley, Carl Holty; New School for Social Research, with Amedee Ozenfant; Art College of Western England, Bristol, 1944; Ecole Regionale de Beaux-Arts, Reims, 1945; ASL, 1946, with Will Barnet, Jose de Creeft; privately with Amedee Ozenfant, 1946–49 (and served concurrently as his assistant). US Air Force, 1942–45. TAUGHT: NYU; Brooklyn College; New Paltz; School of Visual Arts, NYC. MEMBER: SAGA; Boston Printmakers; Society for Aesthetic Realism. COMMISSIONS: International Graphic Arts Society, 1958; A.A.A. Gallery, NYC, 1959, 61, 64. AWARDS: L. C. Tiffany Grant, 1956, 59; Audubon Artists, Medal for Graphics, 1960; Library of Congress, Pennell P.P.; PAFA, Hon. Men., 1959. ADDRESS: 498 Broome Street, NYC. DEALERS: The Terrain Gallery; A.A.A. Gallery, NYC. ONE-MAN EXHIBITIONS: (first) Outline Gallery, Pittsburgh, 1943; "67" Gallery, NYC, 1945; The Terrain Gallery, 1956; Philadelphia Art Alliance, 1959; Kornbluth Gallery, Paterson, N.J., 1964. GROUP: Yale U., 1949, 60; WMAA Annuals, 1948, 50, 61, 63; Brooklyn Museum; Boston/MFA; Los Angeles/County MA; Chicago/AI; Walker; Baltimore/MA; Detroit/Institute; Documenta II, Kassel, 1959; II Inter-American Paintings and Prints Biennial, Mexico City, 1960; USIA, Contemporary American Prints, circ. Latin America, 1959–60; MOMA, Recent Painting USA:The Figure, circ., 1962–63; Graphics:USA, Moscow, 1964. COLLECTIONS: Boston/MFA; Caracas; Long Beach State College; MMA; MOMA; National Gallery; Otis Art Institute; Peabody Museum; Syracuse U.; US State Department; Victoria and Albert Museum; Walker; Yale U.

How to Use This Book
....and something of its history

A major problem in the organizing of art exhibitions and the preparation of catalogues has been the general unavailability of information about American artists of the past quarter-century. There is a growing demand for such information; heretofore it has been necessary to contact a wide variety of sources (museums, libraries, dealers, the artists themselves) to gather any substantial quantity of data. From questionnaires, personal interviews, and more than a year of intensive research, have been brought together herein significant particulars on the careers of 689 artists, chosen for inclusion on the basis of the following criteria: representation in museum, public, and private collections; representation in major American and international exhibitions; influence as a teacher; recognition they have received from fellow-artists, dealers, critics, and others with a professional interest in the fine arts. December 1964 was chosen as the cut-off point for all data, except for obituary data through February 1966.

Each artist's entry is organized on the following plan:[1] Where he studied art, and with whom; where he has taught;[2] professional organizations to which he belongs; his participation (if any) in the Federal Art Project;[3] commissions he has executed; his scholarships and awards;[4] his spouse (if prominent in art); his address and dealers(s) of record; important one-man, retrospective, and group exhibitions;[5] selected bibliography.

Naturally, many artists have won the same awards, have been represented in the same exhibitions and collections, and are mentioned in the same books. Repetition of the complete data for each case would have made this volume far too large; therefore the data has been compressed into a series of keys, found in the front of the book, and a keyed, annotated bibliography, found at the back. Any abbreviations the reader finds in the A–Z section are explained in one or another of those keys (or in the footnotes on this page).

---

[1] Additional miscellaneous data are interspersed where significant and available.
[2] If he is still teaching, the dates are left open-ended: 1953–
[3] The Federal A.P. refers to a Government program of direct subsidies, classes, competitions, and public works projects during the Depression.
[4] The abbreviation P.P. in this category stands for "purchase prize" or "purchase award."
[5] The abbreviation "circ." in this category indicates that the exhibition circulated among various institutions.

The often long and complex names of museums and public collections have generally been abbreviated, and codified in the Key to Museums and Institutions. Common-sense methods have been used, most often acronyms (MOMA for The Museum of Modern Art, and similar familiar examples), and reductions, either merely to the name of the city (Mons, for the Musee des Beaux-Arts, Mons, Belgium) or to a combination of city and key-word (Albany/Institute for Albany Institute of History and Art), or city and acronym (Akron/AI for Akron Art Institute).

In the key entitled Galleries, addresses are given for the galleries which function as dealers for the artists in this volume; the many other galleries named in the "exhibitions" portions of the individual entries are identified therein by city.

The use of boldface type in the "bibliography" portion of the entries distinguishes the writings of the artist himself, and the most comprehensive material about him in the writings of others.

The Index of Artists in the front of this volume offers both a guide to pronouncing the artists' names, and a breakdown of the types of work for which they are best known.

Example:
... **ONE-MAN EXHIBITIONS:** (first) Boris Mirski Gallery, 1946; Blank Gallery, Washington, D.C., 1949. **GROUP:** Toledo/MA; Corcoran, 1950; NAD, 1951; Venice Biennials. **COLLECTIONS:** Springfield, Mass./MFA; Montclair/AM. **BIBLIOGRAPHY:** Baur 1, 5, **6**, 7.

Explanation:
The address of Boris Mirski Gallery is given in the Gallery list at the front of this book; the Blank Gallery was located in Washington, D.C., at the time of this exhibition, and may yet be found there if it is still in business, but it does not function as a dealer for any of the artists herein. Toledo/MA is for Toledo Museum of Art, and may be found alphabetically under T in the Key to Museums; similarly (under C) Corcoran for The Corcoran Gallery of Art and (under N) NAD for The National Academy of Design; the location of the Venice Biennials is found in the Key as Venice/Contemporaneo, under V. Springfield, Mass./MFA stands for Museum of Fine Arts, Springfield, Mass., and is found under S for Springfield; Montclair/AM stands for Montclair Art Museum, found under M. The bibliographic notation shows that this particular artist, among others, is referred to in the four books having those numbers among the seven books by Baur in the Bibliography, with boldface No. 6 being a monograph.

KRASNER, LEE. b. 1911, Brooklyn, N.Y. STUDIED: Cooper Union; NAD; Hofmann School, 1938. FEDERAL A.P.: Mural painting. COMMISSIONS: 2 Broadway Building, NYC (86-ft. mural). m. Jackson Pollock (1944). ADDRESS: Springs, East Hampton, N.Y. DEALER: Marlborough-Gerson Gallery Inc. ONE-MAN EXHIBITIONS: (first) Betty Parsons Gallery, 1950; The Stable Gallery, 1955; Martha Jackson Gallery, 1958; The Howard Wise Gallery, NYC, 1961, 62. GROUP: MacMillin Gallery, NYC, French and American Painting, 1942; Howard Putzell Gallery, Hollywood, 1945; Marlborough Fine Arts Ltd., London, The New, New York Scene, 1961; PAFA, 1962; WMAA; PMA. COLLECTIONS: WMAA. BIBLIOGRAPHY: Hunter 5; Janis and Blesh 1; Janis, S.

KRIESBERG, IRVING. b. March 13, 1919, Chicago, Ill. STUDIED: Chicago Art Institute School, 1941, BFA; Escuela Nacional de Artes Plasticas, Mexico City, 1941–44. TAUGHT: Brooklyn College; Yale U.; New School for Social Research. Made experimental animated film, "Pastoral," 1954. FEDERAL A.P.: Mural in Chicago, 1940–41. AWARDS: Ford Foundation, P.P., 1946. ADDRESS: 44 E. Broadway, Roslyn, N.Y. DEALER: The Graham Gallery. ONE-MAN EXHIBITIONS: Curt Valentine Gallery, NYC; Jewish Museum, 1961; Detroit/Institute, 1954; St. Louis/City, 1954; MOMA, 1953; Chicago/AI, 1946. GROUP: Chicago/AI, 1946; MOMA, New Talent; MOMA, Fifteen Americans, circ., 1952; Detroit/Institute, 1953; St. Louis/City, 1954. COLLECTIONS: Baltimore/MA; Brandeis U.; MOMA; Santa Barbara/MA; WMAA.

KROLL, LEON. b. December 6, 1884, NYC. STUDIED: ASL, with John Henry Twachtman; NAD; Academie Julian, Paris, with Jean Paul Laurens. Traveled France, USA. TAUGHT: NAD and ASL, 1911– ; Maryland Institute, 1919–21; Chicago Art Institute School, 1924–25; PAFA, 1929–30. MEMBER: NAD; AAAL; NIAL. FEDERAL A.P.: Mural Division. COMMISSIONS (murals): US Justice Department, Washington, D.C., 1936–37; Worcester (Mass.) War Memorial Building, 1938–41; Johns Hopkins U.; US Military Cemetery, Omaha Beach, France. AWARDS: Chicago/AI, The Mr. & Mrs. Frank G. Logan Prize, 1919, 32, 35; NAD, Benjamin Altman Prize, 1923, 32, 35; Chicago/AI, Potter Palmer Gold Medal, 1924; PAFA, Joseph E. Temple Gold Medal, 1927; Carnegie, First Prize, 1936; Chevalier of the Legion of Honor; and more than 20 others. ADDRESS: 15 West 67 Street, NYC. DEALER: Kraushaar Galleries. ONE-MAN EXHIBITIONS: (first) NAD, 1910; Buffalo/Albright, 1929; Cleveland/MA, 1945; French & Co. Inc., 1947; The Milch Gallery, 1947, 59; Toronto (three-man), 1930; Worcester/AM, 1937. GROUP: The Armory Show, 1913; Chicago/AI; Cleveland/MA; St. Louis/City; U. of Nebraska; WMAA; Detroit/Institute; Baltimore/MA; MMA. COLLECTIONS: Baltimore/MA; Britannica; Carnegie; Chicago/AI; Cleveland/MA; Corcoran; Dayton/AI; Denver/AM; Detroit/Institute; U. of Illinois; Indianapolis/Herron; Los Angeles/County MA; MMA; MOMA; Minneapolis/Institute; Municipal U. of Omaha; U. of Nebraska; PAFA; SFMA; St. Louis/City; San Diego; WMAA; West Palm Beach/Norton; Wilmington. BIBLIOGRAPHY: Baur 7; Biddle 3; Boswell 1; Brown; Bruce and Watson; Bryant; Cheney, M. C.; Coke; Eliot; Hall; Index of 20th Century Artists; Jackman; Jewell 2; Kent, N.; Kroll 1, 2; Mather 1; McCurdy, ed.; Mellquist; Narodny; Neuhaus; Pagano; Poore; Watson 1.

KRUSHENICK, NICHOLAS. b. May 31, 1929, NYC. STUDIED: ASL; Hofmann School, NYC. US Army, 1947–48. Co-founder of Brata Gallery, NYC. AWARDS: Longview Foundation Grant. ADDRESS: 131 West 21 Street, NYC. ONE-MAN EXHIBITIONS: (first) Camino Gallery, NYC, 1956; Brata Gallery, NYC, 1958, 60; The Graham Gallery, 1962, 64; Cinema I and Cinema II, NYC, 1964. GROUP: Wagner College, 1958; The Howard Wise Gallery, Cleveland, 1960; Barnard College, 1962; Galerie Creuze, Paris, 1958; Tokyo/Modern, 1959; MOMA, Contemporary Painters and Sculptors as Printmakers, 1964; Lincoln, Mass./De Cordova, 1962; WMAA Annual, 1963; Los Angeles/County MA, Post Painterly Abstraction, 1964. COLLECTIONS: Kalamazoo/Institute; MOMA; Provincetown/Chrysler.

KUHN, WALT. b. October 27, 1877, Brooklyn, N.Y.; d. July 13, 1949, NYC. STUDIED: Academie Colarossi, Paris, 1901; Academy of Fine Arts, Munich, 1901, with H. von Zugel; Artists Sketch Class, NYC, 1905. TAUGHT: New York

School of Art, 1908–09. Executive Secretary, Association of American Painters and Sculptors, sponsor of The Armory Show, NYC, 1913. Founder of the Penguin Club, 1917–19. Designed sets and directed many revue skits for Broadway in the 1920's. ONE-MAN EXHIBITIONS: (first) Madison Gallery, NYC, 1910, also 1911; Montross Gallery, NYC, 1914, 15, 22, 24, 25; DeZayas Gallery, NYC, 1920; Grand Central, NYC, 1927; M. Knoedler & Co., 1928; The Downtown Gallery, 1928; Marie Harriman Gallery, NYC, 1930–42; Colorado Springs/FA, 1947; Durand-Ruel Gallery, NYC, 1944, 45, 46, 48; Maynard Walker Gallery, 1954, 57, 62. RETROSPECTIVE: Cincinnati/AM, 1960; Albany/Institute, 1958; Phillips (two-man), 1944; A.F.A., circ., 1951; Fort Worth, 1964. GROUP: WMAA; Chicago/AI; Detroit/Institute; Cincinnati/AM; MOMA. COLLECTIONS: Buffalo/Albright; Cincinnati/AM; Colorado Springs/FA; Columbus; Currier; Denver/AM; Des Moines; Detroit/Institute; Gallery of Modern Art, NYC; Indianapolis/Herron; Kansas City/Nelson; MMA; MOMA; U. of Nebraska; Ogunquit; Phillips; WMAA; Wellesley College; Wichita/AM. BIBLIOGRAPHY: Adams; Baur 7; Bazin; Biddle 3; Bird; Blesh 1; Brown; Bulliet 1; Cahill and Barr, eds.; Cheney, M. C.; Eliot; Flanagan; Genauer; Goodrich and Baur 1; Hunter 5; *Index of 20th Century Artists;* Janis, S.; Jewell 2; Kootz 1; Kuhn 1, 2; McCurdy, ed.; Mellquist; Mendelowitz; Newmeyer; Pagano; Phillips 2; Poore; Richardson; Ringel, ed.; Smith, S. C. K.; Wight 2.

KUNIYOSHI, YASUO. b. September 1, 1893, Okayama, Japan; d. May 14, 1953, NYC. To USA 1906. STUDIED: Los Angeles School of Art, three years; NAD; Robert Henri School, 1910; Independent School of Art, 1914–16, with Homer Boss; ASL, 1916–20, with Kenneth Hayes Miller. Traveled Europe, Japan, USA. TAUGHT: ASL, 1933–53; New School for Social Research, 1936–53; Brooklyn Museum School. MEMBER: Salons of America, 1922–38 (Director); Hamilton Easter Field Foundation; American Artists Congress; An American Place (President, 1939–44); Artists Equity (President, 1947–50, Hon. President until his death). FEDERAL A.P.: Graphics Division, two years, *ca.* 1936. COMMISSIONS: Radio City Music Hall, NYC (mural). AWARDS: Carnegie, Hon. Men.,

Yasuo Kuniyoshi
Somebody Tore My Poster. 1943

1931, Second Prize, 1939, and First Prize, 1944; Los Angeles/County MA, Second Prize, 1934; PAFA, Joseph E. Temple Gold Medal, 1934; PAFA, J. Henry Schiedt Memorial Prize, 1944; Guggenheim Foundation Fellowship, 1935; Golden Gate International Exposition, San Francisco, 1939, First Prize; VMFA, P.P., 1944; Chicago/AI, Norman Wait Harris Bronze Medal and Prize, 1945; La Tausca Competition, Fifth Award, 1947, 48; *Look* Magazine poll of "Ten Best Painters," February, 1948; MMA, Second Prize, 1950. ONE-MAN EXHIBITIONS: The Daniel Gallery, NYC, 1922, also 1928, 30; Tokyo/Modern and Osaka/Municipal, 1931–32; The Downtown Gallery, 1933, 36, 39, 40, 41, 45, 48, 50, 52, 55, 61;

ASL, 1936; Baltimore/MA, 1939; Boston Museum School, 1950; Woodstock (N.Y.) Art Gallery, 1956. RETROSPECTIVE: The Downtown Gallery, benefit for United China Relief, 1942; WMAA, 1948; Tokyo/Modern, 1954; Boston U., 1961. GROUP: Society of Independent Artists, NYC; Penguin Club, NYC, 1917; MOMA, Paintings by 19 Living Americans, 1929; MOMA, Twentieth Century Portraits, 1942; The U. of Chicago, 1948; Portland, Me./MA, 1949; XXVI Venice Biennial, 1952; U. of Illinois; U. of Nebraska. COLLECTIONS: AAAL; Agricultural and Mechanical College of Texas; Andover/Phillips; Arizona State College; U. of Arizona; Atlanta/AA; Auburn U.; Baltimore/MA; Britannica; Brooklyn Museum; Buffalo/Albright; Carnegie; Chicago/AI; Cincinnati/AM; Clearwater/Gulf Coast; Cleveland/MA; Columbus; Cranbrook; Dallas/MFA; Des Moines; Detroit/Institute; Hamilton Easter Field Foundation; Fort Worth; U. of Georgia; Hartford/Wadsworth; Honolulu Academy; Houston/MFA; U. of Illinois; Indiana U.; Indianapolis/Herron; Kalamazoo/Institute; Kansas City/Nelson; Library of Congress; MMA; MOMA; U. of Michigan; Milwaukee; U. of Nebraska; Newark Museum; New London; Ogunquit; PMA; Phillips; Portland, Ore./AM; Santa Barbara/MA; Sao Paulo; Tel Aviv; Tokyo/Modern; Utica; VMFA; WMAA; Walker; Washington U.; West Palm Beach/Norton; Wichita/AM; Wilmington; Youngstown/Butler. BIBLIOGRAPHY: American Artists Congress, Inc.; American Artists Group Inc. 3; Barker 1; Baur 7; Bazin; Bethers; Biddle 3; Blesh 1; Boswell 1; Brown; Cahill and Barr, eds.; Cheney, M. C.; Coke; Eliot; Genauer; **Goodrich 7;** Goodrich and Baur 1; **Goodrich and Imgizumi;** Haftman; Hall; Halpert; *Index of 20th Century Artists;* Jewell 2; Kootz 1, 2; **Kuniyoshi;** McCurdy, ed.; Mellquist; Newmeyer; Pagano; Pearson 1, 2; Poore; Pousette-Dart, ed.; Reese; Richardson; Ringel, ed.; Wheeler; Wight 2; Zaidenberg, ed.; Zigrosser 1.

KUNTZ, ROGER. b. January 4, 1926, San Antonio, Tex. STUDIED: Pomona College, 1943–44, 1946–48, BA; Claremont Graduate School, 1948–50, MFA; in France and Italy, 1950. AWARDS: Guggenheim Foundation Fellowship, 1956; Arizona State Fair, Second Prize, 1949, and First Prize, 1950; NAD

Annual, Andrew Carnegie Prize, 1952; Denver/AM, P.P., 1952, 53; Los Angeles/County MA, P.P., 1953, 55, and First Prize, 1954; Jose Drudis Foundation P.P. ($400), 1956; U. of Illinois, P.P., 1955; Los Angeles Art Festival, 1959; Chaffey College, First Award, 1960. ADDRESS: c/o Dealer. DEALER: Felix Landau Gallery. ONE-MAN EXHIBITIONS: Scripps College, 1950, 54; San Diego, 1951; Felix Landau Gallery, 1952, 54, 56, 58, 62, 64; Pasadena/AM, 1953, 63; Urban Gallery, NYC, 1955; Barone Gallery, NYC, 1957; Gump's Gallery, 1957; Sierra Madre (Calif.) Public Library, 1958; San Bernardino Valley College, 1959; Whittier (Calif.) Art Association, 1960; Mount San Antonio College, 1961. GROUP: Los Angeles/County MA, California Centennial Art Exhibition, 1949; Los Angeles/County MA Annuals, 1951, 53, 57; NAD, 1952, 53; Denver/AM, 1952, 53, 54, 55; PAFA, 1952, 55; Corcoran, 1953; Carnegie, 1955, 64; Sao Paulo, 1955; U. of Illinois, 1955, 57; Santa Barbara/MA, I West Coast Biennial, 1958; Long Beach/MA, Arts of Southern California II, 1958; Oakland/AM, Pop Art USA, 1963. COLLECTIONS: Denver/AM; U. of Illinois; Los Angeles/County MA; NAD; Pasadena/AM; Scripps College.

KUPFERMAN, LAWRENCE. b. March 25, 1909, Boston, Mass. STUDIED: Boston Museum School, 1929–31; Massachusetts School of Art, Boston, 1931–35, BS.Ed. TAUGHT: Massachusetts College of Art, 1941– (Head, Department of Painting). MEMBER: SAGA; NAD; Fellow of the Royal Society of Arts, London. COMMISSIONS (murals): SS *Constitution* and SS *Independence,* American Export Isbrandtsen Lines Inc. AWARDS: U. of Illinois, $1,000 P.P., 1953; Rhode Island Arts Festival, First Prize for Painting, 1961. ADDRESS: 38 Devon Road, Newton Center 59, Mass. DEALER: The Pace Gallery, Boston. ONE-MAN EXHIBITIONS: (first) Boris Mirski Gallery, 1944, also 1945, 46, 47; Mortimer Brandt, NYC, 1946; Philadelphia Art Alliance, 1947; Mortimer Levitt Gallery, NYC, 1948, 49, 51, 53; Martha Jackson Gallery, 1955; The Swetzoff Gallery, 1956; Verna Wear Gallery, NYC, 1956; Ruth White Gallery, 1958; Gropper Gallery, Cambridge, Mass., 1958; The Pace Gallery, Boston, 1960, 63; Lincoln, Mass./De Cordova, 1961; Irla Kert Gallery,

Montreal, 1962. **GROUP:** Chicago/AI Annuals; PAFA; WMAA Annuals; Venice Biennial; U. of Illinois; Brooklyn Museum Biennials; MMA; Hartford/Wadsworth; NAD; Carnegie; Musee du Petit Palais, Paris. **COLLECTIONS:** Andover/Phillips; Baltimore/MA; Boston/MFA; Boston Public Library; Brooklyn Museum; Carnegie; Hartford/Wadsworth; Harvard U.; U. of Illinois; Library of Congress; MMA; MOMA; U. of Michigan; Mills College; SFMA; WMAA; Walker. **BIBLIOGRAPHY:** Baur 7; Pousette-Dart, ed.; Reese.

LABAUDT, LUCIEN. b. May 14, 1880, Paris, France; d. December 13, 1943, Assam, India. Primarily self-taught. To London 1903; to USA 1906; became a citizen. French Army, World War I; US War Department, World War II. Artist War Correspondent for *Life* Magazine, 1943. COMMISSIONS (murals): Coit Memorial Tower, San Francisco; George Washington High School, San Francisco; Beach Chalet, San Francisco; US Post Office, Los Angeles; US Court House, Los Angeles; California State Building and Auditorium, Golden Gate International Exposition, San Francisco, 1939. AWARDS: SFMA, Anne Bremer Memorial Prize, 1927; Gump's Gallery, First Prize, 1932; Radical Group, Los Angeles, First Prize, 1937; SFMA, First Municipal P.P., 1937. ONE-MAN EXHIBITIONS: Beaux Arts Gallery, San Francisco; California Palace; Stanley Rose Gallery, Hollywood; Stendahl Gallery, Los Angeles; Oakland/AM; San Joaquin Pioneer Museum and Haggin Art Galleries, Stockton, Calif.; SFMA, 1940; SFMA, Memorial Exhibition, 1944; Lucien Labaudt Gallery, Memorial Exhibition, annually. GROUP: Salon des Artistes Independants, Paris, 1921, 22, 23, 24, 25, 26; Salon d'Automne, Paris, 1924, 25, 26; Paris Salon, 1928; Society of Independent Artists, NYC, 1922–31; MOMA, 1933, 34, 36; Brooklyn Museum, 1936; Carnegie, 1931, 33, 34, 35, 36, 37; SFMA Annuals, 1920–43. COLLECTIONS: SFMA; San Francisco Municipal Art Commission. BIBLIOGRAPHY: Cheney, M. C.

LACHAISE, GASTON. b. March 19, 1882, Paris, France; d. October, 1935, NYC. STUDIED: Ecole Bernard Palissy, Paris, 1895; Academie des Beaux-Arts, Paris, 1898–1904, with G. J. Thomas. Worked for Rene Lalique. To USA 1906. Worked for H. H. Kitson in Boston, 1906–12. COMMISSIONS: Electricity Building, A Century of Progress, Chicago, 1933–34; Rockefeller Center, NYC; Fairmount Park, Philadelphia. ONE-MAN EXHIBITIONS: (first) Bourgeois Gallery, NYC, 1918, also 1920; Stieglitz's Intimate Gallery, NYC, 1927; Joseph Brummer Gallery, NYC, 1928; Philadelphia Art Alliance, 1932; WMAA, 1937; Robert Schoelkopf Gallery, 1964; MOMA, circ. only, 1962; Brooklyn Museum, 1938; M. Knoedler & Co., NYC, 1947; Weyhe Gallery, 1956; Margaret Brown Gallery, Boston, 1957. RETROSPECTIVE: MOMA, 1935; Los Angeles/County MA, 1963. GROUP: MOMA; WMAA; Phillips; Hartford/Wadsworth. COLLECTIONS: Andover/Phillips; Arizona State College; Cincinnati/AM; Cleveland/MA; Hartford/Wadsworth; Harvard U.; Los Angeles/County MA; MMA; MOMA; Museum of the City of New York; New London; PMA; Phillips; Rochester/Memorial; U. of Rochester; Santa Barbara/MA; Smith College; U. of Texas; WMAA. BIBLIOGRAPHY: Baur 7; Biddle 3; Blesh 1; Brumme; Cahill and Barr, eds.; Cheney, M. C.; Elsen; Fierens; **Gallatin 4;** Goodrich and Baur 1; Hunter 5; Lee and Burchwood; McCurdy, ed.; **Nordland;** Parkes; Ringel, ed.; Ritchie 3; Selz, J.; Seuphor 3; Seymour; Sutton.

LANDAU, JACOB. b. December 17, 1917, Philadelphia, Pa. STUDIED: Philadelphia Museum School, with Franklin Watkins, H. C. Pitz; New School for Social Research, 1947–48, 1952–53; in Paris, 1949–52. US Army, 1943–46. TAUGHT: Pratt Institute. MEMBER: Philadelphia Watercolor Club. COMMISSIONS: International

Gaston Lachaise   *Kneeling Woman.*

Graphic Arts Society; A.A.A. Gallery; National Broadcasting Co.; The Limbach Co.; McGraw-Hill Inc. **AWARDS:** The Print Club, Philadelphia, Lessing J. Rosenwald P.P., 1955, 59; L. C. Tiffany Grant, 1962; PAFA, Watercolor Prize, 1963. **ADDRESS:** 2 Pine Drive, Roosevelt, N.J. **DEALER:** Cober Gallery. **ONE-MAN EXHIBITIONS:** (first) Galerie Le Bar, Paris, 1952; Cober Gallery, 1961, 63; Zora Gallery, Los Angeles, 1964; Philadelphia Art Alliance, 1954; Samuel S. Fleisher Art Memorial, Philadelphia, 1959; U. of Maine, 1961; A.A.A. Gallery, NYC, 1960. **GROUP:** Cober Gallery, The Insiders, 1960; NAD Annual, 1953; Brooklyn Museum Biennials, 1960, 62; PAFA Annuals, 1961, 63; Boston/MFA, 1955; Seattle/AM, 1957; MOMA, Recent Painting USA:The Figure, circ., 1962–63; SAGA; A.A.A. Gallery, NYC, 100 Prints of the Year, 1962; St. Paul Gallery,

Drawings, USA, 1961; USIA, Graphic Arts—USA, circ. U.S.S.R., 1963; Library of Congress, 1963; PCA/USIA, 30 Contemporary Prints, circ. Europe, 1964; Corcoran, 1964. **COLLECTIONS:** Brooklyn Museum; U. of Kentucky; Library of Congress; MMA; MOMA; U. of Maine; U. of Minnesota; Montclair/AM; Norfolk; PAFA; PMA; Princeton U.; Rutgers U.; San Antonio/McNay; Syracuse U.; VMFA; Yale U.

LANDON, EDWARD. b. March 13, 1911, Hartford, Conn. **STUDIED:** Hartford Art School; ASL, with Jean Charlot; privately in Mexico with Carlos Merida. Traveled Europe, Scandinavia, Mexico. **TAUGHT** privately (serigraphy). Subject of a film, "How to Make a Serigraph," produced by the Harmon Foundation. Charter **MEMBER** and past President, National Serigraph

Society; member: Boston Printmakers; American Color Print Society; The Print Club, Philadelphia. FEDERAL A.P.: Easel painting and murals. AWARDS: Fulbright Fellowship (Norway), 1950, 51; Northwest Printmakers Annual, 1944, 46, 52; Brooklyn Museum, 1947; American Color Print Society, 1947; San Francisco Art Association, 1949; National Serigraph Society, 1947, 54, 57, 58; Boston Printmakers. ADDRESS: Bondville, Vt. DEALER: Doris Meltzer Gallery. ONE-MAN EXHIBITIONS: (first) Boston/MFA, 1934; Smith College, 1941; Norlyst Gallery, NYC, 1945; Unge Kunstneres Samfund, Oslo, 1950; The Print Club, Philadelphia, 1953; Fine Arts Gallery, Hartford, 1954; Doris Meltzer Gallery, 1957, 58. GROUP: Brooklyn Museum; Northwest Printmakers Annuals; American Color Print Society; National Serigraph Society; MOMA; Library of Congress; MMA; and many others. COLLECTIONS: Bezalel Museum; Bibliotheque Nationale; Brooklyn Museum; Buffalo/Albright; Library of Congress; Kansas City/Nelson; MMA; MOMA; PMA; SFMA; Tel Aviv; Turku Museum, Finland; Victoria and Albert Museum; Worcester/AM. BIBLIOGRAPHY: American Artists Congress, Inc.; **Landon;** Reese.

LANGLAIS, BERNARD. b. July 23, 1921, Old Town, Me. STUDIED: The Corcoran School of Art; Skowhegan School; Brooklyn Museum School; Academie de la Grande Chaumiere; Academy of Art, Oslo. US Navy, 1942–48. AWARDS: Fulbright Fellowship (Norway); Ford Foundation, P.P. ADDRESS: 114 West 29 Street, NYC. ONE-MAN EXHIBITIONS: (first) Roko Gallery, 1956; Area Gallery, NYC, 1959; U. of Maine, 1960; Leo Castelli Inc., 1961; Allan Stone Gallery, 1962; Grippi and Waddell Gallery, 1964. GROUP: A.F.A., circ., 1961–62; ART:USA:58 and ART:USA:59, NYC, 1958, 59; Boston Arts Festival, 1960, 61; Martha Jackson Gallery, New Media—New Forms, I & II, 1960, 61; WMAA Annuals, 1960, 63; Houston/MFA, New Media, 1961; Yale U., Best of Contemporary Painting from New York Galleries, 1960; MOMA, The Art of Assemblage, circ., 1961; Carnegie, 1961; Chicago/AI Annuals, 1960, 61, 64; Colby College, Maine and Its Artists, 1963. COLLECTIONS: Chicago/AI; Colby College; U. of Maine; The Olsen Foundation Inc.; Provincetown/Chrysler; The Singer Company Inc.; WMAA. BIBLIOGRAPHY: Janis and Blesh 1; Seitz 2.

LANING, EDWARD. b. April 26, 1906, Petersburg, Ill. STUDIED: The U. of Chicago; ASL, with Boardman Robinson, Max Weber, John Sloan, Kenneth Hayes Miller; Academy of Fine Arts, Rome. Traveled USA, Europe, North Africa. TAUGHT: Cooper Union, 1938–41; Kansas City Art Institute and School of Design, 1945–50; Pratt Institute, 1952–56; ASL, 1952– . MEMBER: NAD; ASL; National Society of Mural Painters. FEDERAL A.P. (murals): Ellis Island; New York Public Library; US Post Offices, Rockingham, N.C., and Bowling Green, Ky. COMMISSIONS: *Life* Magazine (paintings); murals for Sheraton Corporation hotels in Los Angeles, Dallas, Louisville, Niagara Falls, NYC. AWARDS: Guggenheim Foundation Fellowship, 1945; Fulbright Fellowship, 1950; AAAL Grant; VMFA, 1945; Chicago/AI, 1945. ADDRESS: 30 East 14 Street, NYC. DEALER: The Griffin Gallery. ONE-MAN EXHIBITIONS: (first) Dudensing Gallery, NYC, 1932; The Midtown Galleries; Hewitt Gallery, NYC, 1950; Kansas City/Nelson, 1945; The Griffin Gallery, 1963. GROUP: WMAA; MMA; Chicago/AI; Cleveland/MA; VMFA; NAD; Audubon Artists. COLLECTIONS: Kansas City/Nelson; MMA; WMAA. BIBLIOGRAPHY: Boswell 1; Cheney, M. C.; Hall.

LANSNER, FAY. b. June 21, 1921, Philadelphia, Pa. STUDIED: Wanamaker Institute, 1939–41; Stella Elkins Tyler School of Fine Arts, Temple U., 1945–47; Columbia U., 1947–48; ASL, 1947–48, with Vaclav Vytlacil; Hofmann School, 1948; Atelier Fernand Leger, Paris, 1950; Academie Andre Lhote, Paris, 1950. Traveled Europe extensively; resided Paris, 1950–52. ADDRESS: 317 West 80 Street, NYC. DEALER: The Kornblee Gallery. ONE-MAN EXHIBITIONS: (first) Galerie Huit, Paris, 1951; Le Gerrec, Paris, 1952; Peretz Johannes Gallery, NYC, 1952; Hansa Gallery, NYC, 1955, 56, 58; Hood College, 1961; David Herbert Gallery, NYC, 1961; The Zabriskie Gallery, 1963; The Kornblee Gallery, 1963. GROUP: Finch College, Paul Magriel Collection; Southampton/Parrish; Houston/MFA, The Emerging Figure, 1961; Louis Alexander Gallery, NYC, Recent American Drawings,

1962; Stanhope Gallery, Boston, Works on Paper.

LANYON, ELLEN. b. December 21, 1926, Chicago, Ill. STUDIED: Chicago Art Institute School, The U. of Chicago, Roosevelt College (with Max Kahn, Kathleen Blackshear, Joseph Hirsch, 1944–48, BFA); State U. of Iowa, with Mauricio Lasansky, Eugene Ludins, 1948–50, MFA; Courtauld Institute, 1950–51. Traveled Europe, USA. TAUGHT: Chicago Art Institute Junior School, 1952–54; Rockford College, 1954; Saugatuck Summer School of Painting, 1961–62; occasionally privately. A founder and active member of the Chicago/AI Exhibition Momentum, 1948–52. AWARDS: Fulbright Fellowship (England), 1950; Chicago/AI, Watson F. Blair Prize, 1958; Chicago/AI, Mr. & Mrs. Frank H. Armstrong Prize, 1946, 55; Chicago/AI, Pauline Palmer Prize, 1962, 64; Chicago/AI, Martin B. Cahn Award, 1961; Denver/AM, P.P., 1950; Library of Congress, Pennell P.P., 1950. ADDRESS: 2131 North Hudson, Chicago, Ill. DEALERS: B. C. Holland Gallery; The Zabriskie Gallery. ONE-MAN EXHIBITIONS: (first) Superior Street Gallery, Chicago, 1948; Stewart Richard Gallery, San Antonio, 1962; Fairweather-Hardin Gallery, 1962; The Zabriskie Gallery, 1962, 64; B. C. Holland Gallery, 1964. GROUP: The Downtown Gallery, Chicago Artists, 1954; Chicago/AI, Prints from the Graphic Workshop, 1955; Chicago/AI Annuals, 1946, 47, 51, 53, 55, 57, 58, 60, 61, 62; Corcoran, 1961; Denver/AM, 1951, 52; Chicago/AI, Exhibition Momentum, 1948, 50, 52, 54, 56; Omaha/Joslyn, 1949, 58; Library of Congress, 1950, 52; MMA, 1952; MOMA, Young American Printmakers, 1953; MOMA, Recent Painting USA:The Figure, circ., 1962–63; PMA, 1946, 47, 50, 54; U. of Illinois, 1953, 57. COLLECTIONS: Chicago/AI; Denver/AM; U. of Illinois; Institute of International Education; Library of Congress; The Singer Company Inc.

LASANSKY, MAURICIO. b. October 12, 1914, Buenos Aires, Argentina. STUDIED: Superior School of Fine Arts, Buenos Aires. Traveled Europe, Latin America. To USA 1943; citizen 1952. TAUGHT: Director, Free Fine Arts School, Villa Maria, Argentina, 1936; Taller Manualidad, 1939; Atelier 17, NYC; State U. of Iowa, 1954– . AWARDS: Guggenheim Foundation Fellowship (USA), 1943, renewed 1944; Guggenheim Foundation Fellowship (Spain and France), 1963, 64; The Print Club, Philadelphia, P.P., 1945, 48; Library of Congress, Pennell P.P., 1945, 48, 50, 56, 59, 62, 63; Denver/AM, P.P., 1946, 47; Brooklyn Museum, P.P., 1948, 58; Northwest Printmakers Annual, P.P., 1948, 51, 55, 59, 61; Printmakers of Southern California, P.P., 1952; Bradley U., P.P., 1952; Des Moines, P.P., 1946, 49, 51, 57, 58; Silvermine Guild, P.P., 1958; Walker Biennial, P.P., 1958; De Pauw U., P.P., 1959; Kansas City/Nelson, P.P., 1960; Pasadena/AM, P.P., 1962; Ford Foundation, P.P., 1962; Seattle/AM, Seattle International, First Prize, 1944; Iowa State Fair, First Prize, 1947; Society of American Etchers and Engravers, NYC, 1947; PAFA, Alice McFadden Eyre Medal, 1948, 57; Walker, First and Second Prizes, 1949; The Print Club, Philadelphia, Charles M. Lea Prize, 1951, 57, 62; Des Moines, IV Annual, Edmundson Award, 1952; Des Moines, V Annual, Special Commendation, 1953; Des Moines, Prize in Painting, 1955; Des Moines, Younkers Professional Award, 1956; I Inter-American Paintings and Prints Biennial, Mexico City, Posada Award, 1958, II Inter-American Paintings and Prints Biennial, Mexico City, Special Hon. Men. with Gold Medal, 1960; PAFA, Hon. Men. and one-man exhibition, 1961; Hon. DFA, Iowa Wesleyan College, 1959. ADDRESS: 404 South Summit, Iowa City, Iowa. DEALER: The Contemporaries. ONE-MAN EXHIBITIONS: (first) Fort General Roca, Rio Negro, Argentina, 1935; SFMA, 1945, 50; Whyte Gallery, Washington, D.C., 1945; Chicago/AI, 1947; U. of Louisville, 1948; Walker, 1949; Houston/MFA, 1949; Milwaukee, 1949; Purdue U., 1949; Santa Barbara/MA, 1950; Northwestern U., 1950; Cornell U., 1951; Tulane U., 1952; Memphis/Brooks, 1953; Madrid/Nacional, 1954; Oakland/AM, 1958; USIA, Intaglios (one-man and his students), circ. Latin America and USA, 1959–61; PAFA Annual, 1961. RETROSPECTIVE: State U. of Iowa, 1957; A.F.A./Ford Foundation, circ., 1960–62. GROUP: Carnegie, American Prints, 1949; Sao Paulo, 1951; U. of Illinois, Graphic Art, USA, 1954; France/National, 50 Ans d'Art aux Etats-Unis, circ. Europe, 1955; Gallery of Modern Art, Ljubljana, Yugoslavia, I, II, and V International Exhibitions of Prints, 55, 57, 63; Michigan State U., 20 American Printmakers, 1956;

Achenbach Foundation, Prints Since the 14th Century, 1957; SAGA, 1957; U. of California, Berkeley, Modern Master Prints, 1958; PAFA, 1959, 60; ICA, Boston, 100 Works on Paper, circ. Europe, 1959; Yale U., American Prints, 1950–60, 1960; I & II Inter-American Paintings and Prints Biennials, Mexico City, 1958, 60; PCA, American Prints Today, circ., 1959–62; USIA, Graphic Arts—USA, circ. U.S.S.R., 1963. COLLECTIONS: Albion College; American Life and Casualty Insurance Co.; Argentina/Nacional; Barcelona; Bradley U.; Brooklyn Museum; Buenos Aires/Municipal; Cedar Rapids/AA; Chicago/AI; Colorado Springs/FA; Cordoba/Municipal; Cordoba/Provincial; U. of Delaware; De Pauw U.; Des Moines; Detroit/Institute; First National Bank, Iowa City; Flint/Institute; U. of Georgia; Gettysburg College; IBM; Illinois State Normal U.; U. of Illinois; Indiana U.; Iowa Wesleyan College; State College of Iowa; State U. of Iowa; Kansas City/Nelson; La Plata; Library of Congress; Louisiana State U.; Luther College; MOMA; Madrid/Nacional; U. of Maine; Melbourne/National; Mendoza; U. of Michigan; Millikin U.; U. of Minnesota; Museo Rosario; NYPL; National Gallery; U. of Nebraska; New Britain; Oakland/AM; Omaha/Joslyn; PAFA; PMA; Pasadena/AM; Portland, Ore./AM; Rio Cuarto; SFMA; St. Louis/City; Salt Lake City Public Library; Seattle/AM; Silvermine Guild; Southwest Missouri State College; Springfield, Mo./AM; Syracuse U.; Time Inc.; USIA; U. of Utah; Walker; Washburn U. of Topeka; Washington U.; U. of Washington; Wesleyan U.; Yale U. BIBLIOGRAPHY: Hayter 1, 2; Reese; Zigrosser 2.

LASSAW, IBRAM. b. May 14, 1913, Alexandria, Egypt. To USA 1921; citizen 1928. STUD-

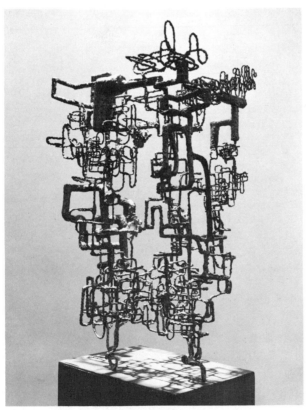

Ibram Lassaw   *Counterpoint Castle. 1957*

IED: City College of New York; Clay Club, 1926–30; Beaux-Arts Institute of Design, NYC, 1930–31; Ozenfant School of Art, NYC. Traveled Europe. US Army, 1942–44. TAUGHT: American U., 1950; Duke U., 1962–63; and privately. A founder and MEMBER of American Abstract Artists (President, 1946–49). FEDERAL A.P.: 1933–42. COMMISSIONS: Beth El Temple, Springfield, Mass.; Beth El Temple, Providence, R.I.; Temple of Aaron, St. Paul; Temple Anshe Chesed, Cleveland; Kneses Tifereth Israel Synagogue, Port Chester, N.Y.; House of Theology of the Franciscan Fathers, Centreville, Ohio; Washington U., 1959; New York Hilton Hotel; Yale & Towne Inc. ADDRESS: Fireplace Road, Springs, East Hampton, N.Y. DEALER: The Kootz Gallery. ONE-MAN EXHIBITIONS: (first) The Kootz Gallery, 1951, also 1952, 54, 58, 60, 63, 64; Duke U., 1963. RETROSPECTIVE: MIT, 1957. GROUP: Salon des Realites Nouvelles, Paris, 1950; MOMA, Abstract Painting and Sculpture in America, 1951; MOMA, Sculpture of the XXth Century, 1953; XXVII Venice Biennial, 1954; Chicago/AI, 1954; WMAA, The New Decade, 1954–55; U. of Illinois, 1955, 57, 59, 61; WMAA Annuals, 1936–46; IV Sao Paulo Biennial, 1957; Brussels World's Fair, 1958; MOMA, Twelve Americans, circ., 1956; Documenta II, Kassel, 1959; Cleveland/MA, Paths of Abstract Art, 1960; Carnegie, 1961; Seattle World's Fair, 1962; WGMA, Sculptors of Our Time, 1963; American Abstract Artists Annuals, 1937– . COLLECTIONS: Baltimore/MA; Buffalo/Albright; Carnegie; Chase Manhattan Bank; Hartford/Wadsworth; Harvard U.; MOMA; Metalcraft Corp.; Newark Museum; Rio de Janeiro; WMAA; Washington U.; Worcester/AM. BIBLIOGRAPHY: Baur 5, 7; Blesh 1; Brumme; Giedion-Welcker 1; Goodrich and Baur 1; Goossen 2; Henning; Hunter 5; McCurdy, ed.; Mendelowitz; Myers 2; Ritchie 1, 3; Seuphor 3.

LAUFMAN, SIDNEY. b. October 29, 1891, Cleveland, Ohio. STUDIED: Chicago Art Institute School, with Reynolds, Buehr; ASL, with Robert Henri. Traveled Europe; resided France, 1920–33. TAUGHT: ASL, 1938–50; Brandeis U., 1959–60. MEMBER: NAD; Woodstock Artists Association. FEDERAL A.P.: Easel painting. AWARDS: Chicago/AI, The Mr. & Mrs. Frank G. Logan Prize, 1932; Carnegie, Third Prize, 1934; NAD, Benjamin Altman Prize, 1937, 63; NAD, Special Landscape Prize, 1949; NAD, Samuel F. B. Morse Gold Medal, 1953; NAD Annual, Andrew Carnegie Prize, 1959; ASL, Diamond Jubilee P.P., 1950; PAFA, Jennie Sesnan Gold Medal, 1951; Corcoran, Hon. Men., 1951; Youngstown/Butler, First P.P., 1954. ADDRESS: Glasco Turnpike, Woodstock, N.Y. DEALER: The Forum Gallery. ONE-MAN EXHIBITIONS: (first) Galerie Devambez, Paris, 1922; Marie Sterner Gallery, NYC, 1923; Gage Gallery, Cleveland, 1927; Arts Club of Chicago, 1927; The New Gallery, NYC, 1927; Galerie Granoff, Paris, 1930; de Hauke Gallery, NYC, 1931; The Milch Gallery, 1934, 44, 48, 53, 56, 58; East End Gallery, Provincetown, 1960, 61, 62, 63; The Forum Gallery, 1962; Rudolph Gallery, Coral Gables, Fla., 1964; Peabody Museum, 1963; U. of Miami, 1964; Brandeis U., 1960. GROUP: Carnegie; NAD; PAFA; Corcoran; WMAA; Chicago/AI; Youngstown/Butler; and many others since 1922. COLLECTIONS: AAAL; Bezalel Museum; Brandeis U.; Chicago/AI; Cleveland/MA; Indianapolis/Herron; Kansas City/Nelson; MMA; MOMA; Minneapolis/Institute; U. of Oregon; Provincetown/Chrysler; St. Louis/City; Tel Aviv; Toledo/MA; WMAA; Youngstown/Butler. BIBLIOGRAPHY: Hess, T. B.; Zaidenberg, ed.

LAURENT, JOHN. b. November 27, 1921, Brooklyn, N.Y. STUDIED: Syracuse U., Indiana U. (MFA), Academie de la Grande Chaumiere (with Walt Kuhn, Othon Friesz, Stephen Greene). Traveled France, Italy. TAUGHT: Virginia Polytechnic Institute, 1949–53; U. of New Hampshire, 1954– ; Ogunquit School of Painting, 1952– . COMMISSIONS: U. of New Hampshire (mural for Student Union building). AWARDS: L. C. Tiffany Grant; Syracuse U., Traveling Fellowship; Silvermine Guild, Larry Aldrich Prize. ADDRESS: Ogunquit, Me. DEALER: Kraushaar Galleries. ONE-MAN EXHIBITIONS: (first) Kraushaar Galleries, 1955; Smithsonian; U. of New Hampshire, 1956; Lincoln, Mass./De Cordova, 1959; Bowdoin College, 1959; Indiana U.; Currier. GROUP: WMAA Annual; PAFA, 1951, 54; ART:USA:58, NYC, 1958; Boston Arts Festival; U. of Nebraska; MMA; Carnegie; Corcoran; Chicago/AI; Audubon Artists; Newark Museum. COLLECTIONS: Hollins College; Illinois Wesleyan U.;

U. of Illinois; Indiana U.; Lehigh U.; U. of Nebraska; Syracuse U.

LAURENT, ROBERT. b. June 29, 1890, Concarneau, France. STUDIED: British School, Rome, 1908–09, with Frank Burty; also with Hamilton Easter Field, Maurice Sterne, Giuseppe Doratore. US Naval Aviation, World War I. Traveled Europe, Cuba, Canada, Mexico, USA; resided France, Italy. TAUGHT: ASL, fifteen years intermittently (sculpture); The Corcoran School of Art, 1940–42; Vassar College, 1939–40; Indiana U., 1942–60 (Professor Emeritus, 1960–); Goucher College, 1940–41. MEMBER: Sculptors Guild; National Sculpture Society; Audubon Artists; Indiana Artists; New England Sculptors Association, Cambridge, Mass. FEDERAL A.P.: Federal Trade Building, Washington, D.C. (relief); New York World's Fair, 1939; US Post Office, Garfield, N.J. COMMISSIONS: Fairmount Park, Philadelphia (sculpture); Radio City Music Hall, NYC; Indiana U. (a relief, a fountain, and several sculptures); many portrait busts. AWARDS: Chicago/AI, First Prize, and The Mr. & Mrs. Frank G. Logan Medal, 1924, 38; Fairmount Park (Philadelphia), International Sculpture Competition, 1935 (monument); Brooklyn Museum, First Prize, 1942; Audubon Artists, 1945; Indianapolis/Herron, five First Prizes; Louisville/Speed, First Prize, 1954; Artist-in-Residence, American Academy, Rome, 1954–55. ADDRESS: Cape Neddick, Me. DEALER: Kraushaar Galleries. ONE-MAN EXHIBITIONS: (first) The Daniel Gallery, NYC, 1915; Bourgeois Gallery, NYC; Curt Valentine Gallery, NYC; Worcester/AM; Arts and Crafts Club, New Orleans; Vassar College; Corcoran; Indiana U.; Indianapolis/Herron; Kraushaar Galleries; Galleria Schneider, Rome; Art Association of Richmond, Ind.; New England Sculptors Association, Cambridge, Mass. RETROSPECTIVE: Indiana U., Laurent: Fifty Years of Sculpture, 1961. GROUP: Salons of America, NYC; Society of Independent Artists, NYC; Audubon Artists; Sculptors Guild; American Society of Painters, Sculptors and Gravuers; National Sculpture Society; WMAA; MMA; Brooklyn Museum; Newark Museum; Portland, Me./MA; Boston/MFA; Colby College; Riverside Museum; Louisville/Speed; Indianapolis/Herron; Chicago/AI; PMA; American Painting and Sculpture, Moscow, 1959. COLLECTIONS: Barnes Foundation; Brookgreen Gardens; Brooklyn Museum; Chicago/AI; Colby College; Hartford/Wadsworth; IBM; Indiana U.; MMA; MOMA; U. of Nebraska; Newark Museum; Ogunquit; PAFA; Society of the Four Arts; Vassar College; WMAA. BIBLIOGRAPHY: Baur 7; Blesh 1; Brumme; Cahill and Barr, eds.; Cheney, M. C.; Goodrich and Baur 1; *Index of 20th Century Artists;* Parkes; Richardson; Ringel, ed.; *Sculpture of the Western Hemisphere.*

LAWRENCE, JACOB. b. September 17, 1917, Atlantic City, N.J. STUDIED: College Art Association, Harlem Workshop, 1932, with Charles Alston; Federal Art Project class, NYC, 1934–37, with Henry Bannarn; American Artists School, NYC, 1937–39, with Anton Refregier, Sol Wilson, Eugene Morley. Traveled USA, British West Indies, Africa. TAUGHT: Black Mountain College, summer, 1946; Five Towns Music and Art Foundation, Cedarhurst, N.Y., 1956–60; Pratt Institute, 1960. FEDERAL A.P.: Easel painting, 1938–39. COMMISSIONS: *Fortune* Magazine, 1947 (10 paintings). AWARDS: Scholarship to American Artists School, NYC, 1937; Lessing J. Rosenwald Fund Fellowship, 1940, 41, 42; Guggenheim Foundation Fellowship, 1946; PAFA, Hon. Men., 1948; Brooklyn Museum, Hon. Men., 1948; MMA, Sixth P.P., 1942; Chicago/AI, Norman Wait Harris Silver Medal, 1948; NIAL Grant, 1953; Chapelbrook Foundation Grant, 1954. ADDRESS: 385 Decatur Street, Brooklyn, N.Y. DEALER: Terry Dintenfass, Inc. ONE-MAN EXHIBITIONS: (first) Harlem YMCA, NYC, 1938; Baltimore/MA, 1938; Columbia U., 1940; The Downtown Gallery, 1941, 43, 45, 47, 50, 53; Portland, Me./MA, 1943; MOMA, 1944; Institute of Modern Art, Boston, 1945; Trenton/State, 1947; The Alan Gallery, 1957, 60; Terry Dintenfass, Inc. RETROSPECTIVE: A.F.A., circ., 1960. GROUP: WMAA; Brooklyn Museum; Phillips. COLLECTIONS: Andover/Phillips; U. of Arizona; Atlanta U.; Auburn U.; Baltimore/MA; Brooklyn Museum; Buffalo/Albright; Cornell U.; Detroit/Institute; George Washington Carver Junior College; Harmon Foundation Inc.; Howard U.; MMA; MOMA; Phillips; Portland, Me./MA; RISD; Sao Paulo; Southern Illinois U.; Trenton/State; VMFA; Wichita/AM; Worcester/AM. BIBLIOGRAPHY: Eliot; Finkelstein;

Goodrich and Baur 1; Halpert; McCurdy, ed.; Newmeyer; Nordness, ed.; Pearson 2; Richardson.

LAWSON, ERNEST. b. 1873, San Francisco, Calif.; **d.** 1939, Miami Beach, Fla. STUDIED: ASL; Cos Cob, Conn., with John Henry Twachtman, J. Alden Weir; Academie Julian, Paris, with Jean Pierre Laurens, B. Constant. Traveled Europe, USA. TAUGHT: Broadmoor Art Academy, Colorado Springs; Kansas City Art Institute and School of Design. MEMBER: NAD; NIAL; National Arts Club; Century Association. AWARDS: St. Louis Exposition, 1904, Silver Medal; PAFA, Jennie Sesnan Gold Medal, 1907; American Academy of Arts and Sciences, Gold Medal, 1907; NAD, Hallgarten Prize, 1908; Panama-Pacific Exposition, San Francisco, 1915, Gold Medal; NAD, Benjamin Altman Prize, 1916, 21, 28; Corcoran, Second William A. Clark Prize, 1916; NAD, Innes Gold Medal, 1917; PAFA, Joseph E. Temple Gold Medal, 1920; Carnegie, First Prize, 1921; NAD, Saltus Gold Medal for Merit, 1930. ONE-MAN EXHIBITIONS: The Milch Gallery; Ferargil Galleries, NYC; The Babcock Gallery. GROUP: WMAA; MMA; NAD; Corcoran; Brooklyn Museum; Carnegie; PAFA. COLLECTIONS: Barnes Foundation; Brooklyn Museum; Carnegie; Chicago/AI; Columbus; Corcoran; Detroit/Institute; Kansas City/Nelson; MMA; Montclair/AM; National Gallery; Newark Museum; St. Louis/City; San Diego; Savannah/Telfair; Toronto; WMAA; Worcester/AM; Youngstown/Butler. BIBLIOGRAPHY: Baur 7; Bazin; Blesh 1; Born; Brown; Cahill and Barr, eds.; Canaday; Cheney, M. C.; **Du Bois 3**; Eliot; Ely; Gallatin 2; Glackens; Goodrich and Baur 1; Hartmann; Hunter 5; McCourbrey; McCurdy, ed.; Perlman; Phillips 2; Richardson; Ringel, ed.; Sutton.

LEBRUN, RICO. b. December 10, 1900, Naples, Italy; **d.** May 10, 1964, Malibu, Calif. STUDIED: Academy of Fine Arts, Naples, 1919–21. Italian Army, 1917–18. To USA 1924. Traveled USA, Europe. TAUGHT: ASL, 1936–37; Chouinard Art Institute, Los Angeles, 1938–39; H. Sophie Newcomb Memorial College, 1942–43; Jepson Art Institute, Los Angeles, 1947–50; UCLA, summers, 1956, 57; Yale-Norfolk Summer Art School, 1956; Santa Barbara Museum School, 1962; Yale U., 1958–59;

Escuela de Bellas Artes, San Miguel de Allende, Mexico, 1953; American Academy, Rome, 1959–60; Colorado Springs Fine Arts Center, 1945. COMMISSIONS (murals): Pomona College; Pennsylvania Station, NYC, 1936–38. ONE-MAN EXHIBITIONS: Faulkner Gallery, Santa Barbara, 1940, 47; San Diego, 1940; Julien Levy Galleries, NYC, 1944; Jepson Art Institute, Los Angeles, 1947, 49; Philadelphia Art Alliance, 1945, 50; J. Seligmann and Co., 1950, 51; Los Angeles/County MA, 1950, 61; Santa Barbara/MA, 1942, 47, 51, 1956 (three-man, with Channing Peake and Howard Warshaw); de Young, 1942; Frank Perls Gallery, 1955; Colorado Springs/FA, 1945; Chicago/AI, 1955; Whyte Gallery, Washington, D.C., 1956; Pomona Gallery, 1956; Toronto, 1958; Yale U., 1958; Boston U.; Boris Mirski Gallery, 1959, 62; U. of California, Santa Barbara, 1960; Esther Baer Gallery, 1960; Princeton U., 1961; Obelisk Gallery, Washington, D.C., 1962; A.F.A., Drawings, 1949. GROUP: U. of Illinois; WMAA, 1948, 50, 52, 57, 58, 60; MOMA; Chicago/AI; PAFA, 1951, 52, 53, 56; SFMA; Oakland/AM; Carnegie, 1945, 52, 55, 59; XXV Venice Biennial, 1950. COLLECTIONS: Andover/Phillips; Boston/MFA; Britannica; Colby College; de Young; Denver/AM; Harvard U.; U. of Hawaii; U. of Illinois; Kansas City/Nelson; Los Angeles/County MA; MMA; MOMA; Mills College; U. of Nebraska; Pomona College; RISD; Santa Barbara/MA; Syracuse U.; Toronto; Utica; WMAA. BIBLIOGRAPHY: Barker 1; Baur 7; Biddle 3; Frost; Getlein; Goodrich and Baur 1; Mendelowitz; Miller, ed. 1; Nordness, ed.; Pearson 2; Pousette-Dart, ed.; Rodman 1, 2, 3; Sachs; Wight 2.

LECHAY, JAMES. b. July 5, 1907, NYC. STUDIED: U. of Illinois, 1928, BA; privately with Myron Lechay. Traveled Canada, Europe, USA. TAUGHT: State U. of Iowa, 1945– ; Skowhegan School, summer, 1961. FEDERAL A.P.: Easel painting. AWARDS: Chicago/AI, Norman Wait Harris Medal, 1941; PAFA, Lambert P.P., 1942; Society for Contemporary American Art, Presentation Prize, 1942; Chicago/AI, Hon. Men., 1942, 43; Portrait of America Prize, 1945; Iowa State Fair, First Prize, 1946, Second Prize, 1951; Denver/AM, Hon. Men., 1946; Walker, First Prize, 1947; Des Moines, Edmundson Trustee Prize, 1950; Davenport/Municipal, 1950; Des Moines, First

Prize, 1952, 53; Hon. DFA, Coe College, 1961. **ADDRESS:** 1191 Hotz Avenue, Iowa City, Iowa. **DEALER:** Kraushaar Galleries. **ONE-MAN EXHIBITIONS:** Toledo/MA; Cedar Rapids/AA; Springfield, Ill./State; Louisville/Speed; Des Moines; State U. of Iowa; Fort Dodge/Banden; Wesleyan U.; Davenport/Municipal; Kraushaar Galleries. **GROUP:** Toledo/MA; MMA; Corcoran; RAC; WMAA; Carnegie; Arts Club of Chicago; St. Louis/City; Worcester/AM; California Palace; U. of Illinois; Indiana U.; Phillips. **COLLECTIONS:** U. of Arizona; Brooklyn Museum; Chicago/AI; Des Moines; Illinois Wesleyan U.; State College of Iowa; State U. of Iowa; Memphis/Brooks; New Britain; Omaha/Joslyn; PAFA; Tulsa/Philbrook; Wichita/AM.

LEIBER, GERSON. b. 1921, Brooklyn, N.Y. **STUDIED:** Academy of Fine Arts, Budapest; ASL, with Will Barnet, Louis Bosa, Vaclav Vytlacil, Morris Kantor; Brooklyn Museum School, with Gabor Peterdi. US Armed Forces, 1943–47. **TAUGHT:** Creative Graphic Workshop, NYC; Summer Workshop, East Hampton, N.Y. (graphics); Newark (N.J.) School of Fine and Industrial Art, 1959– . **MEMBER:** Boston Printmakers; SAGA; California Society of Etchers; American Color Print Society; ASL. **AWARDS:** L. C. Tiffany Grant (2); Audubon Artists, Gold Medal of Honor; Brooklyn Museum, P.P.; Arden Prize; Francesca Wood Award; A.A.A. Gallery, NYC, National Print Competition, Second Prize; Audubon Artists, Joseph Mayer Award; Henry B. Shope Prize; Hunterdon County (N.J.) Art Center, P.P. **ADDRESS:** 749 West End Avenue, NYC. **DEALERS:** A.A.A. Gallery, NYC; Roko Gallery. **ONE-MAN EXHIBITIONS:** (first) A.A.A. Gallery, NYC, 1961; Roko Gallery, 1963; East Side Gallery, NYC, 1963; Riverdale-on-the-Hudson Museum, Riverdale, N.Y., 1963; Matrix Gallery, NYC, 1960; Queens College; Raleigh/NCMA, 1964; Oakland/AM, 1960. **GROUP:** Library of Congress; Cincinnati/AM, Cincinnati International Biennial of Contemporary Color Lithography; PCA, American Prints Today, circ., 1959–62; Brooklyn Museum; PAFA; WMAA; Oakland/AM; Lincoln, Mass./De Cordova; MMA; Cincinnati/AM. **COLLECTIONS:** Abbot Academy; Brooklyn Museum; Cincinnati/AM; Clairol Inc.; Cooper Union; U. of Delaware; Free Library of Philadelphia; Guild Hall; Ham-

ilton College; Karachi; Library of Congress; Lincoln, Mass./De Cordova; MMA; U. of Maine; Memphis/Brooks; Montclair/AM; NYPL; National Gallery; New York Hilton Hotel; Norfolk; PMA; Rutgers U.; Seattle/AM; Topeka Public Library; USIA; US State Department; Wilmington; Walker; Wesleyan U.; Yale U.

LEKAKIS, MICHAEL. b. March 1, 1907, NYC. Self-taught. US Army Air Corps, 1942–45. Traveled Mexico, Europe, Egypt. **ADDRESS:** 57 West 28 Street, NYC. **DEALER:** The Howard Wise Gallery, NYC. **ONE-MAN EXHIBITIONS:** Artists' Gallery, NYC, 1941; San Antonio/McNay, 1946; The Bertha Schaefer Gallery, 1946, 48; American U., 1949; Signa Gallery, East Hampton, N.Y., 1959; The Howard Wise Gallery, NYC, 1961. **GROUP:** SRGM, Sculpture and Drawings, 1958; Cleveland/MA, 1961; Boston Arts Festival, 1961; WMAA Annuals, 1948, 49, 50, 51, 52, 58, 60, 62; Hartford/Wadsworth, Continuity and Change, 1962; Seattle World's Fair, 1962; MOMA, Americans 1963, circ., 1963–64. **COLLECTIONS:** Dayton/AI; Hartford/Wadsworth; MOMA; Portland, Ore./AM; SRGM; Seattle/AM; Tel Aviv; WMAA.

LEONG, JAMES C. b. November 27, 1925, San Francisco, Calif. **STUDIED:** California College of Arts and Crafts, 1951–53, BFA, MFA; San Francisco State College, 1954, MA. US Army, 1952–53. Traveled Europe, USA. **COMMISSIONS** (murals): Chung Mei Home for Boys, El Cerrito, Calif., 1950; Ping Yuen Federal Housing Project, San Francisco, 1951; San Francisco State College, 1951. **AWARDS:** Fulbright Fellowship; Guggenheim Foundation Fellowship; San Francisco Art Festival, Third Prize, 1951; SFMA, 1962. **ADDRESS:** Piazza del Biscione 95, Interno 4, Rome, Italy. **DEALER:** Royal Athena II. **ONE-MAN EXHIBITIONS:** (first) Hungry i, San Francisco, 1951; Barone Gallery, NYC, 1955, 56, 57, 60; American Gallery, Los Angeles, 1955; Holst Halvorsen Gallery, Oslo, 1956; Galerie Paletten, Oslo, 1957; Erling Haghfelt, Copenhagen, 1957; L'Obelisco, Rome, 1960, 61; Feingarten Gallery, NYC, 1962; Galleria dell'Ariete, Milan, 1962; Royal Athena II, 1963. **GROUP:** SFMA; de Young; WMAA, 1955; American Academy, Rome; MOMA, 1960; Internazionale di Arte Astratta,

Prato, Italy, 1960; Brooklyn Museum, 1961; Carnegie, 1961; Rochester/Memorial, 1962. COLLECTIONS: Brooklyn Museum; Rochester/Memorial.

LESLIE, ALFRED. b. October 29, 1927, NYC. STUDIED with Tony Smith, William Baziotes, Hale Woodruff, John McPherson; NYU, 1956–57. US Coast Guard, 1945–46. TAUGHT: San Francisco Art Institute, summer, 1964; Great Neck (N.Y.) Adult Education Program, 1956–57. Co-director-producer (with Robert Frank and Jack Kerouac) of the film "Pull My Daisy." ADDRESS: 940 Broadway, NYC. ONE-MAN EXHIBITIONS: (first) Tibor de Nagy Gallery, 1951, also 1952, 53, 54, 57; Martha Jackson Gallery, 1959, 60; Holland-Goldowsky Gallery, Chicago, 1960. GROUP: MOMA, 1959; WMAA; Amsterdam/Stedelijk; Walker, 1960; U. of Nebraska, 1958. COLLECTIONS: U. of Alabama; Buffalo/Albright; Cornell U.; Kunsthalle, Basel; MOMA; Sao Paulo; Stockholm/National; WMAA; Walker. BIBLIOGRAPHY: Friedman, ed.; Hunter 1; Janis and Blesh 1.

LEVEE, JOHN. b. April 10, 1924, Los Angeles, Calif. STUDIED: UCLA, BA (Philosophy); New School for Social Research, with Stuart Davis, Yasuo Kuniyoshi, Adja Yunkers, Abraham Rattner; Academie Julian, Paris. Traveled Europe, North Africa, Middle East; resides Paris, 1949– . AWARDS: I Paris Biennial, First Prize, 1959; Deauville Salon, 1951. ADDRESS: 119 rue N. D. des Champs, Paris 6, France. DEALERS: Galerie de France; Andre Emmerich Gallery, NYC; Gimpel Fils Ltd.; Esther Robles Gallery; Rina Gallery. ONE-MAN EXHIBITIONS: (first) Galerie Huit, Paris, 1951; Felix Landau Gallery, 1954; Twenster, Rotterdam, 1953; Gimpel Fils Ltd., 1958, 60; Andre Emmerich Gallery, NYC, 1956, 58, 59, 62; Galerie de France, 1958, 61, 62; Esther Robles Gallery, 1962; Haifa, 1964; Phoenix, 1964. GROUP: Carnegie, 1955, 58; Corcoran, 1956, 58; MOMA, Younger American Painters, circ., 1957–59; WMAA, Young America, 1957; WMAA Annuals, 1958, 59; Arts Club of Chicago, 1958; Brooklyn Museum, 1957, 59; Smithsonian, American Painters in France, circ. USA. COLLECTIONS: Allentown/AM; Amsterdam/Stedelijk; Baltimore/MA; Basel; Carnegie; Cincinnati/AM; Columbus; Dallas/MFA; Des Moines; Djakarta Museum; Haifa; Har-

vard U.; Los Angeles/County MA; NYPL; Oberlin College; Phoenix; Santa Barbara/MA; Smith College; Towner Art Gallery; WGMA; WMAA; Washington U.; Yale U. BIBLIOGRAPHY: Juin; Read 2.

LEVI, JULIAN. b. June 20, 1900, NYC. STUDIED: PAFA, with Henry McCarter, Henry Breckenridge, Arthur B. Carles, Jr.; and five years in France and Italy. TAUGHT: ASL; PAFA; New School for Social Research. AWARDS: PAFA, Cresson Fellowship, 1920; Chicago/AI, The M. V. Kohnstamm Prize, 1942; Chicago/AI, Norman Wait Harris Medal, 1943; Carnegie, Hon. Men., 1945; NAD, The Adolph and Clara Obrig Prize, 1945; U. of Illinois, 1948; PAFA, Fellowship, 1954; NIAL Grant, 1955; elected to the NIAL, 1960. ADDRESS: East Hampton, N.Y. ONE-MAN EXHIBITIONS: Crillon Galleries, Philadelphia, 1933; The Downtown Gallery, 1940, 42, 45, 50; Philadelphia Art Alliance, 1953, 63; The Alan Gallery, 1955; Lee Nordness Gallery, NYC, 1961; Anna Werbe Gallery, Detroit, 1961. RETROSPECTIVE: Boston U., 1962; New Britain. GROUP: Detroit/Institute; PAFA; NAD; U. of Illinois; WMAA; Newark Museum; Youngstown/Butler. COLLECTIONS: U. of Arizona; Britannica; Buffalo/Albright; Chicago/AI; Cranbrook; Des Moines; Detroit/Institute; U. of Georgia; U. of Illinois; S. C. Johnson & Son, Inc.; MMA; MOMA; Michigan State U.; NAD; U. of Nebraska; Newark Museum; New Britain; PAFA; Reed College; Santa Barbara/MA; Scripps College; Springfield, Mass./MFA; Toledo/MA; WMAA; Walker; Wilmington; Youngstown/Butler. BIBLIOGRAPHY: Baur 7; Blesh 1; Halpert; Hess, T. B.; Kootz 2; Nordness, ed.; Pagano; Passloff; Watson 2; Wheeler.

LEVINE, JACK. b. January 3, 1915, Boston, Mass. STUDIED with Denman W. Ross, Harold Zimmerman. Traveled Europe, Mexico; resided Rome, one year. MEMBER: NIAL; American Academy of Arts and Sciences; Artists Equity. FEDERAL A.P.: Easel painting. AWARDS: Carnegie, 1946; Corcoran, 1959; PAFA, 1948; NIAL, 1946; Guggenheim Foundation Fellowship, 1946; Hon. DFA, Colby College. **m.** Ruth Gikow. ADDRESS: 231 West 11 Street, NYC. DEALER: The Alan Gallery. ONE-MAN EXHIBITIONS: (first) The Downtown Gallery, 1938; The Alan Gallery; Ogunquit, 1963. RETROSPEC-

TIVE: ICA, Boston, 1953; WMAA, 1955; Mexico City/Nacional, 1960. GROUP: PAFA; Corcoran; Chicago/AI; WMAA; Boston/MFA; MOMA. COLLECTIONS: Andover/Phillips; Boston/MFA; Chicago/AI; Harvard U.; U. of Kansas; MMA; MOMA; U. of Nebraska; U. of Oklahoma; PAFA; Phillips; Portland, Ore./AM; WMAA; Walker. BIBLIOGRAPHY: Barker 1; Baur 7; Blesh 1; Cheney, M. C.; Christensen; Eliot; Finkelstein; Frost; Genauer; Getlein; Goodrich and Baur 1; Halpert; Hunter 5; Kootz 2; McCurdy, ed.; Mendelowitz; Miller, ed. 1; Munsterberg; Newmeyer; Nordness, ed.; Pousette-Dart, ed.; Read 2; Richardson; Rodman 1, 2, 3; Sachs; Soby 5, 6; Wight 2.

LEVINSON, MON. b. January 6, 1926, NYC. STUDIED: U. of Pennsylvania, 1948, BS.Econ.; self-taught in art. US Army, 1945–46. Traveled Mexico, Europe. COMMISSIONS: MOMA, 1964 (greeting card); Betsy Ross Flag & Banner Co., 1963 (banner). ADDRESS: 91 Central Park West, NYC. DEALER: The Kornblee Gallery. ONE-MAN EXHIBITIONS: (first) The Kornblee Gallery, 1961, also 1963, 64. GROUP: Martha Jackson Gallery, New Media—New Forms, I, 1960; Sidney Janis Gallery, 1964; Chicago/AI, 1964; MOMA, 1962, 63; A.F.A., circ.; Buffalo/Albright, 1964.

LEVITAN, ISRAEL. b. June 13, 1912, Lawrence, Mass. STUDIED: Chicago Art Institute School; Ozenfant School of Art, NYC; Hofmann School, NYC; Zadkine School of Sculpture, Paris. Traveled Europe, USA extensively. TAUGHT: Brooklyn Museum School, 1956–60; Cooper Union, 1955; U. of California, Berkeley, 1962; Philadelphia Museum School, 1962–64; and privately. MEMBER: American Abstract Artists, 1954–57. COMMISSIONS: Interchurch Center, NYC. AWARDS: MacDowell Colony Fellowship, 1956; Guild Hall, First Prize, Sculpture, 1960. ADDRESS: 299 East 10 Street, NYC. DEALER: Grand Central Moderns. ONE-MAN EXHIBITIONS: (first) Artists' Gallery, NYC, 1952; Weyhe Gallery, 1953; Barone Gallery, NYC, 1957, 59, 60; U. of California, Berkeley, 1962; Grand Central Moderns, 1964. GROUP: WMAA Annuals, 1952, 53; PAFA; Paris/Moderne; SFMA; Brooklyn Museum; PMA; Claude Bernard, Paris, Aspects of American Sculpture, 1960; American Abstract Artists, 1953, 54, 55, 56, 57. BIBLIOGRAPHY: Seuphor 3.

LEWANDOWSKI, EDMUND D. b. July 3, 1914, Milwaukee, Wisc. STUDIED: Layton School of Art, 1932–35. TAUGHT: Florida State U., 1949–54; Layton School of Art, 1945–49, 1954– . AWARDS: Hallmark International Competition, 1950, 53, 57; Milwaukee, Medal, 1940. ADDRESS: 1360 North Prospect Avenue, Milwaukee, Wisc. ONE-MAN EXHIBITIONS: Layton School of Art; Minnesota State Fair; Florida State U., 1950. GROUP: Chicago/AI; Carnegie; Corcoran; PAFA; Brooklyn Museum; New York World's Fair, 1939; Phillips. COLLECTIONS: AAAL; Allen-Bradley Co. Inc.; Andover/Phillips; Beloit College; Boston/MFA; Brooklyn Museum; Dartmouth College; Flint/Institute; Florida State U.; Gimbel Bros.; Grand Rapids; Hallmark Collection; Krakow/National; Layton School of Art; MOMA; Marquette U.; U. of Oklahoma; St. Patrick's, Menasha, Wisc.; Shell Oil Co.; US Maritime Commission; Warsaw/National; U. of Wisconsin. BIBLIOGRAPHY: Baur 7; Cheney, M. C.; Halpert; Pousette-Dart, ed.; Ritchie 1.

LEWIS, NORMAN. b. July 23, 1909, NYC. STUDIED: Columbia U., with Augusta Savage. TAUGHT: Junior high school, NYC, 1935; Harlem Art Center, NYC, 1937; Thomas Jefferson School, NYC, 1944–49; Indian Hill Music School, Stockbridge, Mass., 1954. Traveled Europe, North Africa. Organized an art center at Bennett College under Government sponsorship, 1938. Supervised a mural for Thomas Jefferson High School, St. Albans, N.Y., 1939. AWARDS: Carnegie, Popularity Prize, 1955. ADDRESS: 139 West 125 Street, NYC. DEALER: The Willard Gallery. ONE-MAN EXHIBITIONS: The Willard Gallery, 1949, 51, 52, 54, 56; Harlem Artists Guild, 1936; Fisk U., 1939; Baltimore/MA, 1939. GROUP: Carnegie, 1955; XXVIII Venice Biennial, 1956. COLLECTIONS: Andover/Phillips; Utica. BIBLIOGRAPHY: Baur 5; Motherwell and Reinhardt, eds.; Ritchie 1.

LIBERMAN, ALEXANDER. b. 1912, Kiev, Russia. STUDIED: Academie Andre Lhote, Paris, 1929–31 (painting); Academie des Beaux-Arts, Paris, with August Perret (architecture). With the Louvre Museum, made "La Femme Francais," 1936, one of the first color films on painting. US citizen 1946. Art Editor of VU, 1933–37. Joined Vogue Magazine, 1941; became its Art Director, 1943; became Art Director of Conde Nast Publications Inc., USA and Europe, 1944, and the organization's Editorial Director, 1962. **ADDRESS:** 137 East 70 Street, NYC. **DEALER:** Betty Parsons Gallery. **ONE-MAN EXHIBITIONS:** Betty Parsons Gallery, 1960, 62, 63, 64; Robert Fraser Gallery, London, 1964; Bennington College, 1964; MOMA, The Artist in His Studio, 1959. **GROUP:** SRGM, Younger American Painters, 1954; A. Tooth & Sons, Six American Painters, 1961; Chicago/AI, 1961, 62; WMAA, Geometric Abstraction in America, circ., 1962; WMAA Annuals, 1962, 63; III International Biennial Exhibition of Prints, Tokyo, 1962; MOMA, Modern American Drawings, circ. Europe, 1961–62; Corcoran, 1963; Hartford/Wadsworth, 1964; Los Angeles/County MA, Post Painterly Abstraction, 1964; MOMA, Contemporary Painters and Sculptors as Printmakers, 1964; SRGM, American Drawings, 1964; Galerie Denise Rene, Paris, Hard-Edge, 1964; New York World's Fair, 1964–65. **COLLECTIONS:** Andover/Phillips; Buffalo/Albright; Chase Manhattan Bank; Chicago/AI; MOMA; Smith College; Tate; WGMA; WMAA; Woodward Foundation; Yale U.

LICHTENSTEIN, ROY. b. October 27, 1923, NYC. **STUDIED:** The Ohio State U., 1940–43, BFA, 1946–49, MA; ASL, 1940, with Reginald Marsh. US Army, 1943–46. **TAUGHT:** The Ohio State U., 1946–51; New York State College of Education, Oswego, 1957–60; Douglass College, 1960–63. **COMMISSIONS:** New York State Pavilion, New York World's Fair, 1964–65 (mural). **ADDRESS:** 36 West 26 Street, NYC. **DEALER:** Leo Castelli Inc. **ONE-MAN EXHIBITIONS:** (first) Carlebach Gallery, NYC, 1951; John Heller Gallery, NYC, 1952, 53, 54, 57; Leo Castelli Inc., 1962, 63, 64; Ferus Gallery, 1963; Ileana Sonnabend (Gallery), Paris, 1963; Il Punto, Turin, 1964. **GROUP:** Dayton/AI, 1962; Pasadena/AM, New Paintings of Common Objects, 1962; Sidney Janis Gallery, The New Realists, 1962; Galerie Saqqarah, Gstaad, Switzerland, The Figure and the Object from 1917 to the New Vulgarians, 1962; Chicago/AI, 1963; SRGM, Six Painters and The Object, circ., 1963; WGMA, The Popular Image, 1963; ICA, London, The Popular Image, 1963; Houston/MFA, Pop Goes the Easel, 1963; Brandeis U., New Directions in American Painting, 1963. **COLLECTIONS:** Brandeis U.; Buffalo/Albright; Dayton/AI. **BIBLIOGRAPHY:** *Metro.*

LINDNER, RICHARD. b. November 11, 1901, Hamburg, Germany. **STUDIED:** School of Fine and Applied Arts, Nurnberg; Academy of Fine Arts, Munich, 1924; in Berlin, 1927–28. To Paris 1933–39; English Army, 1939–41; to USA 1941; citizen 1948. Traveled Europe, Mexico. **TAUGHT:** Pratt Institute, 1951– . **AWARDS:** William and Noma Copley Foundation Grant, 1957. **ADDRESS:** 333 East 69 Street, NYC. **DEALER:** Cordier & Ekstrom Inc. **ONE-MAN EXHIBITIONS:** Betty Parsons Gallery, 1954, 56, 59; Cordier and Warren, NYC, 1961; Cordier & Ekstrom Inc., 1963, 64; Robert Fraser Gallery, London, 1962. **GROUP:** MOMA, Americans 1963, circ., 1963–64; Walker, 1954; Chicago/AI, 1954, 57; Brooklyn Museum, 1955; WMAA, 1959, 60; Tate, Dunn International, 1964; Yale U., 1955; Documenta III, Kassel, 1964. **COLLECTIONS:** Chicago/AI; MOMA; WMAA. **BIBLIOGRAPHY:** Tillim.

LIPCHITZ, JACQUES. b. August 22, 1891, Druskieniki, Lithuania. **STUDIED:** Academie des Beaux-Arts, Paris, 1909–11, with Jean Antonine Ingalbert, Dr. Richet; Academie Julian, Paris, with Raoul Verlet; Academie Colarossi, Paris. Became French citizen 1924; to USA 1941. Traveled Europe, Middle East, USA. Fire destroyed Manhattan studio, 1952. **COMMISSIONS:** Dr. Albert Barnes, 1922 (5 bas-reliefs); Vicomte Charles de Noailles, Hyeres, France,

Roy Lichtenstein   *In the Car. 1963*

1927 ("Joy of Life"); Paris World's Fair, 1937 ("Prometheus"); Brazilian Ministry of Health and Education, 1943 ("Prometheus Strangling the Vulture"); Notre Dame de Toute-Grace, Assy, Haute-Savoie, France, 1956 (baptismal font); Mrs. John D. Rockefeller III, 1950 (bas-relief); Fairmount Park Association, Philadelphia, 1958 (sculpture); Presidential Scholars Medallion (USA), 1964; U. of Minnesota, Duluth, 1964 (9-ft. statue of Sieur Duluth). AWARDS: Academie Julian, Paris, First Prize for Sculpture, 1909; Paris World's Fair, 1937, Gold Medal; Legion of Honor (France), 1946; PAFA, George D. Widener Memorial Gold Medal, 1952; Hon. DFA, Brandeis U., 1958. ADDRESS: Hastings-on-Hudson, N.Y. DEALER: Marlborough-Gerson Gallery Inc. ONE-MAN EXHIBITIONS: (first) Leonce Rosenberg Gallery, Paris, 1920; Galerie de la Renaissance, Paris, 1930; Joseph Brummer Gallery, NYC, 1935; Musee du Petit Palais, Paris World's Fair, 1937; Buchholz Gallery, NYC, 1942, 43, 46, 48, 51; Galerie Maeght, 1946; Petite Galerie Seminaire, Brussels, 1950; Portland, Ore./AM, 1950; SFMA, 1951, 63; Cincinnati/AM, 1951; Frank Perls Gallery, 1952, 57; Santa Barbara/MA, 1952; XXVI Venice Biennial, 1952; MOMA, 1954; Walker, 1954, 63; Cleveland/MA, 1954; Otto Gerson Gallery, NYC, 1957, 59, 61; Amsterdam/Stedelijk, 1958; Rijksmuseum Kroller-Muller, 1958; Musees Royaux des Beaux-Arts de Belgique, Brussels, 1958; Basel, 1958; Paris/Moderne, 1959; Tate, 1959; Cornell U., 1961; UCLA, 1963; Denver/AM, 1962; Fort Worth, 1963; Buffalo/Albright, 1963; Des Moines, 1964; PMA, 1964; Omaha/Joslyn, 1964; Marlborough-Gerson Gallery Inc., 1964. GROUP: Salon d'Automne, Paris, 1913; WMAA; MOMA; Tate; Paris/Moderne; Chicago/AI. COLLECTIONS: Baltimore/MA; Barnes Foundation; Buffalo/Albright; Carleton College; Chicago/AI; Cleveland/MA; Cornell U.; Currier; Dartmouth College; Des Moines; Detroit/Institute; Harvard U.; Jewish Museum; Los Angeles/County MA; MOMA; U. of Minnesota; Montreal/MFA; U. of Nebraska; New Orleans/Delgado; PMA; Paris/Moderne; Regina/MacKenzie; Rijksmuseum Kroller-Muller; Rouen; SRGM; St. Louis/City; Tate; Tel Aviv; Toronto; Zurich. BIBLIOGRAPHY: Barr 1; Baur 7; Biddle 3; Biederman 1; Blesh 1; Canaday; Cassou; Elsen; Fierens; George 1; Gertz; Giedion-Welcker 1, 2; Goodrich and Baur 1; Greenberg 1; Hayter 1, 2; Henning; Hess, T. B.; **Hope;** Huyghe; Kuh 2; Langui; Lowry; McCurdy, ed.; Mendelowitz; *Metro;* Myers 2; Neumeyer; **Raynal 2;** Read 1; Rodman 1; Rosenblum; Rothschild; Sachs; Salvini; Selz, J.; Seuphor 3; Seymour; Valentine 2; Zervos.

LIPPOLD, RICHARD. b. May 3, 1915, Milwaukee, Wisc. STUDIED: The U. of Chicago and Chicago Art Institute School, 1933–37, BFA (industrial design). TAUGHT: Layton School of Art, 1940–41; U. of Michigan, 1941–44; Goddard College, 1945–47; Trenton Junior College (Head of Art Department), 1947–52; Queens College, 1947–48; Black Mountain College, 1948; Hunter College, 1952– . Designer, Chicago Corporation, 1937–41. Began wire constructions 1942. COMMISSIONS: Harvard U. Graduate Law School, 1950; MMA, 1952–56; Inland Steel Building, Chicago, 1957; Longview Bank, Longview, Tex., 1958; Four Seasons Restaurant, NYC, 1959; Festival of Two Worlds, Spoleto, 1959 (stage set); Benedictine Chapel, Portsmouth, R.I., 1960; Musee du Vin, Chateau Mouton Rothschild, Pouillac, France, 1960; J. Walter Thompson, NYC, 1960; Pan Am Building, NYC, 1961; Philharmonic Hall, Lincoln Center for the Performing Arts, NYC, 1961. AWARDS: Brandeis U., Creative Arts Award, 1958; American Institute of Architects, Chicago Chapter, Honors Award, 1958; American Institute of Architects, New York Chapter, Silver Medal, 1960; Hon. PBK, NYC, 1961; Municipal Art Society of New York, Citation, 1963; ICA, London/Tate, International Unknown Political Prisoner Competition, Third Prize, 1953; elected to the NIAL, 1963. ADDRESS: 27 Frost Creek Drive, Locust Valley, N.Y. DEALER: The Willard Gallery. ONE-MAN EXHIBITIONS: (first) The Willard Gallery, 1947, also 1948, 50, 52; Arts Club of Chicago, 1953; Brandeis U., 1958; Layton School of Art, 1953. GROUP: MOMA, Fifteen Americans, circ., 1952; PMA, Sculpture of the Twentieth Century, 1953; ICA, London/Tate, International Unknown Political Prisoner Competition, 1953; WMAA, The New Decade, 1954–55; France/National, 50 Ans d'Art aux Etats-Unis, circ. Europe, 1955; Brooklyn Museum, Sculpture in Silver, 1955; Newark Museum, Abstract Art, 1910 to Today, 1956. COLLECTIONS: Andover/Phillips;   Detroit/Institute;   Hartford/Wadsworth; MMA; MOMA; Utica; VMFA; WMAA. **BIBLIOGRAPHY:** Baur 7; Blesh 1; Brumme; Flanagan; Giedion-Welcker 1; Hunter 5; McCurdy, ed.; Mendelowitz; *Metro;* Motherwell and Reinhardt, eds.; Neumeyer; Read 1; Ritchie 1, 3; Seuphor 3.

LIPTON, SEYMOUR. b. November 6, 1903, NYC. **STUDIED:** City College of New York, 1922–23; Columbia U., 1923–27. **TAUGHT:** Cooper Union, 1943–44; Newark State Teachers College, 1944–45; Yale U., 1957–59; New School for Social Research, 1940– . **COMMISSIONS:** Temple Israel, Tulsa, Okla.; Temple Beth-El, Gary, Ind.; Manufacturers Hanover Trust Co., NYC; Inland Steel Building, Chicago; Reynolds Metals Co. (NYC); International Business Machines Corp. (Yorktown Heights, N.Y.); Dulles International Airport, Washington, D.C.; Golden Gateway Redevelopment Project, San Francisco; Philharmonic Hall, Lincoln Center for the Performing Arts, NYC. **AWARDS:** Chicago/AI, 1957; IV Sao Paulo Biennial, Top Acquisition Prize, 1957; NIAL, 1958; Guggenheim Foundation, 1960; New School for Social Research, 1960; Ford Foundation Grant, 1961. **ADDRESS:** 302 West 98 Street, NYC. **DEALER:** Marlborough-Gerson Gallery Inc. **ONE-MAN EXHIBITIONS:** ACA Gallery, 1938; Gallery St. Etienne, NYC, 1943; Betty Parsons Gallery, 1948, 50, 52, 54, 58, 62; Watkins Gallery, Washington, D.C., 1951; New Paltz, 1955; Troy, N.Y., 1961; Phillips, 1964. **GROUP:** WMAA Annuals since 1941; IV Sao Paulo Biennial, 1957; XXIX Venice Biennial, 1958; Carnegie, 1958, 61; Brussels World's Fair, 1958; Seattle World's Fair, 1962; New York World's Fair, 1964–65. **COLLECTIONS:** Baltimore/MA; Brooklyn Museum; Buffalo/Albright; Des Moines; Detroit/Institute; Franklin Institute; U. of Kansas; MMA; MOMA; U. of Michigan; New School for Social Research; Phillips; Santa Barbara/MA; Tel Aviv; Toronto; Utica; WMAA; Yale U. **BIBLIOGRAPHY:** Baur 5, 7; Biddle 3; Blesh 1; Brumme; Chaet; Christensen; Elsen; Flanagan; Goodrich and Baur 1; Henning; Hunter 5; Langui; McCurdy, ed.; Mendelowitz; *Metro;* Myers 2; Neumeyer; Ritchie 1, 3; Seuphor 3.

LOBDELL, FRANK. b. 1921, Kansas City, Mo. **STUDIED:** St. Paul School of Art, 1938–39, with Cameron Booth; California School of Fine Arts, 1947–50. US Army, 1942–46. Resided

Paris, 1950–51. **TAUGHT:** California School of Fine Arts, 1957– . **AWARDS:** SFMA, Artists Council Prize, 1948; SFMA, P.P., 1950; SFMA, Nealie Sullivan Award, 1960. **ADDRESS:** 722 Filbert Street, San Francisco, Calif. **DEALERS:** Martha Jackson Gallery; Ferus Gallery. **ONE-MAN EXHIBITIONS:** (first) Lucien Labaudt Gallery, 1949; Martha Jackson Gallery, 1958, 60, 63; de Young, 1959; Ferus Gallery, 1962; Pasadena/AM, 1961. **RETROSPECTIVE:** Pasadena/AM, 1963. **GROUP:** San Francisco Art Association Annual, 1950; III Sao Paulo Biennial, 1955; WMAA, Fifty California Artists, 1962–63. **COLLECTIONS:** Pasadena/AM; SFMA.

LOBERG, ROBERT W. b. December 1, 1927, Chicago, Ill. US Marine Corps, 1946–47. **STUDIED:** Glendale College, 1948, City College of San Francisco, 1948–50, AA, U. of California, Berkeley, 1950–52, BA, 1953–54, MA (painting, with Karl Kasten, Ward Lockwood, John Haley, Erle Loran, James McCray, Glenn Wessels, Worth Ryder, Felix Ruvulo, William H. Calfee, Carl Holty, Kyle Morris); Hofmann School, Provincetown, 1956, with Hans Hofmann. Traveled northern China, Japan, Europe. **TAUGHT:** U. of California, Berkeley, 1955, 56, 58, 59; California College of Arts and Crafts, 1961–62; San Francisco Art Institute, 1962– . **AWARDS:** California State Fair, Hon. Men., 1955; RAC, Prize in Graphics, 1955; RAC, Prize in Watercolors, 1959; Yaddo Fellowship, 1957; MacDowell Colony Fellowship, 1959, 60; SFMA, Anne Bremer Memorial Prize, 1961; San Francisco Art Festival, P.P. in Painting, 1962; La Jolla, Prize in Painting, 1962. **ADDRESS:** 2787 Folsom Street, San Francisco, Calif. **DEALERS:** Staempfli Gallery; David Stuart Gallery. **ONE-MAN EXHIBITIONS:** (first) Artists' Gallery, NYC, 1959; Staempfli Gallery, 1962; David Stuart Gallery, 1962, 64. **GROUP:** Chicago/AI, 1948, 62; RAC; Oakland/AM; SFMA Annuals since 1955; de Young; California Palace; Carnegie, 1959; SFMA, Abstract Expressionism in the West, circ., 1961; SFMA (three-man), 1961; SFMA, Collage in San Francisco, 1962; WMAA, Fifty California Artists, 1962–63; SFMA, New Paintings, 1964. **COLLECTIONS:** San Francisco Municipal Art Commission.

LOEW, MICHAEL. b. May 8, 1907, NYC. **STUDIED:** City College of New York; ASL, 1926–29, with Richard Lahey, Boardman

Robinson; Academie Scandinave, Paris, 1930, with Othon Friesz; Hofmann School, NYC, 1947–49; Atelier Fernand Leger, Paris, 1950, with F. Leger. US Navy "Seabees," Battalion Artist, Pacific theater, 1943–46. Traveled France, Germany, Italy, Africa, Mexico, Central America. TAUGHT: Portland (Ore.) Museum School, 1956–57; U. of California, Berkeley, 1960–61; School of Visual Arts, NYC, 1958– . MEMBER: American Abstract Artists; Federation of Modern Painters and Sculptors. FEDERAL A.P.: Gustave Straubenmuller Junior High School, NYC (series of 5 murals). COMMISSIONS (murals): Hall of Man and Pharmacy Building, New York World's Fair, 1939; US Post Offices, Amherst, Ohio, and Belle Vernon, Pa. AWARDS: Sadie May Fellowship, 1929; Section of Fine Arts, National Mural Competition for Social Security Building and War Department Building, Washington, D.C., Hon. Men., 1941; Ford Foundation, P.P., 1964. ADDRESS: 280 Ninth Avenue, NYC. DEALER: The Stable Gallery. ONE-MAN EXHIBITIONS: (first) Artists' Gallery, NYC, 1949; Rose Fried Gallery, 1953, 55, 57, 59; Portland, Ore./AM, 1956; Holland-Goldowsky Gallery, Chicago, 1960; U. of California, Berkeley, 1960; The Stable Gallery, 1961, 62, 64. GROUP: American Abstract Artists Annuals, 1949– ; Federation of Modern Painters and Sculptors Annuals, 1959– ; ART:USA:59, NYC, 1959; International Association of Plastic Arts, Contemporary American Painting, circ. Europe, 1956–57; A.F.A., Collage in America, circ., 1957–58; Douglass College, 1959; MOMA, Hans Hofmann and His Students, circ., 1963–64; WMAA, 1950, 61; MMA, 1952; Walker, The Classic Tradition, 1953; Salon des Realites Nouvelles, Paris, 1950; WMAA, Geometric Abstraction in America, circ., 1962; Chicago/AI, 1964; Colby College, 100 Artists of the 20th Century, 1964. COLLECTIONS: Atlanta U.; Baltimore/MA; PMA; US Navy; Union Carbide Corp.; WMAA.

LORAN, ERLE. b. October 3, 1905, Minneapolis, Minn. STUDIED: U. of Minnesota; Minneapolis Institute School, with Cameron Booth. Traveled Europe extensively. TAUGHT: U. of California, Berkeley. FEDERAL A.P.: Easel painting, teaching. AWARDS: Chaloner Prize Foundation Award ($6,000), 1926; SFMA, Artists' Fund Prize, 1944; Pepsi-Cola Bronze Medal, 1949; San Francisco Art Association,

P.P., 1956; California Palace, H. S. Crocker Co. Award, 1963; and some 20 others. ADDRESS: 10 Kenilworth Court, Berkeley, Calif. DEALER: Comara Gallery. ONE-MAN EXHIBITIONS: (first) Kraushaar Galleries, 1931; Artists' Gallery, NYC, 1938; SFMA, 1936, 39, 44; Santa Barbara/MA, 1947, 50; Pasadena/AM, 1947; Dalzell Hatfield Gallery, 1949; Catherine Viviano Gallery, 1952, 54; de Young, 1949, 54, 63. GROUP: WMAA, 1937, 41, 44, 48, 51, 52; MOMA, 1935; Chicago/AI, 1938, 39, 43, 44, 46, 48; Carnegie, 1941; MMA, 1951, 53; Sao Paulo, 1955, 56, 61; SFMA, 1936–64; Cranbrook, 1953; U. of Illinois, 1949, 52, 53, 63; California Palace, 1961, 62, 63; Toledo/MA, 1943; Oakland/AM, 1936, 46. COLLECTIONS: Brigham Young U.; Denver/AM; IBM; U. of Minnesota; SFMA; San Diego; Santa Barbara/MA; US State Department; Utah State U. BIBLIOGRAPHY: Bethers; Blanchard; Cheney, M. C.; Flanagan; **Loran 1, 2;** Pousette-Dart, ed.

LOUIS, MORRIS. b. November 28, 1912, Baltimore, Md.; d. September 7, 1962, Washington, D.C. STUDIED: Maryland Institute, 1920–33. ONE-MAN EXHIBITIONS: (first) Martha Jackson Gallery, 1957; French & Co. Inc., 1959, 60; ICA, London, 1960; Bennington College, 1960; Galleria dell'Ariete, Milan, 1960; Galerie Neufville, Paris, 1961; Galerie Schmela, Dusseldorf, 1962; Galerie Lawrence, 1962; Galerie Muller, Stuttgart, 1962; Andre Emmerich Gallery, NYC, 1961, 62. RETROSPECTIVE: SRGM, 1963; XXXII Venice Biennial, 1964. GROUP: The Kootz Gallery, New Talent, 1954; Rome-New York Foundation, Rome, 1960; SRGM, Abstract Expressionists and Imagists, 1961; Seattle World's Fair, 1962; Jewish Museum, Toward a New Abstraction, 1963; Tate, Painting and Sculpture of a Decade, 1954–64, 1964; Corcoran; WMAA, 1962. COLLECTIONS: Allentown/AM; Brandeis U.; Buffalo/Albright; Harvard U.; MOMA; Phillips; SRGM; WGMA.

LOZOWICK, LOUIS. b. December 10, 1892, Russia. STUDIED: The Ohio State U., 1918, BA; NAD, 1912–15. Traveled Europe, Russia, the Orient. TAUGHT: Educational Alliance, NYC; and privately. MEMBER: SAGA; Boston Printmakers. FEDERAL A.P.: Main Post Office, NYC (mural); printmaker. AWARDS: Brewster Prize for Lithography; PMA, International Print Competition, First Prize; Society of American Etchers and Engravers, NYC, Knobloch Prize;

Brooklyn Museum, p.p.; Rochester/Memorial, 150 Years of Lithography, Second Prize; SAGA; Audubon Artists. **Address:** 62 Massel Terrace, South Orange, N.J. **Dealer:** The Zabriskie Gallery. **One-man Exhibitions:** (first) Heller Gallery, Berlin, 1923; Weyhe Gallery; Courvoisier Gallery, San Francisco; Stendahl Gallery, Los Angeles; Casson Gallery, Boston; J. B. Neumann's New Art Circle, NYC; Argus Gallery, Madison, N.J.; The Zabriskie Gallery, 1961; Galerie Zak, Paris; Smithsonian. **Group:** Carnegie, 1930, 39; WMAA Annuals, 1933, 41; Chicago/AI, 1929; Youngstown/Butler, 1960; Corcoran, 1932; MMA, 1942; Brooklyn Museum, 1926; MOMA, 1943; A Century of Progress, Chicago, 1933–34; New York World's Fair, 1939; Boston/MFA. **Collections:** Boston/MFA; Cincinnati/AM; Cleveland/MA; Honolulu Academy; Houston/MFA; Library of Congress; Los Angeles/County MA; MMA; MOMA; Montclair/AM; Moscow/Western; NYPL; Newark Museum; PMA; Rochester/Memorial; Victoria and Albert Museum; WMAA. **Bibliography:** American Artists Congress, Inc.; American Artists Group Inc. 3; Baur 7; Brown; *Index of 20th Century Artists;* Mellquist; Reese.

LUND, DAVID. b. October 16, 1925, NYC. **Studied:** Queens College, with Vaclav Vytlacil, Cameron Booth, 1944–48, BA (major in Painting); NYU, 1948–50, with Hale Woodruff; New School for Social Research, with Yasuo Kuniyoshi. Traveled Europe, southwestern USA, Mexico. **Taught:** Cooper Union, 1955–57, 1959– ; Parsons School of Design, 1963– . **Awards:** Fulbright Fellowship (Rome), 1957–58, renewed 1958–59; WMAA Annual, Ford Foundation Purchase, 1961. **Address:** 470 West End Avenue, NYC. **Dealer:** Grace Borgenicht Gallery Inc. **One-man Exhibitions:** (first) Grand Central Moderns, 1954; Galleria Trastevere di Topazia Alliata, Rome, 1958; Grace Borgenicht Gallery Inc., 1960, 63. **Group:** Tanager Gallery, NYC, Invitational; The Stable Gallery Annual, 1956; Galleria Schneider, Rome, Fulbright Artists, 1958, 59; WMAA, Fulbright Artists, 1958; Hirschl & Adler Galleries, Inc., NYC, Experiences in Art, I, 1959; WMAA, Young America, 1960; WMAA Annual, 1961; WMAA, Forty Artists Under Forty, circ., 1962.

Collections: Baltimore/MA; Chase Manhattan Bank; McDonnell & Co. Inc.; The Pure Oil Co.; Toronto; WMAA.

LYE, LEN. b. June 6, 1901, Christchurch, New Zealand. **Studied:** Wellington Technical College; Canterbury College of Fine Arts. To London 1926; to USA 1946; became a citizen. Traveled Samoa, Europe, USA. **Taught:** City College of New York (film technique). International **awards** for experimental films. Began kinetic constructions in the 1920's. **Address:** 41 Bethune Street, NYC. **Dealer:** The Howard Wise Gallery, NYC. **One-man Exhibitions:** London Film Society ("Tusalava"), 1928; MOMA, Tangible Motion Sculpture, 1961; St. Luke's School, NYC, Wind Wands, 1962. **Group:** Seven & Five Society, London, 1928–33; a Surrealists group, London, 1937; Amsterdam/Stedelijk, Art in Motion, circ. Europe, 1961–62; WMAA Annual, 1962; The Howard Wise Gallery, NYC, On The Move, 1963. **Collections:** WMAA. **Bibliography:** Read 4.

LYTLE, RICHARD. b. February 14, 1935, Albany, N.Y. **Studied:** Cooper Union, with Nicholas Marsicano, Victor Candell; Yale U., with Josef Albers (whom he assisted as teaching fellow in color and drawing), James Brooks, Bernard Chaet, 1957, BFA, 1960, MFA. Traveled Europe, northeastern USA. **Taught:** Yale U., 1960–63; Dean, Silvermine Guild, 1963– . **Awards:** Fulbright Fellowship (Italy), 1958; New Haven Arts Festival, First Prize, 1958; Scholarship to the Cummington School of Fine Arts, 1956. **Address:** RFD #2, Freeman Road, Oxford, Conn. **Dealer:** Grace Borgenicht Gallery Inc. **One-man Exhibitions:** (first) Grace Borgenicht Gallery Inc., 1961, also 1963; Silvermine Guild, 1964. **Group:** MOMA, Sixteen Americans, circ., 1959; Seattle World's Fair, 1962; PAFA, 1963; Brooklyn Museum, 1956; Boston Arts Festival, 1958; Chicago/AI Annuals, 1960, 61; A.F.A., American Art, circ. Europe, 1956–59; Houston/MFA, The Emerging Figure, 1961; Art:USA:Now, circ., 1962– ; WMAA, 1964. **Collections:** Columbia U.; S. C. Johnson & Son, Inc.; Lincoln, Mass./De Cordova; MOMA; Yale U. **Bibliography:** Nordness, ed.

MACDONALD-WRIGHT, STANTON. b. July 8, 1890, Charlottesville, Va. STUDIED: Sorbonne; Academie des Beaux-Arts, Paris; Academie Colarossi, Paris; Academie Julian, Paris; ASL, with W. T. Hedges, J. Greenbaum. Met Morgan Russell in Paris, 1912, and with him founded the Synchromist movement in 1913. Studied the color theories of Michel Eugene Chevruel, Herman von Helmholz, and O. N. Rood. Returned to USA 1916. Traveled Japan, 1937, 1952–53. TAUGHT: U. of California, 1942–50; U. of Hawaii, 1949; U. of Souchern California; Scripps College, 1946; Fulbright Exchange Professor to Japan, 1952–53; lectured on art history and Oriental aesthetics. FEDERAL A.P.: California State Director, 1935–42, and technical advisor to seven Western states. COMMISSIONS (murals): Santa Monica (Calif.) Public Library; Santa Monica City Hall; Santa Monica High School (mosaic). ADDRESS: 336 Bellino Drive, Pacific Palisades, Calif. DEALERS: Esther Robles Gallery; Rose Fried Gallery. ONE-MAN EXHIBITIONS: (first) Photo-Secession, NYC, 1917; Stendahl Gallery, Los Angeles (two-man), 1942; Duveen-Graham Gallery, NYC, 1956; Rose Fried Gallery, 1955. RETROSPECTIVE: Los Angeles/County MA, 1956. GROUP: Salon des Artistes Independants, Paris, 1913–14; The Synchromists, Munich and Paris, 1913; Salon d'Automne, Paris, 1910; MMA; Brooklyn Museum; Honolulu Academy. COLLECTIONS: Boston/MFA; Brooklyn Museum; Carnegie; Chicago/AI; Columbus; Corcoran; Denver/AM; Detroit/Institute; Grand Rapids; Los Angeles/County MA; MMA; MOMA; U. of Minnesota; Newark Museum; Omaha/Joslyn; PMA; Pasadena/AM; San Diego; Santa Barbara/MA; Toledo/MA; WMAA; Walker. BIBLIOGRAPHY: Baur 7; Blanchard; Blesh 1; Brown; Cheney, M. C.; Christensen; Craven 1; Goodrich and Baur 1; Haftman; Hess, T. B.; Hunter 5; Huyghe; Jackman; Janis, S.; McCurdy, ed.; Mellquist; Neuhaus; Read 2; Richardson; Ringel, ed.; Ritchie 1; Seuphor 1, 2; Wright 1, 2.

MacIVER, LOREN. b. February 2, 1909, NYC. STUDIED: ASL, 1919–20. Traveled Europe. Lighting and decor for four Coffee Concerts, MOMA, 1941. MEMBER: NIAL, 1959. FEDERAL A.P.: 1936–39, New York. COMMISSIONS (murals): Moore-McCormack Lines Inc., SS *Argentina*, 1947; American Export Lines, SS *Excalibur, SS Exeter, SS Exochorda, SS Excambion*, 1948. AWARDS: Corcoran, First Prize, 1957; Ford Foundation Grant, 1960. ADDRESS: 61 Perry Street, NYC. DEALER: Pierre Matisse Gallery. ONE-MAN EXHIBITIONS: (first) East River Gallery, NYC, 1938; Pierre Matisse Gallery, 1940, 44, 49, 56, 61; Santa Barbara/MA, 1951; Arts Club of Chicago, 1941; MOMA, circ., 1941; Baltimore/MA, 1945; Vassar College, circ., 1950; Margaret Brown Gallery, Boston, circ., 1951; Phillips, 1951; Corcoran, 1956; Fairweather-Hardin Gallery, 1959. RETROSPECTIVE: WMAA, circ., 1953. GROUP: WMAA Annuals; MOMA, Fourteen Americans, circ., 1946; Corcoran. COLLECTIONS: Andover/Phillips; Baltimore/MA; Bibliotheque Nationale; Brooklyn Museum; Chicago/AI; Corcoran; Detroit/Institute; Hartford/Wadsworth; Los Angeles/County MA; MMA; MOMA; National Gallery; Newark Museum; U. of Oklahoma; PMA; Phillips; Utica; Vassar College; WMAA; Walker; Williams College; Yale U. BIBLIOGRAPHY: Barr 3; Baur 4, 5, 7;

Stanton Macdonald-Wright   *Embarkation. 1962*

Bazin; Blesh 1; Eliot; Flanagan; Genauer; Goodrich and Baur 1; Hunter 5; Janis, S.; McCurdy, ed.; Mendelowitz; Miller, ed. 2; Newmeyer; Nordness, ed.; Pousette-Dart, ed.; Read 2; Richardson; Soby 5, 6; Wight 2.

MALDARELLI, ORONZIO. b. September 9, 1892, Naples, Italy; **d.** January 4, 1963, NYC. To USA 1900. STUDIED: Cooper Union, 1906–08; NAD, 1908, with Leon Kroll, Ivan Olinsky, Hermon McNeil; Beaux-Arts Institute of Design, NYC, 1912, with Solon Borglum, Jo Davidson, John Gregory, Elie Nadelman. TAUGHT: Sarah Lawrence College, 1933–61. MEMBER: NIAL; NAD; Architectural League of New York; National Sculpture Society.

COMMISSIONS: St. Patrick's Cathedral, NYC, 1947; James Weldon Johnson Houses, NYC, 1953–55; State Insurance Fund Building, NYC, 1957–58; Hartford (Conn.) Public Library, 1957–58. AWARDS: Fairmount Park Association, Philadelphia, First Prize, Sculpture, 1930; J. S. Guggenheim Fellowship, 1931–33; Chicago/AI, The Mr. & Mrs. Frank G. Logan Medal, 1941; NIAL Grant, 1948; PAFA, George D. Widener Memorial Gold Medal, 1951; Architectural League of New York, Silver Medal of Honor, 1954, 56. EXHIBITIONS: NAD, 1922, 23, 58, 62, 63; California Palace, 1930; Chicago/AI, 1935, 36, 40, 42, 57; WMAA, 1936, 56, 62; U. of Minnesota, 1937; Society of Independent Artists, NYC, 1941; PAFA, 1943;

Sao Paulo, 1951; MOMA, 1953; U. of Illinois, 1953, 55; Hartford/Wadsworth, 1957; P. Rosenberg and Co., 1959, Memorial Exhibition, 1963. **COLLECTIONS:** Chicago/AI; Dallas/MFA; Fairmount Park Association; MMA; Newark Museum; Ogunquit; PAFA; Sara Roby Foundation; Utica; VMFA; WMAA. **BIBLIOGRAPHY:** Baur 7; Brumme; Cheney, M. C.; Pearson 2; Ritchie 3.

MALLARY, ROBERT. b. December 2, 1917, Toledo, Ohio. STUDIED: La Escuela de las Artes del Libro, Mexico City, 1938; privately with Koloman Sokol (graphics), Mexico City and New York, 1941–42. **COMMISSIONS:** Beverly Hilton Hotel, Beverly Hills, Calif., 1954–55 (mural, with Dale Owen); New York State Pavilion, New York World's Fair, 1964–65. **ADDRESS:** 239 Davenport Avenue, New Rochelle, N.Y. DEALER: Allan Stone Gallery. **ONE-MAN EXHIBITIONS:** SFMA, 1944; Sacramento/Crocker, 1944, 52; Santa Barbara/MA, 1952; Gump's Gallery, 1953; San Diego, 1953;

Robert Mallary   *The Spector. 1961*

Urban Gallery, NYC, 1954; U. of New Mexico, 1956; Jonson Gallery, Albuquerque, N.M., 1957, 58, 59; Santa Fe, N.M., 1958; Allan Stone Gallery, 1961, 62. GROUP: Salon de Grabado, Mexico City, 1942; SFMA, 1945; Los Angeles/County MA Annuals, 1951, 53, 56; Denver/AM Annual, 1955; III & VII Sao Paulo Biennials, 1955, 63; Smithsonian, California Painters, circ. USA, 1956–58; MOMA, Recent Sculpture USA, 1959; MOMA, Sixteen Americans, circ., 1959; SRGM, Guggenheim International, 1960; WMAA Annuals, 1960, 62; MOMA, The Art of Assemblage, circ., 1961; Martha Jackson Gallery, New Media—New Forms, II, 1961; Seattle World's Fair, 1962; Carnegie, 1962; Chicago/AI Annual, 1962; A.F.A., Relief Sculpture, circ., 1964. COLLECTIONS: Brandeis U.; U. of California, Berkeley; Kalamazoo/Institute; Los Angeles/County MA; MOMA; U. of New Mexico; U. of North Carolina; Roswell; Smith College; U. of Texas; WMAA. BIBLIOGRAPHY: Janis and Blesh 1; Seitz 2.

MAN RAY. b. 1890, Philadelphia, Pa. STUDIED: NAD, 1908. Co-founder (with Marcel Duchamp and Francis Picabia) of DADA group, NYC, 1917. Co-organizer (with Katherine S. Dreier and Marcel Duchamp) of Societe Anonyme (Museum of Modern Art), 1920. Published one issue of New York DADA with Marcel Duchamp, 1921. To Paris, 1921, and became a member of the DADA and Surrealist groups, 1924–39. Developed the rayograph technique in photography, 1921. Created abstract and surrealist films: "Le Retour de la Raison," 1923; "Emak Bakia," 1926; "L'Etoile de Mer," 1928; "Les Mysteres du Chateau de Des," 1929. Resided Hollywood, 1940–50; returned to Paris. ADDRESS: 2 Bis rue Ferou, Paris, France. DEALER: Cordier & Ekstrom Inc. ONE-MAN EXHIBITIONS: Galerie Vanleer, Paris, 1929; Galerie Vignon, Paris, 1932; Curt Valentine Gallery, NYC, 1936; Librairie Six, Paris, 1922; Galerie Surrealiste, Paris, 1926; Myrbor Galerie, Paris, 1929; Galerie Beaune, Paris, 1939; The London Gallery, London, 1939; Julien Levy Galleries, NYC, 1945; Copley Gallery, Hollywood, 1948; Frank Perls Gallery, 1941; Paul Kantor Gallery, 1953; Galerie Furstenberg, Paris, 1954; Galleria Schwarz, Milan, 1964; Princeton U., 1963; Cordier & Ekstrom Inc., 1963; Galerie Rive Droite, Paris, 1959.

GROUP: Societe Anonyme, NYC, 1920; Brooklyn Museum, 1926; Springfield, Mass./MFA, 1929; MOMA, 1936; WMAA, 1946; Yale U., 1948. COLLECTIONS: MOMA. BIBLIOGRAPHY: Barr 1; Baur 7; Biddle 3; Blesh 1; Breton 1, 2, 3; Brown; Bryant; Cassou; Christensen; Crespelle; Flanagan; Gascoyne; Guggenheim, ed.; Haftman; Hunter 5; Huyghe; Janis and Blesh 1; Janis, S.; Kyrou; **Man Ray 1, 2, 3**; McCurdy, ed.; Mellquist; Motherwell 1; Raynal 3; Read 2, 4; **Ribemont-Dessaignes**; Ritchie 1; Seitz 2; Soby 1; Waldberg 2, 3; Wright 1; Zervos.

MANSHIP, PAUL. b. December 25, 1885, St. Paul, Minn.; d. February 1, 1966, NYC. STUDIED: St. Paul School of Art, 1892–1903; ASL, 1905; PAFA, 1906–08; American Academy, Rome, 1909–12. Traveled Europe, USA; resided Paris, 1922–26. TAUGHT: PAFA, 1943–46. MEMBER: National Sculpture Society (President, 1939–42); AAAL (President, 1948–53); Century Association (President, 1950–54); (Federal) Commission of Fine Arts (President, 1937–41); Academy of St. Luca, Rome, 1952. COMMISSIONS: Designed coinage for Irish Free State, 1927. AWARDS: NAD, Helen Foster Barnett Prize, 1913, 17; PAFA, George D. Widener Memorial Gold Medal, 1914; NAD, 1920; Panama-Pacific Exposition, San Francisco, 1915, Gold Medal; Philadelphia Sesquicentennial, 1926, Gold Medal; Legion of Honor, 1929; NAD, Saltus Gold Medal for Merit, 1924; Philadelphia Art Week, Gold Medal, 1925; American Independent Artists Medal, 1921; American Institute of Architects, Gold Medal, 1921; Paris World's Fair, 1937, Diplome d'Honneur; National Sculpture Society, Medal of Honor, 1939; NIAL, Gold Medal, 1945; elected to the NIAL, 1920; elected to the AAAL, 1932. ONE-MAN EXHIBITIONS: Architectural League of New York, 1912; A.F.A., 1914; Corcoran, 1920, 37; Leicester Gallery, London, 1921; PMA, 1926; Toronto, 1928; Rochester/Memorial, 1927; Averell House, NYC, 1933; Tate, 1935; VMFA, 1936; Walker, 1958; AAAL, 1945; Arden Gallery, NYC, 1941; Century Association, 1935. RETROSPECTIVE: Smithsonian, 1958. GROUP: Corcoran, 1920; PAFA; NAD; WMAA; MMA; and many others in America and abroad. COLLECTIONS: American Academy, Rome; Andover/Phillips; Chicago/AI; Cochran Memorial Park; Detroit/Institute; Harvard U.; League of Nations; MMA; Minneapolis/Institute; New York Coliseum; Pratt Institute; Rockefeller Center; St. Louis/City; Smith College; West Palm Beach/Norton. **BIBLIOGRAPHY:** Baur 7; **Beggs;** Birnbaum; Brumme; Cahill and Barr, eds.; Cortissoz 1; **Gallatin 7;** *Index of 20th Century Artists;* Jackman; Lee and Burchwood; Mather 1; Mellquist; Mendelowitz; **Murtha;** Pach 1; Poore; **Vitry.**

MANSO, LEO. b. April 15, 1914, NYC. STUDIED: NAD, 1930–34; Educational Alliance, NYC, 1929; New School for Social Research. Traveled Mexico. **TAUGHT:** Cooper Union, 1947– ; Columbia U., 1950–55; NYU, 1950– ; Provincetown Workshop, 1959– (co-founder). **MEMBER:** American Abstract Artists. **AWARDS:** U. of Illinois, P.P., 1951; Audubon Artists, 1952, 57. **ADDRESS:** 460 Riverside Drive, NYC. **DEALER:** Grand Central Moderns. **ONE-MAN EXHIBITIONS:** (first) Norlyst Gallery, NYC, 1947; Guadalajara Institute, Mexico, 1948; Mortimer Levitt Gallery, NYC, 1950; The Babcock Gallery, 1953, 56; Columbia U., 1954; NYU, 1957; Grand Central Moderns, 1957, 60, 61. **GROUP:** WMAA Annuals, 1949, 50, 51, 53, 54, 55, 56; PAFA, 1948, 49, 50, 52, 54; U. of Illinois, 1950, 51, 52, 54, 57; U. of Nebraska Annual; A.F.A., circ.; American Abstract Artists Annual; ART:USA: 58, NYC, 1958; Brooklyn Museum, Watercolor Biennials; MOMA,

The Art of Assemblage, circ., 1961. **COLLECTIONS:** Brandeis U.; Brooklyn Museum; U. of Illinois; NYU; Safad; WMAA; Wesleyan U. **BIBLIOGRAPHY:** Seitz 2.

MARCA-RELLI, CONRAD. b. June 5, 1913, Boston, Mass. **STUDIED:** Cooper Union, one year; mostly self-taught. US Army, 1941–45. Traveled Europe, USA, Mexico. **TAUGHT:** Yale U., 1954–55, 1959–60; U. of California, Berkeley, 1958. **FEDERAL A.P.:** Easel and mural painting; also art teacher. **AWARDS:** Chicago/AI, The Mr. & Mrs. Frank G. Logan Medal, 1954; Ford Foundation, 1959; Detroit/Institute, P.P., 1960; II Inter-American Paintings and Prints Biennial, Mexico City, 1960, Hon. Men.; Chicago/AI, The M. V. Kohnstamm Prize, 1963. **ADDRESS:** Apaquogue Road, East Hampton, N.Y. **DEALER:** The Kootz Gallery. **ONE-MAN EXHIBITIONS:** (first) Niveau Gallery, NYC, 1948, also 1950; The New Gallery, NYC, 1951; The Stable Gallery, 1953–58 (4); Frank Perls Gallery, 1956; La Tartaruga, Rome, 1957; Galleria d'Arte del Naviglio, Milan, 1957, 62; The Kootz Gallery, 1959, 60, 61, 62, 63, 64; Bolles Gallery, San Francisco, 1961; Galerie Schmela, Dusseldorf (two-man, with Robert Motherwell), 1961; Lima, Peru, 1961; Joan Peterson Gallery, 1961; Galerie de France, 1962; Galerie Charles Leinhard, Zurich, 1963; Tokyo Gallery, 1963. **GROUP:** Ninth Street Exhibition, NYC, 1951; WMAA Annuals;

Conrad Marca-Relli　　　*The Blackboard. 1961*

Chicago/AI; U. of Illinois; U. of Nebraska; Carnegie; Venice Biennial; Yale U.; Corcoran; Arts Club of Chicago; Rome-New York Foundation, Rome; Boston Arts Festival; Minneapolis/Institute; PAFA; Montreal/MFA; MOMA; Brussels World's Fair, 1958; Documenta II, Kassel, 1959; American Painting and Sculpture, Moscow, 1959; Sao Paulo Biennial; Seattle World's Fair, 1962. **COLLECTIONS:** Allentown/AM; Buffalo/Albright; Carnegie; Chicago/AI; Cleveland/MA; Detroit/Institute; Hartford/Wadsworth; Harvard U.; Houston/MFA; MMA; MOMA; U. of Michigan; Minneapolis/Institute; U. of Nebraska; PAFA; Rochester/Memorial; SRGM; St. Paul Gallery; WMAA; Waitsfield/Bundy; Walker; Washington U.; Yale U. **BIBLIOGRAPHY: Arnason 1;** Chaet; Goodrich and Baur 1; Henning; Janis and Blesh 1; *Metro;* Nordness, ed.; Rodman 3; Seitz 2; **Tyler.**

MARCUS, MARCIA. b. January 11, 1928, NYC. STUDIED: NYU, 1943–47, BFA; Cooper Union, 1950–52; ASL, 1954, with Edwin Dickinson. Traveled Europe. **ADDRESS:** 703 East Sixth Street, NYC. **DEALER:** The Alan Gallery. **ONE-MAN EXHIBITIONS:** (first) March Gallery, NYC, 1957; Delancey Street Museum, NYC, 1960; Cober Gallery, 1961; The Alan Gallery, 1962. **GROUP:** WMAA, Young America, 1960; WMAA Annual, 1963. **COLLECTIONS:** Newark Museum; WMAA.

MARGO, BORIS. b. November 7, 1902, Wolotschisk, Russia. STUDIED: Polytechnik School, Odessa, 1919; Futemas, Moscow, 1924; Filonoy School, Leningrad, 1927. To USA 1930; citizen 1937. **TAUGHT:** Master Institute of United Arts, Inc., 1932; American U., 1946; U. of Michigan, 1957; Chicago Art Institute School, 1957; Michigan State U., 1959; U. of Illinois, 1960; U. of Minnesota, Duluth, 1962; U. of North Carolina, 1963. MEMBER: SAGA. FEDERAL A.P.: Newark (N.J.) Airport (assisted Arshile Gorky on a mural). **AWARDS:** Chicago/AI, Watson F. Blair Prize, 1947; Portland, Me./MA, P.P., 1960; Brooklyn Museum Print Exhibitions, 1947, 53, 55, 60, 64. m. Jan Gelb. **ADDRESS:** 749 West End Avenue, NYC. DEALER: World House Galleries. **ONE-MAN EXHIBITIONS:** (first) Artists' Gallery, NYC, 1939, also 1941, 42; Norlyst Gallery, NYC, 1943; Mortimer Brandt, NYC, 1946, 47; American U., 1946, 47; J. Seligmann and Co., 1947; Brooklyn Museum, 1947; Smith-

Marcia Marcus   *Double Portrait. 1962*

John Marin   *Green Sea: Rocks and Boat, Cape Split, Maine. 1940*

sonian, 1948; Betty Parsons Gallery, 1950, 53, 55, 57, 60; World House Galleries, 1964. GROUP: MMA, Artists for Victory, 1942; Mortimer Brandt, NYC, Abstract and Surrealist Art in the U.S., circ. Western museums, 1944; NAD, 1946; Carnegie, 1946, 52; Library of Congress, 1946; Chicago/AI, Abstract and Surrealist Art, 1948; WMAA Annuals, 1947, 48, 49, 50, 53, 54, 55; U. of Illinois, 1950, 52; Chicago/AI, 1950, 54; MOMA, XXVth Anniversary Exhibition, 1954; I Sao Paulo Biennial, 1951; Federation of Modern Painters and Sculptors Annual, 1955. COLLECTIONS: Albion College; Baltimore/MA; Brooklyn Museum; Brown U.; Buffalo/Albright; Chase Manhattan Bank; Chicago/AI; Cincinnati/AM; Cornell U., Currier; Dartmouth College; U. of Illinois; Los Angeles/County MA; Louisville/Speed; MIT; MMA; MOMA; U. of Maine; U. of Michigan; U. of Minnesota; NYPL; New Orleans/Delgado; U. of North Carolina; Omaha/Joslyn; PMA; RISD; SFMA; San Jose State College; Sao Paulo; WMAA; Yale U. BIBLIOGRAPHY: Baur 5, 7; Blesh 1; Hayter 1; Janis, S.; Peterdi; Pousette-Dart, ed.; Reese.

MARIN, JOHN. b. December 3, 1870, Rutherford, N.J.; d. October 1, 1953, Cape Split, Me. STUDIED: Hoboken Academy; Stevens Preparatory School; Stevens Institute of Technology; PAFA, 1899–1901, with Thomas Anshutz, Henry Breckenridge; ASL, 1901–03, with Frank V. DuMond. Worked as a freelance architect. Traveled Europe, 1905–11. MEMBER: AAAL, 1945. AWARDS: American Institute of Architects, 1948; Philadelphia Watercolor Club, 1940; MMA, 1952; PAFA, Joseph E. Temple Gold Medal, 1954; Hon. DFA, Yale U., Hon. DFA, U. of Maine, 1950. ONE-MAN EXHIBITIONS: (first) Photo-Secession, NYC, 1909, also 1910, 13, 15; Brooklyn Museum, 1922; Montross Gallery, NYC, 1922, 24; Stieglitz's Intimate Gallery, NYC, 1925, 28; An American Place (Gallery), NYC, 1929–35, 1937–42, 1944–50; The Downtown Gallery, 1939, 48, 1950–54; Cleveland/MA, 1939; ICA, Boston, 1947; de Young, 1949; XXV Venice Biennial, 1950; A.F.A., 1952–54; Detroit/Institute, 1954; Philadelphia Art Alliance, 1954. RETROSPECTIVE: The Daniel Gallery, NYC, 1920; MOMA, 1936; Trenton/State, 1950; U. of Michigan, 1951; Houston/MFA, 1953; AAAL, 1954; UCLA, 1955. GROUP: Salon d'Automne, Paris, 1908; Salon des Artistes Independants, Paris, 1904; The Armory Show, 1913; WMAA; MOMA; Chicago/AI; Detroit/Institute; Cleveland/MA; Walker; Cincinnati/AM; SFMA; Toronto; Dallas/MFA; Utica; Corcoran; MMA. COLLECTIONS: Andover/Phillips; Arizona State U.; Auburn U.; Baltimore/MA; Brooklyn Museum; Buffalo/Albright; Chicago/AI; Cleveland/MA; Colorado Springs/FA; Columbus; Cranbrook;

Denver/AM; Des Moines; Detroit/Institute; Fisk U.; U. of Georgia; Hagerstown/County MFA; Hartford/Wadsworth; Harvard U.; Houston/MFA; IBM; Indiana U.; Indianapolis/Herron; Lane Foundation; MMA; MOMA; U. of Maine; The Miller Co.; National Gallery; U. of Nebraska; Newark Museum; New Britain; Ogunquit; Omaha/Joslyn; PAFA; Phillips; Rochester/Memorial; U. of Rochester; Roswell; SFMA; St. Louis/City; San Antonio/McNay; San Diego; Santa Barbara/MA; Springfield, Mo./AM; Utica; WMAA; Walker; Wellesley College; West Palm Beach/Norton; Wichita/AM; Wilmington; Yale U.; Youngstown/Butler. BIBLIOGRAPHY: American Artists Group Inc. 3; Baldinger; Barker 1; Barr 3; Baur 5, 7; Bazin; Beekman; **Benson;** Bethers; Biddle 3; Blesh 1; Born; Brown; Bryant; Cahill and Barr, eds.; Canaday; Cassou; Cheney, M. C.; Christensen; Coke; Craven 1; Eliot; Elsen; Flanagan; Flexner; Flockhart; Frank, ed.; Frost; Gallatin 1; Gaunt; Goldwater and Treves, eds.; Goodrich 1; Goodrich and Baur 1; Haas; Haftman; Hartmann; **Helm; Helm and Wight;** Hess, T. B.; Hunter 5; Huyghe; *Index of 20th Century Artists;* Janis, S.; Jewell 2; Kootz 1, 2; Kuh 1; Lane; Langui; Lee and Burchwood; Leepa; Mather 1; **McBride;** McCourbrey; McCurdy, ed.; Mellquist; Mendelowitz; Munsterberg; Neuhaus; Newmeyer; **Norman;** Pach 1; Pearson 2; Phillips 1, 2; Pousette-Dart, ed.; Raynal 3, 4; Read 2; Richardson; Ritchie 1; Rodman 2; Rosenblum; Sachs; **Seligmann, ed.;** Soby 5, 6; Sutton; Valentine 2; Wight 2; Wright 1; Zigrosser 1.

MARISOL (Escobar). **b.** May 22, 1930, Paris, France. STUDIED: ASL, 1950, with Yasuo Kuniyoshi; Hofmann School, 1951–54; Academie des Beaux-Arts, Paris, 1949; New School for Social Research, 1951–54. Traveled Venezuela, USA, Europe. AWARDS: Academy of Achievement, San Diego. ADDRESS: 141 East 33 Street, NYC. DEALER: Sidney Janis Gallery. ONE-MAN EXHIBITIONS: (first) Leo Castelli Inc., 1957; The Stable Gallery, 1962, 64. GROUP: MOMA, Americans 1963, circ., 1963–64; WMAA Annuals, 1962, 64; Festival of Two Worlds, Spoleto, 1958; Dallas/MFA, Humor in Art, 1958; Carnegie, 1959, 64; Chicago/AI, Pan American Art, 1959; MOMA, The Art of Assemblage, circ., 1961; U. of Illinois, 1961; A.F.A., Wit and Whimsey in 20th Century Art, circ.,

1962–63; Chicago/AI, 1963; Tate, Painting and Sculpture of a Decade, 1954–64, 1964; The Hague, New Realism, 1964. COLLECTIONS: Brandeis U.; Buffalo/Albright; MOMA; WMAA. BIBLIOGRAPHY: Seitz 2; Seuphor 3.

MARSH, REGINALD. b. March 14, 1898, Paris, France; **d.** July 3, 1954, Dorset, Vt. STUDIED: The Lawrenceville School, 1915–16; Yale U., 1916–20, AB; ASL, 1919, 1920–24, 1927–28, with John Sloan, Kenneth Hayes Miller, George Bridgeman, George Luks. Traveled Europe extensively. Artist War Correspondent for *Life* Magazine, 1943. TAUGHT: ASL; Moore Institute of Art, Science and Industry, Philadelphia, 1953–54. COMMISSIONS: US Post Office, Washington, D.C., 1937; US Customs House, NYC, 1937. AWARDS: NAD, 1943; NIAL, 1946; Chicago/AI, The M. V. Kohnstamm Prize, 1931; Wanamaker Prize, 1934; NAD, The Thomas B. Clarke Prize, 1937; Limited Editions Club, 1938; Chicago/AI, Watson F. Blair Prize, 1940; PAFA, Dana Watercolor Medal, 1941; Corcoran, First William A. Clark Prize, 1945; Salmagundi Club, NYC, T. J. Watson Prize, 1945; NIAL, Gold Medal for Graphics, 1954. ONE-MAN EXHIBITIONS: (first) Whitney Studio Club, NYC, 1924, also 1928; Curt Valentine Gallery, NYC, 1927; Weyhe Gallery, 1928; Marie Sterner Gallery, NYC, 1929; Rehn Galleries, 1930–34, 36, 38, 40, 41, 43, 44, 46, 48, 50, 53; McDonald Gallery, NYC, 1939; Martha Jackson Gallery, 1953; Steeplechase Park, Coney Island, NYC, 1953; Yale U., 1937; Andover/Phillips, 1937; Carnegie, 1946; Print Club of Cleveland (two-man), 1948; Philadelphia Art Alliance, 1950; Moravian College, 1954. RETROSPECTIVE: Gallery of Modern Art, NYC, 1964. GROUP: WMAA, MOMA; MMA; Corcoran; Carnegie. COLLECTIONS: Andover/Phillips; Boston/MFA; Chicago/AI; Hartford/Wadsworth; MMA; U. of Nebraska; PAFA; Springfield, Mass./MFA; WMAA. BIBLIOGRAPHY: American Artists Group Inc. 1, 3; Barker 1; Baur 7; Bazin; Boswell 1; Brown; Bruce and Watson; Cahill and Barr, eds.; Canaday; Cheney, M. C.; Christensen; Craven 2; Eliot; Flanagan; Flexner; **Goodrich** 1, **9;** Goodrich and Baur 1; Hall; Hunter 5; Kent, N.; Kuh 1; **Marsh;** McCourbrey; McCurdy, ed.; Mellquist; Mendelowitz; Newmeyer; Nordmark; Pagano; Pearson 1; Reese; Richardson; Ringel, ed.; **Sasowsky;** Sutton; Wight 2.

Reginald Marsh   *Burlesque. 1945*

MARSICANO, NICHOLAS. b. October 1, 1914, Shenandoah, Pa. STUDIED: PAFA and Barnes Foundation, 1931–34; abroad, 1933–36. TAUGHT: Cooper Union, 1948– ; U. of Michigan, summer, 1950; Yale U., summers, 1951–54; Brooklyn Museum School, 1951–58; Pratt Institute, 1957–60; Cornell U., summer, 1959. AWARDS: PAFA, Cresson Fellowship, and Barnes Foundation Scholarship, 1933–36; V Hallmark International Competition, Second Prize, 1960. ADDRESS: 23 West 16 Street, NYC. DEALER: The Howard Wise Gallery, NYC. ONE-MAN EXHIBITIONS: The Salpeter Gallery, 1948; The Bertha Schaefer Gallery, 1957, 59, 60, 61; San Joaquin Pioneer Museum and Haggin Art Galleries, Stockton, Calif., 1959; Stewart Richard Gallery, San Antonio, 1959; The Howard Wise Gallery, NYC, 1963. GROUP: U. of Nebraska, 1954, 58, 60; Walker, Vanguard, 1955; II Inter-American Paintings and Prints Biennial, Mexico City, 1960; A.F.A., The Figure, circ., 1960; Chicago/AI, 1961, 64; MOMA, Abstract American Drawings and Watercolors, circ. Latin America, 1961–63; PAFA, 1962, 64; MOMA, Recent Painting USA:

The Figure, circ., 1962–63; Dallas/MFA, 1961, 62; WMAA Annuals, 1960, 61, 62. COLLECTIONS: Hallmark Collection; MOMA; James A. Michener Foundation.

MARTIN, FLETCHER. b. April 29, 1904, Palisade, Colo. TAUGHT: ASL, 1947–49; U. of Florida, 1949–52; State U. of Iowa, 1940; Kansas City Art Institute and School of Design, 1941–42; Mills College, 1951; U. of Minnesota, 1954; San Antonio Art Institute, 1957; Los Angeles County Museum of Art, 1958–59; Washington State U., 1960–61. Artist War Correspondent for *Life* Magazine, 1943. FEDERAL A.P.: Mural painting, 1936–37. AWARDS: PAFA, Walter Lippincott Prize, 1947; NAD, Benjamin Altman Prize, 1949. ADDRESS: 224 Mead Mountain Road, Woodstock, N.Y. ONE-MAN EXHIBITIONS: San Diego, 1934; A.A.A. Gallery, NYC, 1948; John Heller Gallery, NYC, 1955, 57; The Midtown Galleries, 1940, 43; Jake Zeitlin Gallery, 1939. GROUP: MOMA, 1942; U. of Minnesota, Duluth. COLLECTIONS: Abbott Laboratories; Andover/Phillips; Brandeis U.; Britannica; Clearwater/Gulf Coast; Cranbrook;

Davenport/Municipal; Denver/AM; Houston/MFA; IBM; State U. of Iowa; Kansas City/Nelson; Library of Congress; Los Angeles/County MA; MMA; MOMA; SFMA; Youngstown/Butler. **BIBLIOGRAPHY:** American Artists Group Inc. 2; Baur 7; **Ebersole;** Kent, N.; Miller, ed. 1; Zaidenberg, ed.

MARTIN, KNOX. b. 1923, Barranquilla, Colombia. STUDIED: ASL. US Navy, three years. **ADDRESS:** 145 Audubon Avenue, NYC. DEALER: Fischbach Gallery. **ONE-MAN EXHIBITIONS:** Charles Egan Gallery, 1954, 61; Avant Garde Gallery, NYC, 1956; Holland-Goldowsky Gallery, Chicago, 1958; Rose Fried Gallery, 1963; Fischbach Gallery, 1964. **GROUP:** WGMA, 1963, Chicago/AI, 1963; Baltimore/MA, 1963; Buffalo/Albright, 1963. **COLLECTIONS:** Austin; U. of California, Berkeley; Corcoran; U. of Illinois; MOMA; NYU; WMAA.

MARTINELLI, EZIO. b. November 27, 1913, West Hoboken, N.J. STUDIED: Academy of Fine Arts, Bologne, Italy, 1931; NAD, 1932–36, with Leon Kroll, Gifford Beal, Robert Aitken (sculpture), Ivan Olinsky. Traveled France, Italy. TAUGHT: Sarah Lawrence College, 1947– ; Parsons School of Design, 1953– ; Philadelphia Museum School, 1946–49; Pennsylvania School of Industrial Art, Philadelphia, 1946–49; Artist-in-Residence, American Academy, Rome, 1964–65. Painted only until 1952; began sculpture in 1938. FEDERAL A.P.: Teacher, NYC; easel painter and unit supervisor, 1937–41. COMMISSIONS: United Nations General Assembly Building, NYC (30-ft. sculpture). AWARDS: L. C. Tiffany Grant, 1936; Guggenheim Foundation Fellowship, 1958, 62; NAD, President's Award; Ford Foundation/A.F.A. Artist-in-Residence, Sarasota, 1964. **ADDRESS:** 121 West 85 Street, NYC. DEALER: The Willard Gallery. **ONE-MAN EXHIBITIONS:** (first) Philip Ragan Gallery, Philadelphia, 1943; The Willard Gallery, 1946, 47, 52, 55; Seattle/AM; U. of Minnesota; Chicago/AI. **GROUP:** Art of This Century, NYC, 1942–44; Chicago/AI, Drawings, 1952; A.F.A., Major Work in Minor Scale, circ., 1957; NIAL, 1959; WMAA, Business Buys American Art, 1960; Chicago/AI, Abstract and Surrealist Art, 1948; WMAA Annuals, 1948, 61, 62; PAFA, 1944, 58, 64; Carnegie, 1959; Contemporary American Drawings, circ. France, 1954; Walker, Expres-

sionism, 1900–1955, 1956; VMFA, American Sculpture Today, 1958; Newark Museum, Survey of American Sculpture, 1962; Brooklyn Museum, 1947; USIA, Eight American Artists, circ. Europe and Asia, 1957–58; Claude Bernard, Paris, Aspects of American Sculpture, 1960. COLLECTIONS: Brooklyn Museum; U. of Illinois; Memphis/Brooks; Newark Museum; PMA; Seattle/AM; United Nations; WMAA; U. of Wisconsin. **BIBLIOGRAPHY:** Seuphor 3.

MASON, ALICE TRUMBULL. b. November 16, 1904, Litchfield, Conn. STUDIED: British School, Rome, 1922; NAD, 1923; privately with C. W. Hawthorne, 1924, and Arshile Gorky, 1926. Traveled Italy and around the world, 1920. MEMBER: American Abstract Artists; Federation of Modern Painters and Sculptors; SAGA; American Color Print Society. AWARDS: Longview Foundation Grant, 1963; The Print Club, Philadelphia, Charles M. Lea Prize, 1945. **ADDRESS:** 334 West 85 Street, NYC. **ONE-MAN EXHIBITIONS:** (first) Museum of Living Art, NYC, 1948; Hansa Gallery, NYC, 1958. **GROUP:** Federation of Modern Painters and Sculptors Annuals; A.A.A. Gallery, NYC, Annuals; Brooklyn Museum, 1949; PMA, "8 x 8," 1945. COLLECTIONS: Brooklyn Museum; Free Library of Philadelphia; ICA, Washington, D.C.; Library of Congress; MMA; NYPL; PMA; The Pennsylvania State U.; WMAA. **BIBLIOGRAPHY:** Reese.

MATULKA, JAN. b. November 7, 1890, Prague, Czechoslovakia. STUDIED: NAD, with G. W. Maynard. Traveled Europe, USA. TAUGHT: ASL, 1929, 31. FEDERAL A.P.: Mural for a hospital in Brooklyn, N.Y. AWARDS: Pulitzer Scholarship for Painting. **ADDRESS:** 439 East 89 Street, NYC. DEALER: Rehn Galleries. **ONE-MAN EXHIBITIONS:** (first) Modern Gallery, NYC, 1927, also 1930; Whitney Studio Club, NYC, 1929; Rehn Galleries, 1928, 29, 31, 32, 33, 35, 56. **GROUP:** WMAA, 1944; MMA; Chicago/AI; Carnegie, 1944. COLLECTIONS: Brooklyn Museum; Chicago/AI; Cincinnati/AM; Detroit/Institute; MMA; SFMA; WMAA. **BIBLIOGRAPHY:** Blesh 1; Hunter 5; Janis, S.

MAYHEW, RICHARD. b. April 3, 1924, Amityville, N.Y. STUDIED: Brooklyn Museum School, with Edwin Dickinson, Reuben Tam. AWARDS: John Hay Whitney Fellowship, 1958;

Ingram Merrill Foundation Grant, 1960; L. C. Tiffany Grant, 1964; NAD, P.P., 1964. **ADDRESS:** 716 Jefferson Street, Brooklyn, N.Y. **DEALER:** Durlacher Brothers. **ONE-MAN EXHIBITIONS:** The Morris Gallery, 1957; Washington Irving Gallery, NYC, 1958; Robert Isaacson Gallery, NYC, 1959, 61, 62; Durlacher Brothers, 1963. **GROUP:** NAD, 1955, 59; Brooklyn Society of Artists Annual, 1956; Chicago/AI, 1961; Youngstown/Butler, 1961; Carnegie, 1961; Brooklyn Museum, 1961; WMAA Annual, 1961; ART:USA:58, NYC, 1958. **COLLECTIONS:** NAD.

MAZUR, MICHAEL B. b. November 2, 1935, NYC. **STUDIED:** Amherst College, 1954–58, BA; Academy of Fine Arts, Florence, Italy, 1956–57; Yale U., with Gabor Peterdi, Rico Lebrun, Josef Albers, Jon Schueler, Bernard Chaet, Nicholas Carone, 1959–61, BFA, MFA; privately with Leonard Baskin (printmaking), 1956–58. **TAUGHT:** Yale U., 1960–61; RISD, 1961– ; Yale U., summer, 1963. **AWARDS:** L. C. Tiffany Grant, 1962; Guggenheim Foundation Fellowship, 1964; NIAL, 1964; Library of Congress, Pennell P.P.; Boston Printmakers, P.P., 1962; Memphis/Brooks, P.P., 1961, 62; SAGA, Second Prize. **ADDRESS:** 8 Arlington Street, Cambridge, Mass. **DEALERS:** The Kornblee Gallery; Boris Mirski Gallery. **ONE-MAN EXHIBITIONS:** (first) The Kornblee Gallery, 1961, also 1962; Boris Mirski Gallery, 1964; The Gallery, Northampton, Mass., 1963; Silvermine Guild, 1964. **GROUP:** USIA, 10 American Printmakers, circ. Europe; MOMA, 60 Modern Drawings, 1963; Library of Congress; Seattle/AM; Kansas City/Nelson; Smith College; The Print Club, Philadelphia; Boston Arts Festival. **COLLECTIONS:** Andover/Phillips; Boston/MFA; Brooklyn Museum; Chicago/AI; Harvard U.; Library of Congress; MOMA; Memphis/Brooks; PMA; Portland, Ore./AM; Smith College; USIA; Westminster Foundation; Yale U.

McCHESNEY, ROBERT P. b. January 16, 1913, Marshall, Mo. **STUDIED:** Washington U., with Fred Conway; Otis Art Institute, Los Angeles. Resided Mexico, one year. **TAUGHT:** California School of Fine Arts, 1949–51; Santa Rosa Junior College, 1957–58. **FEDERAL A.P.:** Federal Building, Golden Gate International Exposition, San Francisco, 1939 (mural). **COM-**

MISSIONS: SS *Monterey* (wall decoration). **AWARDS:** WMAA Annual, P.P., 1955; SFMA, First Prize, 1960; San Francisco Municipal Art Commission, P.P., 1950. **ADDRESS:** 2955 Mountain Road, Petaluma, Calif. **DEALER:** Fredric Hobbs Fine Art Center. **ONE-MAN EXHIBITIONS:** (first) Raymond and Raymond, Inc., San Francisco, 1944; SFMA, 1964; Bolles Gallery, NYC, 1960; Bolles Gallery, San Francisco, 1960, 61; Parson Gallery, Los Angeles, 1960, 61; Myrtle Todes Gallery, Glencoe, Ill., 1958; SFMA, 1949, 53, 57; Gump's Gallery, 1952, 53, 55; Daliel Gallery, Berkeley, 1950; Murquis Gallery, Los Angeles, 1949; Lucien Labaudt Gallery, 1947, 51; Pat Wall Gallery, Monterey, 1946. **GROUP:** Sao Paulo, 1955; WMAA Annual, 1955; Chicago/AI Annuals, 1947, 54, 60, 61; Phillips, 1947; Los Angeles/County MA, 1949; Corcoran, 1957; SFMA, 1945, 50, 53, 60; de Young, 1947, 51, 53, 59, 60, 61; California Palace, 1962, 64. **COLLECTIONS:** SFMA; San Francisco Municipal Art Commission; WMAA.

McCLELLAN, DOUGLAS EUGENE. b. October 10, 1921, Pasadena, Calif. **STUDIED:** Art Center School, Los Angeles; Colorado Springs Fine Arts Center, with Boardman Robinson, Jean Charlot; Claremont Graduate School, MFA. **TAUGHT:** Chaffey College, 1950–59; Otis Art Institute, Los Angeles, 1959– . **AWARDS:** Los Angeles/County MA, P.P., 1950, 53; National Orange Show, 1954. **ADDRESS:** 5062 Rosewood Court, Montclair, Calif. **ONE-MAN EXHIBITIONS:** Felix Landau Gallery, 1953, 55, 57, 59; Pasadena/AM, 1954; U. of California, Riverside, 1955. **GROUP:** MMA, 1950; Library of Congress, 1948; Corcoran, 1953; PAFA, 1953; SFMA, 1949, 52; Carnegie, 1955, 57; Los Angeles/County MA, 1949, 50, 52, 54, 55; Los Angeles County Fair, 1949, 53; Santa Barbara/MA, I Pacific Coast Biennial, 1955; WMAA, 1957. **COLLECTIONS:** Los Angeles/County MA; Los Angeles County Fair Association; Pasadena/AM.

McFEE, HENRY LEE. b. April 14, 1886, St. Louis, Mo. **STUDIED:** Washington U. School of Fine Arts; ASL, Woodstock, N.Y., 1908, with Birge Harrison; Stevenson Art Center, Philadelphia. **AWARDS:** Carnegie, Hon. Men., 1923; Corcoran, Fourth William A. Clark Prize, 1928; Carnegie, First Hon. Men., 1930; PAFA, Joseph E. Temple Gold Medal, 1937; VMFA, p.p., 1935; Los Angeles County Fair, p.p., 1940, 49; Guggenheim Foundation Fellowship, 1941; NIAL, 1945; elected an Associate of the NAD, 1949. **ADDRESS:** c/o Dealer. **DEALER:** Rehn Galleries. **ONE-MAN EXHIBITIONS:** Rehn Galleries, 1927, 29, 33, 36, 50; Pasadena/AM, 1950. **GROUP:** Anderson Galleries, NYC, Forum Exhibition, 1916; Carnegie, 1923–49; Corcoran, 1924, 26, 1928–44; PAFA; Chicago/AI; St. Louis/City; Panama-Pacific Exposition, San Francisco, 1915; Detroit/Institute; Cleveland/MA. **COLLECTIONS:** Brooklyn Museum; Buffalo/Albright; Carnegie; Cleveland/MA; Columbus; Corcoran; Detroit/Institute; Los Angeles County Fair Association; MMA; PMA;

Phillips; St. Louis/City; Taft Museum; VMFA; WMAA. **BIBLIOGRAPHY: Barker 2;** Baur 7; Brown; Cahill and Barr, eds.; Cheney, M. C.; Hall; Hunter 5; Huyghe; *Index of 20th Century Artists;* Janis, S.; Kent, N.; Mellquist; Mendelowitz; **Millier 1;** Pearson 2; Poore; Pousette-Dart, ed.; Richardson; Smith, S. C. K.; Watson 2; Wright 1.

McGARRELL, JAMES. b. February 22, 1930, Indianapolis, Ind. STUDIED: Indiana U., with Alton Pickens, Leo Steppat, AB; UCLA, with John Paul Jones, Gordon Nunes, MA; Skowhegan School; Academy of Fine Arts, Stuttgart. Traveled Germany, France, USA. **TAUGHT:**

James McGarrell   *Mound. 1963*

Reed College, 1956–59; Indiana U., 1959– .
AWARDS: Fulbright Fellowship, 1955; NIAL Grant, 1963; J. S. Guggenheim Fellowship, 1964. **ADDRESS:** 411 E. University, Bloomington, Ind. **DEALERS:** Allan Frumkin Gallery, NYC and Chicago; Frank Perls Gallery. **ONE-MAN EXHIBITIONS:** (first) Frank Perls Gallery, 1955, also 1957, 58, 62, 64; Allan Frumkin Gallery, Chicago, 1960, 62; Allan Frumkin Gallery, NYC, 1961, 64; Portland, Ore./AM, 1959, 62. **GROUP:** WMAA Annuals, 1957, 59, 60; Carnegie, 1959, 64; MOMA, New Images of Man, 1959; Documenta III, Kassel, 1964; U. of Illinois, 1959, 61, 63; III International Biennial Exhibition of Prints, Tokyo, 1962. **COLLECTIONS:** Brooklyn Museum; Chicago/AI; Indiana U.; MOMA; U. of Nebraska; PAFA; Portland, Ore./AM; SFMA; Santa Barbara/MA; WMAA.

McLAUGHLIN, JOHN. b. May 21, 1898, Sharon, Mass. Self-taught in art. US Army Intelligence, 1941–45. Traveled the Orient, resided Japan, for many years beginning 1935. Began to paint 1938. **AWARDS:** Tamarind Fellowship, 1963. **ADDRESS:** Box 95, Dana Point, Calif. **DEALER:** Felix Landau Gallery. **ONE-MAN EXHIBITIONS:** Felix Landau Gallery, 1953, 58, 62; U. of California, Riverside, 1958; Long Beach/MA, 1960; K. Kazimir Gallery, 1964. **RETROSPECTIVE:** Pasadena/AM, 1956. **GROUP:** California State Fair, 1950; Los Angeles/County MA, Contemporary Painting in the United States, 1951; Los Angeles/County MA Annuals, 1949, 50, 54, 55, 56, 57, 58, 59, 60; Sao Paulo, 1955; SFMA, Art in the Twentieth Century, 1955; Corcoran, 1955; Long Beach/MA, Fifteen Americans, circ., 1956; Walker, 1956; Houston/MFA, The Sphere of Mondrian, 1957; VMFA, American Painting, 1958; U. of Nebraska, 1958; Denver/AM, 1958; Los Angeles/County MA, Four Abstract Classicists, circ., 1959–61; ICA, London, 1960; SFMA, Fifty California Artists, circ., 1962; A.F.A., Purist Painting, circ., 1960–61; WMAA, Geometric Abstraction in America, circ., 1962.

McNEIL, GEORGE. b. February 22, 1908, NYC. **STUDIED:** Pratt Institute, 1927–29; ASL, 1930–33; Hofmann School, 1933–36; Columbia U., BA, MA, Ed.D. US Navy, 1943–46. Traveled Cuba, Europe, North Africa, the Orient. **TAUGHT:** Pratt Institute, 1946– ; U. of Wyoming, 1946–48; U. of California, Berkeley,

1955–56. **FEDERAL A.P.:** Designed abstract murals, 1935–40. **AWARDS:** Ford Foundation, P.P., 1963. **ADDRESS:** 226-A Willoughby Avenue, Brooklyn, N.Y. **DEALER:** The Howard Wise Gallery, NYC. **ONE-MAN EXHIBITIONS:** (first) Lyceum Gallery, Havana, 1941; Black Mountain College, 1947; Charles Egan Gallery, 1950, 52, 53, 54; Margaret Brown Gallery, Boston, 1953; Hendler Gallery, Philadelphia, 1954; de Young, 1955; Poindexter Gallery, 1957, 59; The Howard Wise Gallery, NYC, 1960, 62; Nova Gallery, Boston, 1961; U. of Wyoming, 1948; U. of New Mexico, 1948; U. of Colorado, 1948. **GROUP:** American Abstract Artists, 1936; MOMA, New Horizons in American Art, 1936; New York World's Fair, 1939; Chicago/AI, Abstract and Surrealist Art, 1948; MOMA, Abstract Painting and Sculpture in America, 1951; WMAA Annuals, 1953, 57, 61; Carnegie, 1953, 55, 58; Walker, 60 American Painters, 1960; Cleveland/MA, Some Contemporary American Artists, 1961; SRGM, Abstract Expressionists and Imagists, 1961; USIA, American Painting, circ. Latin America, 1961; PAFA, 1962; Hartford/Wadsworth, 1962; Chicago/AI, 1963; MOMA, Hans Hofmann and His Students, circ., 1963–64. **COLLECTIONS:** Havana/Nacional; MOMA; Newark Museum; WGMA; WMAA; Waitsfield/Bundy; Walker. **BIBLIOGRAPHY:** Passloff; Pousette-Dart, ed.; Ritchie 1.

MEEKER, DEAN JACKSON. b. May 18, 1920, Orchard, Colo. **STUDIED:** Chicago Art Institute School, BFA, MFA; Northwestern U.; U. of Wisconsin. **TAUGHT:** U. of Wisconsin, 1946– . **AWARDS:** Milwaukee, Medal of Honor, 1952, 56; Guggenheim Foundation Fellowship, 1959. **ADDRESS:** 309 Parkway, Glen Oak Hills, Madison, Wisc. **ONE-MAN EXHIBITIONS:** Milwaukee, 1950; Lawrence College, 1953; U. of North Dakota, 1954; U. of Wisconsin, 1955; Chicago/AI, 1956; U. of New Mexico, 1956; Los Angeles/County MA, 1957; La Gravure, Paris, 1959. **GROUP:** Boston/MFA, 1954–56; PAFA, 1946–53; Brooklyn Museum, 1951–55; Library of Congress, 1952, 54, 55; Seattle/AM, 1953–55; SFMA, 1952–54; Walker, 1952–54; Chicago/AI, Exhibition Momentum, 1952–54; MMA, 1953; MOMA, 1955; Chicago/AI, 1952; The Hague, 1954; Milwaukee; Connecticut College; U. of Missouri; Los Angeles/County MA, 1959; Lawrence College.

COLLECTIONS: Beloit College; Bibliotheque Nationale; Boston/MFA; Brooklyn College; Carleton College; Cornell U.; Dallas/MFA; Denison U.; Denver/AM; Kansas City/Nelson; Library of Congress; Lincoln, Mass./De Cordova; MOMA; Milwaukee; U. of Oklahoma; PAFA; The Print Club, Philadelphia; SFMA; Seattle/AM; USIA; Victoria and Albert Museum; U. of Wisconsin. BIBLIOGRAPHY: Hayter 1.

MEIGS, WALTER. b. September 21, 1918, NYC. STUDIED: Syracuse U., BFA; State U. of Iowa, MFA; with R. Lotterman; Ecole des Beaux-Arts, Fontainebleau, Diplome. US Army, more than three years, World War II. Traveled France, Greece; resides in Greece. TAUGHT: U. of Nebraska, 1949–53; U. of Connecticut, 1953–61. AWARDS: Boston Arts Festival, Grand Prize, 1956; Silvermine Guild, 1954; and some 20 others. ADDRESS: c/o Mr. Lee Nordness, 831 Madison Avenue, NYC. ONE-MAN EXHIBITIONS: (first) The Downtown Gallery; U. of Nebraska, 1952; The Alan Gallery, 1954; Wesleyan U., 1956; New London, 1956; Boris Mirski Gallery, 1957; Lincoln, Mass./De Cordova, 1959; Lee Nordness Gallery, NYC, 1958, 64. GROUP: Walker Biennial, 1951; Omaha/Joslyn, 1952; Boston Arts Festival; Berkshire Art Festival; Youngstown/Butler, 1957. COLLECTIONS: Amherst College; Birmingham, Ala./MA; Denver/AM; Fort Worth; Hartford/Wadsworth; Lincoln, Mass./De Cordova; The Pennsylvania State U.; Springfield, Mo./AM; USIA; Utica; Youngstown/Butler. BIBLIOGRAPHY: Nordness, ed.

MENKES, SIGMUND. b. May 7, 1896, Lwow, Poland. STUDIED in Europe. AWARDS: Corcoran, 1941; PAFA, Medal, 1945; NIAL, 1955; ART:USA:58, NYC, 1958. ADDRESS: 5075 Fieldstone Road, Riverdale, N.Y. ONE-MAN EXHIBITIONS: Mrs. Cornelius J. Sullivan Gallery, NYC; Durand-Ruel Gallery, NYC, 1941; A.A.A. Gallery, NYC, 1936–54; Le Portique, Paris, 1928. GROUP: Carnegie; Chicago/AI; Corcoran; PAFA; U. of Nebraska; Cleveland/MA; American U.; State U. of Iowa; Cranbrook; MMA; WMAA; Toronto. COLLECTIONS: Abbott Laboratories; Belgrade/National; Britannica; Brooklyn Museum; Cranbrook; Davenport/Municipal; Greece/National; MMA; U. of Miami; Montclair/AM; Musee du Jeu de Paume;

NIAL; PAFA; Tel Aviv; WMAA; Walker; Warsaw/National; Wichita/AM. BIBLIOGRAPHY: Genauer; Pousette-Dart, ed.; Zaidenberg, ed.

MESIBOV, HUGH. b. December 29, 1916, Philadelphia, Pa. STUDIED: Graphic Sketch Club, Philadelphia; PAFA; Barnes Foundation. TAUGHT: Wiltwyck School, Esopus, N.Y. COMMISSIONS: US Post Office, Hubbard, Ohio (mural). AWARDS: PAFA, 1952, 58; Hallmark International Competition, 1952; The Print Club, Philadelphia, 1941, 46. ADDRESS: 377 Saddle River Road, Monsey, N.Y. ONE-MAN EXHIBITIONS: Elizabeth Nelson Gallery, Chicago, 1952; The Morris Gallery, 1954; Bookshop Gallery, Aspen, Colo., 1951, 53; Pied Piper Gallery, Aspen, Colo., 1954; Chinese Gallery, NYC, 1947; Artists' Gallery, NYC, 1956, 58; Sunken Meadow Gallery, Kings Park, N.Y., 1958; Carlen Gallery, Philadelphia, 1940; Philadelphia Art Alliance, 1945; Gallery Mayer, NYC, 1959. GROUP: PAFA, 1943, 1952–55, 57; New York World's Fair, 1939; Harrisburg, Pa.; Carnegie, 1939; Philadelphia Art Alliance, 1940, 41, 45; Brooklyn Museum, 1951, 1953–55; Library of Congress, 1951; WMAA, 1956, 57, 58, 59; Corcoran, 1959; MOMA, 1961. COLLECTIONS: Barnes Foundation; Carnegie; Free Library of Philadelphia; MMA; NYU; PAFA; Phillips; U. of Wyoming.

MESTROVIC, IVAN. b. August 15, 1883, Vrpolje, Croatia; **d.** January 17, 1962, Notre Dame, Ind. STUDIED: Privately with Otto Koenig in Vienna, 1899; Academy of Fine Arts, Vienna, 1900–04, with E. Hellmer, H. Bitterlich, Otto Wagner. Member of Yugoslav Provisional National Assembly, 1919. Traveled Italy, France, Austria, USA. To USA 1947; citizen 1954. TAUGHT: Syracuse U., 1947–55; U. of Notre Dame, 1956–62. MEMBER: AAAL, 1953. COMMISSIONS: Grant Park, Chicago, 1925; Unknown Soldier Memorial, Belgrade, 1934; equestrian figure of King Carol, 1938–39; Vatican commissions, 1942. AWARDS: AAAL, Award of Merit Medal, 1953; Hon. Member, Academy of Fine Arts, Vienna, 1952; American Institute of Architects, Fine Arts Medal, 1955; Hon. DFA from Colgate U., Ohio Wesleyan U., Syracuse U., Marquette U., U. of Notre Dame, and Columbia U. ONE-MAN EXHIBITIONS: Vienna Sezession, 1909; Mestrovic Museum, 1910; Musee du Jeu de Paume, 1933; MMA, 1947.

GROUP: Vienna Sezession, 1903, 04; Salon d'Automne, Paris, 1905; International Exhibition, Rome, 1911; Victoria and Albert Museum, 1915; Musee du Petit Palais, Paris, 1919. COLLECTIONS: Belgrade/National; Brooklyn Museum; Buffalo/Albright; Chicago/AI; Detroit/Institute; Mestrovic Gallery; Mestrovic Museum; U. of Minnesota; Montreal/MFA; Prague/National; St. Antony's College; San Diego; Syracuse U.; Tate; Toronto; Victoria and Albert Museum. BIBLIOGRAPHY: Bulliet 1; Cheney, M. C.; Christensen; Lee and Burchwood; Mendelowitz; Pach 1; Ramsden 2; Salvini; Selz, J.; Taft.

METCALF, JAMES. b. March 11, 1925, NYC. STUDIED: Dayton Art Institute School; PAFA, 1944–46; Central School of Arts and Crafts, London, 1950–53. US Army, 1943–44. Traveled Europe, USA; resides in Paris since 1956. COMMISSIONS: War Memorial for Middletown, Ohio, 1949. AWARDS: William and Noma Copley Foundation Grant, 1957; Clark Foundation Grant. ADDRESS: c/o Dealer. DEALER: Albert Loeb Gallery. ONE-MAN EXHIBITIONS: (first) Galerie Furstenberg, Paris, 1959; Alexander Iolas Gallery, 1961; Galerias Augusta, Barcelona, 1955; Galerie J, Paris, 1962; Galerie Europe, Paris, 1963; Albert Loeb Gallery, 1964. GROUP: Dayton/AI, 1946; Cincinnati/AM, 1947; a gallery in Springfield, Ohio, 1947, 58; Goldsmith's Hall, London, 1952; III Biennial of Spanish-American Art, Barcelona, 1955; V Sao Paulo Biennial, 1959; Exposition Internationale de la Sculpture, Paris, 1961; Un Demi-Siecle de la Sculpture, Paris, 1962; Actualite de la Sculpture, Paris, 1963; Documenta III, Kassel, 1964. COLLECTIONS: U. of Arizona; Museum des 20. Jahrhunderts; New York Hilton Hotel; Yale U. BIBLIOGRAPHY: Hunter 4; Seuphor 3.

MILLER, KENNETH HAYES. b. March 11, 1878, Oneida, N.Y.; **d.** January 1, 1952, NYC. STUDIED: ASL, with H. S. Mowbray, Kenyon Cox, F. L. Mora, Frank V. DuMond. Traveled Europe. TAUGHT: New York School of Art, 1899–1911; ASL, 1911–35, 1937–43, 1945–52. MEMBER: NAD; Artists Equity; NIAL. AWARDS: Chicago/AI, Ada S. Garrett Prize, 1945; NAD, Gold Medal, 1943; NIAL, 1947. ONE-MAN EXHIBITIONS: Montross Gallery, NYC, 1922, 23, 25, 28; Rehn Galleries, 1929, 35; Utica, 1953; ASL,

1953. GROUP: Chicago/AI; The Armory Show, 1913; Buffalo/Albright; RISD; PAFA; Musee de Luxembourg, Paris; Brooklyn Museum; Carnegie; Corcoran; NAD; WMAA. COLLECTIONS: Andover/Phillips; Bibliotheque Nationale; Chicago/AI; Cleveland/MA; Columbus; Hartford/Wadsworth; Library of Congress; Los Angeles/County MA; MMA; MOMA; NYPL; PAFA; Phillips; San Diego; Utica; VMFA; WMAA. BIBLIOGRAPHY: American Artists Group Inc. 1, 3; Baur 7; Blesh 1; Brown; **Burroughs;** Cahill and Barr, eds.; Cheney, M. C.; Goodrich and Baur 1; Hall; *Index of 20th Century Artists;* Hunter 5; Jewell 2; McCurdy, ed.; Mellquist; **Miller;** Pach 3; Pagano; Phillips 2; Reese; Richardson; Wight 2.

MILLER, RICHARD K. b. March 15, 1930, Fairmount, W. Va. STUDIED: American U., with William H. Calfee, 1949–53, BA; Columbia U., with John Heliker, 1956, MA; PAFA, 1948, with Franklin Watkins. Traveled Europe and USA extensively. TEACHES privately. Professional actor-singer. AWARDS: Fulbright Fellowship (Paris), 1953; Gertrude V. Whitney Scholarship, 1948, 56. ADDRESS: 104 East 96 Street, NYC. DEALER: The Graham Gallery. ONE-MAN EXHIBITIONS: (first) Washington, D.C., Public Library, 1945; Trans-Lux Gallery, Washington, D.C., 1948; Watkins Gallery, Washington, D.C., 1951; Bader Gallery, Washington, D.C., 1954, 61; Baltimore/MA, 1955; The Graham Gallery, 1960, 62, 63. GROUP: WMAA Annual; PAFA Annual; WMAA, Fulbright Artists, 1958; Salon National, Paris; Corcoran, 1961; Pan-American Union, Washington, D.C.; U. of Nebraska; San Antonio/McNay, 1960; Carnegie, 1961. COLLECTIONS: U. of Arizona; Columbia U.; Phillips.

MILLMAN, EDWARD. b. January 1, 1907, Chicago, Ill.; **d.** February 11, 1964, Woodstock, N.Y. STUDIED: Chicago Art Institute School, 1923–28, with Leon Kroll; privately with Diego Rivera in Mexico City, 1934–35 (fresco painting). TAUGHT: Florida Gulf Coast Art Center, Inc., 1951; Indiana U., 1951–52; Washington U., 1952; U. of Arkansas, 1953; Cornell U., 1954; Layton School of Art, 1955; U. of Buffalo, 1955, summer, 1956; ASL, 1954–56, summer, 1950; Munson-Williams-Proctor Institute, Utica, N.Y., 1955–56; Rensselaer Polytechnic Institute, 1956–64. COMMISSIONS (murals): US Post Offices in Moline, Ill., 1935, Decatur, Ill., 1936, and St. Louis, Mo. (with Mitchell Siporin), 1939–41; Chicago City Hall. AWARDS: Guggenheim Foundation Fellowship, 1945; Ohio U., First Prize, 1952. ONE-MAN EXHIBITIONS: Chicago/AI, 1956, 62; The Downtown Gallery, 1942; A.A.A. Gallery, NYC, 1948; U. of Kansas City, 1949; Louisiana State U., 1949; Florida State U., 1949; Clearwater/Gulf Coast, 1950; Indiana U., 1951; U. of Arkansas, 1953; Tulsa/Philbrook, 1953; The Alan Gallery, 1954; Cornell U., 1954; Layton School of Art, 1955; Buffalo/Albright, 1955; Utica, 1956; Lee Nordness Gallery, NYC, 1959, 61; Rensselaer Polytechnic Institute, 1961; Galleria d'Arte Annunciata, Milan, 1960. GROUP: WMAA Annuals; Chicago/AI; Brooklyn Museum; and many others. COLLECTIONS: Abbott Laboratories; Brandeis U.; Brooklyn Museum; Chicago/AI; Clearwater/Gulf Coast; Jewish Museum; MOMA; PAFA; U. of Pennsylvania; St. Louis/City; US Navy; Utica; WMAA; Washington U.; Youngstown/Butler. BIBLIOGRAPHY: Bruce and Watson; Nordness, ed.; Pousette-Dart, ed.; Zaidenberg, ed.

MITCHELL, FRED. b. November 24, 1923, Meridian, Miss. STUDIED: Carnegie Institute of Technology, 1942–43; Cranbrook Academy of Art, 1946–48, BFA, MFA; Academy of Fine Arts, Rome. TAUGHT: Positano (Italy) Art Workshop, 1956; Cranbrook Academy of Art, 1955–59; NYU, 1961– . A co-founder of the Tanager Gallery, NYC. COMMISSIONS: Mississippi State College for Women (cast concrete screen). AWARDS: Scholarship to Carnegie Institute of Technology; Traveling Fellowship (Italy), 1948–51. ADDRESS: 128 Front Street, NYC. DEALER: The Howard Wise Gallery, NYC. ONE-MAN EXHIBITIONS: (first) Municipal Gallery, Jackson, Miss., 1942; Tanager Gallery, NYC, 1953; Positano (Italy) Art Workshop, 1956; The Howard Wise Gallery, Cleveland, 1957, 59; The Howard Wise Gallery, NYC, 1960, 63; i Gallery, La Jolla, 1964; Kasha Heman, Chicago, 1964. GROUP: SRGM, Younger American Painters, 1954; Walker, Vanguard, 1955; Carnegie, 1961; Dallas/MFA, 1954; Cranbrook, 1958. COLLECTIONS: Columbus; Cranbrook.

MITCHELL, JOAN. b. 1926, Chicago, Ill. STUDIED: Smith College, 1942–44; Columbia U.; Chicago Art Institute School, 1944–47, BFA; NYU, 1950, MFA. Resides in Paris. ADDRESS: c/o The Stable Gallery. DEALERS: The Stable Gallery; Galerie Lawrence. ONE-MAN EXHIBITIONS: St. Paul Gallery, 1950; The New Gallery, NYC, 1952; The Stable Gallery, 1953, 54, 55, 57, 58, 61; Galerie Neufville, Paris, 1960; B. C. Holland Gallery, 1961; Dwan Gallery; Southern Illinois U.; Jacques Dubourg, Paris, 1962; Galerie Lawrence, 1962; Klipstein & Kornfeld, Berne, 1962; MIT, 1962. GROUP: U. of Illinois, 1950; WMAA, 1950, 55; Chicago/AI; Walker, Vanguard, 1955; Corcoran; Arts Club of Chicago; U. of North Carolina; Minneapolis/Institute. COLLECTIONS: Basel; Buffalo/Albright; Chase Manhattan Bank; Chicago/AI; MOMA; Phillips; Rockefeller Institute; The Singer Company Inc.; Union Carbide Corp.; WMAA; Walker. BIBLIOGRAPHY: Baur 5; Blesh 1; Friedman, ed.; Hunter 1; McCourbrey; *Metro;* Nordness, ed.; Read 2; Seuphor 1.

MITCHELL, WALLACE. b. October 9, 1911, Detroit, Mich. STUDIED: Northwestern U., BA; Cranbrook Academy of Art, with Zoltan Sepeshy; Columbia U., MA. TAUGHT: Cranbrook Academy of Art, 1936– . AWARDS: Springfield, Ill./State, Old Northwest Territory Exhibition; Detroit/Institute, 1945. ADDRESS: Cranbrook Academy of Art, Bloomfield Hills, Mich. ONE-MAN EXHIBITIONS: The Bertha Schaefer Gallery, 1950, 57, 58; Cranbrook, 1947, 53; U. of Minnesota, 1954; Detroit Artists Market, 1938. GROUP: Chicago/AI, 1938–41; Detroit/Institute; Buffalo/Albright, 1939; U. of Nebraska; Springfield, Ill./State, Old Northwest Territory Exhibition. COLLECTIONS: Cranbrook; Detroit/Institute.

MOHOLY-NAGY, LAZLO. b. July 20, 1895, Bacsbarsod, Hungary; **d.** November 24, 1947, Chicago, Ill. STUDIED: U. of Budapest, 1913–14, LLB. TAUGHT: Staatliche Bauhaus, Berlin, 1922; a founding collaborator, with Gyorgy Kepes and Robert Wolff, of the Institute of Design, Chicago, 1938–42; Director of the New Bauhaus, Chicago. Designed for State Opera and the Piscator Theatre, Berlin, 1928. Traveled Europe extensively. To England, 1935, where he produced three volumes of photo documents and a film, "Life of the Lobster." To USA 1937. ONE-MAN EXHIBITIONS: Harvard U., 1950; Amsterdam/Stedelijk; Brno,

Czechoslovakia; Hamburg; Mannheim; Cologne; Budapest/National; Stockholm/National; A.F.A.; The London Gallery, London, 1937. **RETROSPECTIVE:** SRGM, 1947. **GROUP:** WMAA; MOMA; SRGM; Yale U.; Harvard U. **COLLECTIONS:** Chicago/AI; Dayton/AI; Detroit/Institute; Jacksonville/AM; Los Angeles/County MA; MOMA; SFMA; SRGM. **BIBLIOGRAPHY:** Barr 1; Blanchard; Cassou; Frost; Giedion-Welcker 2; Goodrich and Baur 1; Huyghe; Janis and Blesh 1; Janis, S.; Langui; **Moholy-Nagy;** Morris; Motherwell 1; Ramsden 1; Selz, J.; Seuphor 3; Valentine 2.

MOLLER, HANS. b. March 20, 1905, Wuppertal-Barmen, Germany. **STUDIED:** Art School Barmen, 1919–27; Academy of Fine Arts, Berlin, 1927–28. To USA 1928. **TAUGHT:** Cooper Union, 1944–56. **MEMBER:** Federation of Modern Painters and Sculptors. **COMMISSIONS:** William Douglas McAdams Inc., NYC (mural); Percival Goodman, Architect; tapestry design for synagogue ark curtains; A.F.A./Stained Glass Industry (stained glass window). **AWARDS:** Art Directors Club, NYC, Distinctive Merit Award, 1944, 55, 56; Corcoran, Hon. Men., 1949; American Institute of Graphic Art, Certificate of Excellence, 1949 (2), 51; National Religious Art Exhibition, Detroit, First Prize, 1964. **ADDRESS:** 150 East 49 Street, NYC. **DEALER:** The Midtown Galleries. **ONE-MAN EXHIBITIONS:** (first) Bonestell Gallery, NYC, 1942, also 1943; Arts Club of Chicago, 1945; U. of Michigan, 1945; Kleemann Gallery, NYC, 1945, 47, 48, 49, 50; Pen and Palette Gallery, St. Louis, 1949; Macon, Ga., 1949; Atlanta/AA, 1950; Grace Borgenicht Gallery Inc., 1951, 53, 54, 56; Fine Arts Associates, NYC, 1957, 60; Albert Landry, NYC, 1962; The Midtown Galleries, 1964. **RETROSPECTIVE:** The Olsen Foundation Inc., Leetes Island, Conn., Hans Moller: 1926–56, circ., 1956–64. **GROUP:** MMA; Brooklyn Museum; PAFA; Chicago/AI; The Print Club, Philadelphia; Des Moines; Detroit/Institute; Corcoran; U. of Illinois; Walker; Buffalo/Albright; SFMA; WMAA; Colby College; A.F.A. **COLLECTIONS:** Bennington College; Brooklyn Museum; Detroit/Institute; U. of Georgia; IBM; MOMA; Meta-Mold Aluminum Co.; NYPL; PAFA; Phillips; Society of the Four Arts; WMAA; Walker; Washington U.; Wuppertal. **BIBLIOGRAPHY:** Baur 5; Genauer.

MORIN, THOMAS. b. September 22, 1934, Malone, N.Y. **STUDIED:** Massachusetts School of Art, with Lawrence Kupferman, 1952–56, BS.Ed.; Cranbrook Academy of Art, 1956–57, MFA; Academy of Fine Arts, Florence, Italy, 1960–61. Traveled Europe. **TAUGHT:** Cranbrook Academy of Art, 1957–58; Silvermine Guild, 1958–60; RISD, 1961– . **MEMBER:** American Foundrymens Society. **COMMISSIONS:** Brown U. (40 x 8-ft. cast aluminum relief). **AWARDS:** Fulbright Fellowship, 1960; Silvermine Guild, First Prize, 1960; Rhode Island Arts Festival, First Prize. **ADDRESS:** 62 Waterman Street, Providence, R.I. **DEALER:** The Kornblee Gallery. **ONE-MAN EXHIBITIONS:** (first) Margaret Brown Gallery, Boston, 1954; Gallery Four, Detroit, 1957; Kanegis Gallery, Boston, 1958, 60; Silvermine Guild, 1960; The Kornblee Gallery, 1961, 64; Lincoln, Mass./De Cordova, 1963; Providence (R.I.) Art Club, 1963. **GROUP:** Boston Arts Festival, 1953, 54, 55, 58, 59, 60, 62; Audubon Artists Annual, 1962; PAFA, 1958, 64; Detroit/Institute Annuals, 1958–64; ICA, Boston, View, 1960; WMAA Annual, 1961; Hartford/Wadsworth, Eleven New England Sculptors, 1963. **COLLECTIONS:** Brown U.; VMFA.

MORRIS, CARL. b. May 12, 1911, Yorba Linda, Calif. **STUDIED:** Fullerton Junior College, 1930–31; Chicago Art Institute School; Kunstgewerbeschule, Vienna, 1933–34; Academy of Fine Arts, Vienna, 1933–34. **TAUGHT:** ASL, 1937–38; privately, 1940–41; U. of Colorado, summer, 1957. **FEDERAL A.P.:** Director at Spokane, Wash., 1938–39. **COMMISSIONS** (murals): US Post Office, Eugene, Ore., 1941–42; Hall of Religion, Oregon Centennial Exposition, Portland, 1959. **AWARDS:** Austro-American Scholarship, 1935; Werkbund Scholarship, 1939; Seattle/AM, Margaret E. Fuller Award, 1946; SFMA, Anne Bremer Memorial Prize, 1946; Pepsi-Cola Bronze Medal, 1948; SFMA, James D. Phelan Award, 1950; Seattle/AM, Hon. Men., 1939, 46, 47; Seattle/AM, Second Prize, 1943; Denver/AM, P.P., 1946; U. of Illinois, P.P., 1958; Institute of International Education Fellowship (Paris), 1935–36. **ADDRESS:** 919 N.W. Skyline Boulevard, Portland, Ore. **DEALER:** Kraushaar Galleries. **ONE-MAN EXHIBITIONS:** (first) Foundation de Etats-Unis, Paris, 1935; Paul Elder Gallery, San Francisco, 1937; Seattle/AM, 1940; Portland, Ore./AM, 1946, 52, 55; California Palace, 1947; U. of

Oregon, 1947; Santa Barbara/MA, 1956; Opportunity Gallery, NYC, 1948; SFMA, 1958; Reed College, 1956; Zivile Gallery, Los Angeles, 1956; Mills College, 1956; Kraushaar Galleries, 1956, 57, 58; Rotunda Gallery, San Francisco, 1956; U. of Colorado, 1957. RETROSPECTIVE: A.F.A./Ford Foundation, circ., 1960. GROUP: Chicago/AI; Carnegie; Corcoran; MMA; WMAA; SRGM, Younger American Painters, 1954; III Sao Paulo Biennial, 1955. COLLECTIONS: Buffalo/Albright; California Palace; Colorado Springs/FA; U. of Colorado; Denver/AM; Eastern Oregon College; Houston/MFA; U. of Illinois; MMA; Mills College; U. of Oregon; Portland, Ore./AM; Portland State College; Provincetown/Chrysler; Reed College; Rochester/Memorial; SFMA; SRGM; Santa Barbara/MA; Sao Paulo; Seattle/AM; Southern Oregon College; Stanford U.; Toronto; Utica; WMAA; Walker; Wichita/AM. BIBLIOGRAPHY: Nordness, ed.; Pousette-Dart, ed.; Read 2.

MORRIS, GEORGE L. K. b. November 14, 1905, NYC. STUDIED: Groton School, 1924; Yale U., 1928, BA; ASL, with John Sloan, Kenneth Hayes Miller; Academie Moderne, Paris, with F. Leger, Amedee Ozenfant. Traveled around the world, and spends much time in Paris. TAUGHT: ASL, 1943–44; St. John's College, Annapolis, Md., 1960–61. Editor: *Yale Literary Magazine*, 1928; *Plastique*, Paris, 1937–39; *The Miscellany*, 1929–31. MEMBER: American Abstract Artists (a founder, 1936, and President, 1948–50); Federation of Modern Painters and Sculptors. COMMISSIONS: Lenox (Mass.) Elementary School (mosaic). AWARDS: Pepsi-Cola, 1948. ADDRESS: One Sutton Place South, NYC. DEALER: The Downtown Gallery. ONE-MAN EXHIBITIONS: (first) Curt Valentine Gallery, NYC, 1933; The Downtown Gallery, 1943, 44, 47, 50; Pittsfield/Berkshire, 1933; Museum of Living Art, NYC, 1935; Reinhardt Galleries, NYC, 1936; Passedoit Gallery, NYC, 1938; Galerie Pierre, Paris, 1936, 38; Galerie Colette Allendy, Paris, 1946; Yale U.; Mayor Gallery, London, 1936; J. Seligmann and Co., 1938; The Alan Gallery, 1955; ICA, Washington, D.C., 1958. GROUP: WMAA, annually; American Abstract Artists, annually; Federation of Modern Painters and Sculptors, annually; Salon des Realites Nouvelles, Paris. COLLECTIONS: Brandeis U.; Darmstadt/Kunsthalle; U. of Illinois; MMA; U. of Oklahoma; PAFA; PMA; Phillips; Pittsfield/Berkshire; Portland, Ore./AM; WMAA; Wichita/AM; Yale U. BIBLIOGRAPHY: American Abstract Artists, ed.; Arp; Baur 7; Biederman 1; Blanchard; Blesh 1; Cheney, M. C.; Flanagan; Frost; Kootz 2; McCurdy, ed.; **Morris;** Newmeyer; Pagano; Pearson 2; Pousette-Dart, ed.; Read 2; Ritchie 1; Seuphor 1, 3; "What Abstract Art Means to Me."

MORRIS, KYLE R. b. January 17, 1918, Des Moines, Iowa. STUDIED: Northwestern U., 1935–39, BA, 1940, MA; Chicago Art Institute School, 1935–39; Cranbrook Academy of Art, 1947, MFA. US Army Air Force, 1942–45. Traveled Europe. TAUGHT: Stephens College, 1940–41; U. of Texas, 1941–42, 1945–46; U. of Minnesota, 1947–51; U. of California, Berkeley, 1952–54; Cooper Union, 1958. Art Consultant to Sandak, Inc. Editor and Publisher, *Contemporary Slides* (Magazine), 1954–59. Organized the Vanguard, 1955, exhibition for The Walker Art Center. AWARDS: Walker, P.P., 1948; SFMA, Oil Painting Award, 1953; II Inter-American Paintings and Prints Biennial, Mexico City, 1960, Hon. Men.; Ford Foundation, P.P., 1963. ADDRESS: 243 East 17 Street, NYC. DEALER: The Kootz Gallery. ONE-MAN EXHIBITIONS: (first) Pepsi-Cola Opportunity Art Gallery, NYC, 1945; Walker, 1952; Des Moines, 1955; The Stable Gallery, 1955; The Kootz Gallery, 1959, 60, 62, 63; Galleria d'Arte del Naviglio, Milan, 1960. GROUP: WMAA Annuals from 1952; SRGM, Younger American Painters, 1954; U. of Illinois, 1954, 56, 61, 63; Chicago/AI, 1954; U. of Nebraska, 1954; Corcoran, 1956, 58, 61, 63; Minneapolis/Institute, 1957; WMAA, Nature in Abstraction, 1958; Brussels World's Fair, 1958; VMFA, 1958; Rome-New York Foundation, Rome, 1958; PAFA, 1959; Detroit/Institute, 1959; Carnegie, 1961; SRGM, Abstract Expressionists and Imagists, 1961; Brandeis U., 1963. COLLECTIONS: Buffalo/Albright; Chase Manhattan Bank; Continental Grain Company; Des Moines; Detroit/Institute; U. of Illinois; Newark Museum; Reynolds Metals Co.; SRGM; The Singer Company Inc.; Toledo/MA; Union Carbide Corp.; WMAA; Walker; Washington U. BIBLIOGRAPHY: Baur 5.

MOTHERWELL, ROBERT. b. January 24, 1915, Aberdeen, Wash. STUDIED: Stanford U., 1932–37, AB (Philosophy); California School of Fine Arts, *ca.* 1935; Harvard U., 1937–38; U. of Grenoble, summer, 1938; Columbia U., 1940–41; primarily self-taught in art. Traveled extensively, USA, Europe, Mexico. TAUGHT: Hunter College, 1951–57; lectures extensively in American universities and museums. Series of paintings, "Elegy to Spanish Republic," begun 1947. Co-founder of a school, "Subject of the Artist," with William Baziotes, Barnett Newman, and Mark Rothko, NYC, 1948. Art Director, *Partisan Review*, 1962– . Director, *Documents of Modern Art*, NYC. AWARDS: IV Guggenheim International, 1964 ($2,500). m. Helen Frankenthaler. ADDRESS: 173 East 94 Street, NYC. DEALER: Marlborough-Gerson Gallery Inc. ONE-MAN EXHIBITIONS: (first) Art of This Century, NYC, 1944; The Kootz Gallery, 1946, 47, 49, 52; SFMA, 1946; Arts Club of Chicago, 1946; New London, 1953; Bennington College, 1959; Sidney Janis Gallery, 1957, 59, 61, 62; Sao Paulo, 1961; Pasadena/AM, 1962; Berggruen, Paris, 1961; Galleria Odyssia, Rome, 1962; Galerie der Spiegel, Cologne, 1962; Smith College, 1963; MIT, 1963; Galerie Schmela, Dusseldorf (two-man, with Conrad Marca-Relli). GROUP: Venice Biennial; Sao Paulo Biennial; Carnegie; WMAA Annuals; Tate, Dunn International, 1964; Tate, Gulbenkian International, 1964; Documenta II & III, Kassel, 1959, 64; American Painting and Sculpture, Moscow, 1959; Brussels World's Fair, 1958; Chicago/AI Annuals; Boston Arts Festival. COLLECTIONS: Andover/Phillips; Baltimore/MA; Bennington College; Brooklyn Museum; Brown U.; Buffalo/Albright; Cleveland/MA; Fort Dodge/Banden; Harvard U.; Houston/MFA; MMA; MOMA; U. of Minnesota; NYU; U. of Nebraska; Raleigh/NCMA; Rio de Janeiro; Smith College; Smithsonian; Society of the Four Arts; Tel Aviv; Toronto; WMAA; Washington U.; Yale U. BIBLIOGRAPHY: Baur 7; Biederman 1; Blanchard; Blesh 1; Eliot; Finkelstein; Flanagan; Goodrich and Baur 1; Greenberg 1; Haftman; Henning; Hess, T. B.; Hunter 1, 5; Janis and Blesh 1; Janis, S.; McCourbrey; McCurdy, ed.; Mendelowitz; *Metro;* Miller, ed. 2; **Motherwell 1, 2; Motherwell, ed.; Motherwell and Reinhardt, eds.;** Nordness, ed.; Paalen; Ponente; Pousette-Dart, ed.; Read 2; Ritchie 1; Seitz 1, 2; Seuphor 1; Soby 5; "What Abstract Art Means to Me."

MOY, SEONG. b. October 20, 1921, Canton, China. To USA 1931. STUDIED: Federal Art Project School, with Ben Swanson; St. Paul School of Art, 1936–40, with Cameron Booth; ASL, with Vaclav Vytlacil; Hofmann School, 1941–42, with Hans Hofmann; Atelier 17, NYC, 1948–50. US Air Force, 1943–46. TAUGHT: Indiana U., 1953; U. of Minnesota, 1951; Smith College, 1954; Vassar College, 1955; Columbia U., 1959– ; Cooper Union, 1957– ; ASL, 1963– ; Moy Summer School, Provincetown. FEDERAL A.P.: Assistant in graphic shop. COMMISSIONS: International Graphic Arts Society (3 editions); New York Hilton Hotel. AWARDS: John Hay Whitney Fellowship, 1950; Guggenheim Foundation Fellowship, 1955; Minneapolis/Institute, First Prize, 1939; The Print Club, Philadelphia, First Prize, 1948; Brooklyn Museum, P.P., 1953. ADDRESS: 100 La Salle Street, NYC. DEALER: Grand Central Moderns. ONE-

Robert Motherwell   *Summertime in Italy, #8.*

MAN EXHIBITIONS: (first) Carmel (Calif.) Art Association, 1943; Hacker Gallery, NYC, 1950; Grand Central Moderns, 1959; Dubin Gallery, Philadelphia, 1950; U. of Minnesota, 1951; The Howard Wise Gallery, Cleveland, 1958; Ashby Gallery, NYC, 1947; Carlebach Gallery, NYC, 1949; Springfield, Ill./State, 1949; The New Gallery, NYC, 1951, 52, 54; Boris Mirski Gallery, 1955; Yamada Gallery, Kyoto, 1959; The Contemporaries, 1955. GROUP: MMA, 1950; Carnegie, 1955; U. of Minnesota; Brooklyn Museum; Chicago/AI; MOMA; PAFA; Library of Congress; U. of Illinois, 1951, 53, 54; New York World's Fair, 1964–65. COLLECTIONS: Abbott Laboratories; Andover/Phillips; Bibliotheque Nationale; Boston/MFA; Brooklyn Museum; Indiana U.; Library of Congress; MMA; MOMA; Memphis/Brooks; U. of Minnesota; NYPL; PAFA; PMA; Smith College; Smithsonian; Tel Aviv; Victoria and Albert Museum; WMAA; Walker; Worcester/AM.

MOYER, ROY. b. August 20, 1921, Allentown, Pa. STUDIED: Columbia U., BA, MA; U. of Oslo; self-taught in art. Traveled extensively; resided in Europe (mainly Greece), four years. TAUGHT: U. of Salonica, Greece, 1948–51; U. of Toronto, 1953–55. Director, American Federation of Arts. ADDRESS: 201 West 85 Street, NYC. DEALER: The Contemporaries. ONE-MAN EXHIBITIONS: (first) Salonica, Greece, 1949; The Contemporaries, 1958, 59, 61, 62. GROUP: WMAA Annual, 1960; U. of Illinois, 1959. COLLECTIONS: Sara Roby Foundation; Wichita/AM.

MULLER, JAN. b. December 27, 1922, Hamburg, Germany; **d.** January 29, 1958, NYC. Traveled Czechoslovakia, Switzerland, Holland, southern France, 1933–41. To USA 1941. STUDIED: Hofmann School, 1945–50. Cofounder of Hansa Gallery, NYC, 1952. ONE-MAN EXHIBITIONS: (first) Hansa Gallery, NYC, 1953, also 1954, 55, 56, 57, 58; Sun Gallery, Provincetown, 1955, 56; U. of Minnesota, 1960; The Zabriskie Gallery, 1961. RETROSPECTIVE: Hansa Gallery, NYC, 1959; SRGM, 1962. GROUP: 813 Broadway (Gallery), NYC, 1952; Chicago/AI, 1953; U. of Minnesota, 1955; The Stable Gallery Annual, 1956; Jewish Museum, The New York School, Second Generation, 1957; WMAA, Young America, 1957; Carnegie, 1958; Festival of Two Worlds, Spoleto, 1958;

ICA, Boston, 1958, 59; MOMA, New Images of Man, 1959; A.F.A., The Figure, circ., 1960. COLLECTIONS: Charlotte/Mint; MOMA; Newark Museum. BIBLIOGRAPHY: Messer.

MULLICAN, LEE. b. December 2, 1919, Chickasha, Okla. STUDIED: Abilene Christian College, 1937; U. of Oklahoma, 1939; Kansas City Art Institute and School of Design, 1941, with Fletcher Martin. Corps of Army Engineers, 1942–46. ADDRESS: 370 Mesa Road, Santa Monica, Calif. DEALER: The Willard Gallery. ONE-MAN EXHIBITIONS: SFMA, 1949; Dynaton Exhibition, San Francisco, 1951; Santa Barbara/MA, 1958; The Willard Gallery, 1950, 52, 53, 59, 61; Paul Kantor Gallery, 1952, 53, 56; The Swetzoff Gallery, 1950; The Rose Rabow Gallery, 1955. GROUP: Corcoran, 1948; MMA, 1951; Denver/AM Annuals, 1950, 55, 56, 57; Chicago/AI, 1951, 54; Carnegie, 1951; Sao Paulo, 1955; WMAA Annuals, 1952, 56; Santa Barbara/MA, 1957; MOMA, 1957; U. of Illinois, 1953, 55, 57; U. of Nebraska, 1953; Rome-New York Foundation, Rome, 1960; Pasadena/AM, 1961. COLLECTIONS: Colorado Springs/FA; Denver/AM; Detroit/Institute; MOMA; SFMA; San Francisco Municipal Art Commission; Santa Barbara/MA. BIBLIOGRAPHY: Pousette-Dart, ed.; Richardson.

MURCH, WALTER TANDY. b. August 17, 1907, Toronto, Canada. STUDIED: Ontario College of Art, 1924–27, with Arthur Lismer, L. Harris; ASL, 1929–30, with Kenneth Hayes Miller, William Von Schlegell; Grand Central School, NYC, 1930, with Arshile Gorky; and privately with Gorky, 1931–32. US citizen, 1948. Traveled Mexico, Canada, France. TAUGHT: Pratt Institute, 1952–61; NYU, 1961; Boston U., 1961– ; Columbia U., 1964. COMMISSIONS: *Scientific American; Fortune* Magazine. AWARDS: NIAL Grant, 1961; Ford Foundation, P.P. (2); U. of Illinois, P.P., 1949. ADDRESS: 468 Riverside Drive, NYC. DEALER: Betty Parsons Gallery. ONE-MAN EXHIBITIONS: (first) Wakefield Gallery, NYC, 1941; Betty Parsons Gallery, 1947, 49, 51, 54, 57, 59, 62; Mortimer Brandt, NYC, 1946; St. Louis Art Center, 1949; Allan Frumkin Gallery, Chicago, 1953; Worth Avenue Gallery, Palm Beach, Fla., 1955; Choate School, Wallingford, Conn., 1959; Hampton Gallery, Huntington, W. Va., 1964. GROUP: WMAA, The New Decade, 1954–55;

Walter Tandy Murch   *Broken Rock. 1964*

MMA, Edward Root Collection, 1953; XXVIII Venice Biennial, 1956; WMAA Annuals, 1945–64; Chicago/AI, 1945, 46, 54, 56, 58, 59, 60, 62, 63; Corcoran, 1945, 46, 52, 53, 54, 55, 58, 61, 63; PAFA, 1945, 46, 53, 54, 55, 57, 59, 60, 63, 64; ICA, London, American Painting; U. of Illinois, 1951, 52, 54, 61, 63; Detroit/Institute, 1952, 57; A.F.A., Private Worlds, 1959; New School for Social Research, The Creative Process, 1961; Andover/Phillips, 1945; Worcester/AM, 1947; A.F.A., World at Work, 1955; Contemporary American Painting, Tokyo, 1952; PMA, 1954; Dallas/MFA, 1954; Indianapolis/Herron, 1954; Milwaukee, American Painting, 1760–1960, 1960; Minneapolis/Institute, American Painting, 1945–57, 1957; Walker, 1955; NIAL, 1961; ART:USA:59, NYC, 1959; Carnegie, 1964. **COLLECTIONS:** Andover/Phillips; Barnes Foundation; Brooklyn Museum; Buffalo/Albright; Carnegie; Chase Manhattan Bank; Corcoran; First National City Bank; Hallmark Collection; Hartford/Wadsworth; IBM; U. of Illinois; Jay Mfg. Co.; S. C. Johnson & Son, Inc.; Kalamazoo/Institute; Lane Foundation; MMA; Newark Museum; Omaha/Joslyn; PAFA; Toledo/MA; Union Carbide Corp.; Upjohn Co.; Utica; WGMA; WMAA. **BIBLIOGRAPHY:** Baur 7; Flanagan; Goodrich and Baur 1; Nordness, ed.; Pousette-Dart, ed.; Soby 5.

n

NADELMAN, ELIE. b. February 20, 1882, Warsaw, Poland; **d.** December 28, 1946, NYC. Studied: Art Academy, Warsaw, 1901; Academie Colarossi, Paris, 1904; privately with Konstantin Lazczka, 1902. Imperial Russian Army, 1900. Traveled Russia, Europe, USA. To USA 1914. Awards: Sztuka Prize, 1902. One-man Exhibitions: (first) Galerie Drouant, Paris, 1909, also 1913; Scott and Fowles Gallery, NYC, 1917, 25; Photo-Secession, NYC, 1915; M. Knoedler & Co., NYC, 1919, 27; Galerie Bernheim-Jeune, Paris, 1920, 27; Arts Club of Chicago, 1925; MOMA, 1948. Group: Non-Jury Salon, Berlin, 1913; The Armory Show, 1913; Salon des Artistes Independants, Paris, 1905–08; Salon d'Automne, Paris, 1905–08; Photo-Secession, NYC, 1915; Carnegie, 1938; WMAA; MOMA; MMA. Collections: MOMA; Newark Museum; Utica; WMAA. Bibliography: Baur 7; Biddle 3; Birnbaum; Blesh 1; Brumme; Cheney, M. C.; Goodrich and Baur 1; Hunter 5; Huyghe; *Index of 20th Century Artists;* **Kirstein 1, 3;** McCurdy, ed.; Mendelowitz; Motherwell 1; **Murrell 2;** Richardson; Ringel, ed.; Selz, J.

NAKIAN, REUBEN. b. August 10, 1897, College Point, N.Y. Studied: Robert Henri School, with Homer Boss, A. S. Baylinson; ASL, 1912; apprenticed to Paul Manship, 1917–20, and Gaston Lachaise. Traveled Italy, France. Taught: Newark Fine Arts and Industrial Arts College; Pratt Institute, 1949. Commissions: NYU, 1960 (sculpture). Awards: Guggenheim Foundation Fellowship, 1930; Ford Foundation Grant, 1959 ($10,000); Sao Paulo, 1960. Address: c/o Dealer. Dealer: Charles Egan Gallery. One-man Exhibitions: (first) The

Downtown Gallery, 1933, also 1935; Charles Egan Gallery, 1949, 50, 52, 63, 64; Stewart-Marean (Gallery), NYC, 1958; WGMA, 1963; Los Angeles/County MA, 1962; Sao Paulo, 1961. Group: Salons of America, NYC, 1922; Whitney Studio Club, NYC; WMAA; Chicago/AI; PAFA. Collections: MOMA; NYU. Bibliography: Cahill and Barr, eds.; Cheney, M. C.

NATKIN, ROBERT. b. 1930, Chicago, Ill. Studied: Chicago Art Institute School, 1952. Address: 245 West 107 Street, NYC. Dealer: Poindexter Gallery. One-man Exhibitions: Wells Street Gallery, Chicago, 1957, 58; Poindexter Gallery, 1959, 61, 63; Fairweather-Hardin Gallery, 1963; Ferus Gallery, 1960. Group: Chicago/AI, 1955, 57, 59, 62; Chicago/AI, Exhibition Momentum, 1950, 56, 57; WMAA, Young America, 1960; Carnegie, 1961; WGMA, Lyricism in Abstract Art, 1962; ICA, Boston, 1961; International Mitsubishi, Tokyo and other Japanese cities, 1963. Collections: Carnegie; Hartford/Wadsworth; ICA, Boston; SRGM; WMAA; Worcester/AM.

NEAL, REGINALD. b. May 20, 1909, Leicester, England. Studied: Bradley U., 1932, BA; Yale U., 1929–30; State U. of Iowa, summer, 1936; The U. of Chicago, 1939, MA (Art History); Colorado Springs Fine Arts Center, summer, 1941. Taught: Millikin U., 1940–46; U. of Mississippi, 1951–57; New Paltz, 1957–58; Southern Illinois U., 1958–59; Escuela de Bellas Artes, San Miguel de Allende, Mexico, summer, 1944; The Contemporaries Graphic Center, NYC, summer, 1956; Douglass College, 1959– . Commissions: A.A.A. Gallery, NYC (two editions of lithographs). **AWARDS:** Film Council of America, Golden Reel Award, 1956 (American Film Festival, Chicago), for a 30-min. color film, "Color Lithography—An Art Medium." **ADDRESS:** c/o Dealer. **DEALER:** The Amel Gallery. **ONE-MAN EXHIBITIONS:** Decatur, 1944; South Bend Art Center, 1950; A.A.A. Gallery, Chicago, 1950; Davenport/Municipal, 1945, 51; U. of Mississippi, 1951, 55; The Salpeter Gallery, 1953; New Paltz, 1953; Pratt-Contemporaries, NYC, 1960; Allan Stone Gallery, 1962; Primus-Stuart Gallery, Los Angeles, 1962. **GROUP:** MMA; Cincinnati/AM, 1954, 56, 58; Brooklyn Museum; Library of Congress; Houston/MFA, 1956; Oakland/AM; Riverside Museum; Gallery of Modern Art, Ljubljana, Yugoslavia, III & IV International Exhibitions of Prints, 1959, 61. **COLLECTIONS:** Cincinnati/AM; Davenport/Municipal; Decatur; Grenchen; Library of Congress; Memphis/Brooks; Princeton U.; Queens U.; Southern Illinois U. **BIBLIOGRAPHY:** Reese.

NEPOTE, ALEXANDER. b. November 6, 1913, Valley Home, Calif. **STUDIED:** California College of Arts and Crafts, BA; Mills College; U. of California, MA. **TAUGHT:** California College of Arts and Crafts, 1945–50; San Francisco State College, 1950– . **AWARDS:** SFMA, James D. Phelan Award, 1941, 42; Oakland/AM, P.P., 1955; Oakland/AM, 1947, 48; San Mateo County Fair, 1954, 57; San Francisco Art Festival, 1951, 53, 59, 60; Pasadena/AM, P.P., 1957; California State Fair, 1957, 58; California Palace, 1958; Oakland/AM, Silver Medal, 1957. **ADDRESS:** 410 Taylor Boulevard, Millbrae, Calif. **GROUP EXHIBITIONS:** United Nations Conference Exhibition, San Francisco, 1945; Grand Central, NYC, 1948; California Palace, 1947, 48, 52, 1959–61; U. of Illinois, 1951, 52; WMAA, 1951; A.F.A.; MMA, 1952; Sao Paulo, 1955; SFMA, 1955; a gallery in Provincetown, Mass., 1958; ART:USA:58, NYC, 1958; VMFA, American Painting, 1962. **COLLECTIONS:** California Palace; Denver/AM; Los Angeles/County MA; U. of Michigan; Mills College; Oakland/AM; Pasadena/AM; SFMA.

NEUMAN, ROBERT S. b. September 9, 1926, Kellogg, Ida. **STUDIED:** California School of Fine Arts; Mills College, with Max Beckmann;

U. of Idaho; Academy of Fine Arts, Stuttgart, with Willi Baumeister. Traveled Europe, USA. **TAUGHT:** Harvard U., Carpenter Center for Visual Arts, 1963–64; Brown U. **AWARDS:** Fulbright Fellowship, 1953; Boston Arts Festival, Grand Prize, 1961; Guggenheim Foundation Fellowship, 1956–57. **ADDRESS:** c/o Dealer. **DEALER:** Allan Stone Gallery. **ONE-MAN EXHIBITIONS:** Lincoln, Mass./De Cordova, 1963; Gump's Gallery, 1952; Felix Landau Gallery, 1954; La Escondida, Taos, N.M., 1956; Sala Vayreda, Barcelona, 1956; Galleria del Cavallino, Venice, 1957, 60; The Swetzoff Gallery, 1957, 58; Allan Stone Gallery, Harrison, N.Y., 1959; Gres Gallery, Washington, D.C., 1959; The Pace Gallery, Boston, 1960, 62. **GROUP:** California Palace, 1951; SFMA, 1951, 52, 53; Denver/AM, 1952; MMA, 1952; Kyoto, Japan, 1956; ICA, Boston, 1958, 59, 60; Carnegie, 1961; Seattle World's Fair, 1962; WMAA, 1952, 58; U. of Illinois, 1952, 61; PAFA, 1953; Colorado Springs/FA, 1953. **COLLECTIONS:** Boston U.; Carnegie; ICA, Boston; SFMA; Worcester/AM; Yale U.

NEVELSON, LOUISE. b. 1900, Kiev, Russia. To USA 1905. **STUDIED:** ASL, 1929–30, with Kenneth Hayes Miller; Hofmann School, Munich, 1931; assistant to Diego Rivera in Mexico City, 1932–33. Traveled Europe, Central and Latin America. **TAUGHT:** Educational Alliance, NYC; Great Neck (N.Y.) Adult Education Program; New York School for the Deaf. **MEMBER:** Artists Equity (President); Sculptors Guild (Vice President); Federation of Modern Painters and Sculptors (Vice President). **FEDERAL A.P.:** Easel painting. **AWARDS:** ART:USA:59, NYC, Grand Prize, 1959; Chicago/AI, The Mr. & Mrs. Frank G. Logan Prize, 1960. **ADDRESS:** 29 Spring Street, NYC. **DEALER:** The Pace Gallery, NYC and Boston. **ONE-MAN EXHIBITIONS:** (first) Karl Nierendorf Gallery, NYC, 1941, also 1943, 44, 46; Norlyst Gallery, NYC, 1941, 43; Lotte Jacobi Gallery, NYC, 1950; Grand Central Moderns, 1951, 54, 56, 57, 58; Esther Stuttman Gallery, NYC, 1958; Martha Jackson Gallery, 1959, 61; Daniel Cordier, Paris, 1960; David Herbert Gallery, NYC, 1960; Devorah Sherman Gallery, 1960; The Pace Gallery, Boston, 1960, 64; Sidney Janis Gallery, 1963; Hanover Gallery, 1963; Gimpel & Hanover Galerie, Zurich, 1964. **GROUP:** Sezession Gallery (Europe), 1933–38;

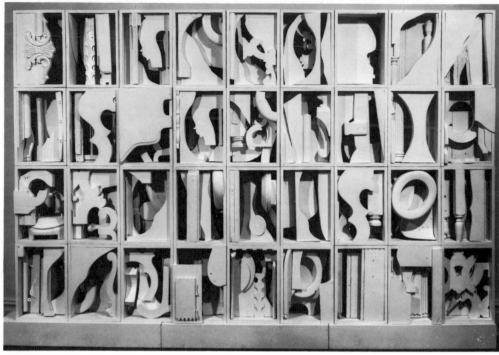

Louise Nevelson   *New Continent. 1962*

Contemporary Arts Gallery, NYC; Jacobsen Gallery, NYC; Society of Independent Artists, NYC; Brooklyn Museum; ACA Gallery; Federal Art Project Gallery, NYC, 1933–38; PAFA, 1944; VMFA, 1957; Riverside Museum, Directions in Sculpture, 1957; A.F.A., Art and the Found Object, circ., 1959; Jeanne Bucher, Paris (three-man), 1958; MOMA, Sixteen Americans, circ., 1959; ART:USA:59, NYC, 1959; Rome-New York Foundation, Rome, Ciphers, 1960; Utica, Art Across America, 1960; A.F.A., Unique Impressions, 1960; XXXI Venice Biennial, 1962; WMAA Annuals, 1947, 57, 61, 64; Federation of Modern Painters and Sculptors Annuals, 1955, 56, 57, 59; A.F.A., Contemporary Trends, circ., 1955–56; American Abstract Artists Annuals, 1956, 57, 59, 60; Documenta III, Kassel, 1964. COLLECTIONS: Birmingham, Ala./MA; Brandeis U.; Brooklyn Museum; Carnegie; Houston/MFA; MOMA; Newark Museum; Queens College; Riverside Museum; Sara Roby Foundation; Rockland Foundation; Tate; WMAA. BIBLIOGRAPHY: Baur 5; Goodrich and Baur 1; Janis and Blesh 1; *Metro;* Neumeyer; Seitz 2; Seuphor 3.

NEVELSON, MIKE. b. February 23, 1922, NYC. STUDIED: NYU; self-taught in art. Traveled Europe, Mediterranean, Africa, Central and Latin America. TEACHES occasionally. ADDRESS: 3 Milltown Road, New Fairfield, Conn. DEALER: The Amel Gallery. ONE-MAN EXHIBITIONS: (first) U. of Maine, 1953; Carl Siembab Gallery, Boston; Roko Gallery; Staempfli Gallery; The Amel Gallery, 1964. GROUP: Colby College; Boston Arts Festival; Carnegie, 1961; WMAA Annual, 1963; Houston/MFA, 1964. COLLECTIONS: Colby College; Hartford/Wadsworth; WMAA.

NEWBILL, AL. b. January 13, 1921, Springfield, Mo. STUDIED: Society of Arts and Crafts, Detroit, with John Caroll; Brooklyn Museum School, with John Ferren; Hofmann School, with Hans Hofmann. Traveled Europe, USA. TAUGHT: Southern Illinois U.; U. of California, Berkeley; Queens College; and privately. ADDRESS: 108 West 28 Street, NYC. ONE-MAN EXHIBITIONS: (first) Creative Gallery, NYC, 1949; Hendler Gallery, Philadelphia; Holland-Goldowsky Gallery, Chicago; Leo Castelli Inc.,

1959; Parma Gallery, NYC, 1960. **GROUP:** Detroit/Institute; Cleveland/MA; Santa Fe, N.M.; Rose Fried Gallery, International Collage Exhibition, 1956. **COLLECTIONS:** Southern Illinois U.

NEWMAN, BARNETT. b. January 29, 1905, NYC. **STUDIED:** City College of New York, 1927, BA; Cornell U., 1922–26; ASL, with Duncan Smith, John Sloan, William Von Schlegell. Traveled USA, Canada, Europe. **TAUGHT:** U. of Saskatchewan, 1959; U. of Pennsylvania, 1962–64. Co-founder of a school, "Subject of the Artist," with William Baziotes, Robert Motherwell, and Mark Rothko, NYC, 1948. **ADDRESS:** 685 West End Avenue, NYC. **ONE-MAN EXHIBITIONS:** (first) Betty Parsons Gallery, 1950, also 1951; Bennington College, 1958; French & Co. Inc., 1959; Allan Stone Gallery (two-man), 1962. **GROUP:** Chicago/AI, Abstract and Surrealist Art, 1948; Minneapolis/Institute, American Painting, 1945–57, 1957; MOMA, The New American Painting, circ. Europe, 1958–59; Documenta II, Kassel, 1959; Kimura Gallery, Tokyo, 1959; SRGM, Abstract Expressionists and Imagists, 1961; SRGM/USIA, American Vanguard, circ. Europe, 1961–62; Seattle World's Fair, 1962; WMAA Annual, 1963; Brandeis U., New Directions in American Painting, 1963; Jewish Museum, Black and White, 1963; Tate, Dunn International, 1964; Chicago/AI Annual, 1964; SRGM, Guggenheim International, 1964; Kunsthalle, Basel, International Painting Since 1950, 1964. **COLLECTIONS:** Basel; MOMA. **BIBLIOGRAPHY:** Greenberg 1; Haftman; Hunter 1; *Metro;* Motherwell and Reinhardt, eds.; Seuphor 1.

NIVOLA, CONSTANTINO. b. July 5, 1911, Orani, Sardinia. **STUDIED:** Instituto Superiore d'Arte, Monza, Italy, with Marino Marini, Marcello Nizzoli, 1930–36, MA. Art Director for Olivetti Company, 1936–39. Traveled Europe, USA. To USA 1939. Art Director, *Interiors* Magazine, 1941–45. **TAUGHT:** Director, Design Workshop of Harvard U. Graduate School, 1953–57; Columbia U., 1961–63. **COMMISSIONS:** Milan Triennial, 1933 (mural, with S. R. Francello); Italian Pavilion, Paris World's Fair, 1937; Olivetti Showroom, NYC, 1953–54 (mural); Four Chaplains Memorial Fountain, Falls Church, Va., 1955; 1025 Fifth Avenue, NYC, 1955 (gardens); William E. Grady Vocational High School, Brooklyn, N.Y., 1957; Mutual Insurance Co. of Hartford, Hartford, Conn., 1957 (façade); P.S. 46, Brooklyn, N.Y., 1959 (murals and sculptures for playground); McCormick Place, Exposition Hall, Chicago, 1960 (façade); Motorola Building, Chicago, 1960 (murals); Saarinen Dormitories, Yale U., 1962 (35 sculptures). **AWARDS:** Philadelphia Decorators Club Award, 1959; Carborundum Major Abrasive Marketing Award, 1962; Municipal Art Society of New York, Certificate of Merit, 1962; Architectural League of New York, Silver Medal of Honor in Sculpture, 1962; Regional Exhibition of Figurative Art, Cagliari, Italy, Gold Medal; Federation of Graphic Arts, Diploma. **ADDRESS:** 123 Waverly Place, NYC. **DEALERS:** The Byron Gallery; Galleria Il Milione. **ONE-MAN EXHIBITIONS:** (first) Sassari Gallery, Sardinia, 1927 (paintings); (first in USA) Tibor de Nagy Gallery, 1950; The Peridot Gallery, 1954, 57; Harvard U., 1956; The Bertha Schaefer Gallery, 1958; Architectural League of New York, 1958; Galleria Il Milione, 1959; Arts Club of Chicago, 1959; A.F.A., circ., 1960; Galleria dell'Ariete, Milan, 1962; The Byron Gallery, 1964; Andrew-Morris Gallery, NYC; Betty Parsons Gallery (two-man, with Saul Steinberg), 1940. **GROUP:** Brooklyn Museum, 1947; American Abstract Artists, 1947; Rome National Art Quadrennial, 1950; Riverside Museum, 1955; WMAA, 1957; Carnegie, 1958; Museum of Contemporary Crafts, 1962; National Gold Medal Exhibition of the Building Arts, NYC, 1962; A.F.A., American Drawing, circ., 1964; MOMA. **COLLECTIONS:** MOMA; WMAA. **BIBLIOGRAPHY:** Giedion-Welcker 1; *Metro;* Seuphor 3.

NOGUCHI, ISAMU. b. November 17, 1904, Los Angeles, Calif. Resided Japan, ages 2–14. **STUDIED:** Columbia U., 1923–25 (pre-medical); apprenticed briefly to Gutzon Borglum; Leonardo da Vinci Art School, NYC; East Side Art School, NYC; apprenticed to Constantin Brancusi, Paris, 1927–29. Traveled Mexico, U.S.S.R., the Orient, Europe, Israel, USA. Designed numerous stage sets for Martha Graham Dance Co. **MEMBER:** National Sculpture Society. **COMMISSIONS:** Connecticut General Life Insurance Co. (gardens and sculpture); First National Bank of Fort Worth, Tex. (piazza and sculpture); John Hancock Building (fountain and sculpture); Chase Manhattan Bank, NYC (garden); Associated Press, NYC (relief), 1938;

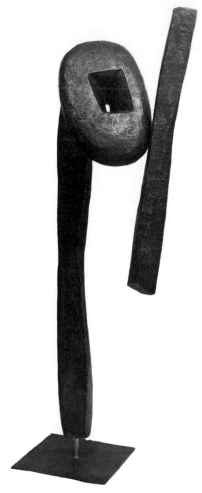

Isamu Noguchi   *The Cry. 1962*

Yale U. Library of Precious Books; Keyo U., Japan (2 gardens); UNESCO Headquarters, Paris (garden); International Business Machines, Armonk, N.Y.; Billy Rose Garden, Jerusalem. **AWARDS:** Guggenheim Foundation Fellowship, 1927; Bollingen Foundation Fellowship, 1950; Chicago/AI, The Mr. & Mrs. Frank G. Logan Medal. **ADDRESS:** 33–38 Tenth Street, Long Island City, N.Y. **DEALER:** Cordier & Ekstrom Inc. **ONE-MAN EXHIBITIONS:** (first) Eugene Schoen Gallery, NYC, 1929; Marie Sterner Gallery, NYC, 1930; Harvard Society for Contemporary Art, 1930; Marie Harriman Gallery, NYC, 1934; Arts Club of Chicago, 1930; Buffalo/Albright, 1930; Reinhardt Galleries, NYC, 1932; John Becker (Gallery), NYC, 1939, 42; Demotte Gallery, NYC, 1932; Mellon Galleries, Philadelphia, 1933; Honolulu Academy, 1934, 39; Sidney Burney Gallery, London, 1934; Western Association of Art Museum Directors, circ., 1934; SFMA, 1942; Cordier & Ekstrom Inc., 1963; Daniel Cordier, Paris; Charles Egan Gallery, 1948. **COLLECTIONS:** Brooklyn Museum; Buffalo/Albright; Chicago/AI; Honolulu Academy; Los Angeles/County MA; MMA; MOMA; SRGM; Tate; Toledo/MA; Toronto; WMAA. **BIBLIOGRAPHY:** Baur 5, 7; Biddle 3; Blesh 1; Breton 3; Brumme; Cahill and Barr, eds.; Calas; Cheney, M. C.; Flanagan; Giedion-Welcker 1; Goodrich and Baur 1; Hunter 5; *Index of 20th Century Artists;* Kuh 2; McCurdy, ed.; Mendelowitz; *Metro;* Miller, ed. 2; Neumeyer; Ritchie 1, 3; Seuphor 3; Seymour; **Takiguchi.**

NOLAND, KENNETH. b. April 10, 1924, Asheville, N.C. STUDIED: Black Mountain College, 1946, with Ilya Bolotowsky; Zadkine School of Sculpture, Paris, 1948–49. US Air Force, 1942–46. **TAUGHT:** The Catholic U. of America; ICA, Washington, D.C.; Emma Lake U., Saskatchewan. **ADDRESS:** Shaftsbury, Vt. DEALERS: Andre Emmerich Gallery, NYC; Galerie Lawrence; Kasmin Ltd. **ONE-MAN EXHIBITIONS:** (first) Galerie Creuze, Paris, 1949; French & Co. Inc., 1959; Galleria dell'Ariete, Milan, 1960; Galerie Lawrence, 1961; Bennington College, 1961; Galerie Charles Leinhard, Zurich, 1962; Galerie Schmela, Dusseldorf, 1962; Andre Emmerich Gallery, NYC, 1961, 62, 63, 64. **GROUP:** Seattle World's Fair, 1962; Corcoran, 1958, 63; XXXII Venice Biennial, 1964; SRGM, Abstract Expressionists and Imagists, 1961; The Kootz Gallery, New Talent, 1954; Jewish Museum, Toward a New Abstraction, 1963; WMAA, Geometric Abstraction in America, circ., 1962; Los Angeles/County MA, New Abstraction, 1964; Tate, Gulbenkian International, 1964. **COLLECTIONS:** Buffalo/Albright; Detroit/Institute; WMAA. **BIBLIOGRAPHY:** *Metro.*

NORDFELDT, B. J. O. b. 1897; **d.** 1955. STUDIED: Chicago Art Institute School; Academie Julian, Paris. Traveled France, Italy, Sweden, 1908–09. **TAUGHT:** Minneapolis Institute School, 1933. **AWARDS:** Milan Triennial, Silver Medal, 1906; Panama-Pacific Exposition, San Francisco, 1915, Silver Medal; Philadelphia Sesquicentennial, 1926, Bronze Medal; Chicago/AI, The Mr. & Mrs. Frank G. Logan Medal, 1926; Brooklyn Society of Etchers, First Prize, 1927; Chicago Society of Etchers, First Prize, 1928; Denver/AM, First Yetter Prize, 1937; Worcester/AM, P.P., 1947; Corcoran, Bronze Medal, 1949. **ONE-MAN EXHIBITIONS:** Scott Thurber Gallery, Chicago, 1912, 13; The Daniel Gallery, NYC, 1914, 17; Montross Gallery, NYC, 1923; Lilienfeld Gallery, NYC, 1937–43; Hudson D. Walker Gallery, NYC, 1940; Passedoit Gallery, NYC, 1944–55; Minneapolis/Institute; U. of Minnesota; Arts Club of Chicago; Wichita/AM; SFMA; The Zabriskie Gallery. **GROUP:** MMA, 1956; Carnegie; Corcoran; WMAA; Brussels World's Fair, 1958; A.F.A., Expressionists in American Painting. **COLLECTIONS:** Atlanta U.; Corcoran; Des Moines; U. of Illinois; MMA; Minneapolis/Institute; U. of Minnesota; U. of Oregon; Rochester/Memorial; Santa Fe, N.M.; U. of Texas;

Kenneth Noland   *Chamfer. 1964*

Toledo/MA; Walker; Wichita/AM; Worcester/AM. **BIBLIOGRAPHY:** Cheney, M. C.; Coke; Hartmann.

NOWACK, WAYNE K. b. May 7, 1923, Des Moines, Iowa. STUDIED: Drake U., 1943–45; State U. of Iowa, with Mauricio Lasansky, James Lechay, Stuart Edie, 1945–47, BA, PBK, 1948, MA (Art History), 1950, MFA (Painting). **TAUGHT:** Union College (N.Y.), 1957– . **AWARDS:** Des Moines, First Prize, 1950; Danforth Foundation Grant, 1962. **ADDRESS:** c/o Dealer. **DEALER:** Allan Stone Gallery. **ONE-MAN EXHIBITIONS:** (first) Des Moines, 1950, also 1957; Albany/Institute, 1961; Union College (N.Y.), 1957; Schenectady Museum Association, 1961. **GROUP:** Des Moines, 1948, 50, 51, 52, 53; Library of Congress Print Annual, 1948; Denver/AM, 1948; Omaha/Joslyn Annuals, 1947, 50; Silvermine Guild, 1954; Utica, 1961; Skidmore College, 1961. **COLLECTIONS:** Des Moines; Drake U.; Fort Worth; State U. of Iowa; Skidmore College; Union College (N.Y.).

O

O'HANLON, RICHARD. b. October 7, 1906, Long Beach, Calif. STUDIED: California College of Arts and Crafts, 1926–27; California School of Fine Arts, 1930–33. Traveled the Orient and around the world. TAUGHT: U. of California, 1947–61. AWARDS: SFMA, Anne Bremer Traveling Scholarship; SFMA, Edgar Walter Memorial Prize, 1940; CSFA, Albert M. Bender Fellowship, 1940; Marin Society Annual, First Prize; SFMA, First Prize, 1950. ADDRESS: 616 Throckmorton Avenue, Mill Valley, Calif. DEALER: The Willard Gallery. ONE-MAN EXHIBITIONS: The Willard Gallery, 1953; Rochester/Memorial; U. of Kentucky. RETROSPECTIVE: SFMA, 1961. GROUP: Carnegie; SFMA; Baltimore/MA. COLLECTIONS: Andover/Phillips; Baltimore/MA; U. of California, Davis; Denver/AM; SFMA; Smith College; WMAA; Walker; Worcester/AM.

OHASHI, YUTAKA. b. August 19, 1923, Hiroshima, Japan. STUDIED: Academy of Arts, Tokyo, 1941–46, BFA; Boston Museum School, 1950–55, with David Aronson, Karl Zerbe. Japanese Army, 1943–45. Traveled Europe, the Orient, USA. TAUGHT: Boston Museum School, 1958; Visiting Critic, Cornell U., 1961. AWARDS: Boston/MFA, James William Paige Fellowship (Europe), 1955–57; J. S. Guggenheim Fellowship (Japan), 1959. ADDRESS: 14 Bank Street, NYC. DEALER: The Swetzoff Gallery. ONE-MAN EXHIBITIONS: (first) Margaret Brown Gallery, Boston, 1955; The Alan Gallery, 1957, 60, 63; The Swetzoff Gallery, 1958, 60, 63, 64; Cornell U., 1961; Dennenchof Studio, Tokyo, 1960. GROUP: Rome-New York Foundation, Rome; ICA, Boston, 1962; SRGM; Chicago/AI; U. of Illinois; Carnegie; ICA, Boston, Contem-

porary Painters of Japanese Origin in America, 1958. COLLECTIONS: Andover/Phillips; Boston/MFA; Cornell U.; Lincoln, Mass./De Cordova; SRGM; U. of Wyoming.

OKADA, KENZO. b. September 28, 1902, Yokohama, Japan. STUDIED: Meijigakuin Middle School; Tokyo U. of Arts, three semesters; in Paris, 1924–27. TAUGHT: Nippon Art College, 1940–42; Musashino Art Institute, 1947–50; Tama College of Fine Arts, Tokyo, 1949–50. To USA 1950; citizen 1960. MEMBER: Nikakai (Group), Japan, 1938– . AWARDS: Nikakai (Group), Japan, 1936; Showa Shorei, 1938; Chicago/AI, 1954, 57; Yomiuri Press, 1947; Carnegie, 1955; Columbia, S.C./MA, First Prize, 1957; XXIX Venice Biennial, 1958; Tate, Dunn International Prize, 1964. ADDRESS: 51 West 11 Street, NYC. DEALER: Staempfli Gallery. ONE-MAN EXHIBITIONS: Nichido Gallery, Tokyo, 1929–35; Hokuso Gallery, 1948, 50; US Army Education Center, Tokyo, 1949, 50; US Army Education Center, Yokohama, 1950; Betty Parsons Gallery, 1953, 55, 56, 59, 62, 63; Corcoran, 1955; Fairweather-Hardin Gallery, 1956; Myrtle Todes Gallery, Glencoe, Ill., 1957; Sao Paulo, 1955; Venice/Contemporaneo, 1958; Ferus Gallery, 1959; MIT, 1962. GROUP: Salon d'Automne, Paris, 1924–27; Nikakai (Group), Japan, 1938– ; WMAA; Chicago/AI; U. of Illinois; XXIX Venice Biennial, 1958; Tate, Dunn International, 1964; III Sao Paulo Biennial, 1955; Corcoran; MOMA. COLLECTIONS: Baltimore/MA; Boston/MFA; Brooklyn Museum; Buffalo/Albright; Carnegie; Chase Manhattan Bank; Chicago/AI; U. of Colorado; Equitable Life Assurance Society; MMA; MOMA; Phillips; Reynolds Metals Co.; Rocke-

Kenzo Okada   *Open.*

feller Institute; SFMA; SRGM; Santa Bar-
bara/MA; Utica; WMAA; Yale U. **Bibliography:** Baur 5; Goodrich and Baur 1; Nordness,
ed.; Ponente; Read 2; Rodman 1.

OKAMURA, ARTHUR. b. February 24, 1932,
Long Beach, Calif. **Studied:** The U. of Chi-
cago, 1951, 53, 57; Chicago Art Institute
School, 1950–54, with Paul Wieghardt; Yale U.,
1954. US Army, 1954. Traveled France, Spain;
resided in Mallorca for a year. **Taught:** Chi-
cago Art Institute School, 1957; Central YMCA
College, Chicago, 1956–57; Evanston (Ill.) Art
Center, 1956–57; Northshore Art League,
Winnetka, Ill., 1957; Academy of Art, San
Francisco, 1957; California School of Fine Arts,
1958; California College of Arts and Crafts,

1958–59; Saugatuck Summer School of Paint-
ing, 1959, 62; U. of Utah, 1964. **Awards:**
Edward L. Ryerson Traveling Fellowship, 1945;
four-year scholarship to the Chicago Art Insti-
tute School; The U. of Chicago, Religious Arts,
First Prize, 1953; Chicago/AI, Martin B. Cahn
Award, 1957; U. of Illinois, P.P., 1960; WMAA,
Neysa McMein P.P., 1960; NIAL, P.P.; SFMA,
Schwabacher-Frey Award, 1960. **Address:** P.O.
Box 21, Ocean Parkway, Bolinas, Calif. **Deal-
ers:** M. Knoedler & Co., NYC; Feingarten
Gallery, Chicago. **One-man Exhibitions:** (first)
Frank Ryan Gallery, Chicago, 1953; Le Bou-
tique, Chicago, 1953, 54; Feingarten Gallery,
Chicago, NYC, San Francisco, and Los Angeles,
1956–64; Santa Barbara/MA, 1958; Oak-
land/AM, 1959; California Palace, 1961;

Dallas/MFA, 1962; La Jolla, 1963; U. of Utah, 1964. GROUP: Chicago/AI Annuals, 1951–54; U. of Illinois, 1955, 59; Ravinia Festival, Highland Park, Ill., 1956, 64; Los Angeles/County MA, Contemporary Americans, 1957; SFMA, Art in Asia and the West, 1957; A.F.A., New Talent, circ., 1959; Dallas/MFA, 1959; de Young, Fresh Paint, 1958; California Palace, 1959; WMAA, 1960; SFMA, Sculpture and Drawings, 1961; WMAA Annuals, 1962, 63, 64; WMAA, Forty Artists Under Forty, circ., 1962; PAFA, 1954; U. of Nebraska, 1958; WMAA, Friends of the Whitney, 1964; Denver/AM, 1958; USIA, Drawings from California, circ. Europe, 1958–59. COLLECTIONS: Borg-Warner International Corporation; Chicago/AI; The U. of Chicago; Container Corp. of America; Corcoran; Illinois State Normal U.; U. of Illinois; S. C. Johnson & Son, Inc.; Miles Laboratories Inc.; NIAL; Phoenix; SFMA; Santa Barbara/MA; Steel Service Institute; WMAA. BIBLIOGRAPHY: Nordness, ed.

O'KEEFFE, GEORGIA. b. November 15, 1887, Sun Prairie, Wisc. STUDIED: Chatham Episcopal Institute (Va.), 1901; Chicago Art Institute School, 1904–05, with John Vanderpoel; ASL, 1907–08, with William M. Chase; Columbia U., 1916, with Arthur Dow, Alan Bement. Traveled Europe, Mexico, USA, Peru, Japan. TAUGHT: U. of Virginia; Supervisor of Art in public schools, Amarillo, Tex., 1912–16; Columbia College (S.C.); West Texas Normal College. AWARDS: Hon. DFA, College of William and Mary, 1939; Hon. Litt.D., U. of Wisconsin, 1942; elected to the NIAL, 1947. m. Alfred Stieglitz (1924). ADDRESS: Abiquiu, N.M. ONE-MAN EXHIBITIONS: (first) "291," NYC, 1917, also 1926; Anderson Galleries, NYC, 1924; Stieglitz's Intimate Gallery, NYC, 1927, 29; An American Place (Gallery), NYC, 1931, 32, 35, 36, 37, 38, 39, 40, 41, 42, 44, 45, 46, 50; The Downtown Gallery, 1937, 52, 55, 58, 61; College of William and Mary, 1938; La Escondida, Taos, N.M., 1951; Dallas/MFA, 1953; Mayo Hill, Delray Beach, Fla., 1953; Gibbes Art Gallery, Charleston, S.C., 1955. RETROSPECTIVE: Anderson Galleries, NYC, 1923; Chicago/AI, 1943; MOMA, 1946; Dallas/MFA, 1953; Worcester/AM, 1960. GROUP: "291," NYC, 1916; Pomona College, Stieglitz Circle, 1958; MMA, 14 American Masters, 1958; MOMA, Paintings by 19 Living Americans, 1929; U. of Minnesota, 5 Painters, 1937. COLLECTIONS: Andover/Phillips; Arizona State College; U. of Arizona; Auburn U.; Balti-

Georgia O'Keeffe   *Black Door with Red. 1955*

more/MA; Brooklyn Museum; Bryn Mawr College; Buffalo/Albright; Chicago/AI; Cleveland/MA; Colorado Springs/FA; Currier; Dallas/MFA; Detroit/Institute; Fisk U.; U. of Georgia; IBM; Indianapolis/Herron; MMA; MOMA; The Miller Co.; Milwaukee; U. of Minnesota; National Gallery; U. of Nebraska; Newark Museum; U. of Oklahoma; Omaha/Joslyn; PMA; Phillips; Randolph-Macon Woman's College; Rochester/Memorial; Roswell; SFMA; Santa Barbara/MA; Shelburne; Smith College; Springfield, Mass./MFA; Tate; Texas Technological College; Toledo/MA; Utica; WMAA; Walker; Wellesley College; Westminster Academy; West Palm Beach/Norton; Wichita/AM; Wilmington. **BIBLIOGRAPHY:** Barker 1; Baur 5, 7; Bazin; Bethers; Biddle 3; Blanchard; Blesh 1; Boswell 1; Brown; Bulliet 1; Cahill and Barr, eds.; Cheney, M. C.; Christensen; Coke; Craven 1; Eliot; Flanagan; Frank, ed.; Frost; Goodrich and Baur 1; Haftman; Hall; Hunter 5; Huyghe; *Index of 20th Century Artists;* Janis, S.; Jewell 2; Kootz 1; Kuh 1, 2; Lane; Lee and Burchwood; Mather 1; McCourbrey; McCurdy, ed.; Mellquist; Mendelowitz; Neu-

haus; Newmeyer; Nordness, ed.; Pearson 1; Phillips 1, 2; Poore; Pousette-Dart, ed.; **Rich 1, 2;** Richardson; Ringel, ed.; Ritchie 1; Smith, S. C. K.; Soby 6; Sutton.

OLDENBURG, CLAES THURE. b. January 28, 1929, Stockholm, Sweden. STUDIED: Yale U., 1950, BA; Chicago Art Institute School, 1952–55, with Paul Wieghardt. Traveled USA, Europe. Apprentice reporter, City News Bureau, Chicago, 1950–52. Operated the Ray Gun Mfg. Co., NYC. **ADDRESS:** c/o Dealer. **DEALER:** Sidney Janis Gallery. **ONE-MAN EXHIBITIONS:** (first) Judson Gallery, NYC, 1959 (sculpture, drawings, poems); Judson Gallery, NYC (two-man, with Jim Dine), 1959; Reuben Gallery, NYC, 1960; Dwan Gallery, 1963; The Green Gallery, NYC, 1962; Sidney Janis Gallery, 1964; The Pace Gallery, Boston, 1964; Ileana Sonnabend (Gallery), Paris, 1964. **ENVIRONMENTS:** Judson Gallery, NYC, Ray Gun Street, 1960; Ray Gun Mfg. Co., The Store, 1961; Sidney Janis Gallery, Bedroom Ensemble, 1964. **HAPPENINGS:** Judson Gallery, NYC, Snapshots from the City, 1960; Reuben Gallery, NYC,

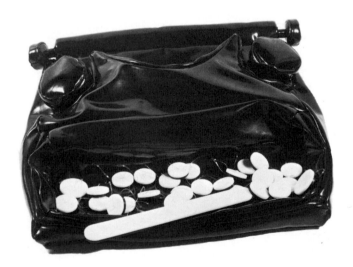

Claes Thure Oldenburg   *Soft Typewriter. 1963*

Blackouts, 1960; Reuben Gallery, NYC, Ironworks and Fotodeath, 1961; Dallas/MFA, Injun, 1962; Ray Gun Mfg. Co., Ray Gun Theatre, 1962; The U. of Chicago, Gayety, 1963; WGMA, Stars, 1963; Los Angeles/County MA, Autobodys, 1963. **GROUP EXHIBITIONS:** Buffalo/Albright, Mixed Media and Pop Art, 1963; Oberlin College, 3 Young Painters, 1963; Chicago/AI, 1962, 63; Brandeis U., New Directions in American Painting, 1963; Cincinnati/AM, An American Viewpoint, 1963; Dallas/MFA; Tate, Dunn International, 1964; ICA, London, The Popular Image, 1963; Martha Jackson Gallery, New Media—New Forms, I & II, 1960, 61; Stockholm/National, American Pop Art, 1964; MOMA, Americans 1963, circ., 1963–64; Oakland/AM, Pop Art USA, 1963; Hartford/Wadsworth, Continuity and Change, 1962; WGMA, The Popular Image, 1963; Philadelphia YM-YWHA Arts Council, Art, A New Vocabulary, 1962; Sidney Janis Gallery, The New Realists, 1962; XXXII Venice Biennial, 1964. **COLLECTIONS:** Brandeis U.; Buffalo/Albright; MOMA; Oberlin College; Stockholm/National. **BIBLIOGRAPHY:** Janis and Blesh 1; *Metro.*

OLITSKI, JULES. b. March 27, 1922, Gomel, U.S.S.R. **STUDIED:** NYU, BA, MA (Art Education); NAD, with Sidney Dickinson; Beaux-Arts Institute of Design, NYC; Academie de la Grande Chaumiere; Zadkine School of Sculpture, Paris; and privately with Chaim Gross. Traveled USA, Europe, Mexico. **TAUGHT:** Chairman of Fine Arts, C. W. Post College of Long Island U., 1956–63; Bennington College, 1963– . **AWARDS:** Carnegie International, Second Prize, 1961; Ford Foundation, P.P., 1964. **ADDRESS:** R. D. 1, Box 16-A, Shaftsbury, Vt. **DEALERS:** Poindexter Gallery; Kasmin Ltd.; Richard Gray Gallery. **ONE-MAN EXHIBITIONS:** (first) Galerie Huit, Paris, 1951; Alexander Iolas Gallery, 1958; French & Co. Inc., 1959, 60; Poindexter Gallery, 1961, 62, 63, 64; Bennington College, 1963; Galleria d'Arte Santa Croce, Florence, Italy, 1963; Galleria Trastevere di Topazia Alliata, Rome, 1963; Galleria Toninelli, Milan, 1963; Richard Gray Gallery, 1964; Kasmin Ltd., 1964. **GROUP:** Carnegie, 1961; WGMA, The Formalists, 1963; Worcester/AM, 1963; IV International Art Biennial, San Marino (Europe), 1963; Brandeis U., 1964; WMAA Annual, 1964; MOMA, Recent Acquisitions,

1963; Los Angeles/County MA, Post Painterly Abstraction, 1964; Chicago/AI, Americans 1964; Festival of Two Worlds, Spoleto, 1963. **COLLECTIONS:** Chicago/AI; MOMA; Provincetown/Chrysler; U. of Saskatchewan.

OLIVEIRA, NATHAN. b. December 19, 1928, Oakland, Calif. **STUDIED:** Mills College, California College of Arts and Crafts (MFA, 1952). US Army, 1953–55. Traveled Europe. **TAUGHT:** San Francisco Art Institute; U. of Illinois, 1961–62; California College of Arts and Crafts, 1955–56; UCLA, 1963–64. **AWARDS:** Chicago/AI, Norman Wait Harris Bronze Medal, 1960; Guggenheim Foundation Fellowship, 1958; L. C. Tiffany Grant, 1957; El Retiro Parquet, Madrid, Arte de America y España, Special Prize, 1963. **ADDRESS:** 1050 Fiske Street, Pacific Palisades, Calif. **DEALERS:** The Alan Gallery; Paul Kantor Gallery. **ONE-MAN EXHIBITIONS:** (first) The Alan Gallery, 1958, also 1959, 60, 63; Paul Kantor Gallery, 1959, 60, 62, 63; U. of Illinois, 1961; Walker, 1961. **RETROSPECTIVE:** UCLA, circ., 1963. **GROUP:** Chicago/AI; Carnegie; WMAA Annuals, 1958, 59, 60, 61; Denver/AM; SFMA; U. of Illinois, 1961, 63; Corcoran Annual; MOMA, New Images of Man, 1959; I Inter-American Paintings and Prints Biennial, Mexico City, 1958; MOMA, Recent Painting USA: The Figure, circ., 1962–63; I Paris Biennial, 1959; Seattle World's Fair, 1962; SRGM, 1961. **COLLECTIONS:** UCLA; Chicago/AI; Illinois Wesleyan U.; S. C. Johnson & Son, Inc.; MOMA; U. of Michigan; SFMA; Walker; Youngstown/Butler. **BIBLIOGRAPHY:** Nordness, ed.; **Wight 4.**

ONSLOW-FORD, GORDON. b. December 26, 1912, Wendover, England. **STUDIED:** Royal Naval College, Dartmouth; Royal Naval College, Greenwich; self-taught in art; frequent visits to the studio of Fernand Leger. Traveled Europe, the Orient, and most of the world; resided in Paris, 1936–39, and Mexico, 1941–47. **TAUGHT:** Series of lectures, New School for Social Research, 1940–41; California College of Arts and Crafts, 1956–58. **ADDRESS:** P.O. Box 128, Inverness, Calif. **DEALER:** The Rose Rabow Gallery. **ONE-MAN EXHIBITIONS:** (first) Karl Nierendorf Gallery, NYC, 1940; SFMA (two-man, with Richard Bowman), 1959; The Rose Rabow Gallery, 1964. **GROUP:** SFMA, 1948, 60; de Young, 1962. **COLLECTIONS:** SRGM;

Nathan Oliveira   *Seated Figure with Pink Background. 1960*

WMAA. **Bibliography:** Breton 2; **Onslow-Ford;** Paalen; Ragon 1.

OPPER, JOHN. b. October 29, 1908, Chicago, Ill. **Studied:** Western Reserve U., 1931, BS; Columbia U., 1942, MA, 1952, Ed.D.; Cleveland Institute of Art, 1926–28; Chicago Art Institute School, 1928–29; Hofmann School, 1936. Traveled Europe. **Taught:** U. of Wyoming; U. of North Carolina; Columbia U.; NYU. **Member:** American Abstract Artists, since 1936. **Federal A.P.:** Easel painting. **Address:** 32 King Street, NYC. **Dealer:** The Stable Gallery. **One-man Exhibitions:** (first) Artists' Gallery, NYC, 1938, also 1940; SFMA, 1939; San Diego, 1939; Charles Egan Gallery, 1955; The Stable Gallery, 1959, 60, 61. **Group:** Carnegie; MOMA; MMA; Brooklyn Museum; Chicago/AI; Baltimore/MA. **Collections:** MOMA; Union Carbide Corp.

ORTMAN, GEORGE EARL. b. October 17, 1926, Oakland, Calif. **Studied:** California College of Arts and Crafts, 1947–48; Atelier 17, NYC, 1949, with S. W. Hayter; Academie Andre Lhote, Paris, 1950; Hofmann School, 1950–51. **Taught:** School of Visual Arts, NYC; Fairleigh Dickinson College. **Address:** 62 East 90 Street, NYC. **Dealers:** The Howard Wise Gallery, NYC; The Swetzoff Gallery. **One-man Exhibitions:** (first) Tanager Gallery, NYC, 1953; Wittenborn Gallery, NYC, 1956; The Stable Gallery, 1957, 60; The Swetzoff Gallery, 1961, 62; The Howard Wise Gallery, NYC, 1962, 63, 64; Fairleigh Dickinson U., 1962; David Mirvish Gallery, Toronto, 1964. **Group:** Salon du Mai, Paris, 1950; SFMA Annual, 1952; Martha Jackson Gallery, New Media—New Forms, I, 1960; Claude Bernard, Paris, 1960; WMAA, Young America, 1960; Chicago/AI Annuals, 1961, 62; WMAA, Geometric Abstraction in America, circ., 1962; Seattle World's Fair, 1962; MOMA, Hans Hofmann and His Students, circ., 1963–64; Amsterdam/Stedelijk, 1963; Jewish Museum, Toward a New Abstraction, 1963; SFMA, Directions—Painting U.S.A., 1963; WMAA Annual, 1963; A.F.A., Contemporary Wall Sculpture, circ., 1963–64. **COLLECTIONS:** Allentown/AM; MOMA; NYPL; NYU; Omaha/Joslyn; WMAA; Walker; Worcester/AM. **BIBLIOGRAPHY:** Janis and Blesh 1.

OSSORIO, ALFONSO. b. August 2, 1916, Manila, Philippine Islands. STUDIED in England, 1924; Harvard U., 1938; RISD, 1938–39. To USA 1929. US Army, 1943–46. **ADDRESS:** The Creeks, Southampton, N.Y. **DEALER:** Cordier & Ekstrom Inc. **ONE-MAN EXHIBITIONS:** (first) Wakefield Gallery, NYC, 1941, also 1943; Studio Paul Facchetti, Paris, 1951; Mortimer Brandt, NYC, 1945; Betty Parsons Gallery, 1951, 53, 56, 58, 59, 61; Galerie Stadler, Paris, 1960, 61; Cordier & Ekstrom Inc., 1961, 64. **GROUP:** WMAA; MOMA. **COLLECTIONS:** Finch College; WMAA. **BIBLIOGRAPHY: Seitz 2; Tapie 1, 2.**

OSVER, ARTHUR. b. July 26, 1912, Chicago, Ill. STUDIED: Northwestern U., 1930–31; Chicago Art Institute School, with Boris Anisfeld. Traveled and resided in France and Italy for several years. **TAUGHT:** Brooklyn Museum School, 1947; Columbia U., 1950–51; U. of Florida, 1954; Cooper Union, 1955, 58; Yale U.,

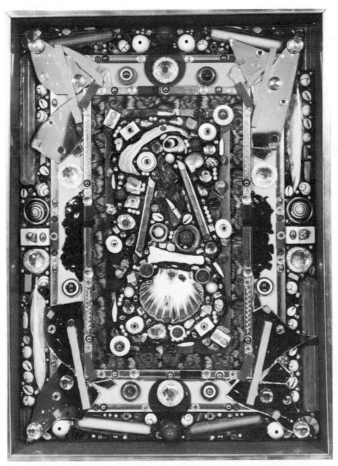

Alfonso Ossorio   *Undistracted. 1963*

1956–57; American Academy, Rome, 1957–58; Washington U., 1960– . MEMBER: Artists Equity; Audubon Artists. FEDERAL A.P.: Teaching, painting. COMMISSIONS: *Fortune* Magazine, 1960 (cover). AWARDS: Chicago/AI, James Nelson Raymond Traveling Fellowship ($2,000), 1936; VMFA, John Barton Payne Medal; Pepsi-Cola $500 Award, 1947; PAFA, Joseph E. Temple Gold Medal, 1947; U. of Illinois, P.P., 1949; Guggenheim Foundation Fellowship, 1948, renewed 1949; Prix de Rome, 1952, renewed 1953; Audubon Artists, Emily Lowe Prize, 1961; Art Directors Club, Chicago, Medal, 1961. ADDRESS: 465 Foote Avenue, St. Louis, Mo. DEALER: Fairweather-Hardin Gallery. ONE-MAN EXHIBITIONS: (first) Mortimer Brandt, NYC, 1943; Grand Central Moderns, 1947, 49, 51, 57; U. of Chattanooga, 1958; Syracuse U., 1959; Hamline U., 1950; U. of Florida, 1951, 55; Fairweather-Garnett Gallery, Evanston, 1955; Fairweather-Hardin Gallery, 1955, 57, 62; Philadelphia Art Alliance, 1959. GROUP: Chicago/AI; PAFA; MMA; PMA; WMAA; MOMA; Carnegie; Corcoran; Phillips; Detroit/Institute; Brooklyn Museum; VMFA; Des Moines; Walker; Venice Biennial; Tokyo/Modern. COLLECTIONS: Abbott Laboratories; Cincinnati/AM; Colorado Springs/FA; Davenport/Municipal; Des Moines; U. of Georgia; Houston/MFA; IBM; U. of Illinois; Inland Steel Co.; S. C. Johnson & Son, Inc.; MMA; MOMA; U. of Michigan; Montclair/AM; U. of Nebraska; New Orleans/Delgado; PAFA; PMA; Peabody Museum; Phillips; Rio de Janeiro; Rochester/Memorial; St. Louis/City; Syracuse/Everson; Toledo/MA; WMAA; Walker; Washington U.; Wilmington. BIBLIOGRAPHY: Bethers; Nordness, ed.

p

PACE, STEPHEN. b. 1918, Charleston, Mo.
STUDIED: Evansville Museum School, 1937–41,
with Robert Lahr; Escuela de Bellas Artes,
San Miguel de Allende, Mexico, 1945–46; ASL,
1948–49, with Cameron Booth, Morris Kantor;
Academie de la Grande Chaumiere, 1950;
Academy of Fine Arts, Florence, Italy, 1951;
Hofmann School, 1951. US Army, 1943–46.
Traveled Mexico, Europe, Canada, USA.
TAUGHT: Washington U., 1959; Pratt Institute,
1962– . AWARDS: Dolia Laurian Fund Award,
1954; Hallmark International Competition,
1961. ADDRESS: 345 West 29 Street, NYC. ONE-
MAN EXHIBITIONS: (first) Evansville, 1946;
Hendler Gallery, Philadelphia, 1953; Artists'
Gallery, NYC, 1954; Poindexter Gallery, 1956,
57; HCE Gallery, 1956, 57, 58, 59; Washing-
ton U., 1959; Dilexi Gallery, San Francisco,
1960; Holland-Goldowsky Gallery, Chicago,
1960; The Howard Wise Gallery, Cleveland,
1960; Dwan Gallery, 1961; The Howard Wise
Gallery, NYC, 1960, 61, 63, 64; MIT, 1961.
GROUP: Brooklyn Museum, 1953, 55; PAFA,
1954; Walker, Vanguard, 1955; Carnegie, 1955;
WMAA Annuals, 1953, 54, 56, 57, 58, 61;
International Biennial Exhibition of Paintings,
Tokyo; Walker, 60 American Painters, 1960;
Cleveland/MA, Paths of Abstract Art, 1960;
Hallmark Art Award, 1960; Brandeis U. (two-
man), circ., 1961; USIA, American Paintings,
circ. Latin America, 1961; Corcoran, 1963;
MOMA, Hans Hofmann and His Students,
circ., 1963–64; U. of Texas, Recent Amer-
ican Painting, 1964. COLLECTIONS: Evansville;
James A. Michener Foundation; Province-
town/Chrysler; Southern Illinois U.; WMAA;
Waitsfield/Bundy. BIBLIOGRAPHY: Henning.

PACHNER, WILLIAM. b. April 7, 1915,
Brtnice u Jihldy, Moravia, Czechoslovakia.
STUDIED: Kunstgewerbeschule, Vienna, 1930–
33. Staff Artist, Narodni Galerie, Prague,
1933–35. To USA 1939. Art Director, *Esquire*
Magazine, 1940–43. TAUGHT: Florida Gulf
Coast Art Center, Inc., 1953–57; Tampa Art
Institute, Inc., 1957; Director of own school,
1957– . AWARDS: NIAL Grant, 1949; Mead
Painting of the Year, $1,000 Prize, 1958; New
Orleans/Delgado, First Prize, 1958; Youngs-
town/Butler, First Prize, 1959; Guggenheim
Foundation Fellowship, 1960. ADDRESS: c/o
Dealer. DEALER: The Krasner Gallery. ONE-
MAN EXHIBITIONS: (first in USA) Weyhe Gal-
lery, 1948; Ganso Gallery, NYC, 1951, 55;
A.A.A. Gallery, NYC, 1949; Ringling, 1954; The
Krasner Gallery, 1959; Barry Stephens Gallery,
NYC, 1945. RETROSPECTIVE: A.F.A./Ford
Foundation, circ., 1959. GROUP: Carnegie,
1948; WMAA, 1948–51, 58, 60; Corcoran, 1949,
51; PAFA, 1950, 59; ART:USA:58, NYC, 1958;
U. of Nebraska; U. of Michigan; Detroit/Insti-
tute, 1959. COLLECTIONS: Ain Harod; Bran-
deis U.; State College of Iowa; Milwaukee;
Provincetown/Chrysler; Ringling; WMAA;
Witte; Youngstown/Butler. BIBLIOGRAPHY:
Zaidenberg, ed.

PACKARD, DAVID. b. May 29, 1928, Albany,
N.Y. STUDIED: PAFA, 1946–48, with Walker
Hancock; Syracuse U., with Ivan Mestrovic,
1951–56, BFA. TEACHES privately. AWARDS:
William and Noma Copley Foundation Grant,
1962; New Horizons in Sculpture, First Prize
($2,000), Chicago, 1962. ADDRESS: 2050 Hall-
stead Street, Chicago, Ill. DEALER: Main Street

Gallery. ONE-MAN EXHIBITIONS: (first) Main Street Gallery, 1960, also 1962, 64; Milwaukee, 1963. GROUP: Ravinia Festival, Highland Park, Ill., 1961; PAFA, 1953; Audubon Artists, 1953, 62; Springfield, Ill./State, 1962; Ball State Teachers College, Drawings and Sculpture Annual, 1963. COLLECTIONS: Syracuse U.

PADOVANO, ANTHONY. b. July 10, 1933, NYC. STUDIED: Brooklyn Museum School; Pratt Institute, with Alexander Kostellow; Columbia U., with Oronzio Maldarelli, 1957, BFA; Carnegie Institute of Technology. Traveled Italy, Switzerland; resided Rome, two years. TAUGHT: U. of Connecticut, 1962–64; Columbia U., 1964– . MEMBER: Silvermine Guild; American Association of University Professors. AWARDS: Prix de Rome, 1960–62; Guggenheim Foundation Fellowship, 1964; III International Exhibition of Figurative Art, Rome, First Prize, 1962; Silvermine Guild, Olivetti Prize for Sculpture, 1963, 64; Ford Foundation, P.P., 1964. ADDRESS: 555 West 171 Street, NYC. DEALERS: Richard Feigen Gallery, NYC; I.F.A. Gallery. ONE-MAN EXHIBITIONS: (first) Geejon Gallery, NYC, 1957; Lincoln, Mass./De Cordova, 1954 (drawings); Sculptor Studio, Washington, D.C., 1958; Galleria George Lester, Rome, 1962; U. of Connecticut, 1962, 63; Ruth White Gallery, 1962; Richard Feigen Gallery, NYC, 1964. GROUP: American Academy, Rome, 1960, 61, 62; Palazzo dell'Esposizione, Rome, 1961, 62; WMAA Annual, 1962; Lincoln, Mass./De Cordova, New England Sculpture, 1964; Finch College, 1964; Carnegie, 1952; Portland, Me./MA, 1959; Baltimore/MA, 1963; Waitsfield, Bundy Sculpture Competition, 1963. COLLECTIONS: American Academy, Rome; Silvermine Guild.

PALMER, WILLIAM C. b. January 20, 1906, Des Moines, Iowa. STUDIED: ASL, 1924–26, with Boardman Robinson, Henry Schnakenberg, A. Tucker, Thomas Hart Benton, Kenneth Hayes Miller, and privately with Miller, 1928–29; Ecole des Beaux-Arts, Fontainebleau, with M. Baudoin. US Army, 1943–45. TAUGHT: Munson-Williams-Proctor Institute, Utica, N.Y., 1941– ; ASL, 1936–40; Hamilton College, 1941–47. FEDERAL A.P.: Mural painter and supervisor, 1933–39; murals for: US Post Office Department Building, Washington, D.C.,

1936; Queens General Hospital, Jamaica, N.Y., 1934–36; US Post Offices at Arlington, Mass., 1938, and Monticello, Iowa, 1935. COMMISSIONS (murals): First National City Bank, Socony Building, NYC; Homestead Savings and Loan Association, Utica, N.Y., 1957. AWARDS: Paris Salon, Medal, 1937; Audubon Artists, 1947; NAD, 1946; AAAL Grant, 1953. ADDRESS: Butternut Hill, Clinton, N.Y. ONE-MAN EXHIBITIONS: (first) The Midtown Galleries, 1932, also 1937, 40, 44, 50, 52, 54, 57, 59, 62; Des Moines, 1948, 49; Cazenovia Junior College, 1949; Utica, 1956. GROUP: Corcoran; VMFA; Carnegie, 1936; Brooklyn Museum; Chicago/AI; Toledo/MA; WMAA; New York World's Fair, 1939; MOMA; Kansas City/Nelson; Audubon Artists. COLLECTIONS: AAAL; Andover/Phillips; Britannica; Cranbrook; Dallas/MFA; Des Moines; MMA; Rochester/Memorial; Utica; WMAA. BIBLIOGRAPHY: Boswell 1; Bruce and Watson; Palmer; Watson 2.

PAONE, PETER. b. October 2, 1936, Philadelphia, Pa. STUDIED: Philadelphia Museum School, 1958, BA, Art Ed.; Barnes Foundation, 1953–54. Traveled Europe. TAUGHT: Philadelphia Museum School, 1958–59; Positano (Italy) Art Workshop, 1961; Pratt Institute, 1959–64. AWARDS: L. C. Tiffany Grant, 1962; PMA, P.P., 1959; Library of Congress, Pennell P.P., 1962; The Print Club, Philadelphia, P.P., 1963; Syracuse U., P.P., 1964. ADDRESS: 2223 Green Street, Philadelphia, Pa. DEALERS: The Forum Gallery; Delphic Arts. ONE-MAN EXHIBITIONS: (first) Dubin Gallery, Philadelphia, 1957; Gallery Ten, New Hope, Pa., 1959; The Print Club, Philadelphia, 1958, 61, 62; Grippi Gallery, NYC, 1959, 60, 61, 62; Fort Worth, 1964. GROUP: PMA, 1959, 62; Brooklyn Museum, 1962; Escuela Nacional de Artes Plasticas, Mexico City, 1963; Dallas/MFA, Four Young Artists, 1964; III Paris Biennial, 1963; Syracuse/Everson, American Printmakers, 1964; New York World's Fair, 1964–65. COLLECTIONS: Fort Worth; Free Library of Philadelphia; General Mills Inc., Library of Congress; MOMA; PMA; Princeton U.; The Print Club, Philadelphia; Carl Sandburg Memorial Library; Syracuse U. BIBLIOGRAPHY: Rodman 3.

PARIS, HAROLD P. b. August 16, 1925, Edgemere, N.Y. STUDIED: Atelier 17, NYC, 1949;

Creative Graphic Workshop, NYC, 1951–52; Academy of Fine Arts, Munich, 1953–56. Traveled Europe. TAUGHT: U. of California, Berkeley. AWARDS: L. C. Tiffany Grant, 1949; Guggenheim Foundation Fellowship, 1953; Fulbright Fellowship (Germany), 1953. ADDRESS: c/o Dealer. DEALER: Royal Marks Gallery. ONE-MAN EXHIBITIONS: (first) Argent Gallery, NYC; Philadelphia Art Alliance; Village Art Center, NYC; Wittenborn Gallery, NYC; Esther Stuttman Gallery, NYC; Newcomb Gallery, NYC; Pratt Graphic Art Center; Silvan Simone Gallery, Los Angeles; U. of California, Berkeley; Paul Kantor Gallery; Bolles Gallery, San Francisco; Humboldt State College. GROUP: MMA; Brooklyn Museum; MOMA; Boston/MFA; PMA; Vienna Sezession; The Hague; Amerika Haus, Munich; California Palace; Baltimore/MA; Ottawa/National; WMAA; Smithsonian; Barcelona; Salon de la Jeune Sculpture, Paris; New Orleans/Delgado; Pasadena/AM. COLLECTIONS: California Palace; Chicago/AI; U. of Delaware; Library of Congress; MOMA; Memphis/Brooks; NYPL; U. of North Dakota; Oakland/AM; Ottawa/National; PMA; SFMA; U. of Wisconsin.

PARK, DAVID. b. March 17, 1911, Boston, Mass.; d. September 20, 1960, Berkeley, Calif. STUDIED: Otis Art Institute, Los Angeles, 1928, assistant to Ralph Stackpole, 1929. TAUGHT: Various private schools, San Francisco, 1931–36; Winsor School, Boston, 1936–41; California School of Fine Arts, 1943–52; U. of California, Berkeley, 1955–60. Designed sets and costumes for the U. of California, Berkeley, production of the opera *The Sorrows of Orpheus*, by Darius Milhaud, 1958. FEDERAL A.P.: Mural painting, San Francisco. AWARDS: SFMA, 1935, 51, 53, 55, 57; Oakland/AM, Gold Medal, 1957; PAFA, Walter Lippincott Prize, 1960. ONE-MAN EXHIBITIONS: SFMA, 1935, 40; Delphic Studios, NYC, 1936; New Gallery, Boston, 1939; Albany/Institute (two-man, with Dorothy Dehner), *ca.* 1944; California Palace, 1946; Paul Kantor Gallery, 1954; RAC, 1955; U. of California College of Architecture, 1956; Oakland/AM, 1957; de Young, 1959; Staempfli Gallery, 1959, 61, 63; U. of California, Berkeley, circ., 1964. GROUP: U. of Illinois, 1952, 57, 59, 61; III Sao Paulo Biennial, 1955; ART:USA:58 and ART:USA:59, NYC, 1958, 59; WMAA Annual, 1959; Indiana U., New Im-

David Park   *Ethiopia. 1959*

agery in American Painting, 1959; PAFA, 1950; A.F.A., The Figure, circ., 1960; Chicago/AI; Corcoran; SRGM/USIA, American Vanguard, circ. Europe, 1961–62. COLLECTIONS: U. of California, Berkeley; ICA, Boston; U. of Illinois; Indian Head Mills, Inc.; Oakland/AM; SFMA; WMAA. BIBLIOGRAPHY: Goodrich and Baur 1.

PARKER, RAYMOND. b. 1922, Beresford, S. D. STUDIED: State U. of Iowa, 1946, BA, 1948, MFA. TAUGHT: Hunter College, 1955– ; U. of Southern California, summer, 1959; State U. of Iowa; U. of Minnesota. AWARDS: Ford Foundation, P.P., 1963. ADDRESS: 52 Carmine Street, NYC. DEALER: The Kootz Gallery. ONE-MAN EXHIBITIONS: Walker, 1950; Paul Kantor Gallery, 1953, 56; Memphis/Brooks, 1953; Louisville/Speed, 1954; Union College (N.Y.), 1955; Widdifield Gallery, NYC, 1957, 59; U. of Southern California, 1959; Dwan Gallery, 1960, 62; Galerie Lawrence, 1960; The Kootz Gallery, 1960, 61, 62, 63, 64; Galleria dell'Ariete, Milan, 1961; SRGM, 1961; Bennington College, 1961; Des Moines (three-man), 1962. GROUP: Minnesota State Historical Society, St. Paul, Centennial Minnesota; Walker Biennial, 1949, 51; MOMA, New Talent; WMAA Annuals, 1950, 52, 58; MMA, American Paintings Today, 1950; Oberlin College, 1951; Walker, Vanguard, 1955; Tokyo/Modern, 1957; Walker, 60 American Painters, 1960; II Inter-American Paintings and Prints Biennial, Mexico City, 1960; U. of Illinois, 1961, 62; SRGM, Abstract Expressionists and Imagists, 1961; Seattle World's Fair, 1962; Corcoran, 1963; Jewish Museum, Toward a New Abstraction, 1963. COLLECTIONS: Allentown/AM; Brandeis U.; Buffalo/Albright; Dayton/AI; Des Moines; Fort Worth; Hartford/Wadsworth; State U. of Iowa; Los Angeles/County MA; MOMA; Minneapolis/Institute; Minnesota State Historical Society; SRGM; Tate; WMAA; Walker. BIBLIOGRAPHY: Friedman, ed.; Metro.

PARKER, ROBERT ANDREW. b. May 14, 1927, Norfolk, Va. STUDIED: Chicago Art Institute School, with Paul Wieghardt, Rudolph Pen, Max Kahn, 1948–52, BA.Ed.; Atelier 17, NYC, 1952–53, with Peter Grippe. US Army Air Force, 1945–46. Traveled Europe, Africa, Central and Latin America. TAUGHT: New York School for the Deaf, 1952–55; School of Visual Arts, NYC, 1959–63. COMMISSIONS: US Pavilion, New York World's Fair, 1964–65 (mural); sets for the MOMA production of The Mighty Casey, opera by William Schuman; illustrated 8 Poems, by Marianne Moore (MOMA, 1962). AWARDS: Chicago/AI, Maurice L. Rothchild Scholarship, 1961; NIAL, Richard and Hinda Rosenthal Foundation Award, 1962. ADDRESS: Kent Cliffs Road, Carmel, N.Y. DEALER: World House Galleries. ONE-MAN EXHIBITIONS: (first) The Little Gallery, Chicago, 1949; Roko Gallery, 1953, 54, 57, 58, 59; Palmer House Galleries, Chicago, 1957; World House Galleries, 1961, 62, 64; Felix Landau Gallery, 1961; Nexus Gallery, Boston, 1957; Raymond Burr Gallery, Los Angeles, 1962; J. L. Hudson Art Gallery, 1963; Obelisk Gallery, Washington, D.C., 1963; Nashville, 1961; St. Paul Gallery, 1961; Katonah (N.Y.) Library, 1957, 63. GROUP: MMA, American Watercolors, Drawings and Prints, 1952; MOMA, Young American Printmakers, 1953; La Napoule, France, 5 Masters of Line, 1957; WMAA Annuals, 1955, 56, 59; WMAA, Young America, 1957; A.F.A., New Talent, circ., 1956; USIA, Contemporary Graphic Art in the USA, circ. Europe and Asia, 1957–59; WMAA, Forty Americans Under Forty, circ., 1962; Brooklyn Museum, 1963. COLLECTIONS: Brooklyn Museum; MOMA; U. of Michigan; Montclair/AM; Nashville; Newark Museum; Phoenix; Raleigh/NCMA; WMAA.

PASILIS, FELIX. b. 1922, Batavia, Ill. STUDIED: Hofmann School, 1949–52; American U., 1946–48, with William H. Calfee. A co-founder of Hansa Gallery, NYC. AWARDS: Longview Foundation Grant; Walter K. Gutman Foundation Grant. ADDRESS: 95 East 10 Street, NYC. DEALER: The Greer Gallery. ONE-MAN EXHIBITIONS: Hansa Gallery, NYC, 1952, 53; Urban Gallery, NYC, 1954, 55; Tibor de Nagy Gallery, 1956; The Zabriskie Gallery, 1957; The Green Gallery, NYC, 1961; RJ Gallery, NYC, 1962; The Greer Gallery, 1963. GROUP: 813 Broadway Gallery, NYC, 1951; The Stable Gallery, 21 Young Americans, 1955; Carnegie, 1955, 58, 61; Jewish Museum, The New York School, Second Generation, 1957; Staten Island, Richard Brown Baker Collection, 1959; Yale U., 1961. COLLECTIONS: Agricultural and Mechanical College of Texas; Charlotte/Mint; MIT.

PATTISON, ABBOTT. b. May 15, 1916, Chicago, Ill. STUDIED: Yale U., 1937, BA, 1939, BFA. US Navy, four years. TAUGHT: Chicago Art Institute School, 1946–50; U. of Georgia, 1954–55; Skowhegan School, summers, 1955, 56; Northshore Art League, Winnetka, Ill., 1947–62. AWARDS: Yale U. Traveling Fellowship; MMA, $1,500 Prize; Chicago/AI (5); Waitsfield, Bundy Sculpture Competition, Second Prize; and some dozen others. ADDRESS: 334 Woodland Avenue, Winnetka, Ill. DEALER: Ontario-East Gallery. ONE-MAN EXHIBITIONS: (first) Chicago/AI, 1946; Sculpture Center; Santa Barbara/MA; La Jolla; U. of Georgia; U. of Florida; U. of Pittsburgh; U. of Wisconsin; Lee Nordness Gallery, NYC; Feingarten Gallery, Chicago. GROUP: MMA; WMAA; PMA; Cleveland/MA; Detroit/Institute; Los Angeles/County MA; Oakland/AM; Santa Barbara/MA; Chicago/AI. COLLECTIONS: Andover/Phillips; Brandeis U.; California Palace; Chicago/AI; Corcoran; Davenport/Municipal; Evansville; U. of Georgia; La Jolla; U. of Notre Dame; Phoenix; Provincetown/Chrysler; WMAA.

PEAKE, CHANNING. b. October 24, 1910, Marshall, Colo. STUDIED: California College of Arts and Crafts, 1928; Santa Barbara School of Art, 1929–31; ASL, 1935–36, with Rico Lebrun. A founder of the Santa Barbara (Calif.) Mu-

seum of Art. Operates a large ranch in Lompoc, California; first president, American Quarter Horse Association. COMMISSIONS (murals): Germanic Museum, Harvard U., 1936 (assistant to Louis Rubenstein); Pennsylvania Station, NYC, 1936–38 (assistant to Rico Lebrun); Santa Barbara (Calif.) Public Library, 1958 (with Howard Warshaw). ADDRESS: Rancho Jabali, Lompoc, Calif. DEALER: Felix Landau Gallery. ONE-MAN EXHIBITIONS: Frank Perls Gallery, 1952; Santa Barbara/MA, 1953, 56 (three-man, with Rico Lebrun and Howard Warshaw); de Young (three-man), 1953; J. Seligmann and Co. (two-man, with Howard Warshaw), 1957. GROUP: PAFA; U. of Illinois, 1953, 55; Colorado Springs/FA; Los Angeles/County MA. COLLECTIONS: Santa Barbara/MA.

PEARLSTEIN, PHILIP. b. May 24, 1924, Pittsburgh, Pa. STUDIED: Carnegie Institute of Technology, with Sam Rosenberg, Robert Lepper, Balcomb Greene; NYU, BA, MFA. TAUGHT: Pratt Institute, 1959– . MEMBER: Tanager Gallery, NYC. AWARDS: Fulbright Fellowship (Italy), 1958. ADDRESS: 317 West 89 Street, NYC. DEALER: Allan Frumkin Gallery, NYC and Chicago. ONE-MAN EXHIBITIONS: (first) Tanager Gallery, NYC, 1955, also 1959; The Peridot Gallery, 1956, 57, 59; Allan Frumkin Gallery, Chicago, 1960; Allan Frumkin Gallery, NYC, 1961, 62, 63; Kansas City/Nel-

Philip Pearlstein   *Two Female Nudes on Yellow Drape. 1964*

son, 1962. GROUP: The Kootz Gallery, Emerging Talent, 1954; WMAA Annuals, 1955, 56, 58, 62; The Stable Gallery Annuals, 1955, 56, 57; U. of Nebraska, 1956, 57; Walker, Expressionism, 1900–1955, 1956; Carnegie, 1955; Walker, 1958; Chicago/AI, 1959, 62; U. of Colorado, 1962; Boston U., 1964. COLLECTIONS: Colgate U.; NYU; U. of Nebraska; Newark Museum; WMAA.

PEARSON, HENRY CHARLES. b. October 8, 1914, Kinston, N.C. STUDIED: U. of North Carolina; Yale U., BA, MFA; ASL, 1953–55, with Reginald Marsh, Will Barnet, Robert Hale. US Army and Air Force, 1942–53. Traveled USA, the Orient. TAUGHT: Boston Museum School, and privately. MEMBER: American Abstract Artists. AWARDS: Raleigh/NCMA, 1957; Tamarind Fellowship, 1964. ADDRESS: 1810 Second Avenue, NYC. DEALER: Stephen Radich Gallery. ONE-MAN EXHIBITIONS: (first) Workshop Gallery, NYC, 1958; Stephen Radich Gallery, 1961, 62, 64. GROUP: PAFA, 1956, 64; Scranton/Everhart, Contemporary Americans, 1956; American Abstract Artists Annuals, 1958–64; A.F.A., Drawings from the WMAA Annual, 1960, circ., 1961–62; A.F.A., Purist Painting, circ., 1960–61; WMAA, Geometric Abstraction in America, circ., 1962. COLLECTIONS: Kansas City/Nelson; MOMA.

PEIRCE, WALDO. b. December 17, 1884, Bangor, Me. STUDIED: Phillips Academy; Harvard U., 1908, AB; Academie Julian, Paris, 1911. Traveled Europe, North Africa, Spain. COMMISSIONS (murals): US Post Offices, Westbrooke, Me., Troy, N.Y., and Peabody, Mass.; Field Service Building, NYC, 1961. AWARDS: Pomona College, 1939; Pepsi-Cola, 1944; Carnegie, First Hon. Men., 1944. ADDRESS: Searsport, Me. ONE-MAN EXHIBITIONS: (first) Wildenstein & Co., NYC, 1926; Wildenstein & Co., NYC (two-man), 1941; The Midtown Galleries, 1939, 41, 44, 45, 49, 60. RETROSPECTIVE: Rockland/Farnsworth, 1950. GROUP: Salon du Mai, Paris, 1912, 13, 14; Salon d'Automne, Paris, 1922. COLLECTIONS: Andover/Phillips; U. of Arizona; Augusta, Me./State; Bangor Public Library; Britannica; Brooklyn Museum; Harvard U.; MMA; U. of Maine; U. of Nebraska; PAFA; Pepsi-Cola Co.; Rockland/Farnsworth; Upjohn Co.; WMAA. BIBLIOGRAPHY: American Artists Group Inc. 3; Baur 7; Bazin; Bethers;

Boswell 1; Eliot; **Hale;** Hall; Mellquist; **Peirce; Varga.**

PENNEY, JAMES. b. September 6, 1910, St. Joseph, Mo. STUDIED: U. of Kansas, with Albert Bloch, Karl Mattern, R. J. Eastwood, 1931, BFA; ASL, 1931–34, with George Grosz, Charles Locke, William Von Schlegell, Thomas Hart Benton, John Sloan. Traveled USA, Mexico, Europe, Canada. TAUGHT: Hamilton College, 1948– ; Vassar College, 1955–56; Munson-Williams-Proctor Institute, Utica, N.Y., 1948–55; Bennington College, 1946–47; Bennett College, 1945–46; Hunter College, 1941–42; U. of Kansas, 1938–39; School for Art Studies, NYC, 1947; Kansas State U., summer, 1955; California College of Arts and Crafts, summer, 1960. MEMBER: ASL; National Society of Mural Painters; Audubon Artists. FEDERAL A.P. (murals): Greenpoint Hospital, Brooklyn, N.Y. (with Moses Soyer); Flushing (N.Y.) High School; P.S. 231, NYC; Far Rockaway (N.Y.) High School; New York World's Fair, 1939. COMMISSIONS (murals): Nebraska State Capitol, 1962–63 (3); US Post Offices, Union, Mo., and Palmyra, Mo.; Section of Fine Arts, Washington, D.C., 1939; Dunham Hall, Hamilton College, 1959. AWARDS: Kansas City/Nelson, Medal, 1931; Pepsi-Cola, Award and Medal, 1948; Western New York Printmakers Annual, First Prize, 1950; AAAL, Childe Hassam Award, 1953; Utica, P.P., 1955, 57; Our Town Competition, 1958; Kansas State U., P.P., 1951, 53, 57; Section of Fine Arts, 1939, 40, 41; Yaddo Fellowship, 1956, 61. ADDRESS: 101 Campus Road, Clinton, N.Y. DEALER: Kraushaar Galleries. ONE-MAN EXHIBITIONS: (first) Eighth Street Playhouse, NYC, 1936; Kraushaar Galleries, 1950, 54, 57, 61; Hudson D. Walker Gallery, NYC, 1939; Utica, 1951; Colgate U., 1952, 54; Union College (N.Y.), 1955; Wells College, 1953; Vassar College, 1956; Syracuse U., 1957; Wichita/AM, 1955; Kansas State College, 1955; Mulvane Art Museum, 1937; U. of Kansas, 1934, 37; Bennington College, 1946; Cazenovia Junior College, 1962. RETROSPECTIVE: Utica, 1955; Hamilton College, 1962. GROUP: Carnegie; Brooklyn Museum; PAFA; American Watercolor Society; New York World's Fair, 1939; Pepsi-Cola; Audubon Artists; U. of Illinois; Chicago/AI; WMAA Annuals; California Palace; Kansas City/Nelson; Cleveland/MA; National Gallery; Newark Museum; Walker; Fort Worth; Colby College; Toledo/MA; Atlanta/AA. **Collections:** Clearwater/Gulf Coast; Columbus; Continental Grain Company; Des Moines; Exeter; Fort Worth; Howard U.; Kansas City/Nelson; Kansas State College; Lehigh U.; Lincoln Life Insurance Co.; U. of Nebraska; New Britain; Springfield, Mass./MFA; Syracuse U.; Upjohn Co.; Utica; Wichita/AM. **Bibliography:** Baur 5.

PEREIRA, I. RICE. b. August 5, 1901, Boston, Mass. **Studied:** ASL, with Richard Lahey, Jan Matulka. Traveled Europe, North Africa; resided London, Paris. **Taught:** Pratt Institute. **Federal** A.P.: Easel painting, teaching. **Awards:** Pepsi-Cola, 1943. **Address:** 121 West 15 Street, NYC. **One-man Exhibitions:** ACA Gallery, 1933, also 1934, 35, 46, 49; East River Gallery, NYC, 1939; Howard U., 1938; Julien Levy Galleries, NYC, 1939; Art of This Century, NYC, 1944; Arts Club of Chicago, 1945; SFMA, 1947; Barnett Aden Gallery, Washington, D.C., 1948; Andover/Phillips, 1949; Santa Barbara/MA, 1950; Portland, Ore./AM, 1950; de Young, 1950; Syracuse U., 1951; Baltimore/MA, 1951; Ball State Teachers College, 1951; Durlacher Brothers, 1951; Phillips, 1952; Dayton/AI, 1952; Adele Lawson Gallery, Chicago, 1954; Hofstra College, 1954; U. of Michigan, 1954; Philadelphia Art Alliance, 1955; Corcoran, 1956; Adele Lawson Gallery, NYC, 1956; Lee Nordness Gallery, NYC, 1958, 59, 61; Rome-New York Foundation, Rome, 1960; A.A.A. Gallery, Washington, D.C., 1961; The Amel Gallery, 1961; Galerie Internationale, NYC, 1964. **Retrospective:** WMAA, circ., 1953. **Group:** Venice Biennial; Tate; ICA, London; MOMA, Fourteen Americans, circ., 1946; Darmstadt/Kunsthalle; Lille; Internationale Kunstausstellung, Berlin, 1951; USIA, 20th Century Highlights, circ., 1957–58; Chicago/AI Annuals; PAFA; Carnegie; I Sao Paulo Biennial, 1951. **Collections:** Allentown/AM; Andover/Phillips; Arizona State College; U. of Arizona; Atlanta U.; Ball State Teachers College; Baltimore/MA; Boston/MFA; Boston U.; Brandeis U.; The Catholic U. of America; Chicago/AI; Connecticut College; Dallas/MFA; Detroit/Institute; Finch College; Goucher College; Hartford/Wadsworth; Harvard U.; Howard U.; State U. of Iowa; S. C. Johnson & Son, Inc.; Kansas

City/Nelson; MMA; MOMA; The Miller Co.; U. of Minnesota; Newark Museum; New London; New Orleans/Delgado; New Paltz; Norfolk; Phillips; Phoenix; SFMA; SRGM; Smith College; Syracuse U.; Toledo/MA; Utica; Vassar College; WMAA; Walker; Worcester/AM; Youngstown/Butler. **Bibliography:** Baur 4, 5, 7; Bazin; Flanagan; Genauer; Goodrich and Baur 1; Janis, S.; Kootz 2; Mendelowitz; Miller, ed. 2; Nordness, ed.; Pearson 2; Pousette-Dart, ed.; Read 2; Richardson; Ritchie 1; Soby 5, 6; Wight 2.

PERLIN, BERNARD. b. November 21, 1918, Richmond, Va. **Studied:** New York School of Design, 1934–36; NAD, 1936–37, with Leon Kroll; ASL, 1936–37, with Isabel Bishop, William Palmer, Harry Sternberg. Traveled Europe, Mediterranean, the Orient; resided Italy, 1948–54. **Taught:** Brooklyn Museum School, 1947–48. **Commissions:** US Treasury Department; US Post Office Department, 1940. **Awards:** Kosciuszko Foundation, 1938; Chaloner Prize Foundation Award, 1948; Fulbright Fellowship, 1950; Guggenheim Foundation Fellowship, 1954, 59; NIAL, 1964. **Address:** Shadow Lake Road, Ridgefield, Conn. **Dealer:** Catherine Viviano Gallery. **One-man Exhibitions:** M. Knoedler & Co., 1948; Catherine Viviano Gallery, 1955, 58, 63. **Group:** Chicago/AI Annuals, 1948, 54, 59; Carnegie, 1949, 52; MMA, 1950; WMAA Annuals, 1951, 55; WMAA, The New Decade, 1954–55; Corcoran, 1953, 59; U. of Illinois, 1955, 59; Cincinnati/AM, 1958; Detroit/Institute, 1960; PAFA, 1960; Palazzo di Venezia, Rome, 1950; ICA, London, 1950; XXVIII Venice Biennial, 1956; Brussels World's Fair, 1958. **Collections:** California Palace; Chicago/AI; Denver/AM; Detroit/Institute; S. C. Johnson & Son, Inc.; Kansas City/Nelson; MOMA; Princeton U.; Springfield, Mass./MFA; Tate; WMAA. **Bibliography:** Baur 7; Eliot; Goodrich and Baur 1; McCurdy, ed.; Mendelowitz; Pousette-Dart, ed.; Rodman 1, 2.

PETERDI, GABOR. b. September 17, 1915, Budapest, Hungary. **Studied:** Academy of Fine Arts, Budapest, 1929; Academie Julian, Paris, 1931; Academie Scandinave, Paris, 1932; Academy of Fine Arts, Rome, 1930; Atelier 17, Paris, 1935. **Taught:** Brooklyn Museum School, 1948–53; Yale U., 1954– . **Awards:** Prix de

Gabor Peterdi   *Morning After. 1959*

Rome, 1930; Paris World's Fair, 1937, Gold Medal (jointly with Lurçat); Brooklyn Museum, 1950, 52, 60; American Color Print Society, 1951; Oakland/AM, 1957, 60; PAFA, Gold Medal, 1957; Boston Printmakers, 1959; Seattle/AM, P.P., 1960; Pasadena/AM, P.P., 1960; Bay Printmakers Society, Oakland, Adell Hyde Morrison Memorial Medal, 1960; PAFA, Pennell Memorial Medal, 1961; Ford Foundation Grant, 1960. **Address:** 108 Highland Avenue, Rowayton, Conn. **Dealer:** Grace Borgenicht Gallery Inc. **One-man Exhibitions:** (first) Ernst Museum, Budapest, 1930, also 1934; Bratislava, Czechoslovakia, 1930; Prague/National, 1930; Rome/Nazionale, 1930; Jeanne Bucher, Paris, 1936; Julien Levy Galleries, NYC, 1939; Norlyst Gallery, NYC, 1943, 44; Laurel Gallery, NYC, 1948, 49; Philadelphia Art Alliance, 1950, 55; Smithsonian, 1951; Silvermine Guild, 1952; Grace Borgenicht Gallery Inc., 1952, 55, 59, 61; NYPL, 1956; Kanegis Gallery, Boston, 1956, 57, 59, 61; The Howard Wise Gallery, Cleveland, 1959; Boston/MFA, 1959; Achenbach Foundation, 1960;

St. George's Gallery, London, 1958. **Group:** Salon des Surindependants, Paris, 1936, 38; Library of Congress, 1943, 47; The Print Club, Philadelphia, 1948; Brooklyn Museum, 1948, 49, 64; WMAA, 1949; MOMA, 1949; Yale U., 1949; Corcoran, 1949; PAFA, 1949, 61; Silvermine Guild; NYPL; Chicago/AI; Achenbach Foundation; U. of Nebraska; Minneapolis/Institute; Oakland/AM; U. of Illinois. **Collections:** Abilene Christian College; Achenbach Foundation; Albion College; Beloit College; Berea College; Boston/MFA; Brandeis U.; Brooklyn Museum; Brown U.; Budapest/National; Chicago/AI; Clearwater/Gulf Coast; Columbia, S.C./MA; Cranbrook; Currier; Dartmouth College; U. of Georgia; Honolulu Academy; Illinois Wesleyan U.; U. of Illinois; Indiana U.; MMA; MOMA; Memphis/Brooks; Michigan State U.; U. of Michigan; Minneapolis/Institute; NYPL; U. of Nebraska; Northwestern U.; Oakland/AM; U. of Oklahoma; Oregon State U.; PAFA; Pasadena/AM; Prague/National; Princeton U.; RISD; Rome/Nazionale; Rutgers U.; Sao Paulo; Smith

College; Smithsonian; Texas Wesleyan College; Vassar College; WMAA; Yale U. **BIBLIOGRAPHY:** Baur 5; Chaet; Goodrich and Baur 1; Hayter 1; **Johnson; Peterdi.**

PFRIEM, BERNARD. b. September 7, 1916, Cleveland, Ohio. STUDIED: John Huntington Polytechnical Institute, 1934–36; Cleveland Institute of Art, 1936–40. US Air Force, 1942–46. Traveled Europe, Mediterranean; resided Mexico, 1940–42, Paris, 1952–63. TAUGHT: Chicago Art Institute School, 1938–40; Peoples Art Center (MOMA), 1946–51; Cooper Union. Assistant to Jose Clemente Orozco on frescoes, Jiquilpan (Michoacan), Mexico, and to Julio Castellanos on murals, Mexico City. AWARDS: Agnes Gund and Mary Ranney Traveling Fellowship, 1940; William and Noma Copley Foundation Grant, 1959. ADDRESS: 448 West Broadway, NYC. DEALERS: Alexander Iolas Gallery; Galerie du Dragon. ONE-MAN EXHIBITIONS: (first) Alexander Iolas Gallery, 1951, also 1961, 63; Obelisk Gallery, Washington, D.C., 1962; Galerie du Dragon, 1960; American Cultural Center, Paris, 1954. RETROSPECTIVE: Cleveland Institute of Art, 1963. GROUP: Carnegie, 1942; WMAA Annual, 1951; Salon du Mai, Paris, 1962; Cleveland Institute of Art, 1939, 40, 41. COLLECTIONS: Chase Manhattan Bank; MOMA. BIBLIOGRAPHY: Waldberg 1, 2.

PINEDA, MARIANNA. b. May 10, 1925, Evanston, Ill. STUDIED: Bennington College; U. of California, Berkeley; privately with George Stanley in Los Angeles (sculpture); Cranbrook Academy of Art, with Carl Milles; privately with Raymond Puccinelli in San Francisco, with Oronzio Maldarelli in New York, and Ossip Zadkine in Paris. AWARDS: Buffalo/Albright, 1948; Walker, P.P., 1951; Boston Arts Festival, 1957, 60. **m.** Harold Tovish. ADDRESS: 164 Rawson Road, Brookline, Mass. DEALER: The Swetzoff Gallery. ONE-MAN EXHIBITIONS: (first) Slaughter Gallery, 1951; Walker, 1952; The Swetzoff Gallery, 1953; Lincoln, Mass./De Cordova, 1954. GROUP: MOMA; WMAA, 1953, 54, 57; MMA, 1957; Chicago/AI, 1957, 60; Buffalo/Albright, 1948; Boston Arts Festival, 1957, 58, 60; U. of Illinois, 1957. COLLECTIONS: Andover/Phillips; Boston/MFA; Dartmouth College; Hartford/Wadsworth; Utica; Walker; Williams College.

PITTMAN, HOBSON L. b. January 14, 1900, Tarboro, N.C. STUDIED: Rouse Art School, Tarboro, 1912–16, Penn State College, 1921–22, Carnegie Institute of Technology, 1924, Columbia U., 1925–26 (with Molly Rouse, Albert Heckman, Doris Rosenthal, Harold Dickson). Traveled Europe, North Africa, USA; summered in Woodstock, N.Y., 1920–30. TAUGHT: Friends Central School, Philadelphia, 1931–58; PAFA; The Pennsylvania State U.; Philadelphia Museum School. MEMBER: Philadelphia Watercolor Club; International Institute of Arts and Letters; NAD (past member, Artists Equity). COMMISSIONS: *Holiday* Magazine (cover); De Beers Diamonds (painting); Radio Corporation of America (2 paintings for music advertisements). AWARDS: Golden Gate International Exposition, San Francisco, 1939, Hon. Men.; PAFA, J. Henry Schiedt Memorial Prize, 1943; PAFA, Dawson Memorial Medal, 1944; California Palace, American Exhibition, Second Prize, 1947; Corcoran, William A. Clark Prize, 1947; Carnegie, Third Prize, 1949; Youngstown/Butler, First Prize, 1950; Corcoran, Second William A. Clark Prize, 1953; Guggenheim Foundation Fellowship, 1956. ADDRESS: 560 New Gulph Road, Bryn Mawr, Pa. DEALERS: M. Knoedler & Co.; The Milch Gallery. ONE-MAN EXHIBITIONS: (first) Edward Side Gallery, Philadelphia, 1928; Hudson D. Walker Gallery, NYC, 1938; The Milch Gallery, 1947, 54; San Antonio/McNay; PAFA, 1960; Raleigh/NCMA, 1950. RETROSPECTIVE: Raleigh/NCMA, 1963; Youngstown/Butler, 1942. GROUP: Carnegie; PAFA; Corcoran; Venice Biennial; Chicago/AI; WMAA; MMA; PMA; Golden Gate International Exposition, San Francisco, 1939; New York World's Fair, 1939; Tate, American Painting, 1946; Raleigh/NCMA; Youngstown/Butler. COLLECTIONS: Andover/Phillips; Britannica; Brooklyn Museum; Cleveland/MA; Carnegie; Corcoran; Cranbrook; Eaton Paper Co.; Florence, S. C., Museum; IBM; Indianapolis/Herron; MMA; MOMA; Memphis/Brooks; Montclair/AM; U. of Nebraska; North Carolina/State; Oklahoma; PAFA; PMA; The Pennsylvania State U.; Phillips; Phoenix; Raleigh/NCMA; St. Albans School, Washington, D.C.; Santa Barbara/MA; Toledo/MA; Twentieth Century Fox Film

Corp.; VMFA; WMAA; Wilmington; Youngstown/Butler. **BIBLIOGRAPHY:** American Artists Congress, Inc.; Baur 7; Genauer; Hall; **Pittman;** Watson 2.

POLLACK, REGINALD. b. July 29, 1924, Middle Village, N.Y. STUDIED: ASL, with William Harrison, Moses Soyer, Boardman Robinson. US Navy, 1941–45. Resided France, 1948–59, 1960–61. **TAUGHT:** Yale U., 1962–63; Cooper Union, 1963–64. **AWARDS:** Prix Neumann, Paris, 1952; Prix Othon Friesz, Paris, Mention, 1954, 57; Paris/Moderne, Prix de Peintres Etrangers, Second Prize, 1958. **ADDRESS:** 331 West 19 Street, NYC. DEALER: The Peridot Gallery. **ONE-MAN EXHIBITIONS:** (first) Charles Fourth Gallery, NYC, 1948; The Peridot Gallery, 1949, 52, 55, 56, 57, 59, 60; Galerie Saint-Placide, Paris, 1952; Dwan Gallery, 1960. **GROUP:** WMAA, 1953, 55, 56, 58; U. of Nebraska, 1957; Chicago/AI; Carnegie; NIAL; PAFA; Salon du Mai, Paris; U. of Illinois; Salon des Artistes Independants, Paris, 1952, 53, 54. **COLLECTIONS:** Bezalel Museum; Brooklyn Museum; Collection de l'Etat; U. of Glasgow; Haifa; MOMA; U. of Nebraska; Newark Museum; Rockefeller Institute; WMAA; Worcester/AM.

POLLOCK, JACKSON. b. January 28, 1912, Cody, Wyo.; **d.** August 11, 1956, Southampton, N.Y. STUDIED: ASL, 1929–31, with Thomas Hart Benton. FEDERAL A.P.: Easel painting, 1938–42. **m.** Lee Krasner (1944). **ONE-MAN EXHIBITIONS:** (first) Art of This Century, NYC, 1943, also 1946, 47; Arts Club of Chicago, 1945, 51; Sidney Janis Gallery, 1952, 54, 55, 57; Museo Civico Correr, Venice; Galleria d'Arte del Naviglio, Milan, 1950; Studio Paul Facchetti, Paris, 1952; Zurich, 1953; IV Sao Paulo Biennial, 1957. **RETROSPECTIVE:** MOMA, 1956. **GROUP:** XXIV, XXV, and XXVIII Venice Biennials, 1948, 50, 56; MOMA, Fifteen Americans, circ., 1952; I Sao Paulo Biennial, 1951; Galerie de France, American Vanguard, 1952; MOMA, 12 Modern American Painters and Sculptors, circ. Europe, 1953–55; SRGM, 75 Paintings from The Solomon R. Guggenheim Museum, circ. Europe, 1957; WMAA, The New Decade, 1954–55; PAFA; Chicago/AI; Brooklyn Museum; Buffalo/Albright. **COLLECTIONS:** Andover/Phillips; Baltimore/MA; Brooklyn Museum; Buffalo/Albright; Carnegie; Dallas/MFA; Hartford/Wadsworth; State U. of Iowa; Los Angeles/County MA; MMA; MOMA; Omaha/Joslyn; Rio de Janeiro; SFMA; SRGM; Utica; Washington U.; Yale U. **BIBLIOGRAPHY:** Barr 3; Baur 5, 7; Bazin; Beekman; Biddle 3; Blesh 1; Brion 1; Canaday; Christensen; Eliot; Elsen; Flanagan; Gaunt; Goodrich and Baur 1; Greenberg 1; Haftman; Henning; Hess, T. B.; Hunter 1, 5; Janis and Blesh 1;

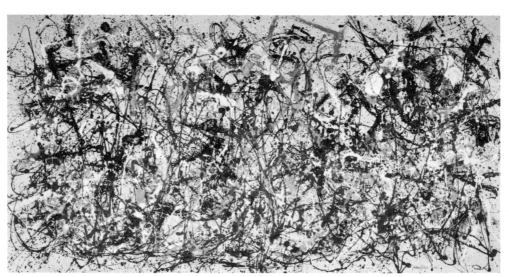

Jackson Pollock   *Autumn Rhythm.*

Janis, S.; Langui; Leepa; Lowry; McCourbrey; McCurdy, ed.; Mendelowitz; Motherwell, ed.; Neumeyer; **O'Hara 2;** Paalen; Ponente; Pousette-Dart, ed.; Ragon 1, 2; Read 2, 5; Restany 2; Richardson; Ritchie 1; **Robertson 2;** Rodman 1, 2, 3; Seuphor 1; Soby 5; Tapie 1.

PONCE DE LEON, MICHAEL. b. July 4, 1922, Miami, Fla. STUDIED: NAD; ASL, with Cameron Booth, Vaclav Vytlacil, Will Barnet, Harry Sternberg; PAFA; Brooklyn Museum School, with Ben Shahn, Gabor Peterdi, John Ferren; U. of Mexico City, BA. US Air Force, three years. Traveled Mexico, Norway and Europe extensively. TAUGHT: Vassar College; Cooper Union; Pratt Graphic Art Center; Hunter College. MEMBER: SAGA. COMMISSIONS: US Post Office Department (design for fine arts commemorative stamp). AWARDS: Bradley U., p.p., 1954; Dallas/MFA, p.p., 1954; SAGA, Gold Medal, 1954; L. C. Tiffany Grant, 1953, 55; The Print Club, Philadelphia, 1958; U. of Nebraska; Oakland/AM, Gold Medal; Fulbright Fellowship, 1956, 57; Audubon Artists, Gold Medal of Honor. ADDRESS: 30 East 14 Street, NYC. ONE-MAN EXHIBITIONS: (first) Galeria Proteo, Mexico City, 1954; Oslo/National; Oakland/AM. GROUP: MMA; MOMA; Brooklyn Museum; Walker; Victoria and Albert Museum; PAFA; SAGA; Portland, Me./MA; Audubon Artists; Denver/AM; Bradley U.; Chicago/AI; I Inter-American Paintings and Prints Biennial, Mexico City, 1958; NAD; Boston/MFA; U. of Illinois. COLLECTIONS: Achenbach Foundation; Brooklyn Museum; Cincinnati/AM; Columbia, S.C./MA; Dallas/MFA; Indiana U.; Library of Congress; MOMA; Melbourne/National; Mexico City/Nacional; NYPL; NYU; National Gallery; U. of Nebraska; Oslo/National; PAFA; SFMA; US State Department; United Nations; Victoria and Albert Museum; Walker.

POONS, LARRY. b. October 1, 1937, Tokyo, Japan. STUDIED: New England Conservatory of Music, 1955–57; Boston Museum School, 1958. ADDRESS: 108 Front Street, NYC. DEALER: Leo Castelli Inc. ONE-MAN EXHIBITIONS: (first) The Green Gallery, NYC, 1963, also 1964. GROUP: WGMA, 1963; Sidney Janis Gallery, The Classic Spirit, 1964; SRGM, American Drawings, 1964. COLLECTIONS: Buffalo/Albright; MOMA.

POOR, HENRY VARNUM. b. September 30, 1888, Chapman, Kans. STUDIED: Stanford U., AB, PBK, 1910; U. of London, Slade School, 1910, with Walter Sickert; Academie Julian, Paris, 1911, with Jean Paul Laurens. US Army, 1918. TAUGHT: Stanford U.; Mark Hopkins Art School, 1917; Colorado Springs Fine Arts Center, 1937; Skowhegan School. Active 1920–30 only as a potter: there are no paintings from this period. COMMISSIONS (murals): Penn State College, 1940; Justice Department, Washington, D.C., 1935; Interior Department, Washington, D.C., 1937; Deerfield (Mass.) Academy; Mt. Sinai Hospital, NYC. AWARDS: Architectural League of New York, Gold Medal of Honor, 1938; Syracuse/Everson, First Prize, 1937; Chicago/AI, Norman Wait Harris Silver Medal, 1932; Carnegie, Third Prize, 1933. ADDRESS: South Mountain Road, New City, N.Y. DEALER: Rehn Galleries. ONE-MAN EXHIBITIONS: (first) H. Kevorkian, NYC, 1920; Montross Gallery, NYC, 1921–31; Rehn Galleries, 1933– . GROUP: WMAA; Carnegie; Chicago/AI; U. of Illinois. COLLECTIONS: Andover/Phillips; Brooklyn Museum; Cleveland/MA; Columbus; U. of Kansas; MMA; U. of Nebraska; Newark Museum; SFMA; San Diego; WMAA; Wichita/AM. BIBLIOGRAPHY: Baur 7; Biddle 3; **Boswell 1, 2;** Bruce and Watson; Cahill and Barr, eds.; Cheney, M. C.; Genauer; Goodrich and Baur 1; Hall; Kent, N.; Mellquist; Nordmark; **Poor 1, 2;** Richardson.

PORTER, DAVID. b. May 18, 1912, Chicago, Ill. STUDIED: Chicago Art Institute School, briefly. Traveled USA, Mexico, Italy, France, Switzerland. TAUGHT: Privately, 1952–57; Ogunquit, 1964; Dartmouth College, 1964. Co-author of the Broadway play *Mrs. Patterson.* Operated the David Porter Gallery, Washington, D.C., 1942–46. AWARDS: Guild Hall, Hon. Men., 1951; Provincetown Arts Festival, First Prize, 1958; Sassoferrato (Italy) International, Second Gold Medal, 1960, and First Prize, Gold Medal of President Gronchi, 1961; Guild Hall, First Prize, 1964. ADDRESS: 541 East 72 Street, NYC. DEALERS: The Marble Arch Gallery, NYC; Mary Harriman Gallery Inc.; Mickelson's Gallery. ONE-MAN EXHIBITIONS: (first) Hugo Gallery, NYC, 1952; Deerfield (Mass.) Academy, 1953; Galerie Herve, NYC, 1955; The New Gallery, NYC, 1957; Obelisk Gallery, Washington, D.C., 1958; Tirca Karlis Gallery,

1959; Galleria L'Incontro, Rome, 1960; Modern Art Gallery, Palermo, Sicily, 1960; Ann Ross Gallery, White Plains, N.Y., 1961, 62; Southampton/Parrish, 1962; Alan Auslander Gallery, NYC, 1962; Ferrill Galleries, Santa Fe, N.M., 1963; Royal Athena II, 1964; Mickelson's Gallery, 1964; Dartmouth College, 1964. GROUP: Ninth Street Exhibition, NYC, 1951; Guild Hall, 1951, 54, 55, 56, 58, 64; WMAA Annual, 1951; Chicago/AI, 1952; U. of Illinois, 1952, 53; Carnegie, 1958; Corcoran, 1959; Dayton/AI, Modern Americans, 1959. COLLECTIONS: American Airlines; Guild Hall; Hempstead Bank; Miami/Modern; Norfolk; Provincetown/Chrysler; Southampton/Parrish; WMAA. BIBLIOGRAPHY: Janis and Blesh 1.

PORTER, FAIRFIELD. b. June 10, 1907, Winnetka, Ill. STUDIED: Harvard U.; ASL, with Boardman Robinson, Thomas Hart Benton. Traveled Europe, U.S.S.R., Scandinavia, USA, Canada. TAUGHT occasionally. Editorial Associate, *Art News* (Magazine), 1951–58; Art Critic, *The Nation* (Magazine), 1959. MEMBER:

International Association of Art Critics. AWARDS: Longview Foundation (for art criticism), 1959. ADDRESS: 49 South Main Street, Southampton, N.Y. DEALER: Tibor de Nagy Gallery. ONE-MAN EXHIBITIONS: (first) Community House, Winnetka, Ill., 1939; Tibor de Nagy Gallery, annually, 1951– ; U. of Alabama, 1963; RISD, 1959. GROUP: WMAA Annuals, 1961–64; Dayton/AI, 1961; MOMA, 1961; Yale U., 1961–62; PAFA, 1962; NIAL, 1962; U. of Nebraska, 1963; Colby College, Maine and Its Artists, 1963; Chicago/AI. COLLECTIONS: Corcoran; Hartford/Wadsworth; MOMA; U. of Nebraska; Santa Fe, N.M.; WMAA; Woodward Foundation. BIBLIOGRAPHY: McCourbrey; **Porter.**

POUSETTE-DART, NATHANIEL. b. September 7, 1886, St. Paul, Minn.; **d.** October 17, 1965, Valhalla, N.Y. STUDIED: ASL; W. M. Chase School, NYC, 1918; with Robert Henri; PAFA, 1920–24, with Thomas Anshutz. Traveled Europe, southern USA. TAUGHT: Minnesota College; College of Saint Catherine;

Fairfield Porter　　　*The Bay. 1964*

various art schools in NYC. MEMBER: Federation of Modern Painters and Sculptors (Past President); Art Directors Club, NYC (an organizer and Past President); American Society for Aesthetics; Architectural League of New York; Fellowship of The Pennsylvania Academy of the Fine Arts. AWARDS: PAFA, Cresson Fellowship (2); Westchester (N.Y.) Art Society, First Prize, 1963; Nantucket, First Prize, 1963. ONE-MAN EXHIBITIONS: (first) Stevens Art Gallery, St. Paul, 1910; American-British Art Center, NYC, 1934; Kenneth Taylor Gallery, Nantucket, 1959; Sunken Meadow Gallery, Kings Park, N.Y., 1961. RETROSPECTIVE: Anderson Galleries, NYC, 1926. BIBLIOGRAPHY: Blesh 1; Pousette-Dart; Pousette-Dart, ed.

POUSETTE-DART, RICHARD. b. June 8, 1916, St. Paul, Minn. STUDIED: Bard College, 1936. TAUGHT: New School for Social Research, 1959–61. AWARDS: S. R. Guggenheim Fellowship, 1951; Ford Foundation Grant, 1959. ADDRESS: Suffern, N.Y. DEALER: Betty Parsons Gallery. ONE-MAN EXHIBITIONS: (first) Artists' Gallery, NYC, 1941; The Willard Gallery, 1943, 45, 46; Art of This Century, NYC, 1947; Betty Parsons Gallery, 1948, 49, 50, 51, 53, 55, 58, 59, 61, 64. RETROSPECTIVE: WMAA, 1963. GROUP: Buffalo/Albright, Expressionism in American Painting, 1952; SRGM, Abstract Expressionists and Imagists, 1961; WMAA, Nature in Abstraction, 1958; WMAA, The New Decade, 1954–55; Carnegie, 1958, 61; I Inter-American Paintings and Prints Biennial, Mexico City, 1958; Documenta II, Kassel, 1959; Chicago/AI, Abstract and Surrealist Art, 1948; MOMA, The Art of Assemblage, circ., 1961; MOMA, Abstract Painting and Sculpture in America, 1951; U. of Illinois, 1951, 52, 53; Hartford/Wadsworth, Continuity and Change, 1962; WMAA Annuals, 1949, 51, 53, 55–59, 1961. COLLECTIONS: Equitable Life Assurance Society; MOMA; Union Carbide Corp.; WMAA. BIBLIOGRAPHY: Baur 5; Blesh 1; Goodrich and Baur 1; Janis and Blesh 1; Motherwell and Reinhardt, eds.; Nordness, ed.; Pousette-Dart, ed.; Ragon 2; Ritchie 1; Seitz 2.

POZZATTI, RUDY. b. January 14, 1926, Telluride, Colo. STUDIED: U. of Colorado, with Wendell Black, Ben Shahn, Max Beckmann, 1948, BFA, 1950, MFA. US Army, 1943–46. Traveled Europe, U.S.S.R., Mexico; resided Italy. TAUGHT: Indiana U., 1956–60; U. of Colorado, 1948–50, summers, 1951, 54; U. of Nebraska, 1950–56; Cooper Union, summer, 1955; The Ohio State U., summer, 1959; Yale-Norfolk Summer Art School, 1957. MEMBER: SAGA. COMMISSIONS: International Graphic Arts Society (3 editions); Print Club of Cleveland; New York Hilton Hotel. AWARDS: Youngstown/Butler, P.P., 1951, 52; St. Louis/City, Vladimir Golschmann Prize, 1952; St. Louis/City, Henry V. Putzell Prize, 1955; PAFA, Alice McFadden Eyre Medal, 1957; The Print Club, Philadelphia, Mildred Boericke Award, 1955; U. of Illinois, Graphic Art Exhibition, First Prize, 1949; Walker, P.P., 1951; Library of Congress, Pennell P.P., 1958; Boston Printmakers, Paul J. Sachs Award, 1958, 61; PAFA, P.P., 1959 (2); AAAL, P.P., 1960; SAGA, 100 Prints of the Year, First Prize, 1963; Fulbright Fellowship (Italy), 1952–53; and many others. ADDRESS: 117 South Meadowbrook, Bloomington, Ind. DEALER: Weyhe Gallery. ONE-MAN EXHIBITIONS: (first) Chicago/AI. 1953; Martha Jackson Gallery, 1954; Philadelphia Art Alliance, 1953; Kansas City/Nelson, 1955; Weyhe Gallery, 1957; Clarke College, 1957; Carleton College, 1957; U. of Maine, 1956; Cleveland/MA, 1955; U. of Nebraska, 1956; Gump's Gallery, 1956, 60; U. of Minnesota, 1958; Louisville/Speed, 1958; Ohio U., 1960; Walker, 1960; J. Seligmann and Co., 1961; U. of Louisville, 1963; Jane Haslem Gallery, Durham, N.C., 1963. GROUP: The Print Club, Philadelphia, 1954; U. of Oklahoma, 1956; WMAA, Fulbright Artists, 1958; U. of Michigan, 1959; The Pennsylvania State U., 10 American Printmakers, 1959; WMAA, Young America, 1960; Syracuse U., 1962; PCA, American Prints Today, circ., 1962; U. of Kentucky, Graphics IV, 1962; IBM Gallery of Arts and Sciences, NYC, 30 American Printmakers, circ., 1964. COLLECTIONS: Achenbach Foundation; Albion College; Allegheny College; Alverthorpe Gallery; Ball State Teachers College; Baltimore/MA; Bibliotheque Nationale; Boston/MFA; Bradley U.; Brooklyn Museum; U. of California, Berkeley; Cleveland/MA; U. of Colorado; Concordia Teachers College; Davidson, N.C.; U. of Delaware; De Pauw U.; Duke U.; Eastern Michigan U.; Harvard U.; Indiana U.; Indianapolis/Herron; State College of Iowa; Jacksonville/AM; Kansas City/Nelson; Kansas State College; La Jolla; Library of

Congress; Louisville/Speed; U. of Louisville; MMA; MOMA; U. of Maine; Marshall U.; U. of Michigan; NYPL; National Gallery; Nebraska State Teachers College; U. of Nebraska; Oakland/AM; Oberlin College; The Ohio State U.; Oklahoma City U.; U. of Oklahoma; Omaha/Joslyn; PAFA; PMA; U. of Puerto Rico; SFMA; St. Louis/City; St. Mary's College (Ind.); Seattle/AM; Sioux City Art Center; Springfield, Mo./AM; Syracuse U.; Texas Western College; US State Department; Utica; Victoria and Albert Museum; Walker; Washburn U. of Topeka; Wichita/AM; College of William and Mary; U. of Wisconsin; Youngstown/Butler; Youngstown U. **BIBLIOGRAPHY:** Chaet; **Print Club of Cleveland.**

PRESTOPINO, GREGORIO. b. June 21, 1907, NYC. STUDIED: NAD, with C. W. Hawthorne. Traveled Europe, southwestern USA, Mexico. **TAUGHT:** New School for Social Research, 1949– ; Brooklyn Museum School, 1946–49; Veterans Art Center, MOMA, 1946–48. FEDERAL A.P.: Easel painting. **AWARDS:** NIAL Grant, 1961; PAFA, Joseph E. Temple Gold Medal, 1946; Pepsi-Cola, Third Prize, 1946; Youngstown/Butler, First Prize, 1958; Cannes Film Festival, First Prize (for the art film "Harlem Wednesday"), 1958. **ADDRESS:** 20 Farm Lane, Roosevelt, N.J. ONE-MAN EXHIBITIONS: (first) ACA Gallery, 1943, also 1946, 48, 50, 51, 53, 54, 57; Lee Nordness Gallery, NYC, 1959, 60, 61, 62, 64; Rex Evans Gallery, 1961; Witte. GROUP: WMAA Annuals; MOMA; Corcoran; PAFA; New York World's Fair, 1939; Golden Gate International Exposition, San Francisco, 1939; Chicago/AI; Venice Biennial; USIA. COLLECTIONS: U. of Alabama; Andover/Phillips; Chicago/AI; U. of Hawaii; IBM; U. of Illinois; S. C. Johnson & Son, Inc.; MOMA; Mary Washington College; U. of Nebraska; U. of Oklahoma; Phillips; Rochester/Memorial; WMAA; Walker; Youngstown/Butler. **BIBLIOGRAPHY:** Genauer; Nordness, ed.; Pousette-Dart, ed.

PRICE, CLAYTON S. b. May 24, 1874, Bedford, Iowa; **d.** May 1, 1950, Portland, Ore. STUDIED: Washington U. School of Fine Arts, 1905–06. Traveled Canada, western USA. PWA, 1933–34. FEDERAL A.P.: Easel painting, intermittently 1935–40. AWARDS: Seattle/AM, Katherine Baker Memorial Award, 1929; Portland, Ore./AM, P.P., 1950; Hon. MA, Reed College, 1948. ONE-MAN EXHIBITIONS: (first) Beaux Arts Gallery, San Francisco, 1925; Berkeley (Calif.) League of Fine Art, 1927; Oregon Society of Artists, Portland, 1929; Curt Valentine Gallery, NYC, 1945; Reed College, 1948; Portland, Ore./AM, 1949; The Willard Gallery, 1949. RETROSPECTIVE: Portland, Ore./AM, Price Paintings 1900–42, 1942; Portland, Ore./AM, Memorial Exhibition, circ., 1951. GROUP: MOMA, Fourteen Americans, circ., 1946; Detroit/Institute, 1944. COLLECTIONS: Andover/Phillips; Beach Public School; Detroit/Institute; Los Angeles/County MA; MMA; U. of Oregon; Pendleton High School; Portland, Ore./AM; Reed College; Seattle/AM; US Treasury Department; Utica. **BIBLIOGRAPHY:** Baur 7; Blesh 1; Janis, S.; Miller, ed. 2; Richardson.

q

QUIRT, WALTER. b. November 24, 1902, Iron River, Mich. STUDIED: Layton School of Art, 1921–23. Traveled Mexico, Canada. TAUGHT: Layton School of Art, 1924–29; U. of Minnesota, 1945–47, 1952– . FEDERAL A.P.: Easel painting, 1936–37. COMMISSIONS: Bellevue Hospital, NYC, 1939 (mural). AWARDS: Detroit/Institute, Cranbrook Prize, 1946. ADDRESS: 2816 West 42 Street, Minneapolis, Minn. DEALER: The Greer Gallery. ONE-MAN EXHIBITIONS: (first) Julien Levy Galleries, NYC, 1936, also 1939; The Pinacotheca, NYC, 1942; A.A.A. Gallery, NYC, 1943; Durlacher Brothers, 1944, 45; U. of Minnesota, 1949, 59; The New Gallery, NYC, 1951; Duveen-Graham Gallery, NYC, 1957; The Greer Gallery, 1963. RETROSPECTIVE: A.F.A./Ford Foundation, circ., 1960. GROUP: MOMA; WMAA; California Palace; St. Louis/City; Hartford/Wadsworth; Walker; Minneapolis/Institute; Newark Museum; U. of Illinois. COLLECTIONS: Andover/Phillips; Hartford/Wadsworth; U. of Illinois; State U. of Iowa; La Jolla; MOMA; U. of Minnesota; Newark Museum; WMAA; Walker; Washington U. BIBLIOGRAPHY: Baur 7; Biddle 3; **Coates;** Janis, S.; Kootz 2.

QUISGARD, LIZ WHITNEY. b. October 23, 1929, Philadelphia, Pa. STUDIED: Johns Hopkins U.; U. of Baltimore; Maryland Institute, 1947–49; privately with Morris Louis, 1957–60. AWARDS: Maryland Institute, Fellow of the Rinehart School of Sculpture, 1964–65; Baltimore/MA, Second Prize, 1958. ADDRESS: 603 Evesham Avenue, Baltimore, Md. DEALER: Andre Emmerich Gallery, NYC. ONE-MAN EXHIBITIONS: (first) Ef Gallery, Baltimore, 1954; Main Gallery, Maryland Institute, 1955; Martick's Gallery, Baltimore, 1956, 58; Johns Hopkins U., 1958; Jefferson Place Gallery, 1961; Key Gallery, NYC, 1961; Andre Emmerich Gallery, NYC, 1962. GROUP: Baltimore/MA, 1951, 52, 53, 58; Peale Museum, Baltimore, 1947, 56; Corcoran, 1957, 64; PAFA Annual, 1964; Youngstown/Butler, 1956. COLLECTIONS: U. of Arizona; U. of Baltimore.

RABKIN, LEO. b. July 21, 1919, Cincinnati, Ohio. STUDIED: U. of Cincinnati, BA, B.Ed.; Art Academy of Cincinnati; NYU, with Robert Iglehart, Hale Woodruff, Tony Smith, William Baziotes, MA. TAUGHT: NYC public school system. MEMBER: American Abstract Artists. AWARDS: Ford Foundation, P.P., 1961; Silvermine Guild, Watercolor Award, 1961, 64. ADDRESS: 61 Sullivan Street, NYC. ONE-MAN EXHIBITIONS: (first) Stairway Gallery, NYC, 1954; Muriel Latow Gallery, NYC, 1961; Gotham Gallery, New Hope, Pa., 1961; Louis Alexander Gallery, NYC, 1962, 63. GROUP: Brooklyn Museum, Watercolor Biennial; Hirschl & Adler Galleries, Inc., NYC, Experiences in Art, I & II, 1959, 60; Martha Jackson Gallery, New Media—New Forms, I & II, 1960, 61; MOMA, New Talent; WMAA Annuals, 1959, 61; A.F.A., Affinities, circ., 1962; MOMA, Abstract American Drawings and Watercolors, circ. Latin America, 1961–63; American Abstract Artists Annuals, 1963, 64. COLLECTIONS: Geigy Chemical Corp.; MOMA; NYU; SRGM; Savings Bank Association of New York State; The Singer Company Inc.; WMAA; Woodward Foundation.

RACZ, ANDRE. b. November 21, 1916, Cluj, Rumania. STUDIED: U. of Bucharest, 1935, BA; Atelier 17, NYC, 1943–45; New School for Social Research, 1943–45. To USA 1939; citizen 1948. Traveled Europe, Latin America, Mexico. TAUGHT: U. of Chile, 1947; U. of Kentucky, 1960; Columbia U., 1951– . MEMBER: American Association of University Professors; SAGA. AWARDS: Guggenheim Foundation Fellowship, 1956; Fulbright Fellowship (Chile), 1957; SAGA, Mrs. A. W. Erickson Prize, 1953; Noyes Memorial Prize, 1955; Ford Foundation, P.P., 1962; U. of Kentucky, P.P., 1959. ADDRESS: P.O. Box 43, Demarest, N.J. DEALER: Ruth White Gallery. ONE-MAN EXHIBITIONS: (first) New School for Social Research, 1942; A.F.A., circ., 1948–51; and exhibits in NYC nearly every year. RETROSPECTIVE: NYPL, 1954; Museo de Bellas Artes, Santiago, Chile, 1957; U. of Kentucky, 1960. GROUP: MOMA; WMAA Annuals; Brooklyn Museum; Corcoran; Library of Congress; MOMA, 50 Years of American Art, circ. Europe, 1955; I Inter-American Paintings and Prints Biennial, Mexico City, 1958; I International Religious Art Biennial, Salzburg, 1958. COLLECTIONS: Bibliotheque Nationale; Brooklyn Museum; Cordoba/Provincial; George Washington U.; U. of Kentucky; Library of Congress; MMA; MOMA; Melbourne/National; U. of Minnesota; NYPL; National Gallery; Oslo/National; PMA; SFMA; Salzburg; Smith College; Smithsonian; WMAA; Youngstown/Butler. BIBLIOGRAPHY: Baur 7; Hayter 2; Janis, S.

RAFFAELE, JOSEPH. b. February 22, 1933, NYC. STUDIED: Cooper Union, 1951–54, with Sidney Delevante, Leo Manso; Yale U., with Josef Albers, James Brooks, BFA. Traveled Europe; resided Rome and Florence, Italy, 1958–60. AWARDS: Yale-Norfolk Summer Art School Fellowship, 1954, 55; Fulbright Fellowship, 1958; L. C. Tiffany Grant, 1961. ADDRESS: 56 West 12 Street, NYC. DEALER: The Stable Gallery. ONE-MAN EXHIBITIONS: (first) Kanegis Gallery, Boston, 1958; Numero Galleria d'Arte, Florence, Italy, 1959; D'Arcy Gallery, 1962, 63. GROUP: Brooklyn Museum; MOMA.

RATTNER, ABRAHAM. b. July 8, 1895, Poughkeepsie, N.Y. STUDIED: George Washington U.; The Corcoran School of Art; PAFA, 1916–17; Academie des Beaux-Arts, Paris; Academie Julian, Paris; Academie Ranson, Paris; Academie de la Grande Chaumiere, 1920. US Army, 1917–19. Traveled Europe, USA; resides New York and Paris. TAUGHT: New School for Social Research, 1947–55; Yale U., 1949; American Academy, Rome, 1951; U. of Illinois, 1952–54; ASL, 1954; Michigan State U., 1956–58; Sag Harbour Summer Art Center, 1956; PAFA, 1954; Brooklyn Museum School, 1950–51. COMMISSIONS: Fairmount Temple, Cleveland, 1957; Loop Synagogue, Chicago, 1958; St. Francis Monastery, Chicago, 1956; Duluth (Minn.) Synagogue; De Waters Art Center, Flint, Mich., 1958; US Navy Department, Washington, D.C. AWARDS: PAFA, Cresson Fellowship, 1919; PAFA, Joseph E. Temple Gold Medal, 1945; Pepsi-Cola, Second Prize, 1946; La Tausca Competition, First Prize, 1947; Carnegie, Hon. Men., 1949; U. of Illinois, P.P., 1950; Corcoran, First Prize, 1953; NIAL, 1958. ADDRESS: 8 West 13 Street, NYC. DEALER: The Downtown Gallery. ONE-MAN EXHIBITIONS: (first) Galerie Bonjean, Paris, 1935; Julien Levy Galleries, NYC, 1936–41; Courvoisier Gallery, San Francisco, 1940; Arts Club of Chicago, 1940; P. Rosenberg and Co., 1943, 44, 46, 48, 50, 52, 56; Philadelphia Art Alliance, 1945; Stendahl Gallery, Los Angeles, 1943; Santa Barbara/MA, 1943; Arts and Crafts Club, New Orleans, 1952; Renaissance Society, Chicago, 1957; The Downtown Gallery, 1957, 58, 60; Corcoran, 1958; North Shore Congregation Israel, Chicago, 1958; WMAA (four-man), 1959; Galerie Internationale, NYC, 1961; Chicago/AI, 1955. RETROSPECTIVE: U. of Illinois, 1952; A.F.A., circ., 1960; Baltimore/MA, 1946; Vassar College, 1948. GROUP: PAFA; Corcoran; Chicago/AI; U. of Illinois; Carnegie; MMA; WMAA; Buffalo/Albright; Baltimore/MA; Detroit/Institute; Des Moines; New School for Social Research. COLLECTIONS: Arizona State College; Ball State Teachers College; Baltimore/MA; Bezalel Museum; Brandeis U.; Britannica; Buffalo/Albright; CIT Corporation; Chicago/AI; Cornell U.; Dartmouth College; Des Moines; Detroit/Institute; Fort Worth; Hartford/Wadsworth; U. of Illinois; Jewish Museum; Johnson College; MMA; Manufacturers Hanover Trust Co.; Mar-

quette U.; Michigan State U.; Musee du Jeu de Paume; U. of Nebraska; Newark Museum; New School for Social Research; U. of Oklahoma; PAFA; PMA; Phillips; St. Louis/City; Santa Barbara/MA; Vassar College; WMAA; Walker; Washington U.; Williams College; Yale U.; Youngstown/Butler. BIBLIOGRAPHY: Baur 5, 7; Biddle 3; Eliot; Frost; Genauer; Getlein; Goodrich and Baur 1, 2; Hayter 1, 2; Janis, S.; Kootz 2; Leepa; Mendelowitz; Newton 1; Nordness, ed.; Pagano; Pearson 2; Pousette-Dart, ed.; Read 2; Richardson; Wight 2.

RAUSCHENBERG, ROBERT. b. October 22, 1925, Port Arthur, Tex. STUDIED: Kansas City Art Institute and School of Design, 1946–47; Academie Julian, Paris, 1947; Black Mountain College, 1948–49, with Josef Albers; ASL, 1949–50, with Vaclav Vytlacil, Morris Kantor. US Navy. Traveled Italy, North Africa, 1952–53. TAUGHT: Black Mountain College, 1952. Designs stage sets and costumes for the Merce Cunningham Dance Co. (since 1955); Technical Director since early 1960's. AWARDS: XXXII Venice Biennial, First Prize, 1964; Gallery of Modern Art, Ljubljana, Yugoslavia, V International Exhibition of Prints, First Prize, 1963. ADDRESS: 809 Broadway, NYC. DEALER: Leo Castelli Inc. ONE-MAN EXHIBITIONS: Betty Parsons Gallery, 1951; The Stable Gallery, 1953; Galleria d'Arte Contemporanea, Florence, Italy, 1953; L'Obelisco, Rome, 1963; Charles Egan Gallery, 1955; Leo Castelli Inc., 1958, 59, 60, 61, 63; La Tartaruga, Rome, 1959; Galerie 22, Dusseldorf, 1959; Daniel Cordier, Paris, 1961; Galleria dell'Ariete, Milan, 1961; Dwan Gallery, 1962; Ileana Sonnabend (Gallery), Paris, 1963. RETROSPECTIVE: Jewish Museum, 1963; Whitechapel Art Gallery, London, 1964. GROUP: The Stable Gallery Annuals, 1951–56; Jewish Museum, The New York School, Second Generation, 1957; A.F.A., Collage in America, circ., 1957–58; Houston/MFA, Collage International, 1958; Carnegie, 1958, 61; A.F.A., Art and the Found Object, circ., 1959; Documenta II, Kassel, 1959; V Sao Paulo Biennial, 1959; I Paris Biennial, 1959; Daniel Cordier, Paris, Exposition InteRnatiOnale de Surrealisme, 1959; MOMA, Sixteen Americans, circ., 1959; Martha Jackson Gallery, New Media—New Forms, I & II, 1960, 61; A.F.A., School of New York—Some Younger American Painters, 1960; Des Moines,

Robert Rauschenberg   *Kite. 1963*

Six Decades of American Painting, 1961; WMAA Annuals, 1961, 63, 64; MOMA, The Art of Assemblage, circ., 1961; SRGM/USIA, American Vanguard, circ. Europe, 1961–62; SRGM, Abstract Expressionists and Imagists, 1961; Galerie Rive Droite, Paris, Le Nouveau Realisme, 1961; MOMA, Abstract Watercolors and Drawings:USA, circ. Latin America and Europe, 1961–62; Stockholm/National, 4 Americans, circ., 1962; Salon du Mai, Paris, 1962; Seattle World's Fair, 1962; Art:USA:Now, circ., 1962– ; III International Biennial Exhibition of Prints, Tokyo, 1962; Chicago/AI, 1963; Corcoran, 1963; SRGM, Six Painters and The Object, circ., 1963; WGMA, The Popular Image, 1963; Musee Cantonal des Beaux-Arts, Lausanne, I Salon International de Galeries Pilotes, 1963; Tate, Dunn International, 1964; ICA, London, The Popular Image, 1963; El Retiro Parquet, Madrid, Arte de America y España, 1963; Gallery of Modern Art, Ljubljana, Yugoslavia, V International Exhibition of Prints, 1963; Brandeis U., New Directions in American Painting, 1963; Jewish Museum, Black and White, 1963; Hartford/Wadsworth, Black, White, and Gray, 1964; New York State Pavilion, New York World's Fair, 1964–65. COLLEC-

TIONS: Buffalo/Albright; Cornell U.; Goucher College; S.C. Johnson & Son, Inc.; The Singer Company Inc.; Tate; WMAA. **BIBLIOGRAPHY:** Elsen; Friedman, ed.; Janis and Blesh 1; *Metro;* Newmeyer; Nordness, ed.; Rodman 3; Seitz 2.

REDER, BERNARD. b. June 29, 1897, Czernowitz, Bukovina, Austria; **d.** September 7, 1963, NYC. Austrian Army, 1914–18. STUD- IED: Academy of Fine Arts, Prague, 1919, with Peter Bromse, Jan Stursa. Traveled Cuba, USA, Europe extensively. To USA 1943; citizen 1948. **AWARDS:** International architectural competi- tion to house the monument to Christopher Columbus in Santo Domingo, 1927; Ford Foun- dation Grant, Program in Humanities and the Arts ($10,000), 1960. **ONE-MAN EXHIBITIONS:** (first) The Rudolphinium, Prague, 1928 (water- colors); Manes Gallery, Prague, 1935; Galerie de Berri, Paris, 1940; Lyceum Gallery, Havana, 1942; U. of Ravenna, 1942; Weyhe Gallery, 1943; Philadelphia Art Alliance, 1950; Bezalel Museum, 1950; Tel Aviv, 1950; The Print Club, Philadelphia, 1950; Grace Borgenicht Gallery Inc., 1951, 52, 53; Dominion Gallery, Mont- real, 1953; Chicago/AI, 1953; Galleria d'Arte Moderna L'Indiano, Florence, Italy, 1956, 57; The Contemporaries, 1956; Palazzo Torrigiani, Florence, Italy, 1957; World House Galleries, 1959, 61. **RETROSPECTIVE:** WMAA, 1961. **GROUP:** WMAA, European Artists in America, 1945; MOMA, 1949, 51; U. of Illinois, 1953; Chicago/AI; PMA, 1949. **COLLECTIONS:** Balti- more/MA; Brooklyn Museum; Chicago/AI; Harvard U.; Jewish Museum; MMA; MOMA; NYPL; National Gallery; PMA; Sao Paulo. **BIBLIOGRAPHY:** Goodrich and Baur 1.

Bernard Reder   *Bust of Flower Girl. 1955*

REINHARDT, AD. b. December 24, 1913, Buffalo, N.Y. STUDIED: Columbia U., with Meyer Schapiro, 1931–35, BA, 1936–37; NYU, Institute of Fine Arts, 1945–51, with Alfred Salmony; NAD, 1936–37, with Francis Criss, Carl Holty. US Navy, photographer, 1944–45. Traveled Europe and Asia extensively. TAUGHT: Brooklyn College, 1947– ; California School of Fine Arts, 1950; Yale U., 1952–53; U. of Wyoming, 1951; Hunter College, 1959– ; Syracuse U., 1957. Worked for *PM* (newspaper), NYC, 1944–47. Articles in *Art International, Art News, College Art Journal, It Is* (magazines). MEMBER: American Abstract Artists, 1937–47; Asia Society; Chinese Art Society. FEDERAL A.P.: Easel painting, 1936–39. ADDRESS: 209 East 19 Street, NYC. DEALERS: Betty Parsons Gallery; Dwan Gallery; Iris Clert. ONE-MAN EXHIBITIONS: (first) Columbia U., 1943; Artists' Gallery, NYC, 1944; Mortimer Brandt, NYC, 1945; Brooklyn Museum School, 1946; Betty Parsons Gallery, 1946, 47, 48, 49, 50, 51, 52, 53, 55, 56, 59, 60; Iris Clert, 1963; Syracuse U., 1957; Leverkusen, 1961; Dwan Gallery, 1961, 63; ICA, London, 1964. GROUP: MOMA, Abstract Painting and Sculpture in America, 1951; MOMA, Americans 1963, circ., 1963–64; American Abstract Artists Annuals; WMAA; New York World's Fair, 1939; WMAA, The New Decade, 1954–55; Brussels World's Fair, 1958; SRGM, Abstract Expressionists and Imagists, 1961; Seattle World's Fair, 1962; Tate, 1964. COLLECTIONS: Baltimore/MA; Buffalo/Albright; Dayton/AI; Leverkusen; Los Angeles/County MA; MOMA; U. of Nebraska; Oslo/National; PMA; SFMA; Toledo/MA; WMAA; Yale U. BIBLIOGRAPHY: Blesh 1; Hess, T. B.; Janis and Blesh 1; Janis, S.; **Motherwell and Reinhardt, eds.;** Nordness, ed.; Pousette-Dart, ed.; Ritchie 1; Rodman 1.

REINHARDT, SIEGFRIED GERHARD. b. July 31, 1925, Eydkuhnen, Germany. STUDIED: Washington U., AB. TAUGHT: Washington U., 1955– . AWARDS: Scholarship, John Herron Art Institute, 1943; 20th Century Book Club Award, 1945; St. Louis Artists' Guild, 1951, 53, 54, 55, 57, 58; St. Louis/City, 1951, 53, 55, 56; Cincinnati/AM, 1958; International Exhibition of Sacred Art, Trieste, 1961. ADDRESS: 635 Craig Woods Drive, Kirkwood 22, Mo. DEALER: The Midtown Galleries. ONE-MAN EXHIBITIONS:

Eleanor Smith Gallery, St. Louis, 1942, 43, 47; St. Louis Artists' Guild, 1951, 58; Southern Illinois U., 1951, 52; Art Mart, Clayton, Mo., 1953; Stevens-Gross Gallery, Chicago, 1952; Texas Western College, 1954; Illinois State Normal U., Normal, Ill., 1954; Schweig Gallery, St. Louis, 1956; Hewitt Gallery, NYC, 1957; The Midtown Galleries, 1961. GROUP: Washington U., 1950; ICA, Boston, 1958; USIA, circ. Europe, 1959; St. Louis/City, 1943, 45, 47, 49, 51, 53, 58, 61; Chicago/AI, 1947, 54; MMA, 1950; Los Angeles/County MA, 1951, 55; WMAA, 1951–55, 1960; Walker, 1954; Dallas/MFA, 1954; Beloit College, 1954; A.F.A. (stained glass), circ.; Cincinnati/AM, 1955, 58, 61; PAFA, 1958; ART:USA:58, NYC, 1958; Kansas State College, 1958; Boston/MFA, 1960, 61; Columbus, 1961; Trieste, 1961. COLLECTIONS: AAAL; Abbott Laboratories; Beloit College; Cincinnati/AM; Concordia Teachers College; Kansas City/Nelson; RISD; St. Louis/City; Southern Illinois U.; WMAA. BIBLIOGRAPHY: Nordness, ed.; Pousette-Dart, ed.

RESNICK, MILTON. b. January 8, 1917, Bratslov, Russia. Resided Paris, 1946–48. TAUGHT: Pratt Institute, 1954–55; U. of California, Berkeley, 1955–56. FEDERAL A.P.: Teacher. ADDRESS: 80 Forsyth Street, NYC. DEALER: The Howard Wise Gallery, NYC. ONE-MAN EXHIBITIONS: (first) Poindexter Gallery, 1955, also 1957, 59; de Young, 1955; Ellison Gallery, Fort Worth, 1959; Holland-Goldowsky Gallery, Chicago, 1959; The Howard Wise Gallery, Cleveland, 1960; The Howard Wise Gallery, NYC, 1960, 61, 64; Feiner Gallery, NYC, 1964. GROUP: WMAA Annuals, 1957, 59, 61, 63; Carnegie, 1958; Walker, 60 American Painters, 1960; SRGM, Abstract Expressionists and Imagists, 1961; USIA, Contemporary American Prints, circ. Latin America, 1961–62; Chicago/AI Annual, 1962; PAFA Annual, 1962; Seattle World's Fair, 1962; SFMA, Directions—Painting U.S.A., 1963. COLLECTIONS: Akron/AI; U. of California, Berkeley; Cleveland/MA; Hartford/Wadsworth; MOMA; WMAA; Waitsfield/Bundy. BIBLIOGRAPHY: Goodrich and Baur 1; Hunter 1; Nordness, ed.; Passloff.

REYNAL, JEANNE. b. April 1, 1903, White Plains, N.Y. Privately educated; apprenticed to Atelier Boris Anrep, Paris, 1930–38. Traveled the world extensively. COMMISSIONS: Ford Foundation, 1959; Our Lady of Florida Monastery, 1962. AWARDS: SFMA, Emanuel Walter p.p., 1945. ADDRESS: 240 West 11 Street, NYC. ONE-MAN EXHIBITIONS: (first) SFMA, 1942; Arts Club of Chicago, 1943; Baltimore/MA, 1943. GROUP: WMAA Annuals, 1950–56; Seattle World's Fair, 1962; MOMA; SFMA, 1944, 45; Hartford/Wadsworth, 1962. COLLECTIONS: Andover/Phillips; Denver/AM; Ford Foundation; MOMA; Mills College of Education; NYU; SFMA; WMAA. BIBLIOGRAPHY: Ashton 1; Breton 3; Calas; Janis and Blesh 1; Ritchie 1.

RICE, DAN. b. June, 1926, Long Beach, Calif. STUDIED: UCLA, 1943; U. of California, Berkeley, 1946; Black Mountain College, with Franz Kline, Robert Motherwell, Ben Shahn, Jack Tworkov. US Navy, 1943–46. ADDRESS: c/o Dealer. DEALER: Catherine Viviano Gallery. ONE-MAN EXHIBITIONS: Catherine Viviano Gallery, 1960, 62, 63. GROUP: U. of Virginia; Buffalo/Albright; Mary Washington College. COLLECTIONS: Dillard U.; Princeton U.

RICHENBURG, ROBERT B. b. July 14, 1917, Boston, Mass. STUDIED: Boston Museum School; George Washington U.; Boston U.; The Corcoran School of Art; Ozenfant School of Art, NYC; Hofmann School; ASL, with Reginald Marsh, George Grosz. US Army, 1942–45. TAUGHT: Schrivenham American U.; City College of New York, 1947–52; Brooklyn-Queens Central YMCA, 1947–51; Cooper Union, 1954–55; NYU, 1960–61; Pratt Institute, 1951–64; Cornell U., 1964– . AWARDS: Boston Museum School, Scholarship; Art In America (Magazine), New Talent. ADDRESS: 927 East State Street, Ithaca, N.Y. DEALER: Tibor de Nagy Gallery. ONE-MAN EXHIBITIONS: (first) Hendler Gallery, Philadelphia, 1954; Artists' Gallery, NYC, 1957; Artists' Gallery, Provincetown, 1958; Hansa Gallery, NYC, 1958; Dwan Gallery, 1960; Santa Barbara/MA, 1961; RISD (four-man), 1960; Dayton/AI, 1962; Tibor de Nagy Gallery, 1959, 60, 61, 62, 63, 64; Cornell U., 1964. GROUP: SRGM, 1949; Eighth Street Exhibition, NYC; Ninth Street Exhibition, NYC; MOMA, The Art of Assemblage, circ., 1961; SRGM, Abstract Expressionists and Imagists, 1961; WMAA Annuals, 1961, 64; Baltimore/MA, 1961; Dayton/AI, 1962; Kansas City/Nelson, 1962; U. of Illinois, 1963;

Corcoran, 1963; MOMA, Hans Hofmann and His Students, circ., 1963–64; U. of Nebraska; A.F.A., New Talent, circ., 1964. COLLECTIONS: Allentown/AM; MOMA; Norfolk; Provincetown/Chrysler; WMAA. BIBLIOGRAPHY: Seitz 2.

RICKEY, GEORGE. b. June 6, 1907, South Bend, Ind. To Scotland, 1913. STUDIED: Trinity College, Glenalmond, Scotland, 1921–26; Balliol College, Oxford, 1926–29, BA, 1941, MA with honors; Ruskin School of Drawing and of Fine Art, Oxford, 1928–29; Academie Andre Lhote and Academie Moderne, Paris, 1929–30; NYU, 1945–46; State U. of Iowa, 1947, with Mauricio Lasansky; Institute of Design, Chicago, 1948–49. Traveled Europe and Mexico extensively; resided Paris, 1933–34. US Army Air Corps, 1941–45. TAUGHT: Groton School, 1930–33 (History Department); Knox College, 1940–41; Muhlenberg College, 1941, 1946–48; U. of Washington, 1948; Indiana U., 1949–55; Tulane U., 1955–62; U. of California, Santa Barbara, 1960; Rensselaer Polytechnic Institute, 1961– . Editorial Department, Newsweek Magazine, 1936. Director, The Kalamazoo Institute of Arts, 1939–40. Shifted emphasis from painting to sculpture, 1950. COMMISSIONS (murals): Olivet College, 1938–39; US Post Office, Selinsgrove, Pa., 1938; Knox College, 1940–41; (sculpture): Belle Boas Memorial Library, Baltimore Museum, 1955; Union Carbide Corp., Toronto, 1960; The Joseph H. Hirshhorn Collection, NYC, 1962; Hamburger Kunsthalle, 1963; Westland Center, Detroit, 1964; Keene Teachers College, 1964; Lytton Savings and Loan Association, Oakland, Calif., 1964; The Singer Company Inc., 1964; Hood College, 1964. AWARDS: Guggenheim Foundation Fellowship, 1960, 61. ADDRESS: RD #2, East Chatham, N.Y. DEALERS: Staempfli Gallery; David Stuart Gallery; Galerie Springer. ONE-MAN EXHIBITIONS: (first) Caz-Delbo Gallery, NYC, 1933; Denver/AM, 1935, 43, 45, 48; Indianapolis/Herron, 1953 (first sculpture shown); The Little Gallery, Louisville, 1954; Kraushaar Galleries, 1955, 59, 61; New Orleans/Delgado, 1956; Amerika Haus, Hamburg, 1957; Orleans Gallery, New Orleans, 1960; Santa Barbara/MA, 1960; U. of Oklahoma, 1961; Phoenix, 1961; Primus-Stuart Gallery, Los Angeles, 1962; Galerie Springer, 1962; Grand Rapids, 1962; Hyde Park Art

Center, Chicago, 1963; Williams College, 1963; U. of Rochester, 1963; Dartmouth College, 1963; ICA, Boston, 1964. **GROUP:** Salon des Artistes Independants, Paris, 1930; MMA, National Sculpture Exhibition, 1951; PAFA, 1953, 54; WMAA, 1952, 53; U. of Nebraska, 1955; U. of Minnesota, 1955; Chicago/AI, Exhibition Momentum, 1954, 55; MOMA, Recent Sculpture USA, 1959; Santa Barbara/MA, 1960; Amsterdam/Stedelijk, Art in Motion, circ. Europe, 1961–62; Battersea Park, London, International Sculpture Exhibition, 1963; Documenta III, Kassel, 1964. **COLLECTIONS:** Andover/Phillips; Atlanta/AA; Ball State Teachers College; Baltimore/MA; Bethlehem Steel Corp.; Dartmouth College; Hamburg; Kansas City/Nelson; Montclair/AM; Raleigh/NCMA; Union Carbide Corp.; WMAA. **BIBLIOGRAPHY:** Rodman 1.

RIVERS, LARRY. b. 1923, NYC. US Army Air Corps, 1942–43. **STUDIED:** Juilliard School of Music, NYC, 1944–45; Hofmann School; NYU, 1947–48. Traveled Europe, USA, U.S.S.R. Active as a professional jazz musician. Began sculpture 1953. Appeared on "$64,000 Question" (CBS-TV) as an art expert, and ran his winnings to $32,000 on "$64,000 Challenge," 1957–58. **COMMISSIONS:** Outdoor billboard for First New York Film Festival, 1963. **AWARDS:** Corcoran, Third Prize, 1954. **ADDRESS:** Main Street, Southampton, N.Y. **DEALER:** Marlborough-Gerson Gallery Inc. **ONE-MAN EXHIBITIONS:** (first) Jane Street Gallery, NYC, 1949; Tibor de Nagy Gallery, 1951, 52, 53, 54, 57, 58, 59, 60, 62; The Stable Gallery, 1954 (sculpture); Martha Jackson Gallery, 1960 (sculpture); Dwan Gallery, 1960; Gimpel Fils Ltd., 1962, 64; Galerie Rive Droite, Paris, 1962;

Larry Rivers   *The Last Civil War Veteran. 1961*

Marlborough-Gerson Gallery Inc.; Brandeis U. **GROUP:** WMAA Annuals, 1954, 58, 60, 61, 63; MOMA, Twelve Americans, circ., 1956; Sao Paulo, 1957; Carnegie, 1958, 61; WMAA, Business Buys American Art, 1960; II Inter-American Paintings and Prints Biennial, Mexico City, 1960; Seattle World's Fair, 1962; PAFA, 1963; WMAA, Between the Fairs, 1964. **COLLECTIONS:** Brooklyn Museum; Corcoran; Kansas City/Nelson; MMA; MOMA; Minneapolis/Institute; New Paltz; RISD; Raleigh/NCMA; Seagram Collection; Tate; Victoria and Albert Museum; WMAA. **BIBLIOGRAPHY:** Friedman, ed.; Gaunt; McCurdy, ed.; *Metro;* Nordness, ed.; Rodman 1; Soby 6.

ROBINSON, BOARDMAN. b. September 6, 1876, Somerset (Nova Scotia), Canada; **d.** September 6, 1952, Colorado Springs, Colo. To USA 1894. **STUDIED:** Boston Normal Art School, 1894–97, with E. W. Hamilton; Academie Colarossi, Academie des Beaux-Arts, and Academie Julian, Paris, 1898–1900. Traveled the world extensively. **TAUGHT:** ASL, 1919–22, 1924–26; Fountain Valley School, Colorado Springs, 1930–44; Michigan State College, 1945; Colorado Springs Fine Arts Center, 1937–39. Illustrated many editions of classics, as well as popular books. Drew cartoons for the *Morning Telegraph,* 1907–10, and the *New York Tribune* (four years). **COMMISSIONS** (murals): Justice Department Building, Washington, D.C., 1937 (18); Kaufmann Department Store, Pittsburgh, 1928–29; Colorado Springs/FA, 1936; US Post Office, Englewood, Colo., 1940. **ONE-MAN EXHIBITIONS:** Thumb Box Gallery, NYC, 1916; M. Knoedler & Co., 1919; Weyhe Gallery, 1924; ASL, 1929; Delphic Studios, NYC, 1930; Hudson D. Walker Gallery, NYC, 1940; Chicago/AI, 1942. **RETROSPECTIVE:** Kraushaar Galleries, 1946; Colorado Springs/FA, 1943; Dallas/MFA, 1946. **GROUP:** WMAA; Chicago/AI; Colorado Springs/FA; Cleveland/MA; Los Angeles/County MA; MMA; NAD. **COLLECTIONS:** AAAL; U. of Arizona; Chicago/AI; Cleveland/MA; Colorado Springs/FA; Cranbrook; Dallas/MFA; Denver/AM; U. of Georgia; Harvard U.; IBM; Los Angeles/County MA; MMA; Minneapolis/Institute; NYPL; NYU; U. of Nebraska; Newark Museum; New Britain; PMA; U. of Vermont; WMAA; Wichita/AM. **BIBLIOGRAPHY:** Baur 7; **Biddle 2,** 3; Brown;

Bruce and Watson; Cahill and Barr, eds.; Cheney, M. C.; **Christ-Janer;** Gallatin 2; Genauer; *Index of 20th Century Artists;* Mather 1; Mellquist; Poore; Richardson.

ROBUS, HUGO. b. May 10, 1885, Cleveland, Ohio; **d.** January 14, 1964, NYC. **STUDIED:** Cleveland Institute of Art, 1904–08; NAD, 1910–11; Academie de la Grande Chaumiere, 1912–14, with Antoine Bourdelle. **TAUGHT:** Myra Carr Art School, *ca.* 1915–17; Columbia U., summers, 1942, 43, 46, 48, 50, 52, 53, 55, 56; Brooklyn Museum School, 1955–56; Hunter College, 1950–58; Munson-Williams-Proctor Institute, Utica, N.Y., 1948. Changed from painting to sculpture, 1920. **FEDERAL A.P.:** 1937–39. **AWARDS:** MMA, Artists for Victory, Second Prize, 1942; PAFA, George D. Widener Memorial Gold Medal, 1950; PAFA, Alfred G. B. Steel Memorial Prize, 1953; NIAL, Citation and Grant, 1957. **ONE-MAN EXHIBITIONS:** (first) Grand Central, NYC, 1946, also 1948; Utica, 1948; Corcoran, 1958; The Forum Gallery, 1963. **RETROSPECTIVE:** A.F.A./Ford Foundation, 1961. **GROUP:** WMAA; PAFA; MMA; Corcoran. **COLLECTIONS:** Cleveland/MA; Corcoran; Fairleigh Dickinson U.; IBM; MMA; MOMA; Utica; WMAA. **BIBLIOGRAPHY:** Baur 7; Brumme; Goodrich and Baur 1; Mendelowitz; Pearson 2.

ROCKLIN, RAYMOND. b. August 18, 1922, Moodus, Conn. **STUDIED:** MOMA School, 1940; Cooper Union, 1951, with Milton Hebald, John Hovannes, Warren Wheelock; Educational Alliance, NYC, with Sam Ostrowsky; Temple U., 1942. Traveled Europe, USA. **TAUGHT:** U. of California, Berkeley, 1959–60; American U., 1956; Ball State Teachers College, 1964. **MEMBER:** American Abstract Artists; Federation of Modern Painters and Sculptors. **AWARDS:** Fulbright Fellowship (Italy), 1952; Yaddo Fellowship, 1956. **ADDRESS:** 118 East 10 Street, NYC. **DEALER:** The Bertha Schaefer Gallery. **ONE-MAN EXHIBITIONS:** (first) Tanager Gallery, NYC, 1956; American U., 1956; Ball State Teachers College, 1964; Pomona College, 1960; Santa Barbara/MA, 1960; Oakland/AM, 1956; U. of California, Berkeley, 1959; Dilexi Gallery, San Francisco, 1960; The Bertha Schaefer Gallery (two-man), 1960. **GROUP:** WMAA, Young America; WMAA, New Talent, 1957; U. of Illinois, 1959; WMAA Annual,

1960; Claude Bernard, Paris, 1960; American Abstract Artists Annuals; U. of Nebraska, 1960. COLLECTIONS: Provincetown/Chrysler; Skowhegan School; Temple Israel, St. Louis; WMAA. BIBLIOGRAPHY: Seuphor 3.

ROESCH, KURT. b. September 12, 1905, near Berlin, Germany. STUDIED: Jaeckel School, Berlin, 1924; Academy of Fine Arts, Berlin, 1925–26, with Karl Hofer, and 1928–29, with Hofer and Meid. To USA 1933. Traveled Europe, USA; resided Paris, Berlin, NYC. TAUGHT: New School for Social Research, 1934–36; Sarah Lawrence College, 1934–   ; Skowhegan School. AWARDS: Prize of the League of German Artists, 1931; Medal of the Academy of Fine Arts, Berlin, 1932; MMA, Artists for Victory, Sixth Prize, 1942; First New Hampshire Art Association Annual, J. W. Hill Co. Award, 1947. ADDRESS: RFD #1, Box 160, Katonah, N.Y. DEALER: Rose Fried Gallery. ONE-MAN EXHIBITIONS: Berlin Sezession, 1928; Gallery A. Flechtheim, Berlin, 1930; New School for Social Research, 1934; U. of Minnesota, 1936; Buchholz Gallery, NYC, 1939, 41, 43, 45, 46; Curt Valentine Gallery, NYC, 1949, 53. GROUP: U. of Illinois; Carnegie; Documenta, Kassel; PMA; New Hampshire Art Association Annuals, 1947, 48, 49; MMA. COLLECTIONS: Buffalo/Albright; Colby College; Fort Worth; MMA; MOMA; U. of Minnesota; NYPL; U. of Nebraska; RAC; Sarah Lawrence College. BIBLIOGRAPHY: Janis, S.; Pousette-Dart, ed.

ROGALSKI, WALTER. b. April 10, 1923, Glen Cove, N.Y. STUDIED: Brooklyn Museum School, 1947–51, with Xavier Gonzalez, Arthur Osver, C. Seide, Gabor Peterdi. US Marine Corps, 1941–42. TAUGHT: Pratt Graphic Art Center; Brooklyn Museum School; Pratt Institute. MEMBER: SAGA. AWARDS: Brooklyn Museum, P.P., 1951, 52; New Britain, P.P.; Northwest Printmakers Annual, P.P.; Dallas/MFA, P.P., 1953. ADDRESS: 15 Cross Street, Locust Valley, N.Y. ONE-MAN EXHIBITIONS: Korman Gallery, NYC, 1954, 55; Cleveland/MA, 1954. GROUP: U. of Minnesota, 1950; Brooklyn Museum, 1951, 52, 54, 60; Library of Congress, 1951; MOMA, New Talent; Seattle/AM, 1952; Dallas/MFA, 1953; The Print Club, Philadelphia, 1958, 60; Riverside Museum, 1959; The Terrain Gallery, 1961; SAGA, 1961; A.A.A. Gallery,

NYC, 1961; Merrick (Long Island) Art Gallery, 1961. COLLECTIONS: Brooklyn Museum; Cleveland/MA; Dallas/MFA; Harvard U.; MOMA; NYPL; New Britain; Seattle/AM; Yale U. BIBLIOGRAPHY: Rogalski.

ROHM, ROBERT. b. 1934, Cincinnati, Ohio. STUDIED: Pratt Institute, 1956; Cranbrook Academy of Art, 1960, B. Industrial Design. TAUGHT: Pratt Institute. MEMBER: Sculptors Guild. AWARDS: Guggenheim Foundation Fellowship, 1964; PAFA, Hon. Men., 1959; Columbus, Sculpture Prize, 1957, 59. ADDRESS: c/o Dealer. DEALER: Royal Marks Gallery. ONE-MAN EXHIBITIONS: (first) Royal Marks Gallery, 1964; Aspen (Colo.) Art Gallery; Columbus (two-man), 1958. GROUP: Columbus, 1958; WMAA Annual, 1963; PAFA, 1961; Aspen (Colo.) Art Gallery, 1963; Silvermine Guild, 1962; Waitsfield, Bundy Sculpture Competition, 1963. COLLECTIONS: Columbus; Fontana-Hollywood Corp.

RONALD, WILLIAM. b. August 13, 1926, Stratford (Ont.), Canada. STUDIED: Ontario College of Art, 1951, with Jock Macdonald. US citizen 1963. AWARDS: SRGM, Award for Canadian Painting, 1956; Hallmark International Competition, 1952; Canada Foundation Scholarship, 1954. ADDRESS: P.O. Box 231, Kingston, N.J. DEALER: The Kootz Gallery. ONE-MAN EXHIBITIONS: (first) Hart House, U. of Toronto, 1954; Greenwich Gallery, Toronto, 1957; Liang Galleries, Toronto, 1960; Douglass College, 1960; The Kootz Gallery, 1957, 58, 59, 60, 61, 63; Isaacs Gallery, Toronto, 1961, 63; Princeton U., 1963. GROUP: Smithsonian, 1956; Toronto Gallery, Toronto, Four Young Canadians, 1956; Carnegie, 1958, 61; Brussels World's Fair, 1958; V Sao Paulo Biennial, 1959; WMAA Annual, 1959; U. of Illinois, 1961, 63; Corcoran, 1962. COLLECTIONS: Baltimore/MA; U. of British Columbia; Brooklyn Museum; Buffalo/Albright; Carnegie; Chicago/AI; International Minerals & Chemicals Corp.; MOMA; Montreal/MFA; NYU; U. of North Carolina; Ottawa/National; Phoenix; Princeton U.; Queens U.; RISD; SRGM; Toronto; WGMA; Walker; Williams College.

ROOD, JOHN. b. February 22, 1906, Athens, Ohio. Self-taught in art. Traveled the world extensively. TAUGHT: Ohio U., 1945; U. of

Minnesota, 1944– . Published a literary magazine, *Manuscript*, 1933–36. MEMBER: Artists Equity (President, 1959–63). COMMISSIONS: Minneapolis Public Library; Wellesley College; St. Marks Cathedral, Minneapolis; Hamline U. ADDRESS: 1650 Dupont Avenue South, Minneapolis, Minn. DEALER: Feingarten Gallery, Chicago and Los Angeles. ONE-MAN EXHIBITIONS: (first) Passedoit Gallery, NYC, 1937, also 1940, 41, 42, 43, 44, 45; Colgate U., 1941; Durand-Ruel Gallery, NYC, 1944; Newark Museum; 1944; Minneapolis/Institute, 1945; U. of Minnesota, 1945, 46; Ward Eggleston Gallery, NYC, 1946, 47 (paintings); A.A.A. Gallery, Chicago, 1949; Galleria del Fiori, Milan, 1956; L'Obelisco, Rome, 1956. GROUP: WMAA; U. of Minnesota; Walker; Corcoran; Cranbrook. COLLECTIONS: Andover/Phillips; Corcoran; Cranbrook; Minneapolis/Institute; U. of Minnesota; Ohio U.; Walker. BIBLIOGRAPHY: Brumme; **Rood**; Seuphor 3.

ROSATI, JAMES. b. 1912, Washington, Pa. Violinist with the Pittsburgh Symphony for two years. TAUGHT: Cooper Union; Pratt Institute; Yale U., 1960– ; Dartmouth College, 1963. FEDERAL A.P.: Sculptor. COMMISSIONS: St. John's Abbey, Collegeville, Md. (sculpture). AWARDS: Brandeis U., Creative Arts Award, 1960; Chicago/AI, The Mr. & Mrs. Frank G. Logan Medal and Prize, 1962; Carborundum Major Abrasive Marketing Award, 1963; Guggenheim Foundation Fellowship, 1964. ADDRESS: 252 West 14 Street, NYC. DEALER: Marlborough-Gerson Gallery Inc. ONE-MAN EXHIBITIONS: (first) The Peridot Gallery, 1954; Otto Gerson Gallery, NYC, 1959, 62; Dartmouth College, 1963. GROUP: Ninth Street Exhibition, NYC, 1951; WMAA Annuals, 1952, 53, 54, 60, 62; Carnegie, 1958, 61, 64; Claude Bernard, Paris, 1960; International Outdoor Sculpture Exhibition, Otterlo, Holland, 1961; A.F.A., Contemporary Sculpture, 1960; Chicago/AI, 1961, 62; Seattle World's Fair, 1962; WMAA, First Five Years, 1962; Festival of Two Worlds, Spoleto, 1962; Battersea Park, London, International Sculpture Exhibition, 1963; New York World's Fair, 1964–65. COLLECTIONS: NYU; WMAA; Yale U. BIBLIOGRAPHY: Seuphor 3.

ROSENBORG, RALPH M. b. June 9, 1913, Brooklyn, N.Y. TAUGHT: Brooklyn Museum

School, 1936–38; Ox-Bow Summer School, Saugatuck, Mich., 1949; U. of Wyoming; U. of North Carolina. AWARDS: AAAL, 1960. ADDRESS: 165 Lexington Avenue, NYC. ONE-MAN EXHIBITIONS: Karl Nierendorf Gallery, NYC; The Willard Gallery, 1941; J. Seligmann and Co., 1948, 50; Passedoit Gallery, NYC, 1959; Artists' Gallery, NYC, 1939; Chinese Gallery, NYC, 1946, 47; Albert Landry, NYC, 1960; Davis Gallery, NYC, 1954; Barone Gallery, NYC; International Gallery, Baltimore, 1964; The Pinacotheca, NYC, 1945. GROUP: Corcoran; WMAA; U. of Illinois; MOMA; Phillips; Chicago/AI; VMFA; Brooklyn Museum; Seattle/AM; Detroit/Institute. COLLECTIONS: Brandeis U.; Colby College; Cornell U.; U. of Georgia; MMA; MOMA; Montclair/AM; Newark Museum; U. of Oregon; Phillips; SRGM; St. Louis/City; Smith College; Yale U. BIBLIOGRAPHY: American Artists Congress, Inc.; Janis, S.; Motherwell and Reinhardt, eds.

ROSENQUIST, JAMES. b. November 29, 1933, Grand Forks, N.D. STUDIED: U. of Minnesota, with Cameron Booth; ASL. ADDRESS: 328 East 89 Street, NYC. DEALER: Leo Castelli Inc. ONE-MAN EXHIBITIONS: (first) The Green Gallery, NYC, 1962, also 1964; Ileana Sonnabend (Gallery), Paris, 1964; Leo Castelli Inc.; Dwan Gallery, 1964. GROUP: Hartford/Wadsworth, 1962; Dallas/MFA, 1962; Chicago/AI, 1962; WGMA, The Popular Image, 1962; SRGM, Six Painters and The Object, 1963; Buffalo/Albright, Mixed Media and Pop Art, 1963; New York State Pavilion, New York World's Fair, 1964–65; ICA, U. of Pennsylvania, The Atmosphere of '64, 1964. COLLECTIONS: Brandeis U. BIBLIOGRAPHY: *Metro*.

ROSENTHAL, BERNARD. b. August 9, 1914, Highland Park, Ill. STUDIED: U. of Michigan, 1936, BA; Chicago Art Institute School; Cranbrook Academy of Art, with Carl Milles. Corps of Army Engineers, 1942–46. Traveled Mexico, USA. TAUGHT: UCLA, 1953; California School of Art, 1947–48. FEDERAL A.P.: US Post Office, Nakomis, Ill. (relief). COMMISSIONS: Elgin Watch Building, New York World's Fair, 1939; Museum of Science and Industry, Chicago, 1941; General Petroleum Building, Los Angeles, 1949; 260 Beverly Drive, Beverly Hills, 1950 (bronze reliefs, 3 storeys high); Bullock's Westwood, Los Angeles, 1951; RKO Studios,

Hollywood, 1952; UCLA Elementary School, 1952; J. W. Robinson Department Store, Beverly Hills, 1952; Capri Theatre, San Diego, 1954; 1000 Lake Shore Drive, Chicago, 1954 (30-ft. relief); Beverly Hilton Hotel, Beverly Hills, 1955; Temple Emanuel, Beverly Hills, 1955; Century City (Alcoa Development), 1963. AWARDS: SFMA, Sculpture Award, 1950; Los Angeles/County MA, P.P., 1950; Los Angeles All-City Show, Sculpture Prize, 1951; Audubon Artists, Sculpture Award, 1953; PAFA, Hon. Men., 1954; Los Angeles/County MA, Sculpture Award, 1957; American Institute of Architects, Southern California Chapter, Honor Award, 1959; Ford Foundation, P.P., 1963; Tamarind Fellowship, 1964. ADDRESS: 358 East 57 Street, NYC. DEALER: The Kootz Gallery. ONE-MAN EXHIBITIONS: (first) Pat Wall Gallery, Monterey, 1947; A.A.A. Gallery, Chicago, 1947; Scripps College, 1948; SFMA, 1950; A.A.A. Gallery, NYC, 1950; Santa Barbara/MA, 1952; Long Beach/MA, 1952; Catherine Viviano Gallery, 1954, 58, 59; Carnegie, 1959; The Kootz Gallery, 1961, 63. GROUP:

MMA; MOMA; Sao Paulo Biennial; Brussels World's Fair, 1958; Chicago/AI; WMAA; PAFA; Sculptors Guild; Audubon Artists; Walker; ICA, Boston; Yale U. COLLECTIONS: Arizona State College; Baltimore/MA; Buffalo/Albright; U. of Illinois; Lincoln, Mass./De Cordova; Long Beach/MA; Los Angeles/County MA; Lytton Savings and Loan Association; MOMA; Milwaukee; NYU; Newark Museum; Santa Barbara/MA; Springfield, Ill./State. BIBLIOGRAPHY: Rodman 2.

ROSZAK, THEODORE. b. May 1, 1907, Poznan, Poland. STUDIED: Columbia U., 1925–26; Chicago Art Institute School, 1922–29, with John W. Norton, Boris Anisfeld; NAD, 1925–26, with C. W. Hawthorne. Traveled Latin America, Europe extensively. TAUGHT: Chicago Art Institute School, 1927–29; Design Laboratory, NYC, 1938–40; Sarah Lawrence College, 1940–56; lectured at many museums and universities. Began abstract constructions 1936, free-form sculpture 1946. MEMBER: Commission of Fine Arts, Washington, D.C. (appointed for 1963–

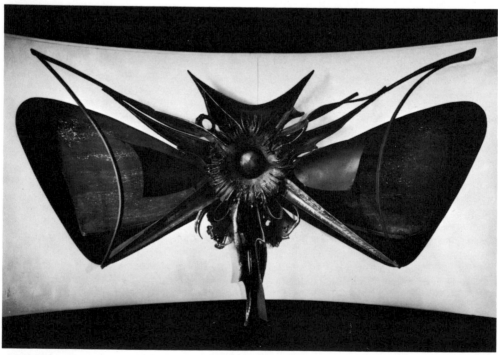

Theodore Roszak   *American Monarch. 1964*

67); Advisory Committee on the Arts, US State Department (appointed for 1963–67). FEDERAL A.P.: Easel painting. COMMISSIONS: Yale & Towne Inc.; MIT (spire and bell tower); Reynolds Metals Co. (aluminum sculpture memorial); American Embassy, London; Maremont Building, Chicago; New York World's Fair, 1964–65. AWARDS: World's Fair, Poland, 1929, Silver Medal; Chicago/AI, Joseph N. Eisendrath Prize, 1934; Chicago/AI, The Mr. & Mrs. Frank G. Logan Medal, 1947, 51; ICA, London/Tate, International Unknown Political Prisoner Competition, 1953; I Sao Paulo Biennial, 1951; PAFA, George D. Widener Memorial Gold Medal, 1958; Chicago/AI, Campana Prize, 1961; Ball State Teachers College, Griner Award, 1962; elected to the NIAL. ADDRESS: One St. Luke's Place, NYC. DEALER: Pierre Matisse Gallery. ONE-MAN EXHIBITIONS: (first) Allerton Galleries, Chicago, 1928; Artists' Gallery, NYC, 1941; Julien Levy Galleries, NYC, 1941; Nicholas Roerich Museum, 1935; Albany/Institute, 1936; Pierre Matisse Gallery, 1957, 62; ICA, Boston, circ., 1959; XXX Venice Biennial, 1960. RETROSPECTIVE: WMAA, circ., 1956. GROUP: Chicago/AI Annuals, 1931, 32, 35, 37, 38, 41; WMAA Annuals, 1932, 33, 34, 35, 36, 37, 38, 41, 57, 58, 59, 62, 64; A Century of Progress, Chicago, 1933–34; PAFA, 1946, 64; MOMA, Fourteen Americans, circ., 1946; A.F.A., Tradition and Experiment in Modern Sculpture, circ., 1950–51; Documenta I & II, Kassel, 1955, 59; Brussels World's Fair, 1958; Carnegie, 1958; NIAL, 1958, 59; Tate, 1959; American Painting and Sculpture, Moscow, 1959; Seattle World's Fair, 1962; Silvermine Guild, 1962; Museum des 20. Jahrhunderts, 1962; MOMA, 1963; Cleveland/MA, 1964. COLLECTIONS: U. of Arizona; Baltimore/MA; Chicago/AI; Cleveland/MA; U. of Colorado; U. of Illinois; Industrial Museum, Barcelona; MOMA; U. of Michigan; SRGM; Sao Paulo; Tate; WMAA; Walker; West Palm Beach/Norton; Yale U. BIBLIOGRAPHY: Arnason 4; Baur 7; Blesh 1; Brumme; Gertz; Giedion-Welcker 1; Goodrich and Baur 1; Hunter 5; Kepes 2; Kuh 1; Langui; McCurdy, ed.; Mendelowitz; *Metro;* Miller, ed. 2; Myers 2; Neumeyer; Ritchie 1, 3; Rodman 3; Seuphor 3; Seymour.

ROTH, FRANK. b. February 22, 1936, Boston, Mass. STUDIED: Cooper Union, 1954; Hof-

mann School, 1955. Traveled Europe, Mexico. TAUGHT: School of Visual Arts, NYC; State U. of Iowa, 1964. AWARDS: Chaloner Prize Foundation Award, 1961; Guggenheim Foundation Fellowship, 1964. ADDRESS: 240 East 15 Street, NYC. DEALERS: Grace Borgenicht Gallery Inc.; Galerie Anderson-Mayer; Hamilton Galleries. ONE-MAN EXHIBITIONS: (first) Artists' Gallery, NYC, 1958; Grace Borgenicht Gallery Inc., 1960, 62, 63, 64; Galerie Anderson-Mayer, 1964; The American Gallery, NYC, 1962. GROUP: WMAA, Young America, 1960; WMAA Annuals, 1958, 60; Carnegie, 1959; Corcoran, 1962; Chicago/AI, 1959; Walker, 60 American Painters, 1960; Buffalo/Albright, 1958. COLLECTIONS: Buffalo/Albright; Chase Manhattan Bank; Manufacturers Hanover Trust Co.; McDonald & Company; Michigan State U.; Santa Barbara/MA; Tate; Walker; WMAA.

ROTHKO, MARK. b. September 25, 1903, Dvinska, Russia. To USA 1913. STUDIED: Yale U., 1921–23; ASL, 1925, with Max Weber. Traveled Europe, USA. TAUGHT: Center Academy, Brooklyn, N.Y., 1929–52; California School of Fine Arts, summers, 1947, 49; Brooklyn College, 1951–54; U. of Colorado, 1955; Tulane U., 1956. A co-founder of the Expressionist group The Ten, 1935. Co-founder of a school, "Subject of the Artist," with William Baziotes, Robert Motherwell, and Barnett Newman, NYC, 1948. FEDERAL A.P.: 1936–37. ADDRESS: 118 East 95 Street, NYC. DEALER: Marlborough-Gerson Gallery Inc. ONE-MAN EXHIBITIONS: (first) Contemporary Arts Gallery, NYC, 1933; Portland, Ore./AM, 1933; Art of This Century, NYC, 1945; Betty Parsons Gallery, 1946, 47, 48, 49, 50, 51; Santa Barbara/MA, 1946; RISD, 1954; Chicago/AI, 1954; Sidney Janis Gallery, 1955, 58; Houston/MFA, 1957; XXIX Venice Biennial, 1958; Phillips, 1960; MOMA, 1961; Whitechapel Art Gallery, London, 1961; Amsterdam/Stedelijk, 1961; Palais des Beaux Arts, Brussels, 1962; Kunsthalle, Basel, 1962; Paris/Moderne, 1962; Marlborough Fine Art Ltd., London, 1964. GROUP: PAFA, 1940; XXIV Venice Biennial, 1948; MOMA, Abstract Painting and Sculpture in America, 1951; 10th Inter-American Conference, Caracas, 1954; 3rd International Contemporary Art Exhibition, New Delhi, 1957; Documenta II, Kassel, 1959; Carnegie, 1958,

Frank Roth　　　*Spector. 1964*

61; Federation of Modern Painters and Sculptors Annuals; WMAA, 1945–50; MOMA, Fifteen Americans, circ., 1952; MOMA, The New American Painting, circ. Europe, 1958–59; Walker, 60 American Painters, 1960. COLLECTIONS: U. of Arizona; Baltimore/MA; Brooklyn Museum; Buffalo/Albright; Chicago/AI; Kansas City/Nelson; MOMA; Paris/Moderne; Phillips; Rio de Janeiro; SFMA; Tate; Utica; Vassar College; WMAA. BIBLIOGRAPHY: Barker 1; Barr 3; Baur 7; Blesh 1; Eliot; Elsen; Goodrich and Baur 1; Greenberg 1; Haftman; Henning; Hess, T. B.; Hunter 1, 5; Janis and Blesh 1; Janis, S.; McCourbrey; McCurdy, ed.; *Metro;* Motherwell, ed.; Ponente; Read 2; Restany 2; Richardson; Ritchie 1; Rodman 1, 2; Seitz 1; **Selz, P. 2;** Seuphor 1; Soby 5.

RUBEN, RICHARDS. b. November 29, 1924, Los Angeles, Calif. STUDIED: Chouinard Art Institute, Los Angeles, 1944–46; Bradley U., 1951, BFA. US Army, 1942–44. TAUGHT: Chouinard Art Institute, Los Angeles, 1954–61; Pomona College, 1958–59; Pasadena Museum School; UCLA, 1958–62; Arts and Crafts Center, Pittsburgh, 1949; Cooper Union, 1962–　. AWARDS: L. C. Tiffany Grant, 1954; International Arts Festival, Newport, R.I., First Prize, 1951; Bradley U., P.P., 1952; Brooklyn Museum, First Prize, 1953, 54; SFMA, Anne Bremer Memorial Prize, 1954. ADDRESS: 61 West 27 Street, NYC. DEALER: Poindexter Gallery. ONE-MAN EXHIBITIONS: Felix Landau Gallery, 1952, 54; Pasadena/AM, 1954, 55, 61; Oakland/AM, 1957; Paul Kantor Gallery, 1958; Grand Central Moderns, 1958; Ferus Gallery, 1960, 61, 63; Poindexter Gallery, 1962, 64; California Palace, 1961. GROUP: Carnegie, 1955; Sao Paulo, 1955; SRGM, Younger American Painters, 1954; Los Angeles/County MA, 1948, 53, 55, 57; Brooklyn Museum, 1957, 59; I Paris Biennial, 1959; PAFA, 1954; Santa Barbara/MA, 1955, 58; Corcoran, 1953; U. of Illinois, 1952, 56; El Retiro Parquet, Madrid, Arte de America y España, 1963; WMAA, 50 California Artists, 1962–63; WMAA Annual, 1964; Bradley U., 1952, 53; Dallas/MFA, 1953. COLLECTIONS: Boston/MFA; Bradley U.; Brooklyn Museum; Los Angeles/County MA;

Oakland/AM; Pasadena/AM; Raleigh/NCMA; W. & J. Sloane, Inc.; U. of Southern California; Stanford U.

RUVOLO, FELIX. b. April 28, 1912, NYC. Throughout his youth, family resided in Italy, where he first attended art school (Catania). STUDIED: Chicago Art Institute School. Traveled Europe, Mexico, Canada, USA. **TAUGHT:** U. of California, Berkeley, 1950– ; Chicago Art Institute School, 1945–47; Mills College, summer, 1948; U. of Southern California, 1963. FEDERAL A.P.: Easel painting. **COMMISSIONS:** Merchandise Mart, Chicago (murals). **AWARDS:** Chicago/AI, P.P., 1942, 46, 47; SFMA, P.P., 1950, 51; U. of Illinois, P.P., 1949; California Palace, Gold Medal, 1946; Milwaukee, Kearney Memorial Prize, 1946; Pepsi-Cola, 1947, 48; Hallmark International Competition, 1949; SFMA, Anne Bremer Memorial Prize, 1942; and some two dozen others. **ADDRESS:** 78 Strathmoor Drive, Berkeley, Calif. **ONE-MAN EXHIBITIONS:** (first) Durand-Ruel Gallery, NYC, 1946; Grand Central Moderns, 1948; de Young, 1947, 58; Mills College, 1947; Catherine Viviano Gallery, 1949, 50, 52, 54; Poindexter Gallery, 1957, 58. **GROUP:** U. of Illinois, 1947, 61; MOMA, Abstract Painting and Sculpture in America, 1951; Walker, 60 American Painters, 1960; Chicago/AI Annuals; MMA; Corcoran; PAFA; WMAA; Buffalo/Albright, Expressionism in American Painting, 1952. **COLLECTIONS:** Auckland; U. of California, Berkeley; Chicago/AI; Denison U.; Denver/AM; Des Moines; U. of Illinois; Mills College; SFMA; U. of Southern California; Tulsa/Philbrook; Walker. **BIBLIOGRAPHY:** Genauer; Pousette-Dart, ed.; Ritchie 1.

SAGE, KAY. b. June 25, 1898, Albany, N.Y.; **d.** January 7, 1963, Woodbury, Conn. Self-taught. Resided Italy, 1900–14, 1919–37, Paris, 1937–39. m. Yves Tanguy. ONE-MAN EXHIBITIONS: (first) Galleria Il Milione, 1936; Pierre Matisse Gallery, 1940; SFMA, 1941; Julien Levy Galleries, NYC, 1944, 47; L'Obelisco, Rome, 1953; Galerie Nina Dausset, Paris, 1953; Catherine Viviano Gallery, 1950, 52, 56, 58; Hartford/Wadsworth (two-man), 1954. RETROSPECTIVE: Catherine Viviano Gallery, 1960. GROUP: Salon des Surindependants, Paris, 1938; International Surrealist Exhibition, NYC, 1942; Brussels World's Fair, 1958; WMAA, 1946–55; Carnegie, 1946–50; Chicago/AI, 1945, 47, 51; Toledo/MA, 1947, 49; California Palace, 1949, 50; U. of Illinois, 1949, 51. COLLECTIONS: California Palace; Chicago/AI; MMA; MOMA; SFMA; WMAA; Wesleyan U. BIBLIOGRAPHY: Breton 3; Goodrich and Baur 1; Pearson 2; Seitz 2; Waldberg 3.

SALEMME, ATTILIO. b. October 18, 1911, Boston, Mass.; **d.** January 24, 1955, NYC. Self-taught. US Marine Corps, 1927–28. Traveled USA. COMMISSIONS (murals): Moore-McCormack Lines Inc., 1949; 200 East 66 Street, NYC, 1950. AWARDS: Chicago/AI, Flora Mayer Witkowsky Prize, 1949; William and Noma Copley Foundation Grant, 1954; MMA, P.P., 1950. ONE-MAN EXHIBITIONS: (first) "67" Gallery, NYC, 1945; Carlebach Gallery, NYC, 1947; Passedoit Gallery, NYC, 1948; Saidenberg Gallery, 1950; Grace Borgenicht Gallery Inc., 1953; Duveen-Graham Gallery, NYC, 1955; Catherine Viviano Gallery, 1960; Staempfli Gallery, 1963; ICA, Boston, 1958; Walker, 1958. RETROSPECTIVE: WMAA, 1960.

GROUP: Carnegie; WMAA Annuals; Chicago/AI Annuals; U. of Illinois, 1955. COLLECTIONS: Brooklyn Museum; MMA; MOMA; WMAA. BIBLIOGRAPHY: Goodrich and Baur 1; Kent, N.; McCurdy, ed.; Newmeyer; Pousette-Dart, ed.

SAMARAS, LUCAS. b. September 14, 1936, Kastoria, Macedonia, Greece. To USA 1948; citizen 1955. STUDIED: Rutgers U., 1955–59, BA; Columbia U. Graduate School, 1959–62. AWARDS: Woodrow Wilson Fellow, Columbia U. ADDRESS: 233 East 77 Street, NYC. ONE-MAN EXHIBITIONS: Rutgers U., 1955, 58; Reuben Gallery, NYC, 1959; The Green Gallery, NYC, 1961, 64. GROUP: Martha Jackson Gallery, New Media—New Forms, II, 1961; MOMA, The Art of Assemblage, circ., 1961; MOMA, Lettering by Hand, 1962; Corcoran, 1963. COLLECTIONS: MOMA. BIBLIOGRAPHY: Seitz 2.

SANDER, LUDWIG. b. July 18, 1906, NYC. STUDIED: NYU, BA; Hofmann School, Munich, two semesters. Traveled Europe, 1927, 1931–32. US Army, World War II. TAUGHT: Colorado College, summers, 1951, 52, 53; Bard College, 1956–58. AWARDS: Hallmark International Competition; Longview Foundation Grant. ADDRESS: 68 East 12 Street, NYC. DEALER: The Kootz Gallery. ONE-MAN EXHIBITIONS: (first) Morton Gallery, NYC, 1930; Hacker Gallery, NYC, 1952; Leo Castelli Inc., 1959, 61; The Kootz Gallery, 1962, 64. GROUP: Ninth Street Exhibition, NYC, 1951; Chicago/AI Annuals, 1961, 62; SRGM, Abstract Expressionists and Imagists, 1961; MOMA, Recent American Painting and Sculpture, circ.

Ludwig Sander   *Corinth XI. 1962*

USA and Canada, 1961–62; WMAA, Geometric Abstraction in America, circ., 1962; Seattle World's Fair, 1962; Los Angeles/County MA, Post Painterly Abstraction, 1964; XXXII Venice Biennial, 1964. COLLECTIONS: Baltimore/MA; Brandeis U.; Buffalo/Albright; Chase Manhattan Bank; Geigy Chemical Corp.; MIT; SRGM; Union Carbide Corp.; WMAA; Walker.

SATO, TADASHI. b. February 6, 1923, Maui, Hawaii. STUDIED: Honolulu Academy School; Brooklyn Museum School; Pratt Institute, with Stuart Davis, John Ferren, Ralston Crawford. AWARDS: Brooklyn Museum School, Scholarship, 1948; Dallas/MFA, Hon. Men., 1953; John Hay Whitney Fellowship, 1954; Honolulu Community Foundation Scholarship, 1955; Albert Kapp Award, 1958. ADDRESS: P.O. Box 476, Lahaina, Maui, Hawaii. DEALER: The Willard Gallery. ONE-MAN EXHIBITIONS: Gima's Art Gallery, Honolulu, 1950; Library of Hawaii, Honolulu, 1950; 442nd Infantry Memorial Hall, Honolulu, 1950, 52; Gallery 75, NYC, 1955; The Gallery, Honolulu, 1956; The Willard Gallery, 1958, 59, 61; McRoberts & Tunnard Gallery, London, 1961. GROUP: U. of Nebraska, 1954; SRGM, 1954; SFMA, 1957; Silvermine Guild, 1958. COLLECTIONS: U. of Arizona; Ball State Teachers College; Buffalo/Albright; Fort

Worth; Honolulu Academy; Omaha/Joslyn; SRGM; WMAA. BIBLIOGRAPHY: Read 3.

SAUL, PETER. b. August 16, 1934, San Francisco, Calif. STUDIED: Stanford U.; California School of Fine Arts, 1950–52; Washington U., with Fred Conway, 1952–56, BFA. Traveled Europe; resided Holland, 1956–58, Paris, 1958–62, Rome, 1962–64. AWARDS: *Art In America* (Magazine), New Talent, 1962; William and Noma Copley Foundation Grant, 1962. ADDRESS: c/o Dealer. DEALER: Allan Frumkin Gallery, NYC and Chicago. ONE-MAN EXHIBITIONS: Allan Frumkin Gallery, Chicago, 1961, 63, 64; Allan Frumkin Gallery, NYC, 1962, 63, 64; Galerie Breteau, Paris, 1962, 63, 64; La Tartaruga, Rome, 1963; Rolf Nelson Gallery, 1963; Notizie Gallery, 1964. GROUP: Salon des Jeunes Peintres, Paris, 1959, 60; Dayton/AI, International Selection, 1961; U. of Colorado, 1962; Chicago/AI, 1962, 63, 64; SFMA, Directions—Painting U.S.A., 1963; U. of Michigan, 1963; Musee Cantonal des Beaux-Arts, Lausanne, I Salon International de Galeries Pilotes, 1963; Abbey Saint-Pierre, Ghent, Forum, 1963; Brandeis U., Recent American Drawings, 1964; The Hague, New Realism, 1964. COLLECTIONS: Chicago/AI; MOMA; Oberlin College.

SAUNDERS, RAYMOND. b. October 28, 1934, Homestead, Pa. STUDIED: U. of Pennsylvania, 1954–57; Barnes Foundation, 1953–55; PAFA, 1953–57; Carnegie Institute of Technology, 1959–60, BFA; California College of Arts and Crafts, 1960–61, MFA. Traveled Mexico, Europe, USA. AWARDS: PAFA, Cresson Fellowship, 1956; AAAL Grant, 1963; Eakins Prize; Prix de Rome, 1964. ADDRESS: c/o Dealer. DEALER: Terry Dintenfass, Inc. ONE-MAN EXHIBITIONS: (first) Pittsburgh Playhouse Gallery, 1953, also 1955; Terry Dintenfass, Inc., 1962, 64. GROUP: PAFA Annuals; SFMA Annuals; New School for Social Research; WMAA Annuals; NAD. COLLECTIONS: Allentown/AM; Howard U.; PAFA; WMAA.

SAVELLI, ANGELO. b. October 30, 1911, Pizzo Catanzaro, Italy. STUDIED: Academy of Fine Arts, Rome, with Ferruccio Ferrazzi, Diploma di Decorazione. To USA 1954. Traveled Europe, USA. A co-founder of The Art Club, Rome, with Gino Severini, Enrico Pramolini, Fazzini and others, 1944. Commissions: Sora, Italy (church façade, fresco); F.A.U., Rome (mural); Italian Line (paintings for SS *Leonardo da Vinci* and SS *Michelangelo*). Awards: Fellowship from the Italian Ministry of Education, 1948; Bergamo, First Prize, 1941, 42; Battistoni, First Prize, 1958. Address: 186 Bowery, NYC. One-man Exhibitions: (first) Galleria Roma, Rome, 1941; La Spiga, Milan, 1942; Galleria Ritrove, Rome, 1943; Galleria San Marco, Rome, 1944, 51; Galleria Cronache, Bologna, Italy, 1946; Oblo, Capri, 1946; Galleria d'Arte del Naviglio, Milan, 1947, 54, 61; Galleria Sandri, Venice, 1947; Centre d'Art Italien, Paris, 1952; Numero Galleria d'Arte, Florence, Italy, 1953; The Contemporaries, 1955; D'Amecourt Gallery, Washington, D.C., 1956; Leo Castelli Inc., 1958; Galleria del Cavallino, Venice, 1958; Galleria Selecta, Rome, 1959; U. of Minnesota, 1960; Peter H.

Deitsch Gallery, 1962; D'Arcy Gallery, 1963; Philadelphia Art Alliance, 1963; XXXII Venice Biennial, 1964. Group: Rome National Art Quadrennial, 1943– ; XXV, XXVI, and XXVII Venice Biennials, 1950, 52, 54; Rose Fried Gallery, International Collage Exhibition, 1956; Hartford/Wadsworth, Graphics, 1956; A.F.A., Collage in America, circ., 1957–58; Library of Congress, 1959; Brooklyn Museum, 1962, 63; Gallery of Modern Art, Ljubljana, Yugoslavia; A.F.A., Moods of Light, circ., 1963–64; Sidney Janis Gallery, 1964. Collections: Cincinnati/AM; MOMA; U. of Minnesota; NYPL; PMA; U. of Pennsylvania; Rome/Nazionale; Turin/Civico.

SCARPITTA, SALVATORE. b. 1919, NYC. To Italy 1936, to study; returned to NYC 1959. Address: 333 Park Avenue South, NYC. Dealer: Leo Castelli Inc. One-man Exhibi-

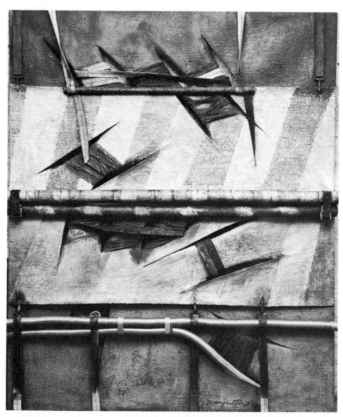

Salvatore Scarpitta   *Sun Dial for Racing. 1962*

TIONS: Galleria Il Pincio, Rome, 1951; Gaetano Chiurazzi, Rome, 1949; La Tartaruga, Rome, 1955, 57, 58; Galleria d'Arte del Naviglio, Milan, 1956, 58; Leo Castelli Inc., 1959, 60, 63; Dwan Gallery, 1961; Galerie Schmela, Dusseldorf, 1963; Musee Royaux des Beaux-Arts, Brussels, 1964. GROUP: Galleria Roma, Rome, 1944; Rome National Art Quadrennial, 1948; XXVI, XXVIII, and XXIX Venice Biennials, 1952, 56, 58; Columbus, 1960; Martha Jackson Gallery, New Media—New Forms, I & II, 1960, 61; Houston/MFA, Ways and Means, 1961; Corcoran, 1963; Musee Cantonal des Beaux-Arts, Lausanne, I Salon International de Galeries Pilotes, 1963; Maryland Institute, 1964; Chicago/AI, 1964. COLLECTIONS: Amsterdam/Stedelijk; Buffalo/Albright; Los Angeles/County MA; MOMA; Tel Aviv. BIBLIOGRAPHY: Janis and Blesh 1; *Metro.*

SCHANKER, LOUIS. b. 1903, NYC. STUDIED: Educational Alliance, NYC; Cooper Union; ASL. Traveled France, USA. TAUGHT: New School for Social Research; Bard College. FEDERAL A.P.: 1940–41. ADDRESS: 121 East 61 Street, NYC. ONE-MAN EXHIBITIONS: (first) Contemporary Arts Gallery, NYC, 1933; Kleemann Gallery, NYC; The Willard Gallery, 1944, 45, 46, 48, 50; Grace Borgenicht Gallery Inc., 1952, 55; Hacker Gallery, NYC, 1950; New School for Social Research, 1938; Mortimer Brandt, NYC, 1945; Brooklyn Museum, 1943; Artists' Gallery, NYC, 1939. GROUP: WMAA; Brooklyn Museum; MMA; Utica; Chicago/AI; U. of Michigan. COLLECTIONS: Brooklyn Museum; Chicago/AI; MMA; U. of Michigan; NYPL; Newark Museum; PMA; Phillips; Toledo/MA; Utica; Wesleyan U. BIBLIOGRAPHY: American Artists Congress, Inc.; Baur 7; Cheney, M. C.; Hayter 1; Pousette-Dart, ed.

SCHAPIRO, MIRIAM. b. 1923, Toronto, Canada. STUDIED: State U. of Iowa, 1944–49, BA, MA, MFA. AWARDS: Tamarind Fellowship, 1963. m. Paul Brach. ADDRESS: 235 West 76 Street, NYC. DEALER: Andre Emmerich Gallery, NYC. ONE-MAN EXHIBITIONS: Andre Emmerich Gallery, NYC, 1958, 60, 61, 63; Illinois Wesleyan U., 1951; U. of Missouri, 1950. GROUP: MOMA, New Talent; U. of Nottingham (England), Abstract Impressionists, 1958; International Biennial Exhibition of Paintings,

Tokyo; Carnegie, 1959; WMAA, 1959; MOMA, Abstract American Drawings and Watercolors, circ. Latin America, 1961–63; Jewish Museum, Toward a New Abstraction, 1963; SFMA, Directions—Painting U.S.A., 1963; Walker, Denver/AM; Brooklyn Museum; Chicago/AI. COLLECTIONS: Albion College; Illinois Wesleyan U.; St. Louis/City; Stephens College.

SCHLEMOWITZ, ABRAM. b. July 19, 1911, NYC. STUDIED: Beaux-Arts Institute of Design, NYC, 1928–33; ASL, 1934; NAD, 1935–39. TAUGHT: Contemporary Art Center, YMHA, NYC, 1936–39; Pratt Institute, 1962–63; U. of California, Berkeley, 1963–64. Organizing chairman of the New Sculpture Group, 1957–58. AWARDS: Guggenheim Foundation Fellowship, 1963. ADDRESS: 128 West 23 Street, NYC. DEALER: The Howard Wise Gallery, NYC. ONE-MAN EXHIBITIONS: The Howard Wise Gallery, NYC, 1961, 62. GROUP: Betty Parsons Gallery, American Abstract Artists, 1959; Claude Bernard, Paris, 1960; The Stable Gallery, Sculpture Annuals, 1960, 61; Museum of Contemporary Crafts, Collaboration: Artist and Architect, 1962; Riverside Museum, 12 New York Sculptors, 1962; New School for Social Research, Humanists of The 60's, 1963; MOMA, Art in Embassies, circ. internationally, 1963–64. COLLECTIONS: U. of California, Berkeley; Provincetown/Chrysler.

SCHMIDT, JULIUS. b. 1923, Stamford, Conn. STUDIED: Oklahoma A. and M. College, 1950–51; Cranbrook Academy of Art, 1952, BFA, 1955, MFA; Zadkine School of Sculpture, Paris, 1953; Academy of Fine Arts, Florence, Italy, 1954. Traveled Europe, USA. TAUGHT: Cranbrook Academy of Art, 1952, 1962– ; Silvermine Guild School of Art, summers, 1953, 54; Cleveland Institute of Art, 1957; Kansas City Art Institute and School of Design, 1954–59; RISD, 1959–60; U. of California, Berkeley, 1961–62. AWARDS: Cranbrook, Mid-American Biennial, First Prize and P.P.; Guggenheim Foundation Fellowship, 1963. ADDRESS: Cranbrook Academy of Art, Bloomfield Hills, Mich. DEALER: Marlborough-Gerson Gallery Inc. ONE-MAN EXHIBITIONS: Silvermine Guild, 1953; Kansas City Art Institute and School of Design, 1956; Santa Barbara/MA, 1961; Otto Gerson Gallery, NYC, 1961, 63. GROUP: PAFA, 1958; Detroit/Institute, 1958; Chicago/AI, 1960;

Julius Schmidt　　　*Untitled. 1962*

MOMA, Sixteen Americans, circ., 1959; WMAA Annuals, 1960, 61, 62, 63; Claude Bernard, Paris, Aspects of American Sculpture, 1960; New School for Social Research, Mechanism and Organism, 1961; Carnegie, 1961; MOMA, American Painting and Sculpture, circ., 1961; Dayton/AI, 1961; SRGM, The Joseph H. Hirshhorn Collection, 1962; Battersea Park, London, International Sculpture Exhibition, 1963; Sao Paulo, 1963; Walker, Ten American Sculptors, 1964; Boston Arts Festival, 1961; SFMA, 1962. COLLECTIONS: Chicago/AI; U. of Illinois; Kansas City/Nelson; MOMA; U. of Nebraska; WMAA; Washington U.

SCHNAKENBERG, HENRY. b. September 14, 1892, New Brighton (Staten Island), N.Y.

STUDIED: ASL, 1914, with Kenneth Hayes Miller. US Army, 1917–19. Traveled Mexico, Europe. TAUGHT: ASL, 1939. COMMISSIONS (murals): US Post Offices, West New York, N.J., and Amsterdam, N.Y. AWARDS: Hon. DFA, U. of Vermont; elected to the NIAL, 1952. ADDRESS: P.O. Box 41, Newtown, Conn. DEALER: Kraushaar Galleries. ONE-MAN EXHIBITIONS: (first) Whitney Studio Club, NYC, 1921; Alfredo Valente Gallery, NYC, 1926; Hartford/Wadsworth (two-man), 1955; Kraushaar Galleries, 1929, 35, 37, 40, 41, 42, 46, 48, 50, 54, 56, 60, 63. GROUP: MMA; WMAA; U. of Nebraska; Chicago/AI; Brooklyn Museum; Newark Museum. COLLECTIONS: Brooklyn Museum; California Palace; Chicago/AI; Dallas/MFA; Hartford/Wadsworth; MMA; Minneapolis/Institute; Montclair/AM; U. of Nebraska; Newark Museum; New Britain; SFMA; Springfield, Mass./MFA; WMAA; Wichita/AM. **Bibliography:** Baur 7; Cheney, M. C.; **Goodrich 5;** Goodrich and Baur 1; Hall; *Index of 20th Century Artists;* Kent, N.; Mellquist; Pearson 1; Richardson.

SCHRAG, KARL. b. December 7, 1912, Karlsruhe, Germany. **Studied:** Humanistisches Gymnasium, Karlsruhe, 1930; Ecole des Beaux-Arts, Geneva, 1931; Atelier Lucien Simon, Paris; Academie Ranson, Paris, with Roger Bissiere; Academie de la Grande Chaumiere, 1931–35; ASL, with Harry Sternberg; Atelier 17, NYC, with S. W. Hayter. To USA 1938; citizen 1944. Traveled Europe, Mexico. **Taught:** Brooklyn College, 1953; Columbia U., 1958; Cooper Union, 1954– ; Director of Atelier 17, NYC, 1950. **Member:** Artists Equity; SAGA; ASL. **Awards:** Brooklyn Museum Biennials, P.P., 1947, 50; SAGA, P.P., 1954; The Print Club, Philadelphia, Charles M. Lea Prize, 1954; American Color Print Society, 1958; Syracuse State Fair, Nelson Rockefeller Award, 1963; American Color Print Society, Florence Tonner Prize, 1960, 63, and Sonia Wather

Karl Schrag   *Black Trees at Noon. 1960*

Award, 1964. **Address:** 127 East 95 Street, NYC. **Dealer:** Kraushaar Galleries. **One-man Exhibitions:** (first) Galerie Arenberg, Brussels, 1938; Kraushaar Galleries, 1947, 50, 52, 56, 59, 62, 64; U. of Alabama, 1949; Smithsonian, 1945; Philadelphia Art Alliance, 1952; U. of Maine, 1953; State U. of New York, Oneonta, 1958; Gesellschaft der Freunde Junger Kunst, Baden-Baden, Germany, 1958. **Retrospective:** A.F.A./Ford Foundation, circ., 1960–62. **Group:** SAGA; PAFA; The Print Club, Philadelphia; Brooklyn Museum; Musee du Petit Palais, Paris, 1949; Graphische Sammlung Albertina; WMAA, 1943, 55, 57; SFMA, 1941, 45, 46; Carnegie, 1944, 47; Chicago/AI; Instituto Nacional de Bellas Artes, Mexico City, 1958. **Collections:** Bibliotheque Nationale; Brandeis U.; Brooklyn Museum; Chicago/AI; Cleveland/MA; Dartmouth College; Hartford/Wadsworth; U. of Illinois; Karlsruhe; Library of Congress; Los Angeles/County MA; MMA; MOMA; NYPL; National Gallery; Oakland/AM; Omaha/Joslyn; PMA; RISD; Smithsonian; Utica; WMAA; Yale U. **Bibliography:** Gordon; Hayter 1, 2; Reese.

SCHUCKER, CHARLES. b. January 9, 1908, Gap, Pa. **Studied:** Maryland Institute, 1928–34. **Taught:** NYU, 1947–54; Pratt Institute, 1956–64. **Member:** Yaddo Board of Directors. **Federal A.P.:** Easel painting in Chicago, 1938–42. **Awards:** Henry Walters Traveling Fellowship; Guggenheim Foundation Fellowship, 1953; Audubon Artists, Prize for Oil Painting. **Address:** 33 Middagh Street, Brooklyn, N.Y. **One-man Exhibitions:** (first) Rennaissance Society, Chicago; Albert Roullier Gallery, Chicago; Chicago/AI: The Chicago Artists Room; Macbeth Gallery, NYC, 1946, 49, 53; Passedoit Gallery, NYC, 1955, 58; Katonah (N.Y.) Art Gallery, 1955; The Howard Wise Gallery, NYC, 1962. **Group:** MOMA, Painting and Sculpture from 16 American Cities, 1933; Carnegie, 1949; Walker, Contemporary American Painting, 1950; MMA, American Paintings Today, 1950; PAFA, 1951, 52, 53; California Palace Annual, 1952; Chicago/AI, 1954; SFMA, Art in the Twentieth Century, 1955; WMAA, Nature in Abstraction, 1958; WMAA Annuals, 1952, 53, 54, 55, 56, 57, 60, 61, 63; Corcoran; Brooklyn Museum; Riverside Museum. **Collections:** AAAL; Brooklyn Museum; Newark Museum; New Britain; WMAA. **Bibliography:** Baur 5; Goodrich and Baur 1.

SCHUELER, JON. b. September 12, 1916, Milwaukee, Wisc. STUDIED: U. of Wisconsin, 1934–38, BA (Economics), 1939–40, MA (English Literature); Bread Loaf School of English, Middlebury, Vt., 1941; California School of Fine Arts, 1948–51, with David Park, Elmer Bischoff, Richard Diebenkorn, Hassel Smith, Clyfford Still, Clay Spohn. US Air Force, 1941–43. Traveled Europe, Great Britain, USA extensively. TAUGHT: U. of San Francisco, 1947–49 (English Literature); Yale U., 1960–62, and summer school, 1960, 61; Maryland Institute, 1963– . COMMISSIONS: New York Hilton Hotel, 1962 (lithograph). ADDRESS: 901 Broadway, NYC. ONE-MAN EXHIBITIONS: (first) Metart Gallery, San Francisco, 1950; The Stable Gallery, 1954, 62, 64; Leo Castelli Inc., 1957, 59; B. C. Holland Gallery, 1960; Hirschl & Adler Galleries, Inc., NYC, 1960; Maryland Institute, 1962, 64; Cornell U., 1962; Columbia U. School of Architecture, 1962. GROUP: Walker, 1955; WMAA Annuals, 1956, 59, 61, 63; A.F.A., School of New York—Some Younger American Painters, 1960; Corcoran, 1958, 62; Walker, 60 American Painters, 1960; WMAA, 50 Years of American Art, 1964. COLLECTIONS: New York Hilton Hotel; Union Carbide Corp.; WMAA. BIBLIOGRAPHY: Baur 5; Friedman, ed.; Goodrich and Baur 1.

SCHWABACHER, ETHEL. b. May 20, 1903, NYC. STUDIED: ASL, 1927–28, with Robert Laurent, Max Weber; and privately with Arshile Gorky, 1934–36. Resided Europe, 1928–34. ADDRESS: 1192 Park Avenue, NYC. ONE-MAN EXHIBITIONS: (first) Passedoit Gallery, NYC, 1935, also 1947; Betty Parsons Gallery, 1953, 56, 57, 60, 62; Greenross Gallery, NYC, 1964. GROUP: Corcoran, 1958; Carnegie, 1961; Walker, 1960; WMAA Annuals, 1947, 49, 51, 52, 54, 56, 57, 59, 61, 63; Brooklyn Museum, 1956, 60; A.F.A., 1953; WMAA, Nature in Abstraction, 1958; Buffalo/Albright, 1962; Mexico City/Nacional, 1960. COLLECTIONS: Buffalo/Albright; Rockefeller Institute; WMAA. BIBLIOGRAPHY: Baur 5; Goodrich and Baur 1; Schwabacher.

SCHWARTZ, MANFRED. b. November 11, 1909, Lodz, Poland. STUDIED: ASL, with George Bridgeman, John Sloan. Traveled Europe, Algeria. TAUGHT: NYU; Skowhegan School; Brooklyn Museum School; New School for Social Research; Pratt Institute. MEMBER: Federation of Modern Painters and Sculptors. ADDRESS: 22 East Eighth Street, NYC. ONE-MAN EXHIBITIONS: (first) Lilienfeld Gallery, NYC, 1940; Durand-Ruel Gallery, NYC, 1947, 48, 49; Otto Gerson Gallery, NYC, 1955, 57; Albert Landry, NYC, 1962, 63; Brooklyn Museum, Drawings and Pastels, 1959. RETROSPECTIVE: Brooklyn Museum, Manfred Schwartz: 20-Year Retrospective, 1961. GROUP: Cincinnati/AM; Brooklyn Museum; WMAA. COLLECTIONS: Brooklyn Museum; MMA; MOMA; U. of Minnesota; Newark Museum; New School for Social Research; PMA; Rochester/Memorial; WMAA. BIBLIOGRAPHY: Genauer.

SEGAL, GEORGE. b. November 26, 1924, NYC. STUDIED: NYU, 1950, BS; Rutgers U., 1963, MFA. TAUGHT: New Jersey high schools, 1957–63. AWARDS: Walter K. Gutman Foundation Grant, 1962. ADDRESS: RFD #4, Box 323, North Brunswick, N.J. DEALER: Sidney Janis Gallery. ONE-MAN EXHIBITIONS: (first) Hansa Gallery, NYC, 1956, also 1957, 58, 59; The Green Gallery, NYC, 1960, 62, 64; Rutgers U., 1958; Ileana Sonnabend (Gallery), Paris, 1963; Galerie Schmela, Dusseldorf, 1963. GROUP: Boston Arts Festival, 1956; Jewish Museum, The New York School, Second Generation, 1957; WMAA Annuals, 1960, 64; A.F.A., The Figure, circ., 1960; Sidney Janis Gallery, The New Realists, 1962; Stockholm/National, American Pop Art, 1964; VII Sao Paulo Biennial, 1963; Jewish Museum, Recent American Sculpture, 1964. COLLECTIONS: Buffalo/Albright; Charlotte/Mint; MOMA; Schwebber Electronics.

SELEY, JASON. b. May 20, 1919, Newark, N.J. STUDIED: Cornell U., 1936–40, BA; ASL, with Ossip Zadkine, 1943–45; Academie des Beaux-Arts, Paris, 1950. Traveled Europe; resided Haiti, 1946–49. TAUGHT: Hofstra College, 1953– . MEMBER: Federation of Modern Painters and Sculptors; Sculptors Guild; New Sculpture Group. COMMISSIONS: Haitian Government, 1949; Episcopal Cathedral, Port-au-Prince, Haiti, 1952. AWARDS: US State Department Grant, 1947–49; Fulbright Fellowship (France), 1949; Silvermine Guild, First Prize for Sculpture, 1962. ADDRESS: 428 East 13 Street, NYC. DEALER: The Kornblee Gallery. ONE-MAN EXHIBITIONS: (first) Le Centre d'Art,

Port-au-Prince, Haiti, 1946, also 1947, 48, 49; American-British Art Center, NYC, 1947, 48; A.A.A. Gallery, NYC, 1955; Hofstra College, 1957; Barone Gallery, NYC, 1960; The Kornblee Gallery, 1962, 64. **GROUP:** WMAA Annuals, 1952, 53, 62; MOMA, Recent Sculpture USA, 1959; MOMA, The Art of Assemblage, circ., 1961; SRGM, The Joseph H. Hirshhorn Collection, 1962; MOMA, Americans 1963, circ., 1963–64; Newark Museum, 1958, 61, 64; Festival of Two Worlds, Spoleto, 1962; Battersea Park, London, International Sculpture Exhibition, 1963; Documenta III, Kassel, 1964. **COLLECTIONS:** Chase Manhattan Bank; MOMA; Newark Museum. **BIBLIOGRAPHY:** Seitz 2.

SELIGER, CHARLES. b. June 3, 1926, NYC. Self-taught in art. **TAUGHT:** Mt. Vernon (N.Y.) Art Center, 1950–51. **ADDRESS:** 616 East Lincoln Avenue, Mt. Vernon, N.Y. **DEALER:** The Willard Gallery. **ONE-MAN EXHIBITIONS:** (first) Art of This Century, NYC, 1945, also 1946; Carlebach Gallery, NYC, 1948, 49; de Young, 1949; Art Center School, Los Angeles, 1949; The Willard Gallery, 1951, 53, 55, 57, 59, 61, 63; Otto Seligman Gallery, 1955, 63; Haydon Calhoun Gallery, 1963. **GROUP:** VMFA, 1946; Chicago/AI, Abstract and Surrealist Art, 1948; XXIV Venice Biennial, 1948, Guggenheim Collection; Cornell U., Young Painters, 1951; USIA, American Painting, circ. Europe, 1956; Brooklyn Museum, 1949; WMAA, 1952, 55, 56; Chicago/AI, 1952; Utica, 1957; MOMA, Abstract Painting and Sculpture in America, 1951; Rome-New York Foundation, Rome, 1960. **COLLECTIONS:** Andover/Phillips; Baltimore/MA; Chicago/AI; The Hague; Iowa State U.; MOMA; Newark Museum; Seattle/AM; Tel Aviv; US State Department; Utica; Vancouver; Vassar College; WMAA. **BIBLIOGRAPHY:** Baur 7; Read 2, 3; Richardson; Ritchie 1.

SELIGMANN, KURT. b. July 20, 1900, Basel, Switzerland; **d.** January 2, 1962, NYC. **STUDIED:** Ecole des Beaux-Arts, Geneva, 1920; Academy of Fine Arts, Florence, Italy, 1927. To USA 1939; became a citizen. **TAUGHT:** Brooklyn Museum School. Designed sets for modern dance and ballet groups. Authority on magic. **ONE-MAN EXHIBITIONS:** Jeanne Bucher, Paris, 1932, 35; Zwemmer Gallery, London, 1933;

Mitzowko-Shi, Tokyo, 1935; New School for Social Research, 1940; Arts Club of Chicago, 1946; Wakefield Gallery, NYC; Mexico City/Nacional, 1943; Karl Nierendorf Gallery, NYC, 1939, 41; Durlacher Brothers, 1944, 46, 48, 50, 53; Alexander Iolas Gallery, 1953; Fine Arts Associates, NYC, 1960; D'Arcy Gallery, 1964; Walker, 1958; Ruth White Gallery, 1960, 61. **GROUP:** WMAA; MOMA; Chicago/AI; Detroit/Institute; U. of Illinois; MMA; NYPL; PAFA. **COLLECTIONS:** Aubusson; Bibliotheque Nationale; Brooklyn Museum; Buffalo/Albright; Chicago/AI; Collège des Musees Nationaux de France; U. of Illinois; Kunstkredit; Lodz; MMA; MOMA; Mexico City/Nacional; NYPL; PAFA; Smith College; WMAA. **BIBLIOGRAPHY:** Blesh 1; Breton 2; Dorner; Flanagan; Frost; Goodrich and Baur 1; Huyghe; Jakovski; Janis and Blesh 1; Janis, S.; Kuh 1; Pearson 2; Pousette-Dart, ed.; Richardson; Sachs; **Seligmann**; Waldberg 3.

SENNHAUSER, JOHN. b. December 10, 1907, Rorschach, Switzerland. **STUDIED:** Technical Institute, Treviso, Italy; Academy of Fine Arts, Venice; Cooper Union. Traveled Europe, USA. **TAUGHT:** Leonardo da Vinci Art School, NYC, 1936–39; Contemporary School of Art, NYC, 1939–42. **MEMBER:** American Abstract Artists; Federation of Modern Painters and Sculptors; International Institute of Arts and Letters. **COMMISSIONS:** Murals for banks and private buildings in NYC and other cities. **AWARDS:** WMAA, p.p., 1951; Tulsa/Philbrook, p.p., 1951. **ADDRESS:** 35–26 79th Street, Jackson Heights, N.Y. **DEALER:** The Salpeter Gallery. **ONE-MAN EXHIBITIONS:** (first) Leonardo da Vinci Art School Gallery, NYC, 1936; Contemporary Arts Gallery, NYC, 1939; Theodore A. Kohn Gallery, NYC, 1942; Artists' Gallery, NYC, 1947, 50, 52; Brown U., 1954; U. of Maine, 1955; Black Mountain College, 1956; The Zabriskie Gallery, 1956, 57; Knapik Gallery, NYC, 1961; The Salpeter Gallery, 1964. **GROUP:** Brunswick U.; Bennington College; Worcester/AM; Walker; Dallas/MFA; NAD; PAFA; Chicago/AI; Museum of Non-Objective Art, NYC; Corcoran; U. of Illinois; Brooklyn Museum; Baltimore/MA; Salon des Realites Nouvelles, Paris. **COLLECTIONS:** SRGM; Tulsa/Philbrook; Utica; WMAA. **BIBLIOGRAPHY:** Pousette-Dart, ed.

SERISAWA, SUEO. b. April 10, 1910, Yokohama, Japan. STUDIED: Otis Art Institute, Los Angeles, 1932–33, with George Barker; Chicago Art Institute School, 1943. TAUGHT: Kann Art Institute, 1947–51; Scripps College, 1950–51; and privately. AWARDS: California State Fair, 1940, 49; PAFA, Medal, 1947; Pepsi-Cola, 1948. ADDRESS: 3950 San Rafael Avenue, Los Angeles, Calif. DEALER: Felix Landau Gallery. ONE-MAN EXHIBITIONS: Tone-Price Gallery, West Hollywood, 1940; Los Angeles/County MA, 1941; Dayton/AI, 1945; Occidental College, 1952; Pasadena/AM, 1951; Dalzell Hatfield Gallery, 1948; Felix Landau Gallery, 1959. GROUP: MMA, 1950; Los Angeles/County MA; California Palace; SFMA; U. of Illinois; Chicago/AI; San Diego; Santa Barbara/MA, I & II Pacific Coast Biennials, 1955, 57; PAFA; WMAA Annuals; Corcoran; Sao Paulo Biennial; International Biennial Exhibitions of Paintings, Tokyo; U. of Nebraska; Carnegie; Walker. COLLECTIONS: Arizona State College; Eilat; Los Angeles/County MA; MOMA; Pasadena/AM; San Diego.

SHAHN, BEN. b. September 12, 1898, Kovno, Lithuania. To USA 1906. STUDIED: NYU; City College of New York, 1919–22 (Biology); NAD, 1922; ASL. Traveled Europe, Japan, North Africa, USA. Photographer and designer for Farm Security Administration, 1935–38. Designed posters for Office of War Information, 1942, and for CIO, 1944–46. Designed sets for "Ballets:USA" and for the Festival of Two Worlds, Spoleto, 1958. COMMISSIONS: Community Building, Roosevelt, N.J., 1938–39; US Post Offices, Bronx, N.Y., 1938–39 (with Bernarda Bryson), and Jamaica, N.Y., 1939; Social Security Building, Washington, D.C., 1940–42; William E. Grady Vocational High School, Brooklyn, N.Y., 1957 (mosaic). AWARDS: PAFA, Pennell Memorial Medal, 1939, 53; PAFA, Alice McFadden Eyre Medal, 1952; PAFA, Joseph E. Temple Gold Medal, 1956; *Look* Magazine poll of "Ten Best Painters," 1948; II Sao Paulo Biennial, 1953; XXVII Venice Biennial, 1954; Harvard U., Medal, 1956; American Institute of Graphic Art, Medal, 1958; North Shore (Long Island, N.Y.) Art Festival, Annual Award, 1959. ADDRESS: Roosevelt, N.J. DEALER: The Downtown Gallery. ONE-MAN EXHIBITIONS: The Downtown Gallery, 1930, 32, 33, 44, 49, 51, 52, 55, 57, 59, 61; Julien Levy Gal-

leries, NYC, 1940; MOMA, 1947; Arts Council of Great Britain, circ., 1947; Albright Art School, 1950; Perls Galleries, 1950; Arts Club of Chicago, 1951; Santa Barbara/MA, circ., 1952; Houston/MFA, 1954; Detroit/Institute (three-man), 1954; Chicago/AI, 1954; XXVII Venice Biennial, 1954; Southern Illinois U., 1954; American Institute of Graphic Art, 1957; St. Mary's College (Ind.), 1958; Bucknell U., 1958; Katonah (N.Y.) Art Gallery, 1959; Leicester Gallery, London, 1959, 64; U. of Louisville, 1960; U. of Utah, 1960; Library of the New Haven (Conn.) Jewish Community Center, 1961; Institute of Modern Art, Boston, Documentary, 1957; Amsterdam/Stedelijk, 1961; Rome/Nazionale, 1962; MOMA, Ben Shahn, circ. Europe, 1962. RETROSPECTIVE: MOMA, 1947; ICA, Boston, 1948. GROUP: Corcoran; Carnegie; WMAA; Chicago/AI; U. of Nebraska; Brooklyn Museum; MOMA; Buffalo/Albright. COLLECTIONS: Abbott Laboratories; Andover/Phillips; Arizona State College; U. of Arizona; Auburn U.; Baltimore/MA; Brandeis U.; Brooklyn Museum; Buffalo/Albright; California Palace; Carnegie; Chicago/AI; Container Corp. of America; Cranbrook; Dartmouth College; Des Moines; Detroit/Institute; Fort Wayne/AM; U. of Georgia; Grand Rapids; Hartford/Wadsworth; Harvard U.; U. of Illinois; Indiana U.; Inland Steel Co.; Jewish Museum; MMA; MOMA; Mary Washington College; U. of Michigan; Museum of the City of New York; U. of Nebraska; Newark Museum; U. of Oklahoma; Omaha/Joslyn; PAFA; Phillips; Sara Roby Foundation; St. Louis/City; Santa Barbara/MA; Smith College; Springfield, Mo./AM; Syracuse U.; Terry Art Institute; VMFA; WMAA; Walker; Wellesley College; Wesleyan U.; Wichita/AM; Youngstown/Butler. BIBLIOGRAPHY: Barr 3; Baur 7; Bazin; Biddle 3; Blesh 1; Canaday; Christensen; Eliot; Finkelstein; Flanagan; Flexner; Gaunt; Goodrich and Baur 1; Haftman; Hunter 5; Kepes 2; Kuh 1, 2; Langui; Lee and Burchwood; McCurdy, ed.; Mendelowitz; *Metro;* Munsterberg; Newmeyer; Newton 1; Nordness, ed.; Pearson 1, 2; Pousette-Dart, ed.; Read 2; Richardson; Rodman 1, 2, 3; Sachs; **Shahn; Soby 2, 3, 4, 5;** Sutton; Wight 2.

SHAW, CHARLES. b. May 1, 1892, NYC. STUDIED: Yale U., Ph.D.; Columbia U. School of Architecture; ASL, with Thomas Hart Benton; and privately with George Luks. US Army, World War I. Traveled Europe extensively, Scandinavia, West Indies. Author of children's books, poetry, and articles for *Vanity Fair, The Bookman, Smart Set,* and other magazines. MEMBER: American Abstract Artists; Federation of Modern Painters and Sculptors; Fellow of the International Institute of Arts and Letters. COMMISSIONS: *Vanity Fair* (Magazine) (covers); Shell-Mex Ltd. (poster). AWARDS: Nantucket, First and Second Prizes; Century Association, Hon. Men., 1964. ADDRESS: 340 East 57 Street, NYC. DEALER: The Bertha Schaefer Gallery. ONE-MAN EXHIBITIONS: (first) Curt Valentine Gallery, NYC, 1934, also 1938; Museum of Living Art, NYC, 1935; SRGM, 1940; Passedoit Gallery, NYC, 1945, 46, 50, 51, 54, 56, 57, 58, 59; Albert Landry, NYC, 1960, 61; The Bertha Schaefer Gallery, 1963, 64; U. of Louisville, 1963; Nantucket, 1954, 55, 56, 57, 58, 59; Art Association of Newport (R.I.), 1960, 62. GROUP: American Abstract Artists, annually since 1936; Federation of Modern Painters and Sculptors, since 1940; PMA, "8 x 8," 1945; WMAA Annuals; MOMA, Abstract Painting and Sculpture in America, 1951; WMAA, Geometric Abstraction in America, circ., 1962; Chicago/AI; Carnegie; Walker; SFMA; International Association of Plastic Arts, Contemporary American Painting, circ. Europe, 1956–57; U. of Illinois; Corcoran. COLLECTIONS: Atlanta U.; Baltimore/MA; Boston/MFA; Brooklyn Museum; California Palace; Chase Manhattan Bank; Chicago/AI; Cincinnati/AM; Cleveland/MA; Corcoran; Dayton/AI; Denver/AM; Detroit/Institute; Fort Worth; U. of Georgia; Hartford/Wadsworth; Los Angeles/County MA; U. of Louisville; MMA; MOMA; NYU; Nantucket; Newark Museum; U. of North Carolina; PMA; Paris/Moderne; Phillips; Pittsfield/Berkshire; Provincetown/Chrysler; RISD; Raleigh/NCMA; Riverside Museum; Rockefeller Institute; SFMA; SRGM; WMAA; Walker; Wichita/AM; Williams College; Yale U. BIBLIOGRAPHY: Baur 7; Cheney, M. C.; Kootz 2; Pousette-Dart, ed.; Ritchie 1.

SHEELER, CHARLES. b. July 16, 1883, Philadelphia, Pa.; d. May 7, 1965. STUDIED: Pennsylvania School of Industrial Art, Philadelphia, 1900–03; PAFA, 1903–06, with William M. Chase. Traveled Europe, USA. TAUGHT: Phillips Academy, 1946; Currier Gallery School, 1948. Collaborated with Paul Strand on the film "Mannahatta." COMMISSIONS: Ford Motor Co., photographed the Ford Plant, 1927. AWARDS: Chicago/AI, Norman Wait Harris Medal, 1945; PAFA, Alumni

Charles Sheeler   *California Industrial. 1957*

Award, 1957; Hallmark International Competition, 1958 ($1,000); AAAL, Award of Merit Medal, 1962. ONE-MAN EXHIBITIONS: (first) Modern Gallery, NYC, 1918 (photographs); DeZayas Gallery, NYC, 1920 (paintings); The Daniel Gallery, NYC, 1922; Whitney Studio Club, NYC, 1924; J. B. Neumann Gallery, NYC (two-man), 1926; Art Center, NYC, 1926; The Downtown Gallery, 1931, 38, 40, 41, 43, 46, 49, 51, 56, 58; Arts Club of Chicago, 1932; Harvard U. (three-man), 1934; Society of Arts and Crafts, Detroit, 1935; Cincinnati/AM (four-man), 1941; Dayton/AI, 1944; Andover/Phillips, 1946; Currier, 1948; Houston/MFA (two-man), 1951; Walker, 1952; Detroit/Institute (three-man), 1954; State U. of Iowa, 1963; Katonah (N.Y.) Art Gallery, 1960. RETROSPECTIVE: MOMA, 1939; UCLA, circ., 1954; Allentown/AM, 1961; MIT, 1959. GROUP: NAD, 1906; PAFA, 1907, 1908–10; The Armory Show, 1913; Anderson Galleries, NYC, Forum Exhibition, 1916; Society of Independent Artists, NYC, 1917; Brooklyn Museum, 1923, 25; Cincinnati/AM, 1924, 1927–31, 34, 35, 39; Whitney Studio Club Annuals, NYC, 1925, 27, 30; Cleveland/MA, 1926, 1927–29, 31, 32, 34; Royal Academy, London, 1930; St. Louis/City, 1931–34, 41, 42, 44, 45; Carnegie, 1931, 33, 35, 37, 40, 41, 43, 45, 48, 52; WMAA, 1932, 34, 36, 42; XVII & XXVIII Venice Biennials, 1934, 56; Chicago/AI, 1935, 37, 38, 41, 46, 48, 49, 51, 54. COLLECTIONS: Albany/Institute; Andover/Phillips; Arizona State College; Boston/MFA; Britannica; Brooklyn Museum; Buffalo/Albright; California Palace; Chicago/AI; Cleveland/MA; Colonial Williamsburg; Columbus; Currier; Detroit/Institute; General Motors Corp.; Harvard U.; Kansas City/Nelson; MMA; MOMA; The Miller Co.; Mount Holyoke College; U. of Nebraska; Newark Museum; New Britain; PAFA; PMA; Phillips; RISD; Sara Roby Foundation; Santa Barbara/MA; Smith College; Springfield, Mass./MFA; Tel Aviv; Toledo/MA; Utica; VMFA; WMAA; Walker; Wesleyan U.; West Palm Beach/Norton; Wichita/AM; Williams College; Worcester/AM; Yale U.; Youngstown/Butler. BIBLIOGRAPHY: Barker 1; Barr 3; Baur 7; Bazin; Beam; Biddle 3; Blesh 1; Born; Boswell 1; Brown; Bulliet 1; Cahill and Barr, eds.; Cheney, M. C.; Christensen; **Dochterman;** Dorner; Eliot; Flanagan; Flexner; Frank, ed.; Frost; Goldwater and Treves, eds.; Goodrich and Baur 1; Haftman; Hall; Halpert; **Hirsch;** Hunter 5; Huyghe; *Index of 20th Century Artists;* Janis and Blesh 1; Janis, S.; Jewell 2; Kootz 1, 2; Kouvenhoven; Kuh 1; Mather 1; McCourbrey; McCurdy, ed.; Mellquist; Mendelowitz; Neuhaus; Newmeyer; Nordness, ed.; Pagano; Phillips 1, 2; Poore; Pousette-Dart, ed.; Ringel, ed.; Rosenblum; **Rourke;** Sachs; Soby 5; Wight 2; **Williams, W. C.**

SHEETS, MILLARD. b. June, 1907, Pomona, Calif. STUDIED: Chouinard Art Institute, Los Angeles, 1925–29, with F. T. Chamberlain, Clarence Hinkle. Traveled Europe, Central America, Mexico, USA. TAUGHT: Scripps College, 1932–35, 1938–62; Chouinard Art Institute, Los Angeles, 1928–35; U. of Hawaii, 1935; Stickney Art Institute, Pasadena, 1930; U. of Southern California, 1934–35; Los Angeles County Art Institute, 1953– . COMMISSIONS (murals): Pomona (Calif.) First Federal Savings and Loan Association; Our Lady of the Assumption Church, Ventura, Calif. (interior and exterior); YMCA, Pasadena; State Mutual Building and Loan Association, Los Angeles; J. W. Robinson Department Store, Los Angeles; Bullock's, Los Angeles; South Pasadena Junior High School. AWARDS: Witte, Edgar B. Davis Prize; Los Angeles/County MA, First Prize, 1932; California State Fair, 1930, 1932 (First Prize), 33, 38; Chicago/AI, 1938; Los Angeles/County MA, 1932, 45; Arizona State Fair, 1928, 29, 30; California Watercolor Society, 1927. ADDRESS: Claremont, Calif. DEALER: Dalzell Hatfield Gallery. ONE-MAN EXHIBITIONS: (first) Los Angeles, Calif., 1929; Corcoran; Los Angeles/County MA; California Palace; San Diego; Fort Worth, 1931, 34; Milwaukee; Baltimore/MA; Buffalo/Albright; Albany/Institute; Witte, 1931, 34; New Orleans/Delgado; Memphis/Brooks; Springfield, Mass./MFA; U. of Oklahoma; Rochester/Memorial. GROUP: Chicago/AI, 1931–35; NAD Annuals, 1932–35; Denver/AM, 1935; Sao Paulo, 1955; WMAA; Carnegie; Oakland/AM; Buffalo/Albright; Kansas City/Nelson; U. of Nebraska; A Century of Progress, Chicago, 1933–34. COLLECTIONS: Albany/Institute; Brooklyn Museum; de Young; Los Angeles/County MA; Los Angeles Public Library; Montpelier/Wood; U. of Oklahoma;

SFMA; The White House, Washington, D.C.; Witte. **Bibliography:** Cheney, M. C.; Hall; **Millier 2;** Pagano.

SHINN, EVERETT. b. November 6, 1876, Woodstown, N.J.; **d.** January 2, 1953, NYC. **Studied:** PAFA. Wrote and produced a number of melodramas in NYC. **Member:** The Eight. **Commissions** (murals): Trenton (N.J.) City Hall; Spring Garden Institute, Philadelphia. **Awards:** Chicago/AI, Watson F. Blair Prize, 1939; elected to the NIAL, 1951. **One-man Exhibitions:** James Vigeveno Gallery, Los Angeles, 1945, 47, 48; American-British Art Center, NYC, 1945, 46, 49; Davis Gallery, NYC, 1959; Ferargil Galleries, NYC, 1943; 56th Street Gallery, NYC, 1930; The Graham Gallery, 1952, 58; M. Knoedler & Co., 1903; One-Ten Gallery, NYC, 1939; Metropolitan Gallery, NYC, 1931; Morton Gallery, NYC, 1935; U. of Pennsylvania, 1959. **Group:** Macbeth Gallery, NYC, The Eight, 1908; The Armory Show, 1913; Brooklyn Museum, The Eight, 1943; Syracuse/Everson, The Eight, 1958; PMA, 1945; U. of Pittsburgh, 1959. **Collections:** Boston/MFA; Brooklyn Museum; Buffalo/Albright; Chicago/AI; Detroit/Institute; MMA; New Britain; Phillips; WMAA. **Bibliography:** Baur 7; Biddle 3; Blesh 1; Brown; Canaday; Cheney, M. C.; Eliot; Flanagan; Flexner; Gallatin 8; Glackens; Goodrich and Baur 1; Hartmann; Hunter 5; Kent, N.; McCourbrey; McCurdy, ed.; Mellquist; Mendelowitz; Neuhaus; Pagano; Perlman; Richardson; Sutton.

SIMON, SIDNEY. b. June 21, 1917, Pittsburgh, Pa. **Studied:** Carnegie Institute of Technology; PAFA; U. of Pennsylvania, with George Harding, BFA; Barnes Foundation. US Army artist, 1943–46. **Taught:** Cooper Union, 1947–48; Brooklyn Museum School, 1950–52, 1954–56; Parsons School of Design, 1962–63; Skowhegan School, 1946–58 (Vice President and Director). **Member:** Artists Equity (National Director, Treasurer, Vice President, 1946–60); Century Association; Architectural League of New York. **Federal A.P.:** US Post Office, Fleminsburgh, Ky. (mural). **Commissions:** Fort Belvoir, Va., 1942 (3 murals); Temple Beth Abraham, Tarrytown, N.Y.; Walt Whitman Junior High School, Yonkers, N.Y.;

Federation of Jewish Philanthropies; "The Family," sculpture group for the film "David and Lisa," 1962 (with Robert Cook and Dorothey Greenbaum); Protestant Council of New York (Family of Man Medal, presented to President John F. Kennedy, 1963); "The Circus," sculpture for Woodland House, Hartford, Conn., 1963; stage set for NYC production of *Ulysses in Nighttown,* by James Joyce, 1959. **Awards:** PAFA, Cresson Fellowship; Edwin Austin Abbey Fellowship, 1940; Prix de Rome, Hon. Men., 1940; Chicago/AI, Posner Painting Prize; PAFA, Fellowship, 1960; Chautauqua Institute, Babcock Memorial Award, 1963. **Address:** 4 St. Marks Place, NYC. **Dealer:** Grippi and Waddell Gallery. **One-man Exhibitions:** (first) PAFA, 1946; Niveau Gallery, NYC, 1949; Grand Central Moderns, 1951, 53; Rockland Foundation, 1955; Motel of the Mountain, 1959; Market Fair, Nyack, N.Y., 1960; Grippi Gallery, NYC, 1963. **Group:** WMAA Annuals, 1950, 52, 53, 54, 55, 59, 62, 63; PAFA, 1948–53, 1962; Corcoran, 1955; MMA, American Painters Under 35, 1950; International Biennial Exhibition of Paintings, Tokyo; Brooklyn Museum, 1953; U. of Nebraska Annuals, 1954, 55; NAD Annuals, 1944–60; MOMA, The Art of Assemblage, circ., 1961; A.F.A., Educational Alliance Retrospective, 1963. **Collections:** Century Association; Chautauqua Institute; Colby College; MMA; The Pentagon; US State Department. **Bibliography:** Seitz 2.

SIMPSON, DAVID. b. January 20, 1928, Pasadena, Calif. **Studied:** California School of Fine Arts, with Leonard Edmondson, Clyfford Still, 1956, BFA; San Francisco State College, 1958, MA. US Navy, 1945–46. **Taught:** American River Junior College, 1959–61; Contra Costa College, 1961– . **Address:** 209 Scenic Avenue, Point Richmond, Calif. **Dealers:** Robert Elkon Gallery; David Stuart Gallery. **One-man Exhibitions:** (first) David Cole Gallery, Sausalito, Calif., 1959; Santa Barbara/MA, 1960; de Young, 1961; Joachim Gallery, Chicago, 1961; Robert Elkon Gallery, 1961, 63, 64; David Stuart Gallery, 1963; Esther Robles Gallery, 1960. **Group:** Carnegie, 1961; Los Angeles/County MA, Post Painterly Abstraction, 1964; Chicago/AI; Walker. **Collections:** MOMA; Oakland/AM; SFMA.

SINTON, NELL. b. June 4, 1910, San Francisco, Calif. STUDIED: California School of Fine Arts, with Maurice Sterne, Spencer Macky, Ralph Stackpole. Traveled Europe, India, the Orient, USA, Mexico. ADDRESS: 1020 Francisco Street, San Francisco, Calif. DEALERS: Staempfli Gallery; Bolles Gallery, San Francisco. ONE-MAN EXHIBITIONS: (first) California Palace, 1949; Santa Barbara/MA, 1950; SFMA (two-man), 1957; Bolles Gallery, San Francisco and New York, 1962; SFMA (four-man), 1962. GROUP: MMA, 1952; ART:USA:58, NYC, 1958; Vancouver, 1958; Denver/AM, 1958, 60; SFMA; de Young; California Palace; Oakland/AM; Scripps College, 1961; Los Angeles/County MA, 1961; A.F.A. COLLECTIONS: Chase Manhattan Bank; Oakland/AM; SFMA.

SIPORIN, MITCHELL. b. May 5, 1910, NYC. STUDIED: Crane Junior College; Chicago Art Institute School; privately with Todros Geller; American Academy, Rome, 1949–50. US Army, 1942–45. Traveled Mexico, Latin America, Africa, Europe. TAUGHT: Boston Museum School, 1949; Columbia U., 1951; Brandeis U., 1951– . MEMBER, Brandeis U. Creative Arts Award Commission; Fellow, American Academy, Rome. FEDERAL A.P.: Mural painting. COMMISSIONS: Bloom Township High School, Chicago, 1938 (mural); Lane Technical High School, Chicago, 1940 (mural); US Post Offices, Decatur, Ill., 1940, and St. Louis, Mo. (with Edward Millman), 1940–42 (mural); Berlin Chapel, Brandeis U. (ark curtain). AWARDS: Chicago/AI, Bertha Aberle Florsheim Prize, 1942; Guggenheim Foundation Fellowship, 1945, 46; PAFA, Pennell Memorial Medal, 1946; Chicago/AI, The Mr. & Mrs. Frank G. Logan Medal, 1947; State U. of Iowa, First P.P., 1947; Prix de Rome, 1949; Hallmark International Competition, Second Prize, 1949; Boston Arts Festival, Second Prize, 1954, and Third Prize, 1955; AAAL, 1955; Youngstown/Butler, First Prize for Watercolors, 1961. ADDRESS: 300 Franklin Street, Newton, Mass. ONE-MAN EXHIBITIONS: The Downtown Gallery, 1940, 42, 46, 47, 57; Springfield, Mass./MFA; Chicago/AI, 1947; Philadelphia Art Alliance, 1949; Jewish Community Center, Cleveland, 1953; Boris Mirski Gallery, 1952; The Alan Gallery, 1954; Lincoln, Mass./De Cordova, 1955; U. of Vermont, 1956; Park Gallery, 1960; Lee Nordness Gallery, NYC,

1960. GROUP: MOMA, Americans 1942, circ., 1942; A Century of Progress, Chicago, 1933–34; MOMA, New Horizons in American Art, 1936; New York World's Fair, 1939; Golden Gate International Exposition, San Francisco, 1939; MOMA/USIA, Pintura Contemporanea Norteamericana, circ. Latin America, 1941; Paris/Moderne, 1946; Carnegie, 1944–49; Chicago/AI, 1942–46; WMAA, 1942–57; ICA, Boston, American Painting in Our Century, circ., 1949; Contemporary American Drawings, circ. France, 1956; Art:USA:Now, circ., 1962– . COLLECTIONS: Andover/Phillips; U. of Arizona; Auburn U.; Brandeis U.; Britannica; Chicago/AI; Cranbrook; U. of Georgia; Harvard U.; U. of Illinois; State U. of Iowa; S. C. Johnson & Son, Inc.; MMA; MOMA; NYPL; U. of Nebraska; Newark Museum; U. of New Mexico; PMA; Smith College; WMAA; Wichita/AM. BIBLIOGRAPHY: Baur 7; Goodrich and Baur 1; Halpert; Miller, ed. 1; Nordness, ed.; Pagano; Pousette-Dart, ed.; Wight 2.

SLOAN, JOHN. b. August 2, 1871, Loch Haven, Pa.; **d.** September 7, 1951, Hanover, N.H. STUDIED: Spring Garden Institute, Philadelphia; PAFA, 1892, with Thomas Anshutz. TAUGHT: ASL, 1914–26, 1935–37; George Luks School, 1934; Archipenko School of Art, 1932–33. Art Editor of *The Masses* (Magazine), 1912–16. Organized a group called The Eight. MEMBER: Society of Independent Artists, NYC (President, 1918–42); NIAL. AWARDS: Carnegie, Hon. Men., 1905; PAFA, Carol H. Beck Gold Medal, 1931; Panama-Pacific Exposition, San Francisco, 1915, Medal; Philadelphia Sesquicentennial, Medal, 1926; MMA, 1942 ($500); NIAL, Gold Medal, 1950. ONE-MAN EXHIBITIONS: (first) Whitney Studio Club, NYC, 1916; Hudson Guild, NYC, 1916; Kraushaar Galleries, 1917, 26, 27, 30, 37, 39, 43, 48, 52, 60; Corcoran, 1933; Montross Gallery, NYC, 1934; WMAA, 1936, 52; Santa Fe, N.M., 1951; PMA, 1948; Carnegie, 1939; The U. of Chicago, 1942; Currier, 1940; Bowdoin College, 1962; Kennedy Gallery, NYC (two-man), 1964; Wilmington, 1961. RETROSPECTIVE: Wanamaker Gallery, Philadelphia, 1940; Dartmouth College, 1946; Andover/Phillips, 1946. GROUP: Macbeth Gallery, NYC, The Eight, 1908; The Armory Show, 1913; WMAA; MMA; Brooklyn Museum, The Eight, 1943; PMA; Syracuse/Everson, The Eight, 1958; Chicago/AI; Detroit/Institute; PAFA; Carnegie; Corcoran. **COLLECTIONS:** Barnes Foundation; Boston/MFA; Brooklyn Museum; Carnegie; Chicago/AI; Cincinnati/AM; Cleveland/MA; Corcoran; Detroit/Institute; Hartford/Wadsworth; IBM; MMA; NYPL; Newark Public Library; PMA; The Pennsylvania State U.; Phillips; U. of Rochester; San Diego; Santa Fe, N.M.; WMAA; Walker. **BIBLIOGRAPHY:** Baur 7; Bazin; Beam; Blesh 1; Boswell 1; **Brooks;** Brown; Bryant; Cahill and Barr, eds.; Canaday; Cheney, M. C.; Coke; Craven 1, 2; **Du Bois 4;** Eliot; Ely; Finkelstein; Flanagan; Flexner; **Gallatin** 2, **5;** Glackens; **Goodrich 6;** Goodrich

and Baur 1; Haftman; Hall; Hartmann; Hunter 5; Huyghe; *Index of 20th Century Artists;* Jackman; Jewell 2; Kent, N.; Kouvenhoven; Mather 1; McCourbrey; McCurdy, ed.; Mendelowitz; Newmeyer; Pach 1, 3; Pagano; Pearson 1; Perlman; Phillips 2; Poore; Pousette-Dart, ed.; Reese; Richardson; Ringel, ed.; Sachs; **Sloan, H. F.; Sloan, J.** 1, **2, 3, 4, 5;** Smith, S. C. K.; Sutton; Wight 2.

SMITH, DAVID. b. 1906, Decatur, Ind.; **d.** May 24, 1965, Bennington, Vt. STUDIED: Ohio U., 1924; ASL, 1926–30, with John Sloan, Jan Matulka. Traveled Europe, U.S.S.R., 1935;

David Smith   *Cubi XVII Dec. 4–63. 1963*

resided Voltri and Spoleto, Italy, 1962. **TAUGHT:** Sarah Lawrence College, 1948; U. of Arkansas, 1953; Indiana U., 1954; U. of Mississippi, 1955. Created a series of 15 bronze "Medals of Dishonor," 1937–40. **AWARDS:** Guggenheim Foundation Fellowship, 1950, 51; Brandeis U., Creative Arts Award, 1964. **ONE-MAN EXHIBITIONS:** East River Gallery, NYC, 1938; Neumann-Willard Gallery, NYC, 1940; Skidmore College, 1939, 43, 46; The Willard Gallery, 1940, 43, 46, 47, 50, 51, 54, 55, 56; Kalamazoo/Institute, 1941; Walker, 1942, 43, 52; Buchholz Gallery, NYC, 1946; Cooling Gallery, London, 1946; Utica, 1947; Kleemann Gallery, NYC, 1952; Tulsa/Philbrook, 1953; Cincinnati/AM, 1954; MOMA, 1957; Fine Arts Associates, NYC, 1957; The Kootz Gallery, 1953; Otto Gerson Gallery, NYC, 1957, 61; French & Co. Inc., 1959, 60; MOMA, circ. only, 1960; Everett Ellin Gallery, Los Angeles, 1960; ICA, U. of Pennsylvania, 1964; Marlborough-Gerson Gallery Inc., 1964. **GROUP:** Sao Paulo, 1959; XXIX Venice Biennial, 1958; Documenta II & III, Kassel, 1959, 64; WMAA; Chicago/AI; MOMA; Carnegie. **COLLECTIONS:** Baltimore/MA; Brandeis U.; Carnegie; Cincinnati/AM; Chicago/AI; Detroit/Institute; MMA; MOMA; U. of Michigan; U. of Minnesota; SFMA; St. Louis/City; Utica; WMAA; Walker. **BIBLIOGRAPHY:** Baur 5, 7; Blesh 1; Brumme; Gertz; Giedion-Welcker 1; Goodrich and Baur 1; Greenberg 1; Henning; Hunter 5; Janis and Blesh 1; Kuh 1, 2; McCurdy, ed.; Mendelowitz; *Metro;* Motherwell, ed.; Motherwell and Reinhardt, eds.; Myers 2; Passloff; Ritchie 1, 3; Rodman 1, 3; Seitz 2; Seuphor 3; Seymour.

SMITH, HASSEL W., JR. b. April 24, 1915, Sturgis, Mich. STUDIED: Northwestern U., BS; California School of Fine Arts, with Maurice Sterne. Traveled Europe, USA, Mexico. **TAUGHT:** California School of Fine Arts, 1945, 47, 48, 52; San Francisco State College, 1946; U. of Oregon, 1947–48; U. of California, Berkeley, 1963–65; Presidio Hill School, San Francisco, 1952–55. **AWARDS:** Abraham Rosenberg Foundation Fellowship, 1941. **ADDRESS:** 1293 Hurlburt, Sebastopol, Calif. DEALERS: Andre Emmerich Gallery, NYC; Gimpel Fils Ltd.; David Stuart Gallery; Dilexi Gallery, San Francisco. **ONE-MAN EXHIBITIONS:** (first) California Palace, 1947, also 1952; California School of

Fine Arts, 1956; New Arts Gallery, Houston, 1960, 61; Ferus Gallery, 1960; Gimpel Fils Ltd., 1961; Pasadena/AM, 1961; Dilexi Gallery, San Francisco, 1962; U. of Minnesota, 1962; Galleria dell'Ariete, Milan, 1962; David Stuart Gallery, 1963; Andre Emmerich Gallery, NYC, 1961, 62, 63. **GROUP:** California Palace; Pasadena/AM; WMAA Annuals; Los Angeles/County MA; Oakland/AM; SFMA; U. of California, Berkeley. **COLLECTIONS:** Buffalo/Albright; New Paltz; SFMA; St. Louis/City; Tate; WMAA.

SMITH, LEON POLK. b. May 20, 1906, Chickasha, Okla. STUDIED: East Central State College, AB; Columbia U., with Eugene Ludins, MA. Traveled Mexico, Europe, Canada, USA, Venezuela. **TAUGHT:** Georgia University System, Teachers Colleges, 1939–41; Rollins College, 1949–51; Oklahoma public schools, 1933–39; State Supervisor, Delaware, 1941–43; Mills College of Education, 1951–58. **AWARDS:** Guggenheim Foundation Fellowship, 1944; Longview Foundation Grant, 1959. **ADDRESS:** 47 East 19 Street, NYC. DEALER: Galerie Chalette. **ONE-MAN EXHIBITIONS:** (first) Uptown Gallery, NYC, 1940; Rose Fried Gallery, 1942, 46, 49; Charles Egan Gallery, 1945; Savannah/Telfair, 1941; Santa Fe, N.M., 1943; Betty Parsons Gallery, 1957, 59; The Stable Gallery, 1960, 62; Caracas, 1962; Galerie Muller, Stuttgart, 1964. **GROUP:** WMAA, 1959; Helmhaus Gallery, Zurich, Konkrete Kunst, 1960; SRGM, Abstract Expressionists and Imagists, 1961; WMAA Annual, 1962; WMAA, Geometric Abstraction in America, circ., 1962; Chicago/AI, 1962; Dallas/MFA, "1961," 1962; Corcoran, 1963. **BIBLIOGRAPHY:** American Artists Group Inc. 2; Seuphor 1.

SNELGROVE, WALTER. b. March 22, 1924, Seattle, Wash. STUDIED: U. of Washington; U. of California, Berkeley, with James McCray, M. O'Hagan, BA, MA; California School of Fine Arts, with Hassel Smith. US Navy, 1943–47. Traveled Europe; resided Florence, Italy. **TAUGHT:** U. of California, 1951–53. **AWARDS:** U. of California, James D. Phelan Traveling Scholarship, 1951; SFMA, M. Grumbacher Award, 1959; Oakland/AM, First Prize, 1962. **ADDRESS:** 2702-A Dana, Berkeley, Calif. DEALER: Gump's Gallery. **ONE-MAN EXHIBITIONS:** (first) Oakland/AM, 1959; California

Palace; Santa Barbara/MA; Gump's Gallery. **GROUP:** de Young; SFMA; RAC; Oakland/AM; Denver/AM, 1964; Los Angeles/County MA; WMAA, Fifty California Artists, 1962–63; VMFA; U. of Illinois, 1963; Carnegie, 1964; U. of Washington. **COLLECTIONS:** A.F.A.; California Palace; Oakland/AM; Stanford U.

SOLOMON, HYDE. b. May 3, 1911, NYC. STUDIED: Columbia U., with Meyer Schapiro; American Artists School, NYC, 1938; Pratt Institute; ASL, 1943, with Ossip Zadkine. Traveled Europe. **TAUGHT:** Princeton U., 1959–62; Goddard College, summers, 1954, 55. **MEMBER:** American Abstract Artists. **AWARDS:** MacDowell Colony Fellowship, 1949, 50, 51, 52; Yaddo Fellowship, 1951, 56, 57, 58, 59, 62, 63, 64. **ADDRESS:** 320 East 42 Street, NYC. **DEALER:** Poindexter Gallery. **ONE-MAN EXHIBITIONS:** (first) Vendome Galleries, NYC, 1941; Jane Street Gallery, NYC, 1945, 48; The Peridot Gallery, 1954, 55, 56; Poindexter Gallery, 1956, 58, 60, 63; Princeton U., 1959; Rutgers U., 1961; Skidmore College, 1962. **GROUP:** MOMA; Walker; WMAA; Brooklyn Museum; Newark Museum; Yale U.; Hartford/Wadsworth; PMA; The Kootz Gallery, New Talent, 1950; WMAA, Nature in Abstraction, 1958. **COLLECTIONS:** Brandeis U.; Chase Manhattan Bank; Ford Foundation; Hartford/Wadsworth; Mitsui Bank of Japan; Newark Museum; Utica; WMAA; Walker. **BIBLIOGRAPHY:** Baur 5.

SOLOMON, SYD. b. July 12, 1917, Uniontown, Pa. STUDIED: Academie des Beaux-Arts, Paris, 1945; Chicago Art Institute School, 1934. **TAUGHT:** Art Institute of Pittsburgh, 1947; Ringling School of Art, 1951–57; Famous Artists Schools, Inc., 1954– ; Sarasota School of Art, 1956–60. **AWARDS:** Youngstown/Butler, First P.P., 1957; Audubon Artists, Gold Medal of Honor, 1957; Hallmark International Competition, 1952; Ringling, First Prize, 1962; American Institute of Architects, Medal of Honor, 1959; Silvermine Guild, 1962. **ADDRESS:** 2428 Portland Street, Sarasota, Fla. **DEALER:** Saidenberg Gallery. **ONE-MAN EXHIBITIONS:** Farnham, England; Stetson U.; Clearwater/Gulf Coast; U. of Miami; A.A.A. Gallery, NYC; U. of Florida, 1957–63; Bezalel Museum; Haifa; Tel Aviv; Ringling; Saidenberg Gallery, 1959–62, 1964; James David Gallery, Miami, 1962; Guild Hall, 1963. **GROUP:** MMA, 1952;

U. of Florida, 1953; Hallmark Art Award, 1952; Corcoran, 1959; WMAA Annual, 1959; New Orleans/Delgado, 1951, 57; Youngstown/Butler, 1954, 56; Chicago/AI, 1961; NAD, 1959; AAAL, 1959; Carnegie, 1956; Dallas/MFA, 1954; Houston/MFA, 1955. **COLLECTIONS:** Atlanta/AA; Baltimore/MA; Birmingham, Ala./MA; Brandeis U.; Clearwater/Gulf Coast; Florida Southern College; Friends of Art; Georgia Institute of Technology; Hartford/Wadsworth; Mead Corporation; New Orleans/Delgado; PMA; Provincetown/Chrysler; Ringling; U. of South Florida; WMAA; Youngstown/Butler. **BIBLIOGRAPHY:** Pousette-Dart, ed.

SONENBERG, JACK. b. December 28, 1925, Toronto, Canada. STUDIED: Washington U., with Fred Becker, Paul Burlin, BA. Traveled USA, Great Britain. **TAUGHT:** School of Visual Arts, NYC. **COMMISSIONS:** International Graphic Arts Society; New York Hilton Hotel. **AWARDS:** L. C. Tiffany Grant (printmaking), 1962; Silvermine Guild, First Prize, 1962; St. Paul Art Center, Drawing USA, P.P.; Bradley U., Print Annual, P.P. **ADDRESS:** 217 East 23 Street, NYC. **DEALER:** The Byron Gallery. **ONE-MAN EXHIBITIONS:** (first) Washington Irving Gallery, NYC, 1958; Roko Gallery, 1961; Carl Siembab Gallery, Boston, 1959; Feingarten Gallery, Los Angeles, 1962; Feingarten Gallery, NYC, 1963; Des Moines, 1964. **GROUP:** Brooklyn Museum; PAFA; Chicago/AI; New York World's Fair, 1964–65; Silvermine Guild; WMAA, American Prints Today, 1959; SRGM; Des Moines. **COLLECTIONS:** Bradley U.; MMA; NYPL; PMA; SRGM; St. Paul Gallery; Washington U.

SOYER, MOSES. b. December 25, 1899, Tombov, Russia. To USA 1913; citizen 1925. STUDIED: Cooper Union; NAD; Educational Alliance, NYC; Ferrer School, San Francisco, with Robert Henri, George Bellows. Traveled Europe, Russia. **TAUGHT:** Contemporary School of Art, NYC; New School for Social Research; Educational Alliance, NYC; and elsewhere. **MEMBER:** NAD; Artists Equity; Audubon Artists. **FEDERAL A.P.:** US Post Office, Philadelphia, Pa.; Greenpoint Hospital, Brooklyn, N.Y. (mural, with James Penney); 10 portable murals for libraries. **AWARDS:** AAAL, Childe Hassam Award (2); NAD Annual, Andrew

Carnegie Prize. **Address:** 50 West Ninth Street, NYC. **Dealer:** ACA Gallery. **One-man Exhibitions:** (first) J. B. Neumann's New Art Circle, NYC, 1928; Macbeth Gallery, NYC, 1940, 41, 43; Boyer Gallery, NYC; Kleemann Gallery, NYC, 1935; ACA Gallery, 1944, 47. **Group:** MMA; WMAA; Brooklyn Museum; Detroit/Institute; Youngstown/Butler; NAD. **Collections:** Brooklyn Museum; Detroit/Institute; U. of Kansas; Library of Congress; MMA; NAD; Newark Museum; PMA; Phillips; Toledo/MA; WMAA; Youngstown/Butler. **Bibliography:** Brown; Cheney, M. C.; Finkelstein; Mendelowitz; **Smith, B.;** Wheeler; **Willard.**

SOYER, RAPHAEL. b. December 25, 1899, Tombov, Russia. To USA 1912. **Studied:** Cooper Union; NAD, 1919–21; ASL, with Guy Du Bois. **Taught:** ASL; American Art School, NYC; New School for Social Research. **Member:** NIAL; NAD. **Federal A.P.:** Easel painting. **Commissions:** US Post Office, Kingsessing Station, Philadelphia (mural). **Awards:** Carnegie, Hon. Men. (3); Chicago/AI, The M. V. Kohnstamm Prize, 1932; Chicago/AI, Norman Wait Harris Gold Medal, 1932; PAFA, Carol H. Beck Gold Medal, 1934; Chicago/AI, Norman Wait Harris Bronze Medal, 1940; PAFA, Joseph E. Temple Gold Medal, 1943; PAFA, Walter Lippincott Prize, 1946; Corcoran, William A. Clark Prize and Corcoran Gold Medal, 1951; ART:USA:59, NYC, $1,000 Prize, 1959. **Address:** 410 Central Park West, NYC. **Dealer:** The Forum Gallery. **One-man Exhibitions:** The Daniel Gallery, NYC, 1929; L'Elan Gallery, NYC, 1932; Curt Valentine Gallery, NYC, 1933, 34, 35, 37, 38; Frank K. M. Rehn Gallery, NYC, 1939; Treasury Section, Fine Arts Division, 1939; A.A.A. Gallery, NYC, 1940, 41, 48, 53, 55; Weyhe Gallery, 1944; Philadelphia Art Alliance, 1949; ACA Gallery, 1960; Alfredo Valente Gallery, NYC, 1961; Bernard Crystal Gallery, NYC, 1962; The Forum Gallery, 1964. **Group:** Salons of America, NYC, 1926; PAFA, 1934, 43, 46; Corcoran, 1937, 51; VMFA, 1938; Chicago/AI, 1940; Brooklyn Museum, 1941; Carnegie, 1944; Phillips, 1944; Dallas/MFA, 1945; California Palace, 1945; MOMA, 1946; NAD, 1951, 52; WMAA Annu-

Raphael Soyer   *Nude with Self Portrait. 1960*

als, 1932– COLLECTIONS: Andover/Phillips; U. of Arizona; Boston/MFA; Brooklyn Museum; Buffalo/Albright; Columbus; Corcoran; Detroit/Institute; Hartford/Wadsworth; MMA; MOMA; Montclair/AM; U. of Nebraska; Newark Museum; Oslo/National; Phillips; Provincetown/Chrysler; WMAA. BIBLIOGRAPHY: American Artists Congress, Inc.; American Artists Group Inc. 3; Bazin; Biddle 3; Boswell 1; Brown; Cheney, M. C.; Finkelstein; Goodrich and Baur 1; **Gutman;** Hall; Kent, N.; Mellquist; Mendelowitz; Nordness, ed.; Pagano; Reese; **Soyer 1, 2;** Wheeler; Zigrosser 1.

SPEICHER, EUGENE. b. April 5, 1883, Buffalo, N.Y.; **d.** 1962. STUDIED: Buffalo Fine Arts Academy, 1902–06; ASL, 1907–08, with Frank V. DuMond, William M. Chase; Robert Henri School, 1909, with Robert Henri. Traveled Europe extensively. MEMBER: NIAL; NAD; National Arts Club. AWARDS: ASL, Kelley Prize, 1907; NAD, Thomas R. Proctor Prize, 1911; Salmagundi Club, Joseph S. Isadora Prize, 1913; NAD, Hallgarten Prize, 1914, 15; Panama-Pacific Exposition, San Francisco, 1915, Silver Medal; PAFA, Carol H. Beck Gold Medal, 1920; Carnegie, Third Prize, 1921; Second Prize, 1923; Chicago/AI, Potter Palmer Gold Medal, 1926; Corcoran, Second William A. Clark Prize, 1928; Corcoran, First Prize; VMFA, P.P.; Hon. DFA, Syracuse U., 1945. ONE-MAN EXHIBITIONS: Montross Gallery, NYC, 1918; M. Knoedler & Co., 1920; Carnegie, 1924; Rehn Galleries, 1925, 29, 34, 41, 43; Boston Arts Club, 1925; Des Moines, 1926; Denver/AM, 1948; Wildenstein & Co., NYC, 1954; AAAL, Memorial Exhibition, 1963. RETROSPECTIVE: Buffalo/Albright, 1950. GROUP: WMAA; PAFA; Carnegie; Century Association, Robert Henri and Five Pupils, 1946; MOMA; Chicago/AI. COLLECTIONS: ASL; Andover/Phillips; Boston/MFA; Britannica; Brooklyn Museum; Buffalo/Albright; Cincinnati/AM; Cleveland/MA; Corcoran; Decatur; Des Moines; Detroit/Institute; Galveston; Harvard U.; IBM; Indianapolis/Herron; Kansas City/Nelson; Los Angeles/County MA; MMA; MOMA; Minneapolis/Institute; Phillips; RISD; St. Louis/City; Toledo/MA; VMFA; WMAA; West Palm Beach/Norton; Worcester/AM; Yale U. BIBLIOGRAPHY: Baur 7; Bazin; Biddle 3; Blesh 1; Boswell 1; Brown; Bryant; **Burchfield 3;** Cahill and Barr, eds.; Cheney, M. C.;

Eliot; Goodrich and Baur 1; Hall; *Index of 20th Century Artists;* Jackman; Jewell 2; Kent, N.; **Mather** 1, 2; McCurdy, ed.; Mellquist; Mendelowitz; Narodny; Neuhaus; Pagano; Phillips 2; Poore; Richardson; Sachs; Smith, S. C. K.; **Speicher;** Watson 1; Zaidenberg, ed.

SPOHN, CLAY E. b. November 24, 1900, San Francisco, Calif. STUDIED: Augusta Military Academy (Va.), 1917–18; U. of California, Berkeley, 1919–22; California College of Arts and Crafts, 1910–12, 1916, 20; privately with Armin Hansen, 1921; San Francisco Art Institute, 1921, 27; ASL, 1922–24, with Guy Du Bois, George Luks, Boardman Robinson, Kenneth Hayes Miller, Kimon Nicolaides; Academie Moderne, Paris, 1926, with Othon Friesz. Traveled Europe, USA, Mexico, Canada. TAUGHT: San Francisco Art Institute; Mount Holyoke College; School of Visual Arts, NYC, 1964– ; and privately. FEDERAL A.P. (murals, 1935–42): Shriner Hospital, San Francisco; Volunteer Fire Department, Carmel, Calif.; Contra Costa County (Calif.) Community Center. ADDRESS: 245 Grand Street, NYC. DEALER: Stables Gallery. ONE-MAN EXHIBITIONS: (first) Art League Gallery, San Francisco, 1929, also 1931; SFMA, 1942; Rotunda Gallery, San Francisco, 1946. GROUP: de Young, *ca.* 1937–38; San Francisco Art Association, intermittently 1929–38; SFMA, Art of Our Time, 1945; California Palace, 1945, 48, 50; American Abstract Artists Annual, 1949; Denver/AM, 1952; U. of Illinois, 1953. COLLECTIONS: SFMA.

SPRINCHORN, CARL. b. May 13, 1887, Broby, Sweden. To USA 1903. STUDIED: New York School of Art, 1903–10, with William M. Chase, Robert Henri; Academie Colarossi, Paris, 1914–15. Traveled France, Scandinavia, Caribbean, USA. TAUGHT: Art League of Los Angeles, 1912–14. Manager, Robert Henri School, 1907–10. Director, The New Gallery, NYC, 1922–25. ADDRESS: Pioneer Acres, Beaver Dam Road, Selkirk, N.Y. ONE-MAN EXHIBITIONS: (first) George S. Hallman Gallery, NYC, 1916; M. Knoedler & Co., NYC, 1917; Marie Sterner Gallery, NYC, 1922–32; Frank K. M. Rehn Gallery, NYC, 1927; Ainslie Gallery, NYC, Philadelphia, Detroit, 1930; Mrs. Cornelius J. Sullivan Gallery, NYC, 1933–37; Macbeth Gallery, NYC, 1941–53; American Swedish Historical Museum; Worcester/AM; Arts

Club of Chicago. **Group:** PAFA; Corcoran; Brooklyn Museum; Phillips; PMA. **Collections:** American Swedish Historical Museum; Atlanta/AA; Boston/MFA; Brooklyn Museum; Dayton/AI; Harvard U.; MMA; U. of Maine; Museum of the City of New York; New Britain; PMA; Phillips; RISD; Virginia State College. **Bibliography:** Blesh 1.

SPRUANCE, BENTON. b. June 25, 1904, Philadelphia, Pa. **Studied:** U. of Pennsylvania, 1924; PAFA, 1925–29. **Taught:** Beaver College, 1933– ; Philadelphia Museum School. **Member:** NAD; SAGA; The Print Club, Philadelphia; Philadelphia Art Alliance. **Commissions:** Municipal Court Building, Philadelphia (mural). **Awards:** PAFA, Cresson Fellowship, 1928; Guggenheim Foundation Fellowship, 1951; Audubon Artists, First Prize, 1948; PAFA, First Prize, 1948; National Color Print Society, First Prize, 1948; Library of Congress, First Pennell p.p., 1948; PAFA, Alice McFadden Eyre Medal, 1944; PAFA, Pennell Memorial Medal, 1937. **Address:** 45 West Walnut Lane, Philadelphia, Pa. **One-man Exhibitions:** Rehn Galleries, 1949; Carnegie, 1949; Philadelphia Art Alliance, 1951; Mount Holyoke College, 1951. **Group:** PAFA; Library of Congress; NYPL; PMA; WMAA; Carnegie. **Collections:** Carnegie; Library of Congress; NYPL; National Gallery; PAFA; PMA. **Bibliography:** American Artists Group Inc. 3; Bethers; Cheney, M. C.; Hall; Reese; Zigrosser 1.

SPRUCE, EVERETT. b. December 25, 1908, Conway, Ark. **Studied:** Dallas Art Institute, 1925–29, with O. H. Travis, T. M. Stell, Jr. **Taught:** Dallas Museum School, 1936–40 (Assistant Director and Instructor); U. of Texas, 1940– . **Awards:** Scholarship, Dallas Art Institute; Texas State Fair, D. D. Feldman Award, 1955; Pepsi-Cola, 1946; La Tausca Competition, 1947; Dallas/MFA, First Prize, 1935, 55; Houston/MFA, First Prize, 1946; Carnegie, Hon. Men., 1946; PAFA, J. Henry Schiedt Memorial Prize, 1947; Corcoran, Hon. Men., 1949. **Address:** 15 Peak Road, Austin, Tex. **One-man Exhibitions:** Dallas/MFA, 1932, 58; Joseph Sartor Gallery, Dallas, 1934; Delphic Studios, NYC, 1936; Hudson D. Walker Gallery, NYC, 1938; Witte, 1943; Mortimer Brandt, NYC, 1943; Santa Barbara/MA, 1945;

Mortimer Levitt Gallery, NYC, 1945, 46, 48, 50, 51; Arts Club, Washington, D.C., 1948; San Antonio/McNay, 1959. **Retrospective:** A.F.A., 1959. **Group:** Corcoran, 1939, 41, 43, 45, 51; Carnegie, 1948, 49, 51; MOMA, 1942; Dallas/MFA, 1932, 35, 38, 40; U. of Illinois, 1948, 50, 51, 52; Bordighera, 1955; Denver/AM, 1946; Pepsi-Cola, 1946. **Collections:** U. of Alabama; Austin; Baltimore/MA; California Palace; Colorado Springs/FA; Dallas/MFA; Des Moines; de Young; Illinois Wesleyan U.; Kansas City/Nelson; MMA; MOMA; NYPL; U. of Nebraska; Newark Museum; New Orleans/Delgado; North Texas State U.; Ohio Wesleyan U.; PAFA; Phillips; Rio de Janeiro; Southern Methodist U.; Tulane U.; WMAA; Walker; Wichita/AM; Witte. **Bibliography:** Baur 7; Goodrich and Baur 1; Hall; Miller, ed. 1; Pearson 1; Pousette-Dart, ed.

SQUIER, JACK. b. February 27, 1927, Dixon, Ill. **Studied:** Oberlin College; Indiana U., with Robert Laurent, Leo Steppat, 1950, BS; Cornell U., with John Hartell, 1952, MFA. Traveled Central and Latin America extensively. **Taught:** Cornell U., 1958– . **Address:** 120 Eastwood Terrace, Ithaca, N.Y. **Dealer:** The Alan Gallery. **One-man Exhibitions:** (first) The Alan Gallery, 1956, also 1959, 62, 64; Cornell U., 1959, 64; Lima, Peru, 1963. **Group:** WMAA; MOMA; Houston/MFA; Andover/Phillips; Boston/MFA; Brussels World's Fair, 1958; U. of Illinois; Chicago/AI; Boston Arts Festival; Carnegie; Claude Bernard, Paris; Buffalo/Albright. **Collections:** Cornell U.; WMAA.

STAMOS, THEODOROS. b. December 31, 1922, NYC. **Studied:** American Artists School, NYC, with Simon Kennedy, Joseph Konzal. Traveled Europe, Near East. **Taught:** Black Mountain College; Cummington School of Fine Arts; ASL. **Commissions:** Moore-McCormack Lines Inc., SS *Argentina* (mural). **Awards:** L. C. Tiffany Grant, 1951; NIAL, 1956; Brandeis U., Creative Arts Award, 1959. **Address:** 80 West 82 Street, NYC. **Dealer:** Andre Emmerich Gallery, NYC. **One-man Exhibitions:** (first) Wakefield Gallery, NYC, 1940; Mortimer Brandt, NYC, 1945; Phillips, 1950, 54; Betty Parsons Gallery, 1947, 56; Philadelphia Art Alliance, 1957; San Antonio/McNay, 1960; Gimpel Fils Ltd., 1960; Galleria d'Arte

Theodoros Stamos   *Solstice Over Field. 1961*

del Naviglio, Milan, 1961; Andre Emmerich Gallery, NYC, 1958, 59, 60, 63. **RETROSPECTIVE:** Corcoran, 1959. **GROUP:** WMAA Annual, 1963; International Biennial Exhibition of Paintings, Tokyo; SRGM, Abstract Expressionists and Imagists, 1961; Carnegie, 1955, 58, 61; WMAA, Nature in Abstraction, 1958; Documenta II, Kassel, 1959; MOMA, The New American Painting, circ. Europe, 1958–59; Venice Biennial. **COLLECTIONS:** U. of Arizona; Baltimore/MA; Buffalo/Albright; California Palace; Chase Manhattan Bank; Colorado Springs/FA; Cornell U.; Des Moines; Detroit/Institute; Hartford/Wadsworth; U. of Illinois; State U. of Iowa; MIT; MMA; MOMA; Memphis/Brooks; Michigan State U.; NYU; Phillips; Phoenix; Rio de Janeiro; SFMA; San Antonio/McNay; Tel Aviv; Utica; Vassar College; WMAA;

Walker; Wellesley College; Youngstown/Butler. **BIBLIOGRAPHY:** Barker 1; Baur 5, 7; Biddle 3; Blesh 1; Eliot; Goodrich and Baur 1; Haftman; Janis and Blesh 1; McCurdy, ed.; Mendelowitz; Nordness, ed.; Pousette-Dart, ed.; Read 2; Richardson; Ritchie 1; Seuphor 1; Soby 5.

STANKIEWICZ, RICHARD P. b. October 18, 1922, Philadelphia, Pa. **STUDIED:** Hofmann School, 1948–49, with Hans Hofmann; Atelier Fernand Leger, Paris, 1950–51; Zadkine School of Sculpture, Paris, 1950–51. Traveled Europe, USA. An organizer of Hansa Gallery, NYC, 1952. **MEMBER:** International Institute of Arts and Letters. **ADDRESS:** Star Route, Huntington, Mass. **DEALER:** The Stable Gallery. **ONE-MAN EXHIBITIONS:** (first) Hansa Gallery, NYC, 1953, also 1954, 55, 56, 57, 58; The Stable Gallery, 1959, 60, 61, 62, 63; Galerie Neufville, Paris, 1960; Allan Frumkin Gallery, Chicago, 1958; The Pace Gallery, Boston, 1961; Walker (two-man, with Robert Indiana), 1963. GROUP: WMAA, 1956, 60, 62; WMAA, Young America, 1957; PAFA, 1954; Houston/MFA, Irons in the Fire, 1957; XXIX Venice Biennial, 1958; Carnegie, 1958, 61; A.F.A., Recent Sculpture, USA, 1959; MOMA, Sixteen Americans, circ., 1959; Claude Bernard, Paris, Aspects of American Sculpture, 1960; Amsterdam/Stedelijk, 1961; Chicago/AI, 1961, 62; VI Sao Paulo Biennial, 1961; MOMA, The Art of Assemblage, circ., 1961; Stockholm/National, 4 Americans, circ., 1962; Seattle World's Fair, 1962; SRGM, The Joseph H. Hirshhorn Collection, 1962; WMAA, Forty Artists Under Forty, circ., 1962; MOMA, Hans Hofmann and His Students, circ., 1963–64; Battersea Park, London, International Sculpture Exhibition, 1963; Jewish Museum, Recent American Sculptors, 1964. COLLECTIONS: Buffalo/Albright; Chicago/AI; Dayton/AI; MOMA; SRGM; Stockholm/National; WMAA; Walker. BIBLIOGRAPHY: Blesh 1; Friedman, ed.; Goodrich and Baur 1; Janis and Blesh 1; Lowry; *Metro;* Seitz 2; Seuphor 3.

STASIK, ANDREW. b. March 16, 1932, New Brunswick, N.J. STUDIED: NYU; Columbia U., BA; State U. of Iowa; Ohio U., MFA. TAUGHT: New School for Social Research; Ohio U.; Ball State Teachers College; Pratt Graphic Art Center. Editorial Staff, *Artist's Proof* Magazine. AWARDS: Gallery of Modern Art, Ljubljana, Yugoslavia, III International Exhibition of Prints, 1959, Le Prix Internationale de 100,000 dn.; Achenbach Foundation, Open Award for All Media, 1961; The Print Club, Philadelphia, Collins Prize; Cleveland/MA, First Prize in Lithography, 1958; Bay Printmakers Society, Oakland, P.P., 1958; Cleveland/MA, First Prize in Serigraphy, 1958; Pasadena/AM, P.P., 1958. ADDRESS: 4001 48th Street, Long Island City, N.Y. DEALER: The Contemporaries. ONE-MAN EXHIBITIONS: Yoseido Gallery, Tokyo, 1961; Samuel S. Fleisher Art Memorial, Philadelphia, 1961; Miami/Modern, 1960; Ross Widen Gallery, Cleveland, 1960; Ball State Teachers College, 1959; Avant Garde, NYC, 1958; Ohio U., 1956. GROUP: Gallery of Modern Art, Ljubljana, Yugoslavia, III & IV International Exhibitions of Prints, 1959, 61; Cincinnati/AM Biennials, 1956, 58, 60, 62; A.F.A., Prints of the World, 1962; The Print Club, Philadelphia, 1962; Brooklyn Museum, Print Biennial; Library of Congress; PCA, American Prints Today, circ., 1959–62; MOMA, Prize-Winning American Prints, circ. Canada. COLLECTIONS: Ball State Teachers College; Cali-

Richard P. Stankiewicz   *Untitled. 1960*

fornia Palace; Cincinnati/AM; Library of Congress; MOMA; NYU; National Gallery; U. of Nebraska; Oakland/AM; PMA; Pasadena/AM; Rockefeller Brothers Fund.

STEFANELLI, JOSEPH. b. March 20, 1921, Philadelphia, Pa. STUDIED: Philadelphia Museum School, 1938–40; PAFA, 1941–42; ASL, 1946–48; Hofmann School, 1948–49. Artist for *Yank* Magazine, 1942–46 (field drawings made during World War II are in the permanent collection of the War Archives Building, Washington, D.C.). ADDRESS: 158 West 22 Street, NYC. DEALER: The Fischbach Gallery. ONE-MAN EXHIBITIONS: Artists' Gallery, NYC, 1950, 54; The New Gallery, NYC, 1952; Hendler Gallery, Philadelphia, 1953; Ganymede Gallery, NYC, 1956; Poindexter Gallery, 1957, 58, 60; Hacker Gallery, NYC, 1962; Thibaut Gallery, NYC, 1963. GROUP: Ninth Street Exhibition, NYC, 1951; PAFA; WMAA; Corcoran; Carnegie; U. of Illinois; Buffalo/Albright; Walker; Chicago/AI; MOMA. COLLECTIONS: Baltimore/MA; Chicago/AI; Cornell U.; NYU; Norfolk; Provincetown/Chrysler; Sarah Lawrence College; Walker.

STEG, J. L. b. February 6, 1922, Alexandria, Va. STUDIED: Rochester Institute of Technology; State U. of Iowa, BFA, MFA. Traveled Europe, Mexico. TAUGHT: Cornell U., 1949–51; Tulane U., 1951– . MEMBER: SAGA. AWARDS: Carnegie Exchange Fellowship (Italy); VIII Lugano Drawing and Print Show, 1,000-Franc Award; Brooklyn Museum, P.P.; Seattle/AM, P.P.; Dallas/MFA, P.P.; Birmingham, Ala./MA, P.P.; U. of Minnesota, P.P.; Syracuse State Fair, P.P.; Library of Congress, Pennell P.P.; New Orleans/Delgado, P.P.; The Print Club, Philadelphia, P.P. ADDRESS: 7919 Spruce Street, New Orleans, La. DEALER: A.A.A. Gallery, NYC. ONE-MAN EXHIBITIONS: (first) Weyhe Gallery, 1945; Utica, 1951; Philadelphia Art Alliance, 1957; Davenport/Municipal, 1958; Dallas/MFA; Orleans Gallery, New Orleans; A.A.A. Gallery, NYC; U. of South Florida; Baton Rouge; Studio-Craft Gallery, Miami. GROUP: ART:USA, NYC; New York World's Fair, 1964–65; Oakland/AM; USIA; and other major print exhibitions. COLLECTIONS: Albion College; Bezalel Museum; Brooklyn Museum; Carnegie; Cleveland/MA; Dallas/MFA; U. of Delaware; Harvard U.; IBM; Library of Con-

gress; MOMA; U. of Minnesota; NYPL; U. of Nebraska; New Orleans/Delgado; PMA; Princeton Print Club; The Print Club, Philadelphia; Print Club of Rochester; Randolph-Macon College; Remington-Rand Corp.; Sao Paulo; Seattle/AM; Smithsonian; USIA; US State Department; Utica; Worcester/AM.

STEIN, RONALD. b. September 15, 1930, NYC. STUDIED: Cooper Union, with Will Barnet; Yale U., with Josef Albers, BFA; Rutgers U., MFA. Traveled Europe, North Africa. TAUGHT: Worcester Museum School, 1959–60; Rutgers U., 1960–61. COMMISSIONS: Uris Buildings Corp. (80-ft. mosaic mural for No. 2 Broadway, NYC). AWARDS: Yale U. Traveling Fellowship. ADDRESS: 76 East 79 Street, NYC. DEALER: Tibor de Nagy Gallery. ONE-MAN EXHIBITIONS: (first) Boris Mirski Gallery, 1956; Gallery Mayer, NYC, 1960, 61; Irving Galleries, Inc., Milwaukee, 1961; Nashville, 1961; Tibor de Nagy Gallery, 1964. GROUP: Chicago/AI, 1956, 57; Carnegie, 1959; Corcoran, 1961; Pan-Pacific Exhibition, circ. Japan, 1961; MOMA; ICA, Boston, 1961; Lincoln, Mass./De Cordova, 1958; New York World's Fair, 1964–65. COLLECTIONS: A.F.A.; Carnegie; Guild Plastics Co.; Hartford/Wadsworth; Nashville; New York Hilton Hotel; North Shore State Bank; SRGM; Uris Buildings Corp.

STEINBERG, SAUL. b. June 15, 1914, Ramnicul-Sarat, Rumania. STUDIED: U. of Milan, 1932–40. To USA 1942; citizen 1943. US Navy, 1943–46. COMMISSIONS: Terrace Plaza Hotel, Cincinnati, 1948 (mural). ADDRESS: 3 Washington Square Village, NYC. ONE-MAN EXHIBITIONS: Wakefield Gallery, NYC, 1943; Galerie Maeght, 1953; Basel, 1954; Amsterdam/Stedelijk, 1953; Sao Paulo, 1952; Galerie Blanche, Stockholm, 1953; Frank Perls Gallery, 1952; Arts Club of Chicago, 1953; Kestner-Gesellschaft, Hannover, 1954; A.F.A., circ., 1953–55; ICA, London, 1957; Betty Parsons Gallery (two-man, with Constantino Nivola), 1940. GROUP: MOMA, Fourteen Americans, circ., 1946; ICA, London, 1952; Chicago/AI, 1949; L'Obelisco, Rome, 1951. COLLECTIONS: Buffalo/Albright; Detroit/Institute; Harvard U.; MMA; MOMA; Utica; Victoria and Albert Museum. BIBLIOGRAPHY: Baur 7; Biddle 3; Kepes 2; *Metro;* Miller, ed. 2; Richardson; Rodman 1; Sachs; **Steinberg, S. 1, 2, 3.**

STELLA, FRANK. b. May, 1936, Malden, Mass. STUDIED: Phillips Academy, with Patrick Morgan; Princeton U., with William Seitz, Stephen Greene. **ADDRESS:** 10 East 16 Street, NYC. DEALER: Leo Castelli Inc. ONE-MAN EXHIBITIONS: Leo Castelli Inc., 1960, 62, 64, and two-man, 1962; Ferus Gallery, 1963; Galerie Lawrence, 1961. GROUP: Oberlin College, 3 Young Painters, 1959; MOMA, Sixteen Americans, circ., 1959; SRGM, Abstract Expressionists and Imagists, 1961; Houston/MFA, Ways and Means, 1961; Seattle World's Fair, 1962; A.F.A., Explorers of Space, circ., 1961–62; WMAA, Geometric Abstraction in America, circ., 1962; Chicago/AI, 1963; Corcoran, 1963; WGMA, The Formalists, 1963; Jewish Museum, Toward a New Abstraction, 1963; Musee Cantonal des Beaux-Arts, Lausanne, I Salon International de Galeries Pilotes, 1963; Brandeis U., New Directions in American Painting, 1963; WMAA Annual, 1964; Jewish Museum, Black and White, 1963; Hartford/Wadsworth, Black, White, and Gray, 1964. COLLECTIONS: Buffalo/Albright; MOMA; Pasadena/AM; WMAA.

STELLA, JOSEPH. b. June 13, 1877, Muro Lucano, Italy; **d.** November 5, 1946, NYC. To USA 1896; citizen 1923. STUDIED medicine and pharmacology, 1896; ASL, 1897; New York School of Art, 1898–1900, with William M. Chase. Traveled Europe, USA. MEMBER: Societe Anonyme. AWARDS: One-year scholarship to New York School of Art, 1899. ONE-MAN EXHIBITIONS: (first) Carnegie, 1910; Italian National Club, NYC, 1913; Bourgeois Gallery, NYC, 1920; Societe Anonyme, NYC; Dudensing Gallery, NYC, 1924; The New Gallery, NYC, 1926; Curt Valentine Gallery, NYC, 1926, 28, 31, 35; Des Moines Art Association, 1926; Angiporto Galleria, Naples, 1929; Galerie Sloden, Paris, 1930; Washington Place, Paris, 1932; Cooperative Gallery, Newark, 1937; A.A.A. Gallery, NYC, 1941; M. Knoedler & Co., NYC, 1942; ACA Gallery, 1943; The Zabriskie Gallery, 1958, 59, 60, 61; MOMA, circ., 1960 (drawings); Robert Schoelkopf Gallery, 1963. RETROSPECTIVE: Newark Museum, 1939; WMAA, 1963. COLLECTIONS: Indiana State College; Iowa State Education Association; MMA; MOMA; U. of Nebraska; Newark Museum; WMAA; Walker; Yale U. BIBLIOGRAPHY: Baur 3, 5, 7; Bethers; Biddle 3; Blanchard;

Blesh 1; Brown; Cahill and Barr, eds.; Christensen; Dreier 2; Eliot; Elsen; Flanagan; Frost; Goodrich and Baur 1; Haftman; Hess, T. B.; Hunter 5; Janis and Blesh 1; Janis, S.; Kuh 1; McCourbrey; McCurdy, ed.; Mellquist; Mendelowitz; Poore; Richardson; Ritchie 1; Rosenblum; Seitz 2; Soby 5.

STERN, GERD. b. October 12, 1928, Saarbrucken, Germany. STUDIED: Black Mountain College, with M. C. Richards. Traveled USA, Latin America. COMMISSIONS: Immaculate Heart College; Associated Coin Amusement Company, Los Angeles (flashing mural). ADDRESS: Maverick Road, Woodstock, N.Y. DEALERS: Allan Stone Gallery; David Stuart Gallery. ONE-MAN EXHIBITIONS: (first) SFMA, 1963; U. of British Columbia, 1964. GROUP: Dwan Gallery, Boxes, 1964; SFMA; U. of Rochester; Los Angeles/County MA; International Arts Festival, Newport, R.I. COLLECTIONS: Associated Coin Amusement Company; Immaculate Heart College; SFMA.

STERNBERG, HARRY. b. July 19, 1904, NYC. STUDIED: ASL; and privately with Harry Wickey. TAUGHT: ASL, 1933– ; New School for Social Research, 1950–51; Brigham Young U., 1958. Directed and produced a film, "The Many Worlds of Art," 1960. FEDERAL A.P. (murals): US Post Offices, Sellersville, Pa., and Chester, Pa. (1935–37). AWARDS: Guggenheim Foundation Fellowship, 1936; Fifty Prints of the Year, 1930; Fine Prints of the Year, 1932, 33, 34; 100 Prints of the Year, 1938; The Print Club, Philadelphia, 1942; Audubon Artists, 1955. ADDRESS: 9 St. James Place, Glen Cove, N.Y. ONE-MAN EXHIBITIONS: ACA Gallery, 1947, 50, 56, 58, 60; U. of Minnesota, 1957; Weyhe Gallery, 1941; Keppel & Co., NYC, 1937; Garelick's Gallery, Detroit, 1958; Brigham Young U., 1958; Idyllwild Art School, 1958; Gallery Eight, Santa Barbara, 1961; Salt Lake Art Center, Salt Lake City, 1961. GROUP: WMAA; Chicago/AI; Walker; U. of Minnesota; de Young; Brooklyn Museum; MOMA. COLLECTIONS: Andover/Phillips; Auckland; Bibliotheque Nationale; Brooklyn Museum; Cleveland/MA; de Young; Harvard U.; Library of Congress; MMA; MOMA; U. of Minnesota; NYPL; Phillips; U. of Southern California; Tel Aviv; Victoria and Albert Museum; WMAA; Walker. BIBLIOGRAPHY:

American Artists Congress, Inc.; American Artists Group Inc. 3; Hayter 1; *Index of 20th Century Artists;* Mellquist; Reese; **Smith, A.; Sternberg 1, 2;** Zigrosser 1.

STERNE, HEDDA. b. August 4, 1916, Bucharest, Rumania. STUDIED: U. of Bucharest; Kunsthistorisches Institut der Universitat, Vienna; and at academies in Paris. To USA 1941. Traveled Europe extensively, Mexico, Latin America. AWARDS: Chicago/AI, Second Prize, 1957; Fulbright Fellowship, 1963. ADDRESS: 179 East 71 Street, NYC. DEALER: Betty Parsons Gallery. ONE-MAN EXHIBITIONS: (first) Wakefield Gallery, NYC, 1943; Mortimer Brandt, NYC, 1945; Betty Parsons Gallery, 1947, 48, 50, 53, 54, 57, 58, 61, 63; L'Obelisco, Rome, 1953, 61; Sao Paulo, 1953; Vassar College, 1956; Arts Club of Chicago, 1955; Saidenberg Gallery, 1956. GROUP: Art of This Century, NYC, 1943, 44; Corcoran, 1955, 56, 58, 63; MOMA, 1955; WMAA, The New Decade, 1954–55; Carnegie, 1955, 58, 61, 64; Chicago/AI, 1954, 55, 57, 60; XXVIII Venice Biennial, 1956; RISD, 1955; Smithsonian, 1956; Stanford U., 1955, 56; U. of Illinois, 1955, 60; VMFA, American Painting, 1958; PAFA, 1958; Rome-New York Foundation, Rome, 1959, 61; II Inter-American Paintings and Prints Biennial, Mexico City, 1960; WMAA Annuals; PAFA Annuals; State U. of Iowa, 1958, 59; U. of Colorado, 1960. COLLECTIONS: Buffalo/Albright; Carnegie; Chase Manhattan Bank; Chicago/AI; Detroit/Institute; U. of Illinois; Inland Steel Co.; MMA; MOMA; U. of Nebraska; PAFA; Rockefeller Institute; Toledo/MA; US State Department; United Nations; VMFA; WMAA. BIBLIOGRAPHY: Motherwell and Reinhardt, eds.; Pousette-Dart, ed.; Read 3.

STERNE, MAURICE. b. 1878, Libau, on the Baltic; **d.** 1957, NYC. To USA 1889. STUDIED: Cooper Union, 1892; NAD, 1894–99, with Thomas Eakins. Traveled Europe, India, Burma, Java, Egypt. MEMBER: National Fine Arts Commission, 1945–51. COMMISSIONS: Justice Department, Washington, D.C. (mural); Fairmount Park, Philadelphia (monument); Rogers-Kennedy Memorial, Worcester, Mass., 1926. AWARDS: Mooney Traveling Scholarship, 1904; Chicago/AI, The Mr. & Mrs. Frank G. Logan Prize, 1928; Corcoran, William A. Clark Prize and Corcoran Gold Medal, 1930; Carnegie, Hon. Men., 1930; Golden Gate International Exposition, San Francisco, 1939; NAD Annual, Andrew Carnegie Prize, 1957. ONE-MAN EXHIBITIONS: Paul Cassirer Gallery, Berlin, 1910; Berlin Photograph Co., NYC, 1910, 15; Bourgeois Gallery, NYC, 1917, 22; Scott and Fowles Gallery, NYC, 1926; Reinhardt Galleries, NYC, 1928, 30; Chicago/AI, 1917; Boston Arts Club, 1919; SFMA, 1936, 38; Honolulu Academy, 1939. RETROSPECTIVE: MOMA, 1933; Phillips, 1952. GROUP: Rome National Art Quadrennial, 1925; Chicago/AI; Corcoran; WMAA; SFMA; Brooklyn Museum; Newark Museum. COLLECTIONS: Carnegie; Chicago/AI; Cleveland/MA; Cologne; Corcoran; Detroit/Institute; MMA; Phillips; RISD; San Diego; Yale U. BIBLIOGRAPHY: Baur 7; Biddle 3; Birnbaum; Blesh 1; Brown; Cahill and Barr, eds.; Cheney, M. C.; Coke; Eliot; Genauer; Goodrich and Baur 1; Hall; *Index of 20th Century Artists;* Jackman; Jewell 2; **Kallem;** Kent, N.; Kootz 1; Mather 1; McCurdy, ed.; Mendelowitz; Neuhaus; Parkes; Phillips 2; Richardson; Ringel, ed.; Sachs.

STILL, CLYFFORD. b. November 30, 1904, Grandin, N.D. STUDIED: Spokane U., 1933, BA; Washington State College, MA. TAUGHT: Washington State College, 1935–45; College of William and Mary, 1944; California School of Fine Arts, 1946–50; "Subject of the Artist," NYC, 1947–48; U. of Pennsylvania, 1963; Hunter College, 1952; Brooklyn Museum School, 1952; Yaddo, 1934, 35. Encouraged California students to form a group which became the Metart Gallery. ADDRESS: Westminster, Md. ONE-MAN EXHIBITIONS: (first) SFMA, 1943; Metart Gallery, San Francisco, 1950; Art of This Century, NYC, 1946; ICA, U. of Pennsylvania, 1964. RETROSPECTIVE: Buffalo/Albright, 1959. GROUP: MOMA, Fifteen Americans, circ., 1952; MOMA, The New American Painting, circ. Europe, 1958–59; Documenta II, Kassel, 1959. COLLECTIONS: Baltimore/MA; Buffalo/Albright; MOMA. BIBLIOGRAPHY: Blesh 1; Finkelstein; Flanagan; Gaunt; Greenberg 1; Haftman; Hess, T. B.; Hunter 1, 5; McCurdy, ed.; *Metro;* Ponente; Read 2; Richardson; Seuphor 1.

STOUT, MYRON S. b. December 5, 1908, Denton, Tex. STUDIED: North Texas State U.,

1930, BA; Columbia U., with C. J. Martin, MA; Academia San Carlos, Mexico City, 1933; Hofmann School. US Army and Air Force, 1943–45. Traveled France, Italy, Mexico. **Address:** 4 Brewster Street, Provincetown, Mass. **One-man Exhibitions:** (first) The Stable Gallery, 1954; Hansa Gallery, 1957, 1958 (three-man). **Group:** WMAA Annual, 1958; WMAA, Geometric Abstraction in America, circ., 1962; A.F.A., New Talent, circ., 1960; Carnegie, 1959; ICA, Boston, 100 Works on Paper, circ. Europe, 1959; Jewish Museum, 1964; ICA, Boston, Paintings, USA, 1959. **Collections:** Brooklyn Museum; Carnegie; MOMA; Woodward Foundation.

STUEMPFIG, WALTER. b. 1914, Germantown, Pa. **Studied:** PAFA, 1931–35. **Taught:** PAFA, 1946– . **Member:** NIAL. **Awards:** PAFA, Cresson Fellowship, 1933. **Address:** Gwynedd Valley, Pa. **One-man Exhibitions:** Philadelphia Art Alliance, 1942; de Young, 1946; Artists' Gallery, Philadelphia, 1947; Woodmere Art Gallery, Philadelphia, 1953; U. of Miami, 1960; MIT, 1960; Art Association of Newport (R.I.), 1961; Durlacher Brothers, 1943–62; Maynard Walker Gallery, 1962. **Group:** PAFA; PMA. **Collections:** Chicago/AI; Corcoran; Harvard U.; MMA, MOMA; PMA; WMAA. **Bibliography:** Bazin; Eliot; Hunter 5; Mendelowitz; Nordness, ed.; Soby 5; Wight 2.

SUGARMAN, GEORGE. b. May 11, 1912, NYC. **Studied:** Zadkine School of Sculpture, Paris, 1955–56. Traveled Mexico, USA, Europe; resided Paris, 1951–55. **Taught:** Hunter College, 1960– . **Commissions:** Geigy Chemical Corp. (wall sculpture). **Awards:** Carnegie, Second Prize, 1961; Longview Foundation Grant, 1960, 61, 63. **Address:** 127 Greene Street, NYC. **Dealer:** Stephen Radich Gallery. **One-man Exhibitions:** (first) Union Dime Savings Bank, NYC, 1958; Widdifield Gallery, NYC, 1960; Stephen Radich Gallery, 1961, 64. **Group:** New York World's Fair, 1964–65; Walker, Ten American Sculptors, 1964; Sao Paulo, 1963; A.F.A., Sculpture for the Home, circ., 1962; Seattle World's Fair, 1962; Hartford/Wadsworth, 1962; Chicago/AI, 1962; Carnegie, 1961; A.F.A., Sculpture in Wood, circ., 1941–42; Claude Bernard, Paris, 1960; Silvermine Guild, 1958; Salon de la Jeune Sculpture, Paris,

1952, 54; Salon des Realites Nouvelles, Paris, 1954; Jewish Museum, Recent American Sculpture, 1964. **Collections:** Geigy Chemical Corp.; S. C. Johnson & Son, Inc.; Kalamazoo/Institute; MIT. **Bibliography:** Janis and Blesh 1.

SUMMERS, CAROL. b. December 26, 1925, Kingston, N.Y. **Studied:** Bard College, with Stefan Hirsch, Louis Schanker, 1951, BA. US Marine Corps, 1944–48. **Taught:** Hunter College, 1963–64. **Member:** PCA. **Awards:** Italian Government Travel Grant, 1955; L. C. Tiffany Grant, 1955, 61; J. S. Guggenheim Fellowship, 1959; Fulbright Fellowship (Italy), 1961. **Address:** 268 Seventh Avenue, NYC. **Dealers:** The Contemporaries; A.A.A. Gallery, NYC. **One-man Exhibitions:** (first) The Contemporaries, 1954, also 1961; MOMA, circ., 1964– . **Group:** Major national print exhibitions. **Collections:** Baltimore/MA; Bibliotheque Nationale; Boston/MFA; Bradley U.; Brooklyn Museum; Chicago/AI; Cincinnati/AM; Cornell U.; Free Library of Philadelphia; U. of Kentucky; Library of Congress; Los Angeles/County MA; Lugano; MMA; MOMA; Milwaukee-Downer College; U. of Minnesota; NYPL; National Gallery; U. of Nebraska; New Britain; Ohio U.; PMA; Seattle/AM; U. of Tennessee; U. of Utah; Victoria and Albert Museum; Walker.

SUTTMAN, PAUL. b. 1933, Enid, Okla. **Studied:** Adelphi College, with Robert Cronbach; U. of New Mexico, with Adja Yunkers, Robert Mallory; Cranbrook Academy of Art, with Tex Schwetz, Maija Groten; BFA, MFA. Traveled Europe, Latin America; resided Mexico, Italy. **Taught:** U. of Michigan, 1958–62. **Commissions:** Roswell (N.M.) Museum and Art Center (bronze relief for façade); Hughes, Hatcher & Suffrin Building, Detroit, 1964; National Educational Television, 1961 ("The Bronze Man," a film illustrating casting techniques). **Awards:** Cranbrook, Horace H. Rackham Research Grant (Florence, Italy), 1960; Fulbright Fellowship (Paris), 1963. **Address:** c/o Terry Dintenfass, Inc. **Dealers:** Terry Dintenfass, Inc.; Park Gallery. **One-man Exhibitions:** (first) Park Gallery, 1959, also 1961; Terry Dintenfass, Inc., 1961, 64; Roswell, 1961; U. of Michigan, 1962. **Group:** Youngstown/Butler; Detroit/Institute; U. of Michigan; Santa Barbara/MA; de Young; U. of New Mexico. **COLLECTIONS:** Detroit/Institute; Layton School of Art; MOMA; U. of Michigan; Roswell; Walker.

SUZUKI, JAMES HIROSHI. b. September 19, 1933, Yokohama, Japan. STUDIED: Privately with Yoshio Markino; Portland (Me.) School of Fine and Applied Art, 1952; The Corcoran School of Art, 1953–54. To USA 1952. Traveled USA, Japan. **TAUGHT:** U. of California, Berkeley, 1962–63. **AWARDS:** Corcoran, Eugene Weiss Scholarship, 1954; John Hay Whitney Fellowship, 1958; Silvermine Guild, Larry Aldrich Prize, 1959. **ADDRESS:** 2728 Grove Street, Berkeley, Calif. DEALERS: The Graham Gallery; Nihonbashi Gallery. **ONE-MAN EXHIBITIONS:** (first) The Graham Gallery, 1957, also 1958, 59, 61, 62; U. of California, Berkeley, 1963; Nihonbashi Gallery, 1963; Seido (Gallery), Kyoto, 1963. **GROUP:** Corcoran, 1956, 58, 60; WMAA; Baltimore/MA; SFMA, 1963, 64; Tokyo/Modern, 1964; Syracuse/Everson, 1958; ICA, Boston, Contemporary Painters of Japanese Origin in America; Cincinnati/AM; Silvermine Guild, 1959; Des Moines; U. of Nebraska, 1960; Hartford/Wadsworth, 1959; A.F.A., Cross-Currents, circ., 1957–58; Houston/MFA, Waning Moon and Rising Sun, 1959. **COLLECTIONS:** Corcoran; Hartford/Wadsworth; Kamakura; McDonnell & Co. Inc.; Rockefeller Institute; Tokyo/Modern; Toledo/MA.

t

TAKAI, TEIJI, b. February 2, 1911, Osaka, Japan. STUDIED: Shinano Bashi Art School, Osaka, 1929. Traveled north and central China. TAUGHT: Kodo Art School, Tokyo. MEMBER: "Nika" (Japanese Modern Art Group), 1939 (accepted for exhibition 1931); Kodo Art Group, 1947. To USA 1954. AWARDS: Niki Prize, 1938; Okada Prize, 1941; Japanese Government Prize, 1943; Fukushima Prize, 1963. ADDRESS: 235 West 103 Street, NYC. DEALER: Poindexter Gallery. ONE-MAN EXHIBITIONS: Takashimaya Gallery, Tokyo; Diamaru, Osaka, 1949–54; Collectors Gallery, NYC, 1956; Poindexter Gallery, 1959, 61, 63. GROUP: WMAA Annuals, 1960, 62; Carnegie, 1961, 64; Columbia, S.C./MA, 1963; ICA, Boston, 1958; Corcoran, 1960, 62. COLLECTIONS: Corcoran; Friends of Art; WMAA.

TAKAL, PETER. b. December 8, 1905, Bucharest, Rumania. STUDIED in Paris and Berlin. To USA 1939; citizen 1944. COMMISSIONS (graphic art): International Graphic Arts Society, 1956 ("City at Dawn"), 1959 ("Dawn"), 1963 ("Winter"); Print Club of Cleveland, 1956 ("City Roofs"), 1957 ("Trees and Fields"); The Contemporaries, 1957 ("Two Windows"); A.A.A. Gallery, NYC, 1958 ("Meditation"). AWARDS: The Print Club, Philadelphia, Max Katzman Award, 1957; Silvermine Guild, Nancy A. Fuller Award, 1959; Yaddo Fellowship, 1961; Pasadena/AM Annual, P.P., 1962; Tamarind Fellowship, 1963–64. ADDRESS: Saylorsburg, Pa. DEALERS: The Contemporaries; Weyhe Gallery; R. M. Light & Co., Inc.; Mary Harriman Gallery Inc. ONE-MAN EXHIBITIONS: (first) Gallery Gurlitt, Berlin, 1932; Galerie Zak, Paris, 1933; Galerie Jeanne Castel, Paris,

1935, 37; Galerie Charpentier, Paris, 1939; Galerie Derche, Casablanca, 1937; Chauvin Gallery, Algiers, 1939; Galeria de Arte Mexicano, Mexico City, 1959; Palazzo Strozzi, Florence, Italy, 1960; Duveen-Graham Gallery, NYC, 1955, 58, 1957–58 (circ. American museums and colleges); Smithsonian, circ. USA, 1959–60; Kestner-Museum, circ. Germany, 1961–62; La Jolla, 1957; Santa Barbara/MA, 1941, 57; Dallas/MFA, 1957; de Young, 1942; Los Angeles/County MA, 1957; Minneapolis/Institute, 1957; Kansas City/Nelson, 1958; Philadelphia Art Alliance, 1962; Carstairs Gallery, NYC, 1940; Karl Nierendorf Gallery, NYC, 1942; Artists' Gallery, NYC, 1954; Wittenborn Gallery, NYC, 1956; The Contemporaries, 1959, 60, 62; Weyhe Gallery, 1964; Katherine Kuh Gallery, Chicago, 1937, 39, 41; Sabersky Gallery, Los Angeles, 1961; Mary Harriman Gallery Inc., 1964. GROUP: MOMA, Recent Drawings USA, 1956; PCA, American Prints Today, circ., 1959–62; WMAA Annuals, 1955, 56, 57, 58, 59, 60, 62, 63, 64; Brooklyn Museum, Print Biennials; PAFA, 1953, 59, 60, 63; Library of Congress Print Annuals, 1955, 58, 59, 60, 62; ICA, Boston, 100 Works on Paper, circ. Europe, 1959; The Print Club, Philadelphia, 1956, 57, 58, 61, 62, 63; St. Paul Art Center, Drawing USA, 1963; SAGA Annual, 1963; Gallery of Modern Art, Ljubljana, Yugoslavia, IV International Exhibition of Prints, 1961; Boston Printmakers, 1956, 57, 58, 59, 62, 63; MOMA, circ. Europe and Far East, 1961 (drawings); Salon d'Automne, Paris, 1933, 34, 35; A.F.A. COLLECTIONS: Achenbach Foundation; Albion College; Andover/Phillips; Baltimore/MA; Berlin National; Bibliotheque Nationale; Bremen; Brooklyn Museum; UCLA;

Chicago/AI; Cincinnati/AM; Cleveland/MA; Dallas/MFA; de Young; Exeter; Fort Worth; Grenoble; Indianapolis/Herron; Kassel; Kestner-Museum; La Jolla; Library of Congress; Lincoln, Mass./De Cordova; Los Angeles/County MA; MMA; MOMA; U. of Maine; Mills College; U. of Minnesota; The Morgan Library; NYU; National Gallery; Omaha/Joslyn; Oran; PMA; Paris/Moderne; Pasadena/AM; RISD; Riverside Museum; SFMA; Sacramento/Crocker; St. Louis/City; Stuttgart; Topeka Public Library; USIA; US State Department; WMAA; Walker; U. of Wisconsin; Yale U. **BIBLIOGRAPHY:** Kent, N.

TALBOT, WILLIAM H. M. b. January 10, 1918, Boston, Mass. STUDIED: PAFA, 1936–38, 1940–41, with Walker Hancock; privately with George Demitrios, Boston, 1938–39; Academie des Beaux-Arts, Paris, 1945–46, with Marcel Gaumont. US Army, 1941–46. Traveled USA extensively, Mexico, Canada, Europe (esp. Greece), Egypt, Sudan. TAUGHT: Birch Wathen School, NYC, 1947–48; Visiting Lecturer, U. of Michigan, 1949. MEMBER: Sculptors Guild; Federation of Modern Painters and Sculptors; Architectural League of New York. COMMISSIONS: Bryn Mawr College, 1948; Fitchburg (Mass.) Youth Library, 1950; National Council of State Garden Clubs, St. Louis, Mo., 1957–59; Johnson Rehabilitation Center, Barnes Hospital, St. Louis, Mo., 1964. AWARDS: PAFA, Cresson Fellowship, 1941; Prix de Rome, 1941; Connecticut Academy of Fine Arts, Howard Penrose Prize, 1950. ADDRESS: Washington, Conn. ONE-MAN EXHIBITIONS: (first) Carroll-Knight Gallery, St. Louis, 1949; Andrew-Morris Gallery, NYC, 1963; Earlham College, 1964. GROUP: Sculptors Guild Annuals; Federation of Modern Painters and Sculptors Annuals; PAFA Annuals; Fairmount Park Association, Philadelphia, Sculpture International; Boston Arts Festival; WMAA; PMA; St. Louis/City; Dallas/MFA; Lincoln, Mass./De Cordova; Andover/Phillips; U. of Michigan, 1949; New York World's Fair, 1964–65. COLLECTIONS: Bryn Mawr College; Earlham College; Rumsey Hall School; WMAA.

TAM, REUBEN. b. January 17, 1916, Kapaa, Hawaii. STUDIED: U. of Hawaii, 1937, B.Ed.; New School for Social Research; Columbia U.; California School of Fine Arts. TAUGHT: Brook-

lyn Museum School, 1946– . AWARDS: Guggenheim Foundation Fellowship, 1948; Golden Gate International Exposition, San Francisco, 1939, First Prize; U. of Illinois, P.P.; Honolulu Academy School, First Prize in Painting, 1939; Brooklyn Museum, First Prize, 1952, 58. ADDRESS: 549 West 123 Street, NYC; summers: Monhegan Island, Me. DEALER: The Alan Gallery. ONE-MAN EXHIBITIONS: (first) California Palace, 1940; Sacramento/Crocker, 1941; Honolulu Academy, 1941; The Downtown Gallery, 1945, 46, 49, 53; The Alan Gallery, 1955, 57, 59, 61, 64; U. of Illinois, 1949, 51, 53, 55, 59. GROUP: MMA, American Painters Under 35, 1950; WMAA Annuals; Carnegie; Chicago/AI Annuals; U. of Illinois, 1961; PAFA; Walker; Brooklyn Museum; Corcoran; WMAA, Artists of Maine. COLLECTIONS: AAAL; Britannica; Brooklyn Museum; Buffalo/Albright; Dallas/MFA; Des Moines; Fort Worth; U. of Georgia; IBM; U. of Illinois; S. C. Johnson & Son, Inc.; MMA; MOMA; Massillon Museum; NYPL; U. of Nebraska; Newark Museum; The Pennsylvania State U.; Utica; WMAA; Wichita/AM; Youngstown/Butler. BIBLIOGRAPHY: Bethers; Nordness, ed.; Pousette-Dart, ed.

TANGUY, YVES. b. January 5, 1900, Paris, France; d. January 15, 1955, Woodbury, Conn. French Army, 1920–22. Traveled Africa, USA. To USA 1939; citizen 1948. m. Kay Sage. ONE-MAN EXHIBITIONS: (first) Galerie Surrealiste, Paris, 1928; Galerie des Cahiers d'Art, Paris, 1935, 47; Stanley Rose Gallery, Hollywood, 1935; Julien Levy Galleries, NYC, 1936; Howard Putzell Gallery, Hollywood, 1936; Palais des Beaux Arts, Brussels (three-man), 1937; Bucher-Myrbor Galerie, Paris, 1938; Guggenheim Jeune Gallery, London, 1938; Pierre Matisse Gallery, 1939, 42, 43, 45, 46, 50; Hartford/Wadsworth, 1939; SFMA, 1946; Arts Club of Chicago, 1940; "G" Place Gallery, Washington, D.C., 1943; Musee du Luxembourg, Paris, 1947; Copley Gallery, Hollywood, 1948; Galerie Nina Dausset, Paris, 1949; ICA, Washington, D.C., 1952; Kunsthalle, Basel, 1952; Galerie Maeght, 1947; L'Obelisco, Rome, 1953; Hartford/Wadsworth (two-man), 1954; MIT (two-man); Bodley Gallery, NYC, 1960; Petit Galerie, Paris, 1961. RETROSPECTIVE: MOMA, 1955. GROUP: Chicago/AI; Hartford/Wadsworth; WMAA; MOMA, Fantastic Art, DADA, Surrealism, 1936. COLLECTIONS:

Buffalo/Albright; Chicago/AI; Hartford/Wadsworth; U. of Illinois; MMA; MOMA; PMA; WMAA; Washington U. **Bibliography:** Baur 7; Blanchard; Blesh 1; **Breton** 1, 2, 3, 4; Canaday; Christensen; Flanagan; Ford; Gascoyne; Genauer; Goodrich and Baur 1; Guggenheim, ed.; Haftman; Hunter 5; Huyghe; Janis, S.; Kuh 1; Langui; McCurdy, ed.; Mendelowitz; Pearson 2; Pousette-Dart, ed.; Ramsden 1; Raynal 3; Read 4; Richardson; Sachs; Seitz 2; **Soby** 1, 8; **Tanguy;** Waldberg 3; Zervos.

TANIA (Schreiber). b. January 11, 1924, Warsaw, Poland. **Studied:** McGill U., 1941–42; Columbia U., 1942–44, MA; ASL, 1948–51, with Yasuo Kuniyoshi, Morris Kantor, Vaclav Vytlacil, Harry Sternberg. Traveled. Europe extensively, Canada, USA, Caribbean. **Taught:** NYU, 1963– . **Address:** 209 East 19 Street, NYC. **Dealer:** The Bertha Schaefer Gallery. **One-man Exhibitions:** (first) Albert Landry, NYC, 1959, also 1961, 62; The Bertha Schaefer Gallery, 1963, 64. **Group:** NYU, 3 Artists; U. of Illinois; U. of Virginia, Color and Space; WGMA, The Formalists, 1963; Oakland/AM; World House Galleries, International, 1964. **Collections:** Brandeis U.; Morgan State College; NYU.

TAUBES, FREDERIC. b. April 15, 1900, Lwow, Poland. **Studied:** Academy of Fine Arts, Munich, 1918, with Franz von Stuck, Max Doerner; Bauhaus, Weimar, 1922, with Josef Itten; and in Berlin and Italy. Traveled Europe extensively, USA. To USA 1930. **Taught:** U. of Illinois, 1940–41; Mills College, 1938; U. of Hawaii, 1939; Cooper Union, 1943; U. of Wisconsin, 1943; and in Great Britain and Canada. Associate Editor, *The Artist* Magazine. **Address:** Haverstraw, N.Y. **One-man Exhibitions:** (first) Vienna/Stadt, 1921; The Midtown Galleries; San Diego; Los Angeles/County MA; SFMA; Sacramento/Crocker; Honolulu Academy; U. of Nebraska; Kansas City/Nelson; Mills College; Seattle/AM. **Group:** Carnegie, 1936–46; Corcoran, 1936–46; PAFA, 1935–44; VMFA, 1938–46; Chicago/AI, 1935–46; Memphis/Brooks. **Collections:** American Locomotive Co.; Atlanta/AA; Britannica; de Young; IBM; Indiana U.; Kansas City/Nelson; MMA; Mills College; SFMA; San Diego; Santa Barbara/MA; Standard Oil Co.; Stony Brook. **Bibliography:** Allen, ed.; Boswell 1; **Boswell,**

ed.; Kent, N.; Pagano; **Taubes** 1, 2, 3, 4, 5, 6, 7, 8, 9, 10, 11, 12, 13; Watson 2.

TCHELITCHEW, PAVEL. b. September 21, 1898, District of Kaluga, near Moscow, Russia; **d.** July 31, 1957, Grotta Ferrata, Italy. **Studied:** U. of Moscow; Kiev Academy, 1918–20. Traveled Europe, USA, North Africa, U.S.S.R. To USA 1934; citizen 1952. Designed sets and costumes for ballets by Balanchine, Massine, and others. **One-man Exhibitions:** (first) Claridge Gallery, London, 1928; A. Tooth & Sons, 1933, 35, 38; Julien Levy Galleries, NYC, 1934, 37, 38; Arts Club of Chicago, 1935, 38; Durlacher Brothers, 1942, 45, 51; Hanover Gallery, 1949; Institute of Modern Art, Buenos Aires, 1949; Detroit/Institute, 1952; Galerie Rive Gauche, Paris, 1954, 56; Galleria d'Arte del Naviglio, Milan, 1955. **Retrospective:** Durlacher Brothers, 1948; Gallery of Modern Art, NYC, 1964. **Group:** Many national and international exhibitions. **Collections:** Hartford/Wadsworth; Kansas City/Nelson; MMA; MOMA; U. of Michigan; Santa Barbara/MA; Tretyakov Art Gallery; Yale U. **Bibliography:** Bazin; Canaday; Flanagan; Ford; Frost; Holme 1; Huyghe; **Kirstein** 2; **Kirstein, ed.;** Kuh 1; McCurdy, ed.; Mendelowitz; Pousette-Dart, ed.; Richardson; **Soby** 1, 7; Wight 2.

THIEBAUD, WAYNE. b. November 15, 1920, Mesa, Ariz. **Studied:** San Jose State College; Sacramento State College, BA, MA. US Army Air Force, 1942–45. Traveled Europe, Mexico, USA. **Taught:** Sacramento City College, 1951–60; Sacramento State College, 1954–55; California School of Fine Arts, 1958; U. of California, Davis, 1960– . Produced 11 educational motion pictures. **Commissions:** Sacramento (Calif.) Municipal Utility Building, 1959 (mosaic mural); California State Fair, 1950, 52, 55. **Awards:** California State Fair, Art Film Festival, First Prize, 1956; Film Council of America, Golden Reel Award, 1956 (American Film Festival, Chicago); Scholastic Art Awards for the films "Space" and "Design," 1961; Creative Research Foundation, $1,000 Grant, 1961; Columbia Records Award, 1959 ($6,000). **Address:** 1970 Fifth Avenue, Davis, Calif. **Dealer:** Allan Stone Gallery. **One-man Exhibitions:** (first) Sacramento/Crocker, 1951; Artists Co-op. Gallery, Sacramento, 1957, 58; SFMA, 1961; de Young, 1962; Allan Stone

Gallery, 1962, 63, 64; Galleria Schwarz, Milan. **GROUP:** SFMA Annual; Chicago/AI Annual; WMAA Annual; Los Angeles/County MA; California Palace; Denver/AM; ICA, London; Pasadena/AM, New Paintings of Common Objects, 1962; Houston/MFA, Pop Goes the Easel, 1963; and print exhibitions abroad. **COLLECTIONS:** Achenbach Foundation; Bryn Mawr College; Buffalo/Albright; California State Library; Corcoran; Dallas/MFA; Houston/MFA; Immaculate Heart College; Library of Congress; MOMA; U. of Miami; U. of Nebraska; Newark Museum; Sacramento/Crocker; Sacramento State College; San Jose State College; Shasta College; WGMA; WMAA.

THOMAS, ROBERT C. b. April 19, 1924, Wichita, Kans. **STUDIED:** Zadkine School of Sculpture, Paris, 1948–49; U. of California, Santa Barbara, 1950, BA; California College of Arts and Crafts, 1952, MFA; and privately with David Green, Pasadena, 1946–47. US Air Force, 1943–46. Traveled Spain, France, Italy. **TAUGHT:** U. of California, Santa Barbara, 1954– . **AWARDS:** Walnut Creek (Calif.) Pageant, Third Prize for Sculpture, 1951; San Francisco Art Association Annual, Bank of America Award, 1952; RAC, First Prize, 1952; San Francisco Art Association, American Trust Co. Award, 1953; RAC, First Prize, Sculpture, 1953; California State Fair, Second Prize and Silver Medal, 1954; Santa Barbara/MA, III Pacific Coast Biennial, P.P., 1959; Los Angeles Art Festival, Bronze Medal, 1949; and others. **ADDRESS:** 38 San Mateo Avenue, Goleta, Calif. **DEALERS:** Esther Robles Gallery; Esther Baer Gallery. **ONE-MAN EXHIBITIONS:** (first) U. of California, Santa Barbara, 1949; Coit Lane Gallery, Santa Barbara, 1950; Paul Desch Gallery, Santa Barbara, 1952; Santa Barbara/MA, 1955, 1959 (two-man), 1963 (three-man); Esther Robles Gallery, 1959, 60, 61, 63; La Jolla, 1960; Esther Baer Gallery, 1961. **GROUP:** Salon des Artistes Independants, Paris, 1949; Salon du Mai, Paris, 1949; City of Los Angeles Annual, 1949; Los Angeles/County MA, 1950, 55, 56; RAC, 1951, 53; SFMA, 1952, 53, 56, 57; California State Fair, 1954, 57, 58, 59, 60, 62; Oakland/AM, 1954, 55, 56, 58; Denver/AM, 1959, 62; La Jolla, 1962; Ball State Teachers College, 1962, 63. **COLLECTIONS:** Santa Barbara/MA.

TOBEY, MARK. b. December 11, 1890, Centerville, Wisc. STUDIED: Chicago Art Institute School, 1908, with Frank Zimmerer, Prof. Reynolds. Traveled Europe, Mexico, USA, the Orient extensively. **TAUGHT:** Cornish School, Seattle, intermittently 1923–29; Dartington Hall, Devonshire, England, 1931–38. **FEDERAL A.P.:** Easel painting, 1938. **AWARDS:** Seattle/AM, Katherine Baker Memorial Award, 1940; MMA, Artists for Victory, $500 Prize, 1942; Portrait of America, Fourth Prize, 1945; NIAL, 1956; Guggenheim International, $1,000 Award, 1956; American Institute of Architects, Fine Arts Medal, 1957; XXIX Venice Biennial, 1958, First Prize of the Commune of Venice; *Art In America* Magazine, 1958 ($1,000); elected to American Academy of Arts and Sciences, 1960 (fails to accept election). **ADDRESS:** c/o The Willard Gallery. **DEALERS:** The Willard Gallery; Otto Seligman Gallery. **ONE-MAN EXHIBITIONS:** (first) M. Knoedler & Co., NYC, 1917; Arts Club of

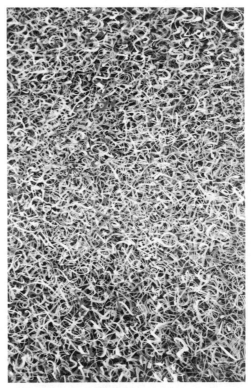

Mark Tobey   *Toward the Whites.*

Chicago, 1928, 40; Romany Marie's Cafe Gallery, NYC, 1929; Cornish School, Seattle, 1930; Contemporary Arts Gallery, NYC, 1931; Paul Elder Gallery, San Francisco, 1934; Beaux Arts Gallery, London, 1934; Stanley Rose Gallery, Hollywood, 1935; Seattle/AM, 1942; The Willard Gallery, 1944, 45, 47, 49, 50, 51, 53, 54, 57; Margaret Brown Gallery, Boston, 1949, 54, 56; California Palace, circ., 1951; The U. of Chicago, 1952; Zoé Dusanne Gallery, 1952; Otto Seligman Gallery, 1954, 57, 62; Chicago/AI, 1955; Gump's Gallery, 1955; Jeanne Bucher, Paris, 1955, 59; Paul Kantor Gallery, 1955; ICA, London, 1955; Victoria (B.C.), 1957; Galerie Stadler, Paris, 1958; St. Albans School, Washington, D.C., 1959; Frederic Hobbs Fine Art Center, 1960; Mannheim, 1960; Galerie Beyeler, Basel, 1961; Royal Marks Gallery, 1961; Seattle World's Fair, 1962; Phillips, 1962; Portland, Ore./AM (three-man), 1950. RETROSPECTIVE: Seattle/AM, circ., 1959; Musee des Arts Decoratifs, Paris, 1961; MOMA, 1962. GROUP: MOMA, Paintings by 19 Living Americans, 1929; New York World's Fair, 1939; Chicago/AI, 1940, 46, 47, 48, 51; MMA, 1942, 44, 45; MOMA, Romantic Painting in America, 1943; Brooklyn Museum, 1945, 51; Seattle/AM, 1945, 50, 51, 52, 53, 55, 56, 58; WMAA, 1945, 46, 47, 49, 62; Tate, 1946; MOMA, Fourteen Americans, circ., 1946; Utica, circ., 1947; XXIV, XXVIII, and XXIX Venice Biennials, 1948, 56, 58; U. of Illinois, 1949, 50, 51, 55, 59; SFMA, 1949; Walker, Contemporary American Painting, 1950; MMA, American Paintings Today, 1950; MOMA, Abstract Painting and Sculpture in America, 1951; Ueno Art Gallery, Tokyo, 1951; U. of Minnesota, 40 American Painters, 1940–50, 1951; I & III Sao Paulo Biennials, 1951, 55; Carnegie, 1952, 55, 58, 61; International Biennial Exhibition of Paintings, Tokyo; Pavillion Vendome, Aix-en-Provence, 1954; France/National, 50 Ans d'Art aux Etats-Unis, circ. Europe, 1955; Darmstadt/Kunsthalle, circ., 1956; III International Contemporary Art Exhibition, New Delhi, 1957; USIA, Eight American Artists, circ. Europe and Asia, 1957–58; WMAA, Nature in Abstraction, 1958; Brussels World's Fair, 1958; American Painting and Sculpture, Moscow, 1959; Documenta II, Kassel, 1959; Walker, 60 American Painters, 1960; Seattle World's Fair, 1962. COLLECTIONS: Andover/Phillips; Baltimore/MA; Boston/MFA; Brooklyn Museum; Buffalo/Al-

bright; Carnegie; Chicago/AI; Detroit/Institute; Hartford/Wadsworth; MMA; MOMA; Milwaukee; Phillips; Portland, Ore./AM; SFMA; St. Louis/City; Seattle/AM; Utica; WMAA; West Palm Beach/Norton. BIBLIOGRAPHY: Alvard; Baur 5, 7; Beekman; Biddle 3; Blesh 1; Eliot; Gaunt; Goodrich and Baur 1; Haftman; Henning; Hess, T. B.; Hunter 1, 5; Janis, S.; Kuh 2; Langui; Leepa, McCurdy, ed.; Mendelowitz; *Metro;* Miller, ed. 2; Neumeyer; Nordness, ed.; Ponente; Pousette-Dart, ed.; Ragon 1, 2; Read 2; Restany 2; Richardson; Ritchie 1; **Roberts;** Rodman 1, 3; **Seitz 1, 4;** Seuphor 1; Soby 5; Tapie 1; **Thomas; Tobey.**

TOMLIN, BRADLEY WALKER. b. August 19, 1899, Syracuse, N.Y.; **d.** May 11, 1953, NYC. STUDIED: Studio of Hugo Gari Wagner, 1913; Syracuse U., 1917–21; Academie Colarossi, Paris, and Academie de la Grande Chaumiere, 1923. Traveled Europe. TAUGHT: Buckley School, 1932–33; Sarah Lawrence College, 1932–41; Dalton Schools, NYC, 1933–34. MEMBER: Federation of Modern Painters and Sculptors; Whitney Studio Club, NYC; Woodstock Artists Association. AWARDS: Scholarship to Wagner Studio, 1913; Syracuse U., Hiram Gee Fellowship; Scholarship to L. C. Tiffany Foundation, Oyster Bay, N.Y.; Carnegie, Hon. Men., 1946; U. of Illinois, P.P., 1949. ONE-MAN EXHIBITIONS: Skaneateles and Cazenovia, N.Y., 1922; Anderson Galleries, NYC, 1923; Montross Gallery, NYC, 1926, 27; Frank K. M. Rehn Gallery, NYC, 1931, 44; Betty Parsons Gallery, 1950, 53; Phillips, 1955. RETROSPECTIVE: WMAA, circ., 1957. GROUP: MMA, 1953; France/National, 1955; MOMA, Abstract Painting and Sculpture in America, 1951; MOMA, Fifteen Americans, circ., 1952; U. of Minnesota, 1951; U. of Illinois, 1949, 51; WMAA, The New Decade, 1954–55. COLLECTIONS: Andover/Phillips; Cranbrook; U. of Illinois; MMA; Phillips; Utica; WMAA. BIBLIOGRAPHY: Baur 7; Blesh 1; Flanagan; Goodrich and Baur 1; Haftman; Hess, T. B.; Hunter 1, 5; McCourbrey; McCurdy, ed.; Mendelowitz; Motherwell and Reinhardt, eds.; Pagano; Ponente; Pousette-Dart, ed.; Read 2; Ritchie 1; Seuphor 1.

TOOKER, GEORGE. b. August 5, 1920, NYC. STUDIED: Phillips Academy, 1936–38; Harvard U., 1942, AB; ASL, with Reginald Marsh,

George Tooker   *The Table.*

Paul Cadmus, Kenneth Hayes Miller, Harry Sternberg. US Marine Corps, 1942–43. Traveled France, Italy, Great Britain. **AWARDS:** NIAL Grant, 1960. **ADDRESS:** Hartland, Vt. **DEALER:** Durlacher Brothers. **ONE-MAN EXHIBITIONS:** (first) Hewitt Gallery, NYC, 1951, also 1955; Robert Isaacson Gallery, NYC, 1960, 62; Durlacher Brothers, 1964. **GROUP:** WMAA; MOMA; MMA, 1950, 52; Chicago/AI, 1951; Corcoran, 1951; XXVIII Venice Biennial, 1956; ICA, London; PAFA, 1952; Carnegie, 1958; Festival of Two Worlds, Spoleto, 1958. **COLLECTIONS:** S. C. Johnson & Son, Inc.; MMA; MOMA; Sara Roby Foundation; WMAA; Walker. **BIBLIOGRAPHY:** Goodrich and Baur 1; Mendelowitz; Newmeyer; Nordness, ed.; Pousette-Dart, ed.; Rodman 1.

TOVISH, HAROLD. b. July 31, 1921, NYC. **STUDIED:** Columbia U., 1940–43; Zadkine School of Sculpture, Paris, 1949–50; Academie de la Grande Chaumiere, 1950–51. Traveled France, Italy. **TAUGHT:** U. of Minnesota, 1951–54; New York State College of Ceramics, 1947–49; Boston Museum School, 1957– . **MEMBER:** Artists Equity. **AWARDS:** Minneapolis/Institute, First Prize, Sculpture, 1954;

Boston Arts Festival, First Prize for Drawing, 1958, First Prize for Sculpture, 1959; NIAL Grant. **m.** Marianna Pineda. **ADDRESS:** 164 Rawson Road, Brookline, Mass. **DEALERS:** The Swetzoff Gallery; Terry Dintenfass, Inc. **ONE-MAN EXHIBITIONS:** (first) Walker, 1953; The Swetzoff Gallery, 1957, 60; Fairweather-Hardin Gallery, 1960. **GROUP:** MMA, Artists for Victory, 1942; Toledo/MA, Sculpture Today, 1947; Walker, 1951; WMAA Annuals, 1952, 54, 57, 60; Minneapolis/Institute, 1952, 54; Chicago/AI, 1959; Denver/AM, 1955; SFMA, 1952; Carnegie, 1958; MOMA, Recent Sculpture USA, 1959; Venice Biennial; SRGM, The Joseph H. Hirshhorn Collection, 1962; Lincoln, Mass./De Cordova, 1964. **COLLECTIONS:** Andover/Phillips; Boston/MFA; Chicago/AI; Minneapolis/Institute; U. of Minnesota; SRGM; WMAA; Walker; Worcester/AM.

TOWNLEY, HUGH. b. February 6, 1923, West Lafayette, Ind. **STUDIED:** U. of Wisconsin, 1946–48; privately with Ossip Zadkine, Paris, 1948–49; Central School of Arts and Crafts, London, 1949–50, with Victor Passmore; Brown U., MA. Traveled France, Great Britain, Holland. **TAUGHT:** Layton School of

Art, 1951–56; Beloit College, 1956–57; Boston U., 1957–61; Brown U., 1961– . MEMBER: Artists Equity, Boston, 1961. COMMISSIONS: Sobin Chemical Co., Boston, 1963; YMCA, Milwaukee, 1956. AWARDS: Chicago/AI, Exhibition Momentum, 1952, 53; SFMA Annual, 1952; ICA, Boston, View, 1960; ICA, Boston, Selections, 1961; Rhode Island Arts Festival, 1962, 63; Silvermine Guild, 1963; Berkshire Art Association Annual, 1961, 63; MIT, Summer Fellowship, 1956; Yaddo Fellowship, 1964; Kalamazoo Art Center, Lithographic Workshop, Fellowship, 1964. ADDRESS: 6 Walley Street, Bristol, R. I. DEALER: The Pace Gallery, NYC. ONE-MAN EXHIBITIONS: (first) Gallerie Apollinaire, London, 1951; U. of Wisconsin, 1955; Milwaukee, 1957; The Swetzoff Gallery, 1958, 59; Arts Council of Winston-Salem (N.C.), 1958; Connecticut College, 1960; The Pace Gallery, Boston, 1960, 64; The Pace Gallery, NYC, 1964; U. of Connecticut, 1964; Studio 40, The Hague (two-man), 1950; Beloit College (two-man), 1956. GROUP: USIA, Americans in Paris, circ. Europe, 1949; Chicago/AI, Exhibition Momentum, 1952, 53, 56, 57; SFMA Annual, 1952; Chicago/AI, 1964; MOMA, New Talent; Walker, 1956; WMAA, Young America, 1957; WMAA Annual, 1962; Boston Arts Festival, 1958, 61, 64; Carnegie, 1958; ICA, Boston, View, 1960; ICA, Boston, Selections, 1961; U. of Illinois, 1961, 63; Silvermine Guild, 1959, 60, 62, 63, 64; Hartford/Wadsworth, Eleven New England Sculptors, 1963; Lincoln, Mass./De Cordova, 1964. COLLECTIONS: Andover/Phillips; Boston/MFA; Harvard U.; Milwaukee; SFMA; Utica; WMAA; Williams College.

TREIMAN, JOYCE. b. May 29, 1922, Evanston, Ill. STUDIED: Stephens College, 1941, AA; State U. of Iowa, with Philip Guston, Lester Longman, 1943, BFA. Traveled Mediterranean, Near East. TAUGHT: U. of Illinois, 1958–60; UCLA, 1960. AWARDS: Graduate Fellowship to State U. of Iowa, 1943; Denver/AM, P.P., 1948; Springfield, Ill./State; Chicago/AI, Mr. & Mrs. Frank H. Armstrong Prize, 1949; Chicago/AI, The Mr. & Mrs. Frank G. Logan Prize, 1951; Chicago/AI, Pauline Palmer Prize, 1953; Chicago/AI, Martin B. Cahn Award, 1959, 60; Ford Foundation, P.P., 1960; Pasadena/AM, 1962; La Jolla, 1962; L. C. Tiffany Grant, 1947; Tupperware Art Fund, 1955; Ford Founda-

tion/A.F.A. Artist-in-Residence, 1963; Tamarind Fellowship, 1962. ADDRESS: 712 Amalfi Drive, Pacific Palisades, Calif. DEALERS: The Forum Gallery; Fairweather-Hardin Gallery; Felix Landau Gallery. ONE-MAN EXHIBITIONS: (first) Paul Theobald Gallery, Chicago, 1942; John Snowden Gallery, Chicago, 1945; Chicago/AI: The Chicago Artists Room, 1947; Fairweather-Garnett Gallery, Evanston, Ill., 1950; Hewitt Gallery, NYC, 1950; Palmer House Galleries, Chicago, 1952; Elizabeth Nelson Gallery, Chicago, 1953; Feingarten Gallery, Chicago, 1955; Cliff Dwellers Club, Chicago, 1955; The Willard Gallery, 1960; Fairweather-Hardin Gallery, 1955, 58, 62, 64; Felix Landau Gallery, 1961; The Forum Gallery, 1963. GROUP: Carnegie, 1955, 57; MMA, American Painters Under 35, 1950; U. of Illinois, 1950, 51, 52, 56, 61, 63; WMAA Annuals, 1951, 52, 53, 58; WMAA, Young America, 1957; Chicago/AI Annuals, 1945–59; Chicago/AI, Directions in American Painting, 1946, 51, 54, 56, 59, 60; Denver/AM, 1943, 48, 55, 58, 60, 64; Library of Congress, 1954; Corcoran, 1957; PAFA, 1958; U. of Nebraska, 1957; MOMA, Recent Painting USA: The Figure, circ., 1962–63; WMAA, Fifty California Artists, 1962–63. COLLECTIONS: Abbott Laboratories; Ball State Teachers College; Chicago/AI; Denver/AM; International Minerals & Chemicals Corp.; State U. of Iowa; Los Angeles/County MA; Oberlin College; U. of Oregon; Orlando; Pasadena/AM; Springfield, Ill./State; Utah State U. BIBLIOGRAPHY: Pousette-Dart, ed.

TSUTAKAWA, GEORGE. b. February 22, 1910, Seattle, Wash. STUDIED: U. of Washington, 1937, BA, MFA. US Army, 1942–46. Traveled Europe, Japan. TAUGHT: U. of Washington, 1946– . COMMISSIONS: Seattle Public Library; Renton Center, Renton, Wash.; Lloyd Center, Portland, Ore.; St. Marks Cathedral, Seattle; Century 21, Seattle World's Fair, 1962 (US Commemorative Medal); Northgate Shopping Center, Seattle; J. W. Robinson Department Store, Anaheim, Calif.; Pacific First Federal Savings and Loan Association, Tacoma, Wash.; Bon Marche Dept. Store, Tacoma, Wash.; Fresno Mall, Fresno, Calif.; Commerce Tower, Kansas City, Mo. (sunken garden). ADDRESS: 3116 South Irving Street, Seattle, Wash. DEALER: Ceeje Galleries. ONE-MAN EXHIBI-

TIONS: (first) Studio Gallery, Seattle, 1947; U. of Washington, 1950, 54; Press Club, Spokane, Wash., 1953; Seattle/AM, 1957; Tacoma; U. of Puget Sound, 1955, 64; Zoé Dusanne Gallery, 1953, 58. **GROUP:** Seattle/AM Annuals, 1933– ; Spokane Art Center of Washington State U., 1954–57; Portland, Ore./AM, 1955, 60; Oakland/AM, 1951; SFMA, 1955, 58, 60; Vancouver, 1955, 57; III Sao Paulo Biennial, 1955; Denver/AM, 1960, 64; Santa Barbara/MA, 1959, 60, 61; Los Angeles/County MA, 1960; Yoseido Gallery, Tokyo, 1956; San Diego, 1960. **COLLECTIONS:** Denver/AM; Santa Barbara/MA; Seattle/AM.

TWARDOWICZ, STANLEY. b. July 8, 1917, Detroit, Mich. **STUDIED:** Skowhegan School, 1946–47, with Henry Poor. Traveled Mexico, Europe. **TAUGHT:** The Ohio State U., 1946–51; Hofstra U., 1964. **AWARDS:** Guggenheim Foundation Fellowship, 1956. **ADDRESS:** 48 Ocean Avenue, Northport, N.Y. **DEALERS:** The Peridot Gallery; Dwan Gallery. **ONE-MAN EXHIBITIONS:** (first) Contemporary Arts Gallery, NYC, 1949, also 1951, 53, 56; Dwan Gallery, 1959, 61; Columbus, 1963; The Peridot Gallery, 1958, 59, 60, 61, 63, 64. **GROUP:** PAFA, 1950; SRGM, 1954; Chicago/AI, 1954, 55; Carnegie, 1955; Sao Paulo, 1960; WMAA, 1954, 55, 57, 64; U. of Nebraska, 1960. **COLLECTIONS:** Columbus; Los Angeles/County MA; MOMA; Milwaukee; Newark Museum.

TWOMBLY, CY. b. 1929, Lexington, Va. **STUDIED:** Boston Museum School; ASL; Black Mountain College, with Franz Kline, Robert Motherwell. Resided Rome, 1957– . **ADDRESS:** c/o Dealer. **DEALER:** Leo Castelli Inc. **ONE-MAN EXHIBITIONS:** The Kootz Gallery, 1951; The Stable Gallery, 1953, 55, 57; La Tartaruga, Rome, 1958, 60, 63; Galleria del Cavallino, Venice, 1958; Galleria d'Arte del Naviglio,

Jack Tworkov   *Thursday. 1960*

Milan, 1958, 60; Galerie 22, Dusseldorf, 1960; Leo Castelli Inc., 1960, 64; Galerie Rudolf Zwirner, Essen, 1961; Galerie J, Paris, 1961; Notizie Gallery, 1962; Musee Royaux des Beaux-Arts, Brussels, 1962; Galleria del Leone, Venice, 1962; Galerie Anne Abels, Cologne, 1963; Galerie Rudolf Zwirner, Cologne, 1963; Galerie D. Benador, Geneva, 1963; Galerie Bonnier, Lausanne, 1963; Galerie Handschin, Basel, 1964. GROUP: Gutai 9, Osaka, 1958; Festival of Two Worlds, Spoleto, 1961; Premio Lissone, 1961; Premio Marzotto, 1962; Amsterdam/Stedelijk, Art and Writing, 1963; Salon du Mai, Paris, 1963; L'Aquila, Aspetti dell'Arte Contemporanea, 1963. BIBLIOGRAPHY: *Metro;* Restany 2.

TWORKOV, JACK. b. August 15, 1900, Biala, Poland. To USA 1913; citizen 1928. STUDIED: Columbia U., 1920–23; NAD, 1923–25, with Ivan Olinsky, C. W. Hawthorne; privately with Ross Moffett, 1924–25; ASL, 1925–26, with Guy Du Bois, Boardman Robinson. TAUGHT: Fieldston School, NYC, 1931; Queens College, 1948–55; American U., 1948–51; Black Mountain College, summer, 1952; Pratt Institute, 1955–58; Yale U., 1963– . FEDERAL A.P.: Easel painting, 1935–41. AWARDS: Cor-

coran, William A. Clark Prize and Corcoran Gold Medal, 1963. ADDRESS: 234 East 23 Street, NYC. DEALER: Leo Castelli Inc. ONE-MAN EXHIBITIONS: (first) ACA Gallery, 1940; Charles Egan Gallery, 1947, 49, 52, 54; Baltimore/MA, 1948; U. of Mississippi, 1954; Walker, 1957; The Stable Gallery, 1957, 58, 59; B. C. Holland Gallery, 1960, 63; Leo Castelli Inc., 1961, 63; Tulane U., 1961; Yale U., 1963. GROUP: PAFA, 1929; MOMA, The New American Painting, circ. Europe, 1958–59; Documenta II, Kassel, 1959; Walker, 60 American Painters, 1960; Carnegie, 1961; SRGM, Abstract Expressionists and Imagists, 1961; SRGM/USIA, American Vanguard, circ. Europe, 1961–62; MOMA, Abstract American Drawings and Watercolors, circ. Latin America, 1961–63; Art:USA:Now, circ., 1962– ; Seattle World's Fair, 1962; WMAA Annual, 1963; Corcoran, 1963; U. of Illinois, 1961. COLLECTIONS: Allentown/AM; American U.; Baltimore/MA; Buffalo/Albright; Cleveland/MA; Hartford/Wadsworth; S. C. Johnson & Son, Inc.; MMA; MOMA; Newark Museum; New Paltz; Rockefeller Institute; Santa Barbara/MA; Union Carbide Corp.; WGMA; WMAA; Walker. BIBLIOGRAPHY: Goodrich and Baur 1; Hess, T. B.; Hunter 1, 5; *Metro;* Nordness, ed.; Pousette-Dart, ed.; Read 2; Rodman 3.

V

VANDER SLUIS, GEORGE. b. December 18, 1915, Cleveland, Ohio. STUDIED: Cleveland Institute of Art, 1934–39; Colorado Springs Fine Arts Center, 1939–40, with Boardman Robinson. US Army, 1942–45. Traveled Europe, USA. TAUGHT: Syracuse U. FEDERAL A.P.: Mural painting, 1939. COMMISSIONS: US Post Offices, Rifle, Colo., 1941, and Riverton, Wyo., 1942; Syracuse U., 1955; J. C. Georg Company, Syracuse, N.Y., 1957. AWARDS: Fulbright Fellowship (Italy), 1951–52. ADDRESS: 960 Lancaster Avenue, Syracuse, N.Y. DEALER: Royal Marks Gallery. ONE-MAN EXHIBITIONS: (first) Salt Lake Art Center, Salt Lake City, Utah, 1942; Columbia U., 1943; Colorado Springs/FA, 1945; Southern Methodist U., 1946; U. of Nebraska, 1947; Hood College, 1948; Galleria d'Arte Contemporanea, Florence, Italy, 1952; Syracuse U., 1955; Syracuse/Everson, 1956, 61; Alfred U., 1957; Colgate U., 1957; Rochester/Memorial, 1959; J. Seligmann & Co., 1959; Cleveland Institute of Art, 1962; Royal Marks Gallery, 1962, 63, 64; Utica, 1963. GROUP: Cleveland/MA, The May Show, 1937, 38, 40, 41; San Francisco Art Association Annuals, 1941, 42; Smithsonian, American Watercolors, 1941; Chicago/AI Annual, 1941; MMA, Artists for Victory, 1942; Pepsi-Cola Co., Paintings of the Year, 1946, 47; Corcoran, 1947, 57; PAFA, 1953; WMAA, 1954; WMAA, Fulbright Artists, 1958; U. of Illinois, 1961; Utica Annuals, 1948, 49, 51, 55, 56, 57, 58, 59, 60, 61, 62, 63, 64. COLLECTIONS: Cleveland/MA; Colgate U.; Colorado Springs/FA; Kansas City/Nelson; New Britain; Rochester/Memorial; Southern Methodist U.; Syracuse/Everson; Syracuse U.; Utica.

VASILIEFF, NICHOLAS. b. November 3, 1892, Moscow, Russia. STUDIED: Academy of Fine Arts, Moscow, with Leonid Pasternack. Traveled Turkey, France, Germany. TAUGHT: Academy of Fine Arts, Moscow, 1918–19; and privately. To USA 1921. COMMISSIONS (murals): a nightclub in Constantinople, Turkey, 1921; Club Troika, Washington, D.C., 1932; a nightclub in Baltimore, Md., 1934. AWARDS: Academy of Fine Arts, Moscow, Gold Medal; La Tausca Competition, 1948 ($3,000); U. of Illinois, P.P., 1954. ADDRESS: P.O. Box 111, Lanesboro, Mass. DEALER: The Amel Gallery. ONE-MAN EXHIBITIONS: (first) Artists' Gallery, NYC, 1938; John Heller Gallery, NYC; The Bertha Schaefer Gallery; The Amel Gallery. GROUP: PAFA; Yale U.; Corcoran; U. of Illinois, 1963; WMAA; Buffalo/Albright; Brooklyn Museum, 1926; Bordighera, 1955; Carnegie; NIAL; Art:USA:Now, circ., 1962– . COLLECTIONS: Albany/Institute; Ball State Teachers College; Brooklyn Museum; Colby College; Corcoran; U. of Florida; Hartford/Wadsworth; U. of Illinois; Kansas City/Nelson; U. of Minnesota, Duluth; Mount Holyoke College; NYU; U. of Nebraska; New Orleans/Delgado; PAFA; PMA; Phoenix; Pittsfield/Berkshire; Rutgers U.; Santa Barbara/MA; Tel Aviv; WMAA; Yale U.; Youngstown/Butler. BIBLIOGRAPHY: Nordness, ed.

VASS, GENE. b. July 28, 1922, Buffalo, N.Y. STUDIED: U. of Buffalo, 1952, BFA; Yale U. Traveled Spain, France, Holland; resided Rome, 1958–59. TAUGHT: U. of Buffalo, 1956–58. ADDRESS: 159 Mercer Street, NYC. ONE-MAN EXHIBITIONS: (first) a gallery in Buffalo,

N.Y., 1957; Appunto Gallery, Rome, 1959; Grace Borgenicht Gallery Inc., 1960, 61. GROUP: Norfolk, Drawing Annual, 1957; Carnegie, 1958, 64; Corcoran, 1959; Buffalo/Albright, 1956–59; U. of Illinois, 1961; U. of Nebraska, 1961; Chicago/AI, 1961; WMAA Annual, 1962; MOMA, Recent American Painting and Sculpture, circ. USA and Canada, 1961–62; PAFA, 1957. COLLECTIONS: Baltimore/MA; Buffalo/Albright; MOMA; St. Paul Gallery; WMAA.

VICENTE, ESTEBAN. b. January 20, 1906, Segovia, Spain. STUDIED: Real Academia de Bellas Artes de San Fernando, Madrid, BA. Resided Paris, 1927–32. To USA 1936. TAUGHT: U. of California, Los Angeles and Berkeley, 1954–55; Queens College; Black Mountain College; High Field School, Falmouth, Mass.; NYU; Yale U.; and in Puerto Rico. AWARDS: Ford Foundation, 1961, 62; Tamarind Fellowship, 1962. ADDRESS: 36 Gramercy Park East, NYC. DEALER: Andre Emmerich Gallery, NYC. ONE-MAN EXHIBITIONS: St. John's College, Annapolis, Md., 1963; B. C. Holland Gallery, 1963; Andre Emmerich Gallery, NYC, 1960, 62, 63; New Arts Gallery, Houston, 1962; Primus-Stuart Gallery, Los Angeles, 1961; Holland-Goldowsky Gallery, Chicago, 1960; U. of Minnesota, 1959; Dayton/AI, 1963; Leo Cas-

telli Inc., 1958; Rose Fried Gallery, 1957, 58; Charles Egan Gallery, 1955; Allan Frumkin Gallery, Chicago, 1953; The Peridot Gallery, 1950, 51; Kleemann Gallery, NYC, 1937. GROUP: Seattle World's Fair, 1962; SRGM, Abstract Expressionists and Imagists, 1961; WMAA Annuals, 1958, 59, 61, 62; MOMA, The Art of Assemblage, circ., 1961; SRGM/USIA, American Vanguard, circ. Europe, 1961–62; International Biennial Exhibition of Paintings, Tokyo; Hartford/Wadsworth, Continuity and Change, 1962; Carnegie, 1958, 59, 61; Chicago/AI, 1960; ICA, Boston, 100 Works on Paper, circ. Europe, 1959; Walker, 60 American Painters, 1960; Columbus, Contemporary American Painting, 1960; Corcoran; Sao Paulo, 1963; The Kootz Gallery, New Talent, 1950; Ninth Street Exhibition, NYC, 1951. COLLECTIONS: Baltimore/MA; Brandeis U.; Chase Manhattan Bank; Dallas/MFA; Geigy Chemical Corp.; Iowa State U.; *Look* Magazine; Reynolds Metals Co.; Shuttleworth Carton Co.; The Singer Company Inc.; Union Carbide Corp.; WGMA; WMAA. BIBLIOGRAPHY: Hess, T. B.; Hunter 5; Janis and Blesh 1; Seitz 2.

VOLLMER, RUTH. b. Munich, Germany. Traveled Europe, Middle East. TAUGHT: Fieldston School, NYC, 1956–61. MEMBER: American Abstract Artists; American Crafts-

Esteban Vicente   *Blue, Red, Black and White. 1961*

men's Council. **COMMISSIONS:** Uris Buildings Corp. (mural for 375 Madison Avenue, NYC); MOMA exhibits. **ADDRESS:** 25 Central Park West, NYC. **DEALER:** Betty Parsons Gallery. **ONE-MAN EXHIBITIONS:** Betty Parsons Gallery, 1960, 63. **GROUP:** U. of Colorado, 1961; American Abstract Artists Annuals, 1963, 64. **COLLECTIONS:** MOMA; NYU; WGMA.

VON WEIGAND, CHARMION. b. March 4, 1899, Chicago, Ill. **STUDIED:** Barnard College; Columbia U.; NYU; self-taught in art. Traveled Europe, Mexico. **MEMBER:** American Abstract Artists (President, 1952–53). **ADDRESS:** 301 East 38 Street, NYC. **DEALER:** The Howard Wise Gallery, NYC. **ONE-MAN EXHIBITIONS:** Rose Fried Gallery, 1942, 48, 56; Saidenberg Gallery, 1952; John Heller Gallery, NYC, 1956; Zoé Dusanne Gallery, 1958; La Cittadella d'Arte Internazionale e d'Avanguardia, Ascona, Switzerland, 1959; The Howard Wise Gallery, NYC, 1961. **GROUP:** Art of This Century, NYC, The Women, 1945; American Abstract Artists Annuals; MMA, 1951; Walker, The Classic Tradition, 1953; WMAA, 1955, 57; Houston/MFA, The Sphere of Mondrian, 1957; Helmhaus Gallery, Zurich, Konkrete Kunst, 1950; Galerie Chalette, Construction and Geometry in Painting, circ., 1960; WMAA, Geometric Abstraction in America, circ., 1962; Amsterdam/Stedelijk, Art and Writing, 1963. **COLLECTIONS:** Carnegie; MOMA; Newark Museum; Seattle/AM; WMAA. **BIBLIOGRAPHY:** Janis and Blesh 1; Seitz 2; Seuphor 1.

VON WICHT, JOHN. b. February 3, 1888, Holstein, Germany. **STUDIED:** Private art school of the Grand Duke of Hesse, 1909–10, BA; School of Fine and Applied Arts, Berlin, 1912. Traveled Europe. To USA 1923; citizen 1936. **TAUGHT:** ASL, 1951–52; John Herron Art Institute, 1953. **MEMBER:** American Abstract Artists; Audubon Artists; Federation of Modern Painters and Sculptors; International Institute of Arts and Letters; SAGA. **FEDERAL A.P.:** Mural painting. **COMMISSIONS:** Pan American Airways Terminal, Miami, Fla.; McGill U.; New York World's Fair, 1939; Pennsylvania Railroad Station, Trenton, N.J. **AWARDS:** Brooklyn Museum, First Prize, 1948, 49, P.P., 1951, 64; SAGA, Mrs. A. W. Erickson Prize, 1953; The Print Club, Philadelphia, William H. Walker Memorial Prize, 1957; Audubon Art-

ists, Gold Medal of Honor, 1958; Ford Foundation, P.P., 1960. **ADDRESS:** 55 Middagh Street, Brooklyn, N.Y. **DEALER:** The Bertha Schaefer Gallery. **ONE-MAN EXHIBITIONS:** (first in USA) Architects Building, NYC, 1936; 608 Fifth Avenue, NYC, 1939; Artists' Gallery, NYC, 1944; Kleemann Gallery, NYC, 1946, 47; UCLA, 1947; Passedoit Gallery, NYC, 1950, 51, 52, 54, 56, 57, 58; Indianapolis/Herron, 1953; The Bertha Schaefer Gallery, 1960, 61, 62, 64; Esther Robles Gallery, 1959; Pasadena/AM, 1959; Liege, 1959; Galerie Neufville, Paris, 1962. **RETROSPECTIVE:** Santa Barbara/MA, 1959. **GROUP:** California Palace, 1964; Brooklyn Museum; Audubon Artists; MMA; WMAA Annuals; Federation of Modern Painters and Sculptors; Corcoran; PAFA; SRGM; Carnegie; NAD; Chicago/AI. **COLLECTIONS:** Baltimore/MA; Boston/MFA; Brandeis U.; Brooklyn Museum; Chase Manhattan Bank; Cincinnati/AM; Jewish Museum; S. C. Johnson & Son, Inc.; Library of Congress; Liege; Lincoln, Mass./De Cordova; MMA; MOMA; Madrid/Nacional; PMA; Paris/Moderne; Provincetown/Chrysler; Riverside Museum; Stockholm/National; Union Carbide Corp.; WMAA; Yale U. **BIBLIOGRAPHY:** Baur 7; Nordness, ed.; Pousette-Dart, ed.

VOULKOS, PETER. b. January 29, 1924, Bozeman, Mont. **STUDIED:** Montana State College, BS; California College of Arts and Crafts, MFA. **TAUGHT:** Archie Bray Foundation, Helena, Mont.; Black Mountain College; Los Angeles County Art Institute; Montana State U.; U. of California, Berkeley; Greenwich House Pottery, NYC; Teachers College, Columbia U. **AWARDS:** RAC, First Prize; National Decorative Art Show, Wichita, Kans., First Prize; Portland, Ore./AM, Northwest Craft Show, First Prize; Pacific Coast Ceramic Show, First Prize; Denver/AM, P.P.; Cranbrook, P.P.; Smithsonian, P.P.; Los Angeles County Fair, P.P.; Pasadena/AM, P.P.; Ford Foundation, P.P.; International Ceramic Exhibition, Ostend, Belgium, Silver Medal, 1959; International Ceramic Exhibition, Cannes, France, Gold Medal; I Paris Biennial, 1959, Rodin Museum Prize in Sculpture. **ADDRESS:** c/o Art Department, U. of California, Berkeley, Calif. **ONE-MAN EXHIBITIONS:** Gump's Gallery; U. of Florida; Historical Society of Montana; Felix Landau Gallery; Chicago/AI;

Bonniers, Inc., NYC; Fresno State College; Scripps College; U. of Southern California; Pasadena/AM; David Stuart Gallery. GROUP: MMA; Scripps College; Syracuse/Everson, National Ceramic Exhibition; U. of Tennessee; Brussels World's Fair, 1958; de Young; Seattle World's Fair, 1962; WMAA; Stanford U.; Denver/AM; Smithsonian; Los Angeles/County MA. COLLECTIONS: Baltimore/MA; Denver/AM; U. of Florida; U. of Illinois; Japanese Craft Museum; Los Angeles/County MA; MOMA; Museum of Contemporary Crafts; Oakland/AM; Pasadena/AM; SFMA; Smithsonian; U. of Wisconsin.

VYTLACIL, VACLAV. b. November 1, 1892, NYC. STUDIED: Chicago Art Institute School, 1908–12; ASL, 1912–14; Hofmann School, Munich, 1922–26. Traveled extensively; resided Europe 16 years. TAUGHT: ASL, 1928–64; U. of California, Berkeley, summers, 1927, 28; California College of Arts and Crafts, summers, 1936, 37; Colorado Springs Fine Arts Center, summers, 1947, 48, 49; Minneapolis Institute School, 1918–22, 1950; Chicago Art Institute School, 1954. MEMBER: Federation of Modern Painters and Sculptors; American Abstract Artists. FEDERAL A.P.: Organized an art school in Harlem, NYC. AWARDS: Chicago/AI, William R. French Memorial Gold Medal. ADDRESS: Sparkill, N.Y. DEALER: The Krasner Gallery. ONE-MAN EXHIBITIONS: (first) Feigl Gallery, NYC, 1942; Phillips; Rochester/Memorial; Baltimore/MA; Minneapolis Institute School. GROUP: American Abstract Artists Annuals; Federation of Modern Painters and Sculptors Annuals; Chicago/AI; Carnegie; PAFA; WMAA; Corcoran; MMA. COLLECTIONS: MMA; PAFA; Phillips; Rochester/Memorial. BIBLIOGRAPHY: Baur 7; Blesh 1; Cheney, M. C.; Janis, S.; Pousette-Dart, ed.

WALD, SYLVIA. b. October 30, 1914, Philadelphia, Pa. STUDIED: Moore Institute of Art, Science and Industry, Philadelphia, 1931–35. Traveled Europe. FEDERAL A.P.: Teacher. AWARDS: MOMA, P.P., 1941; Library of Congress, Pennell P.P., 1944; Brooklyn Museum, P.P., 1951, 54; National Serigraph Society, NYC, First Prize, 1948. ADDRESS: 405 East 54 Street, NYC. DEALERS: Devorah Sherman Gallery; American Art Gallery, Copenhagen. ONE-MAN EXHIBITIONS: (first) ACA Gallery, 1939; U. of Louisville, 1945, 49; Kent State College, 1945; National Serigraph Society, NYC, 1946; Grand Central Moderns, 1957; Devorah Sherman Gallery, 1960. GROUP: WMAA; National Sculpture Society, 1940; City of Philadelphia, Sculpture International, 1940; Chicago/AI, Directions in American Painting, 1941; Brooklyn Museum, Print Biennials; WMAA Annuals, 1948, 55; PAFA Annuals, 1950, 53, 54, 57; MOMA, 1941, 53, 56; Library of Congress, 1943, 52, 58; Smithsonian, Curators Choice—1942–52, circ. USA, 1954; International Print Exhibition, Salzburg and Vienna, 1952; II Sao Paulo Biennial, 1953; MOMA, 50 Years of American Art, circ. Europe, 1955; Brooklyn Museum, 10 Years of American Prints—1947–56, 1956; PCA, American Prints Today, circ., 1959–62; Bordighera, 1957. COLLECTIONS: Aetna Oil Co.; American Association of University Women; Ball State Teachers College; Bibliotheque Nationale; Brooklyn Museum; Howard U.; State U. of Iowa; Library of Congress; Louisville/Speed; U. of Louisville; MOMA; NYPL; National Gallery; U. of Nebraska; Ohio U.; U. of Oklahoma; PMA; Princeton U.; Toronto; Utica; Victoria and Albert Museum; Walker; Worcester/AM. BIBLIOGRAPHY: Peterdi.

WALDMAN, PAUL. b. August 1, 1936, Erie, Pa. STUDIED: Brooklyn Museum School; Pratt Institute. TAUGHT: Brooklyn Museum School, 1963– ; New York Community College, 1963– . ADDRESS: 71 Greene Street, NYC. DEALER: Allan Stone Gallery. ONE-MAN EXHIBITIONS: (first) Allan Stone Gallery, 1963. GROUP: Barnard College, Young Americans, 1962; Louis Alexander Gallery, NYC, Recent American Drawings, 1962; WGMA, Recent American Drawings, 1963; WGMA, Recent American Paintings, 1964; Brandeis U., Recent American Drawings, 1964; Hartford/Wadsworth, Figures, 1964; U. of Colorado, Survey of World Painting and Sculpture, 1964. COLLECTIONS: Colby College; Cornell U.; Finch College; Johns Hopkins U.; U. of Massachusetts; Mount Holyoke College; NYU; Newark Museum; Rutgers U.; The Singer Company Inc.; Stony Brook.

WALKOWITZ, ABRAHAM. b. March 28, 1878, Tyumen, Russia; **d.** January 26, 1965. STUDIED: NAD; Academie Julian, Paris, with Jean Paul Laurens. Traveled Europe extensively. TAUGHT: Educational Alliance, NYC. AWARDS: AAAL, Marjorie Peabody Waite Award, 1962. ONE-MAN EXHIBITIONS: "291," NYC, 1912; Schacht Gallery, NYC, 1944; The Downtown Gallery, 1930; Newark Museum, 1941; Charles Egan Gallery, 1947; Park Gallery, NYC, 1937; Chinese Gallery, NYC, 1946; Hartford/Wadsworth, 1950; Brooklyn Museum, 1939; ACA Gallery, 1955; NYPL, 1942; Jewish Museum, 1949; The Zabriskie Gallery, 1959, 64. GROUP: The Armory Show, 1913; Anderson Galleries, NYC, Forum Exhibition, 1916; NAD, 1904; WMAA. COLLECTIONS: Andover/Phillips; Boston/MFA; Brooklyn

Museum; Columbus; Kalamazoo/Institute; Library of Congress; MMA; MOMA; Newark Museum; Phillips; WMAA. BIBLIOGRAPHY: Baur 7; Biddle 3; Blesh 1; Brown; Cahill and Barr, eds.; Cheney, M. C.; Frank, ed.; Goodrich and Baur 1; Haftman; Hartmann; Hunter 5; Janis, S.; McCourbrey; McCurdy, ed.; Mellquist; Richardson; Walkowitz 1, 2; Wright 1.

WARSHAW, HOWARD. b. August 14, 1920, NYC. STUDIED: ASL, 1938–42. TAUGHT: U. of California, Santa Barbara, 1955– ; Jepson Art Institute, Los Angeles, 1948–52; State U. of Iowa, 1950–51. COMMISSIONS (murals): Wyle Laboratory, El Segundo, Calif., 1955; Santa Barbara (Calif.) Public Library, 1958 (with Channing Peake); U. of California, Santa Barbara, Dining Commons, 1960. ADDRESS: 755 El Bosque Road, Santa Barbara, Calif. DEALER: Felix Landau Gallery. ONE-MAN EXHIBITIONS: The Little Gallery, Beverly Hills, 1944; Gallery of International Art, Los Angeles, 1945; Julien Levy Galleries, NYC, 1946, 1948 (two-man, with Arshile Gorky); Frank Perls Gallery, 1949, 52, 54; Santa Barbara/MA (three-man, with Rico Lebrun and Channing Peake), 1956; J. Seligmann & Co., 1957 (two-man, with Channing Peake), 1958; Felix Landau Gallery, 1957, 59. GROUP: U. of Illinois, 1951, 58; U. of Nebraska, 1958; Carnegie; WMAA, Sao Paulo; Paris/Moderne; MMA; PAFA. COLLECTIONS: Carnegie; Los Angeles/County MA; PAFA; Santa Barbara/MA.

WASHINGTON, JAMES W., JR. b. November 10, 1909, Gloster, Miss. STUDIED painting privately with Mark Tobey in Seattle. Changed from painting to sculpture in 1956. Traveled Mexico, Europe, Middle East. FEDERAL A.P.: Teacher (Vicksburg, Miss.). MEMBER: Sculptors Institute. COMMISSIONS: Island Park School, Mercer Island, Seattle, Wash. (sculpture). AWARDS: SFMA, P.P., 1956; Oakland/AM, P.P., 1957; Seattle World's Fair, 1962, Second Prize. ADDRESS: 1816 26th Avenue, Seattle, Wash. DEALERS: Gordon Woodside Gallery; Haydon Calhoun Gallery. ONE-MAN EXHIBITIONS: (first) Vicksburg (Miss.) YMCA; Hall-Coleman Gallery, Seattle; Lee Nordness Gallery, NYC, 1962. COLLECTIONS: Oakland/AM; SFMA; Seattle/AM.

WATKINS, FRANKLIN C. b. December 30, 1894, NYC. STUDIED: U. of Virginia, 1911–12;

U. of Pennsylvania, 1912–13; PAFA, 1913–14, 1916–17, 1918. US Navy, 1917–18. Traveled Europe, North Africa. TAUGHT: Stella Elkins Tyler School of Fine Arts, Temple U., 1935; PAFA, 1935– ; American Academy, Rome, 1953–54. Designed sets and costumes for a ballet, "Transcendence," 1934. AWARDS: PAFA, Cresson Fellowship, 1917, 18; Carnegie, First Prize, 1931; Chicago/AI, 1938; Art Club of Philadelphia, 1925; Golden Gate International Exposition, San Francisco, 1939; Paris World's Fair, 1937, Bronze Medal; Corcoran, Gold Medal, 1939; PAFA, Carol H. Beck Gold Medal, 1941; Fulbright Fellowship, 1953; PAFA, Gold Medal, 1949; Philadelphia Art Alliance, Medal of Achievement, 1957; Hon. DFA, Franklin and Marshall College, 1954. ADDRESS: 2026 Spruce Street, Philadelphia, Pa. ONE-MAN EXHIBITIONS: (first) Rehn Galleries, 1934, also 1937, 42, 48; Detroit/Institute, 1954; Smith College, 1940; PMA (two-man), 1946. RETROSPECTIVE: MOMA, 1950; PMA, 1964. GROUP: Corcoran; PAFA; Carnegie; Chicago/AI; WMAA. COLLECTIONS: Baltimore/MA; The Budd Co.; Buffalo/Albright; Corcoran; Courtauld Institute; Detroit/Institute; Harvard U.; Kansas City/Nelson; MMA; MOMA; Marquette U.; Newark Museum; PMA; U. of Pennsylvania; Phillips; Randolph-Macon Woman's College; Santa Barbara/MA; Smith College; WMAA; Wichita/AM. BIBLIOGRAPHY: Baur 7; Cahill and Barr, eds.; Clifford; Flexner; Goodrich and Baur 1; Pousette-Dart, ed.; Richardson; Wheeler; Wight 2.

WATTS, ROBERT M. b. June 14, 1923, Burlington, Iowa. STUDIED: U. of Louisville, 1944, B.Mech.Eng.; Columbia U., 1951, AM; ASL, with Stewart Klonis, John McPherson, Alex Katz, Morris Kantor, William Zorach. US Naval Reserve, 1941–46. Traveled Mexico, Europe, Caribbean. TAUGHT: Institute of Applied Arts and Sciences, Brooklyn, 1951–52; Rutgers U., 1952–53; Douglass College, 1953– . Changed from painting to sculpture, 1956; changed to light-sound-motion sculpture, 1957; first Events and Happenings, 1958. Designed costumes for James Waring Dance Co. AWARDS: Rutgers U. Research Fund Grant, 1961, 62, 63. ADDRESS: R. D. 2, Lebanon, N.J. DEALER: The Bianchini Gallery. ONE-MAN EXHIBITIONS: (first) Delacorte Gallery, NYC, 1958 (welded sculpture); Grand Central Moderns, 1960, 61; Douglass College Art Gallery, 1953, 57; U. of Alabama, 1957; Smolin Gallery, 1960 (Magic Kazoo), 1963; The Kornblee Gallery, 1963. GROUP EXHIBITIONS, EVENTS, HAPPENINGS: Newark Museum, New Jersey Artists, 1955; Montclair/AM, New Jersey State Annual, 1955, 56; American Abstract Artists, 1957; Martha Jackson Gallery, New Media—New Forms, II, 1961; Amsterdam/Stedelijk, Art in Motion, circ. Europe, 1961–62; MOMA, The Art of Assemblage, circ., 1961; Fluxus International Festival, 1962–63; WGMA, The Popular Image, 1963; Smolin Gallery, Yam Festival, A Series of Events, 1963; III Paris Biennial, Two Inches (event), 1963; Buffalo/Albright, Mixed Media and Pop Art, 1963; Dwan Gallery, Boxes, 1964; Douglass College, 1964. BIBLIOGRAPHY: Seitz 2.

WAYNE, JUNE. b. March 7, 1918, Chicago, Ill. Self-taught in art. Traveled Europe extensively. Founder and director of Tamarind Lithography Workshop, Inc., funded by the Program in Humanities and the Arts of the Ford Foundation. MEMBER: Artists Equity; Society of Washington Printmakers; The Print Club, Philadelphia; SAGA. FEDERAL A.P.: Easel painting. AWARDS: Los Angeles County Fair, P.P., 1950; Los Angeles/County MA, P.P., 1951; Library of Congress, Pennell P.P., 1953; Pasadena/AM, P.P., 1958, 59; The Print Club, Philadelphia, P.P., 1958; SAGA, Edna Pennypacker Stauffer Memorial Prize, 1963; and others. ADDRESS: 1365 Londonderry Place, Los Angeles, Calif. DEALER: Jake Zeitlin Gallery. ONE-MAN EXHIBITIONS: (first) Boulevard Gallery, Chicago, 1935; Mexico City/Nacional, 1936; Santa Barbara/MA, 1950, 53, 58; SFMA, 1950; Pasadena/AM, 1952; Chicago/AI, 1952; The Contemporaries, 1953; de Young, 1956; California Palace; Achenbach Foundation, 1958; Los Angeles/County MA, 1959; Long Beach/MA, 1959; Philadelphia Art Alliance, 1959. GROUP: Library of Congress; Brooklyn Museum; Seattle/AM; PAFA; U. of Illinois; Los Angeles/County MA; MMA; SAGA Annuals; MOMA, circ. (graphics); MOMA, Young American Printmakers, 1953; California State Fair; San Diego; Denver/AM; WMAA Annuals; Sao Paulo, 1955; Smithsonian; Achenbach Foundation; PCA, American Prints Today, circ., 1959–62; Paris/Moderne; The Japan Print Association, Japan, 1961; and

many others. COLLECTIONS: Achenbach Foundation; Bibliotheque Nationale; Bibliotheque Royale de Belgique; UCLA; U. of California, Santa Barbara; Chicago/AI; Cincinnati/AM; Columbia, S.C./MA; De Pauw U.; Fort Worth; Grunwald Foundation; Iowa State U.; La Jolla; Lehigh U.; Library of Congress; Los Angeles/County MA; MOMA; U. of Minnesota; NYPL; National Gallery; U. of New Mexico; Northwestern U.; PMA; Pasadena/AM; The Print Club, Philadelphia; San Diego; Santa Barbara/MA; Smithsonian; Walker. BIBLIOGRAPHY: Rodman 1, 3.

WEBER, HUGO. b. May 4, 1918, Basel, Switzerland. STUDIED: U. of Basel, 1942–46; Kunstgewerbeschule, Basel; Atelier Suter, Basel; Atelier Gimond, Paris, 1939; and with Aristede Maillol, Jean Arp, Alberto Giacometti, 1939–45. Swiss Army, 1939–41. Traveled USA, Canada, Europe; resided Paris. TAUGHT: Institute of Design, Chicago, 1946–55; Oslo, Norway, 1955; The Pennsylvania State U.; NYU, 1963– . Produced two films, "Vision in Flux," 1951, and "Process Documentation by the Painter," 1954. MEMBER: Abstract and Concrete Artists Alliance, 1947–53. COMMISSIONS: Container Corp. of America (bronze bust of Lincoln). ADDRESS: 797 Greenwich Street, NYC. DEALER: The Howard Wise Gallery, NYC. ONE-MAN EXHIBITIONS: (first) Colorado Springs/FA, 1951; Chicago/AI, 1951; Galerie 16, Zurich, 1952; Institute of Design, Chicago, 1952; Galerie Parnass, Wuppertal, 1952; Allan Frumkin Gallery, Chicago, 1953, 55; Betty Parsons Gallery, 1953, 55, 59; Galerie Hutter, Basel, 1963; American U., Beirut, Lebanon, 1954; B. C. Holland Gallery, 1961; Gres Gallery, Chicago, 1962; The Howard Wise Gallery, NYC, 1962, 63. GROUP: Kunsthalle, Basel, 1945, 56; Chicago/AI Annuals, 1947, 49; Toledo/MA, Sculpture Today, 1947; Salon des Realites Nouvelles, Paris, 1948, 58, 59; Chicago/AI, Directions in American Painting, 1951; SRGM, Younger American Painters, 1954; Salon des Comparaisons, Paris, 1956; Galerie Creuze, Paris, 50 Years of Abstract Painting, 1957; Galerie Arnaud, L'Art Moral, 1957; Palais des Beaux-Arts, Charleroi, Belgium, L'Arte de XXIeme Siecle, 1958; Zurich, 16 Basel Maler, 1960; Salon du Mai, Paris, 1961; Dayton/AI, International Selection, 1963. **COLLECTIONS:** Chicago/AI; Cincinnati/AM.

WEBER, MAX. b. April 18, 1881, Byalestok, Russia; **d.** October, 1961, Great Neck, N.Y. To USA 1891. STUDIED: Pratt Institute, 1898–1900, with Arthur Dow; Academie Julian, Paris, 1905–06, with Jean Paul Laurens; Academie de la Grande Chaumiere; Academie Colarossi, Paris, 1906–07. Traveled Europe extensively. TAUGHT: Lynchburg, Va., public schools, 1901–03; U. of Virginia (summer); State Normal School, Duluth, Minn., 1903–05; helped organize a class under Henri Matisse, Paris, 1907–08; White School of Photography, NYC, 1914–18; ASL, 1920–21, 1925–27; U. of Minnesota, 1931. MEMBER: Society of Independent Artists, NYC (Director, 1918–19);

American Artists Congress (National Chairman, 1937, Hon. National Chairman, 1938–40). AWARDS: Chicago/AI, Potter Palmer Gold Medal, 1928; PAFA, Joseph E. Temple Gold Medal, 1941; Corcoran, Third William A. Clark Prize, 1941; Chicago/AI, Ada S. Garrett Prize, 1941; Pepsi-Cola, Second Prize, 1945, 1946 ($500), 1947 ($750); Carnegie, Fourth Prize, 1946; La Tausca Competition, First Prize, 1946. **ONE-MAN EXHIBITIONS:** (first) Haas Gallery, NYC, 1909; Photo-Secession, NYC, 1911; Murray Hill Gallery, NYC, 1912; Ehrich Galleries, NYC, 1915; Santa Barbara/MA, 1947; WMAA, 1949; Walker, 1949; Pratt Institute, 1959; B'nai B'rith Gallery, Washington, D.C., 1961; Jones Gallery, Baltimore, 1915; Montross Gallery, NYC, 1915, 23; J. B. Neumann Gallery, NYC, 1924, 25, 27, 30, 35, 37;

Max Weber   *Acrobats. 1946*

The Downtown Gallery, 1928, 57, 58; P. Rosenberg and Co., 1942, 43, 45, 46, 47; A.A.A. Gallery, NYC, 1941; Baltimore/MA, 1942; Dayton/AI, 1938; Carnegie, 1943; California Palace, 1949; Jewish Museum, 1956; Weyhe Gallery, 1956; Brandeis U., 1957; Pomona College, Stieglitz Circle, 1958. RETROSPECTIVE: Newark Museum, 1913, 59; Galerie Bernheim-Jeune, Paris, 1924; MOMA, 1930; AAAL, Memorial, 1962; P. Rosenberg and Co., 1944; A.F.A., circ., 1953. GROUP: MOMA, Paintings by 19 Living Americans, 1929; Corcoran; Chicago/AI; MOMA; WMAA. COLLECTIONS: Andover/Phillips; Arizona State College; Baltimore/MA; Bezalel Museum; Brandeis U.; Britannica; Brooklyn Museum; Buffalo/Albright; California Palace; Carnegie; Chicago/AI; Cleveland/MA; Columbus; Cranbrook; Dartmouth College; Des Moines; Detroit/Institute; Fort Worth; Hartford/Wadsworth; Harvard U.; Howard U.; State U. of Iowa; Jewish Theological Seminary; Kansas City/Nelson; La Jolla; Los Angeles/County MA; MMA; MOMA; U. of Nebraska; Newark Museum; U. of North Carolina; PMA; Phillips; Sara Roby Foundation; San Antonio/McNay; San Diego; Santa Barbara/MA; Seattle/AM; Tel Aviv; Utica; Vassar College; WMAA; Walker; West Palm Beach/Norton; Wichita/AM; Youngstown/Butler. BIBLIOGRAPHY: American Artists Congress, Inc.; Barker 1; Baur 7; Bazin; Biddle 3; Blesh 1; Brown; Bulliet 1; **Cahill**; Cahill and Barr, eds.; Cassou; Cheney, M. C.; Christensen; Eliot; Flanagan; Flexner; Frost; Genauer; **Goodrich 8**; Goodrich and Baur 1; Haftman; Hartmann; Hess, T. B.; Hunter 5; *Index of 20th Century Artists;* Janis, S.; Kootz 1, 2; Lee and Burchwood; McCourbrey; McCurdy, ed.; Mellquist; Mendelowitz; Munsterberg; Newmeyer; Pagano; Pearson 1, 2; Phillips 1, 2; Poore; Pousette-Dart, ed.; Read 2; Richardson; Ringel, ed.; Ritchie 1; Rosenblum; Sachs; Smith, S. C. K.; Soby 5; Sutton; **Weber 1, 2**; Wight 2.

WEEKS, JAMES. b. December 1, 1922, Oakland, Calif. STUDIED: San Francisco Art Institute, 1940–42, with David Park; Nebraska State Teachers College, 1943; Hartwell School of Design, 1946–47; Escuela de Pintura y Escultura, Mexico City, 1951. US Army Air Force, 1942–45. TAUGHT: San Francisco Art Institute, 1947–50, 1958, 64; Hartwell School of Design, 1948–50; California College of Arts and Crafts, 1958–59. AWARDS: Abraham Rosenberg Foundation Fellowship, 1952; Howard U., 1961; California Palace, 1961, 62. ADDRESS: 2333 Jones, San Francisco, Calif. DEALERS: Felix Landau Gallery; Poindexter Gallery. ONE-MAN EXHIBITIONS: (first) Lucien Labaudt Gallery, 1951; California Palace, 1953; Gallery 6, San Francisco, 1955; The East-West Gallery, San Francisco, 1958; Poindexter Gallery, 1960, 61, 63; Felix Landau Gallery, 1964. GROUP: Los Angeles/County MA, 1957; Birmingham, Ala./MA, Figure Painting, 1961; California Palace, 1961, 62; Corcoran, 1961; State U. of Iowa, Five Decades of The Figure, 1962; Chicago/AI, 1963; Yale U., 1962; Houston/MFA, 1961, 62; La Jolla, 1963. COLLECTIONS: A.F.A.; Corcoran; Howard U.; Lytton Savings and Loan Association; SFMA.

WEINBERG, ELBERT. b. May 27, 1928, Hartford, Conn. STUDIED: Hartford Art School; RISD, 1951, BFA; Yale U., with Waldemar Raemisch, 1955, MFA. TAUGHT: RISD; Yale U.; Cooper Union. COMMISSIONS: Atlanta, Ga. (copper eagle for a façade); Alavath Achim Synagogue, Atlanta, Ga.; 405 Park Avenue, NYC (terra cotta mural); Jewish Museum, 1959 (sculpture for the garden). AWARDS: Prix de Rome, 1951–53; Guggenheim Foundation Fellowship, 1959; ICA, London/Tate, International Unknown Political Prisoner Competition, Hon. Men., 1953; *Progressive Architecture* Magazine, 1954; Yale U., Silver Medal for Achievement in the Arts, 1959. ADDRESS: 40 Academy Street, New Haven, Conn. DEALER: Grace Borgenicht Gallery Inc. ONE-MAN EXHIBITIONS: Grace Borgenicht Gallery Inc., 1959, 62; Providence (R.I.) Art Club, 1951, 54. GROUP: WMAA, 1935, 36, 57; Andover/Phillips, 1954; Silvermine Guild, 1954; Jewish Museum, 1954; ICA, Boston, 1957; Hartford/Wadsworth, Connecticut Artists, 1957; AAAL, 1958; A.F.A./USIA, Religious Art, circ. Europe, 1958–59; Chicago/AI, 1959, 61; MOMA, Recent Sculpture USA, 1959; Utica, 1960; WMAA Annuals, 1957, 58, 60; Boston Arts Festival, 1961; Carnegie, 1958, 61; PAFA, 1961; U. of Nebraska, 1958, 59, 61; Smithsonian, 1961. COLLECTIONS: Andover/Phillips; 405 Park Avenue, NYC; Hartford/Wadsworth; Jewish Museum; MOMA; RISD; WMAA; Yale U. BIBLIOGRAPHY: Chaet; Rodman 3.

WELLIVER, NEIL. b. July 22, 1929, Millville, Pa. STUDIED: Philadelphia Museum School, 1948–52, BFA; Yale U., with Josef Albers, James Brooks, Burgoyne Diller, Conrad Marca-Relli, 1953–54, MFA. Traveled Asia, Europe. TAUGHT: Yale U.; Cooper Union; U. of Pennsylvania. COMMISSIONS: Painted murals for the architect Paul Rudolph. AWARDS: NAD, Samuel F. B. Morse Fellowship, 1962. ADDRESS: 451 George Street, New Haven, Conn. DEALER: The Stable Gallery. ONE-MAN EXHIBITIONS: (first) Alexandra Grotto, Philadelphia, 1954; Boris Mirski Gallery, 1959; The Stable Gallery, 1962. GROUP: WMAA Annual; A.F.A., Wit and Whimsey in 20th Century Art, circ., 1962–63; Swarthmore College, Two Generations of American Art, 1964; PAFA Annual, 1962; Baltimore/MA, 1963.

WESSELMANN, TOM. b. February 23, 1931, Cincinnati, Ohio. STUDIED: Hiram College; U. of Cincinnati, BA (Psychology); Art Academy of Cincinnati; Cooper Union, with Nicholas Marsicano. ADDRESS: 157 Bleecker Street, NYC. ONE-MAN EXHIBITIONS: (first) Tanager Gallery, NYC, 1961; The Green Gallery, NYC, 1962, 64. GROUP: Sidney Janis Gallery, The New Realists, 1962; Dwan Gallery, 1962, 64; Ileana Sonnabend (Gallery), Paris, 1963; ICA, London, 1963; MOMA, Recent Painting USA: The Figure, circ., 1962–63; WGMA, The Popular Image, 1963; Buffalo/Albright, Mixed Media and Pop Art, 1963; Stockholm/National, 1964; Chicago/AI, 1964. COLLECTIONS: Brandeis U.; Buffalo/Albright; MOMA; U. of Nebraska.

WESTERMANN, H. C. b. December 11, 1922, Los Angeles, Calif. STUDIED: Chicago Art Institute School, 1947–54. US Marine Corps, World War II. Traveled the Orient. ADDRESS: Brookfield Center, Conn. DEALER: Allan Frumkin Gallery, NYC and Chicago. ONE-MAN EXHIBITIONS: (first) Allan Frumkin Gallery, Chicago, 1957, also 1962; Allan Frumkin Gallery, NYC, 1961, 63; Dilexi Gallery, Los Angeles, 1962; Dilexi Gallery, San Francisco, 1963. GROUP: Chicago/AI; Tate, 1964; Houston/MFA; Hartford/Wadsworth; Chicago/AI, Exhibition Momentum; A.F.A.; MOMA, The Art of Assemblage, circ., 1961; MOMA, New Images of Man, 1959; U. of Illinois, 1961; WMAA, 1964. COLLECTIONS: Chicago/AI; Hartford/Wads-

H. C. Westermann   *The Suicide. 1964*

worth; Pasadena/AM. BIBLIOGRAPHY: Janis and Blesh 1; Seitz 2.

WIEGHARDT, PAUL. b. August 26, 1897, Germany. STUDIED: School of Fine Arts, Cologne; Bauhaus, Weimar, with Paul Klee; Academy of Fine Arts, Dresden. TAUGHT: Chicago Art Institute School, 1946– ; Illinois Institute of Technology, 1950– . ADDRESS: c/o Chicago Art Institute School, Chicago 3, Ill. ONE-MAN EXHIBITIONS: Pittsfield/Berkshire, 1941; Harvard U.; St. Paul Gallery; Phillips; M. Knoedler & Co., NYC; Springfield, Mass./MFA; Chicago/AI; Illinois Institute of Technology; Syracuse U.; Milwaukee; Hagen; U. of Arizona; 1920 Art Center, Chicago. GROUP: Salon d'Automne, Paris; Salon des Tuileries, Paris; Salon des Artistes Independants, Paris; Exposition Nationale, Paris; Chicago/AI; PAFA; Library of Congress; Stanford U.; U. of Illinois. COLLECTIONS: Barnes Foundation; Buffalo/Albright; Phillips; Pittsfield/Berkshire; Smith College.

WILDE, JOHN. b. December 12, 1919, Milwaukee, Wisc. STUDIED: U. of Wisconsin, 1947,

MA. TAUGHT: U. of Wisconsin, 1948– . AD-
DRESS: Evansville, Wisc. DEALERS: Durlacher
Brothers; Frank Oehlschlaeger Gallery, Chi-
cago; Bresler Galleries Inc.; Arnold Finkel
Gallery; Lane Gallery; Gump's Gallery. ONE-
MAN EXHIBITIONS: (first) U. of Wisconsin, 1942;
David Porter Gallery, Washington, D.C., 1944;
Kalamazoo/Institute, 1945; Layton School of
Art, 1947; Milwaukee, 1948, 59; Pennsylvania
College for Women, 1949; Hewitt Gallery,
NYC, 1950, 53, 55; Bresler Galleries Inc., 1949,
51, 53, 55, 58, 61, 63; Columbia, S.C./MA,
1960; Newman Brown, Chicago, 1953; Lane
Gallery, 1960; Robert Isaacson Gallery, NYC,
1959, 61; U. of Wisconsin, Milwaukee, 1960;
Durlacher Brothers, 1963. GROUP: Hallmark
Art Award, 1955, 58; WMAA, 1950, 52, 53, 55,
56, 58, 60, 62; MMA, 52 Americans Under 35,
1954; MOMA, Recent Drawings USA, 1956;
Art:USA:Now, circ., 1962– ; Walker, 1947,
49, 51, 62; A.F.A., American Watercolors, 1949;
Chicago/AI, 1940, 41, 42, 51, 52, 54; Den-
ver/AM, 1955, 56; PAFA, 1941, 46, 50, 52, 53,
58, 59, 60, 62; Detroit/Institute, 1959; Youngs-
town/Butler, 1953, 55, 57; Chicago/AI, Abstract and Surrealist Art, 1948; U. of Illinois,
1948, 52, 55, 57, 58, 61, 63; Walker, Reality
and Fantasy, 1954; MMA, 1950; Corcoran,
1953; Carnegie, 1958. COLLECTIONS: Carnegie;
Chicago/AI; De Beers Collection; Detroit/In-
stitute; Hartford/Wadsworth; S. C. Johnson &
Son, Inc.; Marquette U.; Milwaukee; Milwaukee *Journal;* U. of Nebraska; Neenah/Berg-
strom; PAFA; Sara Roby Foundation; St. Paul
Gallery; Santa Barbara/MA; WMAA; Walker;
Washington Federal Bank, Miami; U. of Wisconsin; Worcester/AM. BIBLIOGRAPHY: Nordness, ed.

WILEY, WILLIAM T. b. October, 1937, Bed-
ford, Ind. STUDIED: California School of Fine
Arts, 1956–60, BFA. TAUGHT: U. of California,
Davis, 1962– . AWARDS: SFMA, First Prize,
1960; Oakland/AM, cash award, 1961; Chi-
cago/AI, First Prize and Guest of Honor
Award, 1961; CSFA, Painting Award, 1959,
and Fletcher Award, 1960. ADDRESS: Muri
Beach, Sausalito, Calif. DEALER: Staempfli
Gallery. ONE-MAN EXHIBITIONS: Staempfli
Gallery, 1960; RAC, 1960. GROUP: SFMA,
1959, 60; RAC, 1959, 60; San Francisco Art
Festival, 1960; Chicago/AI, 1961; U. of Illinois,
1961; U. of Nebraska, 1961; California Palace,
1961; WMAA, Young America, 1960; WMAA,
Fifty California Artists, 1962. COLLECTIONS:
SFMA; WMAA.

WILKE, ULFERT S. b. July 14, 1907, Bad
Toelz, Germany. STUDIED: Arts and Crafts
School, Brunswick, 1924–25; privately with

William T. Wiley   *Columbus Rerouted #3. 1963.*

Willy Jaeckel, 1923; Academie de la Grande Chaumiere, 1927–28; Academie Ranson, Paris, 1927–28; Harvard U. Graduate School, 1940–41; State U. of Iowa, 1946–47, MA. Traveled Europe extensively, Japan. US citizen 1943. US Army, 1942–45. TAUGHT: Kalamazoo College, 1940–42; Springfield (Ill.) Art Association, 1946–47; State U. of Iowa, 1947–48; U. of Louisville, 1948–55, 1958–59, 1961–62; U. of Georgia, 1955–56; Douglass College, 1963– . AWARDS: Albrecht Durer Prize, 1928; New Orleans/Delgado, First Prize, 1928; US Army Arts Contest, Gold Medal, 1945; Louisville Art Center Annual Exhibition, First Prize, Painting, 1951; Georgia Museum of Art, P.P., 1956; Guggenheim Foundation Fellowship, 1959, 60. ADDRESS: 100 West 55 Street, NYC. DEALERS: Kraushaar Galleries; David Stuart Gallery. ONE-MAN EXHIBITIONS: (first) a gallery in Germany, 1927; Brunswick Castle, 1929; Anton Ullrich Museum, Brunswick, 1933; Westermann Gallery, NYC, 1939; Harvard U., 1940; Denver/AM, 1943; Springfield (Ill.) Art Association, 1946; Decatur, 1947; Kalamazoo/Institute, 1947; Muhlenberg College, 1947; Memphis Academy of Arts, 1948; U. of Louisville, 1948; Santa Barbara/MA, 1949; Sweet Briar College, 1949; U. of Nebraska, 1949; The Little Gallery, Louisville, 1950, 53; Kunstverein Hannover, 1952; Kraushaar Galleries, 1958, 60; Tulane U., 1958; Yamada Gallery, Kyoto, 1958; de Young, 1959; Dallas/MFA, 1960; American Academy, Rome, 1960; Primus-Stuart Gallery, Los Angeles, 1961; Rutgers U., 1963. GROUP: Academy of Fine Arts, Berlin, 1929, 31; Life Magazine, War Art, circ. USA, 1942; Chicago/AI, 1943–47; MMA, 1952; SRGM, Younger American Painters, 1954; Brooklyn Museum, 1955, 56, 57, 58, 61; Smithsonian, Italy Rediscovered, circ. USA, 1955–56; MOMA, Lettering by Hand, 1962. COLLECTIONS: Aetna Oil Co.; Brandeis U.; Brunswick; Buffalo/Albright; Carnegie; Chase Manhattan Bank; Citizens Fidelity Bank, Louisville; Cooper Union; Dayton/AI; Decatur; U. of Georgia; Hartford/Wadsworth; Honolulu Academy; U. of Illinois; State U. of Iowa; Kultusministerium; Louisiana State U.; Mills College; Minneapolis/Institute; U. of Notre Dame; Nurnberg; Omaha/Joslyn; PMA; Phoenix; Pratt Institute; Seagram Collection; Stanford U. BIBLIOGRAPHY: Seldis and Wilke; Wilke.

WILLIAMS, HIRAM. b. February 11, 1917, Indianapolis, Ind. STUDIED: The Pennsylvania State U., with Hobson Pittman, 1949–50, BS, 1951, M.Ed.; ASL, 1939, with Jean Charlot, Robert Brackman. US Army, 1941–45. TAUGHT: The Pennsylvania State U.; U. of California; U. of Texas; U. of Florida. AWARDS: Guggenheim Foundation Fellowship, 1963; U. of Texas Research Grant, 1958; Texas State Fair, D. D. Feldman Award, 1956, 58, 59. ADDRESS: 2008 N.W. Third Avenue, Gainesville, Fla. ONE-MAN EXHIBITIONS: (first) Nye Gallery, Dallas, 1958, also 1960; Laguna Gloria Gallery, Austin, Tex., 1959; Lee Nordness Gallery, NYC, 1960, 63; Cushman Gallery, Houston, 1959; Felix Landau Gallery, 1959. GROUP: PMA, 1951; Austin, 1955, 57; MOMA, 1960; WMAA Annual, 1960; Corcoran, 1961; SFMA, 1963; Houston/MFA, The Emerging Figure, 1961; Carnegie, 1964; PAFA, 1960, 63; MOMA, Recent Painting USA: The Figure, circ., 1962–63; U. of Illinois. COLLECTIONS: Allentown/AM; Corcoran; S. C. Johnson & Son, Inc.; MOMA; PAFA; The Pennsylvania State U.; Ringling; Wilmington. BIBLIOGRAPHY: Nordness, ed.; Williams, H.

WILSON, JANE. b. April 29, 1924, Seymour, Iowa. STUDIED: State U. of Iowa, with Stuart Edie, James Lechay, Mauricio Lasansky, 1945, BA, PBK, 1947, MA (Painting). Traveled Mexico, USA extensively. TAUGHT: State U. of Iowa. AWARDS: Ingram Merrill Foundation Grant, 1963. ADDRESS: 317 East 10 Street, NYC. DEALER: Tibor de Nagy Gallery. ONE-MAN EXHIBITIONS: (first) Hansa Gallery, NYC, 1953, also 1955, 57; Esther Stuttman Gallery, NYC, 1958, 59; Tibor de Nagy Gallery, 1960, 61, 62, 63, 64; Gump's Gallery, 1963; Esther Baer Gallery, 1964; St. John's College, Annapolis, Md., 1951. GROUP: Chicago/AI, 1946; The Stable Gallery Annuals, 1951, 52; MOMA, New Talent, circ., 1957–59; WMAA Annual, 1962; A.F.A., circ., 1963; MIT; Corcoran; New York World's Fair, 1964–65. COLLECTIONS: Chase Manhattan Bank; Corcoran; Hartford/Wadsworth; MOMA; NYU; Rockefeller Institute; The Singer Company Inc.; Uris Buildings Corp.; WMAA.

WINES, JAMES. b. June 27, 1932, Chicago, Ill. STUDIED: Syracuse U., with Ivan Mestrovic, 1950–55, BA. Traveled Europe, USA; resided

James Wines   *Suspended Disc II. 1963*

Rome, 1956–62. **TAUGHT:** School of Visual Arts, NYC, 1963–64. **COMMISSIONS:** Hoffman-La Roche Pharmaceutical Co. (3 large sculptures for New Jersey offices), to be completed 1965. **AWARDS:** Pulitzer Fellowship, 1953; Prix de Rome, 1956; Guggenheim Foundation Fellowship, 1962; Ford Foundation Grant, 1964. **ADDRESS:** 3 Washington Square Village, NYC. **DEALER:** Marlborough-Gerson Gallery Inc. **ONE-MAN EXHIBITIONS:** (first) Baltimore/MA, 1958; Silvan Simone Gallery, Los Angeles, 1958, 59, 61; National Academy of Istanbul, Turkey, 1956; Otto Gerson Gallery, NYC, 1960, 62; Galleria Trastevere di Topazia Alliata, Rome, 1960, 61; Alphonse Chave, Vence, France, 1960; Syracuse U., 1962; Walker, 1964. **GROUP:** MOMA, Recent Sculpture USA, 1959; WMAA Annuals, 1958, 60, 62; Baltimore/MA, 1952, 53, 54; Syracuse/Everson, 1951, 52, 53, 54, 63; Los Angeles/County MA, 1958; Sacramento Arts Festival, 1958; VII Sao Paulo Biennial, 1963; Uffizi Loggia, Florence, Italy, 1957; Museum des 20. Jahrhunderts; Chicago/AI, 1959, 63; U. of Illinois; Amsterdam/Stedelijk; Carnegie, 1961. **COLLECTIONS:** Amster-

dam/Stedelijk; Chicago/AI; Columbia Broadcasting System; Currier; Kansas City/Nelson; Los Angeles/County MA; Museum des 20. Jahrhunderts; Syracuse/Everson; WMAA; Walker. **BIBLIOGRAPHY:** Goodrich and Baur 1.

WOELFFER, EMERSON. b. July 27, 1914, Chicago, Ill. **STUDIED:** Chicago Art Institute School, with Francis Chapin, Boris Anisfeld, 1935, BA. US Air Force, 1939–42. Traveled USA, Mexico and Europe extensively. **TAUGHT:** Chouinard Art Institute, Los Angeles, 1959– ; New Bauhaus, Chicago, 1941–49; Black Mountain College, 1949; Colorado Springs Fine Arts Center; Southern Illinois U., 1962. **FEDERAL A.P.:** Easel painting and project assistant. **AWARDS:** SFMA, Hon. Men., 1948; Chicago/AI, Pauline Palmer Prize, 1948; Tamarind Fellowship, 1961. **ADDRESS:** 475 Dustin Drive, Los Angeles, Calif. **DEALERS:** David Stuart Gallery; Charles Egan Gallery. **ONE-MAN EXHIBITIONS:** (first) 740 Gallery, Chicago, 1946; Chicago/AI, 1951, Artists' Gallery, NYC, 1951, 54; La Jolla, 1962; Margaret Brown Gallery, Boston, 1951; Paul Kantor Gallery, 1956, 60; Bennington College, 1938; Black Mountain College, 1949; Poindexter Gallery, 1959, 61; Primus-Stuart Gallery, Los Angeles, 1961. **RETROSPECTIVE:** Pasadena/AM, 1962. **GROUP:** MIT, Four Americans, 1952; Carnegie, 1952, 54, 55, 58; WMAA, Six American Painters; WMAA, 1947, 49; ICA, Boston, 1950; Salon des Realites Nouvelles, Paris, 1948; SRGM, 1962; Corcoran, 1952; Houston/MFA, 1957; WMAA, Fifty California Artists, 1962–63. **COLLECTIONS:** Chicago/AI; U. of Illinois; La Jolla; Los Angeles/County MA; MOMA; New Orleans/Delgado; Pasadena/AM; Raleigh/NCMA; WMAA. **BIBLIOGRAPHY:** Woelffer.

WOLFF, ROBERT JAY. b. July 27, 1905, Chicago, Ill. **STUDIED:** Yale U., 1923–26; Academie des Beaux-Arts, Paris, with Henri Bouchard; and privately with Georges Mouveau in Paris. US Army and Air Force, 1942–45; US Naval Reserve. Traveled Europe extensively, 1921–31; resided Paris, 1929–31. **TAUGHT:** A founding collaborator, with Lazlo Moholy-Nagy and Gyorgy Kepes, of the Institute of Design, Chicago, 1938–42; Brooklyn College, 1946– ; MIT, 1961; Harvard U., 1961; U. of Wisconsin, 1955. **MEMBER:** American Abstract Artists, 1937–50. **FEDERAL A.P.:** Illinois State

Supervisor of Painting, 1937. **AWARDS:** Chicago/AI, Robert Jenkins Prize, 1933. **ADDRESS:** Garland Road, New Preston, Conn. **ONE-MAN EXHIBITIONS:** Chicago/AI, 1934 (first sculpture shown); Reinhardt Galleries, NYC, 1935 (sculpture); Quest Gallery, Chicago, 1936 (first paintings shown); Karl Nierendorf Gallery, NYC, 1937; Katherine Kuh Gallery, Chicago, 1938, 39; Kleemann Gallery, NYC, 1947, 48; Saidenberg Gallery, 1953, 54; Grace Borgenicht Gallery Inc., 1956, 58; SRGM, 1952; SFMA, 1940; MOMA, Elements of Design, circ., 1947. **GROUP:** American Abstract Artists Annuals, 1937–50; Corcoran; WMAA; PAFA; U. of Illinois; U. of Nebraska; SFMA; MIT. **COLLECTIONS:** Brooklyn Museum; SRGM. **BIBLIOGRAPHY:** Baur 7; Cheney, M. C.; Janis, S.

WOLFSON, SIDNEY. b. June 18, 1914, Brooklyn, N.Y. **STUDIED:** Pratt Institute, with George Bridgeman, Denman W. Ross, Oronzio Maldarelli, Ogden Pleissner. US Air Force, four years. Traveled Caribbean and Latin America extensively. **ADDRESS:** Salt Point, N.Y. **DEALER:** World House Galleries. **ONE-MAN EXHIBITIONS:** (first) Three Arts Gallery, Poughkeepsie, 1952; Salisbury (Conn.) Public Library; Pittsfield/Berkshire; Betty Parsons Section Eleven (Gallery), NYC, 1959, 61; World House Galleries, 1964. **RETROSPECTIVE:** Bennington College, 1962. **GROUP:** ART:USA, NYC; A. Tooth & Sons, Six American Painters, 1961; WMAA, Geometric Abstraction in America, circ., 1962; Carnegie; Helmhaus Gallery, Zurich, Konkrete Kunst, 1960; U. of St. Thomas, Art Has Many Facets; Syracuse U., Modern Classicism. **COLLECTIONS:** Colgate U.; Stony Brook; WMAA.

WONNER, PAUL JOHN. b. April 24, 1920, Tucson, Ariz. **STUDIED:** California College of Arts and Crafts, 1937–41, BA; ASL, 1947; U. of California, Berkeley, 1950–53, MA, 1955, MLS. US Army, 1941–45. Traveled Europe. **ADDRESS:** 3854 Rambla Orienta, Malibu, Calif. **DEALERS:** Felix Landau Gallery; Poindexter Gallery; Waddington Gallery. **ONE-MAN EXHIBITIONS:** (first) de Young, 1955; San Francisco Art Association, 1956; Felix Landau Gallery, 1959, 60, 62, 63, 64; Santa Barbara/MA, 1960; California Palace, 1961; Poindexter Gallery, 1962, 64; Esther Baer Gallery (two-man), 1964. **GROUP:** SRGM, Younger American Painters, 1954; III Sao Paulo Biennial, 1955; Walker,

Vanguard, 1955; Oakland/AM, Contemporary Bay Area Figurative Painting, 1957; Carnegie, 1958, 64; Festival of Two Worlds, Spoleto, 1958; WMAA Annual, 1959; ART:USA:59, NYC, 1959; Chicago/AI Annuals, 1961, 64; U. of Illinois, 1961, 63; VMFA, American Painting, 1962; MOMA, Recent Painting USA: The Figure, circ., 1962–63; Denver/AM, 1964. **COLLECTIONS:** S. C. Johnson & Son, Inc.; Lytton Savings and Loan Association; *Readers Digest;* SFMA; SRGM. **BIBLIOGRAPHY:** Nordness, ed.

WOOD, GRANT. b. February 13, 1891, Anamosa, Iowa; **d.** February 12, 1942, Iowa City, Iowa. **STUDIED:** State U. of Iowa; Minneapolis School of Design; Academie Julian, Paris. US Army, 1918–19. Traveled Germany, France. **TAUGHT:** Rosedale, Iowa, 1911–12; Jackson, Iowa, 1919–23; Chicago Art Institute School, 1916; State U. of Iowa, 1934–42. **MEMBER:** NAD; National Society of Mural Painters. **FEDERAL A.P.:** Director, Iowa Division, 1934. **COMMISSIONS:** Cedar Rapids (Iowa) Memorial Building, 1926–28 (stained glass window). **AWARDS:** Iowa State Fair, First Prize, 1929, 30, 31, 32; Carnegie, 1934; Hon. Ph.D., U. of Wisconsin; Hon. MA, Wesleyan U.; Hon. DFA, Lawrence College; Hon. DFA, Northwestern U. **ONE-MAN EXHIBITIONS:** Ferargil Galleries, NYC, 1935; Lakeside Press Gallery, Chicago, 1935; Hudson D. Walker Gallery, NYC, 1936. **RETROSPECTIVE:** U. of Kansas, 1959. **GROUP:** Chicago/AI, 1930; Carnegie, 1934; Iowa State Fair; WMAA. **COLLECTIONS:** Abbott Laboratories; Cedar Rapids/AA; Chicago/AI; Dubuque/AA; MMA; U. of Nebraska; Omaha/Joslyn; Terre Haute/Swope; WMAA. **BIBLIOGRAPHY:** Barr 3; Baur 7; Bazin; Beam; Biddle 3; Blanchard; Blesh 1; Boswell 1; Brown; Canaday; Cheney, M. C.; Christensen; Craven 2; Eliot; Finkelstein; Flanagan; **Garwood;** Gaunt; Goodrich and Baur 1; Haftman; Hall; Hunter 5; *Index of 20th Century Artists;* Kent, R., ed.; Kootz 2; Kouvenhoven; Lee and Burchwood; McCurdy, ed.; Mellquist; Mendelowitz; Newmeyer; Pagano; Pearson 1; Reese; Richardson; **Rinard and Pyle;** Wight 2.

WYETH, ANDREW. b. July 21, 1917, Chadds Ford, Pa. **STUDIED** with N. C. Wyeth. **MEMBER:** NAD; Audubon Artists; NIAL; AAAL.

AWARDS: Hon. DFA, Harvard U., 1955; Hon. DFA, Colby College, 1955; Hon. DFA, Dickinson College, 1958; Hon. DFA, Swarthmore College, 1958; AAAL, Medal of Merit, 1947. ADDRESS: Chadds Ford, Pa. DEALER: M. Knoedler & Co., NYC. ONE-MAN EXHIBITIONS: (first) Macbeth Gallery, NYC, 1937, also 1941, 43, 45, 50, 52; M. Knoedler & Co., NYC, 1953; Buffalo/Albright, 1962; Currier, 1951. GROUP: Brussels World's Fair, 1958; PAFA, 1947; A.F.A., 1954; Houston/MFA; MOMA; WMAA; PMA; Wilmington. COLLECTIONS: Andover/Phillips; California Palace; Chicago/AI; Colby College; Currier; Dallas/MFA; Hartford/Wadsworth; Houston/MFA; MOMA; McDonnell & Co. Inc.; Montclair/AM; National Gallery; U. of Nebraska; New London; Omaha/Joslyn; Oslo/National; PMA; Utica; Wilmington; Winston-Salem Public Library. BIBLIOGRAPHY: *Andrew Wyeth;* Barker 1; Baur 7; Bazin; Canaday; Eliot; Flanagan; Gaunt; Hunter 5; McCurdy, ed.; Mendelowitz; Nordness, ed.; Pousette-Dart, ed.; Richardson; Rodman 1, 3; Sachs; Watson 1.

XCERON, JEAN. b. February 24, 1890, Isari, Greece. To USA 1904. STUDIED: The Corcoran School of Art, 1910–16, with George Lohr, Abraham Rattner. Resided Paris, 1927–37. Art reviewer for American newspapers from Paris, 1930–34. MEMBER: American Abstract Artists; Federation of Modern Painters and Sculptors. FEDERAL A.P.: Christian Science Chapel, Rikers Island, NYC, 1941–42 (murals). COMMISSIONS: U. of Georgia, 1947. AWARDS: U. of Illinois, P.P., 1951. ADDRESS: 54 West 74 Street, NYC. DEALER: Rose Fried Gallery. ONE-MAN EXHIBITIONS: (first) Galerie de France, 1931 (sponsored by *Cahiers d'Art*); Galerie Percier, Paris, 1933; Galerie Pierre, Paris, 1934; Garland Gallery, NYC, 1935; Karl Nierendorf Gallery, NYC, 1938; Bennington College, 1944; Sidney Janis Gallery, 1950; Rose Fried Gallery, 1955, 57, 60, 61, 62, 63, 64. RETROSPECTIVE: Jean Xceron, circ. seven museums in the Southwest and West Coast, 1948–49; SRGM, 1952. GROUP: Independent Artists, NYC, 1921–24; Salon des Surindependants, Paris, 1931–35; New York World's Fair, 1939; Golden Gate International Exposition, San Francisco, 1939; SRGM, 1939–52, 1954, 55, 56, 58, 62; American Abstract Artists, 1941–44, 1951–57; Carnegie, 1942, 43, 44, 46, 47, 48, 49, 50; Federation of Modern Painters and Sculptors, 1945, 46, 48, 49, 50, 51, 53, 54, 55, 56; California Palace; WMAA Annuals, 1946, 49, 52, 56; Salon des Realites Nouvelles, Paris, annually, 1947–52; U. of Illinois, 1948, 49, 50, 52, 55, 57; Houston/MFA, The Sphere of Mondrian, 1957; MOMA, circ. Latin America, 1963–64. COLLECTIONS: Andover/Phillips; Brandeis U.; Carnegie; U. of Georgia; U. of Illinois; Karlsruhe; MOMA; NYU; U. of New Mexico; Phillips; Pittsfield/Berkshire; SRGM; Smith College; WMAA; Washington U.; Wellesley College. BIBLIOGRAPHY: Bethers; Blanchard; Hess, T. B.; Janis and Blesh 1; Kootz 2; Pousette-Dart, ed.

YEKTAI, MANOUCHER. b. December 22, 1922, Teheran, Iran. STUDIED with Amedee Ozenfant and Robert Hale, 1945; Academie des Beaux-Arts, Paris, 1946, with Andre Lhote. ADDRESS: 25 East 67 Street, NYC. DEALER: Poindexter Gallery. ONE-MAN EXHIBITIONS: Grace Borgenicht Gallery Inc., 1952, also 1953, 54; A.A.A. Gallery, NYC, 1956; Poindexter Gallery, 1957, 59, 60, 62; Galerie Anderson-Mayer, 1963; Galerie Semiha Huber, Zurich, 1963; Piccadilly Gallery, London, 1963; Felix Landau Gallery, 1963. GROUP: Walker, 60 American Painters, 1960; Carnegie, 1961; USIA, Paris, 1961; MOMA, Recent Painting USA: The Figure, circ., 1962–63; Chicago/AI, Directions in American Painting, 1963; Paris/Moderne, 1963. COLLECTIONS: Baltimore/MA; Charleston/Carolina; MOMA; Syracuse/Everson; Union Carbide Corp.

YOUNGERMAN, JACK. b. March 25, 1926, Louisville, Ky. STUDIED: U. of North Carolina (US Navy Training Program), 1944–46; U. of Missouri, 1947, BA; Academie des Beaux-Arts, Paris, 1947–48. Traveled Europe, Near East; resided Europe, 1947–54. Designed stage sets for *Histoire de Vasco*, produced by Jean-Louis Barrault, Paris, 1956, and *Deathwatch*, by Jean Genet, NYC, 1958. AWARDS: *Art In America* (Magazine), New Talent, 1959. ADDRESS: 123 Fulton Street, NYC. DEALER: Betty Parsons Gallery. ONE-MAN EXHIBITIONS: Galerie Arnaud, 1951; Betty Parsons Gallery, 1957, 60, 61, 64; Galerie Lawrence, 1962; Galleria dell'Ariete, Milan, 1962; Everett Ellin Gallery, Los Angeles, 1963; Gres Gallery, Washington, D.C. (two-man), 1957. GROUP: Galerie Maeght, Les Mains Eblories, 1950; Galerie

Denise Rene, Paris, 1952; Carnegie, 1958, 61; Corcoran, 1959, 62; SRGM, Abstract Expressionists and Imagists, 1961; Kimura Gallery, Tokyo, American Painters, 1960; Chicago/AI, 1961, 62; MOMA, Recent American Painting and Sculpture, circ. USA and Canada, 1961–62; MOMA, Sixteen Americans, circ., 1959; Seattle World's Fair, 1962; International Biennial Exhibition of Paintings, Tokyo. COLLECTIONS: Buffalo/Albright; Chase Manhattan Bank; Chicago/AI; Equitable Life Assurance Society; S. C. Johnson & Son, Inc.; MOMA; Reynolds Metals Co. BIBLIOGRAPHY: Nordness, ed.

YUNKERS, ADJA. b. July 15, 1900, Riga, Latvia. STUDIED art in Leningrad, Berlin, Paris, and London. Traveled the world extensively; resided Paris, 14 years, Stockholm during World War II. Edited and published art maga-

Jack Youngerman   *Palma. 1964*

zines *ARS* and *Creation* in Sweden, 1942–45. To USA 1947; became a citizen. TAUGHT: U. of New Mexico, summers, 1948, 49; New School for Social Research, 1947–54; Cooper Union, 1959– . AWARDS: Guggenheim Foundation Fellowship, 1949; Ford Foundation, 1959; Chicago/AI, Norman Wait Harris Medal, 1961; Tamarind Fellowship, 1961. ADDRESS: 217 East 11 Street, NYC. DEALER: Andre Emmerich Gallery, NYC. ONE-MAN EXHIBITIONS: (first) Maria Kunde Gallery, Hamburg, 1921 or 1922; Galerie Per, Oslo; Tokanten (Gallery), Copenhagen, 1947–54; Kleemann Gallery, NYC; Corcoran; Smithsonian; Chicago/AI; Pasadena/AM; Colorado Springs/FA; Grace Borgenicht Gallery Inc., 1954, 55; Studio Paul Facchetti, Paris; Galleria Schneider, Rome; Zwemmer Gallery, London, 1957–59; Los Angeles/County MA; Rose Fried Gallery; The Howard Wise Gallery, Cleveland; Andre Emmerich Gallery, NYC; Salon des Realites Nouvelles, Paris, 1955. COLLECTIONS: Arts Council of Great Britain; Atlanta/AA; Baltimore/MA; Basel; Bibliotheque Nationale; Bibliotheque Royale de Belgique; Boston/MFA; Brooklyn Museum; UCLA; Carnegie; Cleveland/MA; Colorado Springs/FA; Corcoran; Hamburg; Harvard U.; Johannesburg/Municipal; Library of Congress; Louisville/Speed; MMA; MOMA; Memphis/Brooks; Minneapolis/Institute; NYPL; National Gallery; Oslo/National; PMA; The Print Club, Philadelphia; Rijksmuseum Amsterdam; Riverside Museum; SRGM; Sao Paulo; Springfield, Mass./MFA; Stockholm/National; Victoria and Albert Museum; WMAA; Wellesley College; Worcester/AM. BIBLIOGRAPHY: Goodrich and Baur 1; Nordness, ed.; Read 2.

Z

ZACHARIAS, ATHOS. b. June 17, 1927, Marlborough, Mass. STUDIED: RISD, 1952, BFA; Cranbrook Academy of Art, with Yasuo Kuniyoshi, 1953, MFA. Traveled Greece, eastern USA. TAUGHT: Brown U., 1953–55; Parsons School of Design, 1963– . COMMISSIONS: Fram Corporation, 1963 (painting of explorer ship *Fram*). AWARDS: Scholarship to RISD, 1950; Longview Foundation Grant, 1962; Guild Hall, First and Second Prizes. ADDRESS: 141 Copeces Lane, Springs, East Hampton, N.Y. DEALER: Bob Keene. ONE-MAN EXHIBITIONS: (first) Brown U., 1954; Great Jones Gallery, NYC, 1960; Joachim Gallery, Chicago, 1961; Gallery Mayer, NYC, 1961; Bob Keene, 1961, 62, 63, 64; Louis Alexander Gallery, NYC, 1962. GROUP: Boston Arts Festival, 1954; ART:USA:59, NYC, 1959; Raleigh/NCMA, 1959; Pan-Pacific Exhibition, circ. Japan, 1961. COLLECTIONS: ICA, Boston; Kalamazoo/Institute; RISD.

ZAJAC, JACK. b. December 13, 1929, Youngstown, Ohio. STUDIED: Scripps College, 1949–53, with Millard Sheets, Henry McFee, Sueo Serisawa. Traveled the world extensively. Changed from painting to sculpture, 1955. TAUGHT: Pomona College, 1959. AWARDS: California State Scholarship, 1950; Prix de Rome, 1954, 56, 57; Guggenheim Foundation Fellowship, 1959; AAAL, 1958; Youngstown/Butler, Second Prize, 1950; Pasadena/AM, P.P., 1951; Los Angeles/County MA, P.P., 1953, 58; Limited Editions Club, $2,500 Prize for Etching, 1959; Sarasota Art Association, Prize for Sculpture, 1959; Grace Cathedral, San Francisco, Art in Religion, First Prize, 1960; National Religious Art Exhibition, Birmingham, Mich., 1962. ADDRESS: Via Fratelli Bandiera 10, Rome, Italy. DEALERS: Felix Landau Gallery; Pogliani Gallery; Devorah Sherman Gallery. ONE-MAN EXHIBITIONS: (first) Pasadena/AM, 1951; Felix Landau Gallery, 1951, 53, 54, 56, 58, 60, 62, 63; Santa Barbara/MA, 1953; Scripps College, 1955; Galleria Schneider, Rome, 1955; John Young Gallery, Honolulu, 1956; Il Segno, Rome, 1957; The Downtown Gallery, 1960; Devorah Sherman Gallery, 1960; Roland, Browse and Delbanco, London, 1960; Gallery Marcus, Laguna Beach, Calif., 1961. GROUP: Santa Barbara/MA, 1959; Los Angeles/County MA, 1959, 60; WMAA Annual, 1959; Chicago/AI Annual, 1959; MOMA, Recent Sculpture USA, 1959; Claude Bernard, Paris, Aspects of American Sculpture, 1960; Smithsonian, Drawings by Sculptors, circ. USA, 1961–63; SRGM, The Joseph H. Hirshhorn Collection, 1962; WMAA, American Painters Today, circ., 1962; WMAA, Fifty California Artists, 1962–63; MOMA, Recent Painting USA: The Figure, circ., 1962–63; VMFA, American Painting, 1962. COLLECTIONS: Gibraltar Savings & Loan Association; Home Savings and Loan Association; Kansas City/Nelson; Los Angeles/County MA; Lytton Savings and Loan Association; MOMA; Milwaukee; U. of Nebraska; PAFA; Pasadena/AM; Santa Barbara/MA; State of California; Syracuse U.; Walker. BIBLIOGRAPHY: Seldis and Wilke.

ZERBE, KARL. b. September 16, 1903, Berlin, Germany. STUDIED: Technische Hochschule, Friedberg, 1920; Debschitz School, Munich, with Josef Eberz, 1921–23, DFA. Traveled Europe, USA, Mexico, Canada. To USA 1934;

citizen 1939. **TAUGHT:** Fine Arts Guild, Cambridge, Mass., 1935–37; Boston Museum School, 1937–55; Florida State U., 1954– . **MEMBER:** Artists Equity (President, 1957–59). **FEDERAL A.P.:** Easel painting. **AWARDS:** VMFA, John Barton Payne Medal, 1942; ICA, Boston, First Prize, 1943; Chicago/AI, Watson F. Blair Prize, 1944; Chicago/AI, Norman Wait Harris Silver Medal and Prize, 1946; Carnegie, Third Prize, 1948; PAFA, J. Henry Schiedt Memorial Prize, 1949; Boston Arts Festival, First Prize, 1953; U. of Illinois, P.P., 1955. **ADDRESS:** 1807 Afaphene, Tallahassee, Fla. **ONE-MAN EXHIBITIONS:** (first) Gallery Gurlitt, Berlin, 1922; Marie Sterner Gallery, NYC, 1934, 35, 36, 37; Grace Horne Galleries, Boston, 1936, 38, 39, 40; Vose Gallery, Boston, 1941; Buchholz Gallery, NYC, 1941; The Downtown Gallery, 1943, 46, 48, 51, 52; Mount Holyoke College, 1943; Pittsfield/Berkshire, 1943, 47; Chicago/AI, 1945, 46; Detroit/Institute, 1946; Boris Mirski Gallery, 1948, 55; Philadelphia Art Alliance, 1948, 49; Utica, 1950; The Alan Gallery, 1954; Lee Nordness Gallery, NYC, 1958, 59, 60, 64; Ringling, 1958. **RETROSPECTIVE:** ICA, Boston, circ., 1951–52; A.F.A., circ., 1961–62. **GROUP:** ICA, Boston; Chicago/AI; Carnegie; PAFA; U. of Illinois; WMAA. **COLLECTIONS:** Andover/Phillips; Auburn U.; Baltimore/MA; Boston/MFA; Britannica; Brooklyn Museum; Buffalo/Albright; Chicago/AI; Colby College; Cranbrook; Detroit/Institute; Fort Worth; Frankfurt am Main; U. of Georgia; Harvard U.; IBM; Illinois Wesleyan U.; U. of Illinois; Indianapolis/Herron; State U. of Iowa; Kestner-Museum; Los Angeles/County MA; MIT; MMA; MOMA; Milwaukee; U. of Minnesota; NIAL; U. of Nebraska; Newark Museum; New Britain; Oberlin College; U. of Oklahoma; PMA; Phillips; RAC; RISD; Rio de Janeiro; U. of Rochester; St. Louis/City; San Diego; Sarah Lawrence College; Smith College; Staatliche Graphische Sammlung Munchen; Syracuse U.; Tel Aviv; Utica; WMAA; Walker; Washington U.; U. of Washington; Wichita/AM; Youngstown/Butler. **BIBLIOGRAPHY:** Baur 7; Bethers; Chaet; Genauer; Goodrich and Baur 1; Halpert; Nordness, ed.; Pearson 2; Pousette-Dart, ed.; Richardson; Wight 2.

ZOGBAUM, WILFRID. b. September 10, 1915, Newport, R.I.; **d.** January 7, 1965, NYC.

Wilfrid Zogbaum   *Kroeber Hall. 1962*

STUDIED: Yale U., 1933–34; with John Sloan, NYC, 1934–35; Hofmann School, NYC and Provincetown, 1935–37 (class monitor). US Army, 1941–46. Traveled Europe, the Orient, West Indies, USA. Began sculpture 1954. **TAUGHT:** U. of California, Berkeley, 1957, 1961–63; U. of Minnesota, 1958; Pratt Institute, 1960–61; Southern Illinois U., 1961. **MEMBER:** American Welding Society; Sculptors Guild. **AWARDS:** S. R. Guggenheim Fellowship for Painting, 1937; U. of California Institute for Creative Work in the Arts, 1963. **ONE-MAN EXHIBITIONS:** (first) Alexander Iolas Gallery, 1952 (paintings); The Stable Gallery, 1954, 58; Walker, 1958; Staempfli Gallery, 1960; Obelisk Gallery, Washington, D.C., 1962; Dilexi Gallery, San Francisco, 1962; U. of California, Berkeley, 1962; Grace Borgenicht Gallery Inc., 1963. **GROUP:** American Abstract Artists, 1935–41; Oakland/AM, 1957; Seattle World's Fair, 1962; U. of Nebraska, 1961; MOMA, Modern American Drawings, circ. Europe, 1961–62; WMAA Annuals; Chicago/AI, 1962; Carnegie, 1962; Baltimore/MA, 1961; Turin/Civico, 1962. COLLECTIONS: U. of California; International Institute for Aesthetic Research; New School for Social Research; SFMA; WMAA.

ZORACH, MARGUERITE. b. September 25, 1887, Santa Rosa, Calif. STUDIED in Paris, 1906–10. Traveled Europe, Mexico, Central America, and around the world, 1911–12. TAUGHT: Provincetown, 1913–18; Columbia U., intermittently during the 1940's. COMMISSIONS (murals): US Post Offices, Peterborough, N.H., and Ripley, Tenn. AWARDS: Golden Gate International Exposition, San Francisco, 1939, Silver Medal; Chicago/AI, The Mr. & Mrs. Frank G. Logan Medal, 1920; Hon. Ph.D., Bates College. m. William Zorach. ADDRESS: 276 Hicks Street, Brooklyn, N.Y. DEALER: Kraushaar Galleries. ONE-MAN EXHIBITIONS: (first) The Daniel Gallery, NYC, 1915, also 1917; Montross Gallery, NYC, 1921; Joseph Brummer Gallery, NYC, 1930; The Downtown Gallery, 1935, 38; M. Knoedler & Co., NYC, 1944; Kraushaar Galleries, 1953, 57. GROUP: Salon d'Automne, Paris, 1910; The Armory Show, 1913; WMAA; MOMA. COLLECTIONS: Colby College; Louisville/Speed; MMA; MOMA; Massillon Museum; Newark Museum; WMAA. BIBLIOGRAPHY: Biddle 3; Cheney, M. C.; Goodrich and Baur 1; Hunter 5; Richardson; Ringel, ed.; Wright 1.

ZORACH, WILLIAM. b. February 28, 1887, Eurburg, Lithuania. To USA 1891. STUDIED: Cleveland Institute of Art, 1902–05; NAD, 1908–10; and in Paris, 1910–11. TAUGHT: ASL, 1929– ; The Des Moines Art Center, 1954. MEMBER: NIAL (Vice President, 1955–57); Sculptors Guild. COMMISSIONS: Radio City Music Hall, NYC, 1932; US Post Office, Benjamin Franklin Station, Washington, D.C., 1937; New York World's Fair, 1939; Mayo Clinic, Rochester, Minn., 1954; Municipal Court Building, NYC, 1958; R. S. Reynolds Memorial Award, 1960 (a sculpture). AWARDS: Chicago/AI, The Mr. & Mrs. Frank G. Logan Medal, 1931, 32; Architectural League of New York, Hon. Men., 1939; Bates College, Citation, 1958; NIAL, Gold Medal for Sculpture, 1961; PAFA, George D. Widener Memorial Gold Medal, 1962; Hon. MA, Bowdoin College,

1958. m. Marguerite Zorach. ADDRESS: 276 Hicks Street, Brooklyn, N.Y. DEALER: The Downtown Gallery. ONE-MAN EXHIBITIONS: Taylor Galleries, Cleveland, 1912; The Daniel Gallery, NYC, 1915, 16, 18; O'Brien's Gallery, Chicago, 1916; Dayton/AI, 1922; Rochester/Memorial, 1924; Kraushaar Galleries, 1924, 26, 48; Arts and Crafts Club, New Orleans, 1927; Eastman-Bolton Co., NYC, 1929; The Downtown Gallery, 1931, 32, 33, 36, 43, 44, 47, 51, 55; Passedoit Gallery, NYC, 1937; Ansel Adams Gallery, San Francisco, 1941; Boston Museum School, 1941; Dallas/MFA, 1945; California Palace, 1946; San Diego, 1946; Pasadena/AM, 1946; Ten Thirty Gallery, Cleveland, 1948; Coleman Gallery, NYC, 1949; New Paltz, 1950; Clearwater/Gulf Coast, 1952; Des Moines, 1954; San Antonio/McNay, 1956; Bowdoin College, 1958; Philadelphia Art Alliance, 1961; Coe College, 1961; Queens College, 1961. RETROSPECTIVE: ASL, 1950; WMAA, circ., 1959. GROUP: Salon d'Automne, Paris, 1910; The Armory Show, 1913; Society of Independent Artists, NYC, 1914–16; Anderson Galleries, NYC, Forum Exhibition, 1916; PAFA, New Tendencies, 1918; A Century of Progress, Chicago, 1933–34; American Painting and Sculpture, Moscow, 1959; PAFA; MOMA; WMAA; Corcoran; Chicago/AI. COLLECTIONS: AAAL; Andover/Phillips; Arizona State College; Baltimore/MA; Bezalel Museum; Boston/MFA; Bowdoin College; Brandeis U.; Brooklyn Museum; Buffalo/Albright; Chicago/AI; Cleveland/MA; Colby College; Columbia U.; Columbus; Corcoran; Dallas/MFA; Des Moines; Dubuque/AA; Fairleigh Dickinson U.; Fort Worth; IBM; Los Angeles/County MA; MMA; MOMA; U. of Nebraska; Newark Museum; New Britain; Oberlin College; Ogunquit; PMA; The Pennsylvania State U.; Phillips; Pittsfield/Berkshire; Sara Roby Foundation; Shelburne; Syracuse U.; Tel Aviv; Terre Haute/Swope; Utica; VMFA; WMAA; West Palm Beach/Norton; Wichita/AM; Wilmington. BIBLIOGRAPHY: Baur 7; Beam; Biddle 3; Blesh 1; Brown; Brumme; Bryant; Cahill and Barr, eds.; Cheney, M. C.; Flanagan; Gertz; Goodrich and Baur 1; Hall; Halpert; Hunter 5; *Index of 20th Century Artists;* Jewell 2; Lee and Burchwood; McCurdy, ed.; Mellquist; Mendelowitz; Myers 2; Neuhaus; Parkes; Pearson 2; Phillips 2;

Richardson; Ringel, ed.; Ritchie 3; Seuphor 3; Wheeler; **Wingert**; Wright 1; **Zorach 1, 2.**

ZOX, LARRY. b. May 31, 1936, Des Moines, Iowa. STUDIED: U. of Oklahoma, with Amelio Amero, Eugene Bavinger; Drake U., with Karl Mattern, Leonard Cook; The Des Moines Art Center, with George Grosz, Louis Bouche, Will Barnet. Traveled USA, Mexico, and Canada extensively. TAUGHT: Juniata College, 1964. ADDRESS: 647 Broadway, NYC. DEALER: The Kornblee Gallery. ONE-MAN EXHIBITIONS: (first) The American Gallery, NYC, 1962; The Kornblee Gallery, 1964. GROUP: Des Moines, 1955, 56; WGMA, 1964; A.F.A., Moods of Light, circ., 1963–64; A.F.A., Banners II, 1964. COLLECTIONS: American Republic Insurance Co.

Bibliography

I. = Illustrated; B. = Bibliography; D. = Diagrams; G. = Glossary; P. = Plans. In cases of more than one entry for the same author, the numeral immediately following the position of the author's name is keyed to the Bibliography section of the artists' entries. A supplemental list of Books of General Interest follows the main list.

ADAMS, PHILIP RHYS. *Walt Kuhn.* Cincinnati: The Cincinnati Art Museum, 1960. I. *Monograph.*

ALBERS, JOSEF, 1. *Day and Night.* Los Angeles: Tamarind Lithography Workshop, Inc., 1964. *Boxed folio of 10 lithographs (ed. 20).*

———, 2. *Despite Straight Lines.* New Haven, Conn.: Yale University Press, 1961. I. B. *Captions by Albers; analysis of his graphic constructions by François Bucher.* (German edition, *Trotz der Geraden,* Berne: Benteli, 1961.)

———, 3. *Homage to the Square. Ten Works by Josef Albers.* New Haven, Conn.: Ives-Sillman, 1962. Preface by Richard Lippold. *Ten color silkscreens in folio.*

———, 4. *Interaction of Color.* New Haven, Conn., and London: Yale University Press, 1963. I. *More than 200 color studies, with commentaries.*

———, 5. *Poems and Drawings.* New Haven, Conn.: Readymade Press, 1958. I. (German and English text.)

———, 6. *Poems and Drawings* (2nd ed., rev. and enlarged). New York: George Wittenborn, Inc., 1961. I. (Bilingual text.)

———, 7. *Zeichnungen—Drawings.* New York: George Wittenborn, Inc.; Berne: Spiral Press, 1956. (Text by Max Bill in German and English.) *Twelve b/w plates loose in folio.*

ALFIERI, BRUNO. *Gyorgy Kepes.* Ivrey, Italy: Centro Culturale Olivetti, 1958. I. B. *Monograph.*

ALLEN, CLARENCE CANNING, ed. *Are You Fed Up with Modern Art?* Tulsa, Okla.: The Rainbow Press, 1957. I. *Popular reaction against the new art.*

ALLOWAY, LAWRENCE. *William Baziotes.* New York: The Solomon R. Guggenheim Museum, 1965. I. B. *Retrospective catalogue.*

ALVARD, J. *Mark Tobey.* Paris: Musee des Arts Decoratifs, Palais du Louvre, 1961. I. B. (French and English text.) *Retrospective catalogue.*

AMERICAN ABSTRACT ARTISTS, ed. *American Abstract Artists.* New York: American Abstract Artists, 1946. I. *Documents members and activities.*

AMERICAN ARTISTS CONGRESS, INC. *America Today, a Book of 100 Prints.* New York: Equinox Cooperative Press, 1936. I.

AMERICAN ARTISTS GROUP INC., 1. *Handbook of the American Artists Group.* New York: American Artists Group Inc., 1935. I. B. *Members and organizational information.*

———, 2. *Missouri, Heart of the Nation.* New York: American Artists Group Inc., 1947. I. B. *Midwest art of the 1930's and 1940's.*

———, 3. *Original Etchings, Lithographs and Woodcuts by American Artists.* New York: American Artists Group Inc., 1936. I.

Andrew Wyeth. Buffalo: Buffalo Fine Arts Academy. Albright-Knox Art Gallery, 1963. I. *Exhibition catalogue.*

ARCHIPENKO, ALEXANDER, 1. *Archipenko, 50 Creative Years.* New York: Tekhne, 1960. I. B. *Autobiography.*

———, 2. *Archipentura*. New York: Anderson Galleries, 1928. B. *Exhibition catalogue.*

ARMITAGE, MERLE. *Rockwell Kent.* New York: Alfred A. Knopf, 1932. I. B. *Monograph.*

ARNASON, H. HARVARD, 1. *Marca-Relli.* New York: Harry N. Abrams Inc., 1962. I. *Monograph.*

———, 2. *Philip Guston.* New York: The Solomon R. Guggenheim Museum, 1962. I. B. *Exhibition catalogue.*

———, 3. *Stuart Davis.* Minneapolis: The Walker Art Center, 1957. I. *Exhibition catalogue.*

———, 4. *Theodore Roszak.* Minneapolis: The Walker Art Center, 1956. I. B. *Exhibition catalogue.*

ARP, HANS. *Onze peintres.* Zurich: Editions Girsberger, 1949. I. (French and German text.)

ASHTON, DORE, 1. *The Mosaics of Jeanne Reynal.* New York: George Wittenborn, Inc., 1964. I. *Monograph.*

———, 2. *Philip Guston.* New York: Grove Press Inc., 1960. I. B. *Monograph.*

BAER, DONALD. *Russell Cowles.* Los Angeles: Dalzell Hatfield Gallery, 1946. I. *Monograph.*

BALDES, ALTON PARKER. *Six Maryland Artists.* Baltimore: Balboa Publishers, 1955. I.

BALDINGER, WALLACE S., in collaboration with Harry B. Green. *The Visual Arts.* New York: Holt, Rinehart and Winston, Inc., 1960. I. B. *Includes chapters on the visual arts.*

BALLO, FERDINANDO, ed. *Grosz.* Milan: Rosa e Balio Editori, 1956. I. (German and Italian text.) *Critical essays.*

BARKER, VIRGIL, 1. *From Realism to Reality in Recent American Painting.* Lincoln: University of Nebraska Press, 1959. I. *Essays on the rise of abstract and non-figurative painting.*

———, 2. *Henry Lee McFee.* New York: The Whitney Museum of American Art (American Artists Series), 1931. I. *Monograph.*

BARNES, ALBERT C. *The Art in Painting.* Merion, Pa.: The Barnes Foundation Press, 1925. I. *Dr. Barnes' theories.*

BARR, ALFRED H., JR., 1. *Cubism and Abstract Art.* New York: The Museum of Modern Art, 1936. I. B. *Essays on Cubism and its evolution.*

———, 2. *Edward Hopper.* New York: The Museum of Modern Art, 1933. I. B. *Exhibition catalogue.*

———, 3. *What Is Modern Painting?* New York: The Museum of Modern Art, 1956. I. *Popular introduction to modern art.*

BASKIN, LEONARD. *Leonard Baskin.* Brunswick, Me.: Bowdoin College, 1962. I. B. *Exhibition catalogue.*

BATES, KENNETH. *Brackman, His Art and Teaching.* Noank, Conn.: Noank Publishing Studio, 1951. I. *Monograph.*

BAUR, JOHN I. H., 1. *Charles Burchfield.* New York: The Whitney Museum of American Art, 1956. I. B. *Retrospective catalogue.*

———, 2. *George Grosz.* New York: The Whitney Museum of American Art, 1954. I. B. *Retrospective catalogue.*

———, 3. *Joseph Stella.* New York: The Whitney Museum of American Art, 1963. I. B. *Retrospective catalogue.*

———, 4. *Loren MacIver—Rice Pereira.* New York: The Whitney Museum of American Art, 1953. I. B. *Exhibition catalogue.*

———, 5. *Nature in Abstraction.* New York: The Macmillan Company, for The Whitney Museum of American Art, 1958. I. B. *Nature considered as catalyst for abstraction.*

———, 6. *Philip Evergood.* New York: Frederick A. Praeger, for The Whitney Museum of American Art, 1960. I. B. *Monograph.*

———, 7. *Revolution and Tradition in Modern American Art.* Cambridge, Mass.: Harvard University Press, 1959. I. *Important essays on conservative and advance guard art.*

BAYER, HERBERT. *Book of Drawings.* Chicago: Paul Theobald and Co., 1961. I. B.

BAZALGETTE, LEON. *George Grosz.* Paris: Les Ecrivains Reunis, 1927. I. B. (French text.) *Monograph.*

BAZIN, GERMAIN. *History of Modern Painting.* New York: Hyperion Press, Harper and Brothers, 1951. I. B. *Includes recent American artists of international reputation.*

BEAM, PHILIP C. *The Language of Art.* New York: The Ronald Press, 1958. I. B. *Essays on interpretation.*

BEEKMAN, AARON. *The Functional Line in Painting.* New York: Thomas Yoseloff Inc., 1957. I.

BEGGS, THOMAS M. *Paul Manship.* Washington, D.C.: Smithsonian Institution, 1958. I. *Exhibition catalogue.*

BENSON, E. M. *John Marin, The Man and His Work.* Washington, D.C.: American Federation of Arts, 1935. *Monograph.*

BENTON, THOMAS HART, 1. *An Artist in Amer-*

ica. New York: Robert M. McBride and Co., 1937. I. *Autobiography.*

———, 2. *Thomas Hart Benton.* New York: American Artists Group Inc., 1945. I. *Autobiographical monograph.*

———, 3. *Thomas Hart Benton.* Lawrence: University of Kansas, 1958. I. *Exhibition catalogue.*

BERMAN, EUGENE. *Imaginary Promenades in Italy.* New York: Pantheon Books, 1956. I. *Illustrated essays.*

BETHERS, RAY. *How Paintings Happen.* New York: W. W. Norton and Co., 1951. I. *Artists at work.*

BIDDLE, GEORGE, 1. *An American Artist's Story.* Boston: Little, Brown and Co., 1939. I. *Autobiography.*

———, 2. *Ninety Three Drawings.* Colorado Springs: Colorado Springs Fine Arts Center, 1937. I. *Essays on Boardman Robinson's drawings.*

———, 3. *The Yes and No of Contemporary Art.* Cambridge, Mass.: Harvard University Press, 1957. I. *An artist comments on the contemporary scene.*

BIEDERMAN, CHARLES, 1. *Art as the Evolution of Visual Knowledge.* Red Wing, Minn.: Privately published, 1948. I. B. *History, aesthetics, and theory.*

———, 2. *Letters on the New Art.* Red Wing, Minn.: Privately published, 1951. *Essays.*

BIRCHMAN, WILLIS. *Faces and Facts.* New York: Privately published, 1937. I. *Short biographies with photographs.*

BIRD, PAUL. *Fifty Paintings by Walt Kuhn.* New York: Studio Publications, 1940. I. *Monograph.*

BIRNBAUM, MARTIN. *Introductions.* New York: Frederic Fairchild Sherman, 1919. *New talent in 1919.*

BITTNER, HUBERT. *George Grosz.* New York: A Golden Griffin Book, Arts, Inc., 1959. I. *Monograph.*

BLANCH, ARNOLD, 1. *Arnold Blanch.* New York: American Artists Group Inc., 1945. I. *Autobiographical monograph.*

———, 2. *Methods and Techniques for Gouache Painting.* New York: American Artists Group Inc., 1946. I.

———, 3. *Painting for Enjoyment.* New York: Tudor Publishing Co., 1947. I.

BLANCHARD, FRANCES BRADSHAW. *Retreat from Likeness in the Theory of Painting.* New York: Columbia University Press, 1949. I. B.

From art as illustration to the object as art.

BLESH, RUDI, 1. *Modern Art, USA. Men—Rebellion—Conquest 1900–1956.* New York: Alfred A. Knopf, 1956. I. *Popular study of American art from 1900 to 1956.*

———, 2. *Stuart Davis.* New York: Grove Press Inc., 1960. I. *Monograph.*

BORN, WOLFGANG. *American Landscape Painting, an Interpretation.* New Haven, Conn.: Yale University Press, 1948. I.

BOSWELL, PEYTON, JR., 1. *Modern American Painting.* New York: Dodd, Mead and Co., 1939. I. *Painting in the first 40 years of the twentieth century.*

———, 2. *Varnum Poor.* New York: Hyperion Press, Harper and Brothers, 1941. I. B. *Monograph.*

BOSWELL, PEYTON, JR., ed. *An Appreciation of the Work of Frederic Taubes.* New York: Art Digest Monographs, 1939. I. *Monograph.*

BREESKIN, A. D. *Franz Kline.* Washington, D.C.: Washington Gallery of Modern Art, 1962. I. *Retrospective catalogue.*

BRETON, ANDRE, 1. *Le Surrealisme et la peinture.* Paris: N. R. F., Gallimard, 1928. I. *The Surrealist movement in art.*

———, 2. *Le Surrealisme et la peinture.* New York: Brentano's, 1945. I. *Revised and expanded edition of the above entry.*

———, 3. *Le Surrealisme in 1947.* Paris: Editions Maeght, 1947.

———, 4. *Yves Tanguy.* New York: Pierre Matisse Editions, 1946. I. (French and English text.) *Monograph.*

BRION, MARCEL, 1. *Art abstrait.* Paris: Editions Albin Michel, 1956. I. (French text.) *Development of abstract art in the twentieth century.*

———, 2. *Modern Painting: From Impressionism to Abstract Art.* London: Thames and Hudson, 1958. I.

BROOK, ALEXANDER. *Alexander Brook.* New York: American Artists Group Inc., 1945. I. *Autobiographical monograph.*

BROOKS, VAN WYCK. *John Sloan, a Painter's Life.* New York: E. P. Dutton, 1955. I. *Biography.*

BROWN, MILTON W. *American Painting: From The Armory Show to the Depression.* Princeton, N.J.: Princeton University Press, 1955. I. B.

BRUCE, EDWARD and WATSON, FORBES. *Art in Federal Buildings.* Washington, D.C.: Art in Federal Buildings, Inc., 1936. I. P.

BRUMME, C. LUDWIG. *Contemporary American Sculpture.* New York: Crown Publishers Inc., 1948. I. B.

BRYANT, LORINDA M. *American Pictures and Their Painters.* New York: John Lane Co., 1917. I.

BULLIET, C. J., 1. *Apples and Madonnas.* Chicago: Pascal Covici, Inc., 1927. I. *Critical essays on American artists.*

———, 2. *The Significant Moderns and Their Pictures.* New York: Covici-Friede, Publishers, 1936. I.

BUNCE, LOUIS. *Louis Bunce.* Portland, Ore.: Portland Art Museum, 1955. I. *Exhibition catalogue.*

BURCHFIELD, CHARLES, 1. *Charles Burchfield.* Buffalo: Buffalo Fine Arts Academy, Albright Art Gallery, 1944. I. *Exhibition catalogue.*

———, 2. *Charles Burchfield.* New York: American Artists Group Inc., 1945. I. *Autobiographical monograph.*

———, 3. *Eugene Speicher.* Buffalo: Albright Art Gallery, 1950. I. *Exhibition catalogue.*

BURROUGHS, ALAN. *Kenneth Hayes Miller.* New York: The Whitney Museum of American Art (American Artists Series), 1931. I. B. *Exhibition catalogue.*

BYWATERS, JERRY, 1. *Andrew Dasburg.* Dallas: Dallas Museum of Fine Arts, 1957. I. *Exhibition catalogue.*

———, 2. *Andrew Dasburg.* New York: American Federation of Arts, 1959. I. *Retrospective catalogue.*

CAHILL, HOLGER. *Max Weber.* New York: The Downtown Gallery, 1930. I. *Monograph.*

CAHILL, HOLGER and BARR, ALFRED H., JR., eds. *Art in America, a Complete Survey.* New York: Reynal and Hitchcock, 1935. I. B. *Considers architecture, fine arts, folk art, etc.*

CALAS, NICHOLAS. *Bloodflames, 1947.* New York: Hugo Galleries, 1947. I. *Essays on the advance guard in New York in the 1940's.*

CALDER, ALEXANDER. *Three Young Rats.* New York: The Museum of Modern Art, 1946, 2nd ed. I. *A children's story.*

CALDER, ALEXANDER and LIEDL, CHARLES. *Animal Sketching.* Pelham, N.Y.: Bridgeman Publishers, Inc., 1941, 6th ed. I.

CAMPOS, JULES. *Jose de Creeft.* New York: Erich S. Herrmann, Publisher, 1945. I. *Monograph.*

CANADAY, JOHN. *Mainstreams of Modern Art.* New York: Simon and Schuster, 1959. I. *Popular history of art.*

CASSOU, JEAN. *Gateway to the 20th Century.* New York: McGraw-Hill Book Co., Inc., 1962. I. *Development of nineteenth-century art and indications of its twentieth-century ramifications.*

CHAET, BERNARD. *Artists at Work.* Cambridge, Mass.: Webb Books Inc., 1960. I. *Interviews with artists.*

CHENEY, MARTHA CHANDLER. *Modern Art in America.* New York: Whittlesey House, McGraw-Hill Book Co., Inc., 1939. I.

CHRISTENSEN, ERWIN O. *The History of Western Art.* New York: New American Library, 1959. I.

CHRIST-JANER, ALBERT. *Boardman Robinson.* Chicago: The University of Chicago Press, 1946. I. B. *Monograph.*

CLIFFORD, HENRY. *Franklin Watkins.* Philadelphia: The Philadelphia Museum of Art, 1964. I. B. *Exhibition catalogue.*

COATES, ROBERT M. *Walter Quirt.* New York: American Federation of Arts, 1959. I. *Retrospective catalogue.*

COKE, VAN DEREN. *Taos and Santa Fe. The Artistic Environment. 1882–1942.* Albuquerque: University of New Mexico Press, 1963. I.

CORTISSOZ, ROYAL, 1. *American Artists.* New York: Charles Scribner's Sons, 1923. *Essays on noted artists of the late nineteenth and early twentieth century.*

———, 2. *Guy Pene Du Bois.* New York: The Whitney Museum of American Art (American Artists Series), 1931. I. B. *Monograph.*

CRAVEN, THOMAS, 1. *Modern Art, The Men, The Movements, The Meaning.* New York: Simon and Schuster, 1934. I. *Essays on twentieth-century American figurative artists.*

———, 2. *The Story of Painting: From Cave Pictures to Modern Art.* New York: Simon and Schuster, 1943. I. *Popular history of art.*

———, 3. *Thomas Hart Benton.* New York: Associated American Artists, 1939. I. *Monograph.*

CRESPELLE, J.-P. *Montparnasse vivant.* Paris: Hachette, 1962. I. *The panorama of Montparnasse life.*

CURRY, JOHN STEUART, 1. *John Steuart Curry.* New York: American Artists Group Inc., 1945. I. *Autobiographical monograph.*

————, 2. *John Steuart Curry.* Syracuse, N.Y.: Joe and Emily Lowe Art Center, Syracuse University, 1956. I. *Exhibition catalogue.*

————, 3. *John Steuart Curry.* Lawrence: University of Kansas, 1957. I. *Exhibition catalogue.*

DAUBLER, THEODOR and GOLL, IWAN. *Archipenko-Album.* Potsdam: Gustav Kiepenheuen Verlag, 1921. I. (German text.) *Monograph.*

DAVEY, RANDALL. *Randall Davey.* Santa Fe: Museum of New Mexico, 1957. I. *Exhibition catalogue.*

DAVIDSON, MORRIS, 1. *An Approach to Modern Painting.* New York: Coward-McCann, Inc., 1948. I. *Appreciation of modern art.*

————, 2. *Understanding Modern Art.* New York: Coward-McCann, Inc., 1931. I. *Appreciation and understanding of modern concepts in art.*

DAVIS, STUART. *Stuart Davis.* New York: American Artists Group Inc., 1945. I. *Autobiographical monograph.*

DE CREEFT, JOSE. *Jose de Creeft.* Athens: University of Georgia Press (American Sculptors Series), 1950. I. *Autobiographical monograph.*

DEHN, ADOLF. *Watercolor Painting.* New York: Studio Publications, 1945. I.

DEVREE, CHARLOTTE. *Jose de Creeft.* New York: American Federation of Arts and The Ford Foundation, 1960. I. *Retrospective catalogue.*

DOCHTERMAN, LILLIAN. *The Quest of Charles Sheeler.* Iowa City: State University of Iowa, 1963. I. *Biography.*

DORIVAL, BERNARD. *Twentieth Century Painters.* New York: Universe Books, Inc.; Paris: Editions Pierre Tisne, 1958. I. B. *Painting in Europe and America.*

DORNER, ALEXANDER. *The Way Beyond Art.* New York: New York University Press, 1958. I. *Development of art and its influence in the museums.*

The Drawings of Charles E. Burchfield. Cleveland: Print Club of Cleveland and The Cleveland Museum of Art, 1953. I. *Exhibition catalogue.*

DREIER, KATHERINE S., 1. *Burliuk.* New York: The Societe Anonyme, Inc., 1944. I. *Monograph.*

————, 2. *Western Art and the New Era, an Introduction to Modern Art.* New York: Brentano's, 1923. I. *Early polemic on abstract and non-figurative art.*

DU BOIS, GUY PENE, 1. *Artists Say the Silliest Things.* New York: American Artists Group Inc., 1940. I. *Autobiography.*

————, 2. *Edward Hopper.* New York: The Whitney Museum of American Art (American Artists Series), 1931. I. B. *Monograph.*

————, 3. *Ernest Lawson.* New York: The Whitney Museum of American Art (American Artists Series), 1932. I. B. *Monograph.*

————, 4. *John Sloan.* New York: The Whitney Museum of American Art (American Artists Series), 1931. I. B. *Monograph.*

————, 5. *William Glackens.* New York: The Whitney Museum of American Art (American Artists Series), 1931. I. B. *Monograph.*

————, 6. *William Glackens.* New York: The Whitney Museum of American Art, 1939. *Exhibition catalogue.*

DUCHAMP, MARCEL, 1. *Marcel Duchamp.* Pasadena, Calif.: The Pasadena Art Museum, 1963. I. B. *Exhibition catalogue.*

————, 2. *Marchand du Sel.* Paris: Le Terrain Vague, 1958. I. B. *Essays.*

EBERSOLE, BARBARA. *Fletcher Martin.* Gainesville: University of Florida Press, 1954. I. *Exhibition catalogue.*

ELIOT, ALEXANDER. *Three Hundred Years of American Painting.* New York: Time Inc., 1957. I. B. *Popular history of American art.*

ELLIOTT, JAMES. "Stuart Davis." *Bulletin* of the Los Angeles County Museum of Art, Vol. XIV, No. 3, 1962. I. *Entire issue devoted to this essay.*

ELSEN, ALBERT E. *Purposes of Art.* New York: Holt, Rinehart and Winston, Inc., 1962. I. B. *Elucidation of the art process.*

ELY, CATHARINE BEACH. *The Modern Tendency in American Painting.* New York: Frederic Fairchild Sherman, 1925. I.

ETTING, EMLEN. *Drawing the Ballet.* New York: Studio Publications, 1944. I.

EVANS, MYFANWY, ed. *The Painter's Object.* London: Gerald Howe Ltd., 1937. I. *Critical essays.*

FARRELL, JAMES T. *The Paintings of Will Barnet.* New York: Press Eight, 1950. I. *Monograph.*

FIERENS, PAUL. *Sculpteurs d'aujourd'hui.* Paris: Editions de Chroniques de Jour, 1933. I. (French text.)

FINKELSTEIN, SIDNEY. *Realism in Art.* New York: International Publishers, 1954.

FLANAGAN, GEORGE A. *Understanding and Enjoying Modern Art.* New York: Thomas Y. Crowell Co., 1962. I. B.

FLEXNER, JAMES THOMAS. *A Short History of American Painting.* Boston: Houghton Mifflin Co., 1950. I. B. *Authoritative history of American painting.*

FLOCKHART, LOLITA L. W. *Art and Artists in New Jersey.* Somerville, N.J.: C. P. Hoagland Co., 1938. I.

FORD, CHARLES HENRI. *Poems for Painters.* New York: View Editions, 1945. I. *Poems illustrated by surrealist artists.*

FRANK, WALDO, ed. *America and Alfred Stieglitz.* Garden City, N.Y.: Doubleday, Doran and Co., Inc., 1934. I. *A history of Alfred Stieglitz and his influence.*

FRIEDMAN, B. H., ed. *School of New York: Some Younger Artists.* New York: Grove Press Inc., 1959. I. *Younger artists of promise in the 1950's.*

FRIEDMAN, MARTIN. *Adolph Gottlieb.* Minneapolis: The Walker Art Center, 1963. I. B. *Exhibition catalogue.*

FROST, ROSAMOND. *Contemporary Art: The March of Art from Cezanne Until Now.* New York: Crown Publishers Inc., 1942. I. B.

GABO, NAUM. *Of Divers Arts.* London: Faber and Faber, Ltd., 1962. I. *Critical essays.*

GALLATIN, A. E., 1. *American Watercolourists.* New York: E. P. Dutton, 1922. I.

————, 2. *Certain Contemporaries: A Set of Notes in Art Criticism.* New York: John Lane Co., 1916.

————, 3. *Gallatin Iconography.* n.p.: Privately published, 1934. I. *Genealogy through portraits.*

————, 4. *Gaston Lachaise.* New York: E. P. Dutton, 1924. I. *Critical essay.*

————, 5. *John Sloan.* New York: E. P. Dutton, 1925. I. *Critical essay.*

————, 6. *Paintings by Gallatin.* New York: Wittenborn, Schultz, Inc., 1948. I. B.

————, 7. *Paul Manship.* New York: John Lane Co., 1917. I. B. *Critical essay.*

————, 8. *Whistler, Notes and Footnotes.* New York: The Collector and Art Critic Co., 1907. I. *Critical essays.*

GARWOOD, DARRELL. *Artist in Iowa.* New York: W. W. Norton and Co., 1944. *Biography.*

GASCOYNE, DAVID. *A Short Survey of Surrealism.* London: Cobden-Sanderson, 1935. I. *Essays and documentation.*

GAUNT, WILLIAM. *The Observer's Book of Modern Art from Impressionism to the Present Day.* London: Frederick Warne and Co. Ltd., 1964. I. G.

GENAUER, EMILY. *Best of Art.* Garden City, N.Y.: Doubleday and Co. Inc., 1948. I. *Painting during the 1940's.*

GEORGE, WALDEMAR, 1. *Les Artistes juifs et l'ecole de Paris.* Algiers: Editions du Congres Juif Mondial, 1959. I. (French text.)

————, 2. *John D. Graham.* Paris: Editions Le Triangle, n.d. I. *Critical essay.*

GERSTNER, KARL. *Kalte Kunst.* Switzerland: Verlag Arthur Niggli, 1957. I. (German text.) *Hard edge painting and sculpture.*

GERTZ, ULRICH. *Contemporary Plastic Art.* Berlin: Rembrandt-Verlag, GMBH, 1955. I. (German and English text.) *Post-war painting in Europe, including American influence.*

GETLEIN, FRANK and DOROTHY. *Christianity in Art.* Milwaukee: The Bruce Publishing Co., 1959. I. B.

GIEDION-WELCKER, CAROLA, 1. *Contemporary Sculpture: An Evolution in Volume and Space.* Documents of Modern Art, Vol. 12. New York: George Wittenborn, Inc., 1955. I. B.

————, 2. *Modern Plastic Art: Elements of Reality, Volume and Disintegration.* Zurich: Dr. H. Girsberger, 1937. I. B. *Twentieth-century sculpture.*

GLACKENS, IRA. *William Glackens and the Ashcan Group: The Emergence of Realism in American Art.* New York: Crown Publishers Inc., 1957. I.

GOLDWATER, ROBERT and TREVES, MARCO, eds. *Artists on Art. From the XIV to the XX Century.* New York: Pantheon Books, 1945. I.

GOODRICH, LLOYD, 1. *American Watercolors and Winslow Homer.* New York: The Walker Art Center, for American Artists Group Inc., 1945. I.

————, 2. *The Drawings of Edwin Dickinson.* New Haven, Conn.: Yale University Press, 1963. I.

————, 3. *Edward Hopper.* New York: Penguin Books, 1949. I. *Monograph.*

————, 4. *Edward Hopper.* New York: The Whitney Museum of American Art, 1956. I. B. *Exhibition catalogue.*

————, 5. *H. E. Schnakenberg*. New York: The Whitney Museum of American Art (American Artists Series), 1931. I. B. *Monograph*.

————, 6. *John Sloan*. New York: The Whitney Museum of American Art, 1952. I. B. *Exhibition catalogue*.

————, 7. *Kuniyoshi*. New York: The Whitney Museum of American Art, 1948. I. *Exhibition catalogue*.

————, 8. *Max Weber*. New York: The Whitney Museum of American Art, 1949. I. *Exhibition catalogue*.

————, 9. *Reginald Marsh*. New York: The Whitney Museum of American Art, 1955. I. *Exhibition catalogue*.

GOODRICH, LLOYD and BAUR, JOHN I. H., 1. *American Art of Our Century*. New York: The Whitney Museum of American Art, 1961. I. *Development of American art illustrated through the collection of the WMAA*.

————, 2. *Four American Expressionists*. New York: The Whitney Museum of American Art, 1949. I. *Exhibition catalogue: Doris Caesar, Chaim Gross, Karl Knaths, Abraham Rattner*.

GOODRICH, LLOYD and IMGIZUMI, ATSUO. *Kuniyoshi*. Tokyo: National Museum of Modern Art, 1954. I. (Japanese and English text.) *Retrospective catalogue*.

GOOSSEN, E. C., 1. *Stuart Davis*. New York: George Braziller, Inc., 1959. I. B. *Monograph*.

————, 2. *Three American Sculptors*. New York: Grove Press Inc., 1959. I. *Monograph: Herbert Ferber, David Hare, Ibram Lassaw*.

GORDON, JOHN M. *Karl Schrag*. New York: American Federation of Arts and The Ford Foundation, 1960. I. *Retrospective catalogue*.

GRAHAM, JOHN D. *System and Dialectics of Art*. New York: Delphic Studios, 1937. *Critical essays*.

GREENBERG, CLEMENT, 1. *Art and Culture*. Boston: Beacon Press, 1961. *Critical essays*.

————, 2. *Hofmann*. Paris: The Pocket Museum, Editions George Fall, 1961. I. *Monograph*.

GROSS, CHAIM. *Fantasy Drawings*. New York: Beechhurst Press (A Bittner Art Book), 1956. I. *Drawings*.

GROSSER, MAURICE, 1. *The Painter's Eye*. New York: Rinehart and Co., Inc., 1951. I. *Essays on divers topics*.

————, 2. *Painting in Public*. New York: Alfred A. Knopf, 1948. *Autobiographical*.

GROSZ, GEORGE, 1. *George Grosz*. Berlin: Akademie der Kunste, 1962. I. *Retrospective catalogue*.

————, 2. *George Grosz Drawings*. New York: H. Bittner and Co., 1944. I. *Drawings*.

————, 3. *Die Gezeichneten*. Berlin: Malik Verlag, 1930. I. (German text.) *Drawings*.

————, 4. *A Little Yes and a Big No. The Autobiography of George Grosz*. New York: The Dial Press, 1946. I.

————, 5. *Der Spiesser-Spiegel*. Dresden: Carl Reisser Verlag, 1925. I. (German text.) *Drawings*.

GUEST, BARBARA and FRIEDMAN, B. H. *Goodnough*. Paris: The Pocket Museum, Editions George Fall, 1962. I. *Monograph*.

GUGGENHEIM, PEGGY, ed. *Art of This Century*. New York: Art of This Century, 1942. I. *Documents her New York gallery*.

GUTMAN, WALTER K. *Raphael Soyer, Paintings and Drawings*. New York: Shorewood Publishing Co., Inc., 1960. I. *Monograph*.

HAAS, IRVIN. *A Treasury of Great Prints*. New York: Thomas Yoseloff Inc., 1959. I.

HAFTMAN, WERNER. *Paintings in the Twentieth Century*. New York: Frederick A. Praeger, 1960, 2 vols. I. *A major history of twentieth-century art*.

HALE, ROBERT BEVERLY. *Waldo Peirce*. New York: American Artists Group Inc., 1945. I. *Monograph*.

HALL, W. S. *Eyes on America*. New York: Studio Publications, 1939. I. *Figurative painting in America*.

HALPERT, EDITH GREGOR. *The Downtown Gallery*. New York: The Downtown Gallery, 1943. I. *Documents members of the gallery*.

HAMILTON, GEORGE H. *Josef Albers*. New Haven, Conn.: Yale University Art Gallery, 1956. I. *Exhibition catalogue*.

HAMILTON, RICHARD. *The Bride Stripped Bare by Her Bachelors, Even*. New York: George Wittenborn, Inc., 1960. *Documentary essay on Marcel Duchamp*.

HARTLEY, MARSDEN. *Adventures in the Arts*. New York: Boni and Liveright, Inc., 1921. *Autobiography*.

HARTMANN, SADIKICHI. *A History of American Art*. Boston: L. C. Page and Co., 1932, rev. ed., 2 vols. I. *Important history of American art*.

HAYTER, S. W., 1. *About Prints*. London: Oxford University Press, 1962. I. B. *Print appreciation and techniques.*

———, 2. *New Ways of Gravure*. New York: Pantheon Books, 1949. I. D. *Printmaking techniques.*

HELM, MACKINLEY. *John Marin*. New York: Pellegrini and Cudahy, 1948. I. *Monograph.*

HELM, MACKINLEY and WIGHT, FREDERICK S. *John Marin*. Boston: Institute of Modern Art, 1947. I. *Exhibition catalogue.*

HENNING, EDWARD B. *Paths of Abstract Art*. Cleveland: The Cleveland Museum of Art, 1960. I. *Twentieth-century development of abstract art.*

HESS, HANS. *Lyonel Feininger*. London: Thames and Hudson, 1961. I. B. *Catalogue raisonné.*

HESS, THOMAS B. *Abstract Painting: Background and American Phase*. New York: Viking Press, 1951. I. *Important documentation of abstract painting in America.*

HILDEBRANDT, HANS. *Alexander Archipenko*. Berlin: Ukrainske Slowo Publishers Ltd., 1923. I. (Ukranian and English text.) *Monograph.*

HIRSCH, RICHARD. *Charles Sheeler*. Allentown, Pa.: Allentown Art Museum, 1961. I. *Exhibition catalogue.*

HOFMANN, HANS. *Search for the Real*. Andover, Mass.: Addison Gallery of American Art, 1948. I. *Hofmann's theory of painting.*

HOLME, BRYAN, 1. *Master Drawing in Line*. New York: Studio Publications, 1948. I.

———, 2. *Master Drawings*. New York: Studio Publications, 1943. I.

HOPE, HENRY R. *The Sculpture of Jacques Lipchitz*. New York: The Museum of Modern Art, 1954. I. B. *Exhibition catalogue.*

HOPPER, EDWARD. *Edward Hopper*. New York: American Artists Group Inc., 1945. I. *Autobiographical monograph.*

HOWARD, CHARLES. *Charles Howard*. San Francisco: California Palace of The Legion of Honor, 1946. I. B. *Exhibition catalogue.*

HUNTER, SAM, 1. *Art Since 1945*. New York: Harry N. Abrams Inc., 1958. I. B. *Comprehensive study of world art since 1945.*

———, 2. *Hans Hofmann*. New York: Harry N. Abrams Inc., 1962. I. B. *Monograph.*

———, 3. *James Brooks*. New York: The Whitney Museum of American Art, 1963. I. B. *Retrospective catalogue.*

———, 4. *James Metcalf*. Chicago: William and Noma Copley Foundation, n.d. I. *Monograph.*

———, 5. *Modern American Painting and Sculpture*. New York: Dell Publishing Co., 1959. I. *Concise history of American art since 1900; includes biographies.*

HUYGHE, RENE. *Histoire de l'art contemporain. La Peinture*. Paris: Librairie Felix Alcan, 1936. I. B. (French text.)

IGNATOFF, DAVID. *Kopman*. New York: E. Weyhe, 1930. I. *Monograph.*

Index of 20th Century Artists. New York: The College Art Association, 1933–37, 4 vols. B. *Comprehensive reference on American artists of the 1920's and 1930's.*

JACKMAN, RILLA EVELYN. *American Arts*. Chicago: Rand McNally and Co., 1928. I. B. *Popular essays on the arts.*

JACOBSON, J. Z., ed. *Art of Today: Chicago 1933*. Chicago: L. M. Stein, 1932. I.

JAKOVSKI, ANATOLE. *Arp, Calder, Helion, Miro, Pevsner, Seligmann*. Paris: Chez J. Povolozky, 1933. I. (French text.)

JANIS, HARRIET and BLESH, RUDI, 1. *Collage. Personalities—Concepts—Techniques*. Philadelphia and New York: Chilton Co., 1962. I. G. *Documents development of collage in the world.*

———, 2. *de Kooning*. New York: Grove Press Inc., 1960. I. *Monograph.*

JANIS, SIDNEY. *Abstract and Surrealist Art in America*. New York: Reynal and Hitchcock, 1944. I. *Essays on the two schools of art in the 1940's.*

JENKINS, PAUL and ESTHER, eds. *Observations of Michael Tapie*. New York: George Wittenborn, Inc., 1956. I. *A collection of the critic's commentaries.*

JEWELL, EDWARD ALDEN, 1. *Alexander Brook*. New York: The Whitney Museum of American Art (American Artists Series), 1931. I. B. *Monograph.*

———, 2. *. . . America*. New York: Alfred A. Knopf, 1930. I. *Critical essays.*

———, 3. *Have We an American Art?* New York and Toronto: Longmans, Green and Co., 1939. *Critical essays.*

JOHNSON, UNA E. *Gabor Peterdi*. New York: Brooklyn Museum, 1959. I. *Exhibition catalogue.*

JUIN, HUBERT. *Sieze peintres de la jeune ecole de Paris*. Paris: Le Musee de Poche, 1956. I.

KALLEN, H. M. *Maurice Sterne.* New York: The Museum of Modern Art, 1933. I. B. *Exhibition catalogue.*

KARFIOL, BERNARD. *Bernard Karfiol.* New York: American Artists Group Inc., 1945. I. *Autobiographical monograph.*

KENT, NORMAN. *Drawings by American Artists.* New York: Watson-Guptill Publishing Co. Inc., 1947. I.

KENT, ROCKWELL, 1. *It's Me O Lord.* New York: Dodd, Mead and Co., 1955. I. *Autobiography.*

——, 2. *Rockwell Kent.* New York: American Artists Group Inc., 1945. I. *Autobiographical monograph.*

——, 3. *Rockwellkentiana.* New York: Harcourt, Brace and Co., 1945. I. *Autobiographical monograph.*

KENT, ROCKWELL, ed. *World Famous Paintings.* New York: Wise and Co., 1939. I. *Paintings of all ages.*

KEPES, GYORGY, 1. *Language of Vision.* Chicago: Paul Theobald and Co., 1944. I. *An aesthetic of seeing.*

——, 2. *The New Landscape in Art and Science.* Chicago: Paul Theobald and Co., 1956. I. *Convolutions of science and art.*

KEPES, GYORGY, ed. *The Visual Arts Today.* Middletown, Conn.: Wesleyan University Press, 1960. I. B. *Essays on architecture, fine arts, graphics, typography, etc.*

KIRSTEIN, LINCOLN, 1. *Elie Nadelman Drawings.* New York: H. Bittner and Co., 1949. I. *Drawings.*

——, 2. *Pavel Tchelitchew.* New York: Gallery of Modern Art, 1964. I. B. *Retrospective catalogue.*

——, 3. *The Sculpture of Elie Nadelman.* New York: The Museum of Modern Art, 1948. I. *Retrospective catalogue.*

KIRSTEIN, LINCOLN, ed. *Pavel Tchelitchew Drawings.* New York: H. Bittner and Co., 1947. I. *Drawings.*

KOCH, JOHN. *John Koch in New York.* New York: Museum of the City of New York, 1963. I. B. *Retrospective catalogue.*

KOOTZ, SAMUEL M., 1. *Modern American Painters.* n.p.: Brewer and Warren Inc., 1930. I. *Survey of painting in the 1930's.*

——, 2. *New Frontiers in American Painting.* New York: Hastings House, 1943. I. *Surveys the advance guard in painting.*

KOUVENHOVEN, JOHN A. *Made in America: The Arts in Modern Civilization.* Garden City, N.Y.: Doubleday and Co. Inc., 1948. I. B. *Critical essays on American culture.*

KRAMER, HILTON. *Milton Avery: Paintings, 1930–1960.* New York: Thomas Yoseloff Inc., 1962. I. *Monograph.*

KROLL, LEON, 1. *Leon Kroll.* Cleveland: Print Club of Cleveland and The Cleveland Museum of Art, 1945. I. *Exhibition catalogue.*

——, 2. *Leon Kroll.* New York: American Artists Group Inc., 1946. I. *Autobiographical monograph.*

KUH, KATHERINE, 1. *Art Has Many Faces— The Nature of Art Presented Visually.* New York: Harper and Brothers, 1951. I.

——, 2. *The Artist's Voice, Talks with Seventeen Artists.* New York: Harper and Row, 1962. I.

KUHN, WALT, 1. *The Story of The Armory Show.* n.p.: Privately published, 1938.

——, 2. *Walt Kuhn.* Cincinnati: The Cincinnati Art Museum, 1960. I. *Exhibition catalogue.*

KUNIYOSHI, YASUO. *Yasuo Kuniyoshi.* New York: American Artists Group Inc., 1945. I. *Autobiographical monograph.*

KYROU, ADO. *Le Surrealisme au cinema.* Paris: Le Terrain Vague, 1963. I.

LANDON, EDWARD. *Picture Framing.* New York: American Artists Group Inc., 1945. I.

LANE, JAMES W. *Masters in Modern Art.* Boston: Chapman and Grimes, 1936. I.

LANGUI, EMILE. *Fifty Years of Modern Art.* New York: Frederick A. Praeger, 1959. I. *Critical historical survey.*

LEBEL, ROBERT. *Marcel Duchamp.* New York: Grove Press Inc., 1959. I. B. *Monograph.*

LEE, KATHRYN DEAN and BURCHWOOD, KATHARINE TYLER. *Art Then and Now.* New York: Appleton-Century-Crofts, Inc., 1949. I. *A popular history.*

LEEPA, ALLEN. *The Challenge of Modern Art.* New York: Thomas Yoseloff Inc., 1957. I. *Problems presented by abstract and nonfigurative art.*

LEVY, JULIEN. *Eugene Berman.* New York: American Studio Books, 1947. I. *Monograph.*

LOMBARDO, JOSEF VINCENT. *Chaim Gross.* New York: Dalton House Inc., 1949. I. B. *Monograph.*

LORAN, ERLE, 1. *Cezanne's Composition.* Berke-

ley: University of California Press, 1947. I.
——, 2. *Recent Gifts and Loans of Paint-ings by Hans Hofmann.* Berkeley: University of California Press, 1964. I.

LOWRY, BATES. *The Visual Experience: An Introduction to Art.* Englewood Cliffs, N.J.: Prentice-Hall Inc.; New York: Harry N. Abrams Inc., 1961. I. *Methods for extending the visual experience.*

MACAGY, DOUGLAS. *James Boynton.* New York: Barone Gallery, Inc., 1959. I. *Monograph.*

MAN RAY, 1. *Alphabet for Adults.* Beverly Hills, Calif.: Copley Gallery, 1948. I.

——, 2. *Man Ray.* Pasadena, Calif.: Pasadena Art Institute, 1944. I. *Exhibition catalogue.*

——, 3. *Self Portrait.* Boston: Little, Brown and Co., 1963. I. *Autobiography.*

MARSH, REGINALD. *Anatomy for Artists.* New York: American Artists Group Inc., 1945. I.

MARTIN, J. L., NICHOLSON, B. and GABO, N., eds. *Circle.* London: Faber and Faber, Ltd., 1937. I. B. *Essays on purist art.*

MATHER, FRANK JEWETT, JR., 1. *The American Spirit in Art.* New Haven, Conn.: Yale University Press, 1927. I. *Historical survey with commentary.*

——, 2. *Eugene Speicher.* New York: The Whitney Museum of American Art (American Artists Series), 1931. I. B. *Monograph.*

MCBRIDE, HENRY. *John Marin.* New York: The Museum of Modern Art, 1936. I. B. *Exhibition catalogue.*

MCCAUSLAND, ELIZABETH. *Marsden Hartley.* Minneapolis: University of Minnesota Press, 1952. I. *Biography.*

MCCOURBREY, JOHN W. *American Tradition in Painting.* New York: George Braziller, Inc., 1963. I. B. *Postulates an American tradition.*

MCCURDY, CHARLES, ed. *Modern Art . . . A Pictorial Anthology.* New York: The Macmillan Company, 1958. I. B.

MEDFORD, RICHARD C. *Guy Pene Du Bois.* Hagerstown, Md.: Washington County Museum of Fine Arts, 1940. I. *Exhibition catalogue.*

MEHRING, WALTER. *George Grosz, Thirty Drawings and Watercolors.* New York: Erich S. Herrmann, 1944. I. *Monograph.*

MELLQUIST, JEROME. *The Emergence of an American Art.* New York: Charles Scribner's Sons, 1942.

MENDELOWITZ, DANIEL M. *A History of Amer-ican Art.* New York: Holt, Rinehart and Winston, Inc., 1961. I.

MESSER, THOMAS M. *Jan Muller.* New York: The Solomon R. Guggenheim Museum, 1962. I. *Retrospective catalogue.*

METRO International Directory of Contemporary Art. Milan: Metro, 1964. I. B. (English and Italian text.)

MILLER, DOROTHY C., ed., 1. *Americans 1942. 18 Artists from 9 States.* New York: The Museum of Modern Art, 1942. I. *Documented exhibition catalogue.*

——, 2. *14 Americans.* New York: The Museum of Modern Art, 1946. I. B. *Documented exhibition catalogue.*

——, 3. *The Sculpture of John B. Flannagan.* New York: The Museum of Modern Art, 1942. I. *Retrospective catalogue.*

MILLER, KENNETH HAYES. *Kenneth Hayes Miller.* New York: Art Students League, 1953. I. *Exhibition catalogue.*

MILLIER, ARTHUR, 1. *Henry Lee McFee.* Claremont, Calif.: Scripps College, 1950. I. *Exhibition catalogue.*

——, 2. *Millard Sheets.* Los Angeles: Dalzell Hatfield Gallery, 1935. I. *Monograph.*

MOCSANYI, PAUL. *Karl Knaths.* Washington, D.C.: The Phillips Gallery, 1957. I. B. *Exhibition catalogue.*

MOHOLY-NAGY, SIBYL. *Experiment in Totality.* New York: Harper and Brothers, 1950. I. *Biography: Lazlo Moholy-Nagy.*

MORRIS, G. L. K. *American Abstract Artists.* New York: Ram Press, 1946. I. B. *Documentation of members.*

MOTHERWELL, ROBERT, 1. *The Dada Painters and Poets.* New York: Wittenborn, Schultz, Inc., 1951. Documents of Modern Art, Vol. 8. I. B. *A documented history of this group.*

——, 2. *Robert Motherwell.* Northampton, Mass.: Smith College, 1962. I. *Exhibition catalogue.*

MOTHERWELL, ROBERT, ed. *Possibilities. No. 1.* New York: Wittenborn, Schultz, Inc., 1947. I. *An occasional review concerned with all the arts.*

MOTHERWELL, ROBERT and REINHARDT, AD, eds. *Modern Artists in America.* New York: Wittenborn, Schultz, Inc., 1951. I. B. *The European and American advance guard in the 1940's.*

MUNSTERBERG, HUGO. *Twentieth Century*

Painting. New York: Philosophical Library, 1951. I. *Critical essays.*

MURRELL, WILLIAM, 1. *Charles Demuth.* New York: The Whitney Museum of American Art (American Artists Series), 1931. I. *Monograph.*

———, 2. *Elie Nadelman.* Woodstock, N.Y.: William M. Fischer, 1923. I. *Monograph.*

MURTHA, EDWIN. *Paul Manship.* New York: The Macmillan Company, 1957. I. *Monograph.*

MYERS, BERNARD, 1. *Fifty Great Artists.* New York: Bantam Books, 1953. I. B. *Historical essays.*

———, 2. *Understanding the Arts.* New York: Henry Holt and Co., 1958. I. B. *Art appreciation.*

NARODNY, IVAN. *American Artists.* New York: Roerich Museum Press, 1930. B. *Figurative painting before 1930.*

NEUHAUS, EUGENE. *The History and Ideals of American Art.* Stanford, Calif.: Stanford University Press, 1931. I. B. *Critical essays.*

NEUMEYER, ALFRED. *The Search for Meaning in Modern Art.* Englewood Cliffs, N.J.: Prentice-Hall Inc., 1964. I. *Essays on the understanding of art.*

NEWMEYER, SARAH. *Enjoying Modern Art.* New York: Reinhold Publishing Co., 1955. I. *Popular essays on art appreciation.*

NEWTON, ERIC, 1. *The Arts of Man.* Greenwich, Conn.: New York Graphic Society, 1960. I. *Critical essays.*

———, 2. *In My View.* London: Longmans, Green and Co., 1950. *Critical essays.*

NORDLAND, GERALD. *Gaston Lachaise.* Los Angeles: Los Angeles County Museum of Art, 1963. I. B. *Retrospective catalogue.*

NORDMARK, OLLE. *Fresco Painting.* New York: American Artists Group Inc., 1947. I.

NORDNESS, LEE, ed. *Art:USA:Now.* Lucerne: C. J. Bucher, 1962, 2 vols. I. B. *A collection catalogue with biographies and critical essays.*

NORMAN, DOROTHY. *The Selected Writings of John Marin.* New York: Pellegrini and Cudahy, 1949. I.

O'HARA, FRANK, 1. *Franz Kline.* London: Whitechapel Art Gallery, 1964. I. *Exhibition catalogue.*

———, 2. *Jackson Pollock.* New York: George Braziller, Inc., 1959. I. B. *Monograph.*

OLSON, RUTH and CHANIN, ABRAHAM. *Gabo-*

Pevsner. New York: The Museum of Modern Art, 1948. I. B. *Exhibition catalogue.*

ONSLOW-FORD, GORDON. *Towards a New Subject in Painting.* San Francisco: San Francisco Museum of Art, 1948. I. *The artist's theory of painting.*

PAALEN, WOLFGANG. *Form and Sense. Problems of Contemporary Art No. 1.* New York: Wittenborn and Co., 1945. I. *Essays in aesthetics.*

PACH, WALTER, 1. *Ananias or the False Artist.* New York: Harper and Brothers, 1928. I. *Critical essays.*

———, 2. *The Masters of Modern Art.* New York: B. W. Huebsch, Inc., 1926. I. B. *American and European art before 1926.*

———, 3. *Queer Thing, Painting.* New York: Harper and Brothers, 1938. I. *Autobiography.*

PAGANO, GRACE. *Contemporary American Painting. The Encyclopaedia Britannica Collection.* New York: Duell, Sloan and Pearce, 1945. I.

PALMER, WILLIAM C. *William C. Palmer.* Utica, N.Y.: Munson-Williams-Proctor Institute, 1956. I. *Exhibition catalogue.*

PARKES, KINETON. *The Art of Carved Sculpture.* New York: Charles Scribner's Sons, 1931, 2 vols. I. B.

PASSLOFF, PATRICIA. *The 30's. Painting in New York.* New York: Poindexter Gallery, 1963. I.

PEARSON, RALPH M., 1. *Experiencing American Pictures.* New York: Harper and Brothers, 1943. I. *Appreciation of modern art.*

———, 2. *The Modern Renaissance in American Art.* New York: Harper and Brothers, 1954. I. *Development of modern art in America.*

PEIRCE, WALDO. *Waldo Peirce.* New York: American Artists Group Inc., 1945. I. *Autobiographical monograph.*

PERLMAN, BENNARD B. *The Immortal Eight.* New York: Exposition Press, 1962.

PETERDI, GABOR. *Printmaking: Methods Old and New.* New York: The Macmillan Company, 1959. I.

PHILLIPS, DUNCAN, 1. *The Artist Sees Differently.* New York: E. Weyhe, 1931. I. *Critical essays.*

———, 2. *A Collection in the Making.* New York: E. Weyhe, 1926. I. *Development of the Phillips collection in Washington, D.C.*

PITTMAN, HOBSON. *Hobson Pittman.* Raleigh:

North Carolina Museum of Art, 1963. I. B. *Retrospective catalogue.*

PONENTE, NELLO. *Modern Painting: Contemporary Trends.* Geneva: Skira, 1960. I. B.

POOR, HENRY VARNUM, 1. *An Artist Sees Alaska.* New York: Viking Press, 1945. I.

———, 2. *A Book of Pottery, from Mud into Immortality.* Englewood Cliffs, N.J.: Prentice-Hall Inc., 1958. I. B. *Autobiographical.*

POORE, HENRY R. *Modern Art: Why, What and How?* New York: G. P. Putnam's, 1931. I. *Investigation into the reasons for modern art.*

PORTER, FAIRFIELD. *Thomas Eakins.* New York: George Braziller, Inc., 1959. I. B. *Monograph.*

POUSETTE-DART, NATHANIEL. *Paintings, Watercolors, Lithographs.* New York: Clayton Spicer Press, 1946. I. B. *Monograph.*

POUSETTE-DART, NATHANIEL, ed. *American Painting Today.* New York: Hastings House, 1956. I. *Pictorial documentation of American painting in the mid-1950's.*

PRINT CLUB of CLEVELAND. *The Work of Rudy Pozzatti.* Cleveland: The Cleveland Museum of Art, 1955. I. *Exhibition catalogue.*

PRINT COUNCIL of AMERICA. *Prints.* New York: Holt, Rinehart and Winston, Inc., 1962. I.

RAGON, MICHEL, 1. *L'Aventure de l'art abstrait.* Paris: Robert Laffont, 1956. I. B. (French text.) *Development of abstract art.*

———, 2. *Expression et non-figuration.* Paris: Editions de la Revue Neuf, 1951. I. (French text.) *Expressionism and the development of non-figurative art.*

RAMSDEN, E. H., 1. *An Introduction to Modern Art.* London: Oxford University Press, 1940. I.

———, 2. *Sculpture: Theme and Variations Toward a Contemporary Aesthetic.* London: Lund Humphries, 1953. I. B.

RAYNAL, MAURICE, 1. *A. Archipenko.* Rome: Valori Plastici, 1923. I. (French text.) *Monograph.*

———, 2. *Jacques Lipchitz.* Paris: Edition Jeanne Bucher, 1947. I. (French text.) *Monograph.*

———, 3. *Modern Painting.* Geneva: Skira, 1953. I. B. *Survey of modern painting.*

———, 4. *Peinture moderne.* Geneva: Skira, 1953. I. B. (French text.)

READ, HERBERT, 1. *The Art of Sculpture.* Bollingen Series XXV, No. 3. New York: Pantheon Books, 1956. I. *Documented critical essays on connoisseurship of sculpture.*

———, 2. *A Concise History of Modern Painting.* New York: Frederick A. Praeger, 1959. I. B.

———, 3. *The Quest and the Quarry.* Rome: Rome-New York Art Foundation Inc., 1961. I. *Critical essays.*

———, 4. *Surrealism.* New York: Harcourt, Brace and Co., 1939. I. *Essays on Surrealism.*

———, 5. *The Tenth Muse.* London: Routledge and Kegan Paul, 1957. I. *Critical essays.*

READ, HERBERT and MARTIN, LESLIE. *Gabo.* London: Lund Humphries, 1957. I. B. *Monograph.*

REESE, ALBERT. *American Prize Prints of the 20th Century.* New York: American Artists Group Inc., 1949. I.

RESTANY, PIERRE, 1. *J. F. Koenig.* Paris: Galerie Arnaud, 1960. I. (French and English text.) *Monograph.*

———, 2. *Lyrisme et abstraction.* Milan: Edizioni Apollinairi, 1960. I. (French text.) *Exposition of a lyrical theory in painting leading toward abstraction.*

RIBEMONT-DESSAIGNES, G. *Man Ray.* Paris: Librairie Gallimard, 1924. I. *Monograph.*

RICH, DANIEL CATTON, 1. *Georgia O'Keeffe.* Chicago: The Art Institute of Chicago, 1943. I. *Retrospective catalogue.*

———, 2. *Georgia O'Keeffe.* Worcester, Mass.: The Worcester Art Museum, 1960. *Retrospective catalogue.*

RICHARDSON, E. P. *Painting in America, the Story of 450 Years.* New York: Thomas Y. Crowell Co., 1956. I. B. *Important history of American painting.*

RINARD, PARK and PYLE, ARNOLD. *Grant Wood.* Chicago: Lakeside Press Galleries, 1935. I. *Exhibition catalogue.*

RINGEL, FRED J., ed. *America as Americans See It.* New York: The Literary Guild, 1932. I. *Anthology of the writings of various Americans on American culture.*

RITCHIE, ANDREW CARNDUFF, 1. *Abstract Painting and Sculpture in America.* New York: The Museum of Modern Art, 1951. I. B. *Documented exhibition catalogue.*

———, 2. *Charles Demuth.* New York: The Museum of Modern Art, 1950. I. B. *Retrospective catalogue.*

———, 3. *Sculpture of the Twentieth Century.* New York: The Museum of Modern Art, 1952. I. B.

ROBERTS, COLETTE. *Mark Tobey.* New York: Grove Press Inc., 1959. I. *Monograph.*

ROBERTSON, BRYAN, 1. *Charles Howard.* London: Whitechapel Art Gallery, 1956. I. *Retrospective catalogue.*

———, 2. *Jackson Pollock.* New York: Harry N. Abrams Inc., 1960. I. B. *Monograph.*

RODMAN, SELDEN, 1. *Conversations with Artists.* New York: Capricorn Books, 1961. I.

———, 2. *The Eye of Man.* New York: Devin-Adair, 1955. I. *Polemic devised toward figuration.*

———, 3. *The Insiders.* Baton Rouge: Louisiana State University Press, 1960. I. *A thesis for figurative artists.*

ROGALSKI, WALTER R. *Prints and Drawings by Walter R. Rogalski.* Cleveland: Print Club of Cleveland and The Cleveland Museum of Art, 1954. I. *Exhibition catalogue.*

ROOD, JOHN. *Sculpture in Wood.* Minneapolis: University of Minnesota Press, 1950. I. *Technique.*

ROSENBERG, HAROLD. *Arshile Gorky, The Man, The Time, The Idea.* New York: Horizon Press, Inc., 1962. I. B. *Monograph.*

ROSENBLUM, ROBERT. *Cubism and Twentieth Century Art.* New York: Harry N. Abrams Inc., 1961. I. B. *Chronicles Cubism and its influence.*

ROTHSCHILD, LEON. *Style in Art.* New York: Thomas Yoseloff Inc., 1960. I. *Critical essays.*

ROURKE, CONSTANCE. *Charles Sheeler. Artist in the American Tradition.* New York: Harcourt, Brace and Co., 1938. I. *Biography.*

SACHS, PAUL J. *Modern Prints and Drawings.* New York: Alfred A. Knopf, 1954. I. B.

SALVINI, ROBERTO. *Guida all'arte moderna.* Florence: L'arco, 1949. I. B. (Italian text.)

SASOWSKY, NORMAN. *Reginald Marsh. Etchings, Engravings, Lithographs.* New York: Frederick A. Praeger, 1956. I. *Catalogue raisonné.*

SAWYER, KENNETH. *The Paintings of Paul Jenkins.* Paris: Editions Two Cities, 1961. I. *Monograph.*

SCHMECKEBIER, LAWRENCE E. *John Steuart Curry's Pageant of America.* New York: American Artists Group Inc., 1943. I. *Biography.*

SCHWABACHER, ETHEL K. *Arshile Gorky.* New York: The Whitney Museum of American Art, 1957. I. B. *Biography.*

Sculpture of the Western Hemisphere. New York: International Business Machines Corp., 1942. I. *Catalogue of IBM sculpture collection.*

SEITZ, WILLIAM C., 1. *Abstract Expressionist Painting in America: An Interpretation Based on the Work and Thought of Six Key Figures.* Ph.D. thesis, Princeton University, 1955. Not published; available on microfilm.

———, 2. *The Art of Assemblage.* New York: The Museum of Modern Art, 1961. I. B. *Documented exhibition catalogue.*

———, 3. *Hans Hofmann.* New York: The Museum of Modern Art, 1963. I. B. *Exhibition catalogue.*

———, 4. *Mark Tobey.* New York: The Museum of Modern Art, 1962. I. B. *Retrospective catalogue.*

SELDIS, HENRY J. and Wilke, Ulfert. *The Sculpture of Jack Zajac.* Los Angeles: Gallard Press, 1960. I. B. *Monograph.*

SELIGMANN, HERBERT J., ed. *Letters of John Marin.* New York: An American Place, 1931.

SELIGMANN, KURT. *The Mirror of Magic.* New York: Pantheon Books, 1948. I. *This artist was an authority on magic; his art reflects its influence.*

SELZ, JEAN. *Modern Sculpture.* New York: George Braziller, Inc., 1963. I. B.

SELZ, PETER, 1. *German Expressionist Painting.* Berkeley: University of California Press, 1957. I. B. *Major work documenting the development of German Expressionism and its influence.*

———, 2. *Mark Rothko.* New York: The Museum of Modern Art, 1961. I. B. *Retrospective catalogue.*

SEUPHOR, MICHEL, 1. *Abstract Painting. 50 Years of Accomplishment, from Kandinsky to the Present.* New York: Dell Publishing Co., 1964. I.

———, 2. *L'Art abstrait.* Paris: Editions Maeght, 1949. I. B. (French text.)

———, 3. *The Sculpture of This Century, Dictionary of Modern Sculpture.* London: A. Zwemmer Ltd., 1959. I. B.

SEYMOUR, CHARLES, JR. *Tradition and Experiment in Modern Sculpture.* Washington, D.C.: The American University Press, 1949. I.

SHAHN, BEN. *The Shape of Content*. Cambridge, Mass.: Harvard University Press, 1957. I. *Critical essay*.

SLOAN, HELEN FARR. *The Life and Times of John Sloan*. Wilmington, Del.: Wilmington Society of the Fine Arts, 1961. I.

SLOAN, JOHN, 1. *The Art of John Sloan*. Brunswick, Me.: Walker Art Museum, Bowdoin College, 1962. *Exhibition catalogue*.

——, 2. *The Gist of Art*. New York: American Artists Group Inc., 1939. I. *The artist's theory of painting*.

——, 3. *John Sloan*. Andover, Mass.: Addison Gallery of American Art, Phillips Academy, 1938. I. B. *Exhibition catalogue*.

——, 4. *John Sloan*. New York: American Artists Group Inc., 1945. I. *Autobiographical monograph*.

——, 5. *John Sloan, Paintings and Prints*. Hanover, N.H.: Dartmouth College, 1946. I. *Exhibition catalogue*.

SLUSSER, JEAN PAUL. *Bernard Karfiol*. New York: The Whitney Museum of American Art (American Artists Series), 1931. I. B. *Monograph*.

SMITH, ANDRE. *Concerning the Education of a Print Collector*. New York: Harlow, Keppel and Co., 1941. I.

SMITH, BERNARD. *Moses Soyer*. New York: ACA Gallery, 1944. I. *Monograph*.

SMITH, S. C. KAINES. *An Outline of Modern Painting*. London: The Medici Society, 1932. I. *Early documentation of twentieth-century art*.

SOBY, JAMES THRALL, 1. *After Picasso*. Hartford, Conn.: Edwin Valentine Mitchell; New York: Dodd, Mead and Co., 1935. I. *Critical essays*.

——, 2. *Ben Shahn*. New York: The Museum of Modern Art; West Drayton, England: Penguin Books, 1947. I. *Monograph*.

——, 3. *Ben Shahn*. New York: George Braziller, Inc., 1963. I. B. *Monograph*.

——, 4. *Ben Shahn, His Graphic Work*. New York: George Braziller, Inc., 1957. I. B. *Monograph*.

——, 5. *Contemporary Painters*. New York: The Museum of Modern Art, 1948. I. *Documented exhibition catalogue*.

——, 6. *Modern Art and the New Past*. Nor-man: University of Oklahoma Press, 1957. *Critical essays and documentation*.

——, 7. *Tchelitchew*. New York: The Museum of Modern Art, 1942. I. B. *Exhibition catalogue*.

——, 8. *Yves Tanguy*. New York: The Museum of Modern Art, 1955. I. B. *Exhibition catalogue*.

SOYER, RAPHAEL, 1. *A Painter's Pilgrimage*. New York: Crown Publishers Inc., 1962. I. *A European travelogue*.

——, 2. *Raphael Soyer*. New York: American Artists Group Inc., 1946. I. *Autobiographical monograph*.

SPEICHER, EUGENE. *Eugene Speicher*. New York: American Artists Group Inc., 1945. I. *Autobiographical monograph*.

STEINBERG, LEO. *Jasper Johns*. New York: George Wittenborn, Inc., 1964. I. B. *Monograph*.

STEINBERG, SAUL, 1. *The Art of Living*. New York: Harper and Brothers, 1945. I. *Cartoons*.

——, 2. *The Passport*. New York: Harper and Brothers, 1945. I. *Cartoons*.

——, 3. *Steinberg Dessins*. Paris: N. R. F., Gallimard, 1955. I. *Cartoons*.

STERNBERG, HARRY, 1. *Modern Methods and Materials of Etching*. New York: McGraw-Hill Book Co., Inc., 1949. I.

——, 2. *Silk Screen Color Printing*. New York: McGraw-Hill Book Co., Inc., 1942. I.

SUTTON, DENYS. *American Painting*. London: Avalon Press, 1948. I. *Mid-twentieth-century painting*.

SWEENEY, JAMES JOHNSON, 1. *Alexander Calder*. New York: The Museum of Modern Art, 1951. I. B. *Exhibition catalogue*.

——, 2. *Jacques Villon, Raymond Duchamp-Villon, Marcel Duchamp*. New York: The Solomon R. Guggenheim Museum, 1957. I. B. *Exhibition catalogue*.

——, 3. *Stuart Davis*. New York: The Museum of Modern Art, 1945. I. B. *Exhibition catalogue*.

SWEET, FREDERICK A. *Ivan Albright*. Chicago: The Art Institute of Chicago, 1964. I. *Retrospective catalogue*.

TAFT, LORADO. *Modern Tendencies in Sculpture*. Chicago: The University of Chicago Press, 1921. I.

TAKIGUCHI, SHUZO. *Noguchi.* Tokyo: Bijutsu Shippan-Sha, 1953. I. *Monograph.*

TANGUY, YVES. *Un Recueil de Ses Oeuvres/A Summary of His Work.* New York: Pierre Matisse, 1943. I. B. (French and English text.) *Catalogue raisonné.*

TAPIE, MICHEL, 1. *Un Arte autre.* Paris: Gabriel-Giraud et Fils, 1952. I. (French text.) *Polemic thesis for advance guard painting.*

———, 2. *Ossorio.* Turin: Edizioni d'Arte Fratelli Pozzo, 1961. I. (English and French text.) *Monograph.*

TAUBES, FREDERIC, 1. *Anatomy of Genius.* New York: Dodd, Mead and Co., 1948. I. *Critical essay.*

———, 2. *The Art and Techniques of Portrait Painting.* New York: Dodd, Mead and Co., 1957. I.

———, 3. *Better Frames for Your Pictures.* New York: Studio Publications, 1952. I.

———, 4. *Frederic Taubes.* New York: American Artists Group Inc., 1946. I. B. *Autobiographical monograph.*

———, 5. *The Mastery of Oil Painting.* New York: Studio Publications, 1953. I. *Technique.*

———, 6. *Modern Art, Sweet or Sour?* New York: Watson-Guptill Publishing Co. Inc., 1958. I. *Critical essays.*

———, 7. *The Painter's Question and Answer Book.* New York: Watson-Guptill Publishing Co. Inc., 1948. I. *Technique.*

———, 8. *Paintings and Essays on Art.* New York: Dodd, Mead and Co., 1950. I.

———, 9. *Pen and Ink Drawing, Art and Technique.* New York: Watson-Guptill Publishing Co. Inc., 1956. I.

———, 10. *Pictorial Composition and the Art of Drawing.* New York: Dodd, Mead and Co., 1949. I.

———, 11. *Studio Secrets.* New York: Watson-Guptill Publishing Co. Inc., 1943. I. *Technique.*

———, 12. *The Technique of Oil Painting.* New York: Dodd, Mead and Co., 1941. I.

———, 13. *You Don't Know What You Like.* New York: Dodd, Mead and Co., 1947. I. *Critical essays.*

TAVOLATO, ITALO. *George Grosz.* Rome: Valori Plastici, 1924. I. (French text.) *Monograph.*

THOMAS, EDWARD B. *Mark Tobey.* Seattle: Seattle Art Museum, 1959. I. *Exhibition catalogue.*

TILLIM, SIDNEY. *Richard Lindner.* Chicago: William and Noma Copley Foundation, n.d. I. *Monograph.*

TOBEY, MARK. *Mark Tobey.* New York: The Whitney Museum of American Art, 1951. I. *Exhibition catalogue.*

TYLER, PARKER. *Marca-Relli.* Paris: The Pocket Museum, Editions George Fall, 1960. I. *Monograph.*

VALENTINE, W. R., 1. *Letters of John B. Flannagan.* New York: Curt Valentine, 1942.

———, 2. *Origins of Modern Sculpture.* New York: Wittenborn and Co., 1946. I.

VARGA, MARGIT. *Waldo Peirce.* New York: Hyperion Press, Harper and Brothers, 1941. I. *Monograph.*

VITRY, PAUL. *Paul Manship.* Paris: Editions de la Gazette des Beaux Arts, 1927. I. *Monograph.*

WALDBERG, PATRICK, 1. *Bernard Pfriem.* Chicago: William and Noma Copley Foundation, 1961. I. (French and English text.) *Monograph.*

———, 2. *Main et marveilles.* Paris: Mercure de France, 1961. I. *Essays on Surrealism.*

———, 3. *Surrealism.* Geneva: Skira, 1962. I. B. *Documentation and essays on Surrealism.*

WALKOWITZ, ABRAHAM, 1. *A Demonstration of Objective, Abstract, and Non-Objective Art.* Girard, Kans.: Haldeman-Julius Press, 1945. I. *The artist's theories, illustrated.*

———, 2. *100 Drawings.* New York: B. W. Huebsch, Inc., 1925. I.

WATSON, ERNEST W., 1. *Color and Method in Painting.* New York: Watson-Guptill Publishing Co. Inc., 1942. I. *Studies of various artists' use of color.*

———, 2. *Twenty Painters and How They Work.* New York: Watson-Guptill Publishing Co. Inc., 1950. I.

WATSON, FORBES. *William Glackens.* New York: Duffield and Co., 1923. I. *Monograph.*

WEBER, MAX, 1. *Essays on Art.* n.p.: Privately published, 1916.

———, 2. *Max Weber.* New York: American Artists Group Inc., 1945. I. *Autobiographical monograph.*

WELL, HENRY W., ed. *Selected Poems by*

Marsden Hartley. New York: Viking Press, 1945. I.

"What Abstract Art Means to Me." *Bulletin of The Museum of Modern Art,* Vol. XVIII, No. 3, Spring 1951. I. *Statements by leading artists.*

WHEELER, MONROE. *Painters and Sculptors of Modern America.* New York: Thomas Y. Crowell Co., 1942. I.

WIGHT, FREDERICK S., 1. *Hans Hofmann.* New York: The Whitney Museum of American Art, 1957. I. *Exhibition catalogue.*

———, 2. *Milestones of American Painting in Our Century.* New York: Chanticleer Press, 1949. I. *Historical view of American painting.*

———, 3. *Milton Avery.* Baltimore: Baltimore Museum of Art, 1952. I. *Exhibition catalogue.*

———, 4. *Nathan Oliveira.* Los Angeles: University of California, 1963. I. *Monograph.*

WIGHT, FREDERICK S., BAUR, JOHN I. H. and PHILLIPS, DUNCAN. *Morris Graves.* Berkeley: University of California Press, 1956. I. B. *Exhibition catalogue.*

WIGHT, FREDERICK S. and GOODRICH, LLOYD. *Hyman Bloom.* Boston: Institute of Contemporary Art, 1944. I. *Exhibition catalogue.*

WILENSKI, R. H. *The Modern Movement in Art.* London: Faber and Faber, Ltd., 1955. I. *European and American development of modern art.*

WILKE, ULFERT. *Music to Be Seen.* Louisville, Ky.: Erewhon Press, n.d. I. (English, French, and German text.) *A collection of drawings.*

WILLARD, CHARLOTTE. *Moses Soyer.* Cleveland: World Publishing Co., 1962. I. *Monograph.*

WILLIAMS, HIRAM. *Notes for a Young Painter.* Englewood Cliffs, N.J.: Prentice-Hall Inc., 1963. I.

WILLIAMS, WILLIAM CARLOS. *Charles Sheeler.* New York: The Museum of Modern Art, 1939. I. B. *Exhibition catalogue.*

WINGERT, PAUL S. *The Sculpture of William Zorach.* New York: Pitman Publishing Co., 1938. I. B. *Monograph.*

WOELFFER, EMERSON. *Emerson Woelffer.* Pasadena, Calif.: The Pasadena Art Museum, 1962. I. *Exhibition catalogue.*

WRIGHT, WILLARD HUNTINGTON, 1. *The Forum Exhibition of Modern American Painters.* New York: Anderson Galleries, 1916. I. B.

———, 2. *Modern Painting.* New York: Dodd, Mead and Co., 1927. I. *Essays on modern art.*

ZAIDENBERG, ARTHUR, ed. *The Art of the Artists.* New York: Crown Publishers Inc., 1951. I. *Pictorial documentation of various artists.*

ZERVOS, CHRISTIAN. *Histoire de l'art contemporain.* Paris: Editions Cahiers d'Art, 1938. I. B. *Documented history of contemporary art.*

ZERVOS, CHRISTIAN and RADAMS, PHILIP. *Mary Callery.* New York: Wittenborn and Co., 1961. I. B. *Monograph and catalogue raisonné.*

ZIGROSSER, CARL, 1. *The Artist in America.* New York: Alfred A. Knopf, 1942. I. *Critical essays and biographies.*

———, 2. *Mauricio Lasansky.* New York: American Federation of Arts, 1960. I. *Retrospective catalogue.*

ZORACH, WILLIAM, 1. *William Zorach.* New York: American Artists Group Inc., 1945. I. *Autobiographical monograph.*

———, 2. *Zorach Explains Sculpture, What It Is and How It Is Made.* New York: American Artists Group Inc., 1947. I.

BOOKS OF GENERAL INTEREST

AMERICAN ABSTRACT ARTISTS, ed. *The World of Abstract Art.* New York: George Wittenborn and Co., 1957. I. *Documentation of the group and its members.*

ARNASON, H. HARVARD. *American Abstract Expressionists and Imagists.* New York: The Solomon R. Guggenheim Museum, 1961. B. *Documented exhibition catalogue.*

BARR, ALFRED H., JR., ed. *Masters of Modern Art.* New York: The Museum of Modern Art, 1955. I. B. *Major anthology of modern art.*

BELMONT, I. J. *The Modern Dilemma in Art.* New York: Harbinger House, 1944. I. *Critical evaluation of increasing abstractionism.*

BETHERS, RAY. *Art Always Changes.* New York: Hastings House, 1958, I. *Critical essays.*

CAHILL, HOLGER. *New Horizons in American Art.* New York: The Museum of Modern Art, 1936. I. *Exhibition catalogue related to Federal Art Project.*

CHENEY, SHELDON. *A Primer of Modern Art.*

New York: Boni and Liveright, 1924. I.

——. *The Story of Modern Art.* New York: Viking Press, 1958. I. *Popular history of modern art.*

CIRLOT, JUAN-EDUARDO. *Del Expresionismo a la Abstraccion.* Barcelona: Editorial Seix Barral, S. A., 1955. I. (Spanish text.) *Development of non-figurative art.*

CRANE, AIMEE, ed. *Portrait of America.* New York: Hyperion Press, Harper and Brothers, 1945. I. *Critical essays.*

DAVIDSON, MARSHALL B. *Life in America.* Boston: Houghton Mifflin Co., 1951, 2 vols. *Critical essays and documentation.*

DUFFUS, R. L. *The American Renaissance.* New York: Alfred A. Knopf, 1928. *Critical discussion of American culture.*

FAULKNER, RAY, ZIEGFELD, EDWIN and HILL, GEROLD. *Art Today, an Introduction to the Fine and Functional Arts.* New York: Henry Holt and Co., 1941.

GOODALL, DONALD B. *Partial Bibliography of American Abstract-Expressive Painting, 1943–58.* Los Angeles: University of Southern California, Department of Fine Arts, 1958. *Periodicals and a few books.*

GREGG, FREDERICK JAMES. *For and Against.* New York: Association of American Painters and Sculptors Inc., 1913. *Anthology of commentary on The Armory Show of 1913.*

GRUSKIN, ALAN D. *Painting in the USA.* Garden City, N.Y.: Doubleday and Co., 1946. I. *Survey of American painting in the 1940's.*

GUGGENHEIMER, RICHARD. *Sight and Insight, a Prediction of New Perceptions in Art.* New York: Harper and Brothers, 1945. *Critical discussion.*

HARSHE, ROBERT B. *A Reader's Guide to Modern Art.* San Francisco: The Wahlgreen Co., 1914. *Bibliography.*

KEPPEL, FREDERICK P. and DUFFUS, R. L. *The Arts in American Life.* New York: McGraw-Hill Book Co., Inc., 1933. *Survey of the arts and their development in America.*

McMAHON, A. PHILIP. *The Meaning of Art.* New York: W. W. Norton and Co., 1930. B.

——. *Preface to an American Philosophy of Art.* Chicago: The University of Chicago Press, 1945. B.

MYERS, BERNARD S. *Modern Art in the Making.* New York: McGraw-Hill Book Co., Inc.,

1959. I. B. *Historical development of modern art.*

MYERS, BERNARD S., ed. *Encyclopaedia of Painting. Painters and Painting of the World from Prehistoric Times to the Present Day.* New York: Crown Publishers Inc., 1955. I.

NEUHAUS, EUGENE. *The Appreciation of Art.* Boston: Ginn and Co., 1924. I.

——. *Painters, Pictures, and The People.* San Francisco: Philopolis Press, 1918. I.

PACH, WALTER. *Modern Art in America.* New York: C. W. Kraushaar Art Galleries, 1928. I. *Concise discussion of modern art and its development.*

PARK, ESTHER AILLEEN. *Mural Painters in America: A Biographical Index.* Pittsburg: Kansas State Teachers College, 1949.

PARKER, R. A. *First Papers of Surrealism.* New York: Coordinating Council of French Relief Societies Inc., 1942. *Documented exhibition catalogue.*

PUMA, FERNANDO. *Modern Art Looks Ahead.* New York: The Beechhurst Press, 1947. I. *Popular essays on art.*

RICHARDSON, E. P. *A Short History of Painting in America, the Story of 450 Years.* New York: Thomas Y. Crowell Co., 1963. I. *A basic history of American painting.*

——. *Twentieth Century Painting.* Detroit: Detroit Institute of Arts, 1947, 4th ed. I. B. *Concise essays.*

RICHMAN, ROBERT, ed. *The Arts at Mid-Century.* New York: Horizon Press, Inc., 1954.

SAYLOR, OLIVER M. *Revolution in the Arts.* New York: Brentano's, 1930. *Critical essays.*

SCHNIER, JACQUES. *Sculpture in Modern America.* Berkeley: University of California Press, 1948. I. B.

SEWCALL, JOHN IVES. *A History of Western Art.* New York: Holt, Rinehart and Winston, Inc., 1961. I.

SMITH, RALPH C. *A Biographical Index of American Artists.* Baltimore: The Williams and Wilkins Co., 1930. B.

WATSON, FORBES. *American Painting Today.* Washington, D.C.: American Federation of Arts, 1939. I. *Concerned with the period before World War II.*

YOUNG, A. R., ed. *Art Bibliography.* New York: Teachers College of Columbia University, 1941. *A bibliography for the educator.*